Pro/ENGINEER Wildfire 5.0 for Designers

CADCIM Technologies
525 St. Andrews Drive
Schererville, IN 46375, USA
(www.cadcim.com)

Contributing Author
Sham Tickoo
Professor
Department of Mechanical Engineering Technology
Purdue University Calumet
Hammond, Indiana
USA

CADCIM Technologies

Pro/ENGINEER Wildfire 5.0 for Designers
Sham Tickoo

Published by CADCIM Technologies, 525 St Andrews Drive, Schererville, IN 46375 USA. Copyright © 2010, CADCIM Technologies. All rights reserved. No part of this publication may be reproduced or distributed in any form or by any means, or stored in the database or retrieval system without the prior permission of CADCIM Technologies.

ISBN 978-1-932-709-80-3

NOTICE TO THE READER

Publisher does not warrant or guarantee any of the products described in the text or perform any independent analysis in connection with any of the product information contained in the text. Publisher does not assume, and expressly disclaims, any obligation to obtain and include information other than that provided to it by the manufacturer.

The reader is expressly warned to consider and adopt all safety precautions that might be indicated by the activities herein and to avoid all potential hazards. By following the instructions contained herein, the reader willingly assumes all risks in connection with such instructions.

The Publisher makes no representation or warranties of any kind, including but not limited to, the warranties of fitness for a particular purpose or merchantability, nor are any such representations implied with respect to the material set forth herein, and the publisher takes no responsibility with respect to such material. The publisher shall not be liable for any special, consequential, or exemplary damages resulting, in whole or part, from the reader's use of, or reliance upon, this material.

www.cadcim.com

DEDICATION

*To teachers, who make it possible to disseminate knowledge
to enlighten the young and curious minds
of our future generations*

*To students, who are dedicated to learning new technologies
and making the world a better place to live in*

THANKS

*To the faculty and students of the MET department of
Purdue University Calumet for their cooperation*

To engineers of CADCIM Technologies for their valuable help

Online Training Program Offered by CADCIM Technologies

CADCIM Technologies provides effective and affordable virtual online training on various software packages including Computer Aided Design and Manufacturing (CAD/CAM), computer programming languages, animation, architecture, and GIS. The training is delivered 'live' via Internet at any time, any place, and at any pace to individuals, students of colleges, universities, and CAD/CAM training centers. The main features of this program are:

Training for Students and Companies in a Class Room Setting

Highly experienced instructors and qualified Engineers at CADCIM Technologies conduct the classes under the guidance of Prof. Sham Tickoo of Purdue University Calumet, USA. This team has authored several textbooks that are rated "one of the best" in their categories and are used in various colleges, universities, and training centers in North America, Europe, and in other parts of the world.

Training for Individuals

The cost effective and time saving initiative of CADCIM Technologies strives to deliver the training in the comfort of your home or work place, thereby relieving you from the hassles of traveling to training centers.

Training Offered on Software Packages

We provide basic and advanced training on the following software packages:

CAD/CAM/CAE: CATIA, Pro/ENGINEER Wildfire, SolidWorks, Autodesk Inventor, Solid Edge, NX, AutoCAD, AutoCAD, AutoCAD LT, Customizing AutoCAD, EdgeCAM, and ANSYS

Computer Programming Languages: C++, VB.NET, Oracle, AJAX, and Java

Animation and Styling: Autodesk 3ds Max, 3ds Max Design, Maya, and Alias Design

Architecture and GIS: Autodesk Revit Architecture, Autodesk Civil 3D, and Autodesk Map 3D

For more information, please visit the following link:

http://www.cadcim.com

Note
The free teaching and learning resources, mentioned in the cover page of this textbook, are available only for the faculty who buy the textbook from our web site www.cadcim.com or the university/college bookstores. We need proof of purchase when you request the technical support from us.

Table of Contents

Dedication   iii
Preface   xv

Chapter 1: Introduction to Pro/ENGINEER Wildfire 5.0

Introduction to Pro/Engineer Wildfire 5.0	1-2
Feature-Based Nature	1-2
Bidirectional Associative Property	1-3
Parametric Nature	1-6
System Requirements	1-6
Getting Started with Pro/Engineer Wildfire 5.0	1-7
Important Terms and Definitions	1-8
File Menu Options	1-9
Managing Files	1-20
Menu Manager	1-20
Model Tree	1-20
Understanding the Functions of the Mouse Buttons	1-21
Toolbars	1-22
Navigator	1-26
Browser	1-26
Appearance Gallery	1-27
Rendering in Pro/ENGINEER Wildfire 5.0	1-30
Color Scheme Used in this Book	1-32

Chapter 2: Creating Sketches in the Sketch Mode-I

The Sketch Mode	2-2
Working with the Sketch Mode	2-2
Invoking the Sketch Mode	2-3
The Sketcher Environment	2-3
Working with a Sketch in the Sketch Mode	2-4
Drawing a Sketch Using the **Sketcher Tools** Toolbar	2-5
Placing a Point	2-5
Drawing a Line	2-5
Drawing a Rectangle	2-7
Drawing a Circle	2-7
Drawing an Arc	2-10
Dimensioning the Sketch	2-13
Converting a Weak Dimension into a Strong Dimension	2-13
Dimensioning a Sketch Using the Normal Button or the Normal Option	2-14
Dimensioning the Basic Sketched Entities	2-14
Linear Dimensioning of a Line	2-14
Angular Dimensioning of an Arc	2-14

Diameter Dimensioning	2-14
Radial Dimensioning	2-15
Dimensioning Revolved Sections	2-15
Working With Constraints	2-16
Types of Constraints	2-16
Disabling Constraints	2-17
Modifying the Dimensions of a Sketch	2-18
Using the Modify Button	2-18
Using the Edit Menu	2-18
Modifying a Dimension by Double-Clicking on it	2-19
Modifying Dimensions Dynamically	2-19
Resolve Sketch Dialog Box	2-19
Deleting the Sketcher Entities	2-20
Trimming the Sketcher Entities	2-20
Mirroring the Sketcher Entities	2-21
Inserting Standard/User-Defined Sketches	2-22
Drawing Display Options	2-23
Tutorial 1	2-24
Tutorial 2	2-30
Tutorial 3	2-35
Self-Evaluation Test	2-39
Review Questions	2-40
Exercise 1	2-40
Exercise 2	2-41
Exercise 3	2-41
Exercise 4	2-42

Chapter 3: Creating Sketches in the Sketch Mode-II

Dimensioning the Sketch	3-2
Dimensioning a Sketch Using the Baseline Option	3-2
Replacing the Dimensions of a Sketch Using the Replace Option	3-3
Creating Fillets	3-3
Creating Circular Fillets	3-3
Creating Elliptical Fillets	3-6
Creating a Reference Coordinate System	3-7
Working with Splines	3-7
Creating a Spline	3-7
Dimensioning of Splines	3-8
Modifying a Spline	3-9
Writing Text in the Sketcher Environment	3-11
Moving and Resizing Entities	3-12
Importing 2D Drawings in the Sketch Mode	3-13
Tutorial 1	3-14
Tutorial 2	3-19
Tutorial 3	3-23
Self-Evaluation Test	3-27

Review Questions	3-28
Exercise 1	3-29
Exercise 2	3-29
Exercise 3	3-30

Chapter 4: Creating Base Features

Creating Base Features	4-2
Invoking the Part Mode	4-2
The Default Datum Planes	4-3
Creating a Protrusion	4-4
Extruding a Sketch	4-5
Revolving a Sketch	4-15
Understanding the Orientation of Datum Planes	4-16
Parent-Child Relationship	4-21
Implicit Relationship	4-22
Explicit Relationship	4-22
Nesting of Sketches	4-22
Tutorial 1	4-23
Tutorial 2	4-30
Tutorial 3	4-35
Tutorial 4	4-40
Self-Evaluation Test	4-49
Review Questions	4-50
Exercise 1	4-51
Exercise 2	4-51
Exercise 3	4-52
Exercise 4	4-52

Chapter 5: Datums

Datums	5-2
Default Datum Planes	5-2
Need for Datums in Modeling	5-2
Selection Method in Pro/ENGINEER	5-3
Datum Options	5-5
Datum Planes	5-5
Creating Datum Planes	5-7
Datum Planes Created On-The-Fly	5-13
Datum Axes	5-14
Datum Points	5-19
Creating Cuts	5-25
Removing Material by Extruding a Sketch	5-25
Removing Material by Revolving a Sketch	5-26
Tutorial 1	5-27
Tutorial 2	5-36
Tutorial 3	5-44

Self-Evaluation Test	5-50
Review Questions	5-51
Exercise 1	5-52
Exercise 2	5-53
Exercise 3	5-53
Exercise 4	5-55

Chapter 6: Options Aiding Construction of Parts-I

Options Aiding Construction of Parts	6-2
Creating Holes	6-2
The Hole Dashboard	6-2
Important Points to Remember While Creating a Hole	6-13
Creating Rounds	6-13
Creating Basic Rounds	6-14
Creating a Variable Radius Round	6-22
Points to Remember While Creating Rounds	6-23
Creating Chamfers	6-23
Corner Chamfer	6-23
Edge Chamfer	6-24
Understanding Ribs	6-29
Creating Trajectory Ribs	6-29
Creating Profile Ribs	6-30
Editing Features of a Model	6-32
Editing Definition or Redefining Features	6-33
Reordering Features	6-33
Rerouting Features	6-35
Suppressing Features	6-35
Deleting a Feature	6-36
Modifying a Feature	6-36
Tutorial 1	6-38
Tutorial 2	6-47
Tutorial 3	6-53
Tutorial 4	6-58
Self-Evaluation Test	6-66
Review Questions	6-67
Exercise 1	6-68
Exercise 2	6-69
Exercise 3	6-69

Chapter 7: Options Aiding Construction of Parts-II

Creating Feature Patterns	7-2
Uses of Patterns	7-2
Creating Patterns	7-2
Deleting a Pattern	7-15

Copying Features	7-15
New Refs	7-15
Same Refs	7-16
Mirror	7-16
Move	7-17
Select	7-17
Mirroring a Geometry	7-18
Creating a Section of a Solid Model	7-18
Work Region Method	7-19
Tutorial 1	7-21
Tutorial 2	7-27
Tutorial 3	7-37
Tutorial 4	7-43
Self-Evaluation Test	7-58
Review Questions	7-59
Exercise 1	7-60
Exercise 2	7-61
Exercise 3	7-62
Exercise 4	7-63

Chapter 8: Advanced Modeling Tools-I

Other Protrusion Options	8-2
Sweep Features	8-2
Creating Sweep Protrusions	8-2
Sketching a Trajectory Aligned to an Existing Geometry	8-4
Creating a Sweep Feature by Selecting a Trajectory	8-5
Creating a Thin Sweep Protrusion	8-7
Creating a Sweep Cut	8-7
Blend Features	8-8
Parallel Blend	8-8
Rotational Blend	8-10
General Blend	8-12
Using Blend Vertex	8-12
Shell Feature	8-13
Creating a Constant Thickness Shell	8-14
Creating a Variable Thickness Shell	8-14
Datum Curves	8-16
Creating a Datum Curve by Using the Curve Button	8-16
Creating a Datum Curve by Sketching	8-19
Creating a Curve by Using the Intersect Option	8-19
Creating a Curve by Using the Project Option	8-20
Creating a Curve by Using the Wrap Option	8-23
Creating Draft Features	8-25
Tutorial 1	8-33
Tutorial 2	8-40
Tutorial 3	8-46

Tutorial 4	8-52
Self-Evaluation Test	8-57
Review Questions	8-57
Exercise 1	8-58
Exercise 2	8-59
Exercise 3	8-60
Exercise 4	8-61

Chapter 9: Advanced Modeling Tools-II

Advanced Feature Creation Tools	9-2
Variable Section Sweep Option	9-2
Swept Blend	9-6
Helical Sweep	9-9
Blend Section To Surfaces	9-11
Blend Between Surfaces	9-12
Tutorial 1	9-12
Tutorial 2	9-18
Tutorial 3	9-29
Tutorial 4	9-35
Self-Evaluation Test	9-38
Review Questions	9-39
Exercise 1	9-40
Exercise 2	9-40
Exercise 3	9-41

Chapter 10: Advanced Modeling Tools-III

Advanced Modeling Tools	10-2
Toroidal Bend	10-2
Spinal Bend	10-3
Warp	10-5
Transform Button	10-6
Warp Button	10-9
Spine Button	10-10
Stretch Button	10-11
Bend Button	10-12
Twist Button	10-13
Sculpt Button	10-14
Tutorial 1	10-16
Tutorial 2	10-21
Tutorial 3	10-24
Self-Evaluation Test	10-31
Review Questions	10-32
Exercise 1	10-32
Exercise 2	10-33

Chapter 11: Assembly Modeling

Assembly Modeling	11-2
Important Terms Related to the Assembly Mode	11-2
Top-down Approach	11-2
Bottom-up Approach	11-3
Placement Constraints	11-4
Package	11-4
Creating Top-down Assemblies	11-4
Creating Components in the Assembly Mode	11-4
Creating Bottom-up Assemblies	11-5
Inserting Components in an Assembly	11-5
Assembling Components	11-5
Displaying Components in a Separate Window	11-6
Displaying Components in the Same Window	11-6
Applying Constraints	11-6
Change orientation of constraint button	11-11
Status Area	11-11
Placement Tab	11-11
Move Tab	11-12
Packaging Components	11-13
Creating Simplified Representations	11-15
Redefining the Components of an Assembly	11-19
Reordering Components	11-19
Suppressing/Resuming Components	11-19
Replacing Components	11-20
Assembling Repeated Copies of a Component	11-20
Modifying the Components of an Assembly	11-22
Modifying Dimensions of a Feature of a Component	11-22
Redefining a Feature of a Component	11-22
Creating the Exploded State	11-22
References Tab	11-25
Offset Tab	11-25
Explode Line Tab	11-26
The Bill of Materials	11-26
Tutorial 1	11-28
Tutorial 2	11-41
Self-Evaluation Test	11-51
Review Questions	11-52
Exercise 1	11-53
Exercise 2	11-56

Chapter 12: Generating, Editing, and Modifying Drawing Views

The Drawing Mode	12-2
Generating Drawing Views	12-4
Generating the General View	12-4

Generating the Projection View	12-6
Generating the Detailed View	12-7
Generating the Auxiliary View	12-8
Generating the Revolved Section View	12-8
Generating the Copy and Align View	12-19
Generating the 3D Cross-Section View	12-20
Editing the Drawing Views	12-22
Moving the Drawing View	12-22
Erasing the Drawing View	12-23
Deleting the Drawing View	12-23
Adding New Parts or Assemblies to the Current Drawing	12-23
Modifying the Drawing Views	12-24
Changing the View Type	12-24
Changing the View Scale	12-25
Reorienting the Views	12-25
Modifying the Cross-sections	12-25
Modifying Boundaries of Views	12-25
Adding or Removing the Cross-section Arrows	12-25
Modifying the Perspective Views	12-26
Modifying Other Parameters	12-26
Editing the Cross-section Hatching	12-26
Tutorial 1	12-26
Tutorial 2	12-35
Self-Evaluation Test	12-41
Review Questions	12-42
Exercise 1	12-43

Chapter 13: Dimensioning the Drawing Views

Dimensioning the Drawing Views	13-2
Show Model Annotations Dialog Box	13-2
Adding Notes to the Drawing	13-4
Adding Tolerances in the Drawing Views	13-5
Dimensional Tolerances	13-5
Geometric Tolerances	13-5
Editing the Geometric Tolerances	13-10
Adding Balloons to the Assembly Views	13-10
Adding Reference Datums to the Drawing Views	13-10
Modifying and Editing Dimensions	13-12
Modifying the Dimensions Using the Dimension Properties Dialog Box	13-12
Modifying the Drawing Items Using the Shortcut Menu	13-17
Cleaning Up the Dimensions	13-17
Tutorial 1	13-20
Tutorial 2	13-27
Self-Evaluation Test	13-31
Review Questions	13-32
Exercise 1	13-33

Chapter 14: Other Drawing Options

Sketching in the Drawing Mode	14-2
Modifying the Sketched Entities	14-3
User-Defined Drawing Formats	14-7
Retrieving the User-Defined Formats in the Drawings	14-8
Adding and Removing Sheets in the Drawing	14-9
Creating Tables in the Drawing Mode	14-10
Generating the BOM and Balloons in Drawings	14-11
Tutorial 1	14-14
Tutorial 2	14-25
Self-Evaluation Test	14-34
Review Questions	14-35
Exercise 1	14-36

Chapter 15: Surface Modeling

Surface Modeling	15-2
Creating Surfaces in Pro/ENGINEER	15-2
Creating an Extruded Surface	15-2
Creating a Revolved Surface	15-3
Creating a Sweep Surface	15-4
Creating a Blended Surface	15-4
Creating a Swept Blend Surface	15-5
Creating a Helical Sweep Surface	15-5
Creating a Surface by Blending the Boundaries	15-6
Creating a Surface Using the Variable Section Sweep	15-8
Creating Surfaces the Using the Style Environment of Pro/ENGINEER	15-9
Style Tools Toolbar	15-9
Surface Editing Tools	15-16
Mirroring the Surfaces	15-16
Merging the Surfaces	15-17
Trimming the Surfaces	15-18
Creating the Fill Surfaces	15-19
Creating the Intersect Curves	15-19
Creating the Offset Surfaces	15-21
Adding Thickness to a Surface	15-24
Converting a Surface into a Solid	15-25
Creating a Round at the Vertex of a Surface	15-25
Tutorial 1	15-25
Tutorial 2	15-35
Self-Evaluation Test	15-43
Review Questions	15-43
Exercise 1	15-44
Exercise 2	15-45

Chapter 16: Working with Sheetmetal Components

Introduction to Pro/Sheetmetal	16-2
Invoking the Sheetmetal Mode	16-2
Introduction to Sheetmetal Walls	16-3
Creating the Unattached Flat Wall	16-4
Creating the Unattached Revolve Wall	16-5
Creating the Unattached Blend Wall	16-6
Creating the Unattached Offset Wall	16-8
Creating Reliefs in Sheetmetal Components	16-9
Creating a Flat Wall	16-11
Creating a Twist Wall	16-14
Creating an Extend Wall	16-16
Creating a Flange Wall	16-17
Creating the Bend	16-21
Creating the Unbend	16-25
Creating the Bend Back	16-26
Creating the Conversion	16-27
Creating Cuts in the Sheetmetal Components	16-30
Creating the Flat Pattern	16-30
Tutorial 1	16-31
Tutorial 2	16-40
Self-Evaluation Test	16-47
Review Questions	16-48
Exercise 1	16-48
Exercise 2	16-49

Index   1

Preface

Pro/ENGINEER WILDFIRE 5.0

Pro/ENGINEER, developed by Parametric Technology Corporation, is one of the world's fastest growing solid modeling softwares. Being a parametric feature-based solid modeling tool, it not only unites the 3D parametric features with 2D tools, but also addresses every design-through-manufacturing process. Based mainly on the feedback of the users of solid modeling, this tool is remarkably user-friendly and it allows you to be productive from day one.

This solid modeling tool allows you to easily import the standard format files with an amazing compatibility.

The 2D drawing views of the components are automatically generated in the **Drawing** mode. Using this software, you can generate detailed, orthographic, isometric, auxiliary, and section views. Additionally, you can use any predefined drawing standard files for generating the drawing views. You can display the model dimensions in the drawing views or add reference dimensions whenever you want. The bidirectionally associative nature of this software ensures that any modification made in the model is automatically reflected in the drawing views. Similarly, any modification made in the dimensions of the drawing views is automatically updated in the model.

The **Pro/ENGINEER Wildfire 5.0 for Designers** textbook has been written with the intention of helping the readers effectively use Pro/ENGINEER Wildfire 5.0. The textbook is written with the tutorial-point-of-view and the learn-by-doing theme. The mechanical engineering industry examples and tutorials are used in this textbook to ensure that the users can relate the knowledge of this book with the actual mechanical industry designs. The salient features of this textbook are as follows:

- **Tutorial Approach**

    The author has adopted the tutorial point-of-view and the learn-by-doing theme throughout the textbook. This approach guides the users through the process of creating the models in the tutorials.

- **Real-World Projects as Tutorials**

    The author has used the real-world mechanical engineering projects as tutorials in this textbook so that the reader can correlate them with the real-time models in the mechanical engineering industry.

- **Tips and Notes**
    Additional information related to various topics is provided in the form of tips and notes.

- **Learning Objectives**
    The first page of every chapter summarizes the topics that will be covered in that chapter. This helps the users to easily refer to a topic.

- **Self-Evaluation Test, Review Questions, and Exercises**
    Every chapter ends with a Self-Evaluation test so that the users can assess their knowledge of the chapter. The answers to the Self-Evaluation test are given at the end of the chapter. Also, the Review Questions and Exercises are given at the end of each chapter and they can be used by the Instructors as test questions and exercises.

- **Heavily Illustrated Text**
    The text in this book is heavily illustrated with the help of around 1400 line diagrams and screen capture images that support the tools section and tutorials.

- **Free Companion Website**
    This is an educational resource that is tailored to increase the motivation to learn Pro/ENGINEER Wildfire 5.0. The additional resources for this textbook can be downloaded from the following website: www.cadcim.com

    In this website you will find the resources that aids learning Pro/ENGINEER Wildfire 5.0. If you are a faculty member, please contact the publisher at sales@cadcim.com or the author at stickoo@calumet.purdue.edu to access the Web site that contains teaching resources:

Free Teaching and Learning Resources provided in Companion Website

- **Instructor's Guide:**
    Answers to review questions and solution for exercise are provided only for faculties.

- **PowerPoint Presentations:**
    The contents of the book are arranged in slides so that can be used for your lectures.

- **Drawing Files**
    The drawing files used in illustration and examples are available for free download. For faculty the models used in exercises are also available for free download.

- **Additional Students Projects**
    For the students to practice what they learnt, a set of projects are provided for free download.

Chapter 1

Introduction to Pro/ENGINEER Wildfire 5.0

Learning Objectives

After completing this chapter, you will be able to:
- *Understand the advantages of using Pro/ENGINEER Wildfire 5.0.*
- *Understand the bidirectional associative property.*
- *Know the system requirements of Pro/E.*
- *Learn various important terms and definitions in Pro/E.*
- *Learn various important options in the File menu.*
- *Understand the importance of Model Tree.*
- *Understand the functions of mouse buttons.*
- *Learn about the default toolbars.*
- *Understand the functions of browser.*
- *Understand the Appearance Gallery.*
- *Understand the rendering stages in Pro/ENGINEER.*
- *Change the color scheme of the background in Pro/ENGINEER.*

INTRODUCTION TO Pro/ENGINEER Wildfire 5.0

Welcome to Pro/ENGINEER Wildfire 5.0. If you are a new user of Pro/ENGINEER software package, you are going to join hands with thousands of users of this high-end CAD/CAM/CAE tool worldwide. If you are a user of the previous releases of this software, you are going to upgrade your designing skills with the tremendous improvement in this latest release.

Pro/ENGINEER Wildfire 5.0 is a powerful software used to create complex designs with great precision. The design intent of any three-dimensional (3D) model or an assembly is defined by its specification and its use. You can use the powerful tools of Pro/ENGINEER Wildfire 5.0 to capture the design intent of any complex model by incorporating intelligence into the design. Once you understand the feature-based, associative, and parametric nature of Pro/ENGINEER Wildfire 5.0, you can appreciate its power as a solid modeler.

To make the designing process simple and quick, this software package has divided the steps of designing into different modules. This means each step of the designing is completed in a different module. For example, generally a design process consists of the following steps:

- Sketching using the basic sketch entities.
- Converting the sketch into features and parts.
- Assembling different parts and analyzing them.
- Documenting parts and the assembly in terms of drawing views.
- Manufacturing the final part and assembly.

All these steps are divided into different modes of Pro/ENGINEER Wildfire 5.0; namely, the **Sketch** mode, **Part** mode, **Assembly** mode, **Drawing** mode, and **Manufacturing** mode.

Despite making various modifications in a design, the parametric nature of this software helps preserve the design intent of a model with tremendous ease. Pro/ENGINEER allows you to work in a 3D environment and calculates the mass properties directly from the created geometry. The new feature in this release includes dynamic editing of features, which makes editing easier. You can also switch to various display modes like wireframe, shaded, hidden, and no hidden at any time with ease as it does not affect the model but changes the appearance of the model only. The new release of Pro/ENGINEER Wildfire enables the real-time rendering of solid models. Also, new appearances and scenes have been added to the library. It also includes shadows, reflections, perspective views and animations of the exploded state.

FEATURE-BASED NATURE

Pro/ENGINEER Wildfire 5.0 is a feature-based solid modeling tool. A feature is defined as the smallest building block and any solid model created in Pro/ENGINEER Wildfire 5.0 is an integration of a number of these building blocks. Each feature can be edited individually to bring in any change in the solid model. The use of the feature-based property provides greater flexibility to the parts created. For example, consider the part shown in Figure 1-1. It consists of a counterbore hole at the center and six counterbore holes around it at some Bolt Circle Diameter (BCD).

Introduction to Pro/ENGINEER Wildfire 5.0

Now, consider a case where you need to change all the outer counterbore holes to drill holes keeping the central counterbore hole and the BCD for the outer holes same. Also, you need to change the number of holes from six to eight. In a nonfeature-based software package, you need to delete the entire part and then create a new part as per the new specifications.

Whereas, Pro/ENGINEER Wildfire 5.0 allows you to make this modification by just modifying some values in the same part, see Figure 1-2. This shows that the solid parts created in Pro/ENGINEER Wildfire 5.0 are a combination of various features that can be modified individually at any time.

Figure 1-1 Model displaying the counterbore holes   *Figure 1-2* Model after making the modifications

BIDIRECTIONAL ASSOCIATIVE PROPERTY

There is bidirectional associativity between all modes of Pro/ENGINEER Wildfire 5.0. The bidirectional associative nature of a software package is defined as its ability to ensure that if any modifications are made in a particular model in one mode, the corresponding modifications are also reflected in the same model in other modes. For example, if you make any change in a model in the **Part** mode and regenerate it, the changes will also be highlighted in the **Assembly** mode. Similarly, if you make any change in a part in the **Assembly** mode, after regeneration, the change will also be highlighted in the **Part** mode. This bidirectional associativity also correlates the two-dimensional (2D) drawing views generated in the **Drawing** mode and the solid model created in the **Part** mode of Pro/ENGINEER Wildfire 5.0. This means that if you modify the dimensions of the 2D drawing views in the **Drawing** mode, the change will be automatically reflected in the solid model and also in the assembly after regeneration. Likewise, if you modify the solid model in the **Part** mode, the changes will also be seen in the 2D drawing views of that model in the **Drawing** mode. Thus, bidirectional associativity means that if any modification is made to any one application, it changes the output of all the other modes related to the model. This nature relates the various modes in Pro/ENGINEER.

Figure 1-3 shows the drawing views of the part shown in Figure 1-1 generated in the **Drawing** mode. The views show that the part consists of a counterbore hole at the center and six counterbore holes around it.

Now, when the part is modified in the **Part** mode, the modifications are automatically reflected in the **Drawing** mode, as shown in Figure 1-4. The views in this figure show that all outer counterbore holes are converted into drilled holes and the number of holes is increased from six to eight.

Figure 1-3 Drawing views of the model before modifications

Figure 1-5 shows the Crosshead assembly. It is clear from the assembly that the diameter of the hole is more than what is required (shown using dotted lines). In an ideal case, the diameter of the hole should be equal to the diameter of the bolt.

The diameter of the hole can be changed easily by opening the file in the **Part** mode and making the necessary modifications in the part. This modification is reflected in the assembly, as shown in Figure 1-6. This is due to the bidirectional associative nature of Pro/ENGINEER.

Since all modes of Pro/ENGINEER Wildfire 5.0 are interrelated, it becomes very easy to modify your model at any time. This makes the application software more user-friendly.

Introduction to Pro/ENGINEER Wildfire 5.0

Figure 1-4 Drawing views of the model after modifications

Figure 1-5 Diameter of the hole and the bolt

Figure 1-6 Model after modifying the diameter of the hole

PARAMETRIC NATURE

Pro/ENGINEER Wildfire 5.0 is parametric in nature, which means that the features of a part become interrelated if they are drawn by taking the reference of each other. You can redefine the dimensions or the attributes of a feature at any time. The changes will propagate automatically throughout the model. Thus, they develop a relationship among themselves. This relationship is known as the parent-child relationship. So if you want to change the placement of the child feature, you can make alterations in the dimensions of the references and hence change the design as per your requirement. The parent-child relationship will be discussed in detail while discussing the datums in later chapters.

SYSTEM REQUIREMENTS

The system requirements for Pro/ENGINEER Wildfire 5.0 are given below.

1. Operating System: Windows XP Home Edition, XP Professional Edition, XP Professional x64 Edition, Windows Vista (Professional, Ultimate, and Enterprise Editions), Solaris (64 bit only).

2. Monitor: 1280 x 1024 (or higher) resolution support with 24-bit or more.

3. Processor: 500MHz minimum (2.4GHz or higher recommended).

4. Memory: 256MB RAM minimum (1024MB or higher recommended).

Introduction to Pro/ENGINEER Wildfire 5.0

5. Swap Memory: 500MB minimum (2048MB or higher recommended).

6. Hard disk space: 2.00GB minimum (3.0GB or higher recommend).

7. An ethernet adapter interface card or network card.

8. Microsoft approved 3-button mouse.

9. Microsoft Internet Explorer 6.0 or later.

GETTING STARTED WITH Pro/ENGINEER Wildfire 5.0

Once you have installed Pro/ENGINEER Wildfire 5.0 on your system, there are two options to start it. The first option is to choose the **Start** button at the lower left corner of the screen and then choose **Programs > PTC > Pro ENGINEER > Pro ENGINEER**, as shown in Figure 1-7.

Figure 1-7 Windows screen with the task bar and application icons

The second option to start Pro/ENGINEER Wildfire 5.0 is by double-clicking on its shortcut icon on the desktop of the computer. Note that the icon will be created on the desktop only if the option for displaying the icon on the desktop is selected while installing the software.

Figure 1-8 shows the screen that appears when you start Pro/ENGINEER Wildfire 5.0.

Figure 1-8 Initial screen appearance after starting Pro/ENGINEER Wildfire 5.0

IMPORTANT TERMS AND DEFINITIONS
Some important terms that will be used in this book while working with Pro/ENGINEER Wildfire 5.0 are discussed next.

Entity
An element of section geometry is called an entity. The entity can be an arc, line, circle, point, conic, coordinate system, and so on. When one entity is divided at a point, then the total number of entities is said to be two.

Dimension
It is the measurement of one or more entities.

Constraint
Constraints are logical operations that are performed on the selected geometry to make it more accurate in defining its position and size with respect to the other geometry.

Parameter
It is defined as a numeric value or any definition that defines a feature. For example, all dimensions in a sketch are parameters. The parameters can be modified at any time.

Introduction to Pro/ENGINEER Wildfire 5.0

Relation
A relation is an equation that relates two entities.

Weak Dimensions and Weak Constraints
Weak dimensions and weak constraints are temporary dimensions or constraints that appear in gray color. These are automatically applied to the sketch when it is drawn using the **Intent Manager**. They are removed from the sketch without any confirmation from the user. The weak dimensions or the weak constraints should be changed to strong dimensions or constraints if they seem to be useful for the sketch. This only saves an extra step of dimensioning the sketch or applying constraints to it.

Strong Dimensions and Strong Constraints
Strong dimensions and strong constraints appear in white color. These dimensions and constraints are not removed automatically. All dimensions added manually to a sketch are strong dimensions.

> **Tip**: *When several strong dimensions or constraints conflict, Pro/ENGINEER makes the constraints and dimensions appear in red color, and prompts you to delete one or more of them.*

FILE MENU OPTIONS
The options that are displayed when you choose **File** from the menu bar are discussed next.

Set Working Directory
A working directory is a directory on your system where you can save the work done in the current session of Pro/ENGINEER Wildfire 5.0. You can set any directory existing on your system as the working directory. Before starting the work in Pro/ENGINEER Wildfire 5.0, it is important to specify the working directory. If the working directory is not selected before saving an object file, then the object file will be saved in a default directory. This default directory is set at the time of installing Pro/ENGINEER Wildfire 5.0. If the working directory is selected before saving the object files that you create, it becomes easy to organize them. In Pro/ENGINEER Wildfire 5.0, the working directory can be set in two ways:

Using the Navigator
When you start a Pro/ENGINEER Wildfire 5.0 session, the navigator is displayed on the left of the drawing area. This navigator can be used to select a folder and set it as the working directory.

Right-click on the folder that you need to set as the working directory; a shortcut menu will be displayed, as shown in Figure 1-9. Choose the **Set Working Directory** option from this shortcut menu to set the selected folder as the working directory. To make a new folder, choose the **New Folder** option from the shortcut menu.

Figure 1-9 Shortcut menu

Using the Select Working Directory Dialog Box

To specify a working directory, choose **File > Set Working Directory** from the menu bar; the **Select Working Directory** dialog box will be displayed, as shown in Figure 1-10. Using this dialog box, you can set any directory as the working directory.

Figure 1-10 The **Select Working Directory** *dialog box*

Choose the arrow at the upper left corner of the dialog box, as shown in Figure 1-11; the flyout will be displayed. This flyout displays some of the drives present on your computer along with the **Favorites** folder, as shown in Figure 1-11. The **Favorites** folder contains all directories that you saved as favorites. The procedure to save the favorite directories will be discussed later. When the **Select Working Directory** dialog box is invoked by default, it displays the contents of the default directory. However, you can change the default directory that appears every time you open this dialog box. Various options in the **Select Working Directory** dialog box are discussed next.

Figure 1-11 *The flyout with some drives*

Introduction to Pro/ENGINEER Wildfire 5.0   1-11

> **Tip**: *The **Select Working Directory** dialog box has some of the properties of the Microsoft Windows operating system. You can set the working directory using this dialog box by browsing through directories and folders. You can also rename a file, directory, or a folders name in this dialog box. You can create a new directory using this dialog box.*

File name
The **File name** edit box displays the name of the directory selected in the **Select Working Directory** dialog box. You can select a directory using the flyout as discussed earlier or enter the path of any existing directory in this edit box.

Type
The **Type** drop-down list has two options, **Directories** and **All Files**. If you select the **Directories** option, all directories present are listed, and if you select the **All Files** option, then all files along with the directories are listed in the dialog box.

Organize
When you choose the **Organize** button from the **Select Working Directory** dialog box, a flyout will be displayed. The options in this flyout are used to create a new directory or rename an existing directory. You can also cut, copy, paste, and delete the existing folders using the options in the flyout. Moreover, you can add any existing folder in the **Common Folders** by using the **Add to common folders** option in this flyout, refer to Figure 1-12.

*Figure 1-12 The **Organize** button flyout*

Views
When you choose the **Views** button from the **Select Working Directory** dialog box, a flyout will be displayed. The options in this flyout are discussed next.

> **List**. The **List** option is used to view the contents of the current folder or drive. These include files and folders in the form of a list.

> **Details**. The **Details** option is used to view the contents of the current folder or drive in the form of a table, which displayed the name, size, and date on which it was last modified.

Tools
When you choose the **Tools** button from the **Select Working Directory** dialog box, a flyout will be displayed, as shown in Figure 1-13. The options in this flyout are discussed next.

*Figure 1-13 The **Tools** flyout*

Address Default. When you select this option, the **'Look In' Default** dialog box will be displayed. Figure 1-14 shows this dialog box with the options in the drop-down list. If you select the **Default** option from the drop-down list and then invoke the **File Open** dialog box, it will display the directory that is set as default. If you select the **Working Directory** option from the drop-down list and then invoke the **File Open** dialog box, it will display the working directory that is set. If you select the **In Session** option and then invoke the **File Open** dialog box, the **File Open** dialog box will open with the **In Session** folders selected by default. Similarly, you can set the **Pro/Library** as the working directory.

*Figure 1-14 The **'Look In' Default** dialog box with options in the drop-down list*

Up One Level. The **Up One Level** option allows you to move one level up in the directory. Choose this option; a directory that is one level above the current directory will be displayed. Alternatively, press ALT+Up arrow keys to move one level up. You can also choose the arrow button on the left of the required directory in the address bar to display all folders in it.

Add to Favorites. The **Add to Favorites** option allows you to add the folders in the **Favorites** folder.

Remove from Favorites. The **Remove from Favorites** option allows you to remove the folders from the **Favorites** folder. This option is not enabled by default. To enable this option, you first need to add the folder in the **Favorites** folder using the **Add to Favorites** option.

Sort By. In the **Select Working Directory** dialog box, the **Directories** option in the **Type** drop-down list is displayed by default. From this drop-down list, if you select the **All Files** option and then choose the **Tools** button; a flyout will be displayed with the **Sort By** option.

The **Sort By** option is used to list all files in the directory in an order to facilitate the process of searching a file. When you choose the **Sort By** option, a cascading menu is displayed. In the cascading menu, there are two options, **Model Name** and **Markup/Instance Name**. If you choose the **Model Name** option, the file list will be sorted out alphabetically by the model name in the **Select Working Directory** dialog box. The **Markup/Instance Name** option sorts out the file list by specific markups or instance names in the **Select Working Directory** dialog box.

Common Folders and Folder Tree

The **Common Folders** and **Folder Tree** tabs are available on the left of the **Select Working Directory** dialog box. The **Common Folders** contains folders such as **Desktop**, **My Documents**, **Computer, Working Directory**, and **Favorites**. You can add more folders in the **Common Folders** by using the **Add to common folders** option available in the options of the **Organize** button. The **Folder Tree** contains all the drives available on your computer along with their contents. You can also set the working directory by using the **Folder Tree**. By default, the **Folder Tree** is in the collapsed state. To expand it, you need to click on the arrow that is available on the left of the **Folder Tree**. The **Working Directory** and **Favorites** folders available in the **Common Folders** are discussed next.

Working Directory. This folder is used when you have already set the working directory. You may browse through the directories in the **Select Working Directory** dialog box, but when you choose this folder, the directory selected previously as the working directory is displayed in the list box.

Favorites. This folder is used to save the location of the directories that are to be used frequently. You just need to specify the working directory to be used frequently and save its location by selecting the **Favorites** folder.

If you want to select one of the favorite working directories, then select the **Favorites** folder from the **Common Folders**; the list of all directories that were saved as favorites will be displayed in the list box. Select the required favorite directory and choose **OK**; the selected favorite directory will be set as the current working directory.

Note
*An object in Pro/ENGINEER Wildfire 5.0 is defined as a file that is created using any of its modes such as **Part**, **Drawing**, **Sketch**, and so on.*

New

To create a new object, choose **New** from the **File** menu or choose the **New** button from the **Top Toolchest**; the **New** dialog box will be displayed, as shown in Figure 1-15. This dialog box displays various modes available in Pro/ENGINEER Wildfire 5.0. In this dialog box, by default, the **Part** mode radio button is selected and a default name of the object file is displayed in the **Name** edit box. You can also enter a as desired new name for the object file.

When you select the **Part**, **Assembly**, or **Manufacturing** radio button in this dialog box, the subtypes of the respective modes will be displayed under the **Sub-type** area of this dialog box.

Accept the default settings in the **New** dialog box by choosing the **OK** button; the **New File Options** dialog box will be displayed, as shown in Figure 1-16. Using this dialog box, you can select the predefined templates in Pro/ENGINEER Wildfire 5.0 or create a user-defined template. You can also open an empty template provided in the **New File Options** dialog box. In this case, you need to create the datum planes and the coordinate systems manually.

If, the measuring units for creating models is inches. Select **inlbs_part_solid** from the list in the **Template** area and then choose **OK** from the **New File Options** dialog box. On doing so, the three default datum planes and a coordinate system will be displayed in the drawing area. Also, the **Model Tree** will appear on the left of the screen, as shown in Figure 1-17.

*Figure 1-15 The **New** dialog box*

*Figure 1-16 The **New File Options** dialog box*

Open

The **Open** button is used to open an existing object file. When you choose the **Open** option from the **File** menu or choose the **Open** button from the **File** toolbar in the **Top Toolchest**, the **File Open** dialog box will be displayed, as shown in Figure 1-18. The selected working directory will be displayed in it. Note that the **Preview** area is not displayed by default. To view the **Preview** area, choose the **Preview** button. Most of the options in this dialog box are the same as discussed in the **Select Working Directory** dialog box. The rest of the options in this dialog box are discussed next.

Tools

When you choose this button, a flyout will be displayed. The options available in this flyout are the same as the options discussed in the **Tools** button of the **Select Working Directory** dialog box, except the **All Versions** and **Show Instances** options. These two options are discussed next.

All Versions

This option, when selected, displays all versions of an object file. In Pro/ENGINEER Wildfire 5.0, the file once saved will generate a new version of it with an extension 1. An object file is not copied on another object file but a new version of it is created. Therefore, every time you save an object using the **Save** option, a new version of it is created on the disk in the current working directory.

Introduction to Pro/ENGINEER Wildfire 5.0

Figure 1-17 The initial screen appearance after entering the **Part** mode

Figure 1-18 The **File Open** dialog box with the **Preview** area

Show Instances
The **Show Instances** option, when selected, displays all instances of the object file. Select the required file and then select the **Show Instances** option from the **Tools** button; all the instance of the selected file will be displayed.

File name
In the **File name** edit box, you can enter the name of the existing object file that you want to open.

Type
The **Type** drop-down list contains the file formats of various modes available in Pro/ENGINEER Wildfire 5.0. Also, it contains other file formats that can be imported in Pro/ENGINEER Wildfire 5.0. These file formats include IGES, SET, STEP, DWG/DWF, Medusa, Inventor, Parasolid, Rhino, and so on. By default, the **Pro/ENGINEER Files** option is selected in this drop-down list. As a result, you can open the files created in any mode of Pro/ENGINEER. However, if you select a specific mode from this drop-down list, only the files of the corresponding mode will be displayed. For example, if you select **Part** in the drop-down list, then only the *.prt* files will be displayed. This makes the selection and opening of the files easy.

Preview
The **Preview** button is used to preview the model to be opened. By choosing this button, you can preview the selected model in the **File Open** dialog box. This feature of the **File Open** dialog box helps in previewing the model before actually opening it. You can zoom, pan and rotate the model in the preview. Also, you can change the appearance (shaded, wireframe, no hidden, and hidden line) of the model, switch the model between the orthographic and perspective views, change the orientation type (dynamic, anchored, delayed, velocity, fly through, and standard) of the model, set the number of frames per second, and refit the preview in the preview screen.

> **Note**
> *Assembly files with the file extension .asm can also be previewed by using the **Preview** button. If you are not able to see the preview of the assembly files in the preview area, then choose the **Refresh** button on the upper right of the **File Open** dialog box to resize the assembly according to the preview area.*
>
> *There is no Command prompt in Pro/ENGINEER Wildfire 5.0. However, you are provided with prompts in the message area. Whenever you have to enter any numerical value or text, a **Message Input Window** will be displayed in the message area.*

In Session
The **In Session** folder is available in the **Common Folders**, on the upper left of the **File Open** dialog box. When you choose the **In Session** folder, all the object files that are in the current session will be displayed in the display area. The object files that you open in Pro/ENGINEER Wildfire 5.0 in the current session are stored in its temporary memory. This temporary memory is stored in a folder named **In Session**. Once you exit Pro/ENGINEER Wildfire 5.0, the contents of this folder are deleted automatically. However, the original files are not removed from their actual location.

Erase

The **Erase** option is used to delete the files from the temporary memory stored in the **In Session** folder. To invoke this option, choose **File > Erase** from the menu bar; a cascading menu will be displayed with three options, **Current**, **Not Displayed**, and **Component Reps**. As discussed earlier, all files opened in a session of Pro/ENGINEER Wildfire 5.0 are saved in the temporary memory. You can use the **Erase** option to erase files from the temporary memory. The options that are displayed in the cascading menu are discussed next.

Current

The **Current** option is used to erase the file opened and displayed in the drawing area. On choosing this option, the **Erase Confirm** message box will be displayed, prompting you to confirm the erasing of the file, as shown in Figure 1-19.

*Figure 1-19 The **Erase Confirm** message box*

Not Displayed

This option is used to erase the files that are in the **In Session** folder, but not displayed presently on the screen. On choosing this option, the **Erase Not Displayed** dialog box will be displayed, as shown in Figure 1-20. You can select the files from this dialog box to erase them.

Component Reps

This option removes the unused simplified representations from the **In Session** folder. When you choose this option from the **File** menu, a message will be displayed with the message, All the objects which were not displayed have been erased.

*Figure 1-20 The **Erase Not Displayed** dialog box*

Delete

This option removes the selected file permanently from the hard disk. To invoke this option, choose **File > Delete** from the menu bar. The cascading menu is displayed with two options, **Old Versions** and **All Versions**.

> **Tip**: *Suppose you open an assembly that has a component named Nut. Close the assembly and now open another assembly that has a component named Nut. Now, there are chances that the second assembly you choose to open may open with the Nut that was present in the previous assembly. This is because the component with the file named Nut was already present in the memory of Pro/ENGINEER (in session) before opening the second assembly.*
>
> *To avoid this error of assemblies, you should erase the files in the current session of Pro/ENGINEER before opening the second assembly.*

Old Versions

This option is used to delete all old versions of the current file. When you choose the **Old Versions** option, you are prompted to enter the name of the object file of which the old versions have to be deleted. When the **Message Input Window** is displayed, enter the object file name in this window. All versions of that file will be deleted from the hard disk except the latest version.

All Versions

This option is used to delete all versions including the current file from the hard disk. When you choose the **All Versions** option, a warning is displayed stating that performing this function can result in the loss of data. This option is chosen when the file is opened and is displayed in the drawing area.

Save

The **Save** option is used to save the objects present in the **In Session** folder or an object in the drawing area. When you choose the **Save** option from the **File** menu or the **Save** button on the **File** toolbar, the **Save Object** dialog box will be displayed. Also, the name of the current object will be displayed in the **Model Name** edit box. Choose the **OK** button from the **Save Object** dialog box to save the object.

> **Note**
> *Remember that all object files saved using the **Save** option in the **File** menu should be present in the **In Session** folder. Otherwise, Pro/ENGINEER Wildfire 5.0 will display an error informing you that the file does not exist in the current session.*
>
> *It should be noted here that the file opened currently on the screen may not be in the **In Session** folder, but in the current session. So, the file will be saved without any error.*

Save a Copy

The **Save a Copy** option is used to save a copy of the current object in the same working directory or in some other directory. When you choose this option from the **File** menu, the **Save a Copy** dialog box will be displayed and you need to specify the new name of the object file to be saved as a copy and the name of the target directory in the **Save a Copy** dialog box. You can browse through the directories and select the target directory. The file will be saved in the selected directory.

Using this option, you can also export a file in other file formats such as Inventor file, pdf, ACIS, Wavefront file, and so on. After specifying the name of the new file and the target directory, choose the file format in which you want to export the file from the **Type** drop-down list in the **Save a Copy** dialog box.

Backup

The **Backup** option of the **File** menu is used to create a backup copy of an object file in memory. When you choose this option, the **Backup** dialog box will be displayed, as shown in Figure 1-21.

*Figure 1-21 The **Backup** dialog box*

In the **Model Name** edit box, the name of the file for which you want to take a backup is displayed. In the **Backup To** edit box, the name of the directory is specified where the object will be saved as a backup. If you create the backup of an assembly or a drawing object, Pro/ENGINEER Wildfire 5.0 will save all its dependent files in the specified directory. For example, if you create the backup of a drawing file in a different directory, then the part file of the drawing will also be created automatically in the same directory where backup of the drawing file is created.

Rename

The **Rename** option in the **File** menu is used to rename the currently active object on the screen. To rename an object, choose this option; the **Rename** dialog box will be displayed, as shown in Figure 1-22. Specify the new name of the object in the **New Name** edit box and choose **OK**.

*Figure 1-22 The **Rename** dialog box*

MANAGING FILES

As discussed earlier, a new file is generated whenever you save an object. The number of files generated is directly proportional to the number of times you save that object. So, these files occupy a lot of disk space. The latest version of the object is of use and should be stored. Latest version refers to the highest number that is suffixed with the file name of that object. The rest of the files called old versions should be deleted from the hard disk, if they are not required.

> **Note**
> *To save disk space, you should keep deleting the old versions of a file. This is done using the* **Delete** *option in the* **File** *menu.*

MENU MANAGER

The **Menu Manager** contains a set of menus and submenus cascaded in it. It is displayed for some particular tasks only. For example, if you choose **Edit > Feature Operations** from the menu bar, the **Menu Manager** will be displayed with options to reorder, copy, move, or mirror features. Note that the display of the menus depends on the task chosen.

While using the **Menu Manager**, always complete the option selected by choosing **Done** or **Done Sel** after the current task is over. This is important when you are in the **Drawing** mode of Pro/ENGINEER. If you are directly selecting one option after another, then it is easy to lose track of commands or options in the **Menu Manager**.

MODEL TREE

The **Model Tree** stores and displays all features in a chronicle. You can select any desired feature of a model or an assembly from the **Model Tree** and apply different operations on the selected feature. You can also select the feature by right-clicking on it; a shortcut menu will be displayed. Move the cursor on the shortcut menu and choose the required option from it by using the left mouse button.

When you create a new object file, the **Model Tree** appears and is attached to the drawing area by default. But in this case, the **Model Tree** is attached to the drawing area, and so the drawing area becomes small. You can hide the **Model Tree** by clicking the sash on the right edge of the navigator, as shown in Figure 1-23. The **Model Tree** can slide in or slide out, thus increasing or decreasing the area on the drawing area. It can also be stretched horizontally to cover the drawing area.

Figure 1-23 Partial view of the **Model Tree**

Introduction to Pro/ENGINEER Wildfire 5.0

Tip: *By looking at the **Model Tree**, you can understand the method and approach used to create the model. Using the **Model Tree**, you can modify the features of a model. Generally, when you import a model from a different file format in Pro/ENGINEER, you do not get the features of the model in the **Model Tree** and therefore, you will not be able to modify it.*

Note
*In Pro/ENGINEER, most of the features are created using the **Dashboard**. The **Dashboard** is displayed below the message area and it contains all options to complete the selected operation on the model.*

UNDERSTANDING THE FUNCTIONS OF THE MOUSE BUTTONS

While working with Pro/ENGINEER Wildfire 5.0, it is important to understand the function of the three buttons of the mouse to make efficient use of this device. The various combinations of the keys and three buttons of the mouse are listed below:

1. Figure 1-24 shows the functions of the left mouse button. The left mouse button is used to make a selection. Using CTRL+left mouse button, you can add or remove items from the selection set.

2. Figure 1-25 shows the functions of the right mouse button. The right mouse button is used to invoke the shortcut menus and to query select the items. When you bring the cursor on an item, it is highlighted in cyan color. Now if you hold down the right mouse button, a shortcut menu is displayed. Choose the **Pick From List** option from the shortcut menu; the **Pick From List** dialog box will be displayed. You can make selections from this dialog box.

Figure 1-24 Functions of the left mouse button   *Figure 1-25* Functions of the right mouse button

3. Figure 1-26 shows the functions of the middle mouse button in the 3D mode. The middle mouse button is used to spin the model in the drawing area and view it from different directions.

CTRL+middle mouse button is used to dynamically zoom in and out by moving the mouse. When you press and hold the CTRL key and move the mouse up, the view is reduced, and so you zoom out. When the mouse is moved down, the view is enlarged, and so you zoom in.

When you use CTRL+middle mouse button and move the mouse horizontally, the model is rotated about a point that you specified as center.

SHIFT+middle mouse button is used to pan the object on the screen.

4. Figure 1-27 shows the functions of the middle mouse button in the 2D mode (sketcher environment and **Drawing** mode). The middle mouse button is used to place dimensions in the drawing area. It is also used to confirm an option or to abort the creation of an entity.

The middle mouse button is used to pan in the **Sketch** mode and the **Drawing** mode.

Figure 1-26 *Functions of the middle mouse button in the 3D mode*

Figure 1-27 *Functions of the middle mouse button in the **Sketch** mode*

Note
*When you spin the model with the **Spin Center** on, the model is rotated about the spin center. If the spin center is turned off, then the model is rotated about the cursor.*

TOOLBARS

Before starting work on Pro/ENGINEER Wildfire 5.0, it is very important for you to understand the default toolbars and buttons in the main window. Figure 1-28 shows various default screen components in Pro/ENGINEER Wildfire 5.0.

In Pro/ENGINEER Wildfire 5.0, the toolbars are at two locations, the **Top Toolchest** and the **Right Toolchest**. The area on the top of the drawing area, where the toolbars are present, is called the **Top Toolchest** and the area on the right of the drawing area, where the toolbars are present, is called the **Right Toolchest.** The toolbars that initially appear on the screen are shown in the Figure 1-28. You will notice that all toolbar buttons are not available. These buttons

Introduction to Pro/ENGINEER Wildfire 5.0

are available after you open a new or an existing file. Only those buttons that are required for the current session are activated. As you proceed to enter one of the modes provided by Pro/ENGINEER Wildfire 5.0, you will notice that the toolbar buttons required by that mode are activated. To make the designing easy and user-friendly, this software package provides you with a number of toolbars. Different modes of Pro/ENGINEER Wildfire 5.0 display different toolbars. Some of the frequently used toolbars are shown in Figure 1-28.

Figure 1-28 Items in the main window

Datum Display Toolbar

Figure 1-29 shows the **Datum Display** toolbar. It has five buttons that are used to control the visibility of datum features like the planes, axes, and points. You can also use this toolbar to control the visibility of the coordinate systems and annotation element.

*Figure 1-29 The **Datum Display** toolbar*

> **Tip**: *To add buttons to the toolbar and add toolbars to the **Toolchest**, choose **Tools > Customize Screen** from the menu bar; the **Customize** dialog box is displayed. This dialog box is used to customize the main window of Pro/ENGINEER Wildfire 5.0.*
>
> *Right-click on the **Right Toolchest** to invoke a shortcut menu that has all the names of the toolbar, which are available for the current session. Select any toolbar to display it in the selected **Right Toolchest**.*

File Toolbar

The **File** toolbar has six buttons, as shown in Figure 1-30. These buttons are used to save a file, print the current file, open a new file, or open an existing file. The functions of the **Mail Recipient (as Attachment)** and **Mail Recipient (as Link)** buttons of this toolbar are discussed next.

*Figure 1-30 The **File** toolbar*

The **Mail Recipient (as Attachment)** button is used to send an email with the current model attached with the mail. When you choose this button, the **Send As Attachment** dialog box will be displayed, as shown in Figure 1-31. Next, choose the **OK** button to send the attachment. You can zip an attachment by selecting the **Create a ZIP file containing the attachment** check box.

*Figure 1-31 The **Send As Attachment** dialog box*

The **Mail Recipient (as Link)** button is used to send an email with a link to the current model. This button is available to the users of Windchill.

Help Button

This button, as shown in Figure 1-32, is also known as the **What's This?** button. When you choose this button, a question mark symbol (?) is attached to the cursor. Depending on the location in the main window where you click, the **Pro/ENGINEER Help** window with the help topics is displayed.

*Figure 1-32 The **Help** button*

Model Display Toolbar

Figure 1-33 shows the **Model Display** toolbar. This toolbar has five buttons that are used to set the display mode for viewing a model. The **Wireframe** button is used to display the model as a wireframe model. The visible and the invisible edges of the model will be displayed in this mode. The **Hidden line** button is used to display the visible lines of the model in bright color and the hidden lines in dull

*Figure 1-33 The **Model Display** toolbar*

Introduction to Pro/ENGINEER Wildfire 5.0

color. However, if you plot the model in this display mode, you will notice that the hidden lines are shown as dashed lines in the plot. The **No hidden** button is used to display only the visible edges of the model. When the **Shading** display mode is chosen, the model is displayed as shaded using a default color. However, you have the flexibility to alter the color of your model according to your needs. The last button available in this toolbar is **Enhanced Realism**. This is a toggle button, which enables or disables the realtime rendering as per requirement. The realtime rendering includes the effect of reflections, shadow, and light. You will learn about them later in the chapter.

> **Note**
> *The **Enhanced Realism** button will be available only when you are working on a 3d mode such as the **Part**, **Assembly** or **Manufacturing**.*

View Toolbar

The **View** toolbar, shown in Figure 1-34, has eleven buttons. The first button is **Repaint**, which is used for repainting the screen. This means you can remove any temporary information from the drawing area. The second button is **Spin Center**, which is used to toggle on/off the visibility of the spin center. The third button is **Orient Mode**. This button, when chosen, turns on or off the visibility of the datums and allows you to spin the model using the middle mouse button. The fourth button, **Appearance Gallery**, is newly added in this release and is used to set the appearances of the model. The fifth and sixth buttons are used to zoom in and zoom out the object, respectively. These buttons will be discussed in Chapter 2. The **Refit** button is used to fit the model on the screen. The **Reorient** button is used to orient the model. The next button is **Named View List**, is used to display the saved views. The **Layers** button displays the layers in the navigation area. The **View Manager** button is used to save, retrieve, or delete a view.

*Figure 1-34 The **View** toolbar*

> **Note**
> *If you want to change the predefined unit system, choose **File > Properties** from the menu bar to display the **Model Properties** dialog box. In this dialog box, click on the **change** link on the right of the **Units** option under the **Materials** head; the **Units Manager** dialog box will be displayed with the **System of Units** tab chosen. Next, select the desired unit system from the list box and then choose the **Set** button; the **Changing Model Units** message box will be displayed. Choose the **OK** button message box; the new unit system will be set and displayed with the red arrow on the left.*

NAVIGATOR

The navigator is present on the left of the drawing area and can slide in or out on the drawing area. To make the navigator slide in or out, you need to select the sash present on its right edge. A partial view of the navigator is shown in Figure 1-35. It has the following functions:

1. When you browse files using the navigator, the browser expands and the files in the selected folder are displayed in the browser.

2. When you open a model, the **Model Tree** is displayed in the navigation area.

3. The buttons on the top of the navigator are used to display the different items in the navigation area. The **Model Tree** button is used to display the **Model Tree** in the navigation area. This button is available only when a model is opened. The **Folder Browser** button is used to display the folders that are in the local system. The **Favorites** button is used to display the contents of the **Personal Favorites** folder.

Figure 1-35 Partial view of the navigator

4. Any other locations, if available on your system, can also be accessed by using the navigator.

BROWSER

The Browser is present on the right of the navigator. It can slide in and out of the navigator and can also be stretched horizontally. When the Pro/ENGINEER Wildfire 5.0 session starts, the browser is displayed on the screen. The browser has two tabs. The homepage is linked to *ptc.com*, by default, and the other tab is linked to the PTC's online resources. You can add more tabs in it, switch between tabs, and view the browsing history similar to any other internet explorer. The main advantage of using this browser is that you can work on the Pro/ENGINEER files and navigate through the browser, simultaneously. Figure 1-36 shows the browser with some part files displayed in it. You can also browse to the required folder, change the display of files to thumbnails for previewing the file, dynamically view the models in a pop-up window, or drag and drop the selected file into the Pro/ENGINEER window,

Figure 1-36 Pro/ENGINEER Wildfire 5.0 browser

The functions of the browser are listed next.

1. It is used to preview the Pro/ENGINEER Wildfire 5.0 files and browse the file system.

2. A Pro/ENGINEER file can be opened by using the browser by double-clicking on the file or by dragging it to the drawing area. When you open a file using the browser, the model is displayed on the screen and the browser is closed automatically.

3. You can access the Pro/ENGINEER user community site.

4. You can connect to your client's computer and jointly work with them using the Browser.

APPEARANCE GALLERY

A new library of appearances and real world material have been added in Pro/ENGINEER Wildfire 5.0. You can also add shadows and reflections to the background. This is useful while rendering with a background image. This gives a realistic view of the model.

The **Appearance Gallery** button is available in the **View** toolbar of the **Top Toolchest**. It is used to assign different colors to the model and change its appearances. To change the appearance of the model, click on the down arrow beside the **Appearance Gallery** button;

a palette will be displayed, as shown in Figure 1-37. Select the required appearance from the palette; the **Select** box will be displayed. Select the entities whose appearance you want to change; the appearance of the entities will change. You can assign appearance to the entire model or to the individual face of the model, or entire assembly or individual component of an assembly. Various areas and options in the palette are discussed next.

Search

This option is used for searching any specific appearance you need. To search an appearance, type a keyword related to the appearance to be searched in the **Search** text box and press ENTER; all the appearances matching with the keyword will be searched from all the system libraries and then displayed in the palette. For example, if you type **glass** in the text box, then **ptc-glass** will be displayed in the **My Appearances** area and the **Glass** library is displayed in the **Library** area.

View Options

You can set the display of the appearance icons in the palette by using the **View Options** flyout. These options will be available when you click on the button at the top-right corner of the palette. The icons can be displayed as small thumbnails, large thumbnails, both names and thumbnails, or only names. To set the display of icons, invoke the **View Options** flyout and then choose the required option from it. Choose **Rendered Samples** from this to view the rendered icons of appearances. In this flyout, the **Show Tooltips** option is chosen by default. As a result, tooltips are always displayed for appearances.

Figure 1-37 Appearance Gallery

Clear Appearance

This option is used to remove the selected appearance from the model. To do so, select the appearance and then choose this option. Alternatively, first choose this option and then select the appearance to be removed from the model.

To remove all appearances assigned to a model, click on the black arrow displayed besides the **Clear Appearance** button; a flyout will be displayed. Next, choose the **Clear All Appearances** option from this flyout.

My Appearance

The **My Appearance** area displays all appearances stored in the startup directory. You can also add new appearances to the palette, edit the existing appearance, or delete the selected appearance in the **Appearance** area. To do so, right-click on an appearance icon and then choose the required option from the shortcut menu displayed. Note that you cannot delete the active appearance.

Model

The **Model** area consists of the appearances stored and used in an active model. You can edit the selected appearance, add new appearances, or select the objects to apply the selected appearance by using the shortcut menu as discussed in the **My Appearance** area.

Library

This area displays the predefined appearances in the current library. The library contains appearances from the System library and the Photolux library. Appearances in the library are grouped in various classes such as metals, glass, wood, and so on, based on their similar characteristics. The name of the current library is displayed on the right of the **Library** head. To assign appearances from other libraries, click on the library name; a flyout will be displayed with a tree list of classes and libraries. Browse through the tree and select the required library; all appearances in the selected library will be listed. From the list displayed, you can assign an appearance to the model as well as create a new appearance, as discussed earlier.

More Appearances

Choose the **More Appearances** button; the **Appearance Editor** will be displayed, as shown in Figure 1-38. The **Appearance Editor** provides options for editing the appearance and advanced rendering, thereby providing much more realistic images.

Using the **Appearance Editor**, you can edit the name, description, and keywords of the selected appearance, except the default one. The advanced options are given under two tabs, **Basic** and **Map**. The **Basic** tab provides with various classes and sub-classes of appearances. By default, **Generic** is selected in the **Class** drop-down list. However, you can select the required class and their sub-classes. Also, the properties related to selected class such as color, illumination, reflection, transparency, glossiness, and so on are displayed in the **Properties** area. These properties can be modified by adjusting the sliders given next to them.

The **Map** tab allows you to define and apply texture such as wood, fabrics, metals, and so on to the model. You can preview the changes made to the model on changing the settings in the **Appearance Editor**.

Edit Model Appearances

Choose this button; the **Model Appearance Editor** will be displayed. In this editor, all appearances used in the model will be displayed with their properties. The **Model Appearance Editor** is the same as the **Appearances Editor**. Using this editor, you can modify the properties such as color, texture, shininess, and glossiness.

Figure 1-38 The Appearance Editor

Appearances Manager

Choose this button to display the **Appearances Manager** window. The **Appearances Manager** window displays two panels. The left panel displays the palette with appearances and libraries and the right panel displays the editor with the properties of the active appearance. You can set the required settings in the **Appearances** palette and the **Appearances Editor**. Also, you can open an existing library file, add and save your own textured file.

RENDERING IN Pro/ENGINEER Wildfire 5.0

Rendering is a process of generating two-dimensional image of a three-dimensional scene or an object to make it more realistic. A rendered image makes it easier for visualizing the shape and size of 3D object as compared to a wireframe or a shaded image. Rendering also helps you express your design intent to other people. You need to alter environments, lights, textures, and so on to get a high quality rendered image.

Generally, the rendering process includes the following stages:

Loading a File

The first step is to load a solid model or an assembly to be rendered.

Applying Appearances

Next step is to apply the appearances to the model. You can do so by using the **Appearance Gallery**, which has already been discussed.

Applying Scenes

After applying the appearances, you need to apply scenes to the model. Scenes are the predefined render settings that include lights, rooms, and environmental effects. To set scenes, choose **View > Model Setup > Scene** from the menu bar; the **Scenes** window will be displayed, as shown in Figure 1-39. Using this window, you can apply the predefined settings, edit the current settings, create new scenes, copy a scene, and save the scenes for future use. To apply a scene to the model, double-click on the required scene from the **Scene Gallery** area of the **Scenes** window.

Creating the Rendering Room

A room sets the stage for rendering the model. The room can be cylindrical or rectangular. To create a rendering room, choose the **Room** tab from the **Scenes** window. Using the options in the **Room** tab, you can apply appearances to the wall, ceiling, and floor of the room, set the room orientation with respect to the model, adjust the size of the room and create a background to the room, if required.

Defining Lights

The next step is to define the lighting effects on the model. Adding lights to the model, illuminates the model from various angles. To add lights, choose the **Lights** tab from the **Scenes** window. You can create a light source as well as position them by using the options in the **Lights** tab.

*Figure 1-39 The **Scenes** window*

Shadows get enabled as soon as you add lights to the model. The direction of shadows cast by a light bulb, spot light, skylight or environment type of lights is towards the center of the room.

Adding Effects
Finally, you can add the surrounding effects such as reflection, tone mapping, background, and depth of field. The tone of the image or scene can be set as per the presets such as **Studio Settings**, **Indoor Settings**, and **Outdoor Settings**.

Setting the Perspective View
You can set the perspective view of the model that can be used for rendering the model. To do so, choose **View > Model Setup > Perspective view** from the menu bar. To set the desired angle, invoke the **Perspective** dialog box by choosing **View > Model Setup > Perspective Settings** from the menu bar. Using this dialog box, you can adjust the perspective view settings such as **Walk Through**, **Fly Through**, **From To**, and **Follow Path**. You can also adjust the amount of perspective for viewing the model by adjusting the eye distance and the focal length.

Render the Model

The last step is to render the model. To render the model, choose **View > Model Setup > Render Setup** from the menu bar; the **Render Setup** window will be displayed. Set the required rendering options in this dialog box. Next, you need to render the model with the specified settings. To do so, choose **View > Render Window** from the menu bar. If required, modify the render settings and render the model again.

> **Note**
> *You can toggle between the display of the rendering effects on the model by choosing the **Enhanced Realism** button in the **Model Display** toolbar.*

COLOR SCHEME USED IN THIS BOOK

Pro/ENGINEER allows you to use various color schemes as the background screen color, and also for displaying the entities on the screen. This textbook will follow the white background of Pro/ENGINEER environment for the purpose of printing. However, for better understanding and clear visualization at various places, this book will follow other color schemes too. To change the color scheme of the background screen, choose **View > Display Settings > System Colors** from the menu bar; the **System Colors** window will be displayed, as shown in Figure 1-40. Choose the **Edit** button on the right of the **Blended Background** check box; the **Blended Color** window will be displayed. Choose the color swatch beside the **Top** option to invoke the **Color Editor**. Next, set the R, G, B colors by using the slider bar to extreme right for changing the color to white and then close the **Color Editor**.

Similarly, change the color of the Bottom to white. Choose **OK** from the **Blended Color** window as well as from the **System Colors** window to accept the changes made and then exit the color scheme.

*Figure 1-40 The **System Colors** window*

Chapter 2

Creating Sketches in the Sketch Mode-I

Learning Objectives

After completing this chapter, you will be able to:
- *Use various tools to create geometry.*
- *Dimension a sketch.*
- *Apply constraints to a sketch.*
- *Modify a sketch.*
- *Use the Modify Dimensions dialog box.*
- *Edit the geometry of a sketch by trimming.*
- *Mirror a sketch.*
- *Insert standard/user-defined sketches.*
- *Use the drawing display options.*

THE SKETCH MODE

Almost all models designed in Pro/ENGINEER Wildfire 5.0 consist of datums, sketched features, and placed features. For creating datums and placed features, you do not need to draw sketches. However, to create a three-dimensional (3D) feature, it is necessary to draw its two-dimensional (2D) sketch. When you enter the **Part** mode and select the options to create any sketched feature, the system automatically takes you to the sketcher environment. In the sketcher environment, the sketch of the feature is created, dimensioned, and constrained. The sketches created in the **Sketch** mode are stored in the *.sec* format. Then you return to the **Part** mode to create the required feature.

Note
You will learn about datums and placed features in later chapters.

In Pro/ENGINEER Wildfire, a sketch can be drawn in the **Sketch** mode or in the sketcher environment. A designer can draw a 2D sketch of the product and assign the required dimensions and constraints to it. By assigning the dimensions, the designer can make sure that the 2D sketch of the product or model is satisfying the necessary conditions; then continue to create the 3D model of the product in the **Part** mode.

Working with the Sketch Mode

To create any section in the **Sketch** mode of Pro/ENGINEER Wildfire 5.0, certain basic steps have to be followed. The following points outline the steps to draw a sketch in the **Sketch** mode:

1. Sketch the required section geometry
The different sketcher tools available in this mode can be used to sketch the required section geometry.

2. Add the constraints and dimensions to the sketched section
While sketching the section geometry, weak constraints and dimensions are automatically added to the section. The sketch can also be dimensioned and constrained manually. The dimensions that are applied manually are called strong dimensions. After adding the dimensions, you can modify them as required.

3. Add relations to the sketch if needed
The geometry of the sketch can be controlled by adding relations.

4. Regenerate the section
If the sketch is fully dimensioned and constrained, the sketch is automatically regenerated. Throughout this book, it is assumed that you are sketching in the **Sketch** mode with the **Intent Manager** on. Pro/ENGINEER has the capability to analyze the section, and if the section is not complete for any reason, the section will not be regenerated. You will learn about these reasons as you go through this chapter.

Tip: *Throughout this book, the sketcher environment is referred to the environment in Pro/ENGINEER where you can draw 2D geometries. Apart from the **Sketch** mode, the sketcher environment can be accessed in other modes of Pro/ENGINEER.*

Creating Sketches in the Sketch Mode 2-3

Invoking the Sketch Mode

To invoke the **Sketch** mode, choose **New** from the **File** menu or choose the **New** button from the **File** toolbar; the **New** dialog box will be displayed with other Pro/ENGINEER modes. Select the **Sketch** radio button to start a new file in the **Sketch** mode, see Figure 2-1; a default name of the sketch file appears in the **Name** edit box. You can change the sketch name as required and then choose the **OK** button to enter the **Sketch** mode.

Figure 2-1 The **New** dialog box

THE SKETCHER ENVIRONMENT

When you invoke the **Sketch** mode, the initial screen appeared is similar to the one shown in Figure 2-2. This figure also shows the **Sketcher Tools** toolbar that will be displayed on the right side of the drawing area. The buttons in this toolbar are used to draw sketches. The drawing tools are also available in the **Sketch** menu in the menu bar. When you enter the sketcher environment, the **Intent Manager** is turned on by default. Also, when you are in the selection mode, shortcut menus can be invoked by holding down the right mouse button in the drawing area. The options in these shortcut menus vary depending on the item selected. These shortcut menus also contain the tools to draw the sketches.

Note
*Datum planes are not displayed in the **Sketch** mode.*

*Figure 2-2 Initial screen appearance in the **Sketch** mode*

The navigator is displayed on the left of the drawing area. In navigator, the **Folder Browser** tab is activated by default. It covers a part of the drawing area and therefore, the drawing area is decreased. You can increase the drawing area by clicking on the navigator sash, which is present on the right edge of the navigator.

Note
*The **Folder Browser** tab is divided into two sections, **Common Folders** and **Folder Tree**. The functions of the **Common Folders** and the **Folder Tree** sections have already been discussed in Chapter 1.*

WORKING WITH A SKETCH IN THE SKETCH MODE

When you invoke the sketcher environment, the **One-by-One** button is chosen by default, in the **Sketcher Tools** toolbar. If this button is chosen, the sketcher environment is said to be in the selection mode. In the selection mode, you can select entities of the sketch to edit or to invoke the shortcut menu. The options in the shortcut menu can be used to apply various operations on the selected item.

Note
The sketch is saved with a .sec file extension.

You can create a simple sketch by using the options available in the shortcut menu. To invoke

Creating Sketches in the Sketch Mode

the shortcut menu, hold down the right mouse button in the drawing area. Note that, once the shortcut menu will be displayed, the right mouse button can be released.

DRAWING A SKETCH USING THE SKETCHER TOOLS TOOLBAR

When you are in the sketcher environment, the **Sketcher Tools** toolbar, available on the **Right Toolchest**, contains the buttons to draw a sketch, dimension it, and modify the dimensions. In this section, you will learn how to draw sketched entities using the button available in the **Sketcher Tools** toolbar.

Placing a Point

Points are generally used for dimensioning the vertices that are removed while applying fillets. For example, if the sketch is to be dimensioned using these vertices, you need to place points on them before applying fillets. Now, since a point is placed at the vertex, you can easily use it for dimensioning the sketch. The following steps explain the procedure to sketch a point:

1. Choose the **Point** button from the **Sketcher Tools** toolbar; the system prompts you to select a location for the point.

2. As soon as you select the location of the point by clicking, the point is placed at the desired location in the drawing area.

Note
To increase the number of visible command prompt lines in the message area, select the bottom sash of the message area using the left mouse button and drag it downward, toward the screen.

When you place a single point, no dimensions appear. But, when you place two points, they are dimensioned with respect to each other.

Drawing a Line

To draw lines, there are four buttons in the **Sketcher Tools** toolbar. To view these buttons, choose the black arrow on the right of the **Line** button; a flyout will appear with four buttons. The first button is the **Line** button. This button is used to create a line by selecting two points in the drawing area. The second button in the flyout is the **Line Tangent** button. This button is used to create a tangent line between two entities. The third button is the **Centerline** button, which is used to create a centerline by selecting two points in the drawing area. Centerline is used for creating revolved features, mirroring, and so on. The fourth button is the **Geometry Centerline** button that enables you to create a centerline that can be referenced outside the sketcher environment.

The procedure to create lines by using these buttons is discussed next.

Drawing a Line Using the Line Button

The following steps explain the procedure to create a line using the **Line** button:

1. Choose the **Line** button. Click in the drawing area to start the line; a rubber-band line appears from the selected point with the other end attached to the cursor. The symbols **V** and **H** that appear while drawing the vertical and horizontal lines are called constraints. Constraints are discussed later in this chapter.

2. After specifying the start point for the line, move the cursor in the drawing area to a desired location and click to specify the endpoint of the line; the line appears in yellow color. The rubber-band line continues and you can draw the second line.

3. Repeat step 2 until all lines are drawn. You can end the line creation by pressing the middle mouse button. To abort the line creation, press the middle mouse button again.

Note
If you draw a single line, the color of the line drawn is red. If you draw multiple lines, the color is yellow.

After drawing a line, when you press the middle mouse button to end the line creation, the line drawn is highlighted in red color. In the sketcher environment, the red color of an entity indicates that it is selected. If you press the DELETE key, the line will be erased from the drawing area. After drawing a line, weak dimensions are applied to the sketch and they appear in gray color. These weak dimensions are applied automatically to the sketched entities as you draw them. The concept of weak dimensions is discussed later in this chapter.

Drawing a Line Using the Line Tangent Button

The **Line Tangent** button is used to draw a tangent line between two entities such as arcs, circles, splines, or a combination of these. The following steps explain the procedure to draw a tangent using this button:

1. Choose the black arrow on the right of the **Line** button and then choose the **Line Tangent** button from the **Sketcher Tools** toolbar; you will be prompted to select the start location on an arc or circle.

2. Select the first entity from where the tangent line will be drawn; a rubber-band line appends with the cursor. Also, you will be prompted to select the end location on an arc or circle. As soon as you select the second entity, a line that is tangent to both the selected entities is drawn.

Note
*Whenever you will be prompted to select an entity in the sketcher environment, the **Select** message box will be displayed. You can ignore this dialog box because it appears automatically and disappears without any confirmation.*

Drawing a Line Using the Centerline Button

You can draw horizontal, vertical, or inclined centerlines using the **Centerline** button. This button is available in the flyout that will be displayed when you choose the black arrow on the right of the **Line** button. The centerline in a sketch is used as an axis of rotation, for mirroring, aligning, and dimensioning entities.

Creating Sketches in the Sketch Mode

The steps discussed next explain the procedure to draw a centerline:

1. In the **Sketcher Tools** toolbar, choose the black arrow on the right of the **Line** button and then choose the **Centerline** button; you will be prompted to select the start point.

2. Click in the drawing area to specify the start point. Now, you will be prompted to select the end point.

3. Click in the drawing area to specify the endpoint; a centerline of infinite length is drawn.

Drawing a Line Using the Geometry Centerline Button

The **Geometry Centerline** button is used to create centerlines as a part of the geometry. The centerline created by using this button can be referenced outside the sketcher environment. The steps to create a geometry centerline by using the **Geometry Centerline** button are the same as that of using the **Centerline** tool. To invoke the **Geometry Centerline** tool, choose the black arrow on the right of the **Line** button and then choose the **Geometry Centerline** button from the flyout displayed. Next, specify the start and end points of the geometry centerline; a centerline of infinite length will be created in the drawing area.

Drawing a Rectangle

The following steps explain the procedure to create a rectangle using the **Rectangle** button:

1. Choose the **Rectangle** button from the **Sketcher Tools** toolbar; you will be prompted to select two points to indicate the diagonal of box. Click to specify the first point; a yellow rubber-band box appears with the cursor attached to the opposite corner of the box.

2. Move the cursor to the desired location in the drawing area and then click to specify the second point for the diagonal of the rectangle.

Drawing a Circle

In the **Sketcher Tools** toolbar, there are four buttons to draw a circle and two buttons to draw an ellipse. To view these buttons available for drawing circles and ellipses, choose the black arrow on the right of the **Center and Point** button; a flyout will appear with six buttons. The procedures to create a circle and an ellipse by using various buttons are discussed next.

Drawing a Circle Using the Center and Point Button

As the name suggests, the **Center and Point** button is used to draw a circle by specifying the center of the circle and a point on it. The following steps explain the procedure to draw a circle using this button.

1. Choose the **Center and Point** button; you will be prompted to select the center of a circle.

2. Click in the drawing area to specify the center point of the circle; you will be prompted to select a point on the circle. Also, a yellow rubber-band circle appears with the center at the specified point and the cursor attached to its circumference.

3. Move the cursor to specify the size of circle. Click to complete the creation of the circle; you will be prompted again to select the center of the circle.

4. Repeat steps 2 and 3 until you have drawn all required circles. If you want to abort the process of circle creation, press the middle mouse button.

Drawing a Construction Circle

A construction circle is a circle that is used to align entities, create diametrical or radial dimensions, and to reference the entities. Figure 2-3 shows an application of a construction circle. In the sketch of a flange, centers of the circles lie on a particular bolt circle diameter (BCD) that is defined using a construction circle.

To create a construction circle, draw a circle or select a previously drawn circle. Then, hold the right mouse button to invoke the shortcut menu, as shown in Figure 2-4. Choose the **Construction** option from the shortcut menu; the circle will appear dotted in yellow color, indicating that it is a construction circle.

Figure 2-3 Sketch of a flange

*Figure 2-4 The **Construction** option in the shortcut menu*

Drawing a Circle Using the Concentric Button

The following steps explain the procedure to draw a concentric circle using the **Concentric** button:

1. Choose the **Concentric** button from the flyout in the **Sketcher Tools** toolbar; you will be prompted to select an arc to determine the center. You can select an arc or a circle to specify the center point.

2. Click on an arc or a circle to determine the concentricity of the circle to be drawn. Move the mouse and click at the required location to specify the size of circle.

3. To finish the creation of the circle, press the middle mouse button.

Creating Sketches in the Sketch Mode

> **Tip**: *To convert a construction circle back to a geometric entity, select the construction circle and hold the right mouse button to invoke the shortcut menu. From the shortcut menu, choose the **Geometry** option.*

Drawing a Circle Using the 3 Point Button

The following steps explain the procedure to draw a circle using the **3 Point** button:

1. Choose the **3 Point** button from the flyout in the **Sketcher Tools** toolbar; you will be prompted to specify the first point on the circle.

2. Click to specify the first point at the desired location in the drawing area; you will be prompted to select the second point on the circle. Move the cursor and click to specify the second point in the drawing area.

3. As you select the second point, a yellow rubber-band circle appears with the cursor attached to it and you are prompted to select the third point. Move the mouse to size the circle and click to specify the third point; a circle is drawn and you are prompted again to select the first point on the circle to draw the next circle.

4. You can press the middle mouse button to finish the creation of the circle. Also, you can press the middle mouse button at any stage in the circle creation to abort it.

Drawing a Circle Using the 3 Tangent Button

The **3 Tangent** button is used to draw a circle tangent to three existing entities. This button references other entities to draw a circle. The circle created using this button is drawn irrespective of the points selected on the entities. The following steps explain the procedure to draw a circle using the **3 Tangent** button:

1. Choose the **3 Tangent** button from the flyout in the **Sketcher Tools** toolbar; you will be prompted to select the start location on an arc, circle, or line.

2. Select the first entity; the color of the entity changes to red and you will be prompted to select the end location on an arc, circle, or line. Select the second tangent entity; you will be prompted to select the third location on an arc, circle, or line. Select the third tangent entity; a circle tangent to these three entities is drawn.

3. To end the process of creating the circle, press the middle mouse button.

Drawing an Ellipse Using the Axis Ends Ellipse Button

The following steps explain the procedure to draw an ellipse by using the **Axis Ends Ellipse** button:

1. Choose the **Axis Ends Ellipse** button from the flyout in the **Sketcher Tools** toolbar; you will be prompted to select the start point of the major axis of the ellipse.

2. Click in the drawing area to specify the start point of the major axis; you will be prompted to select the endpoint of the major axis.

3. Click in the drawing area to specify the endpoint; a yellow rubber-band ellipse will appear with the cursor attached to it. Also, you will be prompted to select a point on the minor axis to define the ellipse.

4. Click to specify the point; an ellipse will be created. You can press the middle mouse button to end the creation of the circle.

Drawing an Ellipse Using the Center and Axis Ellipse Button

The following steps explain the procedure to draw an ellipse by using the **Center and Axis Ellipse** button:

1. Choose the **Center and Axis Ellipse** button from the flyout in the **Sketcher Tools** toolbar; you will be prompted to specify the center of the ellipse.

2. Click at the desired location in the drawing area to specify the center point; you will be prompted to select the endpoint of the major axis of the ellipse. Click in the drawing area to specify the point; a yellow rubber-band ellipse will appear with the cursor attached to the ellipse. Move the cursor in the drawing area to size the ellipse.

3. An ellipse is drawn when you click to specify the endpoint on the minor axis of the ellipse. The dimensions for the major radius and the minor radius will be displayed in gray color. The gray color indicates that the dimensions are weak.

Drawing an Arc

To draw an arc there are five buttons in the **Sketcher Tools** toolbar. To view them, choose the black arrow on the right of the **3-Point / Tangent End** button; the flyout appears with five buttons. The procedures to draw arcs using various buttons in the flyout are discussed next.

Drawing an Arc Using the 3-Point / Tangent End Button

The **3-Point / Tangent End** button is used to draw arcs that are tangent from the endpoint of an existing entity, or by defining three points in the drawing area.

When you choose this button to draw an arc from an endpoint, the **Target** symbol will be displayed as soon as you select an endpoint. This **Target** symbol is a green colored circle that is divided into four quadrants. The following steps explain the procedure to draw an arc from the endpoint of an existing entity by using this tool:

1. Choose the **3-Point / Tangent End** button from the **Sketcher Tools** toolbar; you will be prompted to select the start point of the arc.

2. Specify three points in the drawing area to draw an arc. If you want to draw an arc from the endpoint of an existing entity, select the endpoint of that entity. As soon as you select the endpoint, the **Target** symbol appears at the endpoint of the entity. Move the cursor along the tangent direction through a small distance, a yellow rubber-band arc appears with one end attached to the endpoint of the entity and the other end attached to the cursor. Note that when you move the cursor out of the **Target** symbol perpendicular to

Creating Sketches in the Sketch Mode 2-11

the endpoint, an arc is drawn by specifying three points. In this case, the rubber-band arc does not appear, as shown in Figure 2-5.

On the other hand, if you move the cursor out horizontally from one of the quadrants of the **Target** symbol, an arc is drawn tangent to the endpoint, as shown in Figure 2-6.

3. Move the cursor to the desired position in the drawing area to size the arc. Use the left mouse button to complete the arc.

Figure 2-5 *Cursor moved out of the* **Target** *symbol perpendicular to the endpoint*

Figure 2-6 *Cursor moved out of the* **Target** *symbol along the tangent direction*

Tip: *If you do not want to draw a tangent arc, move the cursor out of the* **Target** *symbol perpendicular to the endpoint.*

Drawing an Arc Using the Concentric Button

The **Concentric** button is used to draw an arc concentric to an existing arc. You will have to select an entity to which the arc will be concentric. The entity selected must be an arc or a circle. The following steps explain the procedure to draw an arc using this button:

1. Choose the black arrow on the right of the **3-Point / Tangent End** button, the flyout appear with five buttons. Choose the **Concentric** button from the flyout; you will be prompted to select an arc to determine the center of the arc to be created.

2. As you select an entity, a dotted circle will appear on the screen and you will be prompted to select the start point of the arc. Click to specify the startpoint; a yellow rubber-band arc will appear with one end attached to the start point. As you move the cursor, the length of the arc will change and you will be prompted to select the endpoint of the arc.

3. Click to specify the endpoint; the arc will be created.

You can continue drawing another arc or end the arc creation by pressing the middle mouse button.

Drawing an Arc Using the Center and Ends Button

The following steps explain the procedure to draw an arc using the **Center and Ends** button:

1. Choose the **Center and Ends** button from the flyout in the **Sketcher Tools** toolbar; you will be prompted to select the center of the arc.

2. Click to specify a center point for the arc in the drawing area; a yellow colored center mark appears at that point. Now, you will be prompted to select the start point of the arc. As you move the cursor, a dotted circle appears and is attached to the cursor.

3. Specify the start point of the arc on the circumference of the dotted circle; a yellow rubber-band arc will appear from the start point. The length of this arc will change dynamically as you move the cursor and you will be prompted to select the endpoint of the arc.

4. Move the cursor to size the arc and then click to select the endpoint of the arc; an arc will be drawn between the two specified points.

Note

You can draw only one arc with one center. If you want to draw another arc, you will have to select the center again.

Drawing an Arc Using the 3 Tangent Button

The **3 Tangent** button is used to draw an arc that is tangent to three selected entities. The following steps explain the procedure to draw an arc using this button:

1. Choose the black arrow on the right of the **3-Point / Tangent End** button and then choose the **3 Tangent** button from the flyout in the **Sketcher Tools** toolbar; you will be prompted to select the start location on an arc, circle, or line.

2. As soon as you select the first entity, the color of the entity changes to red and you will be prompted to select the end location on an arc, circle, or line.

3. After doing so, you will be prompted to select a third location on an arc, circle, or line. Select the third entity; an arc is drawn tangent to the three selected entities.

You can continue drawing arcs or press the middle mouse button to abort arc creation.

Drawing an Arc Using the Conic Button

The **Conic** button is used to draw a conic arc. The following steps explain the procedure to draw a conic arc using this button:

1. Choose the **Conic** button from the flyout in the **Sketcher Tools** toolbar; you will be prompted to specify the first endpoint of the conic entity.

2. Click to specify the first point in the drawing area; you will be prompted to specify the second endpoint of the conic entity.

Creating Sketches in the Sketch Mode   2-13

3. Click to specify the second endpoint; a centerline is drawn between the two points and you will be prompted to specify the shoulder point of the conic. Specify a point on the screen; the conic arc is drawn.

Note
If you delete the centerline of the conic arc, the arc will not be deleted.

Note that if the conic arc is the only entity in the drawing area, then you cannot delete its centerline.

DIMENSIONING THE SKETCH

After you draw a sketch, the next step involves the dimensioning of the sketch. The basic purpose of dimensioning in Pro/ENGINEER is to control the size of the sketch and to locate it with some reference. In Pro/ENGINEER, a sketch cannot be regenerated unless it is fully dimensioned and constrained. The phrase "the sketch cannot be regenerated" means that the sketch is not accepted by Pro/ENGINEER.

By default, sketched entities are dimensioned and constrained automatically while sketching. However, sometimes you need to add additional dimensions to the sketch. The **Normal** button in the **Sketcher Tools** toolbar is used to manually dimension the entities. You can also choose **Sketch > Dimension** from the menu bar to display a cascading menu, as shown in Figure 2-7. This menu contains different dimensioning options.

Figure 2-7 Dimensioning options

Note
*When the intent manager is off, the dimensions and constraints are not automatically applied. You need to manually add the dimensions by choosing the **Dimension** option from the **Sketch** menu.*

Converting a Weak Dimension into a Strong Dimension

As discussed earlier, when you draw a sketch, some weak dimensions are automatically applied to the sketch. As you proceed to complete the sketch, these dimensions are automatically deleted from the sketch without any confirmation.

Select a weak dimension from the drawing area; the selected dimension will be highlighted in red. Press and hold the right mouse button to invoke the shortcut menu, as shown in Figure 2-8. Choose the **Strong** option from the shortcut menu and then click outside using the middle mouse button. Alternatively, press CTRL+T to convert the selected dimension to a strong dimension.

You can also choose **Edit > Convert To > Strong** from the menu bar; the color of the selected dimension is changed from gray to orange, indicating that the selected dimension is made permanent.

Figure 2-8 Shortcut menu to convert the weak dimensions to strong

Dimensioning a Sketch Using the Normal Button or the Normal Option

The **Normal** button or the **Normal** option is used for normal dimensioning of the sketch. The following steps explain the procedure to dimension a sketch using this option:

1. Choose the **Normal** button from the **Sketcher Tools** toolbar. Click on the entity you want to dimension; the color of the entity changes from yellow to red.

2. Move the cursor and place the dimension at the desired place by pressing the middle mouse button. You can modify the dimension values using the modifying options that will be discussed later in this chapter.

The remaining options in the cascading menu are not used while sketching and they are discussed in Chapter 3.

DIMENSIONING THE BASIC SKETCHED ENTITIES

Choose the **Normal** button and follow the procedures given below to dimension the sketched entities.

Linear Dimensioning of a Line

You can dimension a line by selecting its endpoints or by selecting the line. After selecting the two endpoints or the line, press the middle mouse button to place the dimension. If the line is inclined and you select the two endpoints to dimension, then the location where you press the middle mouse button is important, because it defines the orientation of the dimension that will be displayed on the screen.

Figure 2-9 shows the three possible orientations of dimension that can be displayed when you dimension a line.

Note
It is not possible to dimension a line in three orientations simultaneously in the sketcher environment. The dimensions in Figure 2-9 are shown for explanation purpose only.

Angular Dimensioning of an Arc

To add angular dimension to an arc, select both ends of the arc by pressing the left mouse button and then select a point on the arc. Next, place the dimension at the desired point by pressing the middle mouse button. The dimension, as shown in Figure 2-10, is displayed. You can modify the dimension using tools that are discussed later.

Diameter Dimensioning

For diameter dimensioning, click on a circle twice. Then place the dimension at the desired location by pressing the middle mouse button. The diameter dimension will be displayed, as shown in Figure 2-11. The same diameter dimensioning technique can also be used for arcs.

Creating Sketches in the Sketch Mode   2-15

Figure 2-9 Approximate locations of the cursor to achieve different dimensions

Figure 2-10 Angular dimensioning

Figure 2-11 Diameter dimensioning

Radial Dimensioning

For radial dimensioning, click on the entity once. Then, place the dimension at the desired location by pressing the middle mouse button. The radial dimension will be displayed, as shown in Figure 2-12.

Dimensioning Revolved Sections

Revolved sections are used to create revolved features such as flanges, couplings, and so on. To dimension a revolved section, click on the entity to be dimensioned. Next, select the centerline about which you want the section to be revolved. Once again, select the original entity that you want to dimension. Now, place the dimension at the desired location by pressing the middle mouse button. The dimension will be displayed, as shown in Figure 2-13. This dimension represents the diameter of a revolved section.

Figure 2-12 Radial dimensioning

Figure 2-13 Dimensioning the revolved sections

Tip: *To add dimension to a revolved section, you can also first select the centerline, next the entity to dimension, and then again the centerline.*

WORKING WITH CONSTRAINTS

In Pro/ENGINEER, the entities in a sketch have to be fully specified in terms of size, shape, orientation, and location. This is achieved by setting constraints. Using constraints in a sketch reduces the number of dimensions in that sketch.

Constraints are the logical operations that are performed on the selected geometry to make it more accurate in defining its position with respect to the other geometry. For example, if a line is nearly parallel to another line, Pro/ENGINEER snaps the parallel line and displays the parallel constraint symbol. Now, if you confirm the line creation, the line is drawn parallel to the other line. You can also apply constraints manually.

Types of Constraints

There are two types of constraints in Pro/ENGINEER, **Geometry** constraints and **Assembly** constraints. Here, you will learn about the **Geometry** constraints and the **Assembly** constraints will be discussed in later chapters.

To apply constraints manually, choose the arrow on right of the **Vertical** button from the **Sketcher Tools** toolbar; a flyout will be displayed as shown in Figure 2-14.

This flyout is used to apply constraints manually. Although the constraints are applied automatically as you draw the sketch, you can use this flyout if you want to manually apply additional constraints to the sketch. The constraints in the flyout are discussed next.

Figure 2-14 Flyout displayed on choosing the arrow on the right of the **Vertical** button

Creating Sketches in the Sketch Mode

Vertical

This constraint forces the selected line segment to become a vertical line. This constraint also forces the two vertices to be placed along a vertical line.

Horizontal

This constraint forces the selected line segment or two vertices that are apart by some distance to become horizontal or to lie in a horizontal line.

Perpendicular

This constraint forces the selected entity to become normal to another selected entity.

Tangent

This constraint forces the two selected entities to become tangent to each other.

Mid-point

This constraint forces a selected point or vertex to lie on the middle of a line.

Coincident

This constraint performs three functions. This constraint can be used to force the two selected points to become coincident to constrain a point on the selected entity, and to make two selected entities collinear, so that they lie on the same line. This constraint aligns two vertices or entities.

Symmetric

This constraint makes a section symmetrical about the centerline. When you select this constraint, you will be prompted to select a centerline and two vertices to make them symmetrical.

Equal

This constraint forces any two selected entities to become equal in dimension. When you select this constraint, you will be prompted to select two lines to make their lengths equal, or you will be prompted to select two arcs, circles, or ellipses to make their radii equal.

Parallel

This constraint is used to force two lines to become parallel. When selected, this constraint prompts you to select two entities that you want to make parallel.

Disabling the Constraints

The need to disable a constraint arises when you are drawing an entity. For example, consider a case where you want to draw a circle at some distance apart from another circle. While drawing it, the system tends to apply the equal radius constraint when the sizes of the two circles become equal. At this moment, if you do not want to apply the equal radius constraint, right-click twice to disable the equal radius constraint; a red line / will appear across the symbol. However, if you right-click once, the constraint will get locked and a circle will appear as its symbol.

MODIFYING THE DIMENSIONS OF A SKETCH

There are four ways to modify the dimensions of a sketch. These methods are discussed next.

Using the Modify Button

You can select one or more dimensions from the sketch to modify them. When you select dimension(s) from a sketch, they are highlighted in red. If you want to select more than one dimension, hold the CTRL key and select the dimensions by clicking on them. You can also use the CTRL+ALT+A keys or define a window to select the dimensions in the sketch. Next, choose the **Modify** button from the **Sketcher Tools** toolbar to modify the dimensions; the **Modify Dimensions** dialog box will be displayed, as shown in Figure 2-15.

To modify dimensions by using this dialog box, you can either enter a value in the edit box or use the thumbwheel available on the right of the edit box. The **Sensitivity** slider is used to set the sensitivity of the thumbwheel.

By default, the **Regenerate** check box is selected. As a result, any modifications in the dimensions are automatically updated in the sketch. If you want to modify the dimensions of the sketch without regenerating the sketch you need to clear this check box. If this check box is cleared, the dimensions will not be modified until you exit this dialog box. This means that Pro/ENGINEER allows you to make multiple modifications before updating the sketch.

*Figure 2-15 The **Modify Dimensions** dialog box*

Note
*It is recommended that you clear the **Regenerate** check box and then modify the dimensions if you need to modify more than one dimension. Also, when the dimensions you specify vary drastically with the original ones.*

The **Lock Scale** check box is used to lock the scale of the selected dimensions. After locking the scale, if you modify any dimension, all other dimensions will also be modified by the same scale.

Using the Edit Menu

The **Modify** option in the **Edit** menu in the menu bar can be used to modify the dimensions. Choose the **Modify** option from the **Edit** menu; the **Select** dialog box will appear on the right of the screen. Now, you can select a dimension from the sketch to modify it. When you select a dimension, the **Modify Dimensions** dialog box will be displayed. By default, the **Regenerate** check box is selected. As a result, the sketch will be regenerated dynamically as you modify the dimension.

Creating Sketches in the Sketch Mode

Modifying a Dimension by Double-Clicking on it

You can also modify a dimension by double-clicking on it. When you double-click on a dimension, the pop-up text field appears. Enter a new dimension value in this field and press ENTER or use the middle mouse button. Remember that you can select a dimension only when you choose **One-by-One** button from the **Sketch Tools** toolbar.

Modifying Dimensions Dynamically

In the sketcher environment, Pro/ENGINEER is always in the selection mode, unless you have invoked some other tool. When you bring the cursor to an entity, the color of the entity changes to cyan. Now, if you hold down the left mouse button, you can modify the entity by dragging the mouse. You will notice that as the entity is modified, the dimensions referenced to the selected entity are also modified.

RESOLVE SKETCH DIALOG BOX

While applying constraints or dimensions, sometimes the system may prompt you to delete one or more highlighted dimensions or constraints. This is because while adding dimensions or constraints, some strong dimensions or constraints conflict with the existing dimensions or constraints. As soon as, a conflict occurs, the **Resolve Sketch** dialog box is displayed, as shown in Figure 2-16 and the constraints or dimensions that conflict are displayed in red. When you select a dimension or a constraint from the **Resolve Sketch** dialog box, the corresponding dimension or constraint in the drawing area is enclosed in a blue box. The buttons in the **Resolve Sketch** dialog box are discussed next.

Undo

When you choose the **Undo** button, the section is brought back to the state that was just before the conflict occurred.

Delete

The **Delete** button is used to delete a selected dimension or constraint that is enclosed within the blue box. Select the dimension or the constraint to delete before you choose the **Delete** button from the **Resolve Sketch** dialog box.

*Figure 2-16 The **Resolve Sketch** dialog box*

Dim > Ref

On choosing the **Dim > Ref** button, the selected dimension is converted to a reference dimension.

> **Note**
> *The reference dimensions are used only for reference. They do not participate in the feature creation.*

Explain

When you choose the **Explain** button, the system provides you with the information about the selected constraint or dimension. The information will be displayed in the message area.

DELETING THE SKETCHER ENTITIES

To delete a sketched entity, select it by defining a window. You can specify a window by picking two points so that the entity or entities are enclosed in the window. After specifying the window, the color of the selected entity changes to red. Hold down the right mouse button in the drawing area to invoke a shortcut menu. Now, choose the **Delete** option from this menu to delete the selected item.

You can also delete an item by selecting it and pressing the DELETE key.

To delete more than one item from the drawing area, press the CTRL key and click to select the entities to be deleted. Press the DELETE key to delete the selected entities. You can also specify a window to select the entities.

> **Note**
> *It is necessary to be in the selection mode while selecting the items. The term "items" used in this chapter refers to dimensions and entities. The **Geometry**, **Dimension**, and **Constraint** filters are available in the drop-down list located in the **Status Bar**. These filters allow you to select exactly the item that you need to select. This means, if you want to select all constraints in the sketch, choose the **Constraint** filter and specify a window to select. You will notice that only the constraints are selected.*

To restore the last deleted item, choose the **Undo Delete** button. This button is available in the **Edit** toolbar on the **Top Toolchest**.

TRIMMING THE SKETCHER ENTITIES

While creating a design, there are a number of places where you need to remove the unwanted and extended entities. You can do this by using the trimming tools that are available in the **Sketcher Tools** toolbar. You can trim entities using three buttons. These buttons are discussed next.

Delete Segment

This button is used to trim the entities that extend beyond the point of intersection. It is also used to delete the selected entities. After choosing the **Delete Segment** button, when you move the cursor over an entity, the entity will be highlighted in cyan color. Press the left mouse button to trim the entity.

Corner

The **Corner** button is used to trim two entities at their corners. Note that when you trim entities using this option, the portion from where you select the entities is retained and the other portion is trimmed. The following steps explain the procedure to trim entities using this button:

Creating Sketches in the Sketch Mode

1. Choose the black arrow on the right of the **Delete Segment** button to display the flyout. From this flyout, choose the **Corner** button; you will be prompted to select two entities to be trimmed.

2. Click to select the two entities on the sides that you want to keep after the trimming action, see Figure 2-17. These two entities must be intersecting entities. The entities are trimmed from the point of intersection.

Figure 2-17 Trimming the lines

Divide

The **Divide** button is used to divide an entity into a number of parts or entities by specifying points on the entity.

When you choose the black arrow on the right of the **Delete Segment** button, a flyout is displayed. You can choose the **Divide** button from this flyout.

The following steps explain the procedure to divide an entity:

1. Choose the **Divide** button from the flyout; you will be prompted to specify a point on an entity.

2. Click to select the entity at the point where you want to divide it; the entity is divided into two different entities. They can now be treated as two separate entities.

3. Similarly, you can break other entities like circles or arcs into several small entities.

MIRRORING THE SKETCHER ENTITIES

The **Mirror** button is used to mirror sketched geometries about a centerline. This button helps to reduce the time used for creation of symmetrical geometries and dimensioning them.

The following steps explain the procedure to mirror the sketched geometry:

1. Sketch a geometry and then sketch a centerline about which you need to mirror the geometry.

2. Select the entities that you need to mirror. The selected entities turn red in color.

3. Choose the **Mirror** button from the **Sketcher Tools** toolbar; you will be prompted to select the centerline about which you need to mirror. Select the centerline; the selected entities will be mirrored about the centerline.

Tip: *In case of symmetrical parts, you can save time involved in dimensioning a sketch by dimensioning half of the section and then mirroring it. Pro/ENGINEER will assume that the mirrored half has the same dimensions as the sketched half.*

INSERTING STANDARD/USER-DEFINED SKETCHES

This button helps you insert certain standard or user defined features such as polygons, profiles, shapes, stars, and other previously created sketches in the **Sketch** mode, thus minimizing the time for repetitive sketching.

The steps that explain the procedure to insert a foreign entity in the **Sketch** mode are given next.

1. Choose the **Palette** button from the **Sketcher Tools** toolbar; the **Sketcher Palette** dialog box will be displayed. The options in this dialog box are used to insert a previously created sketch.

   Note
   *If you have selected a working directory which contains only .sec files, a tab with the name of the working directory will be available in the **Sketcher Palette** dialog box, as shown in Figure 2-18. Also, this tab is chosen by default. On the other hand, if you have selected a working directory which contains other types of files, the same tab will be displayed in the end. In such cases, the **Polygon** tab will be chosen by default.*

   *Figure 2-18 The **Sketcher Palette** dialog box*

2. For inserting a sketch from the working directory tab into the sketch, double-click on the required sketch from the list in the dialog box; a + sign will be attached to the cursor. Click anywhere in the drawing area; the **Move & Resize** dialog box will be displayed, as shown in Figure 2-19. Also, the move, rotate, and scale handles will be displayed on the imported sketch automatically.

3. Enter the scale value in the **Scale** edit box and the rotational angle value in the **Rotate** edit box of the **Move & Resize** dialog box. Alternatively, left-click on the required handle on the sketch and drag; the corresponding

   *Figure 2-19 The **Move & Resize** dialog box*

Creating Sketches in the Sketch Mode

action will take place dynamically. The move handle also acts as the pivot point for rotation and scale. However, you can relocate the pivot point. To move the pivot point, right-click on the pivot point and drag it to the required location and then release the right-click; the pivot point will be relocated.

4. Next, choose the **Accept the changes and close the dialog** button to exit the **Move & Resize** dialog box.

5. Choose the **Close** button from the **Sketcher Palette** dialog box to accept the sketch inserted. Else, repeat the steps 2-4 to continue inserting more sketches in the drawing area.

Similarly, you can add the sketches from the **Polygon, Profiles**, **Shapes**, and **Stars** tab.

DRAWING DISPLAY OPTIONS

While working with complex sketches, sometimes you need to increase the display of a particular portion of a sketch so that you can work on the minute details of the sketch. For example, you are drawing a sketch of a piston and you have to work on the minute details of the grooves for the piston rings. To work on these minute details, you have to enlarge the display of these grooves. You can enlarge or reduce the drawing display using various drawing display tools provided in Pro/ENGINEER. These tools are available in the **View** toolbar. Some of these drawing display options are discussed next. The remaining drawing display options will be discussed in the later chapters.

Zoom In

This button enlarges the view of the drawing on the screen. After choosing the **Zoom In** button, you will be prompted to define a box. The area that you will enclose inside the box will be enlarged and displayed in the drawing area. Note that when you enlarge the view of the drawing, the original size of the entities is not changed. To exit the **Zoom** tool, right-click in the drawing area.

Zoom Out

This button reduces the view of the drawing on the screen, thus increasing the drawing display area. Each time you choose this button, the display of the sketch in the drawing area is reduced.

Refit

This option reduces or enlarges the display such that all entities that comprise the sketch are fitted inside the current display. Note that the dimensions may not necessarily be included in the current display.

Repaint

While working with complex sketches, some unwanted temporary information is retained on the screen. The unwanted information may include the shadows of the deleted sketched entities, dimensions, and so on. This unwanted information can be removed from the drawing area using the **Repaint** button. This option is extensively used while designing in Pro/ENGINEER.

Note

*To remove the temporary information, you can also choose **View** > **Repaint** from the menu bar or CTRL+R to repaint the screen.*

If you have a mouse that has a middle mouse button wheel, then scrolling the wheel will zoom in and out. One more way to zoom in and out is to use the middle mouse button and the CTRL key. When you use CTRL+middle mouse button and drag the mouse upward, the sketch is zoomed out and when you drag the mouse downward, the sketch is zoomed in.

*In the **Sketch** mode, you can pan the sketch using the middle mouse button but in the **Part** mode, use SHIFT+middle mouse button to pan the model.*

TUTORIALS
Tutorial 1

In this tutorial, you will draw the sketch of the model shown in Figure 2-20. The sketch is shown in Figure 2-21.   **(Expected time: 30 min)**

Figure 2-20 Model for Tutorial 1   *Figure 2-21 Sketch of the model*

The following steps are required to complete this tutorial:

a. Start Pro/ENGINEER Wildfire 5.0 session.
b. Set the working directory and create a new sketch file.
c. Draw lines by using the **Line** tool, refer to Figures 2-23 and 2-24.
d. Draw an arc and a circle, refer to Figures 2-25 and 2-26.
e. Dimension the sketch and then modify the dimensions of the sketch, refer to Figure 2-27
f. Save the sketch and close the file.

Starting Pro/ENGINEER
1. Start Pro/ENGINEER Wildfire 5.0 by double-clicking on the Pro/ENGINEER icon on the desktop of your computer. Alternatively, choose **Start > Programs > PTC > Pro ENGINEER > Pro ENGINEER** from the taskbar.

Creating Sketches in the Sketch Mode

Setting the Working Directory

After the Pro/ENGINEER session is started, the first task is to set the working directory. A working directory is a directory on your system where you can save the work done in the current session of Pro/ENGINEER. You can set any existing directory on your system as the working directory. Since it is the first tutorial of this chapter, you need to create a folder with the name *c02*, if it does not exist.

1. Choose the **Set Working Directory** option from the **File** menu; the **Select Working Directory** dialog box is displayed.

2. In this dialog box, browse to *C:\ProE-WF-5.0* folder. If this folder does not exist, create this folder before setting the working directory.

   For selecting *C:\ProE-WF-5.0*, click on the arrow at the right of the **C:** option in the top address box of the **Select Working Directory** dialog box; the contents of the C drive folder are displayed. Now, select *ProE-WF-5.0* from the flyout, as shown in Figure 2-22.

3. Choose the **Organize** button from the **Select Working Directory** dialog box to display the flyout. From the flyout, choose the **New Folder** option; the **New Folder** dialog box is displayed.

Figure 2-22 The flyout displayed by clicking on the arrow

4. Enter *c02* in the **New Directory** edit box and choose **OK** from the **New Folder** dialog box; a new folder named *c02* is created in *C:\ProE-WF-5.0* location.

5. Choose **OK** from the **Select Working Directory** dialog box to set the working directory to *C:\ProE-WF-5.0\c02*; the message **Successfully changed to *C:\ProE-WF-5.0\c02* directory** is displayed in the message area.

Starting a New Object File

Any sketch drawn in the **Sketch** mode is saved with the *.sec* file extension. This file format is one of the file formats available in Pro/ENGINEER.

1. Choose the **New** button from the **File** toolbar or press CTRL+N; the **New** dialog box is displayed. In this dialog box, select the **Sketch** radio button from the **Type** area; the default name of the sketch appears in the **Name** edit box.

2. Enter *c02tut01* in the **Name** edit box and choose the **OK** button.

   You are in the sketcher environment of the **Sketch** mode. When the **Sketch** mode is invoked, the Navigator is displayed on the left in the drawing area.

3. Slide the Navigator to the left by clicking on the sash present on its right edge; the drawing area is increased.

Drawing the Lines of the Sketch

You need to start drawing the sketch with the right vertical line.

1. Choose the **Line** button from the **Sketcher Tools** toolbar.

2. Specify the start point by clicking on the right in the drawing area. One end of the line is attached to the cursor. Move the cursor down to get an approximate size of the line.

   Notice that when the cursor moves vertically downward, a blue colored constraint **V** appears in the drawing area next to the line. Now, if you draw a line, the vertical constraint will be applied to it.

3. Click to specify the endpoint of the line. The vertical constraint **V** is applied to the line, but it is not visible in the drawing area until the line creation is active.

   Also, another rubber-band line is attached to the cursor with its start point at the endpoint of the last line.

4. Move the cursor horizontally toward the left; a horizontal rubber-band line extends to the left as you move the mouse.

   Notice that when the cursor is moves horizontally toward the left, a blue-colored constraint, **H** appears in the drawing area next to the line. Now, if you draw a line, a horizontal constraint will be applied to it.

5. After getting the desired size of the creation of the line, click to end the line. The horizontal constraint **H** is applied to the line, but it is not visible in the drawing area until the line creation is active.

6. Move the cursor upward in the drawing area; a vertical rubber-band line extends as you move the mouse. As you move the cursor upward, notice that at a particular point where the length of the left vertical line is equal to the length of the right vertical line, an L_1 symbol is displayed on both the vertical lines. This symbol suggests that the equal length constraint is applied to two vertical lines.

7. When the L_1 constraint appears on the vertical line, click to specify the endpoint of the vertical line. The rubber-band line is still attached to the cursor.

   You can also apply constraints later. However, to save an extra step of adding the constraints, you will use the constraints that are applied automatically while drawing.

8. Move the cursor to size the line and specify the endpoint of the left inclined line, as shown in Figure 2-23.

9. Press the middle mouse button to end the line creation.

Creating Sketches in the Sketch Mode

10. The line option is still active. Move the cursor close to the top end of the right vertical line; the cursor snaps to the point that is at equal length of the right vertical line. Select the point by clicking.

11. Size the inclined line and specify the endpoint of the right inclined line. Press the middle mouse button twice to end the line creation.

    Figure 2-24 shows the lines that you have drawn. Notice that when you end the line creation by pressing the middle mouse button twice, all the constraints that you have drawn become visible, refer to Figure 2-24. Now, you need to draw the arc and the circle.

    Note
    The labels such as L_2 or L_3 vary from sketch to sketch.

    *The horizontal constraint **H** and the vertical constraint **V** appear in orange color. The orange color of the constraint indicates that the constraint is strong. This means you cannot change the orientation of the line until you delete the constraint applied to the line. The constraints displayed in grey color indicates that they are week constraints, refer to Figure 2-24.*

Figure 2-23 Partial sketch with left inclined line

Figure 2-24 Partial sketch with weak dimensions

Drawing the Arc

1. Choose the **3-Point / Tangent End** button from the **Sketcher Tools** toolbar; you are prompted to select the start point of the arc.

2. Select the endpoint of the left inclined line; the **Target** symbol appears in green color.

3. Move the cursor along the tangent direction through a small distance. A rubber-band arc that is tangent to the inclined line appears. As you move the cursor to the endpoint of the right inclined line, at a particular point, the tangent constraint is applied to both ends of the arc. This is indicated by the symbol **T**, which appears at the endpoints of the inclined lines.

4. As the tangent constraint appears, click to end the arc creation. You will notice that the tangent constraint with the symbol **T** appears at the endpoints of the arc, as shown in Figure 2-25. Press the middle mouse button to end the arc creation.

The tangent constraint **T** appears in orange, which indicates that it is a strong constraint and the tangency of the inclined line with the arc cannot be modified until you delete the tangent constraint.

Note that in Figure 2-24, there are some weak dimensions that are not displayed in Figure 2-25. This is because weak dimensions get deleted without confirming their deletion. Hence, after drawing the arc, some weak dimensions get deleted automatically.

Note
*If the tangent constraint symbol is not displayed on any of the inclined lines, apply the constraint manually by using the flyout that is displayed when you choose the **Vertical** button from the **Sketcher Tools** toolbar (see page 2-16 for more information).*

Dimensioning the Sketch

The right vertical line, the bottom horizontal line, the arc, and the circle are dimensioned automatically and the weak dimensions are applied to them. You will use these dimensions. Hence, there is no need to dimension these entities again.

1. Choose the **Normal** button from the **Sketcher Tools** toolbar.

2. Select the center of the arc and then the bottom horizontal line; both, the center and the line turn red in color.

3. Place the dimension on the right of the sketch by pressing the middle mouse button.

4. Select the center of the arc and then the left vertical line; both the center and the vertical line turn red in color.

5. Press the middle mouse button to place the dimension below the sketch, refer to Figure 2-26.

Figure 2-25 *Sketch with arc*

Figure 2-26 *Sketch with all entities, weak dimensions, and weak constraints*

Creating Sketches in the Sketch Mode

Drawing the Circle

1. Choose the black arrow on the right of the **Center and Point** button to display the flyout. In this flyout, choose the **Concentric** button; you are prompted to select an arc.

2. Select the arc by clicking on it. Move the mouse; a circle appears.

3. To draw the circle, click to select a point inside the sketch.

4. Press the middle mouse button to end the circle creation. The sketch is complete.

Modifying the Dimensions

The sketch is dimensioned with default values. You need to modify these values to the given values.

1. Choose the **One-by-One** button from the Right Toolchest.

2. Select all dimensions by specifying a window around them.

> **Note**
> *You can also use CTRL+ALT+A to select the entire sketch with dimensions.*

3. When all dimensions turn red in color, choose the **Modify** button; the **Modify Dimensions** dialog box is displayed.

   All dimensions in the sketch are displayed in this dialog box. Each dimension has a separate thumbwheel and an edit box. You can use the thumbwheel or the edit box to modify the dimensions. It is recommended that you use the edit boxes to modify the dimensions, if the change in the dimension value is large.

4. Clear the **Regenerate** check box and then modify the values of the dimensions.

   Once you clear this check box, any modification in a dimension value does not update the sketch. It is recommended that you clear the **Regenerate** check box when more than one dimension has to be modified.

   Notice that the dimension that you select in the **Modify Dimensions** dialog box gets enclosed in a blue box in the drawing area.

5. Modify all dimensions according to the dimensions shown in Figure 2-27. After modifying the dimensions, choose the **Regenerate the section and close the dialog** button from the **Modify Dimensions** dialog box; a message **Dimension modifications successfully completed** is displayed in the message area.

The sketch is completed and is shown in Figure 2-27.

Figure 2-27 *The complete sketch with dimensions and constraints*

Tip: *You can modify the location of the dimensions as they appear on the screen by selecting and dragging them to a new location.*

Saving the Sketch

Now, the sketch needs to be saved because you may need the sketch later in the **Part** mode to create a 3D model.

1. Choose the **Save** button from the **File** toolbar; the **Save Object** dialog box is displayed with the name of the sketch that you had entered earlier.

2. Choose the **OK** button; the sketch is saved.

3. After saving the sketch, choose **Window > Close** from the menu bar to close the window.

Tutorial 2

In this tutorial, you will draw the sketch for the model shown in Figure 2-28. The sketch is shown in Figure 2-29. For your reference, all entities in the sketch are labeled alphabetically.

(Expected time: 30 min)

Creating Sketches in the Sketch Mode 2-31

Figure 2-28 *Model for Tutorial 2*

Figure 2-29 *Sketch of the model*

The following steps are required to complete this tutorial:

a. Set the Working directory and create a new object file.
b. Draw the sketch by using the line tool, refer to Figure 2-30.
c. Dimension the required entities and then modify the dimensions of the sketch, refer to Figures 2-31 and 2-32.
d. Save the sketch and close the file.

Setting the Working Directory

The working directory was selected in Tutorial 1, therefore you do not need to select the directory again. But, if a new session of Pro/Engineer is started, you need to set the working directory again by following the steps given below.

1. Open the Navigator (if it is in collapsed state) by clicking on the sash button on the left of the Pro/ENGINEER main window; the Navigator slides out. At the bottom of the Navigator, the **Folder Tree** is displayed. Click on the black arrow on the right of the **Folder Tree**; the **Folder Tree** expands.

2. Click on the plus sign adjacent to the *ProE-WF-5.0* folder in the Navigator; the contents of the *ProE-WF-5.0* folder are displayed.

3. Now, right-click on the *c02* folder to display a shortcut menu. From the shortcut menu, choose the **Set Working Directory** option; the working directory is set to *c02*.

4. Close the Navigator by clicking on the sash located at the right edge of the Navigator; the Navigator slides in.

Starting a New Object File

1. Choose the **New** button from the **File** toolbar; the **New** dialog box is displayed. Select the **Sketch** radio button from the **Type** area of the **New** dialog box; the default name of the sketch appears in the **Name** edit box.

2. Enter *c02tut02* in the **Name** edit box and choose **OK**; you are in the sketcher environment of the **Sketch** mode.

Drawing the Sketch

The sketch in Figure 2-29 consists of only lines. For ease of understanding, all lines in the sketch are labeled alphabetically.

1. Choose the **Line** button from the **Sketcher Tools** toolbar. Select a point close to the lower right corner of the drawing area by clicking and start drawing the horizontal line A. You will notice that as you draw line A, the **H** symbol is displayed on the line. This indicates that the line is horizontally constrained. Move the cursor toward the left and specify the endpoint of the line.

2. Move the cursor vertically upward so that the **V** constraint appears on the line. When you get the appropriate size of the line, click to specify the endpoint of line B; line B is completed.

3. Move the cursor to the right in the drawing area and click to specify the endpoint of line C.

4. Now, to draw line D, move the cursor down and click to specify the endpoint of line D.

5. Move the cursor to size the line and click to specify the endpoint of the inclined line E.

6. The next line you need to draw is line F. Move the cursor vertically downward and click to specify the endpoint of line F.

7. Now, to draw line G, move the cursor horizontally toward the right and click to specify the endpoint of line G.

8. Move the cursor vertically upward and click to specify the endpoint of line H.

9. Now, continue drawing the remaining lines that are shown in Figure 2-29. When the sketch is complete, end the line creation by pressing the middle mouse button. Notice that the sketched entities are dimensioned automatically as you draw them. These dimensions are weak dimensions and appear in gray color.

Applying Constraints to the Sketch

Constraints are applied to the sketch to maintain the design intent of the feature and this might sometimes result in less dimensions in the sketch.

1. Choose the black arrow on the right of the **Vertical** button in the **Sketcher Tools** toolbar; a flyout is displayed.

2. Choose the **Equal** button and select lines F and H. The equal length constraint L_2 is applied to both the lines. The constraint labels such as L_2 or L_3 vary from sketch to sketch.

Creating Sketches in the Sketch Mode

3. Now, select lines J and N; the equal length constraint is applied to both the lines.

4. Select lines C and K; the equal length constraint is applied to both the lines.

5. Select lines A and B; the equal length constraint is applied to both the lines.

6. Choose the **Horizontal** button from the constraints flyout; you are prompted to select a line or two vertices.

7. Select the vertex that is joining lines L and M and the vertex that is joining lines G and H. Both the vertices are aligned horizontally, as shown in Figure 2-30.

8. Select the vertex that is joining lines C and D and the vertex that is joining lines J and K. Both the vertices are aligned horizontally, as shown in Figure 2-31.

Dimensioning the Sketch

Weak dimensions have already been applied to the sketch while drawing. You need to dimension only the angle between lines D and E and lines J and I.

1. Choose the **Normal** button from the **Sketcher Tools** toolbar.

2. Select lines D and E by using the left mouse button; the selected lines turn red in color. Now, press the middle mouse button to place the dimension close to the vertex where lines D and E join.

3. Similarly, dimension the angle between lines J and I.

Figure 2-31 shows the sketch after applying dimensions. If your sketch does not have all dimensions shown in this figure, apply them by using the **Normal** button.

Figure 2-30 Sketch with weak dimensions and constraints

Figure 2-31 Sketch after dimensioning

Modifying the Dimensions

The dimensions that are applied to the sketch need modification in dimension values.

1. Choose the **One-by-One** button from the **Right Toolchest** and then select all dimensions by specifying a window around them.

2. When dimensions turn red in color, choose the **Modify** button; the **Modify Dimensions** dialog box is displayed.

3. Clear the **Regenerate** check box and then modify the values of the dimensions. On clearing this check box, the sketch is not regenerated while you modify the dimensions.

    Notice that the dimension that you select in the **Modify Dimensions** dialog box is enclosed in a blue box in the drawing area.

4. When all dimensions are modified, choose the **Regenerate the section and close the dialog** button from the **Modify Dimensions** dialog box; the message **Dimension modifications successfully completed** is displayed in the message area. The completed sketch is shown in Figure 2-32.

Figure 2-32 Complete sketch with dimensions and constraints

5. Save the sketch as discussed earlier. Next, choose **Window > Close** from the menu bar to exit the **Sketch** mode.

Note
You can also modify dimensions individually. However, individual modification of dimensions is recommended only when there is a minor change in the dimension value or when only one dimension is required to be modified.

Tutorial 3

In this tutorial, you will draw the sketch of the model shown in Figure 2-33. The sketch of the model is shown in Figure 2-34. For your reference, all entities in the sketch are labeled alphabetically. Also, you will print the sketch. **(Expected time: 30 min)**

Figure 2-33 Model for Tutorial 3

Figure 2-34 Sketch of the model

The following steps are required to complete this tutorial:

a. Set the working directory and create a new object file.
b. Draw the sketch by using the sketcher tools, refer to Figures 2-35 through 2-38.
c. Dimension the sketch and then modify the dimensions of the sketch, refer to Figure 2-39.
d. Save the sketch and print it.

Setting the Working Directory

The working directory was selected in Tutorial 1, therefore, you do not need to select the working directory again. But if a new session of Pro/Engineer is started, then you have to set the working directory again by following the steps given next.

1. Open the Navigator by sliding it out. In the Navigator, the **Folder Tree** is displayed at the bottom. Click on the black arrow available on the right of the **Folder Tree**; the **Folder Tree** expands. Click on the plus sign adjacent to the *ProE-WF-5.0* folder in the Navigator; the contents of the *ProE-WF-5.0* folder are displayed.

2. Now, right-click on the *c02* folder to display a shortcut menu. From the shortcut menu, choose the **Set Working Directory** option; the working directory is set to *c02*. Close the Navigator.

Starting New Object File

1. Choose the **New** button from the **File** toolbar; the **New** dialog box is displayed. Select the **Sketch** radio button from the **Type** area of the **New** dialog box. The default name of the sketch appears in the **Name** edit box.

2. Enter *c02tut03* in the **Name** edit box. Choose the **OK** button to enter the sketcher environment of the **Sketch** mode.

Drawing the Circles

1. Choose the **Center and Point** button from the **Sketcher Tools** toolbar and specify the center of the circle.

2. Move the cursor to size the circle and then click to complete the circle.

3. Draw another circle whose center is collinear with the center of the previous circle.

   Figure 2-35 shows the two collinear circles drawn by using the **Center and Point** button from the **Sketcher Tools** toolbar.

Drawing the Tangent Lines

1. Choose the **Line Tangent** button from the **Line** flyout in the **Sketcher Tools** toolbar; you are prompted to select the start location on the arc or the circle.

2. Select the left circle at the top. A rubber-band line appears whose one end is attached to the circle and the other end is attached to the cursor.

3. Click on the top of the right circle; a tangent connecting the two circles is drawn.

4. Similarly, draw a tangent by selecting the two circles at the bottom.

   Figure 2-36 shows the sketch after drawing the tangent lines.

Figure 2-35 Two circles with weak dimensions and constraints

Figure 2-36 Circles joined by tangent lines

Trimming the Circles

As evident from Figure 2-36, the tangents that are drawn intersect the circles at the point where they meet the circle. Therefore, the part of the circle that is not required can be dynamically trimmed.

1. Choose the **Delete Segment** button from the **Sketcher Tools** toolbar.

Creating Sketches in the Sketch Mode

2. Select the two circles individually to trim them at the locations shown in Figure 2-37.

Figure 2-38 shows the two circles after deleting the unwanted portions of the circle.

Figure 2-37 Locations to trim

Figure 2-38 Sketch after trimming

Drawing the Circles

1. Choose the black arrow on the right of the **Center and Point** button to display the flyout. Choose the **Concentric** button from the flyout; you are prompted to select an arc.

2. Select arc P and create circle X concentric to the arc. Similarly, select arc Q to create a concentric circle Y.

   Notice that the radius dimension is applied to the two arcs, whereas the diameter dimension is applied to the circles. This is because by default, the arcs are applied radius dimension and circles are applied diameter dimension.

Dimensioning the Sketch

In order to fully define a sketch, you need to dimension it.

1. Choose the **Normal** button.

2. Select the centers of the two circles and place the dimension at the bottom of the sketch.

Modifying the Dimensions

1. Choose the **One-by-One** button.

2. Select all dimensions by defining a window.

   Note
   You can also use CTRL+ALT+A from the keyboard to select all entities and items in the sketch.

3. When all dimensions turn red in color, choose the **Modify** button; the **Modify Dimensions** dialog box is displayed.

4. Clear the **Regenerate** check box and then modify the values of the dimensions. You will notice that the dimension that you edit in the **Modify Dimensions** dialog box is enclosed by a blue box in the drawing area.

5. When all dimensions are modified, choose the **Regenerate the section and close the dialog** button from the **Modify Dimensions** dialog box; the message **Dimension modifications successfully completed** is displayed in the message area.

   The sketch is completed and is shown in Figure 2-39.

Figure 2-39 Complete sketch with dimensions and constraints

6. Save the sketch as discussed earlier. Next, you need to print the sketch.

Printing the Sketch Using the Plot Option

1. Choose the **Print** button from the **File** toolbar or press CTRL+P; the **Print** dialog box is displayed, as shown in Figure 2-40.

2. Choose the **Commands and Settings** button from this dialog box; a shortcut menu is displayed, as shown in Figure 2-41.

3. Choose the **Add Printer Type** option from the shortcut menu; the **Add Printer Type** dialog box is displayed.

4. From the printers listed in the **Add Printer Type** dialog box, select the printer that is installed on your system and choose the **OK** button.

5. From the **Print** dialog box, choose the **Configure** button; the **Shaded Image Configuration** dialog box is displayed. This dialog box allows you to set the paper size.

Creating Sketches in the Sketch Mode 2-39

*Figure 2-40 The **Print** dialog box*

*Figure 2-41 The **Commands and Settings** shortcut menu*

6. Select the **A** option from the **Size** drop-down list, if not already selected; the dimensions of the sheet are set, by default. Also, select the image resolution and the image depth from the dialog box.

7. Choose the **OK** button from the **Shaded Image Configuration** dialog box.

8. Now, choose the **OK** button from the **Print** dialog box to complete the printing.

Self-Evaluation Test

Answer the following questions and then compare them to those given at the end of this chapter:

1. Dimensions and constraints are automatically applied to a sketch when you draw it. (T/F)

2. In Pro/ENGINEER, you can create lines that are tangent to two circles. (T/F)

3. If the **Intent Manager** is on and you draw a line, the cursor snaps to the endpoint of the previous line. (T/F)

4. You can convert a weak constraint into strong constraint by using the shortcut menu that is displayed when you right-click on the weak constraint. (T/F)

5. While drawing a circle, first you need to specify its diameter. (T/F)

6. The _____ menu in the menu bar has the **Modify** option.

7. A sketch can be modified by changing its _____.

8. The **Intent Manager** is _____ by default when you enter the **Sketch** mode. (on/off)

9. In the **Sketch** mode, the tangent constraint is represented by a _____ symbol.

10. The file created in the **Sketch** mode is saved with a _____ file extension.

Review Questions

Answer the following questions:

1. You can dynamically modify the geometry of a sketch. (T/F)

2. You can use the **Rectangle** button from the **Sketcher Tools** toolbar to draw a square. (T/F)

3. The _____ button is used to apply constraints manually.

4. You cannot undo a previous operation in the sketcher environment. (T/F)

5. You can also use the options in the menu bar to draw a sketch from the **Sketch** menu. (T/F)

6. What is the need of the **Sketch** mode in Pro/ENGINEER?

7. What are the four basic steps required to create a sketch?

8. How many types of lines can be sketched by using the buttons available in the **Sketcher Tools** toolbar?

9. Why the selection of working directory is important before creating a new file?

10. Write all steps involved in creating a sketch that is accepted by Pro/ENGINEER.

Exercises

Exercise 1

In this exercise, you will draw the sketch of the model shown in Figure 2-42. The sketch is shown in Figure 2-43.   **(Expected time: 30 min)**

Creating Sketches in the Sketch Mode 2-41

Figure 2-42 Solid model for Exercise 1

Figure 2-43 Sketch of the model

Exercise 2

In this exercise, you will draw the sketch of the model shown in Figure 2-44. The sketch is shown in Figure 2-45. **(Expected time: 30 min)**

Figure 2-44 Solid model for Exercise 2

Figure 2-45 Sketch of the model

Exercise 3

In this exercise, you will draw the sketch of the model shown in Figure 2-46. The sketch is shown in Figure 2-47. **(Expected time: 30 min)**

Figure 2-46 Solid model for Exercise 3

Figure 2-47 Sketch of the model

Exercise 4

In this exercise, you will draw the sketch for the model shown in Figure 2-48. The sketch is shown in Figure 2-49.

(Expected time: 30 min)

Figure 2-48 Solid model for Tutorial 2

Figure 2-49 Sketch of the model

Answers to Self-Evaluation Test

1. T, **2.** T, **3.** T, **4.** T, **5.** F, **6. Edit**, **7.** dimensions, **8. on**, **9.** T, **10.** *.sec*

Chapter 3

Creating Sketches in the Sketch Mode-II

Learning Objectives

After completing this chapter, you will be able to:
- *Use various options to dimension a sketch.*
- *Create fillets.*
- *Place a user-defined coordinate system.*
- *Create, dimension, and modify splines.*
- *Create text.*
- *Move and resize entities.*
- *Copy a sketch.*
- *Import 2D drawings.*

DIMENSIONING THE SKETCH

In Chapter 2, you learned to dimension a sketch using the **Normal** option from the menu bar or by choosing the **Normal** button from the **Sketcher Tools** toolbar. In this chapter, you will learn the use of the **Baseline** option for dimensioning a sketch.

Dimensioning a Sketch Using the Baseline Option

In Pro/ENGINEER, the **Baseline** option of dimensioning is used to create dimensions in terms of horizontal and vertical location values of an entity with respect to a specified baseline. This type of dimensioning in a drawing can be used for writing a CNC program to manufacture a component.

The **Baseline** option can be used to dimension lines, conics, arcs, and so on. To invoke this option, choose **Sketch > Dimension** from the menu bar; the cascading menu will be displayed, as shown in Figure 3-1 The following steps explain the procedure to create dimensions using the **Baseline** option:

Figure 3-1 Dimensioning options

1. Choose **Sketch > Dimension > Baseline** from the menu bar. Alternatively, choose **Normal > Baseline** from the **Sketcher Tools** toolbar.

2. Select the entity that will act as the baseline (origin or reference). Press the middle mouse button to place the dimension; the dimension **0.00** will be displayed where you place the dimension. Note that since the location value of the baseline is taken as the origin, the dimension value of the baseline entity will become 0.00. The dimension values of all other entities dimensioned with reference to the baseline will be measured from this origin.

   Depending upon the entity selected to act as the baseline, the horizontal or the vertical location value of the entity will be placed. For example, if you select a vertical line, the value of its location will be placed vertically. Similarly, if you select a horizontal line, the value of its location will be placed horizontally.

   For arcs, circles, and splines, there are two options to dimension using the **Baseline** option. When you select the center of a circle or an arc for baseline dimensioning and press the middle mouse button, the **Dim Orientation** dialog box will be displayed, as shown in Figure 3-2. Also, you are prompted to select the orientation. Select the required radio button from this dialog box and choose the **Accept** button; the dimension is placed based on the orientation selected.

   Figure 3-2 The Dim Orientation dialog box

3. Next, choose the **Normal** button from the **Sketcher Tools** toolbar. Select the baseline dimension that was placed earlier and then select the entity to dimension. Now, press the middle mouse button to place the dimension.

Creating Sketches in the Sketch Mode-II

The orientation of the dimension will depend upon the baseline dimension and the entity selected. Figure 3-3 shows a sketch dimensioned using the above-mentioned method. In this figure, the two baselines are dimensioned using the **Baseline** option. Therefore, the dimensions of these lines are displayed as 0.00. The remaining lines are dimensioned by selecting the baseline dimension and then the required entity by using the **Normal** button.

Figure 3-3 Baseline dimensioning of a sketch

Replacing the Dimensions of a Sketch Using the Replace Option

The **Replace** option is used to replace a dimension with a new dimension in a sketch. To use this option, you must have a dimensioned sketch. The following steps explain the procedure to dimension a sketch using the **Replace** option:

1. Choose **Edit > Replace** from the menu bar; you will be prompted to select a dimension to be replaced.

2. Select the dimension to be replaced; the selected dimension will be deleted and you will be prompted to create a replacement dimension. Create the new dimension using the **Normal** tool; the previous dimension is replaced by a new dimension.

CREATING FILLETS

In the sketcher environment, you can create the following two types of fillets:

1. Circular fillets
2. Elliptical fillets

Creating Circular Fillets

A circular fillet is the arc formed at the intersection of two lines, a line and an arc, or two arcs. This type of fillet is controlled by the radius or diameter dimension of the fillet. The resulting fillet will depend on the location where the elements are selected.

Figure 3-4 shows two lines that do not join and Figure 3-5 shows the circular fillet created between them. The circular fillet that is created is an arc with its endpoints tangent to the two lines. This is evident from the **T** symbol that is automatically applied to the endpoints of the fillet arc.

Figure 3-4 *Two lines that do not join*

Figure 3-5 *Fillet created between the two lines*

Figure 3-6 shows two lines that join at a point and Figure 3-7 shows the circular fillet created at the joint. The corner is automatically deleted.

Figure 3-6 *Two lines joining at a point*

Figure 3-7 *Filleted corner*

Figure 3-8 shows two sets of arcs and Figure 3-9 shows the circular fillet created between the two arcs. The location where you select the arcs to create the fillet is important. The fillet is created tangent to the selection points on the arcs. Here, the endpoints of the arcs are selected to create the fillet.

If the points of selection on the two arcs are away from the endpoints of the arcs, then the fillet is created at the selection points. The portion of the arc that extends beyond the fillet should be manually deleted or trimmed. Figure 3-10 shows the points at which the two arcs are selected and Figure 3-11 shows the fillet created at the selection points.

Creating Sketches in the Sketch Mode-II

Figure 3-8 Two sets of arcs

Figure 3-9 Fillet created by selecting the endpoints

Figure 3-10 Points selected on arcs

Figure 3-11 Fillet created

The **Circular** button in the **Sketcher Tools** toolbar is used to create circular fillets. The following steps explain the procedure to create a circular fillet:

1. Choose the **Circular** button from the **Sketcher Tools** toolbar; you are prompted to select two entities.

2. Select the first entity for filleting by using the left mouse button; the yellow color of the first entity changes to red. Now, select the second entity. If it is possible to create a fillet, it will be drawn between the two selected entities as soon as you select the second entity.

3. Repeat step 2 until you have created all fillets.

Creating Elliptical Fillets

An elliptical fillet is the arc in the form of an ellipse that joins two lines, two arcs, or a line and an arc. The geometry of the elliptical fillet depends on the location where you select the entities to create a fillet.

The advantage of elliptical fillets over circular fillets is that the geometry of elliptical fillets can be controlled by dimensions in two directions. Therefore, when an elliptical fillet is dynamically modified, its geometry can be controlled in either the x-direction or the y-direction resulting in more curved geometric shape than a circular fillet.

Figures 3-12 and 3-13 illustrate the elliptical fillet. Notice that a strong tangent constraint **T** is automatically applied when you create a fillet.

Figure 3-12 Arcs to be filleted

Figure 3-13 Elliptical fillet created

An elliptical fillet is created by choosing the **Elliptical** button in the **Sketcher Tools** toolbar. The following steps explain the procedure to create elliptical fillets:

1. Choose the black arrow on the right of the **Circular** button to display a flyout. Choose the **Elliptical** button from this flyout; you are prompted to select two entities.

2. Select the first entity by clicking; the color of the entity changes to red.

3. Select the second entity. As soon as you select the second entity, the elliptical fillet is created. The shape of the elliptical fillet depends upon the specified points. After the fillet is created, you are again prompted to select two entities for elliptical fillet.

4. Repeat steps 2 and 3 until you have created all fillets.

When you select an elliptical fillet to dimension, the **Ellipse Rad** dialog box will be displayed, as shown in Figure 3-14. There are two radio buttons in this dialog box. When the **Major Axis** radio button is selected, the elliptical fillet will be dimensioned radially along the X-direction. The **Minor Axis** radio button, when selected, dimensions the elliptical fillet radially in the Y-direction.

Figure 3-14 The **Ellipse Rad** dialog box

CREATING A REFERENCE COORDINATE SYSTEM

There are two types of coordinate systems, construction and geometric. As discussed earlier the construction entities cannot be referenced outside the Sketcher environment whereas the geometric entities can be. The **Geometry Coordinate System** button in the **Sketcher Tools** toolbar is used to create a coordinate system that will act as a reference for dimensioning. You can dimension the splines using the coordinate system. Thus, it provides you the flexibility to modify the spline points by specifying different coordinates with respect to the coordinate system.

The user-defined coordinate system is used in blend features to align different sections in a blend. It is also used in the **Assembly** mode and **Manufacturing** mode of Pro/ENGINEER.

The following steps explain the procedure to create a coordinate system:

1. Click on the black arrow on the right of the **Point** button in the **Sketcher Tools** toolbar to display a flyout. Choose the **Geometry Coordinate System** button from the flyout; you are prompted to select the location for the coordinate system. The coordinate system symbol is attached to the cursor.

2. Place the coordinate system at the desired points on the screen by clicking the left mouse button. The coordinate system will be placed at as many places as you click in the graphics window. You can end coordinate system creation by using the middle mouse button.

Note
If you add a coordinate system to a sketch, it must be dimensioned. But if the coordinate system is placed at the endpoints of a line, an arc, a spline, or at the center of an arc or a circle, it need not be dimensioned. In other words, a coordinate system must be referenced to an entity in a sketch.

WORKING WITH SPLINES

Splines are curved entities that pass through a number of intermediate points. Generally, splines are used to define the outer surface of a model. This is because the splines can provide different shape to curves and the flexibility to modify the surfaces that result from the splines. Splines find application in automobile and aeroplane body designing.

Creating a Spline

To draw a spline, choose the **Spline** button from the **Sketcher Tools** toolbar.

The steps to create a spline are discussed next.

1. Choose the **Spline** button from the **Sketcher Tools** toolbar; you are prompted to select the location for spline.

2. Use the left mouse button to select the start point for the spline. Similarly, select additional points in the graphics window; a spline will be drawn passing through all specified points. Press the middle mouse button to end the creation of spline. All points through which the spline passes are called interpolation points.

Dimensioning of Splines

When a spline is drawn, the weak dimensions are automatically applied to the spline. A spline can be dimensioned manually in the following ways:

1. Dimensioning the endpoints.
2. Radius of curvature dimensioning.
3. Tangency dimensioning.
4. Coordinate dimensioning.
5. Dimensioning the interpolation points.

Dimensioning the Endpoints

To dimension a spline by selecting the endpoints, you need to follow the steps given below:

1. Choose the **Normal** button from the **Sketcher Tools** toolbar.

2. Select the two endpoints of the spline and place the horizontal or vertical dimension by pressing the middle mouse button. Figure 3-15 shows a spline that is dimensioned by selecting the endpoints.

Radius of Curvature Dimensioning

The radius of curvature of a spline can be dimensioned only if its tangency is defined. In other words, radius of curvature of a spline can be dimensioned only if the spline is tangent to an entity. For dimensioning the radius of curvature of a spline, you need to follow the steps given below:

1. Choose the **Normal** button from the **Sketcher Tools** toolbar.

2. Select the endpoint of the spline where the tangency is defined.

3. Press the middle mouse button to place the dimension. Figure 3-16 shows the radius of curvature dimensioning of a spline.

Tangency or Angular Dimensioning

A spline can be dimensioned angularly with respect to a line tangent to it. This type of dimensioning is also called angular dimensioning. To angular dimension a spline and a line tangent to it, you need to follow the steps given below:

1. Choose the **Normal** button from the **Sketcher Tools** toolbar.

2. Select the spline by clicking the left mouse button.

3. Select the entity tangent to the spline by clicking the left mouse button.

Creating Sketches in the Sketch Mode-II

Figure 3-15 Endpoint dimensioning

Figure 3-16 Radius of curvature

4. Select the interpolation point of the spline that is to be dimensioned tangentially.

5. Press the middle mouse button to place the dimension.

Coordinate Dimensioning

The spline can be dimensioned with respect to a user-defined coordinate system. Choose the **Coordinate System** button from the **Point** flyout in the **Sketcher Tools** toolbar. The coordinate system is attached to the cursor. Place the coordinate system in the graphics window. Now, the spline can be dimensioned with respect to the coordinate system.

Dimensioning the Interpolation Points

A spline can be dimensioned by dimensioning its interpolation points or vertices. This type of dimensioning is used when the designer wants the spline to be standard for all designs. This is because the exact curve can be duplicated if the interpolation points or the vertices of a spline are dimensioned.

> **Tip**: *A dimension can be moved by choosing the **One-by-One** button and then pressing and holding the left mouse button on the dimension and moving it. The dimension text is replaced by a red colored box. You can drag the dimension to the desired location in the graphics window and release the left mouse button to place the dimension at that point.*

Modifying a Spline

In Pro/ENGINEER Wildfire 5.0, a spline can be modified in the following ways:

1. Moving the interpolation points of the spline.
2. Adding points to a spline.
3. Deleting points of a spline.
4. Creating a control polygon and moving its control points.
5. Modifying the dimensions of the spline.

Moving the Points of the Spline

The position of the interpolation points can be dynamically modified. To modify a spline, select an interpolation point on the spline and drag it to modify the shape of the spline.

You can also use the dashboard to modify a spline. To invoke the dashboard, select the spline and hold the right mouse button to invoke the shortcut menu. Choose the **Modify** option from the shortcut menu; the **Modify Spline** dashboard will be displayed at the top of the graphics window with the options and buttons to modify a spline.

The interpolation points of the spline appear in white in the graphics window. Drag the interpolation points to modify the shape of the spline. Choose the **Build Feature** symbol from the dashboard to exit it.

Adding Interpolation Points to a Spline

To add interpolation points on a spline, invoke the dashboard. Now, right-click on the spline to invoke a shortcut menu. Choose the **Add Point** option; a point is added to the spline where the spline was selected. The new point appears in white. You cannot increase the length of the spline by adding points before the start point and after the endpoint of the spline.

Deleting Interpolation Points of a Spline

To delete a point or a vertex, invoke the dashboard. Next, select the vertex to be removed and right-click to invoke the shortcut menu. Choose the **Delete Point** option from the shortcut menu; the selected point is deleted. You can continue deleting vertices or points from a spline until only two end points are left in the spline.

Creating a Control Polygon and Moving its Control Points

When you draw a spline, it is associated with a control frame. The vertices of this frame are called control points. To create a control polygon, choose the **Modify spline using control points** button from the **Modify Spline** dashboard. The control polygon will be displayed in the graphics window. The control points of this polygon can be moved by dragging to modify the spline shape.

Modifying the Dimensions of the Spline

The shape of the spline is controlled by the position of its interpolation points. Hence by modifying the dimensions, the position of the interpolation points are changed, which results in modification of the shape of the spline.

> **Tip**: *To dynamically modify the shape of the sketch, you need to select an entity of the sketch and drag the mouse to modify the sketch. Remember that if the selected entity is constrained, then you cannot modify it. You can modify it only after disabling the constraints.*

WRITING TEXT IN THE SKETCHER ENVIRONMENT

There are various instances when a designer needs to write text on the model. For example, for creating a label, model number, company name, and so on. In Pro/ENGINEER, you can write this text in the sketcher environment.

In the sketcher environment, the text is written using the **Text** button from the **Sketcher Tools** toolbar. The following steps explain the procedure to write text in the sketcher environment:

1. Choose the **Text** button from the **Sketcher Tools** toolbar; you are prompted to select the start point of line to determine the text height and orientation.

2. Specify the start point on the screen by clicking the left mouse button; you are prompted to select the second point of line to determine the text height and orientation.

3. Note that to write the text upright, the second point should be above the start point and in a straight line. If the second point is below the start point, the text will be written down from right to left. Specify the second point on the screen by clicking the left mouse button; the **Text** dialog box will be displayed, as shown in Figure 3-17.

   After specifying the second point, construction line is drawn having height equal to the distance between the two points. The height and orientation of the text depends on the height and angle of the construction line. If the construction line is drawn at an angle, then the text is written at that angle.

4. Enter the text in the **Text line** edit box, which can be up to 79 characters. As you enter the text, the text will be displayed dynamically in the graphics window. You can choose the desired font of the text from the **Font** drop-down list. The aspect ratio and the slant angle of the text can be controlled by using the slider bars.

5. Choose the **OK** button in the **Text** dialog box to exit it.

*Figure 3-17 The **Text** dialog box*

Note

In later chapters of this book, you will learn that there are other methods also to enter the sketcher environment, besides entering through the sketch mode.

MOVING AND RESIZING ENTITIES

The sketches can be scaled or rotated by using the **Move & Resize** button from the **Sketcher Tools** toolbar. To invoke this button, select the sketch and then choose the black arrow on the right of the **Mirror** button from the **Sketcher Tools** toolbar; a flyout is displayed. Choose the **Move & Resize** button from the flyout. On choosing this button, the sketch, which consists of various entities, will act as a single entity. Also, the sketch appears yellow in color and is enclosed within a boundary box, as shown in Figure 3-18.

Figure 3-18 Selected entities enclosed within a boundary box with three handles

There are three handles that facilitate in scaling, rotating, and moving the selected sketch. The rotate handle is used to dynamically rotate the selected entities. The scale handle is used to dynamically scale the selected entities. The base point handle is used to pick the sketch and place it at any other location in the graphics window. To change the location of any of the three handles, right-click on the handle and drag it by pressing and holding the right mouse button; the selected handle will move along with the cursor. Place the symbol at the desired location. The following steps explain the procedure to move and resize a sketch:

1. Select the sketch to be rotated and scaled, and then choose the black arrow on the right of the **Mirror** button from the **Sketcher Tools** toolbar; a flyout will be displayed.

2. From the flyout, choose the **Move & Resize** button; the **Move & Resize** dialog box will be displayed, as shown in Figure 3-19. This dialog box contains the **Translate** and **Rotate/Scale** areas. The options in these areas are used to move, scale, and rotate the sketch dynamically or by entering a value in the respective edit boxes. You can also select a reference about which you want to translate, rotate, or scale the sketch.

3. To move the sketch dynamically, select the move handle and then drag the handle to the required location; the sketch will be repositioned at the new location. You can also select a reference about which you want to move the sketch.

Creating Sketches in the Sketch Mode-II

To dynamically rotate the sketch, select the rotate handle and then move the cursor; the sketch is rotated as you move the cursor. You can also enter the rotation angle in the **Rotate** edit box.

To scale the sketch, select the scale handle and then move the cursor. As you move the cursor, the sketch is scaled dynamically in the graphics window. You can also enter the scale value in the **Scale** edit box.

4. After the sketch has been moved and resized, choose the **Accept the changes and close the dialog** button in the **Move & Resize** dialog box.

Figure 3-19 The Move & Resize dialog box

IMPORTING 2D DRAWINGS IN THE SKETCH MODE

The two-dimensional (2D) drawings when opened in the sketcher environment can be saved in the *.sec* format. The *.sec* file can then be converted to a solid model. The **Data from File** option in the **Sketch** menu in the menu bar is used to import the 2D sketches. This option saves time in drawing the same or similar section again. The file formats from which the data can be imported are shown in Figure 3-20.

Figure 3-20 File formats

When you choose **Sketch > Data from File > File System** from the menu bar, the **Open** dialog box will be displayed, as shown in Figure 3-21. You can use this dialog box to select and open the file.

In the **Open** dialog box, if you select a drawing file that is created in the **Drawing** mode of Pro/ENGINEER Wildfire 5.0, the draft entities in that file are imported. The selected drawing is opened in a sub window. Also, you are prompted to select the entities to copy from the sub window. Select the draft entities and then press the middle mouse button; the sub window disappears and a plus sign gets attached to the cursor indicating that you need to select a point on the Pro/ENGINEER screen to insert the file. Select a point on the screen; the selected entities get inserted and are displayed within an enclosed boundary. Also, the **Move & Resize** dialog box is displayed. Use this dialog box to set the position, scale, and orientation of the sketch. Note that if the *.drw* file does not consist of draft entities, no data will be imported.

In the **Open** dialog box, if you select a *.sec* file that is created in the sketcher environment, the sketch is displayed in the graphics window enclosed within a boundary.

The section imported using the **Data from File** option in the current sketch is an independent copy. The imported section is no longer associated with the source section. The units, dimensions, grid parameters, and accuracy are acquired from the current sketch.

*Figure 3-21 The **Open** dialog box*

Tip: *The display of vertices of the section, the display of dimensions, and the display of constraints can be turned on or off from the **Sketcher** toolbar. This toolbar is in the **Top Toolchest**.*

TUTORIALS
Tutorial 1

In this tutorial, you will import an existing sketch that you had drawn in Tutorial 3 of Chapter 2. After placing the sketch, draw the keyway, as shown in Figure 3-22.

(Expected time: 15 min)

The following steps are required to complete this tutorial:

a. Start Pro/ENGINEER Wildfire 5.0.
b. Set the working directory and create a new object file.
c. Import the section by using the **Data from File** option, refer to Figure 3-23.
d. Draw the keyway and dimension it, refer to Figures 3-24 and 3-25.
e. Modify the dimensions, refer to Figure 3-26.
f. Save the sketch and exit the sketcher environment.

Starting Pro/ENGINEER
1. Start Pro/ENGINEER Wildfire 5.0 by double-clicking on the Pro/ENGINEER icon on the desktop of your computer or by using the **Start** menu.

Creating Sketches in the Sketch Mode-II

Figure 3-22 Sketch for Tutorial 1

Setting the Working Directory

When the Pro/ENGINEER session starts, the first task is to set the working directory. As mentioned earlier, working directory is a directory on your system where you can save the work done in the current session of Pro/ENGINEER. You can set any existing directory on your system as the working directory. Since this is the first tutorial of this chapter, you need to create a folder named *c03* in the *C:\ProE-WF-5.0* folder.

1. Choose the **Set Working Directory** option from the **File** menu; the **Select Working Directory** dialog box is displayed.

2. Select *C:\ProE-WF-5.0*. If this folder does not exists, then first create it prior to setting the working directory.

3. Choose the **Organize** button from the **Select Working Directory** dialog box or right-click in this dialog box to display a shortcut menu. From the shortcut menu, choose the **New Folder** option; the **New Folder** dialog box is displayed.

4. Enter **c03** in the **New Directory** edit box of the **New Folder** dialog box and then choose **OK**; a folder with the name *c03* is created in *C:\ProE-WF-5.0*.

5. Choose **OK** from the **Select Working Directory** dialog box; *C:\ProE-WF-5.0\c03* is set as the working directory.

Starting a New Object File

1. Choose the **New** button from the **File** toolbar; the **New** dialog box is displayed. Select the **Sketch** radio button from the **Type** area of the **New** dialog box; the default name of the sketch appears in the **Name** edit box.

2. Enter *c03tut1* in the **Name** edit box and choose the **OK** button.

   You are in the sketcher environment of the **Sketch** mode. When you enter the sketcher environment, the Navigator is displayed on the left in the graphics window. Slide in the Navigator by clicking on the sash present on its right edge. Now, the drawing area is increased.

Importing the Section

1. Choose **Sketch > Data from File > File System** from the menu bar; the **Open** dialog box is displayed with the working directory as the current directory.

2. Click on the black arrow beside the **ProE-WF-5.0** option in the address bar and choose **c02** from the flyout displayed. Make sure the **Sketch (*.sec)** option is selected in the **Type** drop-down list. Select *c02tut3.sec* and choose the **Open** button from the **Open** dialog box.

3. Move the cursor in the drawing area. Notice that the cursor is attached with a plus mark. Now, click anywhere in the drawing area to place the sketch. The sketch is displayed in the drawing area and the **Move & Resize** dialog box is displayed.

4. Enter **1** in the **Scale** edit box and choose the **Accept changes and close the dialog** button to complete importing the sketch.

5. Choose the **Refit** button from the **View** toolbar. The sketch, similar to the one shown in Figure 3-23, is displayed in the drawing area.

Figure 3-23 Sketch imported and placed in the current file

Drawing the Keyway

To create the keyway, you need to sketch a small rectangle and then the portion of the circle that lies between the horizontal lines and the left vertical line will be removed.

Creating Sketches in the Sketch Mode-II 3-17

1. Choose the **Line** button from the **Sketcher Tools** toolbar.

2. Draw the keyway, as shown in Figure 3-24; the weak dimensions and constraints are automatically applied to the sketch of the keyway.

    The horizontal lines of the keyway and the circle intersect at the points where the lines meet the circle. The portion of the circle that lies between the two horizontal lines of the keyway needs to be deleted from the circle.

3. Choose the **Zoom In** button from the **View** toolbar in the **Top Toolchest**; the cursor is converted into a magnifying glass symbol.

4. Draw a window around the keyway to zoom in it. Now, the display of the keyway is enlarged.

5. Choose the **Delete Segment** button from the **Sketcher Tools** toolbar.

6. Click to select the part of the circle that lies between the two horizontal lines; the selected part is deleted.

7. Choose the **Refit** button from the **View** toolbar to view the full sketch.

Dimensioning the Keyway

Now, you need to apply dimensions to the keyway.

1. Choose the **Normal** button from the **Sketcher Tools** toolbar.

2. Dimension the keyway, as shown in Figure 3-25.

Figure 3-24 Sketch of the keyway with weak dimensions and constraints

Figure 3-25 Sketch after dimensioning the keyway

Modifying the Dimensions

The dimensions of the keyway need to be modified as per the given dimension values.

1. Select the three dimensions of the keyway by pressing CTRL key+left mouse button.

2. Choose the **Modify** button from the **Sketcher Tools** toolbar; the **Modify Dimensions** dialog box is displayed.

3. Clear the **Regenerate** check box and then modify the dimensions of the keyway, refer to Figure 3-26. When you clear the check box, the sketch does not regenerate as you modify the dimensions.

   The dimension that you edit in the **Modify Dimensions** dialog box gets enclosed in a blue box in the sketch.

4. Modify all dimensions. Refer to Figure 3-22 for dimension values.

5. After the dimensions are modified, choose the **Regenerate the section and close the dialog** button from the **Modify Dimensions** dialog box; the message **Dimension modifications successfully completed** is displayed in the message area.

   The sketch after modifying the dimension values of the sketch is shown in Figure 3-26.

Figure 3-26 Sketch after modifying the dimensions

Saving the Sketch

As you may need the sketch later, you must save it.

1. Choose **File > Save** from the menu bar; the **Save Object** dialog box is displayed with the name of the sketch entered earlier.

Creating Sketches in the Sketch Mode-II   3-19

2. Choose the **OK** button; the sketch is saved.

3. After saving the sketch, choose **Window > Close** from the menu bar to exit the **Sketch** mode.

Tutorial 2

In this tutorial, you will draw the sketch for the model shown in Figure 3-27. The sketch is shown in Figure 3-28.   **(Expected time: 30 min)**

Figure 3-27 *Model for Tutorial 2*   *Figure 3-28* *Sketch of the model*

The following steps are required to complete this tutorial:

a. Set the working directory and create a new object file.
b. Draw the sketch using sketcher tools, refer to Figures 3-29 and 3-30.
c. Apply the required constraints and dimensions to the sketched entities, refer to Figure 3-33.
d. Modify the dimensions of the sketch, refer to Figure 3-34.
e. Save the sketch and exit the **Sketch** mode.

Setting the Working Directory

The working directory was selected in Tutorial 1, and therefore there is no need to select the working directory again. But if a new session of Pro/Engineer is started, then you need to set the working directory again by following the steps given next.

1. Open the Navigator by clicking on the sash on the left edge of the Pro/ENGINEER screen; the Navigator slides out. In the Navigator, the **Folder Tree** is displayed at the bottom. Click on the black arrow, which is available on the right of the **Folder Tree**; the **Folder Tree** expands.

2. Click on the plus symbol adjacent to the *ProE-WF-5.0* folder in the Navigator; the contents of the *ProE-WF-5.0* folder are displayed.

3. Now, right-click on the *c03* folder to display a shortcut menu. From this shortcut menu, choose the **Set Working Directory** option; *c03* is set as the working directory.

4. Close the Navigator by clicking the sash on the right edge of the Navigator; the Navigator slides in.

Starting a New Object File
1. Start a new object file in the **Sketch** mode. Name the file as *c03tut2*.

Drawing the Sketch
To draw the outer loop, you need to draw three circles and then draw lines tangent to them.

1. Choose the **Center and Point** button. Draw the circles in a horizontal line, as shown in Figure 3-29.

2. Choose the black arrow on the right of the **Line** button to display a flyout. Choose the **Line Tangent** button from this flyout.

3. Select the left and middle circles on their respective top points; a tangent is drawn from the top of the left circle to the top of the middle circle.

4. Next, select the right and middle circles on their respective top points; a tangent is drawn from the top of the right circle to the top of the middle circle.

5. Similarly, using the **Line Tangent** button, draw the other tangents through the bottom-most points of the left, middle, and right circles, as shown in Figure 3-30.

Figure 3-29 Three circles with weak dimensions and constraints

Figure 3-30 Tangent lines drawn on the circles

Trimming the Circles
The inner portions of the circles are not required. Therefore, you need to trim them.

1. Choose the **Delete Segment** button from the **Sketcher Tools** toolbar.

Creating Sketches in the Sketch Mode-II 3-21

2. Bring the cursor close to the right portion of the left circle; the right part of the circle turns cyan in color. Next, click on it to delete it.

3. Similarly, trim the parts of the middle and right circles that are not required. The sketch after trimming the circles is shown in Figure 3-31.

Drawing the Circles

1. Choose the black arrow on the right of the **Center and Point** button to display a flyout. From this flyout, choose the **Concentric** button; you are prompted to select an arc.

2. Click on the left arc and move the mouse; a circle appears. Select a point inside the sketch to complete the circle. Press the middle mouse button.

> **Tip**: *While drawing a concentric circle, sometimes the circle snaps to the other circle or arc and it becomes difficult to draw a circle of the size you need. In such a case, you can disable the snapping of the circle to the other circle or arc. To do so, use TAB+right-click to disable the snapping or to disable the equal radii constraint that the system tends to apply while drawing the circle.*

Note
You may need to zoom in to select the top arc in the next step.

3. Click on the top arc and move the mouse; a circle appears. Select a point inside the sketch to complete the circle. Press the middle mouse button to end the creation of circle.

4. Click on the right arc and move the mouse; a circle appears. Select a point inside the sketch to complete the circle. Press the middle mouse button to end the creation of circle.

The sketch after drawing all three circles is shown in Figure 3-32.

Figure 3-31 Sketch after trimming the circles   *Figure 3-32 Sketch after drawing all three circles*

Applying the Constraints

1. Choose the arrow on left of the **Vertical** button from the **Sketcher Tools** toolbar; a flyout is displayed.

2. Choose the **Equal** button from the flyout.

3. Select the left arc and then select the right arc to apply the equal radius constraint.

4. Select the left circle and the right circle to apply the equal radius constraint.

5. Again, invoke the Constrain flyout and then choose the **Parallel** button.

6. Click to select the tangent line that connects the left arc and the middle arc at the top and then click to select the tangent line that connects the right arc and the middle arc at the bottom. It is evident from the parallel constraint symbol that the parallel constraint has been applied to the two tangent lines in the sketch.

Dimensioning the Sketch

Pro/ENGINEER applies weak dimensions to the sketch automatically. These dimensions are not the needed dimensions because these dimensions will not help to machine the model. Therefore, you need to dimension the sketch with the dimensions that will be used to machine the model. To do so, follow the steps given next.

1. Choose the **Normal** button from the **Sketch Tool** toolbar.

2. Select the center of the right and left circles; the centers of the circles turn red in color. Now, using the middle mouse button, place the dimension below the sketch. The sketch after applying constraints is as shown in Figure 3-33.

   The rest of the weak dimensions are the needed dimensions.

Modifying the Dimensions

All constraints and dimensions have been applied to the sketch and now dimensions need to be modified.

1. Select all dimensions using the CTRL+ALT+A keys.

2. Choose the **Modify** button; the **Modify Dimensions** dialog box is displayed.

3. Clear the **Regenerate** check box and then modify the values of the dimensions, refer to Figure 3-28 for dimension values.

   When you clear the check box, the sketch does not regenerate while modifying the dimensions. The dimension that you edit in the **Modify Dimensions** dialog box is enclosed in a blue box in the sketch.

Creating Sketches in the Sketch Mode-II

4. After the dimensions are modified, choose the **Regenerate the section and close the dialog** button from the **Modify Dimensions** dialog box; the message **Dimension modifications successfully completed** is displayed in the message area.

The sketch after modifying the dimension values is shown in Figure 3-34.

Figure 3-33 Sketch with constraints

Figure 3-34 Sketch after modifying the dimensions

Saving the Sketch
1. Choose the **Save** button from the **File** toolbar and save the sketch.

Exiting the Sketch Mode
1. After saving the sketch, choose **Window > Close** from the menu bar to exit the **Sketch** mode.

Tutorial 3

In this tutorial, you will draw the sketch of the model shown in Figure 3-35. The sketch is shown in Figure 3-36. **(Expected time: 30 min)**

Figure 3-35 Model for Tutorial 3

Figure 3-36 Sketch of the model

The following steps are required to complete this tutorial:

a. Set the working directory and create a new object file.
b. Draw the sketch using sketcher tools, refer to Figures 3-37 and 3-38.
c. Apply fillets at two corners of the sketch, refer to Figures 3-39 and 3-40.
d. Dimension the sketch, refer to Figure 3-41.
e. Modify dimensions of the sketch, refer to Figure 3-42.
f. Save the sketch and exit the **Sketch** mode.

Setting the Working Directory

The working directory was selected in Tutorial 1, and therefore there is no need to select the working directory again. But if a new session of Pro/Engineer is started, then you have to set the working directory again by following the steps given next.

1. Open the Navigator by clicking on the sash in the left edge of the Pro/ENGINEER window; the Navigator slides out. In the Navigator, the **Folder Tree** is displayed at the bottom. Click on the black arrow that is available at the right-side of the **Folder Tree**; the **Folder Tree** expands.

2. Click on the plus symbol adjacent to the *ProE-WF-5.0* folder in the Navigator. The contents of the *ProE-WF-5.0* folder are displayed.

3. Now, right-click on the *c03* folder to display a shortcut menu. From this shortcut menu, choose the **Set Working Directory** option; *c03* is set as the working directory.

4. Close the Navigator by clicking on the sash on the right edge of the Navigator; the Navigator slides in.

Starting a New Object File

1. Start a new object file in the **Sketch** mode. Name the file as *c03tut3*.

Drawing the Sketch

1. Choose the **Line** button from the **Sketcher Tools** toolbar.

2. Draw the lines with constraints, as shown in Figure 3-37.

3. Choose the **3-Point / Tangent End** button from the **Sketcher Tools** toolbar.

4. Select the endpoint of the left vertical line as the start point of the arc. Complete the arc at the endpoint of the right vertical line.

5. Choose the black arrow on the right of the **Center and Point** button to display a flyout. Choose the **Concentric** button from the flyout; you are prompted to select an arc.

6. Click on the arc; a yellow rubber-band circle appears. Size the circle by moving the cursor and click to complete it. The sketch after drawing the circle is shown in Figure 3-38.

Creating Sketches in the Sketch Mode-II

Figure 3-37 Lines in the sketch with the dimensions turned off for clarity

Figure 3-38 Sketch after drawing the arc and the circle

Note

Choose the **Disp Dims** *button from the* **Sketcher** *toolbar in the* **Top Toolchest** *to turn the dimensions on or off.*

Pro/ENGINEER does not have the options like midpoint, endpoint, or center of an arc or a circle. However, while drawing a sketch, these options are applied in the form of weak constraints. For example, endpoint of any entity snaps the cursor when a new entity is drawn. The middle point constraint appears when you bring the cursor near to the middle point of the line to draw another line.

Filleting the Corners

1. Choose the **Circular** button from the **Sketcher Tools** toolbar; you are prompted to select the two entities to be filleted. The corners that you need to fillet are shown in Figure 3-39.

2. Select the two entities one by one using the left mouse button. The corners of the selected lines are filleted.

The sketch after creating the fillets is shown in Figure 3-40.

Figure 3-39 Corners to be filleted

Figure 3-40 Sketch after creating fillets

Applying the Constraints

1. Choose the black arrow besides the **Vertical** button in the **Sketcher Tools** toolbar; a flyout is displayed.

2. Choose the **Equal** button from the flyout.

3. Click to select the fillets and apply the equal constraint to all fillets.

Dimensioning the Sketch

The weak dimensions are applied to the sketch automatically. These are not the required dimensions and therefore, you need to dimension the sketch manually.

1. Choose the **Normal** button from the **Sketcher Tools** toolbar.

2. Dimension the sketch, as shown in Figure 3-41.

Modifying the Dimensions

You need to modify the dimension values that are assigned to the sketch.

1. Select all dimensions using CTRL+ALT+A.

2. Choose the **Modify** button from the **Sketcher Tools** toolbar; the **Modify Dimensions** dialog box is displayed.

3. Clear the **Regenerate** check box and then modify the values of the dimensions. If this check box is cleared, the sketch does not regenerate while modifying the dimensions.

   The dimension that you edit in the **Modify Dimensions** dialog box is enclosed in a blue box in the sketch.

4. Modify all dimensions. Refer to Figure 3-36 for dimension values.

5. Choose the **Regenerate the section and close the dialog** button from the **Modify Dimensions** dialog box.

   The sketch after modifying the dimension values is shown in Figure 3-42.

Saving the Sketch

1. Choose the **Save** button from the **File** toolbar and save the sketch.

Exiting the Sketch Mode

1. Choose **Window > Close** from the menu bar to exit the **Sketch** mode.

Creating Sketches in the Sketch Mode-II 3-27

Figure 3-41 Sketch after dimensioning

Figure 3-42 Sketch after modifying the dimensions

Self-Evaluation Test

Answer the following questions and then compare them to those given at the end of this chapter:

1. You can increase the length of the spline by adding points before the start point and after the endpoint of the spline. (T/F)

2. While copying the sketched entities, the **Move & Resize** dialog box is also displayed. (T/F)

3. When you modify a weak dimension, it becomes strong. (T/F)

4. You can dimension the length of a centerline. (T/F)

5. The font of the text written in the sketcher environment cannot be modified. (T/F)

6. The _____ of a spline can dynamically be modified.

7. The _____ dialog box is used to modify dimensions.

8. The display of dimensions and constraints can be turned on/off by choosing the _____ and _____ buttons respectively from the **Sketcher** toolbar.

9. The _____ button is used to rotate selected entities.

10. You can delete entities by selecting them and then using the _____ key on the keyboard.

Review Questions

Answer the following questions:

1. How many handles are displayed in the graphics window while moving and resizing entities?

    (a) one (b) two
    (c) three (d) four

2. Which of the following mouse buttons is used to place the dimension?

    (a) left (b) middle
    (c) right (d) mouse is not used for dimensioning

3. Which of the following is the default font for the text in the sketcher environment?

    (a) font (b) filled
    (c) font3d (d) isofont

4. Which of the following toolbars is used to toggle the display of dimensions and constraints in the sketcher environment?

    (a) **Sketcher Tools** (b) **Sketcher**
    (c) **File** (d) **Edit**

5. In which type of dimensioning, the **Dim Orientation** dialog box is displayed while dimensioning the arcs and circles?

    (a) **Normal** (b) **Perimeter**
    (c) **Baseline** (d) None of the above

6. For placing a section in a new sketch, you can use the right mouse button. (T/F)

7. You can create elliptical fillets in Pro/ENGINEER. (T/F)

8. While creating text in the sketcher environment, you need to draw a construction line that will define the height of the text. (T/F)

9. You can modify the dimensions dynamically. (T/F)

10. You can modify a spline by moving its interpolation points. (T/F)

Creating Sketches in the Sketch Mode-II

Exercises

Exercise 1

In this exercise, you will draw the sketch of the model shown in Figure 3-43. The sketch of the model is shown in Figure 3-44. **(Expected time: 30 min)**

Figure 3-43 Solid model for Exercise 1

Figure 3-44 Sketch of the model

Exercise 2

In this exercise, you will draw the sketch of the model shown in Figure 3-45. The sketch of the model is shown in Figure 3-46. **(Expected time: 15 min)**

Figure 3-45 Solid model for Exercise 2

Figure 3-46 Sketch of the model

Exercise 3

In this exercise, you will draw the sketch of the model shown in Figure 3-47. The sketch of the model is shown in Figure 3-48.   **(Expected time: 30 min)**

Figure 3-47 Solid model for Exercise 3

Figure 3-48 Sketch of the model

Answers to Self-Evaluation Test
1. F, **2.** T, **3.** T, **4.** F, **5.** F, **6.** shape, **7. Modify Dimensions**, **8. Disp Dims, Disp Constr**, **9. Move & Resize**, **10.** DEL.

Chapter 4

Creating Base Features

Learning Objectives

After completing this chapter, you will be able to:
- *Use default datums for creating base feature.*
- *Create a solid feature by using the Extrude tool.*
- *Create a thin feature by using the Extrude tool.*
- *Create a solid feature by using the Revolve tool.*
- *Create a thin feature by using the Revolve tool.*
- *Specify the depth of extrusion of a solid feature.*
- *Specify the angle of revolution of a revolved feature.*
- *Orient the datum planes.*
- *Understand the Parent/Child relationship.*
- *Understand the nesting of sketches.*

CREATING BASE FEATURES

The base feature is the first solid feature created while creating a model in the **Part** mode. The base feature is created using the datum planes. However, they can also be created without using the datum planes. But in that case, you do not have proper control over the orientation of feature and direction of feature creation.

While creating the base feature of a model, the designer should be extra careful in specifying its attributes. This is because if the base feature is created wrong, then the features created on it are also created wrong. This results in waste of time and effort. Although Pro/ENGINEER provides you with the options to redefine a feature, doing that also consumes additional time and effort. To create the base feature, you need to enter the **Part** mode.

> **Note**
> *It is recommended that you set the working directory before starting a new file.*

INVOKING THE PART MODE

To invoke the **Part** mode, choose **File > New** from the menu bar or choose the **New** button from the **File** toolbar; the **New** dialog box will be displayed with various modes of Pro/ENGINEER. The **Part** radio button in the **Type** area and the **Solid** radio button in the **Sub-type** area of the **New** dialog box are selected by default. The default name of the part file also appears in the **Name** edit box. You can change the part name as desired and then choose the **OK** button to enter the **Part** mode.

In the **New** dialog box, the **Use default template** check box is selected by default. As a result, the default template provided in Pro/ENGINEER will be used for the part file. This template has certain parameters that will be assigned to the part file that you will create. For example, the units of this model will be Inch lbm Second; the length will be in inch; mass in lb; time in seconds; and temperature in Fahrenheit. After specifying the parameters, if you choose the **OK** button from the **New** dialog box, the **New File Options** dialog box will be displayed, as shown in Figure 4-1.

From the **New File Options** dialog box, you can select the required template file. If you want the default system of units to be mmNs (millimeter Newton sec), then select the **mmns_part_solid** template and choose the **OK** button from this dialog box.

The **Part** mode is the most commonly used mode of Pro/ENGINEER Wildfire 5.0. This is because solid modeling is done in this mode. It should be noted that a solid model is the start of a product development cycle. Product development cycle refers to the development of a product from scratch to its prototype. If you have created a solid model, then it can further be used to generate its drawing views, numerically controlled (NC) machining codes, core and cavity, analyze of the solid model, and so on.

The two-dimensional (2D) sketch drawn in the **Sketch** mode can be converted into a three-dimensional (3D) model in the **Part** mode. The **Part** mode contains the same sketcher environment with similar options to sketch as those available in the **Sketch** mode. There are some sketcher options in the **Part** mode that are not available in the **Sketch** mode because they do not have any use in the **Sketch** mode.

Creating Base Features

*Figure 4-1 The **New File Options** dialog box*

Figure 4-2 shows the initial screen appearance in the **Part** mode. It displays **Model Tree**, three default datum planes, and different toolbars.

> **Tip**: *It is recommended that you always use the datum planes to create a base feature. This is because the model created using the datum planes can be easily oriented. The uses of datum planes are discussed in Chapter 5.*

THE DEFAULT DATUM PLANES

Generally, the three default datum planes act as the first feature in the **Part** mode. These datum planes are used to create the base feature. Also, they are used to draw a 2D sketch and then convert it into a 3D model by using the feature creation tools. The base feature that you create is referenced with default datum planes.

> **Note**
> *Although it is said that the three default datum planes are the first feature in the **Part** mode, in the **Model Tree**, the **RIGHT**, **TOP**, and **FRONT** datum planes appear as three separate features. If you delete any one of them, only that datum plane is deleted.*

These three default datum planes are mutually perpendicular to each other. They are not referenced to each other and are individual features. When a solid model is created, these datum planes adjust their size to the size of the model. You can create any number of datum planes as per your requirement. The creation of additional datum planes is discussed in Chapter 5.

*Figure 4-2 The initial screen appearance in the **Part** mode*

In the releases prior to Release 2000i^2 of Pro/ENGINEER, you had to create the default datum planes. But in recent releases, a default template is provided with the three default datum planes. However, if you do not need the default datum planes, then at the time of creating a new file, you need to clear the **Use default template** check box in the **New** dialog box and select the **Empty** template from the **New File Options** dialog box.

Note
In this chapter, you will learn to use three default datum planes to create the base features. It is important to remember the feature-based nature of Pro/ENGINEER while working on this chapter. The feature-based nature of Pro/ENGINEER has been discussed in Chapter 1.

It is important to create a model in the correct orientation. The correct orientation is the one in which the model will be used later either in assembly or other modes. For example, the Casting component of the Plummer block is modeled in such a way that it always stands vertical.

CREATING A PROTRUSION

Protrusion is defined as a process of adding material defined by a sketched section. In Pro/ENGINEER, there are various options available for adding material to a sketch such as **Extrude**, **Revolve**, **Sweep**, and so on. These options can be chosen from the **Insert** menu in the menu bar. Figure 4-3 shows the options in the **Insert** menu.

Creating Base Features 4-5

The **Base Features** toolbar shown in Figure 4-4 can also be used to invoke the protrusion options. This toolbar is available in the **Right Toolchest** when you are in the **Part** mode.

Figure 4-3 Partial view of the options in the **Insert** menu

Figure 4-4 The **Base Features** toolbar

Extruding a Sketch

The **Extrude** button in the **Base Features** toolbar adds material to the area defined by a sketch drawn. The procedure of creating a base feature by using the **Extrude** button is explained next.

1. When you choose the **Extrude** button from the **Base Features** toolbar or choose **Insert > Extrude** from the menu bar, a dashboard, as shown in Figure 4-5, will be displayed at the top of the drawing area, . This dashboard has all options to define the extrude feature.

Figure 4-5 The **Extrude** dashboard

2. Choose the **Placement** tab from the dashboard to display the slide-down panel. Choose the **Define** button from the slide-down panel to display the **Sketch** dialog box, as shown in Figure 4-6. Alternatively, right-click in the drawing area to display the shortcut menu. Choose the **Define Internal Sketch** option from the shortcut menu; the **Sketch** dialog box will be displayed. You will be prompted to select a sketching plane. Select the datum plane named **FRONT** from the drawing area as the sketching plane.

In the **Sketch** dialog box, the name of the plane that you have selected appears in the **Plane** collector. At the same time, the reference plane is selected by default. The name of the reference datum plane appears in the **Reference** collector of the **Sketch** dialog box. Pro/ENGINEER sets the orientation of the reference plane by default. You can also set the orientation of the reference plane as required by selecting an appropriate option from the **Orientation** drop-down list.

3. After selecting the sketching plane and the reference plane, choose the **Sketch** button in the **Sketch** dialog box.

*Figure 4-6 The **Sketch** dialog box*

Now, you have entered the sketcher environment. The selected datum plane is the sketching plane and is oriented parallel to the screen. In Pro/ENGINEER, the references for the sketch are applied by default. So, you need not select references for the sketches.

If you want to increase the drawing space in the drawing area, close the **Model Tree** by clicking the sash on its right edge, see Figure 4-7.

Figure 4-7 The drawing area after entering the sketcher environment

Creating Base Features

4. Now, choose the **Line** button from the **Sketcher Tools** toolbar to draw the right-half of the I-section and then draw a vertical centerline aligned with the **RIGHT** datum plane. Select all lines on the right-half of the I-section and choose the **Mirror** button from the **Sketcher Tools** toolbar; you will be prompted to select a centerline. Select the centerline to mirror the right-half and to create the I-section, as shown in Figure 4-8. After the I-section is sketched, choose the **Done** button from the **Sketcher Tools** toolbar.

After doing so, the dashboard will be enabled and displayed above the drawing area. The model is created by assuming some default attributes and its preview is displayed in yellow color. The attributes of a model are available on the dashboard and are discussed later in this chapter.

On the dashboard, there is a value edit box containing some default values. These values are the depth of extrusion of the sketch that you have created. Enter the desired value in the value edit box and press ENTER. You can also hold and drag the handle displayed on the model to dynamically specify the depth of extrusion. This drag handle will be visible only after the model is rotated slightly using the middle mouse button.

5. From the dashboard, choose the **Build Feature** button; the required 3D model will be displayed in the drawing area. However, it will appear as a 2D entity. You need to change the display of the model such that the depth of the model can also be viewed. To do so, choose the **Named View List** button from the **View** toolbar and choose the **Default Orientation** option from the flyout displayed. Alternatively, press CTRL+D to change the view to default orientation. Figure 4-8 shows the I-section after extruding it to a certain depth.

Figure 4-8 The I-section extruded to a certain depth

Figures 4-9 and 4-10 show some models created using the **Extrude** button.

Figure 4-9 Model created using the **Extrude** button

Figure 4-10 Model created using the **Extrude** button

The above steps explain how to construct a 3D model using the **Extrude** button. The **Extrude** dashboard and the **Sketch** dialog box that came across while you created the 3D model from an I-section are discussed next.

The Extrude Dashboard

The options and buttons in the **Extrude** dashboard shown in Figure 4-11 are used to extrude a sketch and to specify certain attributes related to the model. These attributes can be assigned to the model before or after the sketch of the model is drawn. The tabs and the buttons available in the dashboard are discussed next.

Figure 4-11 The **Extrude** dashboard

Placement Tab

Choose the **Placement** tab; a slide-down panel will be displayed, as shown in Figure 4-12. The collector in this panel displays **Select 1 item** because the section has not been defined yet. You can select a sketch that is drawn using a datum curve or you can choose the **Define** button to draw a sketch. Choose the **Define** button from this slide-down panel; the **Sketch** dialog box will be displayed.

Figure 4-12 The slide-down panel displayed on choosing the **Placement** tab

Creating Base Features

Options Tab
Choose the **Options** tab; a slide-down panel will be displayed, as shown in Figure 4-13. The slide-down panel is used to specify whether you want the sketch to extrude to one side of the sketching plane or to both sides of the sketching plane. It has **Side 1** and **Side 2** drop-down lists. The options in the **Side 1** drop-down list are discussed next.

Figure 4-13 The slide-down panel displayed on choosing the Options tab

Blind
The **Blind** option is the most commonly used options to define the extrusion depth of the sketch by specifying a depth value. When you select this option from the **Side 1** drop-down list, a default value appears in the dimension edit box that is adjacent to the **Side 1** drop-down list. Enter a value in this dimension edit box and press ENTER to modify the depth of extrusion.

Symmetric
If you select the **Symmetric** option from the **Side 1** drop-down list, the material will be equally added in both the directions of the sketching plane. When you select this option, the **Side 2** drop-down list becomes inactive. This means that you cannot select any option from the **Side 2** drop-down list.

To Selected
The **To Selected** option allows you to select a point, surface, plane, or a curve up to which the section is to be extruded.

The options in the **Side 2** drop-down list are similar to the options in the **Side 1** drop-down list. The **None** option in this drop-down list allows you to extrude the sketch in the first direction only. The **Blind** and **To Selected** options provide the depth of extrusion to the sketch in the second direction.

Properties Tab
Choose the **Properties** tab; the slide-down panel will be displayed. This slide-down panel displays the feature identity in the **Name** collector. When the **i** button is chosen from the slide-down panel, the browser is opened and all the information about the protrusion feature gets displayed. The browser and its properties have been discussed in Chapter 1.

Extrude as solid
This button is chosen by default and is used to create a solid by adding material to the section. When you select a sketch for extrusion using this button, the sketch should be a single closed loop.

> **Tip**: *The features created by using the **To Selected** option do not have a dimension associated with them. Therefore, they cannot be modified by changing the dimension value. However, changing the terminating surface changes the depth of the feature. You will understand it better when you learn the modification of an existing feature.*
>
> *The extrusion depth given using the **Symmetric** option does not appear when you generate dimensions in the drawing views of a model. The drawing views of the model are generated in the Drawing mode of Pro/ENGINEER and are discussed in Chapter 12.*

Extrude as surface

This button is used to create a surface by adding material to the section. Using this button, you can create surface models. The sketch that is drawn for the surface model need not be a closed loop. Surface modeling is discussed in Chapter 15.

Note
*The tabs and the buttons that are available on the **Extrude** dashboard can either be used before drawing the sketch or after drawing it.*

Change depth direction of extrude to other side of sketch

This button is used once the sketch is completed. When you choose this button, it toggles the direction of extrusion with reference to the sketch plane. The direction of extrusion is defined as the direction in which the feature is created with respect to the sketching plane. This direction is displayed by a yellow arrow in the drawing area. When you choose this button, the yellow arrow points in the reverse direction suggesting that the direction of feature creation has been reversed. You can also click on the yellow arrow to flip the direction of extrusion.

Note
The direction of the yellow arrow depends on the type of extrude being created. If material has to be added to a feature, then the arrow, by default, points in the direction toward the user, that is, out of the screen. But, if a cut feature is being created in which material has to be removed from a feature, then, by default, the arrow points into the screen.

If you spin the model using the middle mouse button, then the direction of the arrow can be easily recognized.

Remove Material

The **Remove Material** button is available on the dashboard only after the base feature is created. This is because this button is used to remove the material from an existing feature. Therefore, when you create a base feature, this button is not available. The use of this button is explained in later chapters.

Creating Base Features

Thicken Sketch

The **Thicken Sketch** button is used to create thin parts with specified thickness. When you choose this button, the **Change direction of extrude between one side, other side, or both sides of sketch** button and a dimension edit box appear on the right of this button.

The **Change direction of extrude between one side, other side, or both sides of sketch** button is used to set the direction with respect to the sketch where the thickness should be added. This button appears on the dashboard only when the sketch is completed and you exit the sketcher environment. This button serves three functions. It is used to set the thickness direction to either side of the sketch and even to both sides of the sketch symmetrically. When the sketch is completed, the preview of the model will be displayed in the drawing area. By default, the thickness to the sketch is applied on one side. Now, when you choose the **Change direction of extrude between one side, other side, or both sides of sketch** button, the thickness will be applied to the other side of the sketch. When you choose this button for the second time, the thickness is applied symmetrically to both sides of the sketch.

The dimension edit box that appears when you choose the **Thicken Sketch** button is used to enter the thickness value of the feature to be created. This edit box is available only when you exit the sketcher environment.

Figure 4-14 shows the arrow pointing away from the side of the section wall where the material will be added. If you want to change the direction of the arrow, then choose the **Change direction of extrude between one side, other side, or both sides of sketch** button. Figure 4-15 shows the thickness of the material added to one side of the wall pointed by the arrow.

Figure 4-14 The sketch drawn to thicken

Figure 4-15 Thickness of the material added to one side of the sketch

You can choose the **Change direction of extrude between one side, other side, or both sides of sketch** button so that the thickness of the material added is symmetric to both sides of the section wall, as shown in Figure 4-16. Figure 4-17 shows the model created by using the **Thicken Sketch** button.

Figure 4-16 Thickness of the material added symmetrically to both sides of the sketch

Figure 4-17 Model created using the **Thicken Sketch** button

Pause tool

This button is used to pause the current feature creation. After you choose this button, you can access other available tools such as the **Plane** tool. To resume the current feature creation tool, you can choose the **Resume** button that appears in the place of the **Pause** tool.

Geometry preview/Feature preview

This button has two functions. When the check box on this button is selected, the temporary preview of the created geometry is visible along with its dimensions. When you choose the **Feature Preview** button, the system allows you to preview the feature.

Note that the preview of the feature appears to be a solid model, whereas in the temporary preview the feature appears yellow and translucent.

Note
*By default, the check box in the **Geometry Preview/Feature Preview** button is selected. If this check box is cleared, the temporary preview of the feature will not be displayed.*

Build feature

This button is used to confirm the feature creation and exit the current feature creation tool.

Close

This button is used to abort the creation of feature. When you choose this button, the dashboard is closed.

Note that you can modify the depth of extrusion of the model dynamically after the model is created. To do so, you need to drag the small, white colored square symbol displayed on the model. This method is called dynamic editing and is discussed later. You can also modify the direction of extrusion dynamically. To do so, click on the arrow displayed on the model.

The Sketch Dialog Box

The **Sketch** dialog box will be displayed when you choose the **Define** button from the **Placement** slide-down panel. Alternatively, right-click in the drawing area to display the shortcut menu. Choose the **Define Internal Sketch** option from it; the **Sketch** dialog box will be displayed, as shown in Figure 4-18.

This dialog box is used to select the sketching plane and to set its orientation. As soon as you select the sketching plane, the reference plane and its orientation are selected by default. If you want to change the sketching plane that is already selected, then hold the right mouse button in the drawing area to display a shortcut menu, as shown in Figure 4-19. There are three options in this shortcut menu. By default, the **View Orientation** option is selected. If you choose the **Clear** option, the reference plane and its orientation, which were selected by default, will be cleared and now you can select them manually. Similarly, to change the sketching plane, choose the **Placement** option in the shortcut menu. Again, invoke the shortcut menu and choose the **Clear** option.

*Figure 4-18 The **Sketch** dialog box*

*Figure 4-19 Shortcut menu displayed when the **Sketch** dialog box is invoked*

However, after you select the sketching plane, no matter which reference plane is selected by default, you can select the reference plane manually. The reference you select manually replaces the old reference. If the background of the **Plane** collector or any other collector is displayed in yellow color, then it indicates that you can select its reference from the model. This point should be remembered because this is true with other dialog boxes that are available in Pro/ENGINEER. You will learn more about this later in this book.

The **Flip** button in the **Sketch** dialog box can be used after you select the sketching plane and its orientation. This button is used to set the direction of viewing the sketching plane. When you choose this button, the yellow arrow that is displayed on the sketching plane will change its direction.

> **Tip**: *You can also remove the selected item using the **Sketch** dialog box. To do so, select the item in the dialog box and right-click to invoke a shortcut menu. From this shortcut menu, choose **Remove**.*

In the **Sketch** dialog box, the options in the **Orientation** drop-down list are used to specify the orientation of the horizontal or vertical reference for the sketching plane. Generally, the view is normal to the sketching plane you have selected. In order to orient the sketching plane normal to the viewing direction, you have to specify a plane or a planar surface that is perpendicular to the sketching plane. For example, if you select the **RIGHT** datum plane as the reference plane and then select the **Top** option from the drop-down list, then the **RIGHT** datum plane will be on the top while sketching. The options in this drop-down list are common to other feature creation tools and are available whenever you need to draw a sketch.

Tip: *Remember that if you are creating a protrusion (a material addition process), then no matter what the direction of viewing you choose, the protrusion takes place in the direction toward the user, that is, out of the screen.*

Before you proceed further, you need to understand the three default datum planes that are displayed when you open a new part file. You can view the feature that you have created from different directions. To do so, choose the **Named View List** button from the **View** toolbar in the **Top Toolchest**; a flyout will be displayed, as shown in Figure 4-20. In this flyout, there are some standard preset views provided by Pro/ENGINEER. If you see the feature from the right, your viewing direction will be normal to the **RIGHT** datum plane. If you see the feature from the top, your viewing direction will be normal to the **TOP** datum plane. Similarly, if you see the feature from the front, your viewing direction will be normal to the **FRONT** datum plane.

*Figure 4-20 The **Named View List** flyout*

The options in this flyout list are used to set the orientation of the model in the drawing area.

The options in the **Orientation** drop-down list in the **Sketch** dialog box are very important for the orientation of the base feature. So, you need to select the reference plane very carefully, especially for the base feature. The importance of selecting the reference plane is explained in Figure 4-21. This figure shows two cases, where the sketching plane for both the solid models is same, the same sketch is extruded, and the same option **Top** is selected from the **Orientation** drop-down list in the **Sketch** dialog box, but the reference planes selected are different. The same sketch is used to extrude both the models and the top curve in the sketch is on the top while sketching. Note, the difference in orientation of the resulting models in their default trimetric orientations. The model can be oriented in its default orientation using CTRL+D or by selecting the **Default Orientation** option from the **Named View List** flyout.

Tip: *The **Orientation** dialog box that will be displayed when you choose the **Reorient** button from the **View** toolbar is used to orient the model in the drawing area. This dialog box provides some advanced options to orient the model and also allows you to save the orientation of the model. Using the options in this dialog box, you can dynamically orient a model, by selecting **Dynamic orient** option from the **Type** drop-down list and using available option in it.*

Once a plane has been selected for sketching and the reference plane is oriented, you can enter the sketcher environment. To enter the sketcher environment, choose the **Sketch** button in the **Sketch** dialog box.

Creating Base Features

Figure 4-21 The importance of selecting reference planes

Revolving a Sketch

The **Revolve** button allows you to revolve the sketched section through the specified angle about an axis of the coordinate system or of a geometric centerline. You can also select an existing straight curve or the edge of an existing part. By revolving a sketch, you can add material (protrusion) or remove material (cut). Here, you will learn to use the **Revolve** button to add material. The revolved feature can be revolved on one side of the sketching plane or on both sides of the sketching plane. Besides this, other attributes can be specified to the sketch by using the **Revolve** dashboard. The **Revolve** dashboard is shown in Figure 4-22 and it will be displayed when you choose the **Revolve** button from the **Base Features** toolbar in the **Right Toolchest**.

*Figure 4-22 The **Revolve** dashboard*

Some of the points to be kept in mind while creating a revolve feature are given next.

1. If the revolve feature is a base feature, then the section drawn should be a closed section for revolving the sketch as a solid.

2. Draw a centerline to complete the sketch of the revolved feature or select an axis of the coordinate system or an existing straight curve or an edge of an existing feature as the axis of revolution.

3. The section should be drawn on one side of the centerline.

Revolve as Solid

The **Revolve as solid** button in the **Revolve** dashboard is used to revolve a sketch to create a solid feature. To revolve a sketch using this button, the sketch should be a closed loop. Figures 4-23 and 4-24 show two examples of solid features created by using the **Revolve as solid** button.

Figure 4-23 Example 1

Figure 4-24 Example 2

Revolving a Sketch with Thickness

The **Thicken Sketch** button is used in combination with the **Revolve as solid** button to create revolved features having certain thickness. Unlike in revolving the sketch to create a solid feature, when you revolve a sketch with thickness, the section need not be a closed loop. When you exit the sketcher environment after the section is created, you can specify the side of the section where the material will be added. After specifying the side for the material addition, you can enter the thickness value in the dimension edit box that appears on the dashboard.

Figures 4-25 and 4-26 show the examples of the revolved sketch having some thickness.

UNDERSTANDING THE ORIENTATION OF DATUM PLANES

Consider a case where you need to revolve a sketch through an angle of 270-degree. The trimetric view of the solid model is shown in Figure 4-27. Now, when you start to create the solid model, the first step is to decide the datum plane on which you need to create the sketch.

As evident from the model, the axis of revolution of the model is perpendicular to the **TOP**

Creating Base Features

4-17

Figure 4-25 Example 1

Figure 4-26 Example 2

datum plane. Therefore, the **TOP** datum plane will be selected to be at the top while drawing the sketch. Now, only two options are left for selecting the sketching plane, the **FRONT** and the **RIGHT** datum planes. You can draw the section of the revolved model on any of the two planes. This is because when you view the model, you will notice that the cross-section of the model is parallel to the **RIGHT** datum plane as well as the **FRONT** datum plane.

To draw the cross-section sketch on the two datum planes to achieve the desired orientation of the model is discussed next.

Figure 4-27 The Revolved Feature

Case-1
Drawing a Sketch on the RIGHT Datum Plane

1. When the **Sketch** dialog box is displayed, select the **RIGHT** datum plane as the sketching plane.

   The selected datum plane will get highlighted and the **TOP** datum plane will be automatically selected as the reference plane. The yellow colored arrow will also appear on the sketching plane. This arrow indicates the direction of feature creation. You can change the direction of arrow, but at this stage, accept its default direction.

2. From the **Orientation** drop-down list, select the **Top** option, if not already selected.

   Now, when you draw the sketch, the **RIGHT** datum plane will be parallel to the screen and the **TOP** datum plane will be at the top.

3. Choose the **Sketch** button from the **Sketch** dialog box to enter the sketcher environment.

4. Next, draw the sketch of the cross-section, dimension it, and then modify the dimensions, as shown in Figure 4-28.

Figure 4-28 Sketch with dimensions and constraints

5. Exit the sketcher environment by choosing the **Done** button from the **Sketcher Tools** toolbar.

6. If you have drawn the geometric centerline while sketching, then the preview will be displayed in translucent and yellow color. However, if you have not drawn the centerline, then you will be prompted to select a straight edge or an axis of the coordinate system. In this figure, the geometric centerline is drawn along the Y axis.

7. Select the angle value **270** in the drop-down list available on the dashboard.

8. From the **Named View List** flyout, choose the **Default Orientation** option or press CTRL+D. The model will orient to its default orientation, that is, trimetric view, as shown in Figure 4-29.

But the view that is shown in Figure 4-29 is not the required one. The model is not oriented correctly. This means the direction of feature creation that was selected is not correct in order to get the desired orientation.

Figure 4-29 Default trimetric view of the model

Creating Base Features 4-19

Figure 4-30 shows the sketch drawn on the **RIGHT** datum plane. The sketch is always revolved in the clockwise direction. Remember that the arrow shows the direction in which you will be viewing the sketching plane while in the sketcher environment. Considering the mentioned facts, to orient the sketching plane correctly, the arrow direction should have been flipped by using the **Flip** button in the **Sketch** dialog box. Now, since you have not achieved the desired orientation of the model, exit this feature creation tool, again invoke the **Revolve** button, and this time after you select the sketching plane, choose the **Flip** button to reverse the direction of viewing the sketch. Remember that the case discussed here is applicable when you select the **RIGHT** datum plane as the sketching plane.

*Figure 4-30 Sketch drawn on the **RIGHT** datum plane*

Tip: *You might have difficulty in visualizing the cross-section of a revolved model that has an angle of revolution of 360-degree. This is because the cross-section of the model is not visible. Therefore, you cannot decide the sketch to be drawn for the cross-section of the model.*

Whenever you come across a revolved model, just imagine that if you cut the model along its axis of revolution and remove one quarter of the revolved feature, then the section obtained in one quarter of the revolved feature is the section of the revolved model. Therefore, you need to draw this section in the sketcher environment to create the desired model.

Figure 4-31 shows the sketch on the sketching plane with the direction of the arrow reversed. In this case, the sketch when rotated in the clockwise direction results in the desired orientation of the model, as shown in Figure 4-32.

Case-2
Drawing a Sketch on the FRONT Datum Plane
In this case, you will select the **FRONT** datum plane as the sketching plane and the **RIGHT**

Figure 4-31 Sketch drawn on the **RIGHT** datum plane

Figure 4-32 The desired trimetric view of the model

Tip: *By default, when Pro/ENGINEER creates a revolved model, the material is added in the clockwise direction. You can revolve the model in the counterclockwise direction by using the **Change angle direction of revolve to other side of sketch** button from the **Revolve** dashboard. Also, to revolve the model in the counterclockwise direction, you can enter a negative value for the angle of revolution.*

datum plane as the reference plane. It is recommended that you decide the direction of the arrow at this stage so that you can create the model in the required orientation, refer to Figure 4-27. Figure 4-33 shows the sketch drawn on the **FRONT** datum plane and the default direction of viewing the sketching plane. Remember that the arrow points in the direction along which you view the plane in the sketcher environment. Figure 4-34 shows the default trimetric view of the solid model created in this case.

This is not the desired default orientation of the model. You can still get the desired orientation of the model by choosing the **Change angle direction of revolve to other**

Figure 4-33 Sketch drawn on the **FRONT** datum plane

Figure 4-34 Default trimetric view of the model

Creating Base Features

side of the sketch button from the **Revolve** dashboard, but you should understand the default direction of the yellow arrow on the sketching plane. The desired orientation of the model is shown in Figure 4-35.

Figure 4-36 shows the sketch drawn on the **FRONT** datum plane and the arrow is showing the direction of viewing the sketching plane. The direction of the yellow arrow is reversed by choosing the **Flip** button in the **Sketch** dialog box. Figure 4-37 shows the default trimetric view of the model in this case.

In Figure 4-36, the sketch is revolved in the clockwise direction to create the model shown in Figure 4-37.

Figure 4-35 Desired trimetric view of the model

Figure 4-36 Sketch drawn on the **FRONT** datum plane

Figure 4-37 Default trimetric view of the model

From the two cases discussed, the conclusion is that the arrow that will be displayed when you select the sketching plane is of great importance in orienting the model. Also, the direction of feature creation can be changed once it is created using the **Change angle direction of revolve to other side of the sketch** button from the **Revolve** dashboard.

PARENT-CHILD RELATIONSHIP

Every model created in Pro/ENGINEER is composed of features that in some way or the other are related to other features in the model. The feature that occurs first in the **Model Tree** is called the parent feature and any feature(s) that is related to this feature is called the child feature(s).

There are two types of relationships that can exist between the features, Implicit relationship and Explicit relationship.

Implicit Relationship
This type of relationship exists when the two features are related through equations. These equations are formed using relations.

Explicit Relationship
The explicit relationship is developed when a feature is used as a reference to create another feature. For example, one of the planar surfaces of a feature is used to create another feature, or an edge of a feature is used to dimension the other feature. In this case, the first feature is called the parent feature and the second feature is called the child feature of the first feature. Another example of this type of relationship is, when a hole is referenced to the edges of the surface it is placed on, or to the edges of some other surfaces. In this case, the hole is the child feature of the feature it is referenced to.

Remember that if the parent feature is modified, then the child feature is also modified. Similarly, if the parent feature is deleted, then the child feature is also deleted. For example, if you have used the three default datum planes to create the base feature, and you delete any one of the datum planes, the base feature will also be deleted. In Chapter 6, you will learn how to break the parent-child relationship.

> **Tip**: *If you want to check the parent-child relationship of features in a model, choose **Info > Feature** from the menu bar; you will be prompted to select a feature. After you select the feature, the **Feature Info** window will be displayed. The child features of the selected feature will be displayed in the **Children** area and all parent features will be displayed in the **Parents** area.*

NESTING OF SKETCHES
If more than one closed loop are drawn one inside the other in the sketch of a single feature, it is called nesting of sketches. These sketches are drawn in the sketcher environment. Figure 4-38 shows a sketch in which two circles are created on the base profile.

Advantages of Nesting the Sketches
1. One of the advantages of nesting the sketches is that the number of features used to create a model is reduced. In Figure 4-39, the model has two features. The base feature is the base plate and the second feature is the holes in the model. But, when you nest the two sketches to create the model, you are using only one feature to create the model.

2. There is no parent-child relationship that exists in a nested sketch.

3. The depth of the hole is equal to the depth of extrusion of the base feature. This is because the two circles and the base profile are part of the same sketch. This depends on the designer whether he wants to use the nested sketch to create a part.

Creating Base Features

Figure 4-38 Nested sketch

Figure 4-39 Solid model of the sketch

Disadvantages of Nesting the Sketches

1. In nesting, since the two features on the model are combined into one feature, therefore there is no flexibility in editing the features of a model.

2. If at a later stage, the designer needs to convert the circular holes into elliptical holes with depth as half the depth of extrusion of the base feature, it consumes a lot of time to edit the model.

After understanding the advantages and disadvantages of nesting the sketches, it is recommended to divide a model into separate features. Draw all features as individual features so that the created model is flexible. However, it depends on the need of the designer and the need of the model how the model is approached for creating.

TUTORIALS

Tutorial 1

In this tutorial, you will create the model shown in Figure 4-40. The dimensions of the model are shown in Figure 4-41. **(Estimated time: 30 min)**

The following steps are required to complete this tutorial:

a. Set the working directory and create a new object file in the **Part** mode.
b. First examine the model and then determine the type of protrusion for the model. Select the sketching plane for the model and orient it parallel to the screen.
c. Draw the sketch by using the sketching tools and apply constraints and dimensions, refer to Figures 4-42 through 4-46.
d. Exit the sketcher environment and define the model attributes, refer to Figures 4-47 and 4-48.

Setting the Working Directory

After Pro/ENGINEER session is started, the first task is to set the working directory. A working directory is a directory on your system where you can save the work done in the current session of Pro/ENGINEER. You can set any existing directory on your system as the working directory.

Figure 4-40 The isometric view of the model

Figure 4-41 The front and right views of the model with dimensions

1. Choose the **Set Working Directory** option from the **File** menu; the **Select Working Directory** dialog box is displayed. Browse to the *C:\ProE-WF-5.0* folder.

2. Choose the **Organize** button from the **Select Working Directory** dialog box to display the flyout. Next, choose the **New Folder** option from the flyout; the **New Folder** dialog box is displayed.

3. Enter *c04* in the **New Directory** edit box and choose **OK** from the dialog box. Now, you have created a folder named *c04* in *C:\ProE-WF-5.0*.

4. Next, choose **OK** from the **Select Working Directory** dialog box; the working directory is set to *C:\ProE-WF-5.0\c04* and a message **Successfully changed to *C:\ProE-WF-5.0\c04* directory** is displayed in the message area.

Starting a New Object File

Solid models are created in the **Part** mode of Pro/ENGINEER. The file extension for the files created in this mode is *.prt*.

1. Choose the **New** button from the **File** toolbar; the **New** dialog box is displayed. The **Part** radio button is selected by default in the **Type** area and the **Solid** radio button is selected by default in the **Sub-type** area of the **New** dialog box.

2. Enter the file name as *c04tut1* in the **Name** edit box and choose the **OK** button. The three default datum planes are displayed in the drawing area. Also, the **Model Tree** appears on the left of the drawing area in the Navigator.

4. Close the **Model Tree** by clicking on the sash present at the right edge of the Navigator. Now, the drawing area is increased.

Creating Base Features

Selecting the Extrude Option

The given solid model is created by extruding the sketch to a distance of 75. Therefore, the sketch will be extruded as a solid to create the model.

1. Choose **Insert > Extrude** from the menu bar or choose the **Extrude** button from the **Base Features** toolbar; the **Extrude** dashboard is displayed on the top of the drawing area. All the attributes needed to create the model will be defined after the sketch is drawn.

Selecting the Sketching Plane

To create a sketch for the extruded feature, first you need to select the sketching plane for the model. The **FRONT** datum plane will be selected as the sketching plane. The sketching plane is selected such that the direction of extrusion of the solid model is perpendicular to it. From the trimetric view of the model shown in Figure 4-40, it is evident that the direction of extrusion of the model is perpendicular to the **FRONT** datum plane.

1. Choose the **Placement** tab from the **Extrude** dashboard to display the slide-down panel. Next, choose the **Define** button from the slide-down panel; the **Sketch** dialog box is displayed.

2. Select the **FRONT** datum plane from the drawing area as the sketching plane. As you select the sketching plane, the reference plane and its orientation are set automatically. The reference plane is selected to orient the sketching plane.
   The yellow arrow appeared on the sketching plane indicates the direction of viewing the sketch.

   In the **Sketch** dialog box, the **Reference** box displays **RIGHT:F1(DATUM PLANE)**. This indicates that the **RIGHT** datum plane is selected as the reference plane. In the **Orientation** drop-down list, the **Right** option is selected by default. This means while drawing the sketch, the **RIGHT** datum plane will be on the right. The **RIGHT** datum plane will be perpendicular to the sketching plane and the sketching plane will be parallel to the screen.

3. Choose the **Sketch** button in the **Sketch** dialog box to enter the Sketcher environment.

Drawing the Sketch

You need to draw the sketch of the solid model that will be extruded later to create the 3D model.

1. Choose the **Rectangle** button from the **Sketcher Tools** toolbar.

2. Draw a rectangle by defining its lower left corner and upper right corner. The rectangle is created and weak dimensions are applied to it.

   You will notice that strong vertical and horizontal constraints are applied to the lines composing the rectangle. This is because drawing a rectangle is itself a constraint to the lines composing the rectangle.

3. Choose the **One-By-One** button from the **Sketcher Tools** toolbar.

4. Select the right vertical line; the line turns red. Press the DELETE key to delete it. The sketch after deleting the vertical line is shown in Figure 4-42.

5. Now, draw the lines and arc. Some weak dimensions and constraints are applied to the sketch, as shown in Figure 4-43.

Figure 4-42 The outer loop of the sketch with weak dimensions

Figure 4-43 The sketch before modifying the weak dimensions with all datums turned off

Note
As evident from Figure 4-43, strong constraints are also applied to the sketch while drawing it. However, if these strong constraints are not applied when you draw the sketch, you need to apply these constraints manually.

*The center of the arc and the **TOP** datum plane are aligned by default. In case, they are not aligned, you need to align them. Choose the **Coincident** button from the flyout, which is displayed after choosing the **Vertical** button from the **Sketcher Tools** toolbar. Select the center of the arc and then select the **TOP** datum plane. Now, the center and the datum plane are aligned.*

Applying Constraints to the Sketch

You need to apply equal length constraints to the sketch in order to maintain the design intent of the model.

1. Choose the arrow on the right of the **Vertical** button from the **Sketcher Tools** toolbar; a flyout is displayed.

2. Choose the **Equal** button from the flyout and select the two vertical lines on the right of the sketch. The weak constraint L_2 was applied when the two vertical lines were drawn. Now, the equal length constraint L_2 is applied to both the lines. The constraint labels like L_2 or L_3 vary from sketch to sketch.

Creating Base Features

3. Select the two horizontal lines that are connected to the arc to apply the equal length constraint. The equal length constraint L_2 is applied to both the lines and the constraint symbol L_2 on the two right vertical lines is changed to L_1.

The sketch after applying the equal length constraints is shown in Figure 4-44.

Dimensioning the Sketch

Although some weak dimensions are applied to the sketch, you need to add a dimension to the sketch.

1. Choose the **Normal** button from the **Sketcher Tools** toolbar.

2. Select the center of the arc and the upper right vertical line and then place the dimension by using the middle mouse button, as shown in Figure 4-45.

You need to dimension only these entities because the rest of the weak dimensions are useful dimensions and can be modified directly.

Note
The line numbers displayed in your sketch may be different from the one given in these figures.

If the dimensions in your sketch are different from those shown in Figure 4-45, add the missing dimensions and delete the dimensions that are not required.

Modifying the Dimensions

You need to modify the dimension values of the sketch. The default dimensions shown in Figure 4-45 also include the length and width of the rectangle and the distance of the sketched section from the selected references. It is recommended that you draw the base feature symmetrical with the other two datum planes. As a result, the distance from the **RIGHT** datum plane is 100 (200 divided by 2 is equal to 100).

1. Select the sketch and dimensions using the CTRL+ALT+A keys.

2. Choose the **Modify** button from the **Sketcher Tools** toolbar; the **Modify Dimensions** dialog box is displayed. All dimensions in the sketch are displayed in this dialog box, and each dimension has a separate thumbwheel and an edit box. You can use the thumbwheel or the edit box to modify dimensions. It is recommended to use the edit boxes to modify dimensions, if the desired value is not obtained using the thumbwheel.

3. Clear the **Regenerate** check box; any modification done in a dimension value does not update the sketch during modification. The dimensions get modified after you exit the **Modify Dimensions** dialog box. It is recommended to clear the **Regenerate** check box when more than one dimension has to be modified.

Figure 4-44 Equal length constraints applied to the sketch

Figure 4-45 Dimension added to the sketch

4. Modify all dimensions one by one, as shown in Figure 4-46. You will notice that the dimension you select in the **Modify Dimensions** dialog box is enclosed in a blue box in the drawing area.

5. After modifying the dimensions, choose the **Regenerate the section and close the dialog** button from the **Modify Dimensions** dialog box; the message **Dimension modifications successfully completed** is displayed in the message area.

6. Choose the **Done** button from the **Sketcher Tools** toolbar to exit the sketcher environment.

Specifying the Model Attributes

Next, you need to specify the attributes to create the model.

1. Choose the **Named View List** button from the **View** toolbar; a flyout is displayed. Choose the **Default Orientation** option from the flyout or press CTRL+D; the default trimetric view of the model is displayed in the drawing area.

   This display gives you a better view of the sketch in the 3D space. The model is displayed in yellow and is translucent. Also, the yellow colored arrow is displayed on the model indicating the direction of extrusion. The model may not fit fully in the drawing area.

2. Press CTRL+middle mouse button and drag the mouse downward in the drawing area. Notice that a red rubber band line is attached to the cursor. The length of the rubber band line gives an idea about the extent you need to zoom the model. After the model is in the drawing area, release the middle mouse button and the CTRL key.

   Note
   *Alternatively, to fit the model into the drawing area, choose the **Refit** button from the **View** toolbar in the **Top Toolchest**.*

Creating Base Features   4-29

The model appears, as shown in Figure 4-47. All attributes selected by default in the **Extrude** dashboard will be used to create the model. You need to change only the depth of extrusion.

3. Enter **75** in the edit box present on the **Extrude** dashboard, and press ENTER; the model in the drawing area is displayed with the specified depth of extrusion.

Figure 4-46 Sketch after modifying the dimensions

Figure 4-47 Arrow showing the direction of feature creation

4. Choose the **Build feature** button on the **Extrude** dashboard to confirm the feature creation and exit the current feature creation tool. The trimetric view of the model is shown in Figure 4-48.

Note

*In Figure 4-48, the display of datum planes and the coordinate system are turned off by choosing the **Plane Display** and **Csys Display** buttons, respectively.*

Saving the Model and Closing the File

Figure 4-48 Default trimetric view of the model

1. Choose the **Save** option from the **File** menu or choose the **Save** button from the **File** toolbar; the **Save Object** dialog box is displayed with the name of the object file that you have specified earlier.

2. Choose the **OK** button from **Save Object** dialog box to save the file.

Note

*You can also change the current name of the file before saving it by choosing **File > Rename** from the menu bar. If you do so, the **Rename** dialog box is displayed. Enter the required name of the file in the **New Name** edit box and then choose the **OK** button to accept the new name.*

3. Choose **File > Close Window** or choose **Window > Close** from the menu bar to close the current window.

Tutorial 2

In this tutorial, you will create the model shown in Figure 4-49. The dimensions of the model are shown in Figure 4-50. **(Expected time: 30 min)**

Figure 4-49 The isometric view of the solid model

Figure 4-50 The front section view of the solid model

The following steps are required to complete this tutorial:

a. Create a new object file in the **Part** mode.
b. First examine the model and then determine the type of protrusion required for the model. Next, select the sketching plane for the model.
c. Draw the sketch for the revolved feature and a centerline to revolve it using the sketching tools and apply dimensions, refer to Figures 4-51 through 4-53.
d. Exit the sketcher environment and define the model attributes, refer to Figures 4-54 and 4-55.

Setting the Working Directory

The working directory was selected in Tutorial 1; therefore, there is no need to select it again. But if you are starting a new session of Pro/ENGINEER, you need to set the working directory again by following the steps given below.

1. Open the Navigator by clicking the sash on the left edge of the main window of Pro/ENGINEER; the Navigator slides out. In the Navigator, the **Folder Tree** is displayed at the bottom. Click on the black arrow on the right of the **Folder Tree**; the **Folder Tree** expands.

2. Click on the plus sign adjacent to the *ProE-WF-5.0* folder in the Navigator; the contents of the *ProE-WF-5.0* folder are displayed.

Creating Base Features

3. Now, right-click on the *c04* folder to display a shortcut menu. Choose the **Set Working Directory** option from the shortcut menu; the working directory is set to *c04*.

4. Close the Navigator by clicking the sash at the right edge of the Navigator.

Starting a New Object File

1. Open a new object file in the **Part** mode and then name the file as *c04tut2*.

   The three default datum planes are displayed in the drawing area. However, if the default datum planes were turned off in the previous tutorial, then they will not appear in the drawing area.

2. Turn on the display of datum planes by using the **Plane Display** button.

Selecting the Revolve Option

The given solid model is a revolved feature that will be created by revolving the sketch through an angle of 360-degree about an axis. Therefore, the **Revolve** button will be used to create the model. There are two methods to invoke the **Revolve** option. The first method is to use the menu bar available on the top of the screen and the second method is to use the **Revolve** button available on the **Base Features** toolbar.

1. Choose **Insert > Revolve** from the menu bar or choose the **Revolve** button from the **Base Features** toolbar; the **Revolve** dashboard is displayed at the top of the drawing area.

   Some of the attributes like rotation angle and direction of rotation of the sketch will be defined after the sketch has been created.

Selecting the Sketching Plane

To create the sketch of the model, first you need to select the sketching plane for the model. Note that the axis of revolution of the revolved feature is normal to the **TOP** datum plane in the model. Therefore, any of the other two datum planes, other than the **TOP** datum plane can be selected as the sketching plane. Here, you will select the **FRONT** datum plane as the sketching plane.

1. Choose the **Placement** tab from the dashboard to display the slide-down panel. Choose the **Define** button from the side-down panel; the **Sketch** dialog box is displayed.

2. Select the **FRONT** datum plane as the sketching plane. As you select the sketching plane, the reference plane and its orientation are set automatically. The reference plane is selected in order to orient the sketching plane.

   In the **Sketch** dialog box, the **Reference** collector displays **RIGHT:F1(DATUM PLANE)**. This indicates that the **RIGHT** datum plane is selected as the reference plane. In the **Orientation** drop-down list, the **Right** option is selected by default. As a result, while drawing the sketch, the **RIGHT** datum plane will be on the right.

The **RIGHT** datum plane will be perpendicular to the sketching plane and the sketching plane will be parallel to the screen.

3. Choose the **Sketch** button from the **Sketch** dialog box.

Drawing the Sketch

You need to draw the sketch of the revolved feature. The sketch to be drawn is the cross-section of the revolved feature, which will be revolved about the centerline.

1. Choose the **Line** button from the **Sketcher Tools** toolbar and then draw the sketch, as shown in Figure 4-51. The sketch should be a closed loop and the bottom horizontal line should be aligned to the **TOP** datum plane.

   As you draw the sketch, weak dimensions and strong constraints are applied to the sketch.

2. Choose the black arrow on the right of the **Line** button to display a flyout. From this flyout, choose the **Geometric Centerline** button. Draw centerline for the axis of revolution. The centerline should be drawn such that it is aligned with the **RIGHT** datum plane, see Figure 4-51.

Dimensioning the Sketch

Weak dimensions are automatically applied to the sketch. Since the model is a revolved feature, you need to manually apply the linear diameter dimensions to the sketch. The linear diameter dimensions are applied by using the centerline that was drawn in the sketch.

> **Tip**: *The linear diameter dimensioning is necessary for all revolved features because mostly all revolved models are machined on a lathe. Therefore, while machining a revolved model, it is necessary that the operator of the machine has a drawing of the model that is diametrically dimensioned.*

1. Choose the **Normal** button from the **Sketcher Tools** toolbar.

2. Select the centerline, the first right vertical line, and then again the centerline.

3. Now, use the middle mouse button to place the dimension on the top of the sketch; the diameter dimension is placed.

   The method to dimension a sketch diametrically has been discussed in Chapter 2.

4. Select the centerline, the second right vertical line, and then again the centerline.

5. Place the dimension below the sketch.

6. Select the centerline, the third right vertical line, and then again the centerline. Now, place the dimension below the previous dimension.

Creating Base Features

Dimension the remaining entities in the sketch, as shown in Figure 4-52.

Figure 4-51 Sketch with weak dimensions

Figure 4-52 Sketch after dimensioning

Modifying the Dimensions

When you dimension a sketch, default dimension values are applied to the sketch. You need to modify the dimension values of the dimensions.

1. Select the sketch and dimensions by using the CTRL+ALT+A keys.

2. Choose the **Modify** button from the **Sketcher Tools** toolbar; the **Modify Dimensions** dialog box is displayed.

3. In this dialog box, clear the **Regenerate** check box and then modify the values of the dimensions, as shown in Figure 4-53. If you clear this check box, any modification of the dimension value will not update the sketch. It is recommended that you clear the **Regenerate** check box if more than one dimension has to be modified.

   You will notice that the dimension that you have selected in the **Modify Dimensions** dialog box is enclosed in a yellow box in the drawing area.

4. After modifying all dimensions, choose the **Regenerate the section and close the dialog** button from the **Modify Dimensions** dialog box; the message **Dimension modifications successfully completed** is displayed in the message area.

5. Choose the **Done** button to exit the sketcher environment.

Specifying the Model Attributes

When you exit the sketcher environment, the **Revolve** dashboard above the drawing area is enabled again. Using this dashboard, you can specify the angle of revolution for the revolved feature.

1. Choose the **Named View List** button from the **View** toolbar to display a flyout. Choose the **Default Orientation** option from the flyout or press CTRL+D; the model orients in its default orientation, that is, trimetric view, as shown in Figure 4-54.

The feature will orient in its default orientation, refer to Figure 4-54. This display gives you a better view of the sketch in the 3D space. Model appears in yellow color and is translucent. The drag handle is also available on the model that can be used to modify the angle of revolution dynamically.

Figure 4-53 Sketch after modifying the dimensions

Figure 4-54 Preview of the model in the default trimetric view

All attributes needed to create a solid model are selected by default in the **Revolve** dashboard.

Note
If the model is not fully displayed in the drawing area, you may need to zoom it out.

2. Choose the **Build feature** button in the **Revolve** dashboard. The model appears as the one shown in Figure 4-55.

Saving the Model

1. Choose the **Save** option from the **File** menu or choose the **Save** button from the **File** toolbar; the **Save Object** dialog box is displayed with the name of the object file specified earlier.

Figure 4-55 The default trimetric view of the model

2. Choose the **OK** button to save the file.

Creating Base Features

4-35

Closing the Current Window

The given model is completed and is also saved. Now, you can close the current window.

1. Choose **File > Close Window** from the menu bar or choose **Window > Close** from the menu bar.

Note
*If you need to view the **Model Tree** of the model that you have created, then open it. Click on the sash present at the left edge of the drawing area; the **Model Tree** slides out. To close the sash again, click it again; the **Model Tree** slides in.*

Tutorial 3

In this tutorial, you will create the model shown in Figure 4-56. The dimensions of the sketch are shown in Figure 4-57. The thickness of the model is 1 unit and depth of extrusion is 25 units.

(Expected time: 30 min)

Figure 4-56 The isometric view of the model   *Figure 4-57 The front and the right views*

The following steps are required to complete this tutorial:

a. Create a new object file in the **Part** mode.
b. First examine the model and then determine the type of protrusion for the model. Next, select the sketching plane for the model.
c. Draw the sketch by using the sketching tools and then apply dimensions to it, refer to Figures 4-58 through 4-60.
d. Specify the attributes to create the model and then save it, refer to Figures 4-62 and 4-63.

The working directory was selected in Tutorial 1, and therefore, you do not need to select the working directory again. But if a new session of Pro/ENGINEER is started, then set the working directory using the Navigator.

Starting a New Object File

1. Open a new object file in the **Part** mode and then name it as *c04tut3*.

   If the default datum planes were not turned off in the previous tutorial, they will appear in the drawing area. If the datum planes are not displayed, turn them on by using the **Plane Display** button.

Selecting the Extrude Option

The given thin solid model is created by extruding the sketch to a distance of 25 units. So, you need to use the **Thicken Sketch** button on the **Extrude** dashboard to create the model.

1. Choose **Insert > Extrude** from the menu bar or choose the **Extrude** button from the **Base Features** toolbar; the **Extrude** dashboard is displayed at the top of the drawing area.

   Most of the attributes needed to create the model will be defined after the sketch is drawn.

Selecting the Sketching Plane

From the isometric view of the model shown in Figure 4-56, it is clear that the direction of extrusion of the solid model is perpendicular to the **FRONT** datum plane. Therefore, you need to select the **FRONT** datum plane as the sketching plane.

1. Choose the **Placement** tab from the dashboard to display the slide-down panel. Choose the **Define** button from the slide-down panel; the **Sketch** dialog box is displayed.

2. Select the **FRONT** datum plane as the sketching plane; the reference plane and its orientation are set automatically.

   In the **Sketch** dialog box, the **Reference** collector displays **RIGHT:F1(DATUM PLANE)**. This indicates that the **RIGHT** datum plane is selected as the reference plane. In the **Orientation** drop-down list, the **Right** option is selected by default. As a result, while drawing the sketch, the **RIGHT** datum plane will be on the right.

   The **RIGHT** datum plane will be perpendicular to the sketching plane and the sketching plane will be parallel to the screen.

3. Choose the **Sketch** button in the **Sketch** dialog box to enter the sketching environment.

Drawing the Sketch

Using the sketcher tools, you need to draw the sketch for the thin extruded model.

1. Draw the sketch of the model, as shown in Figure 4-58, by using the **Line** and **3-Point / Tangent End** buttons from the **Sketcher Tools** toolbar.

Creating Base Features 4-37

Figure 4-58 Sketch of the thin extruded model

Applying Constraints to the Sketch

While drawing the sketch, some weak dimensions are applied to the sketch. These dimensions appear in gray color. Although the weak dimensions are applied, you need to apply other constraints to the sketch.

1. Choose the arrow on the right of the **Vertical** button in the **Sketcher Tools** toolbar; a flyout is displayed.

2. Choose the **Coincident** button from the flyout.

3. Select the center of the arc and then the **RIGHT** datum plane; the center of the arc is aligned with the **RIGHT** datum plane.

4. Select the bottom horizontal line and then the **TOP** datum plane. The bottom horizontal line is aligned with the **TOP** datum plane. Skip this point, if the two horizontal lines on the top are aligned with the **TOP** datum plane.

5. Choose the **Equal** button and then select the two horizontal lines on the top to apply the equal length constraint.

6. Choose the **Perpendicular** button and select the left horizontal line and the arc; the perpendicular constraint symbol is applied. Similarly, select the right horizontal line and the arc; the perpendicular constraint symbol is applied. If these constraints have already been applied, the **Resolve Sketch** dialog box is displayed. Choose **Undo** from this dialog box.

The sketch after applying constraints is shown in Figure 4-59.

Note
When you apply constraints to the sketch, some of the weak dimensions are automatically deleted. But, if you need certain constraints that were applied while drawing the sketch, you can use them and need not apply those constraints again.

Modifying Dimensions

You need to modify the dimension values of the weak dimensions.

1. Select the sketch and dimensions by using the CTRL+ALT+A keys.

2. Choose the **Modify** button from the **Sketcher Tools** toolbar; the **Modify Dimensions** dialog box is displayed.

3. In this dialog box, clear the **Regenerate** check box and then modify the values of the dimensions, as shown in Figure 4-60. When you clear the **Regenerate** check box, any modification in a dimension value does not update the sketch. As mentioned earlier, it is recommended that you clear the **Regenerate** check box when more than one dimension has to be modified.

   You will notice that the dimension selected in the **Modify Dimensions** dialog box is enclosed in a blue box in the drawing area.

4. After modifying all dimensions, choose the **Regenerate the section and close the dialog** button from the **Modify Dimensions** dialog box; the message **Dimension modifications successfully completed** is displayed in the message area.

5. Choose the **Done** button to exit the sketcher environment.

Figure 4-59 Sketch after applying constraints

Figure 4-60 Figure after modifying the dimensions

Specifying the Model Attributes

The attributes required to create the model need to be selected from the **Extrude** dashboard.

Creating Base Features   4-39

1. Choose the **Thicken Sketch** button from the **Extrude** dashboard; the model changes to a thin model of default thickness, as shown in Figure 4-61.

2. Choose the **Named View List** button from the **View** toolbar; a flyout is displayed. Choose the **Default Orientation** option from the flyout or you can press CTRL+D.

   The default trimetric view of the model is displayed. The model appears yellow in color and is translucent. If the model does not fit completely on the screen, then you need to zoom out. This display gives you a better view of the model in the 3D space.

   There are two drop-down lists on the **Extrude** dashboard. The drop-down list on the left of the dashboard is used to enter the depth of extrusion and the drop-down list on the right appears only when the **Thicken Sketch** button is selected. This drop-down list is used to specify the thickness value of the thin model.

3. Enter **25** in the left edit box and press ENTER.

4. Enter **1** in the right edit box and press ENTER. The model appears, as shown in Figure 4-62. The model is completed and now you need to exit the **Extrude** dashboard.

Figure 4-61 Arrow showing the direction of material addition with respect to the boundary of the section

Figure 4-62 The default trimetric view of the model

5. Choose the **Build feature** button from the **Extrude** dashboard; the default trimetric view of the model is displayed, as shown in Figure 4-63.

Saving the Model

1. Choose the **Save** option from the **File** menu or choose the **Save** button from the **Top Toolchest**; the **Save Object** dialog box is displayed with the name of the object file specified earlier.

Figure 4-63 The default trimetric view of the solid model

2. Choose the **OK** button. to save the file.

Closing the Current Window

The given model is completed and is also saved. Now, you need to close the current window.

1. Choose **File > Close Window** from the menu bar.

Tutorial 4

In this tutorial, you will create the model shown in Figure 4-64. Figure 4-65 shows the front view and dimensions of the model. Also, you will generate the general drawing view on a format file and then print the file. The thickness of the model is 1 units. **(Expected time: 30 min)**

Figure 4-64 The isometric view of the solid model   *Figure 4-65* The front view of the solid model

The following steps are required to complete this tutorial:

a. Create a new object file in the **Part** mode.
b. First examine the model and then determine the type of protrusion for the model. Next, select the sketching plane for the model.
c. Draw the sketch by using sketching tools, apply dimensions, and modify dimension values, refer to Figures 4-66 through 4-69.
d. Specify the attributes for the model and then save it, refer to Figures 4-70 and 4-71.
e. Insert the isometric view of the model in a format file and then print the file.

The working directory was selected in Tutorial 1, therefore, you do not need to select the directory again. But if a new session of Pro/ENGINEER is started, then set the working directory using the Navigator.

Starting a New Object File

1. Start a new object file in the **Part** mode and then name the file as *c04tut4*.

The default datum planes are displayed, if they are not turned off.

Creating Base Features 4-41

If the default datum planes were not turned off in the previous tutorial, they will appear in the drawing area. If the datum planes are not displayed, turn them on by using the **Plane Display** button.

Selecting the Revolve Option

Now, you need to create a revolved thin model by revolving the sketch through a given angle. Therefore, you need to use the **Thicken Sketch** button in the **Revolve** dashboard to create the model. There are two methods to invoke the **Revolve** option. The first method is to use the menu bar present on the top of the screen and the second method is to use the **Base Features** toolbar.

1. Choose **Insert > Revolve** from the menu bar or choose the **Revolve** button from the **Base Features** toolbar; the **Revolve** dashboard appears on the top of the drawing area.

2. Choose the **Thicken Sketch** button from the dashboard. Make sure that the **Revolve as solid** button is chosen in the dashboard.

   In this tutorial, the **Thicken Sketch** button is chosen before drawing the sketch because the sketch to be drawn is an open section. It is not possible to draw an open sketch with the default attributes selected in the **Revolve** dashboard, that can be accepted by Pro/ENGINEER.

3. Choose the **Placement** tab to display the slide-down panel. Choose the **Define** button from the slide-down panel; the **Sketch** dialog box is displayed.

Selecting the Sketch Plane

Note that in Figure 4-64, the imaginary axis of revolution of the revolved feature is normal to the **TOP** datum plane. Therefore, the **TOP** datum plane will be selected to be at the top while drawing the sketch. Now, you need to decide the sketching plane from the **RIGHT** and **FRONT** datum planes. Any of the two datum planes can be selected as the sketching plane. In this case, the **RIGHT** datum plane will be selected as the sketching plane.

1. Select the **RIGHT** datum plane as the sketching plane. As you select the sketching plane, the reference plane and its orientation are set automatically by default.

   In the **Sketch** dialog box, the **Reference** box displays **TOP:F2(DATUM PLANE)**. This indicates that the **TOP** datum plane is selected as the reference plane. But you need to change the orientation of the plane.

2. From the **Orientation** drop-down list, select the **Top** option.

   The **TOP** datum plane will be perpendicular to the sketching plane and the sketching plane will be parallel to the screen.

3. Choose the **Flip** button to change the direction of the yellow arrow that appears on the sketching plane; the direction of viewing the sketching plane is reversed.

4. Choose the **Sketch** button in the **Sketch** dialog box.

Drawing the Sketch

You need to draw the sketch of the thin extruded model. The sketch can be a closed loop or an open loop. Here, you need to draw an open sketch.

1. Draw a geometric centerline and then draw the sketch, as shown in Figure 4-66. The geometric centerline is the axis of revolution. To fillet the corners, choose the **Circular** button from the **Right Toolchest.**

   While drawing the sketch, weak constraints are applied to the sketch.

Applying Constraints to the Sketch

Weak constraints are applied to the sketch while drawing but you need to apply the constraints to the sketch using the constraints flyout.

1. Choose the arrow on the right of the **Vertical** button from the **Sketcher Tools** toolbar; a flyout is displayed.

2. Choose the **Equal** button from the flyout.

3. Select the two horizontal lines with the constraint symbol L_1 one by one, as shown in Figure 4-67, to apply the equal length constraint.

4. Select the two horizontal lines with the constraint symbol L_2 one by one, as shown in Figure 4-67 to apply the equal length constraint.

5. Select the vertical lines with the constraint symbol L_3, as shown in Figure 4-67, to apply the equal length constraint.

6. Select all fillets to apply equal radii constraint.

Applying Dimensions to the Sketch

The weak dimensions are automatically applied to the sketch. Remember that since the model is a revolved feature, you need to apply the linear diameter dimensions to the sketch manually. You need to apply the linear diameter dimensions by using the centerline drawn in the sketch.

1. Choose the **Normal** button from the **Sketcher Tools** toolbar.

2. Dimension the sketch, as shown in Figure 4-68.

Creating Base Features

Figure 4-66 Sketch for the revolved feature with the weak dimensions turned off for clarity

Figure 4-67 Sketch after applying the constraints with the weak dimensions turned off for clarity

Modifying the Dimensions

You need to modify the dimension values of the weak dimensions.

1. Select the sketch and dimensions by using the CTRL+ALT+A keys.

2. Choose the **Modify** button from the **Sketcher Tools** toolbar; the **Modify Dimensions** dialog box is displayed.

3. In this dialog box, clear the **Regenerate** check box and then modify the values of the dimensions, as shown in Figure 4-69.

   You will notice that the dimension you select in the **Modify Dimensions** dialog box is enclosed in a yellow box in the drawing area.

4. After modifying all dimensions, choose the **Regenerate the section and close the dialog**

Figure 4-68 Sketch after dimensioning with the constraints turned off for clarity

Figure 4-69 Sketch after modifying the dimensions with the constraints turned off for clarity button from the **Modify Dimensions** dialog box; the message **Dimension modifications successfully completed** is displayed in the message area.

5. Choose the **Done** button to exit the sketcher environment.

Specifying the Model Attributes

After completing the sketch, you need to specify the side to which thickness of material will be applied. The thickness can be applied outside the section, inside the section, or symmetrically to both sides of the section boundary. In this model, you need to apply the thickness inside the section.

When you exit the sketcher environment, the model assumes some default attributes and therefore it is not displayed in the drawing area.

1. Enter the thickness value **1** in the drop-down list available on the **Revolve** dashboard, and press ENTER.

2. Enter **270** in the edit box present at the left of the **Revolve** dashboard and press ENTER. The default value of angle of revolution is displayed as 360.

3. Choose the **Named View List** button from the **View** toolbar to display the flyout. From the flyout, choose the **Default Orientation** option or press CTRL+D; the trimetric view of the model after specifying all attributes is displayed, as shown in Figure 4-70.

4. Choose the **Build feature** button from the **Revolve** dashboard. The default trimetric view of the model is shown in Figure 4-71.

Figure 4-70 Model after specifying attributes

Figure 4-71 Default trimetric view of the model

Saving the Model

1. Choose the **Save** option from the **File** menu or choose the **Save** button from the **Top Toolchest**; the **Save Object** dialog box is displayed with the name of the object file specified earlier.

Creating Base Features

2. Press **OK** to save the file.

Starting the Format File

1. Choose the **New** button from the **Top Toolchest**; the **New** dialog box is displayed.

2. Select the **Format** radio button from the **Type** area in the **New** dialog box and name the file as *Format1*. Choose **OK** from the **New** dialog box; the **New Format** dialog box is displayed.

3. Select the **Empty** radio button from the **Specify Template** area and the **Landscape** radio button from the **Orientation** area of the **New Format** dialog box, if they are not selected.

4. Select **A** from the **Standard Size** drop-down list in the **Size** area and then choose **OK** to proceed to the **Format** mode. Note that a sheet of the size A is displayed on the screen. This is evident from the text displayed below the sheet on the screen.

Creating Format

1. Choose **Sketch > Insert > Offset Edge** from the **Ribbon**; the **OFFSET OPER** menu is displayed. Choose the **Ent Chain** option from the **OFFSET OPER** menu and then select all four border lines of the format by drawing a window around them. Press the middle mouse button after making the selection; the **Message Input Window** is displayed at top of the drawing area.

   An arrow is displayed pointing outward. This arrow displays the direction of the offset. Since you need to offset the lines in the opposite direction, you will specify a negative offset distance.

2. Enter the value **-0.25** in the **Message Input Window** and press ENTER. Now, press the middle mouse button twice to exit the **Menu Manager** dialog box.

3. Choose **Table > Table > Table** from the **Ribbon** to display the **TABLE CREATE** menu.

4. Choose **Ascending > Leftward > By Length** from the **TABLE CREATE** menu and then choose **Vertex** from the **GET POINT** submenu.

5. Select the lower right corner of the new rectangle created by offsetting the border lines; the **Message Input Window** is displayed at top of the drawing area. The corner of the new rectangle is selected because the title block will be created such that it is attached to the new rectangle. Now, you need to enter dimensions for the title block.

6. Enter **1.25** as the width of the first column in the **Message Input Window** and press ENTER. Similarly, enter **1.25** as the width of the second column and press ENTER. You are prompted to enter the width for the next column.

7. Enter **1.25** as the width of the third column in **Message Input Window** and press

ENTER. Similarly, enter **1.25** as the width of the fourth column and press ENTER; you are prompted to enter the width for the next column.

8. After entering the width of the column, press the middle mouse button. Now, you are prompted to enter the height of the row. Enter **0.75** as the height of the first row and press ENTER twice; the title block is created.

Note
*You need to double-click on any of the columns of the table to display the **Note Properties** dialog box and enter the text in the respective columns, as required.*

9. Choose the **Save** button from the **File** toolbar; the **Save Object** dialog box is displayed with the name of the file specified earlier.

10. Choose the **OK** button from the **Save Object** dialog box to save the file.

11. Choose **File > Close Window** from the menu bar to close the format file.

Generating the Isometric View in the Format File

Now, you need to create a new drawing file and then generate the isometric view of the model.

1. After saving the model, choose the **New** button from the **File** toolbar; the **New dialog** box is displayed.

2. Select the **Drawing** radio button from the **Type** area; a default name is displayed in the **Name** edit box.

3. Enter *c04tut4* in the **Name** edit box and choose **OK** from the **New** dialog box; the **New Drawing** dialog box is displayed, as shown in Figure 4-72. The name *c04tut4* is displayed in the **Default Model** edit box and the **Use template** radio button is selected by default in the **Specify Template** area of the dialog box.

4. Select the **Empty with format** radio button from the **Specify Template** area and choose the **Browse** button from the **Format** area; the **Open** dialog box is displayed.

5. Select the *Format1.frm* file that you have created and choose **Open**. Next, choose the **OK** button from the **New Drawing** dialog box; the drawing mode is invoked and the format file is displayed in the drawing area.

*Figure 4-72 The **New Drawing** dialog box*

Creating Base Features 4-47

6. Choose **Layout > Model Views > General** from the **Ribbon**.

7. Click once in the drawing area; the default view of the model is displayed in the drawing area and the **Drawing View** dialog box is displayed, as shown in Figure 4-73.

*Figure 4-73 The **Drawing View** dialog box*

8. Select the **Default Orientation** option from the list below the **Model view names** edit box. Also, select the **Isometric** option from the **Default orientation** drop-down list and choose **Apply** from the dialog box. The default view of the model is displayed in the drawing area.

9. Now, select the **Scale** option from the **Categories** list in the **Drawing View** dialog box; the dialog box displayed is as shown in Figure 4-74.

   The **Default scale for sheet** radio button is selected in the **Scale and perspective options** area by default and the default scale value for the sheet is displayed.

10. Select the **Custom scale** radio button and enter **0.04** in the edit box displayed besides the **Custom scale** radio button. Now, choose **Apply** from the **Drawing View** dialog box; the scaled model is displayed in the drawing area.

11. Choose **Close** from the **Drawing View** dialog box to close the dialog box and complete the generation of the isometric view of the model.

*Figure 4-74 The **Drawing View** dialog box with the **Scale** option is selected*

12. Notice that the isometric view of the model is displayed in the drawing area along with the scale factor mentioned at the bottom of the isometric view. If you want to erase the note displayed, choose **Annotate > Insert > Show Model Annotations** from the **Ribbon**. Next, expand the **new_view_1** node and then the **Annotations** node in the drawing tree. Select the draft note node and right-click to invoke a shortcut menu. Choose **Erase** from the shortcut menu to erase the note. The drawing area after erasing the note is similar to the one shown in Figure 4-75.

Saving and Printing the Drawing File

1. Choose **File > Print** from the menu bar; the **Print** dialog box is displayed.

2. Choose the **Commands and Settings** button to display the drop-down list and select the **MS Printer Manager** option from it.

   Note
   *The **MS Printer Manager** option is used to print an active model through the printer installed as the default printer on your computer. It is recommended that you use the laser printer to print the drawing files.*

3. Now, choose the **OK** button from the **Print** dialog box; a new **Print** dialog box is displayed with the default printer installed on your computer selected by default. Select a laser printer from the **Name** drop-down list in the new **Print** dialog box.

Creating Base Features

Figure 4-75 The drawing area after inserting the isometric view of the model

4. Choose the **OK** button from the new **Print** dialog box to print the drawing file.

Closing the Current Window

The given model is completed and also saved. Now, you can close the current window.

1. Choose **File > Close Window** from the menu bar; the window is closed.

Self-Evaluation Test

Answer the following questions and then compare them to those given at the end of this chapter:

1. All features created in the **Part** mode are called the base features. (T/F)

2. You can extrude a sketch to both sides of the sketching plane symmetrically. (T/F)

3. When the sketcher environment is invoked, the references required for creating a sketch are automatically selected. (T/F)

4. The **Sketch** dialog box is used to select the sketching plane. (T/F)

5. After selecting the sketching plane, the yellow arrow displayed on it shows the direction in which you will view the sketching plane. (T/F)

6. The _____ button is selected by default when the **Extrude** dashboard is displayed.

7. The _____ button in the **Revolve** dashboard is used to create a thin revolved model.

8. The **Orientation** dialog box is displayed when you choose the _____ button.

9. After you exit the sketcher environment, the _____ appears on the model to dynamically modify the extrusion depth or the angle of revolution.

10. The **Revolve** button revolves the sketched section about a _____ through the specified angle.

Review Questions

Answer the following questions:

1. By default, a sketch is revolved about a geometric centerline in the _____ direction.

    (a) Clockwise   (b) Counterclockwise
    (c) Right   (d) None of these

2. Which of the following menus in the menu bar contains the **Extrude** option?

    (a) **Edit**   (b) **View**
    (c) **Insert**   (d) **File**

3. How many datum planes are available when you enter the **Part** mode?

    (a) 4   (b) 3
    (c) 2   (d) None of these

4. Which of the following toolbars is used to turn off the display of datum planes?

    (a) **View**   (b) **Sketcher**
    (c) **Model Display**   (d) **Datum Display**

5. Which of the following combinations is used to change the orientation of the model to the default orientation?

    (a) CTRL+D   (b) CTRL+left mouse button
    (c) CTRL+right mouse button (d) None of these

6. Features created by using the **Blind** option do not have a dimension associated with them. Hence, they cannot be modified by changing the dimension value. (T/F)

7. It is recommended not to use the default datum planes to create the base feature. (T/F)

Creating Base Features 4-51

8. The section drawn for revolving as a solid should be a closed loop. (T/F)

9. The revolved section should have a centerline. (T/F)

10. A revolved section can be drawn on both sides of a centerline. (T/F)

Exercises

Exercise 1

Create the model shown in Figure 4-76. The dimensions of the model are shown in Figure 4-77.   **(Expected time: 20 min)**

Figure 4-76 *The isometric view of the model*   *Figure 4-77* *The front and right views of the model*

Exercise 2

Create the model shown in Figure 4-78. The dimensions of the model are shown in Figure 4-79.   **(Expected time: 30 min)**

Figure 4-78 *The isometric view of the model*   *Figure 4-79* *The front view of the model*

Exercise 3

Create the model shown in Figure 4-80. The dimensions of the model are shown in Figure 4-81. **(Expected time: 30 min)**

Figure 4-80 The isometric view of the model

Figure 4-81 The front view of the model

Exercise 4

Create the model shown in Figure 4-82. The dimensions of the model are shown in Figure 4-83. **(Expected time: 30 min)**

Figure 4-82 The isometric view of the model

Figure 4-83 The front view of the model

Answers to the Self-Evaluation Test

1. F, **2.** T, **3.** T, **4.** T, **5.** T, **6. Extrude as solid**, **7. Thicken Sketch**, **8. Reorient view**, **9.** handles, **10.** Geometric Centerline.

Chapter 5

Datums

Learning Objectives

After completing this chapter, you will be able to:
- *Understand three default datum planes.*
- *Understand selection methods in Pro/ENGINEER.*
- *Create datum planes using different constraints.*
- *Create datum planes on-the-fly.*
- *Create datum axes using different constraints.*
- *Create datum points.*
- *Create extrude and revolve cuts.*

DATUMS

Datums are imaginary features with no mass or volume. Datums are available to help you in creating models. They act as reference for sketching a feature, orienting a model, assembling components, and so on. Remember that datums play a very important role in creating complex models in Pro/ENGINEER; therefore, you must have a good understanding of datums. Datums are considered to be features but not model geometry. In Pro/ENGINEER, datums exist as datum plane, datum curve, datum point, datum coordinate system, datum graph, and so on.

Default Datum Planes

When you enter the **Part** mode or the **Assembly** mode, the three datum planes are displayed by default in the drawing area. These datum planes are known as the default datum planes and they are mutually perpendicular to each other. The only difference between the default datum planes of the **Part** mode and those of the **Assembly** mode lies in the names of the datum planes.

The default datum planes in the **Part** mode are named as **FRONT**, **TOP**, and **RIGHT**. In case of the **Assembly** mode, the default datum planes are named as **ASM_FRONT**, **ASM_TOP**, and **ASM_RIGHT**. However, the names of the default datum planes can be changed if required.

To change the name of a default plane, choose **File > Properties** from the menu bar; the **Model Properties** window will be displayed. In this window, click on the **change** link in front of the **Names** line under the **Features and Geometry** head; the **Rename** dialog box will be displayed, as shown in Figure 5-1. Next, double-click on the datum plane you want to rename and enter the desired name to change the default name of the plane. Next, choose **OK** from the **Rename** dialog box and then close the **Model Properties** window.

Alternate method to rename a datum plane is to select it and right-click. On doing so, a shortcut menu will be displayed. Choose **Properties** or **Rename** from it and then enter the desired name for it at the appropriate place.

Figure 5-1 *The Rename dialog box*

Note
The Model Properties window can also be used to set the material, units, and other parameters related to the model.

NEED FOR DATUMS IN MODELING

Generally, most of the engineering components or designs consist of more than one feature. First the base feature of the model is created and then other features of the model are added. Since all features of a model cannot be drawn on a single plane, therefore, to draw rest of

Datums 5-3

Tip: *Whenever you come across any solid model, first try to visualize the number of features in that model and then decide which feature is to be considered as the base feature.*

the features, sometimes, additional planes have to be created or selected. Also, most of the times, the three default datum planes are not enough to create a complex model having many features. For example, Figure 5-2 shows a simple model that consists of two features that require two different planes.

In Figure 5-2, any one of the two features defined on two different planes can be considered as the base feature. However, in this discussion, the feature that is selected as the base feature is shown in Figure 5-3. After creating the base feature, the next feature will be created. For the next feature, a sketching plane has to be defined. Therefore, an additional plane has been created on which you can draw the sketch for the second feature.

Figure 5-2 Model having two extruded features   *Figure 5-3 Base feature of the model*

As shown in Figure 5-4, the plane that is used to create the base feature is highlighted by a mesh. To create the second feature, a new plane is created, which is shown in Figure 5-5. The sketch of the second feature is drawn on this plane.

Note
Throughout the book, at some instances the datum planes are shown by a mesh plane as is evident from Figure 5-4. This view of the datum plane is only for explanation. In Pro/ENGINEER, when you create a datum plane, they do not appear in the form of mesh.

To create various types of datums, you need to select the references on the model. Based on the selection you make on the model, Pro/ENGINEER applies constraints to create the datum.

SELECTION METHOD IN Pro/ENGINEER
The selection method in Pro/ENGINEER Wildfire 5.0 is divided into two types:

1. Selection   2. Collection

Figure 5-4 Plane selected for the base feature

Figure 5-5 Plane selected for the second feature

Selection

In Pro/ENGINEER Wildfire 5.0, selection refers to an action in which you first select entities like edge, plane, face, axis, coordinate system, and so on, and then invoke a feature creation tool. This property of a design package is also known as Object Action. To make your selection process easier, filters are available in Pro/ENGINEER Wildfire 5.0. Filters are available in the **Filter** drop-down list located at the right corner of the **Status Bar** below the **Top Toolchest**. The options in the **Filter** drop-down list change depending upon the mode that is active. The options in this drop-down list, when the **Part** mode is active, are shown in Figure 5-6.

*Figure 5-6 The **Filter** drop-down list*

As you select entities on the model, the number of selected entities appear on the left of the **Filter** drop-down list in the **Status Bar**. When you double-click on the number, the **Selected Items** dialog box will be displayed, as shown in Figure 5-7. All selections that you make on the model are available in this dialog box. You can use the dialog box to remove the selected entities. These selections appear highlighted in red color on the model. To remove a selection on the model, press the CTRL key and then select the entity in red.

By default, the **Smart** filter is selected in the **Filter** drop-down list. The second filter in the **Filter** drop-down list is **Features**. This filter is used to select the features on the model. To redefine a feature, select this option from the drop-down list. The third filter is **Geometry**. This filter allows you to select only the edges, vertices, and surfaces. The fourth filter is **Datums**. This filter allows you to select the datum features. The fifth filter is **Quilts**. This filter allows you to select surfaces. The sixth filter is **Annotation**. This filter is used to select the notes from the drawing area.

*Figure 5-7 The **Selected Items** dialog box*

Datums

5-5

Collection

In Pro/ENGINEER Wildfire 5.0, collection refers to the action when you have invoked a feature creation tool and then select the entities to collect the references in order to create that feature. To make your selection process easy, filters can be used. The filters available in the **Filter** drop-down list depend on the feature creation tool that you have invoked.

DATUM OPTIONS

After discussing the default datum planes, which are the first feature in the **Part** mode, you must know the various other features created using the datum options. Datums are also considered as features having no geometry. Figure 5-8 shows the **Datum** toolbar and Figure 5-9 shows the method of invoking various types of datum options from the menu bar.

*Figure 5-8 The **Datum** toolbar*

Datum Planes

You can create datum planes, other than the three default datum planes by using the menu bar or the **Datum** toolbar. The datum planes can be created anytime when required. The display of the datum planes can be turned on or off by using the **Plane Display** button from the **Datum Display** toolbar. Before discussing the procedure to create datum planes, it is important to understand the use of datum planes. Some of the uses of datum planes in Pro/ENGINEER Wildfire 5.0 are listed below:

1. Datum planes are used as sketching planes to create sketches for the features of a model.

2. Datum planes are used as reference planes for sketching.

3. Datum planes are used as references for placing holes and for assembling components.

4. Datum planes are used as a reference for mirroring features, copying features, creating a cross-section, and for orientation of references.

Pro/ENGINEER provides you with various constraints to create additional

*Figure 5-9 Invoking datum options from the **Insert** menu in the menu bar*

datum planes. Additional datum planes are created with the help of constraints and the filters available in the **Filter** drop-down list. Datums can also be created while you are in the sketcher environment. When you choose **Insert > Model Datum > Plane** from the menu bar or **Plane** button from the **Datum** toolbar, the **DATUM PLANE** dialog box will be displayed, as shown in Figure 5-10. Separate buttons for creating datum axis, datum curve, datum point, datum coordinate system are available in the **Datum** toolbar.

Figure 5-10 shows various options in the **DATUM PLANE** dialog box to create datum planes. The options in different tabs of the **DATUM PLANE** dialog box are discussed next.

Figure 5-10 The DATUM PLANE dialog box with the Placement tab chosen

Tip: *Generally, the three default datum planes are used for creating the base feature. As the part becomes complex or in other words, as the number of features increase, the need for additional datum planes arises.*

Placement Tab

The **Placement** tab in the **DATUM PLANE** dialog box is chosen by default. In this tab, the **References** area displays the references selected to create the datum plane. All valid constraint types for these references are displayed in a drop-down list on the right of the selected reference. These constraints are applied automatically based on the references you select. To change a constraint, select the constraint in the dialog box; you will notice that a drop-down list appears in its place. From this drop-down list, select a different constraint. This drop-down list is available only for those constraints in the dialog box that can be substituted by another constraint. The constraints that are used to create a datum plane are discussed later in the chapter.

The **Offset** area will be available only when you use the **Offset** constraint to create a datum plane. The **Translational** edit box in this area is used to specify the offset distance of the new datum plane. This distance can also be set dynamically on the model by using the drag handle. The **Rotation** edit box will be available only when you create a datum plane at an angle with the selected edge. This edit box is used to specify the rotation angle of the new datum plane. You can also set the rotation angle dynamically by using the drag handle displayed on the model.

Display Tab

The **Display** tab of the **DATUM PLANE** dialog box is shown in Figure 5-11. The **Flip** button in this dialog box is used to change the normal direction of the datum plane being created. Every datum plane has two sides, one is colored brown and the other is black. These colors are visible when the plane is rotated such that its back side comes into view. By default, the arrow on the plane points toward the brown side. The arrow direction and hence the direction of the plane can be changed by using the **Flip** button.

By default, the **Adjust Outline** check box is clear. If you select this check box, it allows you to set the size of the datum plane.

Properties Tab

The **DATUM PLANE** dialog box with the **Properties** tab chosen is shown in Figure 5-12. This tab when selected, allows you to name the datum plane you are creating. By default, the first datum plane you create is named DTM1 and then other datum planes created are successively numbered.

*Figure 5-11 The DATUM PLANE dialog box with the **Display** tab chosen*

*Figure 5-12 The DATUM PLANE dialog box with the **Properties** tab chosen*

Creating Datum Planes

When you create a datum plane, the constraints are applied automatically based on the selection you make on the model. These constraints appear in the **DATUM PLANE** dialog box. Sometimes, while applying constraints to define a datum plane, a single constraint is enough to define the datum plane and sometimes, you may need more than one constraint to do the same. When only one constraint is used to create a datum plane, it is called stand-alone constraint. The stand-alone constraints are sufficient by themselves to constrain a datum plane definition. The constraints that are used to create a datum plane are discussed later in the chapter.

Through Constraint

The **Through** constraint is used to create a datum plane through any specified axis, edge, curve, point/vertex, plane, cylinder, or coordinate system. This constraint can be used in combination with other constraints that are discussed next.

The **Through** constraint can also be used as a stand-alone constraint when you select a plane. Figure 5-13 shows the datum plane constraint combinations using the **Through** constraint. Datum planes can be created using any of the combinations shown in the figure. The possible combinations of datum plane creation are referred to as **Yes** and the combinations that are not possible are referred to as **No** in the figure.

DATUM PLANE CONSTRAINT COMBINATIONS (USING THROUGH CONSTRAINT)		Through			Normal	Parallel	Angle	Tangent	Standalone Constraints
		Axis/Edge/Curve	Point/Vertex	Cylinder	Plane	Plane	Plane	Cylinder	
Through	Axis/Edge/Curve	Yes	Yes	Yes	Yes	Yes	Yes	Yes	No
	Point/Vertex	Yes	Yes	Yes	Yes	Yes	No	Yes	No
	Plane	No	No	No	No	No	No	No	Yes
	Cylinder	Yes	Yes	Yes	Yes	Yes	Yes	Yes	No

Figure 5-13 *Datum plane constraint combinations using the **Through** constraint*

While reading the table shown in Figure 5-13, first preference is given to the text written in the first column and then the text in the first row should be read. For example, if you want to make a datum plane that is passing through a cylinder and normal to a plane then look for **Through** in the first column and then for **Cylinder** in the second column. Now, look for **Normal** in the first row and for **Plane** in the second row. After finding all combinations, trace them in the respective column and row till they intersect. If the result is **Yes**, the creation of a datum plane that passes through a cylinder and is normal to a plane is possible. While reading the table shown in Figure 5-13, remember that the constraints that are not stand-alone have to be applied in pairs.

The options in the **Filter** drop-down list shown in Figure 5-14 are used to make selection on a model. This drop-down list is located at the right corner of the main window just below the **Top Toolchest**. The options in this drop-down list change depending on the operation being performed. For example, when you are creating a datum plane, the options shown in Figure 5-14 are available. Once you exit the datum plane creation, the options in this drop-down list change.

Figures 5-15 and 5-16 show the cylindrical surface and the default datum plane used to create a datum plane at an angle to the selected default datum plane and passes through the center of the cylindrical surface. When you

Figure 5-14 *The **Filter** drop-down list with options*

Datums 5-9

select the cylindrical surface, it is highlighted in red, indicating that it is selected. To make the second selection, select the **Datum Plane** filter from the **Filter** drop-down list. Now, press the CTRL button and then select the datum plane. This method of selecting by pressing the CTRL button is known as collection. Click on the constraint displayed against the selected plane in the **DATUM PLANE** dialog box and select the **Offset** option from the drop-down list. Enter the angle value in the **Rotation** dimension box. Choose the **OK** button to create the datum plane.

Figure 5-15 Selecting a cylindrical surface and a default datum plane to create a datum plane

Figure 5-16 Resulting datum plane passing through the center of a cylinder

Note
The first reference to constrain a datum plane is selected by using the left mouse button. The second reference is selected by using the CTRL+left mouse button.

*Make sure you change the option in the **Filter** drop-down list when you invoke any other tool.*

Normal Constraint

The **Normal** constraint is used to create a datum plane normal to any specified axis, edge, curve, or plane. This constraint is used in combination with other constraints. The **Normal** constraint cannot be used as a stand-alone constraint. Figure 5-17 shows the datum plane constraint combinations using the **Normal** constraint.

DATUM PLANE CONSTRAINT COMBINATIONS (USING NORMAL CONSTRAINT)		Through			Normal	Parallel	Angle	Tangent	Standalone Constraints
		Axis/Edge/Curve	Point/Vertex	Cylinder	Plane	Plane	Plane	Cylinder	
Normal	Axis/Edge/Curve	Yes	Yes	Yes	No	No	No	No	No
	Plane	Yes	Yes	Yes	Yes	Yes	No	Yes	No

Figure 5-17 Datum plane constraint combinations using the **Normal** constraint

The possible combinations of datum plane creation are referred to as **Yes** and the combinations that are not possible are referred to as **No**.

Figure 5-18 shows a planar surface and a cylindrical surface of a solid model. The planar face is selected as the normal surface and the cylindrical face is selected to be tangent to the datum plane. The following steps explain the procedure to create this datum plane:

1. Invoke the **DATUM PLANE** dialog box. Select the first reference shown in Figure 5-18. The **Offset** constraint is automatically applied and will be displayed in the **References** collector.

2. Left-click on the **Offset** constraint in the collector; a drop-down list appears. Select the **Normal** constraint from this drop-down list.

3. Now, use the CTRL+left mouse button to select the second reference shown in Figure 5-18. The **Through** constraint will be displayed in the **References** collector.

4. Change this constraint to **Tangent** from the drop-down list that appears when you click on the constraint in the **References** collector. The datum plane that is created is shown in Figure 5-19.

5. Choose the **OK** button from the **DATUM PLANE** dialog box.

Figure 5-18 Selecting a planar surface and a cylindrical surface to create a datum plane

Figure 5-19 Resulting datum plane

Parallel Constraint

The **Parallel** constraint is used to create a datum plane parallel to any specified datum plane or planar face. This option is used in combination with other constraints. The **Parallel** constraint cannot be used as a stand-alone constraint. Figure 5-20 shows various datum plane constraint combinations using the **Parallel** constraint. The possible combinations of datum plane creation are referred to as **Yes** and the combinations that are not possible are referred to as **No** in Figure 5-20.

Datums

DATUM PLANE CONSTRAINT COMBINATIONS (USING PARALLEL CONSTRAINT)		Through			Normal	Parallel	Angle	Tangent	Standalone Constraints
		Axis/Edge/ Curve	Point/ Vertex	Cylinder	Plane	Plane	Plane	Cylinder	
Parallel	Plane	Yes	Yes	Yes	No	No	No	Yes	No

Figure 5-20 Datum plane constraint combinations using the **Parallel** constraint

Figure 5-21 shows the selection of a default datum plane and an axis to create a datum plane. The resulting datum plane is parallel to the selected datum plane and passes through the axis, as shown in Figure 5-22. The steps explaining the procedure to create this datum plane are given next.

1. Invoke the **DATUM PLANE** dialog box. Select the first reference shown in Figure 5-21; the **Offset** constraint is automatically applied and will be displayed in the **References** collector.

2. Left-click on the **Offset** constraint in the collector; a drop-down list appears. Select the **Parallel** constraint from this drop-down list; the plane is oriented parallel to the selected reference.

3. Now, use CTRL+left mouse button to select the second reference shown in Figure 5-21; the **Through** constraint will be displayed in the **References** collector.

4. Choose the **OK** button from the **DATUM PLANE** dialog box. The datum plane that is created is shown in Figure 5-22.

Figure 5-21 Selecting a datum plane and an axis to create another datum plane

Figure 5-22 Resulting datum plane

Offset Constraint

The **Offset** constraint is used to create a datum plane at an offset distance to any specified plane or coordinate system. This option is used in combination with other constraints. However, the **Offset** constraint can be used as a stand-alone constraint when you select a plane to offset from.

When the **Offset** constraint is applied, the **Translation** dimension box appears in the **DATUM PLANE** dialog box. This dimension box list is used to specify an offset distance. In the case of angular planes the **Translation** dimension box changes to the **Rotation** dimension box in which you need to specify the angle. An arrow appears on the model that shows the positive direction of the offset distance or angle.

Figure 5-23 shows various datum plane constraint combinations using the **Offset** constraint. The possible combinations of datum plane creation are referred to as **Yes** and the combinations that are not possible are referred to as **No** in the Figure 5-23.

DATUM PLANE CONSTRAINT COMBINATIONS (USING OFFSET CONSTRAINT)		Through			Normal	Parallel	Angle	Tangent	Standalone Constraints
		Axis/Edge/Curve	Point/Vertex	Cylinder	Plane	Plane	Plane	Cylinder	
Offset	Plane	Yes	No	Yes	No	No	No	No	Yes
	Coord System	No	No	No	No	No	No	No	Yes

*Figure 5-23 Datum plane constraint combinations using the **Offset** constraint*

Figure 5-24 shows the selection of a default datum plane and an edge to define an offset datum plane. The resulting datum plane is at an offset to the selected datum plane and passes through the edge, as shown in Figure 5-25.

Figure 5-24 Selecting a datum plane and an edge to create a datum plane

Figure 5-25 Resulting datum plane

Datums

The following steps explain the procedure to create this datum plane:

1. Invoke the **DATUM PLANE** dialog box. Select the first reference shown in Figure 5-24. The **Offset** constraint is automatically applied and will be displayed in the **References** collector. Also, the **Translation** dimension box appears.

2. Now, use the CTRL+left mouse button to select the second reference, which is a vertex shown in Figure 5-24; the **Through** constraint will be displayed in the **References** collector.

3. Choose the **OK** button from the **DATUM PLANE** dialog box; the datum plane that is created is shown Figure 5-25.

> **Note**
> *The **OK** button in the **DATUM PLANE** dialog box is enabled only when the datum plane you are creating is fully constrained.*

Tangent Constraint

The **Tangent** constraint creates datum planes tangent to cylindrical features. This constraint is also used with other constraints to create various types of datum planes. Figure 5-26 shows the datum plane constraint combinations using the **Tangent** constraint. The possible combinations of datum plane creation are referred to as **Yes** and the combinations that are not possible are referred to as **No** in the figure.

DATUM PLANE CONSTRAINT COMBINATIONS (USING TANGENT CONSTRAINT)		Through			Normal	Parallel	Angle	Tangent	Standalone Constraints
		Axis/Edge/ Curve	Point/ Vertex	Cylinder	Plane	Plane	Plane	Cylinder	
Tangent	Cylinder	Yes	No	No	Yes	Yes	No	No	No

*Figure 5-26 Datum plane constraint combinations using the **Tangent** constraint*

> **Note**
> *If you want to remove the reference that was selected while creating the datum plane, select the reference in the **Datum Plane** dialog box and press the DELETE key. Alternatively, right-click on the reference in the dialog box and then choose **Remove** from the shortcut menu displayed.*

Datum Planes Created On-The-Fly

The term **On-the-Fly** refers to the creation of a datum plane when the system prompts you to select or create a plane. At this step, if you choose the **Plane** button from the **Datum** toolbar, the datum plane created will be called datum plane on-the-fly. When you create a datum plane on-the-fly, the datum plane is neither visible in the drawing area nor will be displayed under the default display of the **Model Tree** once the feature is completed.

You can try making a datum plane on-the-fly by following these steps:

1. Choose the **Extrude** button; the **Extrude** dashboard will be displayed.

2. In the **Extrude** dashboard, choose the **Placement** tab and then choose the **Define** button to invoke the **Sketch** dialog box.

   Now, you need to select a sketching plane. You can select an existing datum plane, a face as the sketch plane, or you can create a datum plane on-the-fly.

3. Choose the **Plane** button from the **Datum** toolbar. Select the references and constraints to create the datum plane. This datum plane when created is automatically selected as the sketching plane.

When you need to select the references to orient the sketching plane, at this step also you can create a datum plane on-the-fly. Once the datum plane on-the-fly is created, it cannot be referenced by other features.

The datum plane created on-the-fly does not appear in the **Model Tree** under the default display. But it can be seen in the **Model Tree** when you click the plus sign (+) that appears to the left of the feature you have created. The datum plane and the feature that you have created are grouped and appear as a grouped feature in the **Model Tree**. This means that the datum on-the-fly that was created during feature creation belongs to the feature that is created.

Note
Unlike the previous releases of Pro/ENGINEER, now you can create a rotational pattern without creating a datum on-the-fly.

Datum Axes

Datum axis is an imaginary axis that is created in Pro/ENGINEER to help you in creating a model. Datum axes can be created manually. They are also created automatically when any cylindrical feature is created. The display of the datum axis can be turned on or off by using the **Axis Display** button from the **Datum Display** toolbar. The uses of datum axes are given next.

1. Datum axes act as reference for feature creation.

2. They are used in creating a datum plane along with different constraint combinations.

3. They are used in placing features co-axially.

4. They are also used to create rotational patterns. You will learn to create patterns in Chapter 7.

Datum axes are named by default in Pro/ENGINEER. The default name of a datum axis is **A_(Number)**, where **Number** represents the number of datum axis. However, the default name of the datum axes can be changed in the same way as that of the datum planes.

Datums

When you choose **Insert > Model Datum > Axis** from the menu bar or choose the **Axis** button from the **Datum** toolbar, the **DATUM AXIS** dialog box will appear with the **Placement** tab chosen in it, as shown in Figure 5-27. The options in this dialog box are discussed next.

Placement Tab

When you invoke the **DATUM AXIS** dialog box, the **Placement** tab is chosen by default. Under this tab, the **References** collector allows you to select the references that will be used to create the datum axis. The constraints are displayed on the right of the references. These constraints are applied automatically based on the reference you select. The constraints that are used to create a datum axis are discussed later in this chapter.

*Figure 5-27 The **DATUM AXIS** dialog box with the **Placement** tab chosen*

The **Offset references** collector is available only when the **Normal** constraint is used in the **References** collector to define a datum axis. To define the datum axis, you need to select two references. These references can be an edge, datum plane, face, or axis. The references can be specified dynamically on the model by dragging the handles displayed on the datum axis. The handles on the datum axis are displayed only when you select a reference. You can also select the references by using the **DATUM AXIS** dialog box.

There are three drag handles available on the model, as shown in Figure 5-28. The middle handle is used to move the position of the axis you are creating and it appears like a white square. The other two handles are used to specify references for dimensioning and appear like a green square.

Display Tab

The options in this tab are used to control the length of an axis. The **DATUM AXIS** dialog box with the **Display** tab chosen is shown in Figure 5-29. Select the **Adjust Outline** check box to activate the **Length** edit box. By default, the **Length** edit box is in the inactive mode. You need to select the **Adjust Outline** check box to activate it. You can enter a value in this edit box or drag the handles displayed at both ends of the datum axis to modify its length.

Figure 5-28 Solid model with the datum axis and three drag handles

Properties Tab

The **Properties** tab of the **DATUM AXIS** dialog box is shown in Figure 5-30. This tab, when chosen, allows you to name the datum axis you are creating. By default, the first datum axis you create is named A_1 and then additional datum axes created are named successively. As mentioned earlier, a datum axis is created using constraints that are applied automatically, and filters available in the **Filter** drop-down list located in the **Status Bar**. While creating a datum axis, the options available in the **Filter** drop-down list are shown in Figure 5-31. The constraints used to create a datum axis are discussed next.

Figure 5-29 The **DATUM AXIS** dialog box with the **Display** tab chosen

Figure 5-30 The **DATUM AXIS** dialog box with the **Properties** tab chosen

Figure 5-31 Options available in the **Filters** drop-down list

Datum Axis Passing along an Edge

The **Through** constraint is used to create a datum axis passing through any selected edge. This constraint will be displayed in the dialog box when you select an edge, as shown in Figure 5-32. In Figure 5-32, **A_1** is the datum axis created using this option.

> **Note**
> *While creating a datum axis, you may need to create datum points in order to create the datum axis passing through them. Therefore, in the various cases that are discussed next you may need to create datum points. Datum points are discussed later in this chapter.*

Datums

Datum Axis Normal to a Plane

The **Normal** constraint is used to create a datum axis normal to a selected face or datum plane. When you select a face or a datum plane, the **Normal** constraint will be displayed in the dialog box and you are prompted to select two references to place the axis. Notice that three drag handles appear on the model. Use the middle handle to change the location of the axis on the selected face. After you specify its placement location, you need to select two edges, axes, datums, or faces to specify the linear dimension for the placement of the datum axis. Click in the **Offset references** collector; the collector turns green. When you select the first edge for the placement dimensions of the axis, the offset value will be displayed in the **Offset references** collector. You can accept the default dimension or click on it to change its value. Similarly, select the second edge for dimensioning by pressing CTRL+left mouse button and enter the dimension value. Figure 5-33 shows the preview of the datum axis with drag handles. It should be noted that the references for dimensioning can also be selected dynamically using these drag handles.

Figure 5-32 Datum axis created along the edge   *Figure 5-33* Datum axis created normal to the plane

Note
*When you select a reference for creating the datum axis, you are prompted to select the placement references. You need to click in the **Offset references** collector to make it green. The green color of this area in the **DATUM AXIS** dialog box indicates that you can select references to place the axis. Until the **Offset references** collector is made green, you will not be able to select placement references.*

Datum Axis Passing through a Datum Point and Normal to a Plane

The **Normal** constraint creates a datum axis passing through a datum point or vertex and normal to any face or datum plane. When you select a face or a datum plane to which the datum axis will be normal, you will be prompted to select two references to place the axis. Use CTRL+left mouse button to select the datum point or vertex to create an axis passing through it. Choose the **OK** button to exit the **DATUM AXIS** dialog box. Figure 5-34 shows the preview of the datum axis and the datum point.

Datum Axis Passing through the Center of a Round Surface

The **Through** constraint is used to create a datum axis passing through the center of a cylindrical or round surface. To create this datum axis, select the round surface through which you need to pass the datum axis; an axis will be created automatically and will pass through the center. Figure 5-35 shows the preview of the datum axis. In this figure, the selected cylindrical surface is highlighted.

Figure 5-34 Datum axis passing through the datum point and normal to the plane

Figure 5-35 Datum axis passing through the center of a cylinder

Datum Axis Passing through the Edge Formed by Two Planes

The **Through** constraint is used to create a datum axis passing through the intersection edge of two planar faces or planes. When you select the face, the **Normal** constraint is applied automatically. Now, select the second face using the CTRL+left mouse button; the **Through** constraint is applied to both faces automatically and a datum axis is created passing through the edge formed by the two faces or planes. Figure 5-36 shows the preview of the datum axis. The two faces that were selected are also highlighted in this figure.

Figure 5-36 Datum axis created at the edge where the two selected planes meet

Datum Axis Passing through Two Datum Points or Vertices

The **Through** constraint is used to create a datum axis between two datum points or vertices. To create this datum axis, select the first vertex and then select the second vertex using CTRL+left mouse button, ; the datum axis will be created along the two selected datum points or vertices. Figure 5-37 shows the preview of the datum axis with the two vertices highlighted.

Datum Axis Tangent to a Curve and Passing through its Vertex

The **Tangent** and **Through** constraints create a datum axis tangent to a curve and passing through one of its vertex. Select the edge of the cylindrical surface as the first selection. Make sure you do not select the cylindrical surface. After you select a curve or an edge, use CTRL+left mouse button to select one vertex of the edge. The datum axis is created tangent to the curve and passing through its selected vertex. Figure 5-38 shows the preview of the datum axis created by using the **Tangent** and **Through** constraints. The curved edge is also highlighted in this figure.

Figure 5-37 Datum axis created between the two selected vertices

Figure 5-38 Datum axis created tangent to the selected curve

Datum Points

Datum points are imaginary points created in Pro/ENGINEER to aid in creating models, drawings, analyzing models, and so on. The uses of datum points are as follows:

1. To create datum planes and axes.

2. To associate note in the drawings and attach datum targets.

3. To create coordinate system.

4. To specify point loads for mesh generation.

5. To create pipe features.

The default name associated with a datum point in Pro/ENGINEER is **PNT(Number)** where **Number** indicates the number of datum points created in a particular model. However, you can change the default name associated with the datum points.

When you choose **Insert > Model Datum > Point > Point** from the menu bar or choose the **Point** button from the **Datum** toolbar, the **DATUM POINT** dialog box will displayed with various options to create datum points, as shown in Figure 5-39. This dialog box can be used to create more than one datum point. The options in the **DATUM POINT** dialog box are discussed next.

Tip: *On selecting references in the model while creating the datum feature, some constraints appear in the **References** area automatically. You need to choose the required constraint from these constraints to constrain the datum feature. In this process, you will notice that the range of available constraints reduces, thereby enabling you to make a faster decision.*

Placement Tab

The **Placement** tab in the **DATUM POINT** dialog box has the options that change with the reference selected. However, the **References** collector shown in Figure 5-39 is always present.

This area is used to select the references which aid in placing the datum point. The constraints available in the drop-down list in the **References** collector depend on the references you select from the model. This means that the references narrow down the type of constraints you can apply on the datum point that you are creating.

Various cases of creating datum points are discussed next.

*Figure 5-39 The **DATUM POINT** dialog box with the **Placement** tab chosen*

Datum Point on a Face or a Datum Plane

The **On** constraint is used to create datum points on a face or a datum plane. When you select a face or a datum plane to place the datum point, a yellow colored point will be displayed at the selected location on the surface with the three drag handles, as shown in Figure 5-40.

Next, click in the **Offset references** collector to make it green. You are prompted to select two references to specify the linear dimensions for the placement of the datum point. Note that the second selection to select the reference should be made by using CTRL+left mouse button. After you select the two planes or edges for the placement of dimension of the point, a default value will be displayed in the **Offset references** collector. You can accept the default value or change it to the required value. After the datum point is located at the desired position on the face or datum plane, choose the **OK** button to exit the dialog box.

Figure 5-40 Datum point on a face and the three drag handles

Datum Point Offset to a Face or a Datum Plane

The **Offset** constraint creates datum points at an offset distance from a specified face or a datum plane in a specified direction. Select a face or a datum plane from where the offset distance for the placement of the datum point will be measured. The **On** constraint is displayed automatically in the **DATUM POINT** dialog box. From the drop-down list in the **References** collector, change the constraint to **Offset** and make the required settings, as shown in Figure 5-41. Figure 5-42 shows the datum point created at an offset from the sketched face.

Figure 5-41 The **DATUM POINT** dialog box with the **Offset** constraint selected

Figure 5-42 Datum point on the top face with offset **0** and the three drag handles

In the **Offset** edit box under the **References** collector, enter the offset value. You will be prompted to select the planes or the edges for dimensioning the point. Select two planes or edges for dimensioning and enter the distances from the highlighted references.

You can also specify the offset distance dynamically by using the middle drag handle. The two references for dimensioning the datum point can be specified by using the drag handles or selecting directly on the model.

Note
*When you use the **Offset** constraint, the middle drag handle is used to specify the offset distance and when you use the **On** constraint, it is used to specify the location of the datum point on the selected face.*

Datum Point at the Intersection of Three Surfaces

The **On** constraint is used to create a datum point at the intersection of three surfaces. To create this datum point, select the three surfaces; a datum point will be created, as shown in Figure 5-43.

Figure 5-43 The three highlighted surfaces and the datum point at the intersection of the three surfaces

The datum point is created on the vertex that is common to the three surfaces. Remember that the first reference is selected using the left mouse button. The second and third references are selected using CTRL+left mouse button. The **DATUM POINT** dialog box that will be displayed after selecting the three surfaces is shown in Figure 5-44.

Sometimes, more than one intersection point exist with the current selection of references. In such a case, use the **Next Intersection** button in the **DATUM POINT** dialog box to select the other intersection points to create the datum point on them.

Datum Point on a Vertex

The **On** constraint is used to create a datum point on the vertex of a face, an edge, or a datum curve. Invoke the **DATUM POINT** dialog box and then select a vertex to create the datum point. Choose the **OK** button to exit the dialog box.

Note
You can create more than one datum point by simply selecting the desired vertex.

Figure 5-44 The DATUM POINT dialog box

Datum Point at the Center of a Curved Edge

The **Center** constraint creates a datum point at the center of an arc or a curved edge. Invoke the **DATUM POINT** dialog box and select the curve edge. The **On** constraint is applied

Datums

5-23

by default. To modify the constraint, select the constraint in the **References** collector; the drop-down list appears to the right of the constraint. Select the **Center** constraint from it to create the datum point at the center of the curved edge.

Datum Point on an Edge or a Curve

The **On** constraint is used to create a datum point on an edge or a curve. Invoke the **DATUM POINT** dialog box, and select an edge or a curve from the drawing area. The datum point will be placed on the selected edge, as shown in Figure 5-45, and the **DATUM POINT** dialog box will be displayed, as shown in Figure 5-46.

In the **DATUM POINT** dialog box, after the point is placed, the dimension type can be defined. The **Offset** dimension box displays the offset distance of the datum point from one end of the edge. The offset distance is measured as a ratio or a real value from the end of the edge, which can be selected from the drop-down list, refer to Figure 5-46.

In the **Offset reference** area, the **Next End** button is used to flip the end of the edge from where the offset distance is measured. This button is available only when the **End of curve** radio button is selected. If you select the **Reference** radio button, you need to select a reference from which the datum point will be dimensioned.

Figure 5-45 *The highlighted edge and the datum point at some offset distance from one end of edge*

Figure 5-46 *The **DATUM POINT** dialog box*

Note
*The geometry points created in the **Sketcher** environment can also be used as datum points.*

To Create an Array of Datum Points from a Coordinate System

The **Offset Coordinate System** button available in the **Point** flyout of the **Datum** toolbar is used to create an array of datum points at an offset distance from a coordinate system. You can change the array of points by redefining the array. Note that the Datum Coordinate system must be defined before you create an array of datum points.

When you choose this button, the **Offset CSys Datum Point** dialog box will be displayed and you will be prompted to select a coordinate system. After selecting a coordinate system, you can enter the values of coordinates for the datum points, refer to Figure 5-47.

To add a point, click under the **Name** column in the list box; the first row gets activated. Click under the **XAxis** column; the edit box appears in which you can enter an offset value. Similarly, enter the offset values for **Y** and **Z Axis**. To add another point click in the next row. From the **Type** drop-down list, select the type of coordinate system: **Cartesian**, **Cylindrical**, or **Spherical**. The options in the list box change according to the coordinate system selected from the **Type** drop-down list. In Figure 5-47, the coordinates of the three datum points are entered in the **Offset CSys Datum Point** dialog box.

To Create a Datum Point by Clicking

When you choose the **Field** button from the **Point** flyout of the **Datum** toolbar, the **Field Datum Point** dialog box will be displayed, as shown in Figure 5-48. Using this dialog box, you can create a datum point anywhere on the surface of the model. You just need to specify the location of the datum point by using the left mouse button to place a datum point.

Figure 5-47 The **Offset CSys Datum Point** dialog box

Figure 5-48 The **Field Datum Point** dialog box

CREATING CUTS

Cut is a material removal process and this option is available only when at least one base feature exists in the drawing area. The **Remove Material** button available on the dashboard of the feature creation tools is used to create the cuts. In this chapter, you will learn the extrude cut and the revolve cut. The procedure to create a cut on an existing feature is similar to that of adding material or protrusion.

Removing Material by Extruding a Sketch

The **Extrude Cut** is an extruded feature that is created by removing material from an existing feature. The material removed from the feature is defined by a sketch.

After drawing the sketch for the cut feature, you can specify the direction of material removal with respect to the sketch. For example, the yellow arrow in Figure 5-49 shows the direction of material removal. If the direction shown by the arrow is accepted, then the cut feature will be created, as shown in Figure 5-50.

Figure 5-49 Sketch for the extrude cut and arrow showing the direction of material removal

Figure 5-50 Cut feature created on the model

Tip: *In the model shown in Figure 5-49, the sketching plane selected for creation of the extruded cut is not a datum plane but the front face of the base feature. You can also create a datum plane on the surface of an existing feature and select it as the sketching plane. But it is not recommended to create a datum plane if a planar surface of the feature can be used as a sketching plane.*

However, if you choose the **Change material direction of extrude to other side of sketch** button from the **Extrude** dashboard, the arrow will point in the direction shown in Figure 5-51. Entire material on the plane selected for sketching will be removed, leaving the extruded cut feature, as shown in Figure 5-52.

Note

A straight hole can also be created by drawing its cross-section, that is a circle, and then creating an extrude cut. But, Pro/ENGINEER provides predefined placement for a hole feature, which is more desirable than dimensioning the cross-section of a cut feature. Straight holes do not require a sketch if you use the **Hole** *dashboard. The* **Hole** *dashboard is discussed in Chapter 6.*

Figure 5-51 Arrow showing the direction of material removal

Figure 5-52 Cut feature created in the direction shown in the adjacent figure

Removing Material by Revolving a Sketch

The **Revolve Cut** is a revolved feature that is created by removing material from an existing feature. The material that is removed is defined by the sketch you draw. Remember that the geometry center line is necessary in a revolve features. Figure 5-53 shows the section drawn to be revolved. The front surface of the second extruded feature is selected as the sketching plane. Figure 5-54 shows the revolve cut created on the selected surface.

Figure 5-53 The section for revolve cut

Figure 5-54 Revolve cut created

Datums 5-27

TUTORIALS
Tutorial 1

In this tutorial, you will create the model shown in Figure 5-55. The front and right views of the solid model are shown in Figure 5-56. **(Expected time: 30 min)**

Figure 5-55 Model for Tutorial 1

Figure 5-56 Front and right views of the model

The following steps are required to complete this tutorial:

Examine the model and determine the number of features in it, refer to Figure 5-75.
a. Create the base feature, refer to Figures 5-57 and 5-58.
b. Create the second extrude feature, refer to Figures 5-59 through 5-61.
c. Create the third feature on an offset plane, refer to Figures 5-62 through 5-67.
d. Create the circular cut feature, refer to Figures 5-68 through 5-71.

Setting the Working Directory

After starting the Pro/ENGINEER session, the first task is to set the working directory. A working directory is a directory on your system where you can save the work done in the current session of Pro/ENGINEER. You can set any existing directory on your system as the working directory.

1. Choose the **Set Working Directory** option from the **File** menu; the **Select Working Directory** dialog box is displayed. Select the *C:\ProE-WF-5.0* folder from this dialog box.

2. Choose the **Organize** tab from the **Select Working Directory** dialog box to display the flyout. Next, choose the **New Folder** option from the flyout; the **New Folder** dialog box is displayed.

3. Enter **c05** in the **New Directory** edit box and choose **OK** from the dialog box; a folder with the name *c05* is created at *C:\ProE-WF-5.0*.

4. Next, choose **OK** from the **Select Working Directory** dialog box. The working directory is set to *C:\ProE-WF-5.0\c05*. Also, a message **Successfully changed to C:\ProE-WF-5.0\c05 directory** is displayed in the message area.

Starting a New Object File

1. Invoke the **New** dialog box. Next, enter *c05tut1* in the **Name** edit box.

    The three default datum planes are displayed in the drawing area. If required, close the **Model Tree** by clicking on the sash on its right edge so that the drawing area is increased.

Selecting the Sketching Plane for the Base Feature

To create the sketch for the base feature, you need to first select the sketching plane. In this model, you need to draw the base feature on the **FRONT** datum plane, because it is evident from the isometric view of this model that the direction of extrusion for this feature is perpendicular to the **FRONT** datum plane.

Note
You can select any plane as the sketching plane for creating the base feature. The base feature thus created may not have the proper orientation. In this case, the final model will be oriented in the wrong direction. So, you need to be careful while defining the sketching plane for creating the base feature. The desired orientation of the model is shown in Figure 5-55.

1. Choose the **Extrude** button from the **Base Features** toolbar; the **Extrude** dashboard is displayed above the graphics window.

2. Choose the **Placement** tab from the dashboard; a slide-down panel is displayed. Next, choose the **Define** button from this panel; the **Sketch** dialog box is displayed.

3. Select the **FRONT** datum plane as the sketching plane; a yellow arrow is displayed on the **FRONT** datum plane, pointing in the direction of view.

4. Select the **TOP** datum plane from the drawing area and then select the **Top** option from the **Orientation** drop-down list.

    The **TOP** datum plane is selected in order to orient the sketching plane.

5. Choose the **Sketch** button from the **Sketch** dialog box to enter into the sketcher environment.

Creating and Dimensioning the Sketch for the Base Feature

The base feature can be created by drawing the sketch and then extruding it to the given distance.

1. Draw the sketch using various sketcher tools and add required constraints and dimensions to the sketch, as shown in Figure 5-57. When you initially draw the sketch, it is dimensioned automatically and some weak dimensions are assigned to it.

   Tip: *It is recommended that you use the **Modify** button to modify weak dimensions. In the **Modify Dimensions** dialog box that appears on choosing this button, clear the **Regenerate** check box and then modify dimensions by using the thumbwheel or the edit boxes. This way the sketch will not be regenerated while editing.*

2. Modify the dimension values based on those shown in Figure 5-57.

3. After the sketch is completed, choose the **Done** button. Now, you are out of the sketcher environment.

4. Choose the **Named View List** button from the **View** toolbar; a flyout is displayed. Choose the **Default Orientation** option from the flyout; the model orients in its default orientation, the trimetric view, as shown in Figure 5-58. The yellow colored arrow is displayed on the model, indicating the direction of extrusion.

5. In the dimension box of the **Extrude** dashboard, enter **8**; the model looks like the one shown in Figure 5-58.

Figure 5-57 Sketch for the base feature with dimensions and constraints

Figure 5-58 Default orientation of the model and the arrow showing the direction of feature creation

6. Choose the **Build feature** button from the **Extrude** dashboard; the base feature is created. You can use the middle mouse button to spin the model in order to view it from various directions.

Note

*When you choose the **Default Orientation** option from the **Named View List** button, the orientation of the model is trimetric and not isometric. If you want the model to be displayed in the isometric view whenever you choose the **Default** option, use the **Environment** dialog box. The **Environment** dialog box is displayed when you choose **Tools > Environment** from the menu bar. In this dialog box, select the **Isometric** option from the **Standard Orient** drop-down list. Now, the default orientation will be set to isometric.*

Tip: *It is recommended to check the orientation of the base feature of a model when it is completed. To check whether the plane you specified for sketching was correct, choose the **Named View List** button from the **View** toolbar; a flyout is displayed. Next, choose the **FRONT** option from the flyout; the base feature will reorient in the drawing area such that you can view the front view of the base feature.*

Selecting the Sketching Plane for the Second Feature

The second feature is an extrude feature. It will be created on the plane that was used to create the base feature.

1. Choose the **Extrude** button again from the **Base Features** toolbar; the **Extrude** dashboard is displayed above the drawing area.

2. Choose the **Placement** tab from the dashboard. Next, choose the **Define** button from the slide-down panel; the **Sketch** dialog box is displayed.

3. Choose the **Use Previous** button from the **Sketch Plane** area in the **Sketch** dialog box; the **Top** datum plane with default orientation is selected automatically.

   When you choose the **Use Previous** button, the system selects the sketching plane that was used previously to create the base feature. You need to choose this button because the base feature and the second feature are on the same plane, but have different depths of extrusion. But if they had the same depth of extrusion, you could have drawn them on the same plane at the same time as a single feature. The **TOP** datum plane and its orientation are set automatically.

Drawing the Sketch for the Second Feature

The second feature has a rectangular section that will be extruded to a depth of 14 units. To improve the clarity of edges of the base feature, choose the **No hidden** button from the **Model Display** toolbar before you start sketching the second feature.

1. Draw the sketch, as shown in Figure 5-59.

2. The sketch is automatically constrained and some weak dimensions are assigned to it. Add required constraints and modify weak dimensions, refer to Figure 5-59.

3. Choose the **Done** button to exit the sketcher environment; the **Extrude** dashboard is enabled above the drawing area. Choose the **Shading** button from the **Model Display** toolbar to view the shaded model.

Figure 5-59 Sketch for the second feature

Tip: *You can use the **Use** button from the **Sketcher Tools** toolbar to use the bottom edge of the base feature. The edge of the base feature is required to complete the sketch for the second feature. Else, draw an aligned line on the edge.*

4. Use the middle mouse button to orient the model, as shown in Figure 5-60. This orientation of the model gives you a better view of the sketch in the three-dimensional (3D) space. The yellow colored arrow is also displayed on the model, indicating the direction of extrusion.

5. Enter **14** in the dimension box present on the **Extrude** dashboard and press ENTER. The second extruded feature is completed and its preview is displayed in the drawing area.

6. Choose the **Named View List** button from the **View** toolbar; the flyout is displayed. Choose the **Default Orientation** option from the flyout; the model orients in its default orientation, that is, trimetric view.

7. Now, choose the **Build feature** button from the **Extrude** dashboard; the feature is created and orients on the screen, as shown in Figure 5-61. You can also use the middle mouse button to spin the model.

Creating the Datum Plane for the Third Feature

A new datum plane is required to create the next feature. The datum plane will be created at an offset distance of 2 from the front face of the second feature. You need to turn on the display of datum planes it is off.

1. Choose the **Plane** button from the **Datum** toolbar; the **DATUM PLANE** dialog box is displayed.

    Make sure that before opening the dialog box, no selection is made. This can be confirmed from the **Status Bar** that is available above the drawing area. If a selection exists, you can remove it by left-clicking in the empty space of the drawing area.

Figure 5-60 Arrow showing the direction of feature depth

Figure 5-61 Second extruded feature with the base feature

2. Using the left mouse button, select the front face of the second feature, as shown in Figure 5-62. The boundary of the selected front face is highlighted in red.

   In the **DATUM PLANE** dialog box, under the **References** collector, the **Offset** constraint is displayed. This means that by the smart selection property of Pro/ENGINEER Wildfire 5.0, the **Offset** constraint is applied automatically to the datum plane that you are going to create.

   Now, you need to specify the offset distance. If you enter a positive value, the datum plane will be created along the direction of arrow and if you enter a negative value then the datum plane will be created in the direction opposite to that shown by the arrow.

3. In the **Translation** dimension box, under the **Offset** area of the **DATUM PLANE** dialog box, enter **-2** and press ENTER.

   The negative value is entered because the datum plane has to be created in the direction opposite to that shown by the yellow arrow.

4. Choose the **OK** button. The datum plane named **DTM1** is created, as shown in Figure 5-63.

Creating the Third Feature on DTM1

The datum plane **DTM1** is created and can be seen in the **Model Tree** as well as in the drawing area. The sketch of the next feature that will be extruded has to be created on the datum plane **DTM1**.

1. Choose the **Extrude** button from the **Base Features** toolbar; the **Extrude** dashboard is displayed above the drawing area.

2. Choose the **Placement** tab and from the slide-down panel, choose the **Define** button; the **Sketch** dialog box is displayed.

Datums 5-33

Figure 5-62 The front face of the second feature selected

Figure 5-63 The datum plane created

3. Select **DTM1** as the sketching plane for the third feature; a yellow arrow is displayed on the selected datum plane, as shown in Figure 5-64. This arrow shows the direction of viewing the sketching plane.

   The **TOP** datum plane and its orientation are selected by default.

4. Choose the **Sketch** button from the **Sketch** dialog box to enter the sketcher environment. Choose the **No hidden** button from the **Model Display** toolbar to view the visible edges of the model.

5. Sketch the section of the third feature of the model and add constraints and dimensions to the sketch, as shown in Figure 5-65.

Figure 5-64 Arrow on **DTM1** showing the direction of viewing the sketching plane

Figure 5-65 Sketch of the third feature with dimensions and constraints

6. Choose the **Done** button to exit the sketcher environment; the **Extrude** dashboard is enabled above the drawing area.

7. Turn the model display to **Shading**. Use the middle mouse button to orient the model, as shown in Figure 5-66. This orientation gives a better view of the model.

   Notice that the yellow arrow is pointing toward the direction of feature creation. But, you need to extrude the sketch in the opposite direction.

8. Choose the **Change depth direction of extrude to other side of sketch** button from the **Extrude** dashboard to change the direction of arrow.

9. Enter **10** in the dimension box present on the **Extrude** dashboard; the preview of the third feature is displayed in the drawing area.

10. Choose the **Build feature** button from the **Extrude** dashboard to confirm the feature creation.

    Choose the **Named View List** button from the **View** toolbar; a flyout is displayed. Choose the **Default Orientation** option from the flyout; the model orients in its default orientation, that is, trimetric view, as shown in Figure 5-67.

Figure 5-66 Arrow showing the direction of material addition

Figure 5-67 Model after creating the third feature

Selecting the Sketching Plane for the Cut Feature

A through cut will be created on the outer right face of the third feature. The circular section for the cut will be sketched and then using the **Remove Material** button in the **Extrude** dashboard, the circular cut will be created. The sketching plane for the cut feature is shown in Figure 5-68.

Note

*The circular cut feature can also be created using the **Hole** tool, which will be discussed in Chapter 6.*

1. Choose the **Extrude** button from the **Base Features** toolbar; the **Extrude** dashboard is displayed above the drawing area.

Datums

2. Choose the **Remove Material** button from the **Extrude** dashboard.

3. Choose the **Placement** tab from the dashboard; a slide-down panel is displayed. Next, choose the **Define** button from it; the **Sketch** dialog box is displayed.

4. Select the face shown in Figure 5-68 for sketching.

5. Using the left mouse button, select the **TOP** default datum plane and then select the **Top** option from the **Orientation** drop-down list.

6. Choose the **Sketch** button; the system takes you to the sketcher environment.

Sketching the Cut Feature

1. Turn the model display to **No hidden**. Draw the sketch of the cut feature and add dimensions to it, as shown in Figure 5-69.

Figure 5-68 Sketching plane for the hole feature   *Figure 5-69* Sketch and dimensions for cut

2. Choose the **Done** button and turn the model display to **Shading**.

3. Choose the **Named View List** button from the **View** toolbar; a flyout is displayed. Choose the **Default Orientation** option from the flyout; the model orients in its default orientation, that is, trimetric view, as shown in Figure 5-70. Two yellow arrows also appear on the model. One arrow indicates the direction of feature creation and the other arrow indicates the direction along which the material will be removed. Figure 5-70 shows the direction where the arrows are pointing.

Figure 5-70 The two arrows on the cut feature

4. Choose the **Options** tab in the **Extrude** dashboard; the **Depth** slide-down panel is displayed.

5. From the **Side 1** drop-down list, choose the **Through All** option; cut feature is created and can now be previewed in the drawing area.

6. Choose the **Build feature** button from the **Extrude** dashboard to accept the feature creation. The trimetric view of the model is shown in Figure 5-71.

Saving the Model

1. Choose the **Save** button from the **File** toolbar and save the model.

The order of feature creation can be seen in the **Model Tree** shown in Figure 5-72.

Figure 5-71 Completed model for Tutorial 1   *Figure 5-72* The **Model Tree** for Tutorial 1

Tutorial 2

In this tutorial, you will create the model shown in Figure 5-73. This figure also shows the front, top, and right views of the solid model.   **(Expected time: 30 min)**

The following steps are required to complete this tutorial:

Examine the model and determine the number of features in it, refer to Figure 5-73.
a. Create the base feature, refer to Figures 5-74 and 5-75.
b. Create the second feature on the left face of the base feature, refer to Figures 5-76 through 5-80.
c. Create the third and fourth features on the same plane, but with different extrusion depths, refer to Figures 5-81 through 5-88.
d. Save the model.

Datums 5-37

Figure 5-73 The top, front, right, and isometric views of the model

After understanding the procedure for creating the model, you are now ready to create it. Set the working directory, if required.

Starting a New Object File

1. Start a new part file and name it as *c05tut2*.

   Three default datum planes are displayed in the drawing area.

Selecting the Sketching Plane for the Base Feature

To create the sketch for the base feature, you need to first select the sketching plane for the base feature. In this model, you need to draw the base feature on the **TOP** datum plane. This is because the direction of extrusion of the base feature is perpendicular to the **TOP** datum plane.

1. Choose the **Extrude** button from the **Base Features** toolbar; the **Extrude** dashboard is displayed above the drawing area.

2. Choose the **Placement** tab from the dashboard to display a slide-down panel. Choose the **Define** button from it; the **Sketch** dialog box is displayed.

3. Select the **TOP** datum plane as the sketching plane; a yellow arrow is displayed on the

TOP datum plane, pointing in the direction of viewing the sketch. The **RIGHT** datum plane and its orientation are set automatically.

4. Choose the **Sketch** button in the **Sketch** dialog box to enter into the sketcher environment.

Creating and Dimensioning the Sketch for the Base Feature

The sketch for the base feature has a rectangular shape with a slot, as shown in Figure 5-74. When you extrude this sketch, the base feature with the slot will be created, as shown in Figure 5-75.

1. Draw the sketch using various sketcher tools and add required constraints and dimensions to it. Modify these dimensions, as shown in Figure 5-74.

2. Choose the **Done** button from the **Right Toolchest** to exit the sketcher environment.

3. Choose the **Named View List** button from the **View** toolbar; a flyout is displayed. Choose the **Default Orientation** option from the flyout; the model appears with its default orientation, that is, trimetric view.

   The default view of the model is displayed, but it does not fit on the screen. You may need to zoom in the model so that it is displayed properly in the drawing area. This gives you a better view of the sketch in the 3D space. A yellow arrow is also displayed on the model, indicating the direction of extrusion.

4. Enter **16** in the dimension box present on the **Extrude** dashboard; the preview of the base feature is displayed in the drawing area.

5. Choose the **Build feature** button from the **Extrude** dashboard; the base feature is created, as shown in Figure 5-75. You can use the middle mouse button to spin the object to view it from various directions.

Figure 5-74 Sketch of the base feature with dimensions and constraints

Figure 5-75 Base feature of the model

Datums

Selecting the Sketching Plane for the Second Feature

The next feature is an extruded feature and will be created on the left face of the base feature. Therefore, you need to select the left face of the base feature as the sketching plane and then draw the sketch.

1. Choose the **Extrude** button from the **Base Features** toolbar; the **Extrude** dashboard is displayed above the drawing area.

2. Choose the **Placement** tab from the dashboard to display a slide-down panel and then choose the **Define** button from it; the **Sketch** dialog box is displayed.

3. Use the middle mouse button to spin the model to get the view, as shown in Figure 5-76.

4. Now, select the left face of the base feature as the sketching plane; a yellow arrow pointing in the direction of view of the sketching plane appears on the left face of the base feature.

5. Choose the **Flip** button to flip the yellow arrow and to change the direction of viewing the sketching plane, refer to Figure 5-76.

6. Click in the **Reference** area and select the top face of the base feature, as shown in Figure 5-77. Next, select the **Top** option from the **Orientation** drop-down list.

   By selecting the top surface of the base feature, the model will be oriented in such a way that the highlighted planar surface will be at the top while sketching.

7. Choose the **Sketch** button from the **Sketch** dialog box to enter into the sketcher environment.

Figure 5-76 Arrow showing the direction of viewing the model

Figure 5-77 Surface selected to be at top

Creating and Dimensioning the Sketch for the Second Feature

The sketch for the second feature consists of two lines and an arc. The bottom edge of the sketch coincides with the top edge of the base feature. This sketch is extruded to a depth of 16. Before drawing the sketch, turn the model display to **No hidden**.

1. Draw the sketch using various sketcher tools, as shown in Figure 5-78. The sketch is dimensioned automatically and some weak dimensions are assigned to it.

2. Apply constraints and modify weak dimensions to the dimensions shown in Figure 5-78.

Figure 5-78 Sketch of the second feature with dimensions and constraints

3. After the sketch is complete, turn the model display to **Shading** and choose the **Done** button; the **Extrude** dashboard is displayed above the drawing area.

   Use the middle mouse button to orient the model, as shown in Figure 5-79. On doing so, a yellow arrow is displayed on the model, indicating the direction of extrusion.

4. Enter **16** in the dimension box present in the **Extrude** dashboard and press ENTER; its preview is displayed on the screen.

5. Choose the **Build feature** button from the **Extrude** dashboard; the second feature is completed and is shown in Figure 5-80. You can use the middle mouse button to spin the model to view it from various directions.

Selecting the Sketching Plane for the Third Feature

The third feature is an extruded feature and will be created on the back planar surface of the base feature. Therefore, you need to define the back face of the base feature as the sketching plane and then draw the sketch.

1. Choose the **Extrude** button from the **Base Features** toolbar; the **Extrude** dashboard is displayed above the drawing area.

2. Choose the **Placement** tab from the dashboard to display a slide-down panel and then choose the **Define** button from it; the **Sketch** dialog box is displayed.

Datums

5-41

Figure 5-79 Arrow showing the direction of material addition

Figure 5-80 Model with the second extruded feature

3. Use the middle mouse button to spin the model and then select the face of the base feature shown in Figure 5-81, as the sketching plane; a yellow arrow is displayed on the selected face.

4. Choose the **Flip** button to flip the yellow arrow, as shown in Figure 5-81; the arrow points in the direction of viewing the sketching plane.

5. Select the top face shown in Figure 5-82 and then select the **Top** option from the **Orientation** drop-down list. Now, the top face of the base feature is selected to be at top while drawing the sketch.

6. Choose the **Sketch** button to enter the sketcher environment.

Figure 5-81 Arrow showing the direction of viewing the model

Figure 5-82 Face selected to be at top

Creating and Dimensioning the Sketch for the Third Feature

The sketch for the base feature consists of a rectangular section with a semicircular cut at the top. When this section is extruded, a feature with a semicircular slot will be created. Turn the display to **No hidden**.

1. Draw the sketch using various sketcher tools, as shown in Figure 5-83. The sketch is dimensioned automatically and some weak dimensions are assigned to it.

2. Add required constraints and modify weak dimensions to the dimensions shown in Figure 5-83.

3. Choose the **Done** button to exit the sketcher environment; the **Extrude** dashboard is enabled above the drawing area. Turn the display to **Shading**.

4. Use the middle mouse button to orient the model, as shown in Figure 5-84. This orientation of the model gives a better view of the sketch in 3D space. A yellow arrow is displayed on the model, indicating the direction of extrusion.

Figure 5-83 Sketch with dimensions and constraints

Figure 5-84 Arrow showing the direction of material addition

5. Enter **42** in the dimension box present in the **Extrude** dashboard and press ENTER. This feature is completed and its preview can be seen in the drawing area.

6. Choose the **Build feature** button from the **Extrude** dashboard to confirm the feature creation. Choose the **Named View List** button from the **View** toolbar; a flyout is displayed. Choose the **Default Orientation** option from the flyout; the default view of the model is displayed, as shown in Figure 5-85.

Figure 5-85 Model with the third extruded feature

Datums

Selecting the Sketching Plane for the Last Feature

The last feature and the third feature are created on the same plane. But the depth of extrusion is different for both of them. This is the reason they are considered as separate features. Therefore, for sketching this feature, you can use the sketching plane that was used for creating the third feature.

1. Choose the **Extrude** button and then invoke the **Sketch** dialog box.

2. Choose the **Use Previous** button from the **Sketch Plane** area in the **Sketch** dialog box; the sketcher environment gets activated automatically.

   When you choose the **Use Previous** button, the system selects the previous sketching plane that was used to create the base feature.

Creating and Dimensioning the Sketch for the Last Feature

The sketch of the last feature consists of three lines. The bottom edge of the sketch is aligned with the top edge of the base feature and the left edge is aligned with the right edge of the third feature. When this sketch is extruded, it creates a rib shape.

1. Draw the section sketch, as shown in Figure 5-86, by using various sketcher tools. The sketch is dimensioned automatically and some weak dimensions are assigned to it. You can add required constraints to align the lines and points in the sketch with other features, as shown in Figure 5-86. In this figure, the constraint symbol displayed on the line indicates that the edges of the adjacent features are used to close the section.

2. After the sketch is complete, choose the **Done** button; the **Extrude** dashboard is enabled. Use the middle mouse button to orient the model, as shown in Figure 5-87.

Figure 5-86 Sketch and constraints for the last feature

Figure 5-87 Arrow showing the direction of material addition

3. Enter the value **12** in the dimension box present in the **Extrude** dashboard; the feature is completed and its preview can be seen in the drawing area.

4. Choose the **Build feature** button in the **Extrude** dashboard.

The default view of the model is shown in Figure 5-88. To invoke the default view, choose the **Named View List** button from the **View** toolbar; a flyout is displayed. Next, choose the **Default Orientation** option from this flyout.

Saving the Model
1. Choose the **Save** button from the **File** toolbar and save the model. The order of feature creation can be seen from the **Model Tree** shown in Figure 5-89.

Figure 5-88 Final model for Tutorial 2

Figure 5-89 *Model Tree* for Tutorial 2

Tutorial 3

In this tutorial, you will create the model shown in Figure 5-90. This figure also shows the front, top, and right views of the solid model.   **(Expected time: 30 min)**

The following steps are required to complete this tutorial:

Examine the model and then determine the number of features in it, refer to Figure 5-90.
a. Create the base feature, refer to Figures 5-91 and 5-92.
b. Create the second feature, refer to Figures 5-93 through 5-96.
c. Create the hollow cylindrical feature on an offset datum plane, refer to Figures 5-97 through 5-102.

Starting a New Object File
1. Set the working directory, if required, and then start a new part file with the name *c05tut3*.

The three default datum planes are displayed in the drawing area.

Selecting the Sketching Plane for the Base Feature
To create the sketch for the base feature, you first need to select the sketching plane. In this model, you need to draw the base feature on the **FRONT** datum plane because the direction of extrusion is perpendicular to the **FRONT** datum plane.

Datums 5-45

Figure 5-90 The top, front, right, and isometric views of the model

1. Choose the **Extrude** button from the **Base Features** toolbar.

2. Choose the **Placement** tab from the dashboard to display a slide-down panel. Next, choose the **Define** button; the **Sketch** dialog box is displayed.

3. Select the **FRONT** datum plane as the sketching plane.

   A yellow arrow is displayed on the **FRONT** datum plane and it points in the direction of viewing the sketch plane. The **RIGHT** datum plane and its orientation are selected automatically.

4. Choose the **Sketch** button to enter the sketcher environment.

Creating and Dimensioning the Sketch for the Base Feature

The section to be extruded for the base feature is evident from the model. The section sketch is shown in Figure 5-91. When this sketch is extruded, it will create the base feature.

1. Draw the sketch using various sketcher tools, as shown in Figure 5-91.

   The sketch is dimensioned automatically and some weak dimensions are assigned to it.

2. Add required constraints and modify weak dimensions, as shown in Figure 5-91.

3. Choose the **Done** button; the **Extrude** dashboard is displayed.

4. Choose the **Named View List** button from the **View** toolbar; a flyout is displayed. Choose the **Default Orientation** option from the flyout; the model orients in its default orientation, that is, trimetric view and a yellow arrow is also displayed on it, indicating the direction of extrusion.

5. Enter **60** in the dimension box that is present on the **Extrude** dashboard and press ENTER.

6. Choose the **Build feature** button from the **Extrude** dashboard.

   The base feature is completed, as shown in Figure 5-92. You can use the middle mouse button to spin the model to view it from various directions.

Figure 5-91 Sketch with dimensions and constraints for the base feature

Figure 5-92 Base feature of the model

Selecting the Sketching Plane for the Second Feature

The next feature is an extruded feature. The sketching plane for this feature is the top face of the base feature.

1. Choose the **Extrude** button from the **Base Features** toolbar.

2. Choose the **Placement** tab from the dashboard; the slide-down panel is displayed. Choose the **Define** button from the slide-down panel; the **Sketch** dialog box is displayed.

3. Select the top face of the base feature shown in Figure 5-93 as the sketching plane; a yellow arrow pointing in the direction of viewing the sketch is displayed on the top face.

4. Choose the **Flip** button to flip the yellow arrow to point in the direction shown in Figure 5-93.

Datums

5-47

5. Select the **RIGHT** datum plane and then select the **Right** option from the **Orientation** drop-down list.

6. Choose the **Sketch** button to enter the sketcher environment.

Creating and Dimensioning the Sketch for the Second Feature

The next feature to be created is an extrude feature. The section for the extrude feature is shown in Figure 5-94. Before drawing the sketch, turn the model display to **No hidden**.

1. Draw the sketch using various sketcher tools. In the sketch, draw a center line passing through the center of the arc, as shown in Figure 5-94. This center line helps in dimensioning the sketch. Add required constraints and dimensions to the sketch, as shown in Figure 5-94. Before exiting the sketcher environment, turn the model display to **Shading**.

Figure 5-93 Arrow pointing from the sketching plane in the direction of feature creation

Figure 5-94 Sketch with dimensions and constraints

2. Choose the **Done** button; the **Extrude** dashboard is enabled. Use the middle mouse button to orient the model, as shown in Figure 5-95.

3. Enter **10** in the dimension box present on the **Extrude** dashboard and press ENTER.

4. Now, choose the **Build feature** button to confirm the feature creation. The default trimetric view of the extruded feature is shown in Figure 5-96.

Creating a Datum Plane for the Last Feature

To create the hollow cylindrical feature, you need a datum plane. This datum plane will be created at an offset distance of 10 units from the bottom face of the second feature shown in Figure 5-97.

Figure 5-95 Arrow showing the direction of material addition

Figure 5-96 Model with the second extruded feature

Note
The other method to create this feature is to select the top planar surface of the second feature as the sketching plane and extrude the sketch on both sides of the sketching plane. The depth of extrusion will be different at both the sides. If you use this method to create this cylindrical feature, you do not need to create a datum plane.

1. Choose the **Plane** button from the **Datum** toolbar; the **DATUM PLANE** dialog box is displayed.

2. Spin the model using the middle mouse button and then using the left mouse button, select the bottom face of the second feature.

   As you select the face of the second feature, the **Offset** constraint is displayed in the **References** collector of the dialog box.

3. In the **Translation** dimension box, enter **10**.

4. Choose the **OK** button from the **DATUM PLANE** dialog box; the datum plane **DTM1** is created, as shown in Figure 5-98, and is selected as the sketching plane for creating the sketch.

Selecting the Sketching Plane for the Last Feature

The plane **DTM1** will be selected as the sketching plane and the depth of extrusion will be defined from this plane.

1. Choose the **Extrude** button from the **Base Features** toolbar.

2. Choose the **Placement** tab from the dashboard; the slide-down panel is displayed. Choose the **Define** button from the slide-down panel; the **Sketch** dialog box is displayed.

3. Select **DTM1** as the sketching plane; a yellow arrow appears on the datum plane.

Datums

Figure 5-97 Creating the datum plane

Figure 5-98 Model after creating the datum plane

4. Choose the **Flip** button to reverse the direction of viewing the sketch. Now, the arrow points in the direction shown in Figure 5-99.

5. Select the **FRONT** datum plane and choose the **Bottom** option from the **Orientation** drop-down list.

6. Choose the **Sketch** button to enter into the sketcher environment.

Creating and Dimensioning the Sketch for the Last Feature

The sketch for the hollow cylindrical feature will be drawn on the datum plane **DTM1**. The sketch for the hollow cylindrical feature consists of two concentric circles. Before drawing the sketch, turn the model display to **No hidden**.

1. Draw the sketch using various sketcher tools and add required constraints and dimensions to it, as shown in Figure 5-100.

Figure 5-99 Direction of viewing the sketching plane

Figure 5-100 Sketch with dimensions and constraints

2. Choose the **Done** button; the **Extrude** dashboard is displayed. Now, turn the model display to **Shading**.

   Use the middle mouse button to orient the model, as shown in Figure 5-101. This view gives you a better view of the sketch in the 3D space.

3. Enter **60** in the dimension box present on the **Extrude** dashboard and press ENTER.

4. Choose the **Build feature** button to confirm the feature creation. The default trimetric view of the complete model is shown in Figure 5-102.

Saving the Model

1. Choose the **Save** button from the **File** toolbar and save the model.

Figure 5-101 Preview of the feature   *Figure 5-102* Final model of Tutorial 3

Self-Evaluation Test

Answer the following questions and then compare them to those given at the end of this chapter:

1. You can change the default names assigned to datum planes. (T/F)

2. Datum points are also used to associate notes in drawings and attach datum targets to them. (T/F)

3. The constraint combination for creating an offset plane through a cylinder is a valid combination. (T/F)

4. Generally, all features in a model are created on a single sketching plane. (T/F)

5. A sketching plane can be selected on the existing face of a feature. (T/F)

Datums

6. While creating a datum feature, the _____ selected from model helps you choose a constraint from the available constraints to constrain the datum feature.

7. Datum axis is an _____ axis that is created in Pro/ENGINEER.

8. The trimetric view of the model is displayed when you choose the _____ option from the **Named View List** button.

9. When you create a new object file, _____ default datum planes are displayed in the drawing area.

10. The default datum planes in the **Part** mode are named as _____, _____, and _____.

Review Questions

Answer the following questions:

1. Which one of the following is not a type of datum available in Pro/ENGINEER?

   (a) Axis   (b) Plane
   (c) Circle   (d) Curve

2. How many methods are available in Pro/ENGINEER to create a datum plane?

   (a) One   (b) Two
   (c) Three   (d) Four

3. Which one of the following dialog boxes is displayed when you choose the **Point** button from the **Datum** toolbar while extruding a section sketch?

   (a) **DATUM POINT**   (b) **DATUM PLANE**
   (c) **DATUM AXIS**   (d) None of these

4. Which one of the following options is used to spin a model in the drawing area?

   (a) CTRL+ALT   (b) middle mouse button
   (c) left mouse button   (d) CTRL+right mouse button

5. Which one of the following menus in the menu bar is used to set the default orientation of the model to isometric?

   (a) **File**   (b) **Insert**
   (c) **Tool**   (d) None of these

6. Datum planes are considered as feature geometry and have mass and volume. (T/F)

7. To set the default orientation of a model to isometric, you need to use the **Environment** dialog box. (T/F)

8. Generally, the sketching plane for the base feature of any model is decided after viewing the isometric view or drawing views of the model. (T/F)

9. Datum planes are used as a reference for mirroring features, copying features, creating a cross-section, as well as for changing the orientation of the references. (T/F)

10. Unlike the datum planes constraint option, all datum axes constraint options are stand-alone. (T/F)

Exercises

Exercise 1

Create the model shown in Figure 5-103. The dimensions, front view, and right-side view of the model are shown in Figure 5-104. **(Expected time: 45 min)**

Figure 5-103 Isometric view of the model

Figure 5-104 The front and right views of the model

Datums

Exercise 2

Create the model shown in Figure 5-105. The dimensions as well as the front, top, right-side, and isometric views of the model are also shown in figure. **(Expected time: 45 min)**

Figure 5-105 The top, front, right-side, and isometric views of the model

Exercise 3

Create the model shown in Figure 5-106. The top, front, section and two auxiliary views of the model are shown in Figure 5-107. **(Expected time: 1 hr)**

Figure 5-106 The 3D view of the model

Figure 5-107 Top, front section, and two auxiliary views of the model

Hint to create the two side features in Exercise 3:

Feature on the right
1. Create an axis passing through the top face of the base feature and through the **RIGHT** datum plane.

2. Create a datum plane passing through the axis (created in the previous step) and at an angle of 21.5 degrees from the **RIGHT** datum plane.

3. Now, create an offset plane at a distance of 11 from the datum plane (created in the previous step). Select this datum plane as the sketching plane.

Feature on the left
1. Create a datum plane passing through the axis of revolution of the base feature and at an angle of 45 degrees from the **FRONT** datum plane.

2. Create a datum axis passing through the top face of the base feature and through the datum plane (created in the previous step).

3. Create a datum plane passing through datum axis (created in the previous step) and at an angle of 21.5 degrees from the datum plane (created in step1).

4. Create a datum plane offset to a distance of 10 from the datum plane (created in the previous step).

Exercise 4

Create the model shown in Figure 5-108. The dimensions, the left-side view, auxiliary view, and front view of the model are also shown in the Figure 5-109.   **(Expected time: 45 min)**

Figure 5-108 Isometric view of the model

Figure 5-109 Left, auxiliary, and front views of the model

Answers to Self-Evaluation Test
1. T, **2.** T, **3.** T, **4.** F, **5.** T, **6.** geometry, **7.** imaginary, **8. Default Orientation**, **9.** three, **10. TOP, FRONT, RIGHT**.

Chapter 6

Options Aiding Construction of Parts-I

Learning Objectives
After completing this chapter, you will be able to:
- *Create holes.*
- *Create Round, Chamfer, and Rib.*
- *Edit features.*
- *Redefine, Reroute, and Reorder features.*
- *Suppress and delete features.*
- *Modify features.*

OPTIONS AIDING CONSTRUCTION OF PARTS

This chapter explains the feature creation tools provided in Pro/ENGINEER that help in creating a model and editing it. In this chapter, you will also learn to create various types of holes that are required in most of the engineering designs. In previous chapters, you learned to create holes using extrude cut, but in this chapter you will create holes using the **Hole** dashboard. You can create and modify holes in an easier manner using the options in the **Hole** dashboard.

In this chapter you will also learn to create rounds, chamfers, and ribs. The options that are discussed in this chapter increase the efficiency of creating a design using Pro/ENGINEER.

CREATING HOLES

In engineering components, holes can be counterbore, countersink, tapered, or drilled. Pro/ENGINEER allows you to create all these types of holes. Pro/ENGINEER also provides industry standard holes that have standard dimensions. In Pro/ENGINEER Wildfire 5.0, holes are created using the **Hole** dashboard.

The Hole Dashboard

The **Hole** dashboard is displayed when you choose **Insert > Hole** from the menu bar or the **Hole** button from the **Engineering Features** toolbar present in the **Right Toolchest**. You can create two types of holes using the **Hole** dashboard, the **Simple** hole and the **Standard** hole. The **Simple** hole options enable you to create holes using three buttons and these buttons are discussed next.

Creating Simple Holes using Predefined Rectangle Profile

When you invoke the **Hole** dashboard, the **Use predefined rectangle as drill hole profile** button is chosen by default, as shown in Figure 6-1. The options and the buttons available in this dashboard are discussed next.

Figure 6-1 The **Hole** dashboard

Dimension Boxes

The first dimension box in the **Hole** dashboard is used to specify the diameter of the hole.

The second dimension box in the **Hole** dashboard is used to specify the depth of the hole. The options to specify the depth of the hole are the same as those available in the **Extrude** dashboard.

Placement Tab

When you choose the **Placement** tab, the slide-down panel will be displayed, as shown in Figure 6-2. This slide-down panel will be displayed with the parameters that need to

Options Aiding Construction of Parts-I

be specified to define a linear hole. The **Placement** collector in the slide-down panel will be displayed in green color. This indicates that Pro/ENGINEER is prompting you to select the placement plane (primary reference). You can select the placement plane only when this collector is in green color. Once you have selected the primary reference, its name appears in the box. The primary reference can be a plane, axis, or point.

The **Flip** button is used to change the direction of the hole creation with reference to the primary reference. When you choose this button, the direction of the hole creation is reversed and you can view its preview in the drawing area. Remember that the hole will be created only if it is possible to create the hole in the specified direction.

*Figure 6-2 Slide-down panel in the **Placement** tab*

The **Type** drop-down list below the **Placement** collector contains the options that determine the type of placement for the hole. You can use the options in this drop-down list after selecting the placement plane or the primary reference. These options are discussed next.

Linear. When you select this option, you need to specify the distances from two linear references. Generally, these linear references are the edges of the planar surface on the model, any two planar surfaces or axes, or a combination of any of these. Figure 6-3 shows a linear hole on the top face of the block. The procedure to create this hole using the **Hole** dashboard is as follows:

1. Invoke the **Hole** dashboard.
2. Choose the **Placement** tab to open the slide-down panel.
3. Select the top face of the model to place the hole; the preview of the hole will be displayed.
4. Click in the **Offset References** collector to make the secondary selections.
5. Select the left face or the top left edge of the model.
6. Use CTRL+left mouse button to select the front face or the top front edge of the model. Now, you have selected the two references that are needed to dimension the position of hole.
7. Specify the exact location of hole in the edit boxes of the **Offset Reference** collector.
8. Specify the diameter of the hole in the dimension box present on the **Hole** dashboard.
9. From the depth flyout, choose the **Drill to intersect with all surfaces** button.
10. Choose the **Build feature** button to create the hole and exit the **Hole** dashboard.

Note
*To select the secondary references, you need to click in the **Offset References** collector and then select the references on the model.*

*Dimensions of the center of the hole from the selected references are displayed in the drawing area as well as in the **Offset References** collector. You can click on the dimensions to modify them.*

Radial. This option is used to create a hole that can be referenced to an axis. When you select this option, you need to select an axial reference and an angular reference to place the hole. The distance from the axis and the angle from the plane are entered in the boxes under the **Offset References** collector. Figure 6-4 shows a radial hole on a curved surface. The following steps explain the procedure to create this hole.

Figure 6-3 Linear hole on the top face of the block

Figure 6-4 Radial hole on the curved surface

1. Invoke the **Hole** dashboard.
2. Choose the **Placement** tab to open the slide-down panel.
3. Select the curved surface of the model to place the hole; the preview of the hole will be displayed.
4. Click in the **Offset References** collector to make the secondary selections.
5. Select the datum plane that is normal to the curved surface to specify the angular value.
6. Use CTRL+left mouse button to select the top face or the top edge of the model. Now, you have selected the two references that were needed to dimension the hole.
7. Specify the diameter of the hole in the dimension box on the **Hole** dashboard.
8. From the depth flyout, choose the **Drill to intersect with all surfaces** button.
9. Choose the **Build feature** button to create the hole and exit the **Hole** dashboard.

> **Tip**: *Note that since you have selected the curved surface as the placement plane for the hole, therefore, you do not need to select the axis to specify the radial distance. However, if the placement plane is a plane surface, then you do need to select an axis to create a radial hole at some radius from the selected axis.*

Diameter. This option creates a diametrically placed hole. When you select this option, you need to select an axial reference and an angular reference to place it. Figure 6-5 shows a diameter hole on a plane. The following steps explain the procedure to create this hole.

Options Aiding Construction of Parts-I   6-5

1. Invoke the **Hole** dashboard.
2. Choose the **Placement** tab to open the slide-down panel.
3. Select the top face of the model to place the hole; the preview of the hole will be displayed.
4. From the drop-down list, select the **Diameter** option.
5. Click in the **Offset References** collector to make the secondary selections.
6. Select the face shown in Figure 6-5 to specify the angular value.
7. Use CTRL+left mouse button to select the axis of another reference hole that is on the top face. Now, you have selected the two references that are needed to dimension the hole.
8. Specify the distance for the hole measured from the axis of the reference hole and the angle in the **Offset References** collector.
9. From the depth flyout, choose the **Drill to intersect with all surfaces** button.
10. Choose the **Build feature** button to exit the **Hole** dashboard.

Coaxial. This option creates a coaxial hole. When you select this option, you need to select an axis. No dimensions are required to place a coaxial hole. Figure 6-6 shows a coaxial hole on a plane. The procedure to create this hole is explained next.

1. Invoke the **Hole** dashboard.
2. Choose the **Placement** tab to open the slide-down panel.
3. Select the axis of the model to place the hole; the preview of the hole will be displayed.
4. In the **Type** drop-down list, the **Coaxial** option is selected by default.
5. Now, press the CTRL key to select the placement plane or the surface where you want to place the base of the hole.
6. Specify the diameter of the hole in the dimension edit box available on the **Hole** dashboard.
7. From the depth flyout, choose the **Drill to intersect with all surfaces** button.
8. Choose the **Build feature** button to exit the **Hole** dashboard.

Figure 6-5 Diameter dimensioning of the hole

Figure 6-6 Coaxial hole

Tip: *Remember that while placing the linear, diameter, and radial holes using the **Hole** dashboard, you need to define two things. First is the placement plane on which the hole feature will be created and the second is the dimensional references. But for the **Coaxial** hole, you need to select an axis and for the **On Point** hole, you need to select a datum point.*

On Point. This option is available only when you select the datum point as the primary placement reference. The procedure of creating this hole is explained next.

1. Invoke the **Hole** dashboard.
2. Choose the **Placement** tab to open the slide-down panel.
3. Select the datum point to place the hole; the preview of the hole will be displayed.
4. In the **Type** drop-down list, the **On Point** option is selected by default.
5. Specify the diameter of the hole in the first dimension edit box available on the **Hole** dashboard.
6. From the depth flyout, choose the **Drill to intersect with all surfaces** button.
7. Choose the **Build feature** button to exit the **Hole** dashboard.

Shape Tab

When you choose the **Shape** tab, the slide-down panel will be displayed, as shown in Figure 6-7. This slide-down panel can be used to specify the depth and the diameter of the hole. The depth of the hole can be specified in two directions with respect to the placement plane. The options to specify the depth of the hole are similar to those that are available in the **Extrude** dashboard. In the slide-down panel, the sketch of the hole, gives an idea of the shape of the hole and its dimensions. The sketch that is shown in the slide-down panel shows the depth of the hole in the **Side 1** direction. The **Side 2** drop-down list is used to specify the depth of the hole in the direction opposite to **Side 1**. This means the hole can be created on both sides of the placement plane. By default, the **None** option is selected in this drop-down list.

*Figure 6-7 The **Shape** tab slide-down panel*

Note

*The termination options in the **Shape** slide-down panel are similar to those discussed in the **Extrude** dashboard.*

When you specify the placement plane for a hole and then specify two references in case of a linear hole, you can notice four drag handles displayed on the hole. These four drag handles have four different functions to place the hole dynamically on the placement plane. Using these handles, you can set the diameter, depth, and specify two references to place the hole.

Options Aiding Construction of Parts-I

Remember that these drag handles appear only when you select the primary reference, or in other words, the placement plane.

Tip: *The diameter of the hole and its depth in the **Side 1** direction can be specified without using the slide-down panels. The options to specify the diameter and depth in the **Side 1** direction are available on the **Hole** dashboard. When you want to specify the depth in the **Side 2** direction, open the slide-down panel by choosing the **Shape** tab from the **Hole** dashboard.*

Properties Tab
The **Properties** tab of the **Hole** dashboard is shown in Figure 6-8. This tab, when chosen, allows you to name the hole you are creating. By default, the first hole you create is named as HOLE_1 and then every hole created is successively numbered.

*Figure 6-8 The **Properties** tab of the **Hole** dashboard*

Creating Simple Holes using Standard Hole Profile
You need to choose the **Use standard hole profile as drill hole profile** button from the **Hole** dashboard, as shown in Figure 6-9. On choosing this button, you can specify the countersink, counterbore, and depth of the hole. The options and tool buttons available in the dashboard are discussed next.

*Figure 6-9 The **Hole** dashboard*

Placement Tab
The use of the placement options in this tab is same as you did while creating the **Simple** hole using the **Use predefined rectangle as the drill hole profile** button. These placement options have already been discussed.

Shape Tab
The options in the slide-down panel will be displayed when you choose the **Shape** tab from the **Hole** dashboard. These options are different from the options that were available when you created the **Simple** hole using the **Use predefined rectangle as the drill hole profile** button. When you choose the **Shape** tab, the slide-down panel is displayed. The sketch for the hole in the slide-down panel gives an idea about the shape of the hole and its parameters, as shown in Figure 6-10.

*Figure 6-10 The **Shape** tab slide-down panel*

Dimension Edit Boxes

The first dimension edit box in the **Hole** dashboard is used to specify the diameter of the hole.

The second dimension edit box in the **Hole** dashboard is used to specify the depth of the hole. The options to specify the depth of the hole are the same as those available in the **Extrude** dashboard.

Adds countersink

Choose this button to create a countersink hole. A countersink hole has two diameters and the transition between the larger diameter and the smaller diameter is in the form of a cone. In the slide-down panel of the **Shape** tab, the preview of the cross-section with parameters of the countersink hole will be displayed, as shown in Figure 6-11. In the preview of the section, the dimensions can be edited as per the requirement.

Adds counterbore

Choose this button to create a counterbore hole. A counterbore hole is a stepped hole, and it has two diameters, a larger diameter and a smaller diameter. The larger diameter is called counter diameter and the smaller diameter is called drill diameter. In the slide-down panel of the **Shape** tab, the preview of the cross-section with parameters of the counterbore hole will be displayed, as shown in Figure 6-12. In the preview of the section, the dimensions can be edited as required. Note that if both the buttons are chosen, then the hole created will be a combination of the counterbore and countersink holes.

Figure 6-11 Parameters of the countersink hole in the **Shape** tab slide-down panel

Figure 6-12 Parameters of the counterbore hole in the **Shape** tab slide-down panel

Drilled hole shoulder depth

Choose this button to specify the depth of the hole. When you choose the **Drilled hole shoulder depth** button from the **Hole** dashboard, the depth of the hole will be measured upto the shoulder only. In the slide-down panel of the **Shape** tab, the preview of the cross-section with parameters of the hole, whose depth is measured upto the shoulder, will be displayed, as shown in Figure 6-13.

Options Aiding Construction of Parts-I

Drilled hole depth

When you choose the **Drilled hole depth** button from the **Hole** dashboard, the depth of the hole is measured upto the tip of the hole. To invoke this button, choose the black arrow on the right of the **Drilled hole shoulder depth** button; a flyout will be displayed. Choose the **Drilled hole depth** button from the flyout. In the slide-down panel of the **Shape** tab, the preview of the cross-section with parameters of the hole, whose depth is measured upto the tip, will be displayed, as shown in Figure 6-14.

Figure 6-13 Parameters of the hole with depth measured upto the shoulder

Figure 6-14 Parameters of the hole with depth measured upto the tip

Creating Simple Holes using Sketched Profile

This option allows you to sketch the cross-section of the hole that is revolved about a center axis. This option is used to draw custom shapes for the hole. When you choose the **Use sketch to define drill hole profile** button from the **Hole** dashboard, the **Hole** dashboard appears, as shown in Figure 6-15. The tools and options in the dashboard are discussed next.

*Figure 6-15 The **Hole** dashboard with the **Use sketch to define drill hole profile** button chosen*

Activates Sketcher to create section

Choose the **Activates Sketcher to create section** button to open a new window with the sketcher environment. The cross-section for the hole is sketched using the normal sketcher tools available. While drawing the sketch, a center line must be drawn that acts as the axis of revolution for the section of hole. The sketched holes can be blind or through all, depending on the dimensions of its sketch.

When you complete the sketch for the hole and choose the **Done** button to exit the sketcher environment, the **Hole** dashboard will be enabled above the drawing area. Now, you need to specify the placement options to place the hole. The placement options are the same as discussed earlier.

Note
The placement options to place the hole can be specified after drawing the sketch for the hole or before drawing the sketch. The only difference is that when you specify the placement options after drawing the sketch, the preview of the hole is not available in the drawing area. This is because the primary reference is not selected yet. Therefore, it is recommended to specify the placement options before drawing the sketch for the hole.

Opens an existing sketched profile

On the **Hole** dashboard, the **Opens an existing sketched profile** button is used to open an existing sketch that is saved in *.sec* file format. When you choose this button, the **OPEN SECTION** dialog box will be displayed. This dialog box is used to select the *.sec* file to define the shape of the hole.

Placement Tab

The options in the slide-down panel that are displayed when you choose the **Placement** tab from the **Hole** dashboard are the same as those discussed earlier. You can also use the same type of placement options as discussed earlier.

Shape Tab

The options in the slide-down panel that will be displayed when you choose the **Shape** tab from the **Hole** dashboard are different than the options that were available in case of **Straight** holes. When you choose the **Shape** tab, the slide-down panel displays the preview of the sketch that you have drawn in the sketcher environment. You can pan and zoom the sketch in the slide-down panel.

Note
*If you choose the **Shape** tab before drawing the sketch for the hole, then the slide-down panel becomes blank and does not show a sketch.*

Standard Hole

The standard holes can be created by choosing the **Create standard hole** button from the **Hole** dashboard. The holes created using this button are based on industry standard fastener tables.

Note
You need to select the required template for the measurement of holes based on the industry standards. This can be done when you create a new file.

When you choose the **Create standard hole** button from the **Hole** dashboard, the dashboard appears, as shown in Figure 6-16. The tools and options in the dashboard are discussed next.

*Figure 6-16 The **Hole** dashboard*

Options Aiding Construction of Parts-I 6-11

Drop-down Lists

The first drop-down list from the left in the dashboard is used to specify the type of thread on the hole. The options in this drop-down list are **ISO**, **UNC**, and **UNF**. The default option selected in this list depend upon the template selected in the **New File Options** dialog box.

The second drop-down list in the **Hole** dashboard is used to specify the size of the screw that corresponds to the hole.

The third drop-down list in the **Hole** dashboard is used to specify the depth of the hole. The options in this drop-down list are similar to those available in the **Extrude** dashboard.

Adds tapping

Choose this button to tap a hole. Tapping is the process of cutting threads in the hole. In Pro/ENGINEER, these threads are known as cosmetic threads. This means that the threads created will not be visible in the hole. In the slide-down panel of the **Shape** tab, the preview of the cross-section with parameters of the tapped hole will be displayed, as shown in Figure 6-17. In the preview of the section, the dimensions can be edited, as required. The dotted lines represent the threading outside the hole. However, on deactivating the **Adds tapping** button, the **Create drilled hole** and the **Create clearance hole** buttons will be displayed. Choose the required button and then set the parameters in the dashboard to create the desired hole.

Create tapered hole

Choose this button to create tapered threaded holes. The sizes of holes can conform to the ISO, JIS, and ANSI standards. There are three standards in the thread type drop-down list, **ISO_7/1**, **NPT**, and **NPTF**. Set the required standard, specify the screw size, and the drill depth value to create the tapered hole. You can also add countersink or counterbore to the tapered hole, if required.

Figure 6-17 *Parameters of the tapped hole*

Adds countersink

As discussed earlier, this button is used to create a countersink hole. A countersink hole has two diameters and the transition between the bigger diameter and the smaller diameter is in the form of a cone. In the slide-down panel of the **Shape** tab, the preview of the cross-section with parameters of the countersink hole will be displayed, as shown in Figure 6-18. In the preview of the section, the dimensions can be edited as required.

Note that you need to deactivate the **Adds countersink** button and then choose the **Adds counterbore** button to create the counterbore hole. Else, the hole created will be a combination of the countersink and counterbore holes.

Adds counterbore Button

As discussed earlier, this button is used to create a counterbore hole. A counterbore hole is a stepped hole and has two diameters, a larger one and a smaller one. The larger diameter is called counter diameter and the smaller diameter is called the drill diameter. In the slide-down panel of the **Shape** tab, the preview of the cross-section with parameters of the counterbore hole will be displayed, as shown in Figure 6-19. In the preview of the section, the dimensions can be edited as required.

*Figure 6-18 Parameters of the countersink hole in **Shape** tab slide-down panel*

*Figure 6-19 Parameters of the countersink hole in **Shape** tab slide-down panel*

Placement Tab

The options in the slide-down panel that will be displayed when you choose the **Placement** option from the **Hole** dashboard are the same as those that were available in case of the **Simple** hole. You can use the same type of placement options that were available when you created the **Simple** hole.

Shape Tab

The options in the slide-down panel that will be displayed when you choose the **Shape** tab from the **Hole** dashboard are different from the ones that were available in case of **Simple** hole. When you choose the **Shape** tab, the slide-down panel displays the preview of the hole. You can specify the dimensions for the hole in the respective dimension boxes.

Note Tab

This tab displays the specifications of the hole in the text format. This option is available only when you create a **Standard** hole.

Properties Option

This option displays the properties of the hole that you need to create.

Preview the Hole

The **Feature Preview** button is used to preview the hole created before confirming its creation. Changes and modifications in the hole parameters can be made once the hole is previewed.

Note

*The holes created using the **Hole** dashboard are parametric in nature and so, can be modified anytime using the **Model Tree**. The method of modifying the holes using the **Model Tree** is discussed later in this chapter.*

*You can dynamically edit the parameters of the hole as well as relocate the hole after the hole is created. To do so, select the hole and right-click to display a shortcut menu. Choose **Dynamic Edit** from it; all values of parameters and the dynamic edit handles will be displayed on it. You can double-click on the value and enter a new value or drag the edit handles to the required distance.*

Important Points to Remember While Creating a Hole

The points given next should be remembered while creating a hole.

1. While drawing the sketch of a hole, it should have an axis of revolution and at least one entity normal to it. Now, when you place this hole on the primary reference (**Placement** reference), then this normal entity is aligned with the plane (primary reference). If there are two entities normal to the axis, then the normal entity at the top of the sketch is aligned with the placement plane.

2. While creating a hole, the primary reference for the placement of hole can be selected without choosing any option from the **Hole** dashboard. However, if you need to specify the secondary references (**Offset references**), then choose the **Placement** tab from the **Hole** dashboard; the slide-down panel will be displayed. From the slide-down panel, click in the **Offset references** collector and when the **Placement** collector appears white in color, you can select the secondary references.

   Remember when the first reference is selected by using the left mouse button, then the second reference is selected by using CTRL+left mouse button.

3. It is recommended that if you are creating a **Standard** hole then the units of the model should be in mm. This can be achieved by using the appropriate template at the time of creating a new file or by setting the system of units.

4. An application of the **Sketched** hole is a tapered hole. **Sketched** holes are always blind and have depth in one direction only.

5. You cannot select a convex or concave surface as the placement plane. To create a hole on such a surface, you need to create a datum plane passing through the surface and then select this datum plane as the placement plane.

CREATING ROUNDS

The **Round** button is used to create a fillet or a smooth rounded transition between two adjacent faces, with a circular or a conic profile. This feature creation tool can be invoked from the menu bar or from the **Engineering Features** toolbar in the **Right Toolchest**. The **Round** option can add or remove material, depending on the edge selected. You can select the edges or faces and create a round in a single set or define more than one set.

Figures 6-20 and 6-21 show some examples of rounds. From the figures, it is evident that the geometry of the rounds are tangent to the references selected. These references can be edges or surfaces. In Pro/ENGINEER, rounds are created using the **Round** dashboard.

Figure 6-20 Rounds created on the edges

Figure 6-21 Round created on surfaces

Note
The round created after you select references on the model has a circular cross-section and rolling shape. In Pro/ENGINEER, there is more than one shape that a round can have.

Creating Basic Rounds

When you choose the **Round** button from the **Engineering Features** toolbar or **Insert > Round** from the menu bar; the **Round** dashboard will be displayed, as shown in Figure 6-22. Also, you will be prompted to select an edge or a surface set to create the round. Select an edge; the preview of the round with a default radius value and drag handles will be displayed on the selected edge. Similarly, you can go on selecting edges to add rounds to them. But if you select a surface, you are prompted to select another surface to include in the same set. Use CTRL+left mouse button to select another surface; the preview of the round with a default radius value and drag handles will appear on the model, as shown in Figure 6-23. Note that because the radius of all rounds in a set is equal, the drag handles are available on only one edge. You can drag the handles to dynamically specify the radius of the round or specify the radius in the **Round** dashboard. Once all parameters of the round are specified, choose the **Build feature** button to create it. The various options in the **Round** dashboard are discussed next.

Figure 6-22 The **Round** dashboard

Switch to set mode

When you invoke the **Round** dashboard, the **Switch to set mode** button is chosen by default and is used to create rounds by defining sets. When this button is chosen, the dimension box is displayed on its right and it is used to specify the radius of round.

Options Aiding Construction of Parts-I 6-15

Figure 6-23 Preview of the round feature along with the radius of round and the drag handles

> **Tip**: *You can create a round on an edge without invoking the **Round** tool. To do so, choose the **Geometry** option from the **Filter** drop-down list and then select an edge. Hold down the right mouse button and choose the **Round Edges** option from the shortcut menu. The **Round** dashboard is invoked and the preview of the round appears on the edge selected.*

Switch to transition mode Button

The **Switch to transition mode** button is available only when you have defined at least one reference for the round. This button has primarily two applications. The first one is to define the shape of the round that is formed at a vertex and the other is to define a limit up to which the round will be created. Both these applications are discussed next.

> **Tip**: *The need for creating rounds by defining more than one set arises when you want to create rounds that have different radii. The rounds created by using this method will be a single feature and appear as a single feature in the **Model Tree**.*

If the round feature is being created on three intersecting edges, then this button is used to define the shape of the round that is created at the vertex. After choosing the **Round** button, press and hold the CTRL key down and select the three edges, as shown in Figure 6-24. Now, choose the **Switch to transition mode** button from the **Round** dashboard. The various transitions that are possible on the current selection are highlighted on the model, as shown in Figure 6-25. Select the transition that will be displayed at the vertex; a drop-down list will be displayed in the **Round** dashboard. The options available in this dashboard are **Default (Round Only 2)**, **Intersect**, **Corner Sphere**, **Round Only 1**, and **Patch**. Select the desired option to apply the transition.

The **Intersect** option merges the round in such a way that sharp edges are formed at the vertex, as shown in Figure 6-26.

Figure 6-24 Edges selected for creating rounds

Figure 6-25 Various possible transitions

The **Corner Sphere** option results in a smooth spherical merging of rounds at the vertex. If you increase the default radius value of the round feature by dragging the handle while creating the round using the **Corner Sphere** option, handles are displayed on all selected edges. You can drag these handles to dynamically define the length of the fillet along the respective edges. The length values can also be defined in edit boxes that are displayed in the **Round** dashboard. Figure 6-27 shows the round created with the **Corner Sphere** option.

Figure 6-26 Round created using the **Intersect** option

Figure 6-27 Round created using the **Corner Sphere** option

The **Switch to transition mode** button also allows you to select a reference to stop the round on an edge. This means the round will be created on the selected edge up to the selected reference only. After selecting the edge for creating the round, choose the **Switch to transition mode** button to display the two transitions at both the ends. Select any one of them to make it active. Now, select the **Stop at Reference** option from the drop-down list available in the **Round** dashboard. Select a plane that will act as the stopping reference. Note that the edge on the side in which the transition is active will be retained and the round will be created on the other side. Figure 6-28 shows an example of creating a round up to a stopping reference. In this case, four edges have been filleted and the reference plane, which is highlighted by a mesh in the figure, is selected as the stopping reference.

Options Aiding Construction of Parts-I

Note

At a time you can select only one transition to make it active. The stopping references selected will be associated with the active transition only. Therefore, if you want to define the stopping reference for more than one edge, then it has to be done individually for each active transition.

Sets Tab

When you choose the **Switch to set mode** button and then choose the **Sets** tab in the **Round** dashboard, the slide-down panel will be displayed, as shown in Figure 6-29. All references and the geometry of the round are specified in this slide-down panel. The options in this slide-down panel are discussed next.

Figure 6-28 Transition rounds created on four edges and stopped by the highlighted reference plane

First Drop-down List

The first drop-down list that appears in the slide-down panel is used to specify the geometry of the round you need to create. This drop-down list contains the options, as shown in Figure 6-30. These options are discussed next.

*Figure 6-29 The **Sets** tab slide-down panel*

Figure 6-30 First drop-down list

Circular. When you choose this option from the drop-down list, the round that is created has a circular cross-section. This is the most widely used geometry type of rounds. The geometry is controlled by a radius value.

Conic. This type of round has geometry of a conic. When you choose this option, the **Conic Parameter** drop-down list appears on the **Round** dashboard. The geometry of a conic round is controlled by two dimensions: the leg dimension and the conic parameter. The value of the conic parameter lies between 0.05 and 0.95.

In Figure 6-31, the round on the model that is on the left is created using a circular geometry and the round on the model that is on the right is created using a conic geometry.

Figure 6-31 Preview of the round feature along with the radius of round

C2 Continuous. This type of round has a spline geometry. It, when created, maintains the curvature continuity with adjacent surfaces. You can set the sharpness of the spline by specifying a value in the **C2 Shape Factor** edit box in the dashboard. The sharpness value varies between 0.05 - 0.95. You can also set the value of the conic distance in the second edit box in the dashboard. Alternatively, drag the handles on the model preview to adjust the sharpness and conic distance.

D1 x D2 Conic. The round created using this option has a geometry that can be controlled by three dimensions. Figure 6-32 shows the round that is created using the **D1 x D2 Conic** option. This figure shows the two end legs dimensions and the middle dimension is the conic parameter. When you select this option to create a round, the three edit boxes are displayed on the **Round** dashboard. The **Reverse direction of conic distances** button is used to reverse the conic legs dimensions. Figure 6-33 shows the geometry of the conic round and the dimensions of the two legs after choosing this button.

*Figure 6-32 The **D1 x D2 Conic** round*

*Figure 6-33 The **D1 x D2 Conic** round after reversing*

D1xD2 C2. This type of round has spline geometry and it maintains the curvature continuity with adjacent surfaces. In this case also, you can control the geometry by three dimensions as you did in **D1 x D2 Conic.**

Note
The rounds and chamfers are defined in sets when there is a variation in their dimensions. For example, consider a situation, when you may want to create rounds on two sets of edges and the dimensions for both the rounds are different. In this case, you can define two sets of rounds; one set will define the rounds on one edge with some radius value and the second set will define the rounds on the other edge with a different radius value. The sets are also used in a similar way while creating chamfers.

Dimension Box

The edit box that is present below the first drop-down list is available only when you select the **Conic** or **D1 x D2 Conic** options. This is because this dimension box is used to enter the value for the sharpness of the conic round. The value lies between 0.05 and 0.95.

Second Drop-down List

The second drop-down list that is present in the slide-down panel is used to specify the method that Pro/ENGINEER will use to create the round. The options in this drop-down list are **Rolling ball** and **Normal to spine**. These options are discussed next.

Rolling ball. When you select this option, the round is created by rolling a spherical ball along the surfaces to which it will possibly stay tangent. This is the most common type of round that you will create.

Normal to spine. This option creates a round by sweeping an arc or a conic cross-section normal to the selected spine. Remember that in this case, the cross-section remains normal to the spine.

The area to the left of the drop-down lists in the slide-down panel, lists the number of sets formed for creating rounds. This means you can define more than one set to create the rounds. Each set may have different values and references. To add a set, right-click in this area and choose the **Add** option from the shortcut menu or, you can just click on the **New set**. The set selected in this area is the active set. It is recommended that you fully define one set of round and then define the other set.

Full Round

The **Full Round** button creates a complete round between two selected edges or two planar or non-planar surfaces. This button is available only after selecting two references and is not available when you choose the **Conic** or **D1 x D2 Conic** option or the **Normal to spine** option. The following steps explain the procedure to create a full round by selecting two edges.

1. Invoke the **Round** dashboard.
2. Select the first edge and then use CTRL+left mouse button to select the second edge. Note that the edges selected should have a surface between them that can be converted into a round.
3. Make sure the **Circular** and **Rolling ball** options are selected from the first and third drop-down lists, respectively.
4. Choose the **Full Round** button from the slide-down panel that will be displayed when you choose the **Sets** tab from the **Round** dashboard; the round is created.

The following steps explain the procedure to create a full round by selecting the two surfaces.

1. Invoke the **Round** dashboard.
2. Select the first surface and then use CTRL+left mouse button to select the second surface. Note that the edges selected should have a surface between them that can be converted into a round, for example, the top and bottom faces of a rectangular block.
3. If the **Full round** button is not chosen automatically then select it from the slide-down panel that will be displayed when you choose the **Sets** tab from the **Round** dashboard. You are prompted to select a surface to replace it with a full round.
4. Notice that in the slide-down panel, the **Driving surface** display box turns green in color. This indicates that now you can select the driving surface (surface to replace with a full round). Figure 6-34 shows the round created using the **Full round** option between the edge on the upper and the lower faces of the base of the model.

Figure 6-34 Surfaces selected for creating a full round

Through Curve Button

The **Through Curve** button creates a round whose radius is specified by an existing curve.

References Collector

The **References** collector displays the references selected on the model. These references can be deleted by selecting them in the collector and then holding down the right mouse button to display the shortcut menu. Choose the **Remove** or **Remove All** option from this shortcut menu.

Spine Collector
The **Spine** collector displays the spine selected on the model. This collector is active only when you select the **Normal to spine** option from the second drop-down list. The **Spine** collector changes to **Driving surface** collector when you select two surfaces and then choose the **Full Round** button.

The area under the **Spine** collector is used to define the dimension values of the rounds.

Transitions Tab
When you choose the **Transitions** tab, the slide-down panel will be displayed, as shown in Figure 6-35. This slide-down panel displays the transitions if they are present in a round. For example, in Figure 6-28, there are four transitions (each at the four edges).

*Figure 6-35 The **Transitions** tab slide-down panel*

Pieces Tab
When you choose the **Pieces** tab, the slide-down panel will be displayed. It provides the possible locations of the round in the form of pieces. For example, consider a case where you select two faces to fillet. One of the faces has a cut feature such that it has two disjoint surfaces, as shown in Figure 6-36. When you move the cursor over any piece under the **Pieces** area, that piece is highlighted in cyan color on the model. This tab is useful in resolving ambiguity which arises if multiple placement locations for rounds with the current selection of the references exist. This happens if two surfaces intersect each other at more than one place. From the pieces listed in the **Pieces** area, you can select the pieces to exclude by selecting the **Excluded** option from the drop-down list that will be displayed when you click on the **Included** field, as shown in Figure 6-37.

Figure 6-36 Faces selected for creating a round

*Figure 6-37 The **Pieces** slide-down panel*

Options Tab
When you choose the **Options** tab, the slide-down panel will be displayed that has two radio

buttons. These radio buttons allow you to make the round a surface or a solid. When you select the **Surface** radio button, the **Create end surfaces** check box will be enabled. This check box is used to cap all round ends of the model by surfaces.

Properties Tab

When you choose this option, the slide-down panel will be displayed. This slide-down panel displays the feature identity. Click on the **i** button to read the information about the feature. Click on the sash on the right of the **Feature info** window to close it.

Creating a Variable Radius Round

A variable radius round is the one in which the radius round varies through the length of the edge. For example, refer to Figure 6-38, which shows a constant radius round and Figure 6-39, which shows a variable radius round. To create a variable radius round, select the edge. When the preview of the round appears on the edge, hold down the right mouse button anywhere in the drawing window to display a shortcut menu. Choose the **Make variable** option from this shortcut menu. Now, in the slide-down panel that will be displayed when you choose the **Sets** tab, the two default values of the radius are available, which can be modified as per requirement. You can drag the handles displayed at both ends of the selected edge to dynamically modify the radius of round.

Figure 6-38 Constant radius round   *Figure 6-39* Variable radius round

Note
You can also create a variable radius round by selecting two surfaces. In this case, the edge that is common to the two surfaces is converted into a round.

You are also allowed to add additional points between the two end points and define a variable radius in these additional points. To define additional points, choose the **Sets** tab to invoke the slide-down panel. Bring the cursor to the area in the slide-down panel where the radius value and the location of the points are displayed and right-click to invoke the shortcut menu. Choose the **Add radius** option; one additional point appears in the same area of the slide-down panel and also on the selected edge. This point by default is placed on the selected edge by a ratio value with respect to the end point. You can select the **Reference** option from the drop-down list in this area and select a location on the edge to place the point. The location of the point can also be modified by dragging the circular handle displayed on the edge.

Options Aiding Construction of Parts-I 6-23

> **Note**
> *Rounds can be created on one edge, chain of edges, between two surfaces, an edge and a surface, and between two edges.*

Points to Remember While Creating Rounds
The following points should be remembered while creating rounds:

1. To avoid conflict due to the parent-child relationship, other features should not be referenced to the edges created by rounds or to the round surface.
2. Preferably, rounds should be added at the end of model creation. This means, the rounds should be the last features in any solid model.
3. The regeneration time of the model increases if the number of round features in it is increased.
4. Use the shortcut menus extensively while creating rounds to reduce the modeling time.

> **Tip**: *Rounds and chamfers are used in components to reduce the stress concentration at the sharp corners and edges. Therefore, they reduce the chances of failure of a component under a specified loading condition.*

CREATING CHAMFERS

The **Chamfer** tool is used to bevel the selected edges and corners as per some specified parameters. Pro/ENGINEER creates two types of chamfers. The first is the **Corner** chamfer and the second is the **Edge** chamfer. Figure 6-40 shows two types of chamfers. To create a chamfer on a corner, choose **Insert > Chamfer > Corner Chamfer** from the menu bar. To create a chamfer on an edge, choose **Insert > Chamfer > Edge Chamfer** from the menu bar. You can also choose the **Edge Chamfer** button from the **Engineering Features** toolbar to create the edge chamfers.

Figure 6-40 Two types of chamfers

Corner Chamfer
A **Corner** chamfer creates a beveled surface at the intersection of three edges. When you choose the **Corner Chamfer** option from menu bar, the **CHAMFER (CORNER)** dialog box will be displayed, refer to Figure 6-41. Also, you will be prompted to select a corner to chamfer. Select one of the edges that form the corner, the **PICK/ENTER** menu will be displayed, as shown in Figure 6-42.

Note that while selecting the edge, click close to the corner that is to be chamfered. The options in the **PICK/ENTER** menu are used to specify the chamfer distance and these are discussed next.

*Figure 6-41 The **CHAMFER (CORNER)** dialog box*   *Figure 6-42 The **PICK/ENTER** menu*

Pick Point

The **Pick Point** option is used to select a point on the highlighted edge. The selected point denotes the chamfer distance on that edge from the corner. Once the point is selected, the next edge gets highlighted in pink and you are prompted to select a point on it. This step is repeated for the third edge also. Once points have been selected on all three edges, the **PICK/ENTER** menu disappears, indicating that the required information to create a corner chamfer is completed. Choose the **Preview** button from the **CHAMFER (CORNER)** dialog box to preview the chamfer and then choose the **OK** button to create it.

Enter-input

When you use the **Enter-input** option, the **Message Input Window** will be displayed and you will be prompted to enter the length dimension along the highlighted edge. After doing so, the next edge will be highlighted in green, invoke the **Enter-input** option again and enter the value in the **Message Input Window** to set the parameters for the second edge. After you set the parameters for the second edge, the third edge is highlighted, again invoke the **Enter-input** option and specify the value for the third edge. The **PICK/ENTER** menu disappears. Choose **Preview** from the **CHAMFER (CORNER)** dialog box to preview the chamfer and then choose the **OK** button to create it.

Note
*When you are creating the corner chamfer, notice that only the **Edge** filter is available in the **Filter** drop-down list in the **Status Bar**. As mentioned earlier, the filters in this version of Pro/ENGINEER narrow the entities available for selection. Therefore, you can easily select the reference entities on the model.*

Edge Chamfer

An edge chamfer creates a beveled surface along the selected edge. When you choose **Insert > Chamfer > Edge Chamfer** from the menu bar or the **Edge Chamfer** button from the **Engineering Features** toolbar, the **Chamfer** dashboard will be displayed, as shown in Figure 6-43 and you will be prompted to select any number of edges to create a chamfer. The options in this dashboard are discussed next.

Switch to set mode

When you invoke the **Chamfer** dashboard, the **Switch to set mode** button is chosen by default. This button is used to create chamfers by defining either one set or more

Options Aiding Construction of Parts-I

Figure 6-43 The **Chamfer** *dashboard*

than one sets. When this button is chosen, the drop-down list to the right of this button in the **Chamfer** dashboard is also displayed. This drop-down list is used to specify the type of chamfer. The options in the drop-down list are discussed next.

D x D

The **D x D** option creates a chamfer such that the chamfer is created at an equal distance from the selected edge on both the faces connected by the edge. In Figure 6-44, the dimension value 10 is the value of D, where the distance D is measured from the corner.

D1 x D2

The **D1 x D2** option creates a chamfer at two user-defined distances from the selected edge. In Figure 6-45, the dimension value 10 is the value of D1 and the dimension value 16 is the value of D2. The values for D1 and D2 can be entered from the **Chamfer** dashboard. You can choose the **Interchange distance dimensions of the chamfer** button available on the right of the D2 edit box to interchange the two dimensions.

Figure 6-44 Creating chamfers using the **D x D** option

Figure 6-45 Creating chamfers using the **D1 x D2** option

Angle x D

The **Angle x D** option creates a chamfer at a user-defined distance from the selected edge and also at a user-defined angle measured from a specified surface. In Figure 6-46, the angle is 60-degree and the value of D is 15.

45 x D

The **45 x D** option creates a chamfer at the intersection of two perpendicular surfaces. The chamfer created is at an angle of 45-degree from both the surfaces and at a distance D from the edge along each surface. Once the chamfer is created, the distance D can be modified. Figure 6-47 shows this type of chamfer where the value of D is 25.

Figure 6-46 Creating the chamfers using the **Angle x D** option

Figure 6-47 Creating the chamfers using the **45 x D** option

O x O
The **O x O** is used when **Offset Surfaces** is selected from the slide-down panel that is displayed on choosing the **Sets** tab of the **Chamfer** dashboard. In this case, the chamfer is created by offsetting the neighboring surfaces and you need to define the offset distance from the edge.

O1 x O2
The chamfer is created by offsetting the neighboring surfaces independently.

Switch to transition mode

The use of **Switch to transition mode** button in the **Chamfer** dashboard is similar to the one available in the **Round** dashboard. This button will be available only when you have defined at least one reference for the chamfer. Using this button, you can define the shape of the chamfer that is formed at a vertex and also define a limit up to which the chamfer will be created. Both these applications are discussed next.

Note
*After entering into the transition mode, you cannot change the value of **D**. Therefore, it is recommended to set the value of **D** prior to specifying the transition. In case it is required to change the value of **D** after setting the transition, choose the **Switch to set mode** button to return to the set mode and change the value of **D**.*

If the chamfer feature is being created on three intersecting edges, then this button is used to define the shape of the chamfer that is created at the vertex. After choosing the **Edge Chamfer** button, select the three edges. Now choose the **Switch to transition mode** button from the **Chamfer** dashboard; the various transitions that are possible on the current selection are highlighted on the model, as shown in Figure 6-48. Select the transition that will be displayed at the vertex. Now from the drop-down list in the **Chamfer** dashboard, select the desired option, which can be **Default (Intersect)**, **Patch**, or **Corner Plane**.

Options Aiding Construction of Parts-I 6-27

The **Default (Intersect)** option merges the chamfer in such a way that sharp edges are formed at the vertex, as shown in Figure 6-49.

Figure 6-48 Various possible transitions

Figure 6-49 Chamfer created using the **Default (Intersect)** option

The **Patch** option results in a smooth transition of chamfer by creating a fillet at the vertex with respect to a selected surface. After selecting this option from the drop-down list, the **Optional surface** collector will be displayed to its right. Click once in this collector to bring it into the selection mode. Now, select one of the surfaces that form the selected edges. The resulting chamfer created by selecting the top surface of the model as the **Optional surface** is shown in Figure 6-50. Note that the fillet radius will be displayed on the selected surface and can be dynamically modified by dragging the handle displayed on the preview or by entering a value in the **Radius** edit box displayed in the **Chamfer** dashboard.

The **Corner Plane** option can be used only when three chamfers converge at a vertex. By using this option, a plane is created at the point of merger, as shown in Figure 6-51. This plane is in the shape of a triangle and its size depends on the specified value of **D**.

Figure 6-50 Chamfer created using the **Patch** option

Figure 6-51 Chamfer created using the **Corner Plane** option

The **Switch to transition mode** button also allows you to select a reference to stop the chamfer on an edge. As discussed earlier, when you choose this button, the transitions that are possible on the current selection are highlighted on the model. The highlighted piece that you select is not chamfered up to the selected reference. The reference to stop the transition can be selected after you select the **Stop at Reference** option from the drop-down list in the **Chamfer** dashboard. This means the chamfer will be created on the selected edge starting from the opposite end and up to the selected reference only, as shown in Figure 6-52. The reference plane is highlighted by a mesh in the figure.

Figure 6-52 Transition chamfer

Sets Tab

When you choose the **Sets** tab in the **Chamfer** dashboard, the slide-down panel will be displayed, as shown in Figure 6-53. All references and dimensions of the chamfer can be specified in this slide-down panel. The options in this slide-down panel are discussed next.

Set 1 Display Area

This display area displays the number of sets created. To add a set, right-click to invoke a shortcut menu and choose the **Add** option from it or just click on **New set**. It is recommended that you define an additional set only when you have defined the first set completely. You can switch among the sets by selecting them from this area. The set that is highlighted in this area can be previewed in the drawing area.

References collector

The **References** collector displays the edges selected to chamfer. An edge can be removed from the selection set by right-clicking. On doing so, a shortcut menu will be invoked and you can choose the **Remove** option from it.

Figure 6-53 The slide-down panel of the Sets tab

The area below the **References** collector is used to specify the dimension values. The dimension values can also be specified on the dashboard.

Transitions Tab

When you choose the **Transitions** tab, the slide-down panel will be displayed, as shown in Figure 6-54. This slide-down panel displays the transitions, if they are present in a chamfer. For example, in Figure 6-52, there are two transitions (each at the two edges).

*Figure 6-54 The **Transitions** tab slide-down panel*

Options Aiding Construction of Parts-I   6-29

Pieces Tab
The use of **Pieces** tab is the same as discussed in the **Round** dashboard. You can use it to exclude selected pieces in case some ambiguity exists while creating chamfers.

Options Tab
When you choose the **Options** tab, the slide-down panel, which has two radio buttons will be displayed. These radio buttons allow you to change the chamfer as a surface or as a solid.

Properties Tab
When you choose this option, the slide-down panel will be displayed, which shows the feature identity.

UNDERSTANDING RIBS
Ribs are defined as thin wall-like structures used to bind the joints together so that they do not fail under an increased load. In Pro/ENGINEER, the section for the rib is sketched as an open section and can be extruded equally in both directions of the sketch plane or on either side. The procedure of creating a rib is similar to that of creating an extrusion.

In Pro/ENGINEER, you can create two types of ribs: Trajectory Ribs and Profile Ribs. The steps to create both the ribs are almost same. These steps are discussed next.

Creating Trajectory Ribs
Adding Trajectory Ribs to a model is a new feature of Pro/ENGINEER Wildfire 5.0. It is mostly used to strengthen plastic parts that include a base and a shell or a hollow area in between the pocket surfaces. To create a trajectory rib, choose **Insert > Rib > Trajectory Rib** from the menu bar or choose the **Trajectory Rib** button from the **Engineering Features** toolbar in the **Right Toolchest**. On doing so, the **Trajectory Rib** dashboard will be displayed, as shown in Figure 6-55.

Figure 6-55 The *Trajectory Rib* dashboard

To create a trajectory rib, first you need to have a shell feature with a solid base, or a hollow area in between the pocket surface. Next, you need to select a sketching plane and then draw the geometry of the rib feature in the sketcher environment. The profile for the rib feature can be open, closed, or intersecting. Also, the profile must be created in between the hollow area and can include any number of segments.

The procedure to create a trajectory rib feature is discussed next.

1. Choose the **Trajectory Rib** button from the **Engineering Features** toolbar or choose **Insert > Rib > Trajectory Rib** from the menu bar.

2. Choose the **Placement** tab from the dashboard to display a slide-down panel and then choose the **Define** button from the panel; the **Sketch** dialog box will be displayed.
3. Select the sketch plane and specify the reference in the **Sketch** dialog box. The sketch plane will define the top surface of the rib, refer to Figure 6-56.
4. Draw the sketch and exit the sketcher environment; the preview of the rib feature will be displayed with the default width. Also, a yellow arrow will be displayed in the drawing area. This arrow shows the direction of material addition and should point toward the geometry of the model and not away from it. The direction of the arrow can be reversed, if required, by using the **Change depth direction of rib to other side of the sketch** button available in the dashboard.
5. The width of rib can be dynamically modified by dragging the handles displayed on the rib or by entering a value in the edit box available in the dashboard.
6. After specifying all parameters for the rib feature, choose the **Build feature** button; the rib will be created in between the pocket surfaces with the bottom of rib intersecting the base of solid, as shown in Figure 6-57.

Figure 6-56 The sketching plane selected

Figure 6-57 The rib feature created

Creating Profile Ribs

To create a profile rib, choose **Insert > Rib > Profile Rib** from the menu bar; the **Profile Rib** dashboard will be displayed, as shown in Figure 6-58. Alternatively, click on the black arrow on the right of the **Trajectory Rib** from the **Engineering Features** toolbar; a flyout will be displayed. Choose **Profile Rib** from the flyout to invoke the tool.

To create a rib, you first need to select a sketching plane and then draw the geometry of the rib feature in the sketcher environment. The sketch for the rib feature should be an open entity.

Figure 6-58 The **Profile Rib** dashboard

The options and the tools in the **Rib** dashboard are discussed next.

Options Aiding Construction of Parts-I   6-31

References Tab

When you choose the **References** tab, the slide-down panel will be displayed, as shown in Figure 6-59. In the slide-down panel, the **Sketch** collector shows **Select 1 item**. This indicates that the sketch for the rib feature is not drawn. To draw the sketch, choose the **Define** button; the sketch dialog box will be displayed using which you can define the sketch plane and the references.

*Figure 6-59 The **References** tab slide-down panel*

The **Flip** button is used to flip the side where the material should be added. This button will be available only when you draw the sketch and exit the sketcher environment.

Change the thickness option between both sides, side 1, and side 2 Button

This button is available on the **Rib** dashboard only when the sketch of the rib is drawn and you exit the sketcher environment. You have an option to extrude the sketch on either sides or symmetrically on both sides of the sketching plane.

Note
Because the sketch of the rib can be extruded on both sides of the sketching plane, therefore, while creating a rib, you must always select an appropriate sketching plane such that it lies at the center of the rib feature.

The procedure to create a profile rib feature using the **Rib** dashboard is discussed next.

1. Invoke the **Profile Rib** dashboard by choosing the **Profile Rib** button from the **Engineering Features** toolbar or choose **Insert > Rib > Profile Rib** from the menu bar.
2. From the **Profile Rib** dashboard, choose the **References** tab to display the slide-down panel and choose the **Define** button from it.
3. Select the sketch plane and specify the reference in the **Sketch** dialog box. Now, create an open sketch that defines the rib profile. Make sure that the endpoints of the sketch are aligned with the edges of the model.
4. When you exit the sketcher environment, a yellow arrow will be displayed in the drawing area. This arrow shows the direction of material addition and should point toward the geometry of the model and not away from it. The direction of the arrow can be reversed by using the **Flip** button available in the slide-down panel that will be displayed on selecting the **References** tab.
5. If the arrow direction is correct, then you can preview the rib feature on the graphics window. The rib thickness can be dynamically modified by dragging the handles displayed on the rib or by entering a value in the edit box available in the **Rib** dashboard.
6. Now, use the **Change the thickness option between both sides, side 1, and side 2** button to change the direction of extrusion. You can create the rib feature either symmetrically about the sketching plane or on either side of it. Every successive click on this button will change the position of the rib feature with respect to the sketching plane.
7. After specifying all parameters for the rib feature, choose the **Build feature** button.

The profile ribs can be rotational ribs and straight ribs. Rotational ribs are constructed on cylindrical parts and straight ribs are created on planar faces. Figure 6-60 shows a rotational rib and Figure 6-61 shows a straight rib. The options for the creating these ribs are the same. The creation of these ribs depends on the geometry of the feature on which the rib is created.

Figure 6-60 The rotational rib feature

Figure 6-61 The straight rib feature

EDITING FEATURES OF A MODEL

Editing is one of the most important aspects of the product design. Most of the designs require editing during their creation or after they are created. As mentioned earlier, Pro/ENGINEER is a parametric and feature-based solid modeling software. Hence, the features constituting a model can be individually edited. For example, Figure 6-62 shows a cylindrical part that has six counterbore holes created at some bolt circle diameter (BCD).

Now, in case you have to edit the features such that the six holes are to be converted into eight holes and the counterbore holes are to be converted into countersink holes, as shown in Figure 6-63, you just need to use two operations. The first operation will convert six holes into eight holes by using the **Edit** option in the shortcut menu that will be displayed when you select the hole from the **Model Tree** and hold down the right mouse button. Next, choose **Regenerate** to regenerate the model. The second operation will open the **Hole** dashboard and convert the counterbore holes into countersink holes.

Figure 6-62 Six counterbore holes

Figure 6-63 Eight countersink holes

Similarly, you can also edit the datums and the features referenced to these datums. As a parent-child relationship exists between the two, therefore the child feature is also modified when the parent feature is modified. For example, if you have created a feature using a datum plane that is at some offset distance, the feature will be automatically repositioned when the offset value of the datum plane is changed. The following methods explain how to edit the features in Pro/ENGINEER.

Editing Definition or Redefining Features

Editing the definition of features allows you to make changes in the parameters that were used to create it. You can also modify the sketches of the sketched features by editing their definition. To invoke the **Edit Definition** option, there are three methods available in Pro/ENGINEER Wildfire 5.0. These methods are listed next.

1. Select the feature that has to be redefined from the drawing area; the selected feature is highlighted in red. Now, hold down the right mouse button; a shortcut menu will be displayed. Choose the **Edit Definition** option from this menu.

   Tip: *Suppose you have created a cube and the display is selected to be Shaded. Now, you need to select the top face of the cube. By default, in the Filter drop-down list the Smart option is selected. Select the cube on the top face; the whole cube turns red in color. Again click on the top face; it gets selected and is highlighted in red.*

   Sometimes, it becomes difficult to select the desired feature from the model to redefine it. Therefore, you can use the filters in the **Filter** drop-down list in the **Status Bar**.

2. You can also use the **Model Tree** to redefine a feature. Select the feature that has to be redefined from the **Model Tree**; the selected feature is highlighted in red in the drawing area. Now, right-click on the feature listed in the **Model Tree**; a shortcut menu will be displayed. Choose **Edit Definition** from this menu.

3. Select the feature to redefine from the drawing area or from the **Model Tree** and then choose **Edit > Definition** from the menu bar. Remember that the **Definition** option in the **Edit** menu is available only when a feature has been selected.

Reordering Features

Reordering the features is defined as the process of changing the sequence of feature creation in a model. Sometimes after creating a model, it may be required to change the order in which the features of the model were created. A feature can be placed before or after another feature. For this purpose, the **Model Tree** or the **Menu Manager** is used.

If you use the **Model Tree**, you just have to drag and drop the feature that you want to reorder below or above the destination feature.

Choose **Edit > Feature Operations** from the menu bar; the **Menu Manager**, will be invoked as shown in Figure 6-64. It was used extensively in the prior releases of Pro/ENGINEER Wildfire but now, it is mainly used to perform operations on features.

Choose the **Reorder** option from the **FEAT** menu of **Menu Manager**. After choosing the **Reorder** option from the **FEAT** menu of **Menu Manager**, the **SELECT FEAT** submenu will be displayed, as shown in Figure 6-65, and you will be prompted to select the features that you want to reorder. Select the feature to be reordered from the **Model Tree** and then choose the **Done** option from the **SELECT FEAT** submenu or use the middle mouse button to confirm the selection. The message area displays the possible positions where the selected feature can be inserted.

Now, select **BEFORE** or **AFTER** from the **REORDER** submenu, as shown in Figure 6-66. Depending upon this selection, the feature to be reordered will be placed before or after another selected feature. Select another feature and choose the **Done** option from the **Menu Manager** to complete the reordering process.

Figure 6-64 The *FEAT* menu

Figure 6-65 The *SELECT FEAT* submenu

Figure 6-66 The *REORDER* submenu

The example that is discussed here will explain why and when the need for reordering of features in a model arises. Consider the model shown in Figure 6-67. It consists of a rectangular pattern of three columns and two rows. Now, a shell feature is created on this model, which removes the top and the front face, as shown in Figure 6-68.

Figure 6-67 Model with pattern

Figure 6-68 Model after creating the shell feature

Options Aiding Construction of Parts-I 6-35

In Figure 6-68, it is evident that the material equal to the wall thickness of the shell feature is added around the hole features. If this is not desired, the model has to be modified and here the need for reordering the feature arises. You will reorder the features such that the shell feature is inserted before the hole feature and its pattern. When you reorder the features, all features will be automatically adjusted in the new order. The model after reordering the hole feature is shown in Figure 6-69.

Figure 6-69 Model after reordering the features

Rerouting Features

Rerouting of features is required when there is a need of changing its sketch plane. While doing so, you can also redefine the references that were selected while creating the sketch. For rerouting a feature, select the required feature from the **Model Tree** or from the drawing area. Now, choose **Edit > References** from the menu bar. Note that the **References** option is only available after a feature has been selected.

After choosing the **References** option, the **Confirmation** message box is displayed that prompts you whether to roll back the model. If you select **Yes** then all features created after the selected feature will be suppressed and they will not be visible in the model. The suppressed features will be unsuppressed after the rerouting is completed. If **No** is selected, all features will remain active while the selected feature is being rerouted. The desired selection can be made by choosing the appropriate button from the message box.

Now, the **REROUTE** menu will be displayed and also a surface will be highlighted in the drawing area. Also, you will be prompted to select an alternate surface. The highlighted surface can be a sketch plane or a reference that was selected while creating the feature. You can select another plane or surface to replace the highlighted surface. Once a selection is made, another surface gets highlighted for replacement. This process continues till all references are replaced. Finally, the **REROUTE** menu will be automatically closed and the model will be regenerated as per the new references.

Note
While rerouting a feature, if you do not want to replace a highlighted surface then select the same surface again as the alternate surface.

Suppressing Features

Once the feature is suppressed, it will neither be displayed in the drawing area nor in the drawing views. Note that the feature is not deleted; only its visibility is turned off. You can resume the feature anytime by unsuppressing it using the **Model Tree** or using **Edit > Resume** from the menu bar. As soon as you unsuppress the feature, it will be displayed in the drawing area and also in the drawing views. When a model has many features, then suppressing some features decreases its regeneration time. To suppress a feature, right-click on it in the **Model Tree** or select it in the drawing area and then press and hold down the right mouse button to display the shortcut menu. Choose **Suppress** from the shortcut menu to suppress the selected feature; the **Suppress** message box will be displayed prompting you to confirm the suppression of the highlighted features in the drawing area. Confirm the suppression by choosing the **OK** button in this message box. You can also suppress a feature by first selecting it from the **Model Tree** or the drawing area and then choosing **Edit > Suppress > Suppress** from the menu bar. To unsuppress the feature, right-click in the **Model Tree** or in the drawing area, invoke the shortcut menu, and choose the **Resume** option from it.

> **Tip**: *By default, the suppressed features are not displayed in the **Model Tree**. To display the suppressed features, choose **Settings > Tree Filters** from the **Model Tree**; the **Model Tree Items** dialog box will be displayed. Select the **Suppressed Objects** check box and choose the **OK** button. The suppressed features will now be displayed in the **Model Tree** with a small black box displayed on their names.*

Note
If the feature being suppressed has child features, they will also be suppressed on suppressing the parent feature. However, before suppressing the features, the system prompts you to confirm the suppression of the highlighted features in the drawing area.

Deleting a Feature

The feature that is not required can be deleted from the model. Right-click on the feature in the **Model Tree** or in the drawing area to invoke the shortcut menu. From this menu, choose the **Delete** option. Once the feature to be deleted is selected, it gets highlighted, along with its child features. The system confirms you to delete the selected feature. If you confirm the deletion, the feature will be deleted along with its child features.

Modifying a Feature

Once a feature is created, you can still modify it by modifying its dimensions. This editing operation reflects the parametric nature of Pro/ENGINEER. Right-click on the feature in the **Model Tree** or in the drawing area to invoke the shortcut menu. From this menu, choose the **Edit** option; the dimensions of the feature are displayed in the drawing area. These dimensions are the same as those defined while sketching or creating the feature.

In some cases, for example, rounds, holes, and so on, the dimensions of these features were defined as parameters. Therefore, these dimensions are also displayed when you select them to modify. To modify the dimensions, double-click on the dimension in the drawing area; the dimension is converted into an edit box. Type the required value for the selected dimension and press ENTER. Once you modify a dimension, you also need to regenerate the feature. Choose the **Regenerate** button from the **Top Toolchest** or press CTRL+G.

> **Tip**: *You can double-click on a feature in the drawing area to display its dimensions. A dimension can be modified first by double-clicking on it, then entering a new value in the edit box displayed and finally, regenerating it.*

If you want to modify a pattern, it is recommended that you can select the instance as well as the original model. Patterns are discussed in Chapter 7.

Modifying the Sketch of a Feature Dynamically

If you want to modify the sketch of a feature without entering the sketcher environment, then you need to modify it dynamically. To dynamically modify a sketch, follow these steps:

1. Select the feature preferably by using the **Features** filter from the **Filter** drop-down list.

2. When the feature turns red in color, hold down the right mouse button to invoke the shortcut menu.

3. From the shortcut menu, choose the **Edit** option; the dimensions of the sketch appear on the feature.

4. Select the sketch and hold down the right mouse button to invoke the shortcut menu. Choose the **Edit** option from this shortcut menu.

5. Now, bring the cursor close to the sketch. You will notice that the cursor changes to a pointer. The pointer symbol represents that you can select an entity from the sketch and drag it to modify its shape.

6. Modify the shape of the sketch by dragging its entities.

7. Choose the **Regenerate** button from the **Top Toolchest** to apply the modifications.

Modifying the Features Dynamically

Dynamic editing of models is a new feature of Pro/ENGINEER Wildfire 5.0 and it has been introduced to simplify the editing process. This feature enables you to modify the model after it has been created and can be performed any time during the creation. To edit a feature dynamically, select the feature from the drawing area or from the model tree and right-click to invoke a shortcut menu. Next, choose **Dynamic Edit** from the shortcut menu; you can edit the features dynamically.

The following entities displayed on the feature can be modified:

1. Small square boxes are displayed for the options that were defined in the dashboard while creating the feature. These handles enable you to adjust the values by selecting and dragging them to the desired position.
2. The profile used for the feature is also displayed. You can drag the entities and modify the shape of the sketch to modify the feature.
3. All the dimensions that were defined while sketching the model as well as those that were entered in the dashboard are displayed on the feature. You can double-click on the dimension and enter a new value to modify the feature accordingly.

Note that in the process of dynamic modification, the feature gets modified instantaneously and you need not regenerate the model.

TUTORIALS

Tutorial 1

Create the model shown in Figure 6-70. The dimensions, and the front, top, and left-side views of the model are also shown in the figure. **(Expected time: 45 min)**

Figure 6-70 Isometric shaded, left, front, and top views of the model

The following steps are required to complete this model:

Examine the model and determine the number of features in it, refer to Figure 6-70.
a. Create the base feature on the **FRONT** datum plane, refer to Figures 6-68 and 6-69.
b. Create the second extrude feature on the **TOP** datum plane, refer to Figures 6-70 and 6-71.
c. Create the third extrude feature on the front planar surface of the second feature, refer to Figures 6-72 and 6-73.
d. Create the non symmetrically extruded cylindrical feature on the front face of the third feature, refer to Figures 6-74 and 6-75.
e. Create a hole feature that is coaxial to the cylindrical feature, refer to Figure 6-77.
f. Create the round features, refer to Figures 6-78 and 6-79.
g. Create the last feature, which is the rib, refer to Figures 6-80 and 6-81.

When a Pro/ENGINEER session starts, the first task is to set the working directory. As this is the first tutorial of this chapter, you need to select the Working Directory first. Set *C:\ProE-WF-5.0\c06* as the Working Directory. A message **Successfully changed to C:\ProE-WF-5.0\c06 directory** is displayed in the message area.

Options Aiding Construction of Parts-I

Starting a New Object File

1. Start a new part file and name it *c06tut1*.

   The three default datum planes are displayed in the drawing area. Also, the **Model Tree** is displayed on the left of the drawing area.

Creating the Base Feature

To create the sketch of the base feature, you first need to select the sketching plane for it. In this model, you need to draw the base feature on the **FRONT** datum plane because the direction of extrusion of this feature is normal to this plane.

1. Choose the **Extrude** button from the **Base Features** toolbar; the **Extrude** dashboard is displayed.

2. Choose the **Placement** tab to display the slide-down panel and then choose the **Define** button; the **Sketch** dialog box is displayed.

3. Select the **FRONT** datum plane as the sketching plane; the **RIGHT** datum plane and its orientation are selected by default.

4. Select the **TOP** datum plane and then choose the **Top** option from the **Orientation** drop-down list.

5. Choose the **Sketch** button from the **Sketch** dialog box to enter into the sketcher environment.

6. Once you enter into the sketcher environment, create the sketch of the base feature and apply constraints and dimensions, as shown in Figure 6-71. Note that in the sketch, the bottom line of the rectangular section coincides with the **TOP** datum plane.

   As is evident from the sketch of the base feature shown in Figure 6-71 that the **RIGHT** datum plane is located at a distance of 50 from the left edge because later in the tutorial, the rib feature will be created on this plane. The distance of 50 can be calculated from Figure 6-70. As mentioned earlier, that, by default, the sketch for a rib is extruded to both sides of the sketching plane. Therefore, when you create the sketch for the rib feature on the **RIGHT** datum plane, it will extrude on both the sides.

7. After the sketch is completed, choose the **Done** button to exit the sketcher environment; the **Extrude** dashboard is enabled and appears above the drawing area. All model attributes that are selected by default are accepted to create the model.

8. Enter **10** as the depth in the dimension box on the **Extrude** dashboard.

9. Choose the **Named View List** button from the **View** toolbar; a flyout is displayed. Choose the **Default Orientation** option from the flyout; the model orients in its default orientation, that is, the trimetric view.

10. Next, choose the **Build feature** button from the **Extrude** dashboard to create the base feature.

Creating the Second Feature

The second feature is also an extruded feature and will be created on the **TOP** datum plane. Therefore, you need to define the **TOP** datum plane as the sketching plane.

1. Choose the **Extrude** button from the **Base Features** toolbar; the **Extrude** dashboard is displayed.

2. Choose the **Placement** tab; the slide-down panel is displayed. From the slide-down panel, choose the **Define** button; the **Sketch** dialog box is displayed.

3. Select the **TOP** datum plane as the sketching plane.

4. Select the front face of the base feature shown in Figure 6-72 and then select the **Bottom** option from the **Orientation** drop-down list.

5. Choose the **Sketch** button from the **Sketch** dialog box to enter the sketcher environment. After entering the sketcher environment, turn the model display to **No hidden**.

Figure 6-71 Sketch of the base feature with dimensions and constraints

Figure 6-72 Front face of the base feature selected to be at the bottom while sketching

Note
*Before you start sketching a section for any feature, it is recommended that you turn the model display to **No hidden** and turn off the datum plane display using the **Plane Display** button. This is done to improve the clarity of the drawing area while sketching.*

6. Create the sketch for the second feature and apply the constraints and dimensions to it, as shown in Figure 6-73.

You can choose the **Use** button from the **Sketcher Tools** toolbar to use the edge of the base feature. The edge of the base feature is required to close the section for the second feature. However, if you do not use the edge, you will have to draw a line to close the sketch.

Options Aiding Construction of Parts-I

You will then have to align it with the bottom edge and add constraints and dimensions, refer to Figure 6-70.

> **Note**
> *If you do not close the section loop by drawing a line or using the edge of the base feature, a yellow arrow is displayed on exiting the sketcher environment. Using this arrow, you can specify the direction in which the material will be added.*

7. After completing the sketch, turn the model display to **Shading** and choose the **Done** button; the **Extrude** dashboard is enabled above the drawing area.

8. Enter **10** in the dimension box in the **Extrude** dashboard and press ENTER.

9. Choose the **Build feature** button from the **Extrude** dashboard; the second feature is completed and the shaded default trimetric view is displayed, as shown in Figure 6-74.

Figure 6-73 Sketch of the second feature with dimensions and constraints

Figure 6-74 The default trimetric view of the completed second feature and the base feature

Creating the Third Feature

The sketch of the third feature will be drawn on the front planar surface of the second feature and it will be extruded to the given depth.

1. Choose the **Extrude** button from the **Base Features** toolbar.

2. Choose the **Placement** tab. Next, from the slide-down panel, choose the **Define** button; the **Sketch** dialog box is displayed.

3. Select the face of the second feature as the sketching plane, as shown in Figure 6-75.

4. Select the top face of the second feature as the reference and then select the **Top** option from the **Orientation** drop-down list only if these are not selected by default.

5. Choose the **Sketch** button from the **Sketch** dialog box to enter into the sketcher environment.

6. Once you enter in the sketcher environment, turn the model display to **No hidden**. Create the sketch for the third feature and apply constraints and dimensions to it, as shown in Figure 6-73.

Figure 6-75 Planar surface selected as the sketching plane for the third feature

Figure 6-76 Sketch of the third feature with dimensions and constraints

Note
While drawing the sketch of any feature, it is recommended that you first apply the required constraints and then dimension the sketch.

7. Choose the **Done** button; the **Extrude** dashboard is enabled above the drawing area.

8. Enter **10** in the dimension box in the **Extrude** dashboard.

9. Choose the **Build feature** button from the **Extrude** dashboard. Turn the model display to **Shading**. The third feature is completed. You can use the middle mouse button to spin the model to view its different orientations.

Creating the Fourth Feature

The fourth feature of the model is an extruded feature and its sketch is drawn on the front planar surface of the third feature.

1. Choose the **Extrude** button from the **Base Features** toolbar.

2. Choose the **Placement** tab and then from the slide-down panel, choose the **Define** button; the **Sketch** dialog box is displayed.

3. Select the front planar face of the third feature, shown in Figure 6-77, as the sketching plane. The extrusion of the cylindrical feature will be on both sides of the front face.

    The attributes of the feature, like extrusion on both sides and the depth of extrusion will be specified after the sketch of the feature is drawn.

4. Select the top face of the second feature as reference and then select the **Top** option from the **Orientation** drop-down list, if they are not selected by default.

Options Aiding Construction of Parts-I

5. Choose the **Sketch** button from the **Sketch** dialog box to enter into the sketcher environment.

6. Once you enter into the sketcher environment, turn the model display to **No hidden**.

7. Choose the **Concentric** button from the **Sketcher Tools** toolbar to draw the circular section for the fourth feature, refer to Figure 6-78. Select the arc using the left mouse button. As you move the mouse, the yellow rubber-band circle changes its size. Move the cursor close to the arc; the cursor snaps to the arc. Use the left mouse button and select a point on the arc. You will notice that the equal radius constraint is applied to the sketch. Now, exit this tool.

Figure 6-77 Front planar face selected

Figure 6-78 Sketch for the fourth feature

8. After the sketch is completed, choose the **Done** button; the **Extrude** dashboard is enabled above the drawing area.

9. Choose the **Options** option from the **Extrude** dashboard. In the slide-down panel, choose the **Blind** option from both the **Side 1** and **Side 2** drop-down lists.

10. In the dimension box that is on the right of the **Side 1** drop-down list, enter **12**.

11. In the dimension box that is on the right of the **Side 2** drop-down list, enter **13**.

12. Turn the model display to **Shading** and choose the **Build feature** button from the **Extrude** dashboard to create the fourth feature.

Creating the Hole Feature

The hole feature is created using the **Hole** dashboard. The hole will be placed coaxial to the fourth cylindrical feature.

> **Note**
> *For creating a coaxial hole, you need to select the axis of the circular feature. To do so, you need to turn on the display of the axis, if it is not displayed.*

1. Choose the **Hole** button from the **Engineering Features** toolbar; the **Hole** dashboard is displayed, in which the **Create simple hole** button is chosen by default.

2. Choose the **Placement** tab from the **Hole** dashboard; a slide-down panel is displayed.

3. Select the front face of the cylindrical feature, as shown in Figure 6-79, to place the hole.

   As you select the front face of the cylindrical feature, the preview of the hole is displayed in the drawing area. Now, you need to specify the reference for placing the hole.

4. Press the CTRL key and select the axis of the cylindrical feature drawing area.

5. The **Coaxial** option is automatically selected in the drop-down list of the slide-down panel of the **Placement** tab.

6. In the diameter dimension box on the **Hole** dashboard, type **16** and press ENTER.

7. In the depth flyout of the **Hole** dashboard, choose the **Drill to intersect with all surfaces** button.

8. Choose the **Build feature** button from the **Hole** dashboard; the hole is created and the trimetric view of the shaded model with the hole is displayed, as shown in Figure 6-80.

Figure 6-79 Planar face   *Figure 6-80* The default trimetric view

Creating Two Round Features

Now, the two round features will be created. Both the rounds have different radii and will be created by defining two sets.

Options Aiding Construction of Parts-I   6-45

1. Choose the **Round** button from the **Engineering Features** toolbar; the **Round** dashboard is displayed.

2. Choose the **Sets** tab to display the slide-down panel. Let this slide-down panel remain open so that you can view the selections you made on the model.

3. Spin the model and select one of the faces shown in Figure 6-81. Press the CTRL key and then select the other face.

   The preview of the round is created on the edge that connects the two selected faces; the default value of the radius is also displayed.

4. Double-click on the default radius value that is displayed on the preview of the round. In the edit box that appears, enter the value **5** and press ENTER; the first round is created.

5. After spinning the model, select one of the faces shown in Figure 6-82 and then use CTRL+left mouse button to select the second face. You will notice that in the slide-down panel, **Set 1** and **Set 2** appear. This indicates that the second set has been defined.

   The preview of the round is created on the edge that connects the two selected faces. The default value of the radius is also displayed.

Figure 6-81 Faces for creating a round of radius 5

Figure 6-82 Faces for creating a round of radius 15

6. Double-click on the default radius value that is displayed in the preview of the second round. In the edit box that appears, type the value of **15** and press ENTER.

7. Choose the **Build feature** button from the **Round** dashboard.

   The second round is created. In the **Model Tree**, the two rounds created appear as a single feature.

Creating the Rib Feature

Advance planning done while drawing the sketch for the base feature will help you to draw the rib feature now. The location for the **RIGHT** datum plane was calculated while sketching the base feature. The section for the rib feature will be drawn on the **RIGHT** datum plane.

1. Choose **Trajectory Rib > Profile Rib** from the **Engineering Features** toolbar; the **Profile Rib** dashboard is displayed.

2. A rib feature is always sketched from the side view. Now, turn on the display of the datum planes from the **Datum Display** toolbar.

3. Choose the **References** tab; the slide-down panel is displayed. Choose the **Define** button; the **Sketch** dialog box is displayed.

4. Select the **RIGHT** datum plane as the sketching plane from the drawing area.

5. Select the **TOP** datum plane as reference and then select the **Top** option from the **Orientation** drop-down list, only if they are not selected by default.

6. Choose the **Sketch** button to enter into the sketcher environment.

   You will need to turn the model display to **No hidden** before drawing the sketch for the rib feature.

7. Draw the open sketch for the rib feature and apply required constraints and dimensions, as shown in Figure 6-83.

Figure 6-83 Open sketch of the rib feature with dimensions and constraints

8. After the sketch is completed, choose the **Done** button.

Options Aiding Construction of Parts-I

A yellow arrow pointing in the direction of material addition is displayed on the sketch. As the section for the rib feature is open, Pro/ENGINEER allows you to specify the direction where the material should be added. Therefore, you need to change the direction of the arrow toward the model, if it is not already changed.

9. Enter **10** in the dimension box in the **Profile Rib** dashboard.

10. Choose the **Build feature** button from the **Profile Rib** dashboard to complete creating the model and exit this feature creation tool.

    All features in the model have been created and the model is now complete. The trimetric shaded view of the completed model is shown in Figure 6-84.

Saving the Model
1. Choose the **Save** button from the **File** toolbar and save the model. The order of feature creation can be seen from the **Model Tree** shown in Figure 6-85.

Figure 6-84 *The default trimetric view of the model*   *Figure 6-85* *The **Model Tree** for Tutorial 1*

Tutorial 2

In this tutorial, you will create the model shown in Figure 6-86. The dimensions of the model are shown in Figure 6-87.   **(Expected time: 30 min)**

The following steps are required to complete this model:

Examine the model and determine the number of features in it, refer to Figure 6-86.
a. Create the base feature, refer to Figures 6-88 and 6-89.
b. Create the cylindrical feature, refer to Figures 6-90 through 6-92.
c. Create the hole feature coaxially on the cylindrical feature, refer to Figure 6-93.
d. Create the rib feature, refer to Figures 6-94 and 6-95.

Figure 6-86 Isometric view of the solid model

Figure 6-87 Front and right views of the model for Tutorial 2

The working directory has already been selected in Tutorial 1 and therefore, you do not need to select it again. However, if you need to change the working directory, choose **File > Set Working Directory** and then select *c06* in the **Select Working Directory** dialog box.

Starting a New Object File
1. Start a new part file and name it as *c06tut2*.

   The three default datum planes and the **Model Tree** appears in the drawing area.

Creating the Base Feature
1. Choose the **Extrude** button from the **Base Features** toolbar.

2. Choose the **Placement** tab and then from the slide-down panel, choose the **Define** button; the **Sketch** dialog box is displayed.

3. Select the **FRONT** datum plane for drawing the sketch of the base feature.

Options Aiding Construction of Parts-I 6-49

4. Select the **TOP** datum plane from the drawing area and then select the **Top** option from the **Orientation** drop-down list.

5. Choose the **Sketch** button from the **Sketch** dialog box to enter into the sketcher environment.

6. Once you enter into the sketcher environment, create the sketch of the base feature and apply constraints and dimensions to it, as shown in Figure 6-88.

7. After the sketch is completed, choose the **Done** button and exit the sketcher environment; the **Extrude** dashboard is enabled and appears above the drawing area.

8. Specify **38** as the depth in the dimension box that is present on the **Extrude** dashboard; the default trimetric view of the base feature is displayed, as shown in Figure 6-89.

9. Choose the **Build feature** button from the **Extrude** dashboard to exit the feature creation tool.

Note
*In this tutorial, the base feature can also be created by extruding it on both sides of the sketching plane that is the **FRONT** datum plane. This would reduce the step required to create the datum plane, which in turn is used to create a rib feature. However, to familiarize you with creating embedded datum planes, the base feature is extruded on one side of the sketching plane.*

Figure 6-88 Sketch of the base feature with dimensions and constraints

Figure 6-89 The default trimetric view of the base feature

Creating the Second Feature

The second feature is a cylindrical feature that is sketched on the planar surface of the base feature which is shown highlighted in Figure 6-90.

1. Choose the **Extrude** button from the **Base Features** toolbar.

2. Choose the **Placement** tab and then from the slide-down panel, choose the **Define** button; the **Sketch** dialog box is displayed.

3. Select the face of the base feature as the sketching plane shown in Figure 6-90.

4. Select the **TOP** datum plane from the drawing area and then select the **Top** option from the **Orientation** drop-down list.

5. Choose the **Sketch** button from the **Sketch** dialog box to enter into the sketcher environment.

   After invoking the sketcher environment, turn the model display to **No hidden**.

6. Draw the sketch for the second feature. Apply and modify the dimensions, as shown in Figure 6-91.

Figure 6-90 The face of the base feature selected as the sketching plane

Figure 6-91 Sketch and dimensions of the second feature

7. Turn the display of the model to **Shading**. Exit the sketcher environment by choosing the **Done** button; the **Extrude** dashboard is enabled and appears above the drawing area.

8. Enter **17** in the dimension box in the **Extrude** dashboard.

9. Choose the **Build feature** button from the **Extrude** dashboard to exit the feature creation tool. The trimetric view of the model with the second feature is shown in Figure 6-92.

Creating the Hole Feature

The hole feature will be created using the **Hole** dashboard. The coaxial hole will be created on the cylindrical feature. The axis of the cylindrical feature will be used as the axial reference to create the coaxial hole.

Options Aiding Construction of Parts-I 6-51

1. Choose **Insert > Hole** from the menu bar; the **Hole** dashboard is displayed. The **Create simple hole** button in the **Hole** dashboard is chosen by default.

2. Choose the **Placement** tab from the **Hole** dashboard; a slide-down panel is displayed.

3. Select the front face of the cylindrical feature to place the hole.

   As you select the front face of the cylindrical feature, the preview of the hole is displayed in the drawing area. Now, you need to specify the reference for the placement of hole.

4. Hold-down the CTRL key and select the axis of the cylindrical feature from the drawing area.

   The **Coaxial** option is selected automatically in the drop-down list of the slide-down panel.

5. In the diameter edit box of the **Hole** dashboard, enter **20** and press ENTER.

6. From the depth flyout on the **Hole** dashboard, choose the **Drill to intersect with all surfaces** button.

7. Choose the **Build feature** button from the **Hole** dashboard; the hole is created and the trimetric view of the shaded model with the hole is displayed, as shown in Figure 6-93.

Figure 6-92 Model with the second feature   *Figure 6-93* Model with the hole feature

Creating the Rib Feature

To create the rib feature, a datum plane is created on-the-fly. As mentioned earlier, rib features are always drawn from the side view.

1. Choose the black arrow on right of the **Trajectory Rib** button from the **Engineering Features** toolbar; a flyout is displayed. Choose the **Profile Rib** button from this flyout.

2. Choose the **References** tab; a slide-down panel is displayed. Choose the **Define** button; the **Sketch** dialog box is displayed.

3. Choose the **Plane** button from the **Datum** toolbar; the **DATUM PLANE** dialog box is displayed. You may need to move the **Sketch** dialog box to bring the **Plane** button into view.

4. Select the axis of the hole, press the CTRL key, and select the **FRONT** datum plane. You can view your selections in the **References** collector.

5. Click on the **FRONT** reference in the **References** collector; a drop-down list appears on the right of the reference. Select the **Parallel** option from this drop-down list.

6. Choose **OK** from the **DATUM PLANE** dialog box to exit it.

   A datum plane that passes through the selected axis and is parallel to the **FRONT** datum plane will be created. This datum plane is selected automatically as the sketching plane. Now, you need to select the reference plane.

7. Select the **TOP** datum plane and then select the **Top** option from the **Orientation** drop-down list.

8. Choose the **Sketch** button; the system takes you to the sketcher environment.

9. Draw the open sketch of the rib feature and apply dimensions, as shown in Figure 6-94. Exit the sketcher environment by choosing the **Done** button; the **Profile Rib** dashboard is enabled and appears above the drawing area.

10. Choose the **Flip** button on the **References** slide-down panel to flip the arrow; the preview of the rib is displayed on the model. Choose this button only when the preview of the rib is not displayed. Alternatively, click on the yellow arrow to flip the arrow.

11. Enter **8** as the thickness of the rib in the edit box in the **Profile Rib** dashboard. Next, choose the **Build feature** button.

    The trimetric view of the complete model with the rib feature is shown in Figure 6-95.

Saving the Model

1. Choose the **Save** button from the **File** toolbar to save the model and then close the active window.

Options Aiding Construction of Parts-I 6-53

Figure 6-94 Sketch for the rib feature with the model display set to **No hidden**

Figure 6-95 The default trimetric view of the final model

Tutorial 3

In this tutorial, you will create the model shown in Figure 6-96. The solid model, dimensions, and the front and the right views are also shown in this figure. **(Expected time: 45 min)**

Figure 6-96 The isometric, front, and right views of the model

The following steps are required to complete this model:

Examine the model and determine the number of features in it, refer to Figure 6-96.
a. Create the base feature, refer to Figures 6-97 and 6-98.
b. Create the cut feature, refer to Figures 6-99 and 6-100.
c. Create a counterbore hole, refer to Figures 6-101 through 6-103.
d. Create the rounds, refer to Figures 6-104 and 6-105.

Starting a New Object File

1. Start a new part file and name it *c06tut3*.

The three default datum planes and the **Model Tree** appear in the drawing area if they were not turned off previously.

Creating the Base Feature

1. Choose the **Extrude** button from the **Base Features** toolbar.

2. Choose the **Placement** tab; a slide-down panel is displayed. Choose the **Define** button; the **Sketch** dialog box is displayed.

3. Select the **RIGHT** datum plane as the sketching plane.

4. Select the **TOP** datum plane from the drawing area and then select the **Top** option from the **Orientation** drop-down list.

5. Choose the **Sketch** button from the **Extrude** dashboard to enter into the sketcher environment.

6. Once you enter into the sketcher environment, create the sketch of the base feature and apply dimensions and constraints, as shown in Figure 6-97.

Figure 6-97 Sketch of the base feature with dimensions and constraints

Figure 6-98 The default trimetric view of the base feature

Options Aiding Construction of Parts-I

7. Exit the sketcher environment by choosing the **Done** button; the **Extrude** dashboard is enabled and appears above the drawing area.

8. Enter **86** in the dimension box in the **Extrude** dashboard.

9. Choose the **Build feature** button to exit the feature creation tool. The base feature is completed. The default trimetric view of the base feature is shown in Figure 6-98.

Creating the Second Feature

The second feature is an extruded cut feature. This cut feature is created on a datum plane that passes through the center of the base feature.

1. Choose the **Extrude** button from the **Base Features** toolbar.

2. Choose the **Remove Material** button.

3. In the depth flyout, choose the **Extrude on both sides of sketch plane by half the specified depth value in each direction** button.

4. Choose the **Placement** tab; a slide-down panel is displayed. Choose the **Define** button; the **Sketch** dialog box is displayed.

5. Choose the **Plane** button from the **Datum** toolbar; the **DATUM PLANE** dialog box is displayed.

6. Select the **RIGHT** datum plane. In the **Translation** edit box that appears in the dialog box, enter **43**. This value is half of the width of the base feature.

7. Choose **OK** to exit the **DATUM PLANE** dialog box.

8. Select the **FRONT** datum plane and then select the **Left** option from the **Orientation** drop-down list.

9. Choose the **Sketch** button; you will enter into the sketcher environment.

10. Draw the sketch for the cut feature and apply required dimensions and constraints, as shown in Figure 6-99.

    In Figure 6-99, some dimensions appear light in color. These dimensions are weak dimensions and it is not important to convert them into strong dimensions. These dimensions are not important for the creation of this feature. However, the geometry for the cut should be similar to that shown in Figure 6-99.

11. After the sketch is completed, exit the sketcher environment; the **Extrude** dashboard is enabled and appears above the drawing area.

12. Enter a depth value of **55** in the dimension box in the **Extrude** dashboard. The system will accept this depth symmetrical to the sketching plane.

13. Choose the **Build feature** button to exit the feature creation tool. The cut feature is completed now and the default trimetric view of the cut feature along with the base feature is shown in Figure 6-100.

Figure 6-99 Sketch of the cut feature with dimensions and constraints

Figure 6-100 The default trimetric view of the model

Creating the Hole Feature

The hole is created using the **Hole** dashboard.

1. Choose the **Hole** button from the **Engineering Features** toolbar; the **Hole** dashboard is displayed.

2. In the **Hole** dashboard, choose the **Use a sketch to define drill hole profile** button.

3. Choose the **Activates Sketcher to create section** button to enter into the sketcher environment.

4. In the sketcher environment, draw the sketch of the counterbore hole, as shown in Figure 6-101. Make sure that the center line is a geometry centerline. After drawing the sketch, exit the sketcher environment.

5. Select the front face of the base feature to place the hole; the preview of the hole appears on the selected face.

6. Choose the **Placement** tab from the **Hole** dashboard; a slide-down panel is displayed.

7. Click in the **Offset References** collector so that the collector turns green.

8. Select the two references, as shown in Figure 6-102 for dimensioning. Note that the second reference should be selected by using the CTRL key + left mouse button.

Options Aiding Construction of Parts-I 6-57

Figure 6-101 Cross-section of the hole with dimensions and constraints

Figure 6-102 Edges to be selected for placing the hole

9. Modify the dimensions of the references by entering suitable values in the **Placement** slide-down panel. The center of hole is at the distance of **42** from the top edge and **43** from the right edge. After viewing the preview of the hole, you may have to specify a negative value of any one of the distances.

10. Choose the **Build feature** button to completely create the hole and Figure 6-103 shows the hole created.

Creating the Round Features

The round feature is created using the **Simple** option.

1. Choose the **Round** button from the **Engineering Features** toolbar; the **Round** dashboard is displayed.

2. Using the CTRL key, select the edges that are shown in Figure 6-104. The selected edges turn red in color.

Figure 6-103 The default trimetric view

Figure 6-104 Edges selected to create the round feature

3. Enter **3** in the dimension box in the **Round** dashboard or double-click on the default value displayed on the preview of the round and enter the radius value in the edit box displayed. The round is created and its preview appears in the drawing area.

4. Choose the **Build feature** button to exit the round feature creation tool. The trimetric view of the final model with the round feature created is shown in Figure 6-105.

Saving the Model
1. Choose the **Save** button from the **File** toolbar and save the model.

The order of feature creation can be seen from the **Model Tree** shown in Figure 6-106.

Figure 6-105 Final model for Tutorial 3   *Figure 6-106* The **Model Tree** for Tutorial 3

Tutorial 4

Create the model shown in Figure 6-107. The dimensions, top view, front section view, and right section view of the model are shown in Figure 6-108.   **(Expected time: 45 min)**

The following steps are required to complete this model:

Examine the model and determine the number of features in it, refer to Figure 6-107.
a. Create the base feature, refer to Figures 6-109 and 6-110.
b. Create the cut feature, refer to Figures 6-111 through 6-113.
c. Create the cylindrical feature on an offset datum plane, refer to Figure 6-114 through 6-116.
d. Create a counterbore coaxial hole on the cylindrical feature, refer to Figures 6-117 and 6-118.
e. Create straight holes on the top face of base feature, refer to Figures 6-119 and 6-120.

Figure 6-107 Isometric view of the model

Figure 6-108 Top and front section views of the model

Starting a New Object File
1. Start a new part file and name it as *c06tut4*.

   The three default datum planes are displayed in the drawing area if the **Plane display** button is turned on.

Selecting the Sketching Plane for the Base Feature
In this model, you need to draw the base feature on the **FRONT** datum plane because the direction of extrusion of the base feature is perpendicular to the **FRONT** datum plane.

1. Choose the **Extrude** button from the **Base Features** toolbar.

2. Choose the **Placement** tab; a slide-down panel is displayed. Choose the **Define** button; the **Sketch** dialog box is displayed.

3. Select the **FRONT** datum plane as the sketching plane. As you select the sketching plane, the **RIGHT** datum plane and its orientation **Right** are set automatically.

4. Choose the **Sketch** button to enter into the sketcher environment.

Creating and Dimensioning the Sketch for the Base Feature

From the model, the section to be extruded for the base feature is not evident. Therefore, you need to visualize the sketch for the base feature. The sketch is shown in Figure 6-109. When this sketch is extruded, it will create the base feature.

1. Draw the sketch using various sketcher tools, as shown in Figure 6-109.

2. The sketch is dimensioned automatically and some weak dimensions are assigned to it. Add the required constraints to it and modify the weak dimensions, as shown in Figure 6-109.

3. Choose the **Done** button; the **Extrude** dashboard is displayed.

4. Choose the **Named View List** button from the **View** toolbar; a flyout is displayed. Choose the **Default Orientation** option from the flyout; the model orients in its default orientation, which is the trimetric view.

   The default view is displayed which gives you a better view of the sketch in the 3D space. Also, a yellow arrow is also displayed on the model indicating the direction of extrusion.

5. Enter **150** in the dimension box that is present on the **Extrude** dashboard.

6. Choose the **Build feature** button from the **Extrude** dashboard.

   The base feature is completed, as shown in Figure 6-110. You can use the middle mouse button to spin the model to view it from various directions.

Creating the Second Feature

The next feature is an extruded cut feature. The sketching plane for this feature is the bottom face of the base feature. To get the required shape of the base of the model, you need to cut the base feature in such a way that you get the required shape. This sketch and its dimensions can be referred to from the top view of the model shown in Figure 6-108. Before drawing the sketch, change the model display to **No hidden**.

Options Aiding Construction of Parts-I 6-61

Figure 6-109 Sketch with dimensions and constraints

Figure 6-110 Default view of the base feature

1. Choose the **Extrude** button from the **Base Features** toolbar.

2. Choose the **Remove Material** button from the **Extrude** dashboard.

3. Choose the **Placement** tab; a slide-down panel is displayed. Choose the **Define** button from the slide-down panel; the **Sketch** dialog box is displayed.

4. Select the bottom face of the base feature as the sketching plane.

5. Select the **RIGHT** datum plane and from the **Orientation** drop-down list, select the **Right** option.

6. Choose the **Sketch** button to enter into the sketcher environment.

7. Draw the sketch of the cut feature, and apply constraints and dimensions to it, as shown in Figure 6-111.

8. Choose the **Done** button to exit the sketcher environment; the **Extrude** dashboard is displayed above the drawing area.

9. Choose the **Shading** button from the **Model Display** toolbar.

10. Choose the **Named View List** button from the **View** toolbar; a flyout is displayed. Choose the **Default Orientation** option from the flyout; the model orients in its default orientation, which is the trimetric view.

11. Choose the **Change material direction of extrude to other side of sketch** button from the **Extrude** dashboard. The yellow arrow points in the direction shown in Figure 6-112.

Figure 6-111 Sketch with dimensions and constraints for the cut feature

Figure 6-112 Two arrows and the preview of the cut feature

12. Choose the **Options** tab in the **Extrude** dashboard to display the slide-down panel. From the **Side 1** drop-down list, choose the **Through All** option; the model can be previewed in the drawing area.

13. Choose the **Build feature** button from the **Extrude** dashboard to complete the feature creation. The model after creating the cut feature is shown in Figure 6-113.

Creating the Sketching Plane for the Third Feature

You need to create a datum plane to create the third feature. The datum plane will be at a distance of 150 from the bottom face of the model.

1. Choose the **Plane** button from the **Datum** toolbar; the **DATUM PLANE** dialog box is displayed.

2. Spin the model using the middle mouse button and then using the left mouse button, select the bottom face of the model.

   When you select the bottom face of the model, the **Offset** constraint is displayed in the **References** collector of the dialog box. Note that the yellow arrow points in the opposite direction. Therefore, you need to enter a negative value of the offset distance.

3. In the **Translation** dimension box, enter **-150** and press ENTER.

4. Choose the **OK** button from the **DATUM PLANE** dialog box.

   Datum plane **DTM1** is created, as shown in Figure 6-114, and will be selected as the sketching plane for creating the sketch.

Figure 6-113 Model after creating the cut feature   *Figure 6-114 DTM1 created at an offset distance*

Creating the Third Feature

The plane **DTM1** will be selected as the sketching plane and the depth of extrusion will be given from this plane. The third feature is cylindrical in shape and its outer edge is tangent to the edge of the base feature.

1. Choose the **Extrude** button from the **Base Features** toolbar.

2. Choose the **Placement** tab; a slide-down panel is displayed. Choose the **Define** button from the slide-down panel; the **Sketch** dialog box is displayed.

3. Select **DTM1** as the sketching plane; the yellow arrow appears on the datum plane.

4. Select the **FRONT** datum plane, and then from the **Orientation** drop-down list, choose the **Top** option.

5. Choose the **Sketch** button to enter into the sketcher environment.

6. Draw a concentric circle for the cylindrical feature, as shown in Figure 6-115.

7. Choose the **Done** button to exit the sketcher environment.

8. Choose the **Named View List** button from the **View** toolbar; a flyout is displayed. Choose the **Default Orientation** option from the flyout; the model orients in its default orientation, which is the trimetric view.

9. Choose the **Options** tab in the **Extrude** dashboard to display the slide-down panel. From the **Side 1** drop-down list, select the **To Next** option. The model can be previewed in the drawing area.

10. Choose the **Build feature** button from the **Extrude** dashboard to complete the feature creation. The model after creating the feature is shown in Figure 6-116.

Figure 6-115 Sketch for the cylindrical feature

Figure 6-116 Model after creating the cylindrical feature

Creating the Counterbore Hole

The fourth feature is a counterbore hole that can be easily created using the **Hole** feature creation tool.

1. Choose the **Hole** button from the **Engineering Features** toolbar; the **Hole** dashboard is displayed.

2. Choose **Create simple hole** and then **Use standard hole profile as drill hole profile** buttons; some buttons are added to the dashboard.

3. Choose the **Adds counterbore** button from the dashboard.

4. Next, choose the **Shape** tab and enter the values, as shown in Figure 6-117.

5. Select the **To Selected** option from the drop-down list and then select the bottom face of the base feature.

6. Choose the **Placement** tab from the **Hole** dashboard; a slide-down panel is displayed.

7. Select the top face of the third feature and then select the axis of the cylindrical feature by pressing the CTRL key; the preview of the hole can be viewed in the model.

Figure 6-117 Sketch with dimensions

The **Coaxial** option is selected automatically in the **Type** drop-down list of the slide-down panel.

Options Aiding Construction of Parts-I

8. Choose the **Build feature** button to exit the **Hole** dashboard; the model with the counterbore hole is shown in Figure 6-118.

Creating the Datum Axis for the Hole Features

The last feature is a pair of two holes that is on the top face of the base feature. The two holes will be placed coaxially with the two axes that you need to create.

1. Choose the **Axis** button from the **Datum** toolbar; the **DATUM AXIS** dialog box is displayed.

Figure 6-118 Model with counterbore hole

2. Select the curved surface shown in Figure 6-119 to create the datum axis.

3. Choose **OK** from the dialog box to accept the settings and exit.

4. Similarly, create a datum axis on the left of the model. Figure 6-120 shows the model after creating the two datum axes.

Figure 6-119 Surface to be selected for creating the datum axis

Figure 6-120 The two datum axes

Creating Holes

To create the two coaxial holes, you need to invoke the **Hole** dashboard twice. This is because only one hole can be created at a time by using the **Hole** dashboard.

1. Choose the **Hole** button from the **Engineering Features** toolbar; the **Hole** dashboard is displayed.

2. Select the top face of the base feature; the preview of the hole appears on the selected face.

3. Choose the **Placement** tab from the **Hole** dashboard; the slide-down panel is displayed.

4. Select the axis of the feature by pressing the CTRL key.

   The **Coaxial** option is selected automatically in the **Type** drop-down list of the slide-down panel.

5. Enter **20** as the diameter of hole in the dimension box of the **Hole** dashboard.

6. Choose the **Build feature** button to exit the **Hole** dashboard.

7. Again, invoke the **Hole** dashboard and create the second hole similar to the first hole.

   The two holes on the base feature are shown in Figure 6-121.

Saving the Model

1. Choose the **Save** button from the **File** toolbar and save the model. The order of feature creation can be seen from the **Model Tree** shown in Figure 6-122.

Figure 6-121 Model after creating the two holes

Figure 6-122 The **Model Tree** for Tutorial 4

Self-Evaluation Test

Answer the following questions and then compare them to those given at the end of this chapter:

1. A hole created using the **Hole** dashboard is parametric in nature. (T/F)

2. A hole cannot be created on both sides of the sketching plane or the placement plane. (T/F)

3. In Pro/ENGINEER, holes can also be sketched. (T/F)

Options Aiding Construction of Parts-I   6-67

4. The **Full Round** button in the **Sets** slide-down panel allows you to enter the radius of the round. (T/F)

5. The **Model Tree** is used extensively in Pro/ENGINEER for editing a model. (T/F)

6. The profile rib feature is always created from the _____ view.

7. A _____ hole is a stepped hole and has two diameters, a larger one and a smaller one.

8. Straight holes are the holes that have a circular cross-section with a _____ diameter throughout the depth.

9. _____ are defined as thin wall-like structures that are used to bind the joints together so that they do not fail under increased load.

10. By default, the suppressed features are not displayed in the _____.

Review Questions

Answer the following questions:

1. If a feature being suppressed has some child features, then the child features will also be suppressed. (T/F)

2. While in the sketcher mode, the constraints to a sketch should be applied before the dimensions. (T/F)

3. The chamfers created in Pro/ENGINEER are parametric in nature. (T/F)

4. The **Model Tree** can be used to redefine a feature. (T/F)

5. When you redefine a rib feature, the _____ dashboard is displayed.

6. The sketch of a rib feature can be extruded to _____ side(s) of the sketching plane.

   (a) one   (b) both
   (c) either   (d) All of the above

7. _____ is a stepped hole with two diameters.

   (a) Counterbore   (b) Countersink
   (c) Straight   (d) None

8. Which of the following options of the **REROUTE** menu is used to change the sequence in which the features are created?

   (a) **Feature** (b) **Modify**
   (c) **Regenerate** (d) **Reorder**

9. At the intersection of how many edges does a **Corner** chamfer create a beveled surface?

   (a) One (b) Two
   (c) Three (d) None

10. Rounds and chamfers are used in engineering components to reduce the _____ on the corners.

    (a) Stress concentration (b) Tension
    (c) Conduction (d) None

Exercises

Exercise 1

Create the model shown in Figure 6-123. The dimensions and front and top views of the model are shown in Figure 6-124. **(Expected time: 45 min)**

Figure 6-123 Isometric view of the model

Figure 6-124 Top and front views of the model with hidden lines suppressed

Options Aiding Construction of Parts-I

Exercise 2

Create the model shown in Figure 6-125. The dimensions and front and right-side views of the model are shown in Figure 6-126. **(Expected time: 30 min)**

Figure 6-125 Isometric view of the model for Exercise 2

Figure 6-126 Front and right-side views of the model

Exercise 3

Create the model shown in Figure 6-127. The dimensions and front and right-side views of the model are shown in Figure 6-128. **(Expected time: 30 min)**

Figure 6-127 Isometric view of the model for Exercise 3

Figure 6-128 Front and right-side views of the model

Answers to Self-Evaluation Test
1. T, **2.** F, **3.** T, **4.** F, **5.** T, **6.** side, **7.** counterbore, **8.** constant, **9.** Ribs, **10. Model Tree**

Chapter 7

Options Aiding Construction of Parts-II

Learning Objectives

After completing this chapter, you will be able to:
- *Create a Dimension pattern.*
- *Create a Direction pattern.*
- *Create an Axis pattern.*
- *Create a Fill pattern.*
- *Create a Reference pattern.*
- *Create a Table-driven pattern.*
- *Create a Curve-driven pattern.*
- *Create a point pattern.*
- *Control the size of pattern instances using constraints.*
- *Use the Copy option.*
- *Use the Move option.*
- *Use the Mirror option.*
- *Create a section of a model.*

In this chapter, you will learn about various methods for duplicating existing features. In Pro/ENGINEER Wildfire 5.0, you can duplicate a feature by using the following methods:

- **Pattern**
- **Copy**
- **Mirror**

You will also learn to create sections in solid models. A solid model is sectioned for viewing the profile of its cross section and also for creating section drawing views.

CREATING FEATURE PATTERNS

Patterns are one- or two-dimensional incremental array of features created from a single feature called the parent feature or the leader. When a pattern is created, the leader also becomes a part of the pattern. When you pattern a feature, you need to specify the total number of features to be created, including the one that is being patterned and the increment in the dimensions, if required.

Uses of Patterns

Patterns are very helpful in solid modeling as they speed up the model creation process. The uses of patterns in solid modeling are discussed next.

1. Patterns are used to create multiple copies of a feature, and therefore, save time that would otherwise be spent in creating the features individually.

2. All instances in a pattern, including the parent feature, act as a single feature. Therefore, they can be easily suppressed or mirrored.

3. All instances in a pattern are related parametrically. Therefore, you can modify the number of instances in a pattern, the spacing between the instances, and other pattern related parameters.

4. If the dimensions of the parent feature are modified, then the dimensions of the child features are also modified.

Creating Patterns

In Pro/ENGINEER, patterns are created by choosing the **Pattern** button from the **Edit Features** toolbar in the **Right Toolchest**. This button is an object-action tool. This means the **Pattern** button is enabled in the **Edit Features** toolbar only when you have selected the feature to be patterned.

To invoke the pattern tool from the menu bar, choose **Edit > Pattern**; the **Pattern** dashboard will be displayed, as shown in Figure 7-1. The options and tools in the dashboard depend on the type of pattern you create. In Pro/ENGINEER, you can create eight types of pattern. These patterns are **Dimension**, **Direction**, **Axis**, **Fill**, **Table**, **Reference**, **Curve**, and **Point**. The options and tools in the **Pattern** dashboard are discussed next.

Options Aiding Construction of Parts-II

*Figure 7-1 The **Pattern** dashboard*

Drop-down list

In the drop-down list of the **Pattern** dashboard, the **Dimension** option is selected by default. The other options in this drop-down list are **Direction**, **Axis**, **Fill**, **Table**, **Reference**, **Curve**, and **Point.** When you select these options from this drop-down list, the options and tools in the **Pattern** dashboard change accordingly. The types of pattern that can be created in Pro/ENGINEER are discussed next.

Dimension Patterns

In dimension patterns, the existing dimensions of the parent feature are used to create a pattern. This pattern can be created in one direction or in two directions. When you select the option to create the pattern in the second direction, all instances that were created in the first direction can also be created in the second direction. You need to specify the increment value for the instances, which can be positive or negative. Once you have specified the increment value in a direction, the system creates the specified number of instances (including the parent feature) in that direction. Figure 7-2 shows a hole to be patterned and the patterned hole is shown in Figure 7-3.

Figure 7-2 Part with a hole   *Figure 7-3 Hole patterned in two directions*

To create a dimension pattern, use the following steps:

1. Select the feature to be patterned and then choose the **Pattern** button.
2. Click the dimension in the first direction; an edit box will be displayed. Enter the increment in the dimension where you need to place the second instance of the pattern.
3. Enter the number of instances in the **1** edit box of the dashboard. The instances in the first direction are specified and now you need to specify the number of instances and the increment in dimension in the second direction. Note that the dimension in the second direction should be selected only if you need to create instances in the second direction.

4. Click on **Click here to add item** in the **2** collector.; it displays **Select items**. Now, click the dimension in the second direction; an edit box appears. Enter the dimension increment in the edit box.
5. In the **2** edit box, enter the number of instances needed in the second direction. You can view the black dots where the instances of the pattern will be placed.
6. Choose the **Build feature** button to exit the dashboard and to view the pattern.

Direction Patterns

The **Direction** option is used to create the pattern in the specified direction. The direction is specified by selecting an edge, plane, or linear curve. This pattern is different from the **Dimension** pattern in that this pattern does not use the dimensions of the feature to be patterned. When you select this option from the drop-down list, you will be prompted to select the reference for the first direction. An arbitrary dimension that is not the dimension of the parent feature will be displayed in the specified direction. After specifying the first direction, you can specify the second direction to place the instances.

Note that the direction of pattern can be reversed by choosing the **Flip** button in the **Pattern** dashboard. Figure 7-4 shows the linear curve selected to create the direction pattern. The direction is indicated by the arrow. The preview of the pattern instances are shown as black dots and the pattern created is shown in Figure 7-5.

Figure 7-4 Linear curve selected to create the direction pattern

Figure 7-5 Direction pattern created

Note
*The reference that you select for specifying the direction of a **Direction** pattern should belong to a feature created before the feature to be patterned. Otherwise, the desired reference will not be highlighted for selection.*

Axis Patterns

The **Axis** option is used to create rotational patterns. When you choose this option, the **Pattern** dashboard will be displayed, as shown in Figure 7-6. To create this type of pattern, an axis is required. The axis can be a datum axis or the axis of a feature, for example, an axis formed by a revolve feature, like a hole. The parameters that you need to specify to create an axis pattern are shown in Figure 7-7.

Options Aiding Construction of Parts-II

*Figure 7-6 The **Pattern** dashboard with the **Axis** option selected*

Figure 7-7 Parameters to be specified for the axis pattern

Note
Remember that for creating the axis pattern of a feature, the reference axis must be created before the feature that is to be patterned.

To create an axis pattern, use the following steps:

1. Select the feature to be patterned and then select the **Axis** option from the drop-down list in the **Pattern** dashboard; you will be prompted to select an axis about which the pattern will be created.
2. Turn on the display of the axis and then select it.
3. Enter the required angle between each instance and then the number of pattern instances in the edit box.

   The instances in the first direction are specified and now you can specify the number of instances and the increment in dimension in the second direction. Note that the dimension and number of instances in the second direction should be specified only if you need to create instances in the second direction. To create the rotational pattern, as shown in Figure 7-8, you need to create instances in the first direction. The instances in the second direction, along with the instances in the first direction, are shown in Figure 7-9.

Figure 7-8 Rotational pattern created using the axis

Figure 7-9 Pattern created both in circular and linear directions

4. Enter the number of pattern instances in the **2** edit box for the second direction and then enter the radial distance between the pattern instances in the edit box. The pattern is created and now you can view the black dots where the instances will be placed.
5. Choose the **Build feature** button to exit the dashboard and view the pattern.

Fill Patterns

Fill patterns are used to fill the sketched area by a selected feature. This is the easiest and fastest method to create a pattern in the sketched area. When you select the **Fill** option from the drop-down list, the **Pattern** dashboard will appear, as shown in Figure 7-10. The options and tools in this dashboard are discussed next.

Figure 7-10 The **Pattern** dashboard

References tab. When you choose this tab, the slide-down panel will be displayed in which the **Define** button is available. Choose the **Define** button to invoke the **Sketch** dialog box. This dialog box is used to sketch the area that will be filled by the pattern instances. Select the sketching plane and its orientation and then enter the sketcher environment to draw the sketch.

Drop-down list for grid template. This drop-down list is the first drop-down list and is available only when the area to be filled is defined. The options in this drop-down list are used to specify the shape of the fill pattern. The options are Square pattern, Diamond pattern, Hexagon pattern, Concentric circle pattern, Spiral pattern, and along the sketched curves. Generally, it is recommended that the sketch should be similar to the shape of the fill pattern you need. Figures 7-11 through 7-16 show the patterns of various shapes.

Options Aiding Construction of Parts-II 7-7

Figure 7-11 The Square pattern fill in the sketched square

Figure 7-12 The Diamond pattern fill in the sketched square

Figure 7-13 The Hexagon pattern fill in the sketched triangle

Figure 7-14 The Concentric circle pattern fill in the sketched circle

Figure 7-15 The Spiral pattern fill in the sketched circle

Figure 7-16 Along the sketched curves pattern fill in the sketched curve

Dimension boxes. The dimension boxes in the dashboard are used to specify the different parameters of the fill pattern. You can specify the gap between the two members of the pattern, the distance of all members (instances) from the sketched boundary, rotation angle of the pattern, and radial distance between instances, in case of circular and spiral shapes.

*Tip: While creating a **Fill** pattern, you can select the member that you want to remove. This can be done before exiting the **Pattern** dashboard. To remove the member of a pattern, select it in the preview of the **Fill** pattern. The selected member turns white, suggesting that it is removed. To resume the removed member of the pattern, select it once again.*

Reference Patterns

In the reference patterns, an existing pattern is referenced to create a new pattern. In this pattern, the parent feature of the new pattern should be referenced to the parent feature of the existing pattern.

Figure 7-17 shows a rib feature referenced to the parent hole feature. In this figure, the parent rib feature is created on a plane that was created on-the-fly while creating the rib feature. This plane passes through the axis of the parent hole feature. Therefore, a relationship is built between the parent rib feature and the parent hole feature.

To create the reference pattern of the rib feature, select it from the **Model Tree** and choose the **Pattern** button from the **Edit Features** toolbar to invoke the **Pattern** dashboard. The **Reference** option is selected by default in the **Pattern** dashboard. Choose the **Build feature** button; the pattern of the rib feature is created without specifying the increment in dimensions. Figure 7-18 shows the rib feature patterned using the reference of the hole pattern.

Figure 7-17 Rib feature referenced to the parent hole feature

*Figure 7-18 Rib feature patterned using the **Reference** pattern*

Options Aiding Construction of Parts-II

Note
*If the rib feature is not created on an embedded datum plane, the relationship between the hole feature and the rib feature will not exist. Therefore, the rib feature cannot be patterned using the **Reference** option. Ensure that the feature which will be patterned using the **Reference** option, has a relationship with the parent feature, which in this case will be the patterned hole feature.*

Tip: *If you do not want to create an embedded datum plane but still want to create a reference pattern, as shown in Figure 7-18, you need to create a datum plane with a rib feature on it. Group the datum plane and the rib feature. After grouping the two, select the group from the **Model Tree** and choose the **Pattern** button. Now, the reference pattern can be created.*

Table Patterns

Table-driven patterns are created by defining a table. In this table, you need to specify the dimensions of the instances from the edge or faces from where the leader of the pattern is referenced (leader of a pattern is the feature that is selected to create a pattern). When you select the **Table** option from the drop-down list, the **Pattern** dashboard will appear, as shown in Figure 7-19.

*Figure 7-19 The **Pattern** dashboard*

In Figure 7-19, the **Active table** collector shows the active table. You can create more than one table to create a pattern. You can choose the **Edit** button to display the **Pro/TABLE** window shown in Figure 7-20. This button will be available only after you have selected at least one dimension.

To create the table-driven pattern shown in Figure 7-21, follow the steps given below:

1. Create a solid protrusion of dimension 120 X 100 X 15.
2. Create a hole of diameter **5** on the top face of the base feature at a distance of 20 from the left edge and 20 from the bottom edge.
3. Select the hole feature and choose the **Pattern** button from the **Edit Features** toolbar; the **Pattern** dashboard will be displayed and the dimensions of the hole feature will appear on the hole.
4. Select the **Table** option from the drop-down list in the dashboard.
5. Select the dimension **20** that is from the left edge and then use CTRL+left mouse button to select the dimension **20** that is from the bottom edge.
6. Choose the **Edit** button from the **Pattern** dashboard to display the **Pro/TABLE**.
7. In column **C1**, click under **idx** (index number). Enter **1** when the cell is highlighted. The value 1 signifies the first instance.
8. In column **C2**, toward the right of **1**, enter the distance along the first dimension and in column **C3**, enter the distance along the second dimension.
9. Similarly, under the rows below **idx**, enter the dimensions of other instances of the holes, as shown in Figure 7-22. Remember that the distance of each hole is measured from where the leader is dimensioned.

10. Choose **File > Save,** and then choose the **Exit** option to exit the **Pro/TABLE**.
11. Choose the **Build feature** button to exit the feature creation tool.

Figure 7-20 The **Pro/TABLE** window

Figure 7-21 Table-driven pattern

Figure 7-22 Coordinate values of instances

> **Tip**: *Pattern tables can be created from scratch by picking dimensions and filling in all values. In most cases, it is easier and less time-consuming to create a dimensional pattern similar to what you need and then convert it into a table.*

Options Aiding Construction of Parts-II

Generally, table-driven patterns are used when the incremental distances between the instances of the pattern are nonuniform. This pattern is also useful when the coordinate locations of the instances are known.

Curve Driven Pattern

The **Curve** option is used to create patterns along user-defined curves. When you select the **Curve** option from the drop-down list, the **Pattern** dashboard will appear, as shown in Figure 7-23.

*Figure 7-23 The **Pattern** dashboard with the **Curve** option selected*

The **Curve** option can be used where patterns need to be created along user-defined directions and shapes. You have to sketch the curve along which the pattern has to be created. This curve also specifies the direction for the pattern. All instances created using the **Curve** option are identical in size and geometry. The pattern instances also follow the shape of the sketched curve. After choosing the **Curve** option from the drop-down list, you have to sketch a curve for patterning. Then enter the spacing between the patterned instances in the edit box in the pattern dashboard. The preview of the patterned feature can be seen in the drawing area. Figure 7-24 shows the feature to be patterned, along with other parameters for the **Curve** pattern and Figure 7-25 shows the patterned feature.

Figure 7-24 Model with the feature to be patterned and the sketched curve

Figure 7-25 The curve driven pattern

Note
The start point of the curve pattern acts as the start point of the curve. The blue arrow on the curve displays the start point of the curve and direction of the pattern.

Point Pattern

The **Point** option is used to create patterns at sketched points, datum points or coordinate systems. To do so, select the feature to be patterned and invoke the **Pattern** tool, as discussed earlier. Select **Point** from the first drop-down list; the dashboard, as shown in Figure 7-26, will be displayed.

*Figure 7-26 The **Pattern** dashboard with the **Point** option selected*

The two buttons in the dashboard enable you to select the geometry points, geometry coordinate systems, or datum points at which the pattern members will be placed. Select the required entities from the model area and then choose the **Build Feature** button; a pattern will be created at each point or coordinate system, refer to Figures 7-27 and 7-28. Note that the points and the coordinate systems must be drawn first and then you need to invoke the **Pattern** tool. You can also use the geometric points or coordinate systems used in an internal sketch or in an imported feature.

Figure 7-27 Hole on the base feature   *Figure 7-28 Hole patterned on the base feature*

Options Tab
When you choose the **Options** tab, a slide-down panel will be displayed, as shown in Figure 7-29. The options in this slide-down panel are discussed next.

Identical Pattern
The **Identical** option is used to create an identical pattern. You need to select at least one incremental dimension to pattern the feature. Depending on the incremental dimension selected, the resulting pattern will be linear or rotational. A linear pattern

*Figure 7-29 The **Options** slide-down panel*

is created when the driving dimension is linear and a rotational pattern is created when the driving dimension is angular. You can enter a positive or a negative value as the increment in a pattern dimension. All instances of a pattern that are created using this option are identical in size and geometry. This is the reason the patterns created using this option are known as **Identical** patterns. Figure 7-30 shows a hole feature on the base feature and Figure 7-31 shows the holes patterned linearly.

Similarly, Figure 7-32 shows a hole feature on the base feature and Figure 7-33 shows the rotational pattern of the hole feature.

Options Aiding Construction of Parts-II

Figure 7-30 Hole on the base feature

Figure 7-31 Hole patterned on the base feature

Figure 7-32 Hole on the base feature

Figure 7-33 Rotational pattern of hole feature

As evident from Figures 7-31 and 7-33, all instances in the identical patterns are placed on the same placement surface and no feature intersects the edges of the placement surface, any other instance, or any other feature other than the placement surface. Note that you cannot pattern the hole feature on the right flap shown in Figure 7-31 by using the **Identical** option. However, you can use the **General** option.

Variable Pattern

The **Variable** pattern is used when instances vary in size. In this type of pattern, the instances can be placed on different surfaces and can also intersect with the edges of the placement surface. The feature, shown in Figure 7-34, is patterned by using the **Variable** option and the patterned feature created by using this option is shown in Figure 7-35. In Figure 7-35, the length and the diameter of the rod vary in all instances. To create the instances that vary in position and size, you need to select the **Variable** option from the **Options** tab and then select the dimension you want to be variable. Next, choose the **Dimensions** tab and specify the increment value of variation in the slide-down panel. You can add more variable dimensions by pressing and holding the CTRL key. Next, specify the number of instances you want in the pattern. Variable pattern can be created only for the **Dimension**, **Direction**, and **Axis** patterns.

Figure 7-34 A rod on the base feature   *Figure 7-35 Varying pattern of the rod*

General Pattern

You can create the most complex patterns by using the **General** pattern. This option is used to create patterns in which the instances touch each other and intersect with other instances or the edges of a surface. This option of creating patterns is also used when instances intersect with the base feature and the intersection is not visible. Figure 7-36 shows a hole on the base feature and Figure 7-37 shows the hole pattern created using the **General** option. The pattern is shown in Figure 7-37.

Figure 7-36 Hole on the base feature   *Figure 7-37 General pattern*

Note
*If the features that you need to pattern has formed a group and are listed in the **Model Tree** as a group feature, you need to select the desired feature from the group to pattern it.*

*A feature forms a group when it has used other features to form itself. For example, if you create a datum plane on-the-fly and use it as a sketch plane, then after the feature is created, it is listed in the **Model Tree** as a group feature. This group comprises of feature, datum plane, and sketch of feature.*

Options Aiding Construction of Parts-II

Deleting a Pattern

You can delete a pattern created. To do so, select the pattern feature from the **Model Tree** and right-click to invoke the shortcut menu. Choose the **Delete Pattern** option from the shortcut menu. However, note that the parent feature (leader) is not deleted when you delete the pattern by using the **Delete Pattern** option even if it was selected along with other instances for deletion.

If you want to delete the pattern along with the parent feature, choose the **Delete** option from the shortcut menu. The system highlights the pattern in the drawing area and confirms the deletion of the pattern from the user.

COPYING FEATURES

The **Copy** option is used for copying and mirroring the selected features. This option reduces the time required in the model creation and also helps in maintaining its design intent. The **Copy** option is available in the **FEAT** menu. To invoke the **FEAT** menu, choose **Edit > Feature Operations** from the menu bar.

When you choose the **Copy** option from the **FEAT** menu, the **COPY FEATURE** submenu will appear, as shown in Figure 7-38. The options in this submenu are discussed next.

New Refs

The **New Refs** option is used to copy a feature by varying the dimension values and by selecting new references. References can be edges, axes, or placement planes. Choose the **Done** option from the **COPY FEATURE** submenu after the other desired options have been chosen in it; you will be prompted to select the feature to be copied. Select the feature from the drawing area or the **Model Tree** and then choose the **Done** option; the **GP VAR DIMS** menu will be displayed, as shown in Figure 7-39. Using this menu, you can select the dimensions that are to be varied while copying a feature with new references. After making the selection, choose the **Done** option from the **GP VAR DIMS** menu to enter the modified dimensions values in the message input box; the **WHICH REF** menu will be displayed, as shown in Figure 7-40. Finally, choose **Done** to create the copy.

Figure 7-38 The ***COPY FEATURE*** submenu

Figure 7-39 The ***GP VAR DIMS*** menu

Figure 7-40 The ***WHICH REF*** menu

You can copy a feature using the **New Refs** option by two methods. You can keep the same dimensional or placement reference for the copied feature as that of the original feature by using the **Same** option in the **WHICH REF** menu. This means that you can use the same edge or surface as the references for the copied part. The other possibility is that you can use new references for the copied feature. This can be achieved by using the **Alternate** option in the **WHICH REF** menu. This provides you with a greater flexibility to copy the features.

Same Refs

When you use the **Same Refs** option, you have the flexibility to vary the dimensions of the copied features, but the dimensional and placement references of the copied feature are the same as for the source feature. You only need to select the dimensions that will be varied while copying the feature.

Mirror

The **Mirror** option is used to copy a feature by mirroring it about a specified datum plane or a face. When you invoke this option, you will be prompted to select the features to be mirrored. Once you select the features to be mirrored, you will be prompted to select a plane or create a datum about which the features will be mirrored. As soon as you select a datum plane or a planar surface, the selected feature will be mirrored. This option not only reduces the model completion time, but it also helps in maintaining the symmetry in the features of a model. Figure 7-41 shows a rib feature to be mirrored and the datum plane about which the rib feature will be mirrored. Figure 7-42 shows the model after mirroring the rib feature and turning off the visibility of datum plane.

Figure 7-41 Rib feature and the mirror plane   *Figure 7-42* Model after mirroring the rib feature

Tip: *To mirror a feature at an angle of 90 degrees to the parent feature, create a datum plane at an angle of 45 degrees to the parent feature and then use this datum plane to mirror the feature.*

Move

The **Move** option is used to copy the features by translating or rotating them. To invoke the **Move** option, choose **Move > Select > Independent > Done** from the **COPY FEATURE** menu; the **Select** message box will be displayed and you will be prompted to select the features to be translated. Select the features to be translated, and then choose the **OK** button from the **Select** message box; the **MOVE FEATURE** submenu will be displayed, as shown in Figure 7-43. Also, you will be prompted to define the movements by the combining translation and rotation. You can translate or rotate the selected feature by using the options in this submenu.

Figure 7-43 The MOVE FEATURE submenu

Translating the Features

You can select a feature from the drawing area or from the **Model Tree** to copy it while translating. You need to specify a perpendicular plane to define the direction, in which the feature will be copied, and also the offset distance. You can also select multiple features to copy.

Rotating the Features

You can select a feature from the drawing area or from the **Model Tree** and then rotate it about an axis, edge, datum curve, or coordinate system. Using this option, you can select multiple features to copy.

Select

The **Select** option provides the flexibility of choosing the features to be copied. When you use this option, you need to select the features from the drawing area or from the **Model Tree**. You can select any number of features to copy.

All Feat

The **All Feat** option is available only when you copy a feature using the **Mirror** or the **Move** option. When you use this option, all features created are copied. Remember that you need to specify a coordinate system while using this option.

FromDifModel

The **FromDifModel** (From different model) option is used to copy a feature from a different model. This option is available only when you are using the **New Refs** option of the **COPY FEATURE** submenu. This is due to change in the references required to copy from one model to another. Therefore, all references will be new.

FromDifVers

You can copy features from a different version of the current model using the **FromDifVers** (From different versions) option. This option is available only when you are using the **New Refs** and the **Same Refs** options of the **COPY FEATURE** submenu.

FromInheritance

This option is available only when inherited features are present in a model.

Independent

The **Independent** option specifies that the dimensions of the copied features are independent of the dimensions of the parent feature. The features that you copy from a different model or different versions are independent by default. The dimensions of such copied features have no relation with those of the original feature. This is the reason the **Dependent** option is not available while using the **FromDifModel** or the **FromDifVers** options.

Dependent

The **Dependent** option specifies that the dimensions of the copied features are dependent on the dimensions of the parent feature. Therefore, if you make any modification in the section of the parent feature, the changes are automatically reflected in the copied feature.

MIRRORING A GEOMETRY

Pro/ENGINEER Wildfire allows you to mirror a feature across a planar surface. To do so, choose the **Mirror** button from the **Edit Features** toolbar. This button is only available after a feature has been selected. Choose this button; the **Mirror** dashboard will be displayed and you will be prompted to select a datum plane about which the model will be mirrored. Select the required datum plane or a planar surface as the mirroring plane. Next, choose the **Build Feature** button to create the mirrored feature.

This option is slightly different from the **Copy > Mirror** option. You can select the features to be copied by using the **Copy > Mirror** option, whereas, you can mirror the whole feature about a specified datum plane by using the **Mirror** button. The model can be selected by selecting its name available at the top of the **Model Tree**. All features in the mirrored model are related to the parent model. Any modification done in the parent model is reflected in the mirrored model. Figure 7-44 shows a model and a datum plane for mirroring the model and Figure 7-45 shows the resulting mirrored model.

Figure 7-44 Model and datum plane   *Figure 7-45 Resulting mirrored model*

CREATING A SECTION OF A SOLID MODEL

The complex geometry of a model sometimes needs sectioning so that you can see the inner sections of various features that are not visible from outside. These sections are also used for showing sections in the drawing views.

Options Aiding Construction of Parts-II

To create the section view, choose **View > View Manager** from the menu bar; the **View Manager** dialog box will be displayed, as shown in Figure 7-46. Choose the **New** button from the dialog box; the **Rep0001** will be displayed in the **Names** display box. This is the default name given to the section that you will create. If required, you can enter another name in the **Names** display box and press ENTER; the **Menu Manager** with the **EDIT METHOD** menu will be displayed, as shown in Figure 7-47.

Figure 7-46 The **View Manager** dialog box

Figure 7-47 The **Menu Manager** with the **EDIT METHOD** menu

In this menu, the methods of representing a model are listed. Here, you will learn about the **Work Region** method of representing the model.

Work Region Method

This method of representing a model is very similar to removing material (creating cut) from a model. The following steps explain the procedure to create the section of the model shown in Figure 7-48.

1. Choose the **Work Region** option from the **EDIT METHOD** menu; the **SOLID OPTS** submenu will be displayed, as shown in Figure 7-49.
2. Choose **Extrude > Solid > Done** from the **SOLID OPTS** submenu; the **Extrude** dashboard will be displayed.
3. Choose the **Placement** tab and from the slide-down panel, choose the **Define** button; the **Sketch** dialog box will be displayed.
4. Select the top face of the plate as the sketch plane and select the **RIGHT** datum plane to be at the right while drawing the sketch.
5. Choose the **Sketch** button to enter the sketcher environment. Now, you need to draw the section lines, as shown in Figure 7-50. This section is an open loop and the dimensions are not of importance to create this section.

Figure 7-48 Solid model   *Figure 7-49 The **SOLID OPTS** submenu*

6. Exit the sketcher environment and choose the **Extrude to intersect with all surface** button from the depth flyout; the yellow arrow will point in the reverse direction.
7. Choose the **Change material direction of extrude to other side of sketch** button to reverse the direction of arrow.
8. Choose the **Build feature** button from the **Extrude** dashboard. The sectioned model is shown in Figure 7-51.

To resume the view of the complete model, invoke the **View Manager** dialog box. Right-click on **Master Rep** in the **Names** display box to invoke the shortcut menu and select the **Set Active** option from it. Close the **View Manager** dialog box once the complete view of the model is resumed.

Figure 7-50 Sketch of section lines   *Figure 7-51 The sectioned model*

Note

*The created section is saved with the name that is entered in the **Names** display box while creating it. You can create multiple sections and save them with different names. To view a particular section, right-click on its name in the **Names** display box and select the **Set Active** option from the shortcut menu.*

Options Aiding Construction of Parts-II

TUTORIALS

Tutorial 1

In this tutorial, you will create the model shown in Figure 7-52. This figure also shows the top, front, and right views of the model. **(Expected time: 30 min)**

Figure 7-52 The model and its top, front, and right views

The following steps are required to complete this tutorial:

Examine the model to determine the number of features in it. The model consists of four features, refer to Figure 7-52.

a. Create the base feature on the **TOP** datum plane, refer to Figures 7-53 and 7-54.
b. Create the second feature on the right face of the base feature, refer to Figures 7-55 through 7-57.
c. Create the third feature by copying the second feature, refer to Figures 7-58 and 7-59.
d. Create the fourth feature by mirroring the third feature, refer to Figure 7-60.

After starting Pro/ENGINEER session, the first task is to set the working directory. Since it is the first tutorial of this chapter, you need to create a folder with the name *c07*, if it does not exist, and then set it as working directory.

Starting a New Object File

1. Start a new part file and then name it *c07tut1*.

   The three default datum planes are displayed in the drawing area. Also, the **Model Tree** is displayed in the drawing area.

Creating the Base Feature

To create a sketch for the base feature, you need to select the **TOP** datum plane as the sketching plane.

1. Choose the **Extrude** button from the **Base Features** toolbar; the **Extrude** dashboard is displayed above the drawing area.

2. Choose the **Placement** tab; the slide-down panel is displayed. From the slide-down panel, choose the **Define** button; the **Sketch** dialog box is displayed.

3. Select the **TOP** datum plane as the sketching plane; the **RIGHT** datum plane and its orientation **Right** are set automatically.

4. Choose the **Sketch** button to enter the sketcher environment.

5. Next, create the sketch of the base feature and apply constraints and dimensions to it, as shown in Figure 7-53.

   Note that in the sketch, the bottom half of the sketch is mirrored to create the top half of the sketch. This is evident from the constraints of symmetry applied to the sketch in Figure 7-53. Also, as evident from the sketch of the base feature shown in Figure 7-53, the **RIGHT** datum plane is located at a dimension of 18 from the left edge because later in the tutorial, this datum plane will be used as a reference to copy a feature.

6. After the sketch is completed, choose the **Done** button to exit the sketcher environment; the **Extrude** dashboard is enabled and displayed above the drawing area.

7. Enter **9** as the value of the depth in the dimension box in the **Extrude** dashboard.

8. Choose the **Build feature** button from the **Extrude** dashboard.

   Now, the base feature is completed. You need to create the second feature. The default trimetric view of the base feature is shown in Figure 7-54.

Options Aiding Construction of Parts-II   7-23

Figure 7-53 Sketch of the base feature

Figure 7-54 The default trimetric view of the base feature

Note
The two holes are integrated in the base feature. These holes are sketched while drawing the sketch for the base feature. Therefore, the base feature is created as a single feature that includes two holes. The other method is to create the two holes separately on the base feature by using the **Hole** *dashboard. When you create the features separately, the total number of features created will be three.*

Creating the Second Feature

The second feature is also an extruded feature. You will create the second feature on the right face of the base feature. Therefore, you need to select the right face as the sketching plane. Note that the sketch of this feature has to be created keeping in mind some important steps. The feature may not get copied later on if you do not perform the following steps to create the sketch of this feature.

1. Choose the **Extrude** button from the **Base Features** toolbar; the **Extrude** dashboard is displayed above the drawing area.

2. Choose the **Placement** tab to display the slide-down panel. Then, choose the **Define** button from the slide-down panel; the **Sketch** dialog box is displayed.

3. Select the right face of the base feature as the sketching plane.

4. Choose the **Flip** button to reverse the direction of the yellow arrow.

5. Select the **TOP** datum plane as reference and then select the **Top** option from the **Orientation** drop-down list.

6. Choose the **Sketch** button from the **Sketch** dialog box to enter the sketcher environment.

   After entering the sketcher environment, turn the model display to **No hidden** to view the wireframe model without the hidden lines.

7. Choose the **Line** button from the **Sketcher Tools** toolbar and draw the right vertical line starting from the point shown in Figure 7-55. Notice that the endpoint of the right vertical line is not aligned with the edge on the top face of the base feature.

8. Next, draw the horizontal line in continuation with the first line, as shown in Figure 7-55. Since the endpoint of the right vertical line is not aligned with the edge on the top face of the base feature, the horizontal line is also not aligned with that edge.

9. Next, draw the left vertical line in continuation with the horizontal line and then complete the sketch by drawing the arc and the circle, see Figure 7-55.

Figure 7-55 Sketch of the second feature with weak dimensions

10. Choose the **Vertical** button from the **Right Toolchest** to display a flyout. Choose the **Coincident** button and select the bottom horizontal line of the sketch. Now, select the edge on the top face of the base feature as the second entity to apply the constraint. You will notice that the sketch will extend and the horizontal line gets aligned with the top face.

11. If the center points of the arc and the circle are not aligned with the **FRONT** datum plane, align them.

12. Add dimensions to the sketch of the second feature and then modify them, as shown in Figure 7-56. After completing the sketch, turn the model display to **Shading** and choose the **Done** button from the **Sketcher Tools** toolbar; the **Extrude** dashboard is enabled.

13. Enter **9** as the value of the depth in the dimension box in the **Extrude** dashboard.

14. Choose **Build feature** from the **Extrude** dashboard; the default shaded trimetric view of the model after creating the second feature is shown in Figure 7-57.

Figure 7-56 *Adding dimensions to the second feature*

Figure 7-57 *Model after creating the second feature*

Creating the Third Feature

You can create the third feature using two methods. The first method is to draw the sketch of the third feature by defining a sketching plane and then extruding it to the given depth. The second method is to copy the second feature by defining new references. The second method can be used because the third feature is similar to the second feature of the model in geometry and dimensions. In this tutorial, you will use the second method to create the third feature.

1. Invoke the **FEAT** menu by choosing **Edit > Feature Operations** from the menu bar.

2. Choose the **Copy** option from the **FEAT** menu; the **COPY FEATURE** submenu is displayed.

3. Choose **New Refs > Select > Dependent > Done** from the **COPY FEATURE** submenu; the **Select** box is displayed and you are prompted to select the feature to be copied.

4. Select the second feature from the drawing area; the selected feature is highlighted with a red boundary.

5. Choose **OK** from the **Select** message box; the **GP VAR DIMS** submenu is displayed. Since you do not need to vary any dimension of the source feature, you can proceed further without selecting any dimension.

6. Choose **Done** from the **GP VAR DIMS** submenu; the **WHICH REF** submenu is displayed and you are prompted to select a sketching plane reference corresponding to the highlighted surface.

7. Select the face, shown in Figure 7-58, from the drawing area as the surface on which the copied feature will be placed. The **TOP** datum plane is highlighted and you are prompted to select a horizontal sketcher reference corresponding to the highlighted surface.

8. Choose the **Same** option from the **WHICH REF** submenu; the **FRONT** datum plane

is highlighted and you are prompted to select the section dimensioning reference corresponding to the highlighted surface.

9. Select the **RIGHT** datum plane. The edge of the top face of the base feature is highlighted and you are prompted to select the section dimensioning reference corresponding to the highlighted surface.

10. Select the top surface of the first feature; a magenta arrow is displayed and you are prompted to select the upward direction of the horizontal plane for protrusion.

11. Choose **Okay** from the **DIRECTION** submenu and then choose **Done** from the **GRP PLACE** submenu; the feature is copied to the required location on the model, as shown in Figure 7-59.

12. Choose **Done** from the **FEAT** menu to complete the feature creation.

Figure 7-58 Sketching plane reference for the third feature

Figure 7-59 The model after copying the feature with new references

Creating the Fourth Feature

The fourth feature can be created by sketching and extruding it to a given depth. You can also create this feature by placing a mirrored copy of the third feature at the required location. In this tutorial, you will use the second method because it consumes less time.

1. Invoke the **FEAT** menu by choosing **Edit > Feature Operations** from the menu bar. Next, choose the **Copy** option from **FEAT** menu; the **COPY FEATURE** submenu is displayed.

2. Choose **Mirror > Select > Dependent > Done** from the **COPY FEATURE** submenu; the **Select** message box is displayed and you are prompted to select the features to be mirrored.

3. Select the third feature from the drawing area and choose **OK** from the **Select** message box; you are prompted to select a plane or create a datum to mirror about.

Options Aiding Construction of Parts-II

4. Select the **FRONT** datum plane as the mirror plane. The third feature is mirrored about the **FRONT** datum plane. The trimetric view of the final model is shown in Figure 7-60.

5. Choose **Done** from the **FEAT** menu to complete the feature creation.

6. Choose the **Save** button from the **File** toolbar and save the model. The order of feature creation can be seen from the **Model Tree** shown in Figure 7-61. Note that the feature id numbers in your model may be different from the ones shown in this figure.

Figure 7-60 *Default trimetric view of the model*   *Figure 7-61* *The **Model Tree** for Tutorial 1*

Tutorial 2

In this tutorial, you will create the model shown in Figure 7-62. The dimensions of the model in the top view and the front view are shown in Figure 7-63.   **(Expected time: 45 min)**

The following steps are required to complete this tutorial:

Examine the model and determine the number of features in it. The model is composed of nine features, refer to Figure 7-62.
a. Create the base feature on the **FRONT** datum plane, refer to Figures 7-64 and 7-65.
b. Create round features, refer to Figures 7-66 and 7-67.
c. Create the hole feature and then pattern it, refer to Figures 7-68 and 7-69.
d. Create the rib feature on the **FRONT** datum plane, refer to Figures 7-70 and 7-71.
e. Mirror the rib feature, refer to Figure 7-72.
f. Create the extrude feature on the top planar face of the base feature, refer to Figures 7-73 and 7-74.
g. Create the cut feature on the bottom planar face of the base feature, refer to Figures 7-75 and 7-76.
h. Create the hole feature on the top face of the model and then copy it, refer to Figures 7-77 and 7-78.

If required, set the working directory to the *c07* folder.

Figure 7-62 Solid model for Tutorial 2

Figure 7-63 Top view and front views of the model

Starting a New Object File

1. Start a new part file and then name it *c07tut2*.

   The three default datum planes are displayed in the drawing area.

Creating the Base Feature

To create the sketch for the base feature, you first need to select the sketching plane for the base feature. In this model, you need to draw the base feature on the **FRONT** datum plane because the direction of extrusion of this feature is perpendicular to it. The base feature will be created symmetric to the **FRONT** datum plane.

1. Choose the **Extrude** button from the **Base Features** toolbar; the **Extrude** dashboard is displayed above the drawing area.

2. Choose the **Placement** tab; the slide-down panel is displayed. Choose the **Define** button from the panel; the **Sketch** dialog box is displayed.

3. Select the **FRONT** datum plane as the sketch plane.

4. Select the **TOP** datum plane, and then select the **Top** option from the **Orientation** drop-down list.

5. Choose the **Sketch** button to enter the sketcher environment.

6. Next, create the sketch of the base feature and apply constraints and dimensions to the sketch, as shown in Figure 7-64.

   In the sketch, note that the base feature is symmetrical; therefore, a vertical center line is drawn and then the right half of the sketch is mirrored to create the left half. This is evident from the constraints of symmetry applied to the sketch in Figure 7-63. These constraints appear as arrow symbols in the sketch.

   As evident from the sketch of the base feature shown in Figure 7-64, the **TOP** datum plane is aligned with the bottom line segment.

7. After the sketch is completed, choose the Done button to exit the sketcher environment; the **Extrude** dashboard is enabled and appears above the drawing area. Now, you need to extrude the sketch symmetrically to both the sides of the sketching plane in order to create the base feature symmetrical to the **FRONT** datum plane. This is because, later in the tutorial, you need to use the default datum planes as the mirror planes for mirroring the features. On extruding symmetrically, you need not create the datum planes.

8. Choose the **Extrude on both sides of sketch plane by half the specified depth value in each direction** button from the depth flyout in the **Extrude** dashboard.

9. Enter **60** as depth value in the dimension box in the **Extrude** dashboard.

10. Choose the **Build feature** button from the **Extrude** dashboard to exit the feature creation tool.

The base feature is completed and now you need to create the second feature. The default trimetric view of the base feature is shown in Figure 7-65.

Figure 7-64 Sketch with dimensions and constraints for the base feature

Figure 7-65 Default trimetric view of the base feature

Creating the Second Feature

The second feature is a round feature of radius 5.

1. Choose the **Round** button from the **Engineering Features** toolbar; the **Round** dashboard is displayed.

2. Choose the **Sets** tab to display the slide-down panel. Let this slide-down panel remain open so that you can view the selections made on the model.

3. Select one of the edges shown in Figure 7-66. To select the second edge and the subsequent edges, press the CTRL key and then select the edges one-by-one.

   The preview of the round is created on the selected edges; a default value of the radius is also displayed.

4. Double-click on the default radius value that is displayed on the preview of the round; an edit box appears. Enter **5** in it. The first set of rounds is created.

   Now, you need to create the second set of rounds.

5. After spinning the model, select the four vertical edges of the bottom portion of the base feature to round. Remember to use the CTRL key+left mouse button to select the second and subsequent edges.

   You will notice that **Set 1** and **Set 2** appears in the slide-down panel. This indicates that the second set is defined. The preview of the round is created on the edges. The default value of the radius is also displayed.

Options Aiding Construction of Parts-II   7-31

6. Double-click on the default radius value that is displayed along with the preview of the round; an edit box appears. Enter **10** in it.

7. Choose the **Build feature** button from the **Round** dashboard to create the round feature; the round feature is completed. The default trimetric view of the round feature is shown in Figure 7-67. In the **Model Tree,** the two rounds created appear as one feature.

Figure 7-66 Edges selected to create the round features

Figure 7-67 The default trimetric view of the base feature with two sets of round

Creating the Third Feature

The third feature is a through hole and needs to be created by using the **Hole** dashboard.

1. Choose the **Hole** button from the **Engineering Features** toolbar; the **Hole** dashboard is displayed. By default, the **Create simple hole** button is chosen in it.

2. Create the hole, as shown in Figure 7-68, by specifying the placement parameters. The placement parameters can be referred from Figure 7-63.

Creating a Pattern of the Hole Feature

As evident from Figure 7-62, you need to create four instances of the hole. The first instance will be created by using the **Hole** dashboard and the remaining three instances will be created by using the **Pattern** button. You will create a rectangular pattern of the hole feature. You can also create all holes by using the **Hole** dashboard and specify the placement parameters for each of them. However, to save time, it is recommended that you create a pattern of the hole.

1. Select the hole feature and then choose the **Pattern** button from the **Edit Features** toolbar; the **Pattern** dashboard is displayed. Also, you are prompted to select dimensions to vary in the first direction.

2. Make sure the **General** option is selected in the **Options** slide-down panel.

You cannot use the **Identical** option to create the rectangular pattern of the hole feature. This is because when you use the **Identical** option to pattern, the pattern cannot intersect the base feature on which the hole is created. If the top portion of the base feature is created as a separate feature, the hole can be patterned by using the **Identical** option.

3. You need to select the dimension value **10** from the drawing area. Since the two dimensions displayed in the drawing area have the dimension value 10, select the dimension 10 that is along the shorter side of the base feature. After you have selected the dimension in the first direction, the edit box is displayed. Enter **40** in it.

4. Hold the right mouse button to display a shortcut menu. Choose the **Direction 2 Dimensions** option from the shortcut menu.

5. Select the dimension value **10** that is along the longer side of the base feature. After you have selected the dimension in the second direction, the edit box is displayed. Enter **90** in the edit box.

   Note that the number of instances specified in the edit boxes present on the dashboard is 2, by default.

6. Choose the **Build feature** button from the **Pattern** dashboard; the rectangular pattern of the holes is displayed.

   You can use the middle mouse button to spin and display the model, as shown in Figure 7-69.

Figure 7-68 The hole feature on the base feature   *Figure 7-69* Model after creating the hole pattern

Note
*If multiple holes need to be created on a model, it is recommended that you create their pattern, if possible. This is because when you assemble bolts in these holes in the **Assembly** mode, it becomes very easy to assemble them using the reference pattern.*

Creating the Rib Feature

The sketch of the rib feature will be created on the **FRONT** datum plane and the required thickness will be applied to it. This is the fourth feature of the model.

Options Aiding Construction of Parts-II 7-33

1. Choose **Trajectory Rib > Profile Rib** from the **Engineering Features** toolbar; the **Profile Rib** dashboard is displayed.

2. Choose the **References** tab to invoke the slide-down panel. Choose the **Define** button from the slide-down panel; the **Sketch** dialog box is displayed.

3. Select the **FRONT** datum plane as the sketching plane.

4. Select the **TOP** datum plane from the drawing area and then select the **Top** option from the **Orientation** drop-down list.

5. Choose the **Sketch** button to enter into the sketcher environment.

6. Draw the sketch of the rib feature, as shown in Figure 7-70, and then exit the sketcher environment.

   Note
   As evident from Figure 7-70, the top end of the inclined line in the sketch is aligned with the curve and the tangent constraint is applied to the line and the curve. Similarly, the bottom end of the inclined line is also aligned with the two edges. This is the reason, there are no dimensions in the sketch and the sketch for the rib feature is fully constrained.

7. Choose the **Flip** button from the **References** slide-down panel, if the desired direction is not obtained.

8. Specify **8** as the rib thickness in the dimension box in the **Rib** dashboard. Choose the **Build feature** button to create the rib feature.

   The rib feature created is shown in Figure 7-71. You can use the middle mouse button to orient the model to view the correct placement of the rib.

Figure 7-70 Fully constrained sketch for the rib

Figure 7-71 Model after creating the rib feature

Creating a Copy of the Rib Feature

You need to create a copy of the rib feature, as shown in Figure 7-72. The other method to create the same is to create the sketch of the rib feature on the sketching plane. But, this method is time-consuming. Therefore, the rib feature will be copied about the **RIGHT** datum plane.

1. Choose **Edit > Feature Operations** from the menu bar; the **FEAT** menu is displayed.

2. Choose the **Copy** option from the **FEAT** menu; the **COPY FEATURE** submenu is displayed.

3. Choose **Mirror > Select > Independent > Done** from the **COPY FEATURE** submenu; the **Select** message box is displayed and you are prompted to select the features to be mirrored.

4. Select the rib feature from the drawing area and then choose **OK** from the **Select** message box; you are prompted to select a plane or create a datum plane to mirror about.

5. Select the **RIGHT** datum plane as the mirror plane; the selected feature is mirrored about the **RIGHT** datum plane, as shown in Figure 7-72.

Figure 7-72 Model after mirroring the rib feature

6. Choose **Done** from the **FEAT** menu to exit it.

Creating the Protrusion Feature

The sixth feature is an extruded feature. You need to create the extruded feature on the top face of the base feature.

1. Choose the **Extrude** button from the **Base Features** toolbar; the **Extrude** dashboard is displayed.

2. Invoke the **Sketch** dialog box.

3. Select the top face of the base feature as the sketching plane.

4. Select the **RIGHT** datum plane and then select the **Right** option from the **Orientation** drop-down list.

5. Choose the **Sketch** button to enter the sketcher environment.

6. Next, draw the sketch of the extruded feature, as shown in Figure 7-73.

Options Aiding Construction of Parts-II

In Figure 7-73, the tangent and equal radii constraints are applied to the sketch. Also, the center of the top arc and the bottom arc coincide with the intersection of the two datum planes.

7. After the sketch is complete, choose the **Done** button to exit the sketcher environment; the **Extrude** dashboard is enabled and it appears above the drawing area.

8. Enter **3** as the depth value in the dimension box in the **Extrude** dashboard. Choose the **Build feature** button from the **Extrude** dashboard; the extruded feature is completed and the default trimetric view is shown in Figure 7-74.

Figure 7-73 Sketch with dimensions and constraints for the extruded feature

Figure 7-74 The default trimetric view after creating the extruded feature

Creating the Cut Feature

You need to create an extruded cut on the bottom planar surface of the base feature. This is the seventh feature of the model.

1. Choose the **Extrude** button form the **Base Features** toolbar.

2. Select the **Remove Material** button from the **Extrude** dashboard.

3. Choose the **Placement** tab to invoke the slide-down panel. Choose the **Define** button from the slide-down panel; the **Sketch** dialog box is displayed.

4. Select the bottom face of the base feature as the sketching plane.

5. Select the **RIGHT** datum plane and then select the **Right** option from the **Orientation** drop-down list in the **Sketch** dialog box is displayed.

6. Choose the **Sketch** button to enter the sketcher environment.

7. Next, draw the sketch of the cut feature and dimension it, as shown in Figure 7-75.

8. After completing the sketch, choose the **Done** button; the **Extrude** dashboard is enabled and it appears above the drawing area.

9. Enter the value **30** in the dimension box of the **Extrude** dashboard.

10. Choose the **Build feature** button from the dashboard to create the cut feature. You can spin the model by using the middle mouse button. The cut feature is shown in Figure 7-76.

Figure 7-75 Sketch of the cut feature with dimensions

Figure 7-76 Model after creating the cut feature

Creating the Hole

Next, you need to create a through hole on the top extruded feature by using the **Hole** dashboard.

1. Invoke the **Hole** dashboard; the **Create simple hole** button is chosen by default in it. Specify the placement parameters of the hole as given in Figure 7-63 and create the hole. The model after creating the hole is shown in Figure 7-77.

Creating a Copy of the Hole

You need to create a mirror copy of the hole, as shown in Figure 7-78. This is the ninth feature of the model. You need to mirror the hole feature about the **RIGHT** datum plane.

1. Invoke the **FEAT** menu by using the **Edit** menu. Choose the **Copy** option from the **FEAT** menu; the **COPY FEATURE** submenu is displayed.

2. Choose **Mirror > Select > Independent > Done** from the **COPY FEATURE** submenu; the **Select** message box is displayed and you are prompted to select the features to be mirrored.

3. Select the previous hole feature from the drawing area and choose **OK** from the **Select** message box; you are prompted to select a plane or create a datum plane to mirror about.

Options Aiding Construction of Parts-II

4. Select the **RIGHT** datum plane as the mirror plane and choose **Done** from the **FEAT** menu; the hole feature is mirrored about the **RIGHT** datum plane, as shown in Figure 7-78.

Figure 7-77 Hole feature on the extruded feature

Figure 7-78 The copied hole feature

Saving the Model

You need to save the model to use it later.

1. Choose the **Save** button from the **File** toolbar and save the model.

   The order of feature creation of the model can be seen in the **Model Tree**, as shown in Figure 7-79.

Figure 7-79 The **Model Tree** for Tutorial 2

Tutorial 3

In this tutorial, you will create the model shown in Figure 7-80. This figure also shows the top and front views of the model. **(Expected time: 30 min)**

The following steps are required to complete this tutorial:

Examine the model and determine the number of features in it. The model consists of five features, refer to Figure 7-80.

Figure 7-80 The solid model and its top and front views

a. Create the base feature on the **TOP** datum plane, refer to Figures 7-81 and 7-82.
b. Create the cylindrical extrude feature, refer to Figures 7-83 and 7-84.
c. Create the hole feature coaxial with the cylindrical feature, refer to Figure 7-85.
d. Create the hole feature on the top planar surface of the base feature and then pattern it, refer to Figures 7-86 and 7-87.
e. Create the hole feature on the top planar surface of the cylindrical feature, refer to Figure 7-88.
f. Create a rotational pattern of this hole, refer to Figure 7-89.

If required, set the working directory to the *c07* folder.

Starting a New Object File
1. Start a new part file and name it *c07tut3*.

The three default datum planes are displayed in the drawing area.

Creating the Base Feature
To create the sketch for the base feature, you first need to select the sketching plane for the base feature. In this model, you need to draw the base feature on the **TOP** datum plane. This is because the direction of extrusion of this feature is perpendicular to the **TOP** datum plane.

Options Aiding Construction of Parts-II

1. Invoke the **Extrude** dashboard.

2. Invoke the **Sketch** dialog box by using the **Extrude** dashboard.

3. Select the **TOP** datum plane as the sketching plane.

4. Select the **RIGHT** datum plane and then select the **Right** option from the **Orientation** drop-down list, if it is not selected by default.

5. Choose the **Sketch** button to enter the sketcher environment.

6. Next, create the sketch of the base feature and apply the required constraints and dimensions to it, as shown in Figure 7-81.

7. After the sketch is complete, choose the **Done** button to exit the sketcher environment; the **Extrude** dashboard is enabled and it appears above the drawing area.

8. Enter **32** as the depth value in the dimension box of the **Extrude** dashboard and then choose the **Build feature** button from the dashboard.

   The base feature is completed and now you need to create the second feature. The default trimetric view of the base feature is shown in Figure 7-82.

Figure 7-81 Sketch of the base feature with dimensions and constraints

Figure 7-82 Default trimetric view of the base feature

Creating the Second Feature

The second feature is also an extruded feature. You need to create this feature on the top face of the base feature. Therefore, you need to define the top face as the sketching plane for the second feature.

1. Choose the **Extrude** button from the **Base Features** toolbar; the **Extrude** dashboard is displayed.

2. Invoke the **Sketch** dialog box by using the **Extrude** dashboard.

3. Select the top face of the base feature as the sketching plane.

4. Select the **RIGHT** datum plane and then select the **Right** option from the **Orientation** drop-down list, if it is not selected by default.

5. Choose the **Sketch** button to enter the sketcher environment.

6. Create the sketch of the second feature and then dimension it, as shown in Figure 7-83.

7. After creating the sketch, choose the **Done** button; the **Extrude** dashboard is enabled.

8. Enter **58** in the dimension box of the **Extrude** dashboard and choose the **Build feature** button. The model, similar to the one shown in Figure 7-84, is displayed in the drawing area.

Figure 7-83 Sketch of the cylindrical feature with diameter of the cylinder

Figure 7-84 Default trimetric view of the cylindrical feature

Creating the Third Feature

The third feature is a through hole that is coaxial to the cylindrical feature. You need to create the hole feature by using the **Hole** dashboard.

1. Choose the **Hole** button from the **Engineering Features** toolbar; the **Hole** dashboard is displayed. By default, the **Create simple hole** button is chosen in the **Hole** dashboard.

2. Create a hole of diameter 70, as shown in Figure 7-85, by specifying the placement parameters.

Creating the Fourth Feature

The fourth feature is a through hole. You need to create the feature on the top planar surface of the base feature by using the **Hole** dashboard.

1. Choose the **Hole** button from the **Engineering Features** toolbar; the **Hole** dashboard is displayed. By default, the **Create simple hole** button is chosen in the **Hole** dashboard.

2. Create the hole, as shown in Figure 7-86, by specifying the placement parameters.

Options Aiding Construction of Parts-II

Figure 7-85 Coaxial hole on the cylindrical feature

Figure 7-86 Hole on the base feature

Patterning the Hole Feature

Next, you need to create a rectangular pattern of the hole feature that is created on the base feature. You can also create individual holes; however, it is time-consuming and increases the number of features. Therefore, it is recommended that you create a rectangular pattern of the hole feature.

1. Select the hole feature and then choose the **Pattern** button from the **Edit Features** toolbar; the **Pattern** dashboard is displayed and you are prompted to select the dimensions to vary in the first direction.

2. Select the **Identical** option from the **Options** slide-down panel.

   Here, you need to use the **Identical** option because the feature on which the pattern is created does not intersect the pattern.

3. Select the dimension value **25** from the drawing area. Since the two dimensions displayed in the drawing area are both having the value 25; therefore, select the dimension **25** that is along the shorter side of the base feature. After you have selected the dimension in the first direction, an edit box is displayed. Enter **100** in the edit box.

4. Hold down the right mouse button to display the shortcut menu. Choose the **Direction 2 Dimensions** option from the shortcut menu.

5. Select the dimension value **25** that is along the longer side of the base feature. After you have selected the dimension in the second direction, an edit box is displayed.

6. Enter **250** in the edit box. Note that the number of instances, 2, is specified by default, in the instances edit boxes of the dashboard.

7. Choose the **Build feature** button from the **Pattern** dashboard; the rectangular pattern of the hole feature is displayed, as shown in Figure 7-87.

Creating a Hole on the Cylindrical Feature

You need to create the hole on the cylindrical feature diametrically by using the **Hole** dashboard.

1. Choose the **Hole** button from the **Engineering Features** toolbar; the **Hole** dashboard is displayed. By default, the **Create simple hole** button is chosen in the **Hole** dashboard.

2. Choose the **Placement** tab from the **Hole** dashboard to display the slide-down panel.

3. Select the top face of the cylindrical feature as the placement plane.

4. From the drop-down list in the slide-down panel, select the **Diameter** option.

5. Click in the **Offset References** collector and select the axis of the cylindrical feature.

6. Enter **106** in the second dimension box on the right of the **Diameter** option in the **Offset References** collector.

7. Use the CTRL key+left mouse button and select the **FRONT** datum plane from the drawing area. Enter the value **90** in the dimension box of the **Offset References** collector.

8. Enter **15** as the diameter of the hole in the diameter dimension box in the **Hole** dashboard.

9. Choose the **Drill to intersect with all surfaces** option from the depth flyout in the **Hole** dashboard.

10. Choose the **Build feature** button from the **Hole** dashboard; the hole is created, as shown in Figure 7-88.

Figure 7-87 Rectangular pattern of the hole feature

Figure 7-88 Diametrical hole on the cylindrical feature

Creating the Rotational Pattern of the Hole Feature

As the creation of the remaining holes individually on the cylindrical feature is time-consuming, you need to create a rotational pattern of the hole feature.

Options Aiding Construction of Parts-II

1. Select the hole feature and then choose the **Pattern** button from the **Edit Features** toolbar; the **Pattern** dashboard is displayed. Also, the dimensions of the hole feature are displayed in the drawing area and you are prompted to select dimensions to vary in the first direction.

2. Select the **Identical** option from the **Options** slide-down panel.

3. Select the angular dimension **90** from the model; an edit box is displayed.

4. Enter **45** in the edit box and press ENTER. Now, you need to specify the number of instances of the hole feature in the pattern.

5. Enter **8** in the **1** edit box and press ENTER. Choose the **Build feature** button from the dashboard. The rotational pattern is created and the model is completed, as shown in Figure 7-89. You can see the order of feature creation in the **Model Tree**, as shown in Figure 7-90.

Figure 7-89 *The complete model*

Figure 7-90 *The **Model Tree** for Tutorial 3*

Saving the Model

You need to save the model because you may need it later.

1. Choose the **Save** button from the **File** toolbar and save the model.

Tutorial 4

In this tutorial, you will create the model of the cylinder head shown in Figure 7-91. Figure 7-92 shows the top view and the front section view of the model. **(Expected time: 45 min)**

The following steps are required to complete this tutorial:

Examine the model and determine the number of features in it. The model consists of twelve features, refer to Figure 7-91.
a. Create the base feature on the **TOP** datum plane, refer to Figures 7-93 and 7-94.
b. Create the round features on the vertical edges of the base feature, refer to Figure 7-95.
c. Create the cylindrical feature on the bottom face of the base feature, refer to Figure 7-96.

Figure 7-91 Isometric view of the model

Figure 7-92 Top and front-section views of the model

Options Aiding Construction of Parts-II   7-45

d. Create the revolve cut feature on a plane passing through the center of the cylindrical feature, refer to Figures 7-97 and 7-98.
e. Create the fifth feature of the fin that will be patterned later on, refer to Figures 7-99 through 7-101.
f. Create the cut feature that will remove the protrusions of the fins projecting out of the base feature, refer to Figure 7-102.
g. Create a circular cut feature on the top face of the base feature, refer to Figures 7-103 and 7-104.
h. Create a cylindrical feature on the top face of the base feature, refer to Figure 7-105.
i. Create the ninth feature, which is a cut feature, refer to Figures 7-106 and 7-107. This feature is reference patterned to create its other instances, refer to Figure 7-108.
j. Create the tenth feature as a cylindrical feature on the top face of the base feature, refer to Figure 7-109.
k. Create the referenced pattern of the tenth feature, refer to Figure 7-110.
l. The eleventh feature is a coaxial hole. After creating the feature, create a reference pattern of this hole, refer to Figure 7-111.
m. Create the last feature as the coaxial hole that will be created on the eighth feature, refer to Figure 7-112.

If required, set the working directory to the *c07* folder.

Starting a New Object File
1. Start a new part file and name it *c07tut4*.

The three default datum planes are displayed in the drawing area.

Creating the Base Feature
In this model, you need to draw the sketch of the base feature on the **TOP** datum plane. The sketch is a polygon. First, you need to draw the right half of the polygon and then mirror it about the centerline to create the complete polygon.

1. Choose the **Extrude** button from the **Base Features** toolbar.

2. Choose the **Placement** tab to display a slide-down panel. From the slide-down panel, choose the **Define** button; the **Sketch** dialog box is displayed.

3. Select the **TOP** datum plane as the sketching plane.

4. Select the **RIGHT** datum plane and then select the **Right** option from the **Orientation** drop-down list, if it is not selected automatically.

5. Choose the **Sketch** button to enter the sketcher environment.

6. Next, create the sketch of the base feature and apply the constraints and dimensions to it, as shown in Figure 7-93.

7. After the sketch is complete, choose the **Done** button to exit the sketcher environment.

The **Extrude** dashboard is enabled and it appears above the drawing area.

8. Enter **4** as the depth value in the dimension box at the **Extrude** dashboard and then choose **Build feature** button from the dashboard.

The base feature is completed and now you need to create the second feature. The default trimetric view of the base feature is shown in Figure 7-94.

Figure 7-93 Sketch of the base feature with dimensions and constraints

Figure 7-94 Default trimetric view of the base feature

Creating the Second Feature

The second feature is a round feature of radius 15.

1. Choose the **Round** button from the **Engineering Features** toolbar; the **Round** dashboard is displayed.

2. Choose the **Sets** tab to display the slide-down panel.

3. Select one of the four vertical edges at the corners of the base feature. To select the second edge and the subsequent edges, press the CTRL key and then select the edge.

   The preview of the round is created on the selected edges. Also, a default value of the radius is displayed.

4. Double-click on the default radius value displayed along with the preview of the round; a edit box appears. Enter **15** in the edit box. You can also enter the radius value in the dimension box of the **Round** dashboard.

5. Choose the **Build feature** button to create the round feature.

The default trimetric view of the model after creating the round feature is shown in Figure 7-95.

Options Aiding Construction of Parts-II

Creating the Third Feature

The third feature is a cylindrical feature. You need to create the feature on the bottom face of the base feature.

1. Invoke the **Extrude** dashboard and using the **Sketch** dialog box, select the bottom face of the base feature as the sketching plane.

2. Enter the sketcher environment and draw the sketch of the cylindrical feature. Refer to Figure 7-92 for drawing the sketch.

3. Exit the sketcher environment and enter **4** as the depth of extrusion in the dashboard.

4. Exit the **Extrude** dashboard.

The cylindrical feature is completed and is shown in Figure 7-96.

Figure 7-95 Model with round

Figure 7-96 Model after creating the cylindrical feature on the bottom face

Creating the Fourth Feature

The fourth feature is a revolve cut that will be created on the datum plane passing through the center of the cylindrical feature.

1. Invoke the **Revolve** dashboard and choose the **Remove Material** button.

2. Choose the **Placement** tab; the slide-down panel is displayed. Choose the **Define** button from the slide-down panel; the **Sketch** dialog box is displayed. Select the **FRONT** datum plane as the sketching plane.

3. Select the **RIGHT** datum plane and then select the **Right** option from the **Orientation** drop-down list. Next, choose the **Sketch** button.

4. Once you enter the sketcher environment, create the sketch of the revolve cut feature, draw a vertical geometric centerline, and apply constraints and dimensions, as shown in Figure 7-97.

5. After the sketch is completed, exit the sketcher environment.

   The **Revolve** dashboard is enabled and appears above the drawing area. The value for the angle of revolution is 360 by default.

6. Choose the **Build feature** button from the dashboard.

   The revolved cut feature is created and is shown in Figure 7-98.

Figure 7-97 Sketch of the revolved feature with dimensions and constraints

Figure 7-98 Revolved cut feature

Creating the Fifth Feature

The fifth feature is the fin and its pattern. You need to create the sketch of the fin on the **FRONT** datum plane. The pattern of the fin feature will be created by controlling the dimensions of the sketch and constraining it.

This type of pattern can only be created, if dimensions of the feature to be patterned are proper. In the sketch of the feature, a construction entity must exist. This construction entity can be a circle, an arc, or a line. The construction entity is used as the driving entity for the pattern to be created later. The pattern instances are created in such a way that they follow the geometry of the construction entity.

1. Invoke the **Extrude** dashboard and using the **Sketch** dialog box, select the **FRONT** datum plane as the sketching plane.

2. Select the **RIGHT** datum plane and then select the **Right** option from the **Orientation** drop-down list, if it is not selected by default.

3. Choose the **Sketch** button to enter the sketcher environment.

4. Next, draw the arc, refer to Figure 7-99, by using the **Center and Ends** button.

Options Aiding Construction of Parts-II 7-49

> **Note**
> *In the sketch of the fin feature, you need to draw the sketch such that the size of the instances of the pattern can be controlled later. You will use the dimension 6.155 to create the pattern. Also, the vertical height of the fin feature is not specified in the sketch because in that case, the fin feature will not slide along the construction arc but will be locked with the top construction arc.*

5. Select the arc and then hold down the right mouse button to invoke the shortcut menu. From the shortcut menu, choose the **Construction** option; the arc is converted into a construction arc. Next, create the sketch of the fin feature and apply the required constraints and dimensions to it, as shown in Figure 7-99.

Figure 7-99 Sketch for the fin feature with two weak dimensions

6. After the sketch is completed, exit the sketcher environment. Note that the sketch must be closed.

7. Choose the **Extrude on both sides of sketch plane by half the specified depth value in each direction** button from the depth flyout in the **Extrude** dashboard.

8. Enter **135** in the dimension box of the dashboard.

9. Choose the **Build feature** button from the dashboard.

   The default trimetric view of the fin feature is shown in Figure 7-100. Now, you need to pattern the fin feature to create the remaining 12 fins.

10. Select the fin and invoke the **Pattern** dashboard; the dimensions of the fin feature are displayed in the drawing area.

11. Select the dimension value **6.155**; an edit box appears. Enter **9** in this edit box.

12. Enter **13** in the dimension box of the dashboard. These are the number of instances of the fin feature.

13. Choose the **Build feature** button to exit the **Pattern** dashboard. The model after patterning the fin feature is shown in Figure 7-101.

Figure 7-100 *Fin created on the base feature*   *Figure 7-101* *Pattern of the fin feature*

Creating the Sixth Feature

The sixth feature is an extrude cut. You need to create this feature on the bottom face of the base feature. This cut will remove the fins that are projecting out of the base feature.

1. Invoke the **Extrude** dashboard and then choose the **Remove Material** button.

2. Select the bottom face of the base feature as the sketching plane.

3. Select the **RIGHT** datum plane and then select the **Right** option from the **Orientation** drop-down list, if they are not selected by default.

4. Once you enter the sketcher environment, use the edge of the base feature to create the sketch that will be extruded later to create the cut.

5. After the sketch is completed, exit the sketcher environment.

   The **Extrude** dashboard is enabled and it appears above the drawing area.

6. Choose the **Extrude to intersect with all surface** button from the depth flyout.

7. Choose the **Change material direction of extrude to other side of sketch** button from the dashboard to reverse the direction of the yellow arrow. This yellow arrow points in the direction from where the material will be removed. Note that the arrows displayed on the preview should be upward and outward direction. You can click on the arrows to change the direction of the cut.

8. Choose the **Build feature** button from the dashboard. The default trimetric view of the model after creating the cut feature is shown in Figure 7-102.

Options Aiding Construction of Parts-II   7-51

Figure 7-102 Model after trimming the fins by creating the cut feature

Creating the Seventh Feature

The seventh feature is an extrude cut feature. You need to create the feature on the top face of the base feature.

1. Invoke the **Extrude** dashboard and then choose the **Remove Material** button from it.

2. Select the top face of the base feature as the sketching plane.

3. Select the **RIGHT** datum plane and then select the **Right** option from the **Orientation** drop-down list, if they are not selected by default. Next, choose the **Sketch** button.

4. Draw the sketch of the circular cut feature, as shown in Figure 7-103.

5. After the sketch is completed, exit the sketcher environment.

   The **Extrude** dashboard is enabled and it appears above the drawing area.

6. Choose the **Extrude to intersect with all surface** button from the depth flyout.

7. If required, change the depth direction of extrude such that the fins of the model are cut.

8. Choose the **Build feature** button from the dashboard. The top view of the model after creating the circular cut is shown in Figure 7-104.

Creating the Eighth Feature

The eighth feature is a protrusion feature. You need to create this feature on the top face of the base feature.

Figure 7-103 Sketch of the circular cut feature   *Figure 7-104* Model after creating the circular cut

1. Invoke the **Extrude** dashboard and select the top face of the base feature as the sketching plane.

2. Select the **RIGHT** datum plane and then select the **Right** option from the **Orientation** drop-down list, if they are not selected by default.

3. Once you enter the sketcher environment, use the edge of the cut feature to create the sketch of the protrusion feature.

4. After the sketch is completed, exit the sketcher environment.

5. Enter **9** in the dimension box of the **Extrude** dashboard.

6. Choose the **Build feature** button from the dashboard. The model after creating the cylindrical feature is shown in Figure 7-105.

Figure 7-105 Model after creating the cylindrical feature

Options Aiding Construction of Parts-II

Creating the Ninth Feature

The ninth feature is a cut feature. You need to pattern this feature to create its other instances. The cut feature is created on the top face of the base feature.

1. Invoke the **Extrude** dashboard and then choose the **Remove Material** button.

2. Select the top face of the base feature as the sketching plane.

3. Select the **RIGHT** datum plane and then select the **Right** option from the **Orientation** drop-down list.

4. Once you enter the sketcher environment, draw the sketch of the circular cut feature, as shown in Figure 7-106.

5. After the sketch is completed, exit the sketcher environment. The **Extrude** dashboard is enabled and it appears above the drawing area.

6. Choose the **Extrude to intersect with all surface** button from the depth flyout.

7. Change the depth direction of extrude such that the fins of the model are cut.

8. Choose the **Build feature** button from the dashboard. The model after creating the circular cut is shown in Figure 7-107.

Figure 7-106 Sketch of the cut feature

Figure 7-107 Model after creating circular cut

Now, you need to pattern the cut feature to create its other instances.

9. Select the cut feature from the **Model Tree** and then choose the **Pattern** button from the **Edit Features** toolbar. Select the **Dimension** option from the drop-down list, if it is not selected by default.

The **Pattern** dashboard is displayed and you are prompted to select dimensions to vary in the first direction.

10. Select the **General** option from the **Options** slide-down panel, if it is not selected.

11. Select the dimension value **40.5** from the drawing area. After you have selected the dimension in the first direction, an edit box is displayed.

12. Enter **-81** in the edit box.

13. Hold the right mouse button to display the shortcut menu. Choose the **Direction 2 Dimensions** option from the shortcut menu.

14. Select the dimension **16**. After you have selected the dimension in the second direction, the edit box is displayed.

15. Enter **80** in the edit box. Note that in the instances edit boxes in the dashboard, the number of instances, **2**, is specified by default.

16. Choose the **Build feature** button from the **Pattern** dashboard. The rectangular pattern of the cut feature is displayed, as shown in Figure 7-108.

Figure 7-108 Model after patterning the cut feature

Creating the Tenth Feature

The tenth feature is an extrude feature created on the top face of the base feature. You need to pattern this feature to create other instances.

1. Invoke the **Extrude** dashboard.

2. Select the top face of the base feature as the sketching plane.

3. Select the **RIGHT** datum plane and then select the **Right** option from the **Orientation** drop-down list, if they are not selected by default.

Options Aiding Construction of Parts-II

4. Once you enter the sketcher environment, draw the sketch of the protrusion feature using the edges of the cut feature.

5. After the sketch is completed, exit the sketcher environment.

6. Enter **9** in the dimension box of the dashboard.

7. Choose the **Build feature** button from the dashboard. The model after creating the protrusion feature is shown in Figure 7-109.

   Now, you need to create a reference pattern of the protrusion feature to create its other instances.

8. Select the extrude feature from the **Model Tree** and then choose the **Pattern** button from the **Edit Features** toolbar.

   The **Reference** option is selected by default in the drop-down list of the **Pattern** dashboard.

9. Choose the **Build feature** button from the **Pattern** dashboard. The model after creating the pattern is shown in Figure 7-110.

Figure 7-109 Model after creating the cylindrical feature

Figure 7-110 Model after creating the reference pattern of the cylindrical feature

Creating the Eleventh Feature

The eleventh feature is a coaxial hole and is created on the top face of the tenth feature and later it is reference-patterned to create its other instances.

1. Create a hole of diameter 12 on the top face of the protrusion feature created at the lower left corner. You must create a hole that passes through all faces.

Note
While creating the coaxial hole on the top face of the tenth feature, make sure that the axis of the coaxial hole and the axis of the tenth feature are same.

2. Pattern the feature by using the **Reference** option. The model after creating the pattern of the hole feature is shown in Figure 7-111.

Creating the Last Feature

The last feature is a hole of diameter **16** and is created on the top face of the eighth feature. This hole is coaxial with the cylindrical feature on which it is being created. The model after creating the hole feature is shown in Figure 7-112.

Figure 7-111 Model after creating the reference pattern of the hole feature

Figure 7-112 Model after creating the hole on the cylindrical feature

Saving the Model

You need to save the model because you may need it later.

1. Choose the **Save** button from the **File** toolbar and then save the model. The order of feature creation can be seen from the **Model Tree** shown in Figure 7-113.

*Figure 7-113 The **Model Tree** for Tutorial 4*

Options Aiding Construction of Parts-II

Creating a Section View of the Model

1. Choose **View > View Manager** from the menu bar; the **View Manager** dialog box is displayed.

2. Choose the **New** button from the dialog box; **Rep0001** is displayed in the **Names** display box.

3. Press ENTER; the dialog box disappears, and the **Menu Manager** with the **EDIT METHOD** menu is displayed.

4. Choose the **Work Region** option from the **EDIT METHOD** menu; the **SOLID OPTS** menu is displayed.

5. Choose **Extrude > Solid > Done** from the **SOLID OPTS** menu; the **Extrude** dashboard is displayed. Next, invoke the **Sketch** dialog box from the **Extrude** dashboard.

6. Select the bottom most planar face of the model as the sketching plane and then select the **RIGHT** datum plane to be at the right while drawing the sketch.

7. If required, choose the **Flip** button to reverse the direction of the yellow arrow. You need to draw the sketch from the side of the sketch plane where the fins are facing. This is because when you draw the sketch, you need to ensure that the section lines do not cut the fins.

8. While entering the sketcher environment, you need to draw section lines, as shown in Figure 7-114. This section is an open loop and dimensions are not of importance to create it.

Figure 7-114 Sketch of the section lines with weak dimensions

9. Exit the sketcher environment and then choose the **Extrude to intersect with all surface** button from the depth flyout; the yellow arrow will point in the reverse direction.

10. Choose the **Change material direction of extrude to other side of sketch** button to reverse the direction of the arrow.

11. Choose the **Change depth direction of extrude to other side of sketch** button to reverse the direction extrude.

12. Choose the **Build feature** button from the **Extrude** dashboard. The sectioned model is shown in Figure 7-115.

13. Choose the **Done/Return** option from the **EDIT METHOD** menu and then close the **View Manager**.

Figure 7-115 Sectioned model

Self-Evaluation Test

Answer the following questions and then compare them to those given at the end of this chapter:

1. When a pattern is created, the leader or the parent feature also becomes a part of the pattern. (T/F)

2. Once a pattern is created, all instances in the pattern, including the parent feature, act as a single feature. (T/F)

3. In the **Reference** pattern, an existing pattern is referenced to create a new pattern. (T/F)

4. Using the **Pattern** dashboard, you can only create linear patterns. (T/F)

Options Aiding Construction of Parts-II

5. If you select a pattern feature from the **Model Tree** and right-click to display the shortcut menu and then choose the **Delete** option, the whole pattern is deleted including the leader. (T/F)

6. The _____ option is used to delete a pattern except the leader feature.

7. The _____ option is used to mirror the entire geometry about a plane.

8. The _____ option from the **Pattern** dashboard is used to create a pattern in which the dimensions of instances can be varied.

9. The first feature in a pattern is called _____.

10. The _____ menu is used to select the dimensions that you want to vary from the leader while copying.

Review Questions

Answer the following questions:

1. Which of the following options in the **Pattern** dashboard is used to create patterns in which instances touch each other and intersect with other instances or edges of a surface?

    (a) **Identical**   (b) **Variable**
    (c) **General**   (d) None of these

2. Which of the following datums is required to create a rotational pattern?

    (a) Graph   (b) Curve
    (c) Axis   (d) Point

3. Which of the following options in the **Pattern** dashboard cannot be used to create a pattern that intersects an edge of a feature on which the pattern has to be created?

    (a) **Identical**   (b) **Variable**
    (c) **General**   (d) None of these

4. Which of the following options in the **Pattern** dashboard is used to create a pattern that has all instances of different sizes?

    (a) **Identical**   (b) **Variable**
    (c) **General**   (d) None of these

5. Which of the following options in the **COPY FEATURE** submenu is used to create a parent-child relationship between the copied feature and the source feature?

   (a) **FromDifModel** (b) **FromDifVers**
   (c) **Independent** (d) **Dependent**

6. You can mirror features by using datum planes or planar surfaces. (T/F)

7. To create a rotational pattern, you should specify an angular increment. (T/F)

8. The **New Refs** option is available in the **COPY FEATURE** submenu. (T/F)

9. When you copy a feature by using the **New Refs** option, the copied feature is not related with the original feature. (T/F)

10. The features copied from different models or from different versions are always independent. (T/F)

Exercises

Exercise 1

Create the model shown in Figure 7-116. The top, front, right, detailed, and sectioned views of the model are shown in Figure 7-117. **(Expected time: 45 min)**

Figure 7-116 Solid model for Exercise 1

Options Aiding Construction of Parts-II

Figure 7-117 Top, front, right, detailed, and sectioned views of the model

Exercise 2

Create the model shown in Figure 7-118. This figure also shows the top, front, and right view of the model.   **(Expected time: 30 min)**

Figure 7-118 The model and its top, front, and right views

Exercise 3

Create the model shown in Figure 7-119. The top view, front view, and isometric view is shown in the same figure. **(Expected time: 30 min)**

Options Aiding Construction of Parts-II 7-63

Figure 7-119 The model and its top and front views

Exercise 4

Create the model shown in Figure 7-120. The top and sectioned right views are shown in Figure 7-121. **(Expected time: 1hr)**

Note
You will learn about the aligned section view and total aligned section view in Chapter 11.

Figure 7-120 Solid model for Exercise 4

Figure 7-121 Top view and the total aligned sectioned view of the model

Answers to Self-Evaluation Test
1. T, **2.** T, **3.** T, **4.** F, **5.** T, **6. Delete Pattern**, **7. Mirror** tool, **8. Variable**, **9.** leader, **10. GP VAR DIMS**.

Chapter 8

Advanced Modeling Tools-I

Learning Objectives

After completing this chapter, you will be able to:
• *Create sweep features.*
• *Create features by using sweep cut.*
• *Create parallel, rotational, and general blends.*
• *Use blend vertex in blend features.*
• *Create shell features.*
• *Create datum curves.*
• *Create draft features.*

OTHER PROTRUSION OPTIONS

In chapter 4, you learned how to use the **Extrude** and **Revolve** options. In this chapter, you will learn how to use the **Sweep** and **Blend** options. As mentioned in previous chapters, Protrusion and Cut are the two basic options available in Pro/ENGINEER that are used to create a feature.

> **Note**
> *All options available for creating a cut feature are similar to those available for creating a protrusion. Remember that a cut can be created on an existing feature, and therefore, the **Cut** option will be available only when a base feature exists in the drawing area.*

You will also learn about the tools of solid modeling that are used to create a complex model easily. In the next section, you will learn about sweep features.

SWEEP FEATURES

The **Sweep** option extrudes a section along a defined trajectory. The order of operation is to first create a trajectory and then a section. Trajectory is a path along which a section is swept. The trajectory for a sweep feature can be either sketched or selected. The **Sweep** option of protrusion is similar to the **Extrude** option. The only difference being that in the case of the **Extrude** option, the feature is extruded in a direction normal to the sketching plane, but in the case of the **Sweep** option, the section is swept along the sketched or selected trajectory. The trajectory can be open or closed. Normal sketching tools are used for sketching the trajectory. The cross section of the swept feature remains constant throughout the sweep.

> **Note**
> *Some important points to remember while drawing a trajectory and a section for a sweep feature are discussed later in this chapter.*

Creating Sweep Protrusions

The **Sweep** option can be used for adding material (protrusion) as well as for removing material (cut). You can choose the **Sweep** option from the menu bar. To add material that is defined by the section in the specified path, choose **Insert > Sweep > Protrusion** from the **Ribbon**; the SWEEP TRAJ (Sweep Trajectory) menu appears, as shown in Figure 8-1. The options in this menu are discussed next.

Figure 8-1 The SWEEP TRAJ menu

Sketch Traj Option

The **Sketch Traj** (Sketch Trajectory) option is used when you want to sketch the trajectory for the sweep feature. This is the most commonly used option for defining the trajectory. As mentioned earlier, the trajectory can be open or closed. There are some limitations for using closed or open trajectory with closed or open section. These limitations are discussed in the next section. When you choose the **Sketch Traj** option, you are prompted to select a sketching plane. The sketching plane you select will be parallel to the screen when you sketch the trajectory. As you exit the sketching environment after creating the trajectory, you are prompted to sketch the cross-section. Also, a crosshair is displayed to locate the center for the section. Figure 8-2 shows how the section is swept along the sketched trajectory and Figure 8-3 shows the shaded image of the sweep feature.

Advanced Modeling Tools-I   8-3

Figure 8-2 Section swept along the sketched trajectory

Figure 8-3 Shaded image of the sweep feature

The following points specify the combinations of trajectories and sections that can/ cannot be used together to create the sweep:

1. Open section and open trajectory are not possible.

2. Closed section and open trajectory are possible.

3. If the sketched trajectory is a closed loop, then after you exit the sketcher environment, the **ATTRIBUTES** menu is displayed, as shown in Figure 8-4. There are two options in this menu: **Add Inn Fcs** (Add inner faces) and **No Inn Fcs** (No inner faces). The **No Inn Fcs** option is chosen by default.

   Figure 8-4 The **ATTRIBUTES** menu

   By using the **Add Inn Fcs** option, you can use only the open sections, as shown in Figure 8-5. The shaded image of the corresponding sweep feature is shown in Figure 8-6. These two figures explain the use of the **Add Inn Fcs** option.

Figure 8-5 Using the **Add Inn Fcs** option

Figure 8-6 Shaded image of the sweep feature

By using the **No Inn Fcs** option, only closed sections can be created, as shown in Figure 8-7. The shaded image of the corresponding sweep feature is shown in Figure 8-8.

Figure 8-7 *The closed section required for the **No Inn Fcs** option*

Figure 8-8 *Shaded image of the sweep feature*

Select Traj Option

The **Select Traj** (Select Trajectory) option allows you to select a trajectory in the drawing area. The trajectory to be selected can be an existing edge or a datum curve. Creation of datum curves will be discussed later in the chapter. When you choose this option from the **SWEEP TRAJ** menu, the **CHAIN** menu is displayed. The **CHAIN** menu is also discussed later in this chapter.

Figures 8-9 and 8-10 show two examples of selecting the edges of the base feature and then using them as a trajectory to sweep. Also, the corresponding sweep features are shown in the figure.

Figure 8-9 *Sweep along the selected trajectory*

Figure 8-10 *Sweep along the selected trajectory*

Sketching a Trajectory Aligned to an Existing Geometry

When one end of the sketched trajectory is aligned to the adjacent geometry of the existing feature, Pro/ENGINEER provides two options for this type of alignment. The first option is to merge the ends of the sweep feature with the adjacent geometry and the second option

Advanced Modeling Tools-I 8-5

is to leave the ends of the sweep feature free. These options are available in the **ATTRIBUTES** menu that is displayed after you complete the sketch of the trajectory and choose the **Done** button. The **ATTRIBUTES** menu is shown in Figure 8-11.

The **ATTRIBUTES** menu is displayed only when the trajectory is aligned to an edge or surface of the feature that already exists in the drawing area. This means that the **ATTRIBUTES** menu does not appear if the sweep feature you are drawing is the base feature of a model or, in other words, if there is no adjacent geometry to which the trajectory can be merged. The options available in the **ATTRIBUTES** menu are discussed next.

Figure 8-11 The ATTRIBUTES menu

Merge Ends
The **Merge Ends** option merges the end of a sweep feature to the surface to which the end of the trajectory is aligned. For this option the trajectory should be aligned to the adjacent geometry.

Free Ends
The **Free Ends** option leaves the sweep feature partially attached to the adjacent feature even if the end of the trajectory is aligned to the adjacent geometry.

Figure 8-12 shows the use of the **Merge Ends** and **Free Ends** options. In the figure, the trajectory is aligned with the adjacent geometry in both the cases. Figure 8-13 shows the corresponding shaded image.

Figure 8-12 Model with merge and free ends options

Figure 8-13 Shaded image

Creating a Sweep Feature by Selecting a Trajectory
When you choose the **Select Traj** option from the **SWEEP TRAJ** menu, the **CHAIN** menu is displayed, as shown in Figure 8-14. You can use the **CHAIN** menu only if you have created a feature that will be used to select the trajectory. The options in this menu are used to select a trajectory. These options are discussed next.

Tip: *The following points should be remembered while creating a sweep feature:*

1. *Similar to other sketched features, the trajectory of the sweep feature is also sketched after selecting a sketching plane.*

2. *The section for the sweep trajectory is sketched using the normal sketcher tools when the sketch trajectory option is selected.*

3. *At bends in a trajectory, the radius of the bend should be proportionate to the cross-section to be swept to avoid overlapping. If the section size is large and the radius of the curve or bend is small, overlapping takes place and the sweep feature will not be created. Therefore, make sure that the ratio of the size of the section to the size of the trajectory is appropriate.*

One By One
The **One By One** option of the **CHAIN** menu is selected by default. Using this option you can select an edge or curve individually, one by one. You have to hold the CTRL key while selecting the edges. When you select an edge, it is highlighted in red. Before selecting the edge, make sure that the **Select** option in the **CHAIN** menu is highlighted. The edge once selected is confirmed by choosing the **OK** button from the **Select** message box or by using the middle mouse button. The selected edge can be unselected by choosing the **Unselect** option from the **CHAIN** menu.

Tangnt Chain
You can select an edge or edges tangent to a selected edge by using the **Tangnt Chain** option. When you select an edge, all edges tangent to the selected edge are highlighted. If the selected edge is not tangent to any other edge, the function will be this option is the same as that of the **One By One** option. The difference being that you can select only one edge in case you are using the **Tangnt Chain** option. You can also define the start point of the chain.

Figure 8-14 The CHAIN menu

Curve Chain
You can select a chain of curves by using the **Curve Chain** option.

Bndry Chain
The **Bndry Chain** (Boundary Chain) option is used only for surface features. You can define a chain by selecting a quilt and using its one-sided edges. If the quilt has more than one loop, select a specific loop to define the chain.

When you select the edge of the quilt, it is highlighted in blue and the **CHOOSE** menu is displayed, as shown in Figure 8-15.

Figure 8-15 The CHOOSE menu

Advanced Modeling Tools-I   8-7

Surf Chain
Using the **Surf Chain** option, you can define a chain by selecting a surface and using its edges. If the surface has more than one loop, then you are prompted to specify a loop to define the chain. When a surface is selected, the **CHAIN OPT** menu is displayed, as shown in Figure 8-16. Choose either **Select All** or **From-To** from the **CHAIN OPT** menu.

Figure 8-16 The *CHAIN OPT menu*

Intent Chain
The **Intent Chain** option is used to select multiple edges. When a section is extruded, the edges formed by the extrusion consist of intent chains. The intent chains can either be the edges of the section or the edges of the extruded surface. The edges selected should form a closed loop.

Creating a Thin Sweep Protrusion
The **Sweep > Thin Protrusion** option is used to create a thin sweep feature with a specified thickness. This option is similar to the **Extrude > Thin** option that was discussed in Chapter 4. In case of thin features, a certain thickness has to be specified. The thickness is specified on one side of the section or symmetrically to both the sides of the section. The resulting sweep feature will be a hollow sweep feature. Figure 8-17 shows the sections that can be used to create the model shown in Figure 8-18.

Figure 8-17 *Two possible sections to create the same model*

Figure 8-18 *Same model created by using different sections*

Creating a Sweep Cut
The procedure to create a Sweep Cut feature is similar to that of creating the Sweep Protrusion. The only difference is that in case of cut features, the material is removed from an existing feature. The **Cut** option can be invoked by choosing **Insert > Sweep > Cut** from the menu bar. The cut can be a solid swept cut or thin swept cut. Figure 8-19 shows trajectories for the Sweep Cut feature. Figure 8-20 shows the shaded model with the open and closed trajectory sweep cuts.

Figure 8-19 *Trajectories for the Sweep Cut feature*

Figure 8-20 *Shaded model with the open and close trajectory sweep cuts*

BLEND FEATURES

Blend features consists of two or more sections joined through transitional faces at their edges so as to form a continuous feature. The number of entities in each section that are used to create the blend feature should be the same. For example, you cannot blend a circle with a rectangle. This is because a rectangle is composed of four entities and a circle of one. It can be achieved only if the circle is divided into four entities.

In Pro/ENGINEER, the Blend feature is of two types, Protrusion and Cut. The **Blend** option is used where the feature to be created has varying cross sections. To invoke this option, choose **Insert > Blend > Protrusion** or **Insert > Blend > Cut** from the menu bar.

When you choose the **Blend > Protrusion** option, the **BLEND OPTS** submenu is displayed, as shown in Figure 8-21. The options in this menu are discussed next.

Figure 8-21 *The BLEND OPTS submenu*

Parallel Blend

Parallel blends have sections that are drawn parallel to each other with a specified distance between them.

After choosing **Parallel > Regular Sec > Sketch Sec > Done** from the **BLEND OPTS** submenu, the **ATTRIBUTES** menu is displayed, as shown in Figure 8-22. The options in this menu are discussed next.

Straight Option

The **Straight** option is used to connect the vertices of all sections in a blend feature with straight lines.

Figure 8-22 *The ATTRIBUTES menu*

Smooth Option

The **Smooth** option is used to connect the vertices of all sections in a blend feature with smooth curves.

The steps required to be followed to create a Parallel blend feature are as follows:

1. Invoke the **Blend** tool by choosing **Insert > Blend > Protrusion** from the menu bar; the **BLEND OPTS** menu will be displayed.
2. Choose **Parallel > Regular Sec > Sketch Sec > Done** from the **BLEND OPTS** menu; the **ATTRIBUTES** menu will be displayed. Next, choose **Straight > Done** from it; you are prompted to define the sketching plane.
3. Define the required sketching plane and its orientation to draw the sections.
4. Draw the sketch of the first section. After drawing the first section, choose **Sketch > Feature Tools > Toggle Section** from the menu bar to draw the second section. You can also choose the **Toggle Section** option from the shortcut menu. If you choose the **Done** button before drawing the second section, the system prompts you to choose the **Toggle Section** option to continue with the second section. Note that the active section appears in yellow color and the other sections appear in gray.

Note

All sections in a blend feature must have equal number of entities. However, you can blend a point with any section irrespective of the number of entities.

5. Next, enter the depth values between subsequent sections after the completion of all sections in the blend.

Note

*While drawing a section, the start point of all sections should be in the same direction in order to avoid twisted blend features. By default, the start point of any entity drawn to define a section is considered as the **Start Point** of the section. To change the **Start Point** of a section, select the point to be defined as the **Start Point** and hold the right mouse button to display the shortcut menu. Choose the **Start Point** option from this shortcut menu to change the start point.*

6. Choose the **Preview** button to preview the blend feature. Next, choose the **OK** button to accept and exit the tool.

Figure 8-23 shows the three sections that are used to create the blend feature. Figures 8-24 and 8-25 show the parallel blend features with straight edges and smooth edges, respectively, by using the sections shown in Figure 8-23.

Tip: *After defining the sections in a blend feature and before choosing the **Done** button, you can modify the sections by using the **Toggle Section** option.*

Figure 8-23 Three parallel sections

Figure 8-24 Parallel blend with straight edges

Figure 8-25 Parallel blend with smooth edges

Rotational Blend

The rotational blends have sections that are rotated about the Y-axis up to a maximum of 120-degree and the distance between two sections is measured from the coordinate system. An angle called **rotational blend angle** has to be defined between each section. In this type of blend, each section has its own user-defined coordinate system. If the rotational blend angle entered between the two sections is equal to 0-degree, then the **Rotational** blend option functions the same way as the **Parallel** blend option.

Note that all nonparallel blends can be open or close. Therefore, on choosing **Rotational > Regular Sec > Sketch Sec > Done** from the **BLEND OPTS** menu, the **ATTRIBUTES** menu is displayed, as shown in Figure 8-26. The options in this menu are discussed next.

Figure 8-26 The *ATTRIBUTES* menu

Advanced Modeling Tools-I

Tip: *It is recommended that the closed blend features should have at least three sections.*

Open Option
The **Open** option is used when the blend feature to be created has to be kept open.

Closed Option
The **Closed** option is used to create a closed blend feature. In this type of blend feature, Pro/ENGINEER closes the feature by automatically blending the last section with the first section. Figure 8-27 shows the sections used to create a rotational smooth blend feature. Also, it shows the three default datum planes. In Figure 8-27, it is evident that two sections are used to create the blend feature and that these sections are at an angle of 45-degree. It is also evident from the figure that the second section is dimensioned from the coordinate system that was defined in the first section. Figure 8-28 shows the shaded model of the same blend feature.

Figure 8-27 The two sections with dimensions and the default datum planes used to create the blend feature shown in Figure 8-28

Figure 8-28 Shaded model of rotational open blend feature

The following steps briefly explain the procedure of creating the blend feature shown in Figure 8-28:
1. Invoke the **Blend** option and from the **BLEND OPTS** menu, choose **Rotational > Regular Sec > Sketch Sec > Done**; the **ATTRIBUTES** menu is displayed.
2. Choose **Smooth > Open > Done** from the **ATTRIBUTES** menu; you are prompted to select a plane to sketch.
3. Select the **RIGHT** datum plane as the sketch plane and orient the **FRONT** datum plane to be on top.
4. After selecting the sketch plane and its orientation, draw the first section that is a square of side 50. The start point on this square should be at the lower right corner.
5. Place the coordinate system at the lower left corner of the square.
6. Choose the **Done** button to proceed for drawing the next section. Accept the default Y-axis rotation angle of 45-degree for section 2.

7. Draw the second section that is a square of size 25.
8. Place the coordinate system for this section at a distance of 100 toward the left of the lower left corner of the square. Remember that the start point of this section should also lie at the lower right corner of the rectangle.
9. Exit the sketcher environment; the **Confirmation** window appears and you are prompted that do you want to continue to draw the next section.
10. Choose the **No** button from the **Confirmation** window. Choose the **Preview** button to preview the feature and then exit this tool.

General Blend

Using the **General** blend, sections are translated and rotated about the x, y, and z axes. The sections are aligned using the user-defined coordinate system. The coordinate system has to be manually placed in every section sketch that constitutes the blend feature.

USING BLEND VERTEX

As mentioned earlier, each section of the blend feature must have an equal number of entities. However, you can use the **Blend Vertex** option if the numbers of entities in all sections are not equal. For example, to create a blending between a square and a triangle, add blend vertex on a point other than the start point of the triangle. The two vertices of the triangle will blend with the two vertices of the rectangle and the blend vertex in the triangle will be blend with the remaining two vertices in the rectangle, as shown in Figure 8-29.

Figure 8-29 Blending a square with a triangle by using the blend vertex

To add a blend vertex in a sketch, select the point where you want to place the blend vertex. The selected point is highlighted in red. Choose **Sketch > Feature Tools > Blend Vertex**. The blend vertex is placed at the selected point.

Note
*The **Blend Vertex** option can be used either in the first or in the last section of a blend feature.*

Advanced Modeling Tools-I

SHELL FEATURE

The **Shell** option scoops out the material from the model and at the same time removes the selected faces, leaving behind a thin model with some specified wall thickness. The **Shell** option can be invoked by choosing the **Shell** button from the **Engineering Features** toolbar. Alternatively, choose **Insert > Shell** from the menu bar; the **Shell** dashboard will be displayed, as shown in Figure 8-30.

*Figure 8-30 The **Shell** dashboard*

Options Tab

When you choose the **Options** tab from the **Shell** dashboard, a slide-down panel will be displayed, as shown in Figure 8-31.

The **Excluded surfaces** collector lists the surfaces excluded from being removed. If you do not select any surface from being excluded, the entire part will be shelled.

The following steps explain briefly the procedure of creating a shell feature by using the **Excluded surfaces** collector:

1. Invoke the **Extrude** dashboard and then create the extrude feature, as shown in Figure 8-32.
2. Once the **Extrude** feature is created, invoke the **Shell** dashboard by choosing the **Shell** button from the **Engineering Features** toolbar.
3. Select the top face of the model to remove it.
4. Choose the **Options** tab; the slide-down panel is displayed. Activate the **Excluded surfaces** collector by clicking on it.
5. Select the surfaces to be excluded by pressing the CTRL key, refer to Figure 8-32.
6. Choose the **Build feature** button from the **Shell** dashboard to exit it; the shell created by excluding the specified surfaces is shown in Figure 8-33.

*Figure 8-31 The **Options** tab slide-down panel*

Note
*The **Shell** option is used on existing models and hence, this option is available only when a model exists in the drawing area.*

Using the **Shell** dashboard, you can create the following two types of shell:
1. Constant thickness shell
2. Variable thickness shell

Figure 8-32 Selecting surfaces to be excluded   *Figure 8-33* Shell created after excluding surfaces

Creating a Constant Thickness Shell

The constant thickness shell is a shell that has a uniform thickness on all four faces of the model. The following steps explain the procedure to create a constant thickness shell.

1. Invoke the **Shell** dashboard.
2. Select the top face of the model to remove it, as shown in Figure 8-34. This is the face that will be removed from the final model, leaving the specified thickness from the boundary of the selected face.
3. Enter the thickness value of the shell in the dimension edit box present on the dashboard.
4. Choose the **Feature Preview** button from the dashboard to preview the shell feature.
5. Choose the **Build feature** button from the **Shell** dashboard to exit it.

The shell is created on the selected face, as shown in Figure 8-35. The thickness of the shell is uniform on all faces of the model.

Figure 8-34 Face selected to remove   *Figure 8-35* Constant thickness shell feature created on the selected face

Advanced Modeling Tools-I

> **Note**
> *The thickness value entered can be positive or negative. If the value entered is positive, the material is removed, leaving the shell thickness inside the boundary of the selected face. But when the value entered is negative, the shell thickness is added outside the boundary of the selected face.*

Creating a Variable Thickness Shell

The variable thickness shell is a shell that has different thickness values assigned to adjacent faces. The following steps explain the procedure to create a variable thickness shell.

1. Invoke the **Shell** dashboard.
2. Select the top face of the model to remove it, as shown in Figure 8-36.
3. Choose the **References** tab to invoke the slide-down panel. In the slide-down panel, there are two collectors: **Removed surfaces** and **Non-default thickness**. The **Removed surfaces** collector shows the surface id of the face that you have selected to remove. On the other hand, the **Non-default thickness** collector shows the surfaces that you will select to create the variable thickness shell.
4. Click in the **Non-default thickness** collector and then select the adjacent faces shown in Figure 8-36. To select the second and successive faces, you need to use the CTRL+left mouse button. Now, you need to specify different thickness values with reference to the selected face.
5. Enter thickness values in the dimension edit boxes present on the right of the surfaces in the **Non-default thickness** collector or drag the white square to specify the thickness. Alternatively, click on the thickness dimension and enter the new values in the edit boxes displayed.

The shell is created on the selected faces with the thickness values assigned to them, see Figure 8-37.

Figure 8-36 Faces of the model selected for variable thickness and the top face to remove

Figure 8-37 Variable thickness shell

Figure 8-38 shows the model whose top surface is selected to be removed in order to create a shell. Figure 8-39 shows the model after shelling. Notice that the shell thickness is left on the selected face and the remaining material is removed.

Figure 8-38 Solid model

Figure 8-39 Model after shelling the top face

DATUM CURVES

Datum curves are useful in creation of advanced solid and surface features such as the sweep trajectories to create a sweep feature. A datum curve is considered as a feature and is displayed in the **Model Tree**. There are various tools and options to create a datum curve. You can choose the **Curve** button from the **Datum** toolbar to create a datum curve. Alternatively, you can choose the **Intersect**, **Project**, and **Wrap** options from the **Edit** menu to create a datum curve.

Creating a Datum Curve by Using the Curve Button

The **Curve** button is used to create datum curves. When you choose this button from the **Right Toolchest**, the **CRV OPTIONS** menu is displayed, as shown in Figure 8-40. The options in this menu are discussed next.

Thru Points

The **Thru Points** option creates a datum curve by selecting the existing datum points or vertices. The resulting datum curve may be a spline curve or can have a user-defined radius.

When you choose **Done** from this menu, the **CONNECT TYPE** menu will be displayed, as shown in Figure 8-41. The options in this menu are discussed next.

Figure 8-40 The CRV OPTIONS menu

Spline

The **Spline** option creates a datum curve in the form of a spline and passing through the selected datum points or vertices.

Single Rad

The **Single Rad** option creates a datum curve that has a constant radius at the bends. This option is called single radius because the system prompts you to specify a radius value at the bend. The bend is the location on the datum curve that lies between two datum points or vertices.

Advanced Modeling Tools-I

Multiple Rad

As the name suggests, the **Multiple Rad** option allows you to specify radius at every bend that occurs on a datum curve. Using this option, you can specify either the same radius that was specified at the previous bend or a new radius value.

Single Point

The **Single Point** option is used to select the datum points individually. If the datum points are created such that they are a single feature, then, all of them may be selected using this option.

Whole Array

The **Whole Array** option is used to select all datum points that act as a single feature.

Figure 8-41 The *CONNECT TYPE* menu

From File

The **From File** option is used to import a datum curve from IGES, VDA, *.ibl file formats. You can save a model that is in any of the above-mentioned formats and export the geometry in the form of a curve. When you open the exported file to create a datum curve, the geometry of the model is converted to a datum curve.

Use Xsec

The **Use Xsec** option is used to create a datum curve that has the geometry of an existing cross section. The creation of sections is discussed in Chapter 7.

From Equation

The **From Equation** option is used to create datum curves by defining equations using the coordinate systems. When you choose this option, you are prompted to select a coordinate system. Select the default coordinate system from the drawing area; the **SET CSYS TYP** menu is displayed, as shown in Figure 8-42.

You can choose the type of coordinate system from this menu. Choose the coordinate system depending on the equation you want to use to create a datum curve. If you choose the **Cartesian** option from the menu, the **rel.ptd - Notepad** window is displayed, as shown in Figure 8-43.

Figure 8-42 The *SET CSYS TYP* menu

Using this notepad, you can define the equations. The notepad shows the instructions that should be followed while writing an equation in the notepad. These instructions vary and depend on the type of coordinate system you have selected. After you have entered the equations in the notepad, save the file and then exit the notepad.

```
                    rel.ptd - Notepad
                   File  Edit  Format  View  Help
                   /* For cartesian coordinate system, enter parametric
                   equation
                   /* in terms of t (which will vary from 0 to 1) for x, y and
                   z
                   /* For example: for a circle in x-y plane, centered at
                   origin
                   /* and radius = 4, the parametric equations will be:
                   /*      x = 4 * cos ( t * 360 )
                   /*      y = 4 * sin ( t * 360 )
                   /*      z = 0
                   /*-----------------------------------------------------
```

Figure 8-43 The **rel.ptd-Notepad** *window*

Creating a Datum Curve in Spiral Shape

The following steps explain the procedure to create a spiral-shaped datum curve:

1. Choose the **Cylindrical** option from the **SET CSYS TYP** menu; the notepad is displayed. In the notepad the parametric equations to create a circle are given as follows:
   r = 4
   theta = t * 360
   z = 0
   In the above equations, the variable t varies from 0 to 1, r is the radius of the circle, and z is the third equation that is set equal to 0. Now, to understand the given equation of the circle, notice that the radius of the circle is given. The only value that is unknown is theta. The value of theta depends on the variable t. Therefore,
   when t = 0, theta = 0
   when t = 1/2, theta = 180 (semicircle)
   and when t = 1, theta = 360 (circle)
2. Enter the following parametric equation of the spiral curve below the dashed line in the notepad:
   IR = 8
   OR = 80
   TURNS = 10
   r = IR + t * (OR - IR)
   theta = t * 360 * TURNS
   z = 0
   In the above equations, the value of r is selected to vary because in the spiral curve, the value of r always increases from center (at center of spiral, r = 0). The internal radius of the spiral IR = 8, outer radius OR = 80, and number of turns TURNS = 10 are given.

Advanced Modeling Tools-I

3. Choose **File > Save** from the notepad and then exit the notepad.
4. Choose the **Preview** button from the **CURVE: From Equation** dialog box to preview the datum curve.
5. Choose **OK** from this dialog box; the spiral-shaped datum curve appears in the drawing area, as shown in Figure 8-44.

Figure 8-44 Spiral-shaped datum curve

Creating a Datum Curve by Sketching

The **Sketch** button is used to sketch a datum curve using the sketcher tools. This is the most commonly used option to create a datum curve and is drawn in the sketching environment. The sketched curves can consist of one or more sketched entities and of one or more open or closed loops, whereas the datum curves are restricted to a single curve of an open or closed loop.

Creating a Curve by Using the Intersect Option

The **Intersect** option can be invoked by choosing **Edit > Intersect** from the menu bar. This option is object action tool; this means that you need to select a datum plane and then invoke this option. The **Intersect** option creates a datum curve at the intersection of a face of the model and a datum plane, intersection of a face of the model and a quilt surface, intersection of a quilt surface and a datum plane. Note that you cannot create a datum curve at the intersection of two datum planes, two quilts, or two model faces using this option.

When you choose this option, the **Intersect** dashboard appears, as shown in Figure 8-45. You may need to choose the **Intersect** option twice to invoke the **Intersect** dashboard.

To create the ring on the circumference of the cylindrical feature, as shown in Figure 8-46, you need to create a datum curve that is on the circumferential surface of the cylindrical feature.

*Figure 8-45 The **Intersect** dashboard*

Figure 8-46 Ring on the circumference of the cylindrical feature

To create the datum curve that lies on the outer surface, follow these steps:

1. Select the datum plane that is intersecting with the circumferential surface of the cylinder.
2. Choose **Edit > Intersect** from the menu bar; the **Intersect** dashboard is displayed.
3. Choose the **References** tab to open the slide-down panel. In the **Surfaces** collector, the selected datum plane is displayed.
4. Use CTRL+left mouse button to select the top and bottom circumferential surfaces of the cylindrical feature, as shown in Figure 8-47.
5. Choose the **Build feature** button from the dashboard to exit the feature creation tool. The datum curve is created on the circumferential surface of the cylinder, as shown in Figure 8-48.

Figure 8-47 Selections made on the model

Figure 8-48 Datum curve created on the circumferential surface of the cylindrical feature

Advanced Modeling Tools-I

Creating a Curve by Using the Project Option

The **Project** option is used to project a selected or sketched entity on one or more planar or non-planar surfaces or datum planes. The projected datum curve forms a true projection of the selected or sketched entity on the specified surfaces. The dimensions of the original entity may distort while projecting.

Choose **Edit > Project** from the menu bar; the **Project** dashboard is displayed, as shown in Figure 8-49. The tools and options in this dashboard are discussed next.

*Figure 8-49 The **Project** dashboard*

Surfaces Collector

The **Surfaces** collector is used to select the surface on which you need to project the sketched or selected datum curve.

Direction Drop-down List

The **Direction** drop-down list is used to specify the method of projection of the datum curve on the receiving surface or plane. The two options available in this drop-down list are:

1. Along direction
2. Normal to surface

Along direction

This option projects the datum curve in a direction shown by the yellow arrow. To specify the direction of projection, select the default coordinate system, datum plane, edge, or surface. Figure 8-50 shows the top view of the projected datum curves that are overlapping. The datum curve that is selected to project on the receiving surface and the datum curve after projection are of same geometry. This is because, using the **Along direction** option, the true geometry is obtained after projection. Figure 8-51 shows the sketched datum curve after it has been projecting on a receiving surface. The curve is sketched on a datum plane that is parallel to the bottom face of the model.

Normal to surface

This option of projecting a datum curve projects the datum curve normal to the receiving surface. Figure 8-52 shows a datum curve selected to be projected on a receiving surface and the datum curve after projection. Figure 8-53 shows the sketched datum curve after it has been projecting on the receiving surface.

Figure 8-50 Top view of the projected datum curve

Figure 8-51 Projecting a datum curve along the specified direction

Figure 8-52 Top view of the projected datum curve

Figure 8-53 Projecting a datum curve normal to curve

References Tab

When you choose the **References** tab, a slide-down panel is displayed, as shown in Figure 8-54. This slide-down panel is used to select an existing datum curve to be projected or sketch a datum curve to project. The drop-down list in the slide-down panel lists two options, **Project chains** and **Project a sketch**. Using these options, you can project multiple chains or a sketch on a surface or face. These two options are discussed next.

Project chains

The **Project chains** option is used when the datum curve to project exists. Click in the **Chains** collector to make it green in color and then select the datum curve that you need to project. After selecting the datum curve, click in the **Surfaces** collector and select the receiving surface (plane or surface to project on to). Then you need to specify the direction of projection. Remember that if you are using the **Normal to surface** option, then you do not need to specify the direction of projection. The **Direction Reference** collector is displayed while selecting the **Along direction** option from the dashboard, whereas it does not appear while selecting the **Normal to surface** option.

Advanced Modeling Tools-I

Project a sketch
When you select the **Project a sketch** option from the drop-down list in the **References** slide-down panel, the slide-down panel appears, as shown in Figure 8-55.

Figure 8-54 The **References** tab slide-down panel with the **Project chains** option selected

Figure 8-55 The **References** tab slide-down panel with the **Project a sketch** option selected

Click on the **Sketch** collector and then select a curve or sketch to be projected or create a sketch that can be projected on the sketch. To create a new sketch, choose the **Define** button to invoke the **Sketch** dialog box and to select the sketch plane for the curve to be projected. After sketching, exit the sketcher environment and select the surface or plane on which the curve will be projected. If you are using the **Along direction** option to project the curve then you need to click in the **Direction Reference** collector to specify the direction of projection.

Creating a Curve by Using the Wrap Option
This option is used to create a datum curve by wrapping a sketched entity around a solid or a quilt. Choose **Edit > Wrap** from the menu bar, the **Wrap** dashboard is displayed, as shown in Figure 8-56. The tools and options in this dashboard are discussed next.

Figure 8-56 The **Wrap** dashboard

References Tab
When you choose the **References** tab, a slide-down panel is displayed, as shown in Figure 8-57. The **Define** button is used to invoke the **Sketch** dialog box that you can use to select the sketch plane and enter the sketcher environment to draw the curve.

Figure 8-57 The **References** tab slide-down panel

The **Destination** collector in the slide-down panel is used to select the object on which you need to wrap the curve.

Generally, if there is a single feature in the drawing area, then you do not need to select the object to wrap on. Pro/ENGINEER automatically wraps the selected curve or the sketched curve on the object. However, if you want to select a different object to wrap on then you can click in this collector to make it green in color and then select the object.

Options Tab

When you choose the **Options** tab, a slide-down panel is displayed, as shown in Figure 8-58.

The **Ignore intersection surface** check box when selected ignores any intersection surface and wraps the selected curve on the destination object.

The **Trim at boundary** check box when selected trims the extra portion of the curve that is beyond the boundary of the destination object.

*Figure 8-58 The **Options** tab slide-down panel*

Follow the steps given below to sketch and wrap a curve on the rectangular block, as shown in Figure 8-59. It is assumed that the rectangular block of dimension 20x20x50 exists.

1. Choose **Edit > Wrap** from the menu bar to invoke the **Wrap** dashboard.
2. Choose the **References** tab to invoke the slide-down panel.
3. Choose the **Define** button to invoke the **Sketch** dialog box.
4. Choose the datum plane that is passing through the center of the rectangular block as the sketch plane and then choose a reference for orienting the sketch plane.
5. After entering the sketcher environment, draw a line that starts from the bottom of the rectangular block. Its start point is aligned with the center of the rectangular block and with the bottom edge. The endpoint of the line is at a distance of 1000 and at a height of 50 from the bottom of the rectangular block, see Figure 8-60.
6. Place a user-defined coordinate system at the start point of the line.
7. Exit the sketcher environment; the sketched curve is automatically wrapped on the circumference of the cylinder.
8. Choose the **Build feature** button to exit the **Wrap** dashboard.

Figure 8-59 Curve wrapped on the rectangular block

Figure 8-60 Sketch of the curve to be wrapped

Advanced Modeling Tools-I

CREATING DRAFT FEATURES

In Pro/ENGINEER, drafts are created on existing surfaces. They are created by rotating the selected surface by a certain angle. One of the applications of draft features is in moulds and castings where a taper is required to separate the casting from the mould or vice versa. To create a draft, choose the **Draft** button from the **Engineering Features** toolbar; the **Draft** dashboard will be displayed, as shown in Figure 8-61. The options in this dashboard are discussed next.

*Figure 8-61 The **Draft** dashboard*

References Tab

When you choose the **References** tab, the slide-down panel is displayed, as shown in Figure 8-62. The options in this slide-down panel are discussed next.

Draft surfaces Collector

The **Draft surfaces** collector is selected by default. If this collector is clear by default, click in this collector and then select the surface to which you need to add a draft angle. The maximum draft angle that can be added to a surface is 30-degree.

*Figure 8-62 The **References** tab slide-down panel*

Draft hinges Collector

The **Draft hinges** collector is used to select the hinge of the draft surface. The hinge that you select can be an edge, a surface, an axis, or a datum plane. The draft surface is pivoted on the hinge that you select. In other words, the draft surface is rotated about the hinge. The hinge that you select need not intersect the draft surface. Figure 8-63 shows the draft surface and the hinge selected to create the draft and the resultant draft surface is shown in Figure 8-64.

Figure 8-63 Parameters needed to create a basic draft feature

Figure 8-64 Resultant draft feature

Pull direction Collector

The **Pull direction** collector is used to specify the direction of rotation of the draft surface. The direction of pull is shown by the direction of the yellow arrow. Generally, when you select the hinge, the pull direction is selected by default. If the pull direction shown by the yellow arrow is not that is desired, click in the **Pull direction** collector and then select the pull direction. You can change the direction of the yellow arrow by choosing the **Flip** button.

Split Tab

When you choose the **Split** tab, a slide-down panel is displayed, as shown in Figure 8-65. The options in this slide-down panel are discussed next.

*Figure 8-65 The **Split** tab slide-down panel*

Split options Drop-down List

The options in this drop-down list are used to split the surface selected to draft. Using these options the selected surface gets split into two surfaces and different draft angles can be applied to both the surfaces. The options available in the **Split options** drop-down list are discussed next.

No split

This option is used when you do not want to split the surface selected to give the draft angle.

Split by draft hinge

This option is available only when you have selected the hinge for the draft surface. When you select this option, the selected surface is divided into two surfaces at the location on the surface where the hinge intersects it. Figure 8-66 shows the surface that is split into two surfaces at the hinge.

Figure 8-66 Split at draft hinge

Advanced Modeling Tools-I

Split by split object
This option, when chosen activates the **Split object** collector and the **Define** button. This option is used to split the surface selected to draft by drawing a sketch. In this type of split, surface gets split into two surfaces and the sketch defines the profile of the split. Figure 8-67 shows the parameters that you need to define to create a draft by using the split by split object option. Figure 8-68 shows the draft created on the cylindrical surface.

Figure 8-67 Split by split object

Figure 8-68 Resultant model

Side options Drop-down List
The options in this drop-down list are used to specify how to apply the draft once the surface has been split. The options in this drop-down list are discussed next.

Draft sides independently
The two sides of the draft surface that are formed when the surface is split can be given different draft angles. When you choose this option, the edit boxes appear on the **Draft** dashboard. You can enter the values of the draft angle in these edit boxes.

Draft sides dependently
Using this option, you can apply same draft angle on both sides of the split surface.

Draft first side only
Using this option you can apply the draft angle only to the first side of the split surface.

Draft second side only
Using this option you can apply the draft angle only to the second side of the split surface.

Angles Tab
Choose the **Angles** tab from the **Draft** dashboard after you have specified some angle for draft surface. When you choose this option, a slide-down panel is displayed, as shown in Figure 8-69.

*Figure 8-69 The **Angles** tab slide-down panel*

In Pro/ENGINEER, you can create constant as well as variable angle drafts.

Constant Angle Drafts
By default, Pro/ENGINEER creates a constant angle draft feature. This means, the same draft angle is applied to the surface that you have selected.

Variable Angle Drafts
When you apply more than one value of the draft angle to the selected surface, it is called variable angle draft. You need to apply the variable angle draft after you have selected the hinge, the pull direction, and the draft surface.

To create the draft surface shown in Figure 8-70, follow the steps given next. It is assumed that you have created the base feature of the model, as shown in Figure 8-71.

Figure 8-70 Draft feature on the model

Figure 8-71 Base feature

1. Invoke the **Draft** dashboard and click in the first collector from left.
2. Select the top face of the base feature. Notice that in the **Pull direction** collector the direction of pull is selected automatically. Reverse the pull direction by choosing the Reverse pull direction button available on the right of the second collector.
3. Hold the right mouse button to invoke the shortcut menu shown in Figure 8-72.
4. Choose the **Draft Surfaces** option from the shortcut menu and select the cylindrical surface of the base feature to add the draft angle. The drag handle appears on the base feature; you can use it to vary the angle of the draft. The draft angle value of **1** also appears in the drawing area. Also notice the white ball that appears on the edge of the top face (face selected as hinge).
5. Bring the cursor on the white ball and hold the right mouse button to invoke the shortcut menu shown in Figure 8-73.

Figure 8-72 Shortcut menu

Figure 8-73 Shortcut menu

Advanced Modeling Tools-I

6. Choose the **Add Angle** option from the shortcut menu. Notice that now there are two white balls on the edge of the top face. On the first ball the value of **0.5** appears. This value varies from one end of the face to the other end. This value represents the location of the point that you need to use for reference in order to apply the draft angles.
7. Again bring the cursor to any one of the two white balls and invoke the shortcut menu.
8. Choose the **Add Angle** option from the shortcut menu. Another point is added with a location value on the edge.
9. Add eleven such points for locations varying from **0** to **1**.
10. After adding eleven points, double-click on any of the location value that is present in the drawing area; an edit box appears. Enter **0** in this edit box. Similarly, locate all remaining ten points and increment them by 0.1. Figure 8-74 shows the model after relocating all eleven points on the edge.
11. Double-click on the value of the angle that corresponds to the location **0**. The edit box appears, enter a value of **15**.
12. Double-click on the value of the angle that corresponds to the location **0.1** (these values appear above the model and have a default value of 1.0). The edit box appears; enter a value of **5**. Similarly, vary the angle at other locations. Every alternate location should have an angle of **15**. Figure 8-75 shows the preview of the model after modifying the values of the angle at all eleven locations.

Figure 8-74 Location points on the edge

Figure 8-75 Location points with modified angle values

13. After modifying the values of the angle at all locations, choose the **Feature Preview** button from the **Draft** dashboard; the model appears, as shown in Figure 8-76.
14. The model after mirroring the geometry and then shelling with the top and bottom faces removed is shown in Figure 8-77.

Options Tab

When you choose this tab, a slide-down panel is displayed, as shown in Figure 8-78. The options in this slide-down panel are discussed next.

Figure 8-76 Model with the draft feature

Figure 8-77 Model of the lamp shade

Exclude loops Collector

This collector is used to select a surface to which you do not want to add a draft angle. When you select a surface to add a draft angle, all loops that are on the surface are applied the same draft angle. However, using this collector you can select the loop to which you do not want to add a draft angle.

Figure 8-79 shows the surface selected to add a draft angle. You will notice that the surface of the cylindrical feature is selected. If you continue with the draft feature creation and exit the **Draft** dashboard, the draft is created, as shown in Figure 8-80.

Figure 8-78 The **Options** tab slide-down panel

Figure 8-79 Surface for draft

Figure 8-80 The draft created

To exclude the face of the cylindrical feature from the loop, click in the **Exclude loops** collector to turn it green in color. Now, bring the cursor close to the face of the cylindrical feature. The boundary of the face is highlighted in cyan. Select the face to exclude it from the loop.

Advanced Modeling Tools-I

Figure 8-81 shows the draft surface after excluding the face of the cylindrical feature from the loop. Note that the model should be a single feature then only the **Extrude Loops** collector will be active.

Draft tangent surfaces Check Box

When the **Draft tangent surfaces** check box is selected, the draft is applied to the surfaces tangent to the selected surface. In Figure 8-82, the surface shown is selected to add the draft angle. Since the **Draft tangent surfaces** check box is selected, all surfaces tangent to the selected surface and other surfaces are automatically selected. Figure 8-83 shows the resultant model with the draft feature.

Figure 8-81 *Draft after excluding the face of the cylindrical feature*

Figure 8-82 *Single surface selected to draft*

Figure 8-83 *Draft applied to all tangent surfaces*

Extend intersect surfaces Check Box

When this check box is selected, the draft surface extends in the direction of the feature it intersects. Figure 8-84 shows the example of the draft that intersects with the adjacent feature and extends outside the edge of the feature at the bottom. Figure 8-85 shows the feature when the draft surface gets extended.

Figure 8-86 shows another example of extended draft feature. The following steps explain in brief the procedure to create the pencil-shaped model. It is assumed that you have created the model shown in Figure 8-87. The initial model shown is an octagon on the top of which a cylinder is created.

1. Invoke the **Draft** dashboard and select the cylindrical surface to apply draft to it.
2. Select the top face of the cylindrical feature as the hinge. The yellow arrow points in the upward direction.
3. Choose the **Options** tab; a slide-down panel is displayed. Select the **Extend intersect surfaces** check box in it. Also, make sure that the **Draft tangent surfaces** check box is selected.

Figure 8-84 Draft created without selecting the ***Extend intersect surface*** radio button

Figure 8-85 Draft created by selecting the ***Extend intersect surface*** radio button

Figure 8-86 Example of draft created by selecting the ***Extend intersect surface*** radio button

Figure 8-87 Model initially created

4. Use the drag handle and increase the draft angle up to the vertex of the octagon. This can be easily done by viewing the preview of the draft surface as you increase the angle. You may even have to use the edit box present on the dashboard to enter the small increase in angle value. Remember that you will get the desired shape of the intersect only when the draft surface intersects the vertices of the octagonal feature.

Properties Tab

When you choose the **Properties** tab, the slide-down panel displays the feature id of the feature you have created.

Advanced Modeling Tools-I

TUTORIALS

Tutorial 1

In this tutorial, you will create the model shown in Figure 8-88. This figure also shows the top, sectioned front, and right of the solid model with dimensions. The hidden lines are suppressed for clarity. **(Expected time: 45 min)**

Figure 8-88 Top, sectioned front, right, and isometric views of the model.

The following steps are required to complete this tutorial:

Examine the model and determine the number of features in it. The model is composed of six features, refer to Figure 8-88.
a. Create the base feature, refer to Figures 8-89 through 8-91.
b. Create the shell feature of given thickness, refer to Figure 8-92.
c. Create the third and fourth extrude features on the two ends of the swept feature respectively, refer to Figures 8-93 and 8-94.
d. Create the counterbore hole on the third and fourth features, refer to Figures 8-95 and 8-96.
e. Pattern the counterbore holes, refer to Figure 8-97.

When the Pro/ENGINEER session starts, the first task is to set the working directory. This is being the first tutorial of this chapter, you need to create a folder *c08* if it has not been created already and set it as the Working Directory.

Starting a New Object File

1. Start a new part file and name it *c08tut1*.

   The three default datum planes as well as the **Model Tree** are displayed in the drawing area.

Invoking the Sweep Option

You need to use the menu bar present on the top of the screen to invoke the **Sweep** option.

1. Choose **Insert > Sweep > Protrusion** from the menu bar; the **SWEEP TRAJ** menu and the **PROTRUSION: Sweep** dialog box are displayed.

2. Choose the **Sketch Traj** option from the **SWEEP TRAJ** menu; you are prompted to define a sketching plane.

Selecting the Sketching Plane

You need to sketch the trajectory of the sweep feature on the **FRONT** datum plane.

1. Select the **FRONT** datum plane as the sketching plane; a red arrow points in the direction of viewing the sketching plane; the **DIRECTION** submenu is displayed.

2. Choose **Okay** from the **DIRECTION** submenu; the **SKET VIEW** submenu is displayed.

3. Choose **Top** from this submenu and select the **TOP** datum plane.

   After you have selected the planes for orientation, the system takes you to the sketcher environment.

Drawing the Trajectory

From the model, it is evident that the trajectory for the sweep feature is a quarter circle.

1. Choose the black arrow on the right of the **3-Point / Tangent End** button from the **Sketcher Tools** toolbar; a flyout is displayed. Next, choose **Center and Ends** from the flyout.

2. Draw an arc such that the center of the arc lies at the intersection of the **TOP** and **RIGHT** datum planes, as shown in Figure 8-89. As you specify the center of the arc, the cursor snaps to the point of intersection of the two planes. Now, draw the arc and exit this tool.

   The endpoints of the arc are automatically aligned with the **TOP** and **RIGHT** datum planes. You will notice that an arrow is attached at the start point of the trajectory. This arrow points in the direction of sweep.

Advanced Modeling Tools-I

Tip: *To change the start point on the trajectory, select the point where you want the start point. When the point is highlighted in red color, hold the right mouse button to invoke a shortcut menu. From the shortcut menu, choose the **Start Point** option.*

Modifying the Dimensions of the Trajectory

When drawing the arc, a weak radial dimension is assigned to it automatically. You need to modify the dimension as per your requirement.

1. Double-click on the dimension and modify the radial dimension to 26, as shown in Figure 8-90. You will notice the sketch refits on the screen.

2. Choose the **Done** button.

Figure 8-89 The sketch of the required trajectory

Figure 8-90 Dimension for the arc

Drawing the Section for Sweep

After choosing the **Done** button, the direction of viewing is modified such that the start point of the trajectory becomes normal to the screen. Also, a yellow colored cross of infinite length appears on the screen. This cross consists of two perpendicular lines of infinite length. The intersection point of these lines is the start point of the trajectory. The center of the circle should lie at the intersection of these lines. You are also prompted to draw the cross-section for the sweep.

1. Choose the **Center and Point** button from the **Sketcher Tools** toolbar and create a circle such that the center of the circle lies at the intersection of the two infinite perpendicular lines.

   Now, when you draw the circle, the cursor snaps to the intersection point of the cross.

Tip: *When you enter the sketcher environment to define a section for the sweep trajectory, a yellow-colored cross is displayed. The yellow cross determines the orientation of the section with respect to the available trajectory.*

Modifying the Dimensions of the Section

1. Choose the **One-by-One** button from the **Sketcher Tools** toolbar. Next, double-click on the dimension and modify the diameter dimension to 29.

   The sketch gets modified and refits into the screen.

2. Choose the **Done** button.

Previewing the Swept Feature

The sweep feature is completed, and now you can preview it.

1. Choose the **Preview** button from the **PROTRUSION: Sweep** dialog box.

2. Choose the **Named View List** button from the **View** toolbar; a flyout is displayed. Next, choose the **Default Orientation** option from the flyout; the model orients in the drawing area, as shown in Figure 8-91.

   You can use the middle mouse button to change the orientation of the model.

3. Now, choose the **OK** button from the **PROTRUSION: Sweep** dialog box to exit it.

Creating the Shell Feature

The sweep feature is completed. Now, you need to can create the next feature, called shell feature.

Note
*Instead of using the **Shell** option, two concentric circles can be drawn while drawing the section for the sweep feature in order to obtain the desired hollow feature. Alternatively, the **Sweep > Thin Protrusion** option can be used to obtain the same hollow feature. In this tutorial, you will use the **Shell** option.*

1. Choose the **Shell** button from the **Engineering Features** toolbar; the **Shell** dashboard is displayed. Also, you are prompted to select the surfaces to be removed.

2. Select one end surface of the swept feature and then by using CTRL+left mouse button, select the other end surface. The two selected surfaces are highlighted in red.

3. Enter **4** as the thickness value of the shell in the dimension edit box present on the **Shell** dashboard and then press ENTER.

4. Choose the **Build feature** button to create the shell feature and exit the **Shell** dashboard.

   The default trimetric view of the shell feature is shown in Figure 8-92. You can use the middle mouse button to view the model from various directions.

Advanced Modeling Tools-I

Figure 8-91 Trimetric view of the model

Figure 8-92 Shell feature

Creating Extrude Features

The next feature is a protrusion feature with a depth of 5 and is created at both ends of the swept feature. While drawing the circle for the sketch of the extrude feature, remember to use the edge of the shell in order to create a hole in the extruded feature as well.

1. Choose the **Extrude** button from the **Base Features** toolbar; the **Extrude** dashboard is displayed.

2. Choose the **Placement** tab from the dashboard to display the slide-down panel and invoke the **Sketch** dialog box. Select the top face of the swept feature as the sketching plane.

3. Select the **RIGHT** datum plane and then select the **Right** option from the **Orientation** drop-down list. Then enter the sketcher environment.

4. Draw the sketch of the extrude feature and then apply constraints and dimensions to it, as shown in Figure 8-93.

5. Create the extruded feature having a depth extrusion of 5. Similarly, create the next extruded feature at the other end of the swept feature.

    The protrusion features created at both ends of the sweep feature are shown in Figure 8-94.

Creating the Hole Feature

After creating the extruded features at both ends of the swept feature, you need to create the counterbore holes. One hole is to be created on each extruded surface and then they will be patterned on individual planes separately to create the remaining three instances.

1. Choose the **Hole** button from the **Engineering Features** toolbar; the **Hole** dashboard is displayed.

Figure 8-93 Sketch with dimensions and constraints

Figure 8-94 Two extruded features created at both the ends of the sweep feature

2. Choose the **Use standard hole profile as drill hole profile** button from the **Hole** dashboard; two buttons are added to the dashboard.

3. Next, choose the **Adds counterbore** button from the dashboard to add counterbore to the hole. Also, choose **Drill up to next surface** from the depth flyout.

4. Choose the **Shape** tab from the dashboard to enter the counterbore parameters of the hole, as shown in Figure 8-95.

5. Select the top face of the third extruded feature for the placement of hole. The preview of the hole appears in the drawing area.

   Now, you need to specify the placement parameters for the hole. For this purpose, refer to Figure 8-88 and look for dimensions that can help in placing the hole. The two edges are used to dimension the hole.

6. Choose the **Placement** tab and click in the **Offset References** collector to turn it green.

7. Select the front edge and then use CTRL+left mouse button to select the left edge of the third feature for specifying linear references. The hole is at a distance of 5 from both the edges. The default dimensions appear on the hole.

   You can also drag the green handles and place them on the two edges.

8. Double-click on the dimensions and modify the linear distances to 5.

9. Choose the **Build feature** button from the **Hole** dashboard; a hole is created on the selected face.

10. Create another hole on the fourth feature by following the same procedure as discussed above.

Advanced Modeling Tools-I

The isometric view of the model that is completed until now is shown in Figure 8-96.

Figure 8-95 Parameters for the counterbore hole set under the **Shape** tab

Figure 8-96 One hole each on the two extruded features

Creating the Pattern of the Holes

After one hole is placed on each of the two faces, you need to pattern the holes.

1. Select the hole feature from the **Model Tree** or from the drawing area and hold the right mouse button to invoke the shortcut menu. Choose the **Pattern** option from the shortcut menu; the **Pattern** dashboard is displayed.

2. Specify the required parameters in the **Pattern** dashboard and create the pattern of the hole.

   Similarly, create the pattern of the hole on the other extruded feature as well. The default trimetric view of the complete model is shown in Figure 8-97.

Saving the Model

1. Choose the **Save** button from the **File** toolbar and then save the model.

Note
*As discussed in the earlier chapters, the model tree is used to get an idea about the order of feature creation. In the **Model Tree**, the id numbers displayed in front of the features may be different while creating the features.*

Tip: *You can also create a counterbore hole by sketching its profile. To do so, choose the **Use sketch to define drill hole profile** button from the dashboard. Next, choose the **Activates Sketcher to create section** button to activate the sketcher environment.*

*The same sketch can be used for the second hole from the **In Session** folder.*

Figure 8-97 The trimetric view of the complete model

Tutorial 2

In this tutorial, you will create the model of the pencil shown in Figure 8-98 and then change the color of the pencil. Figure 8-99 shows the front, section, and the detail views of the model.   **(Expected time: 30 min)**

Figure 8-98 Solid model of the pencil

The following steps are required to complete this tutorial:

Examine the model and determine the number of features in it. The model is composed of six features, refer to Figure 8-98.
a. Create the base feature, refer to Figures 8-100 and 8-101.
b. Create the second feature that is a cylinder on the top face of the base feature, refer to Figure 8-102.
c. Create the draft feature, refer to Figure 8-103.

Advanced Modeling Tools-I 8-41

Figure 8-99 Top, front, sectioned, and detail views of the model

d. Create the tip of the pencil that is a revolved feature, refer to Figures 8-104 and 8-105.
e. Create the tail end of the pencil that is again a revolved feature, refer to Figures 8-106 and 8-107.
f. Write the text on the pencil by using the sketched datum curves, refer to Figures 8-108 and 8-109.

Make sure that the *c08* folder is the current Working Directory.

Starting a New Object File
1. Start a new part file and name it as *c08tut2*.

The three default datum planes are displayed in the drawing area.

Creating the Base Feature
The base feature of the pencil is a protrusion feature in which a octagon is extruded to a depth of 1500.

1. Choose the **Extrude** button from the **Base Features** toolbar to display the **Extrude** dashboard and invoke the **Sketch** dialog box.

2. Select the **TOP** datum plane as the sketching plane.

3. Select the **RIGHT** datum plane from the drawing area and then select the **Right** option from the **Orientation** drop-down list, only if these options are not selected by default.

4. Draw the sketch of octagon by using the **Palette** button and then apply constraints and dimensions to it, as shown in Figure 8-100.

5. Exit the sketcher environment and extrude the sketch to a depth of 1500. The base feature created looks like, as shown in Figure 8-101.

Figure 8-100 Sketch of the octagonal feature

Figure 8-101 Base feature created by extruding the octangular sketch

Creating the Second Feature

The second feature is a cylindrical feature. You need to draw the feature on the top face of the base feature.

1. Choose the **Extrude** button from the **Base Features** toolbar; the **Extrude** dashboard is displayed. Invoke the **Sketch** dialog box and select the top face of the base feature as the sketching plane.

2. Enter the sketcher environment and draw the sketch of the cylinder. Note that the diameter of the circle is 120. Next, exit the sketching mode.

3. After exiting the sketcher environment, extrude the circle to a depth of 210. The model after creating the cylindrical feature is shown in Figure 8-102.

Creating the Draft Feature

You need to create the draft feature on the cylindrical surface and the draft surface to intersect he base feature. This is because when the draft surface intersects the base feature and is extended, the required shape is obtained at the intersecting edge.

1. Choose the **Draft** button from the **Engineering Features** toolbar; the **Draft** dashboard is displayed.

2. Select the cylindrical surface of the cylinder to apply draft to it.

Advanced Modeling Tools-I

3. Choose the **References** tab to invoke the slide-down panel. Click the **Draft hinges** collector and then select the top face of the cylindrical feature as the hinge; the yellow arrow points in the upward direction.

4. Choose the **Reverse pull direction** button on the right of the **Pull direction** collector to change the direction of the arrow so that it points downward.

5. Choose the **Options** tab to invoke the slide-down panel and then select the **Extend intersect surfaces** check box.

6. Enter **15.3** as the angle value in the edit box present on the **Draft** dashboard.

7. Choose the **Build feature** button from the **Draft** dashboard to complete the draft feature, as shown in Figure 8-103 shows the complete draft feature.

Figure 8-102 Model after creating the cylindrical feature

Figure 8-103 Model after creating the draft feature

Creating the Fourth Feature

The fourth feature is the tip of the pencil, which is a revolved feature.

1. Choose the **Revolve** button from the **Base Features** toolbar; the **Revolve** dashboard is displayed.

2. Invoke the **Sketch** dialog box and select the **FRONT** datum plane as the sketching plane.

3. After entering the sketcher environment, draw the sketch and then apply constraints and dimensions to it, as shown in Figure 8-104. Make sure that the geometry centerline is drawn. Exit the sketcher environment.

   The angle of revolution is 360-degree by default.

5. Choose the **Build feature** button to complete the feature creation. The default trimetric view of the model after creating the fourth feature is shown in Figure 8-105.

Figure 8-104 Sketch for the tip of the pencil

Figure 8-105 Model after creating the tip

Creating the Fifth Feature

The fifth feature, which is a revolve feature, is the bottom portion of the pencil.

1. Choose the **Revolve** button from the **Base Features** toolbar; the **Revolve** dashboard is displayed.

2. Invoke the **Sketch** dialog box and then select the **FRONT** datum plane as the sketching plane.

3. After entering the sketcher environment, draw the sketch and then apply constraints and dimension to it, as shown in Figure 8-106. Make sure that the centerline is also drawn.

4. Exit the sketcher environment; the angle of revolution is set to 360-degree by default.

5. Choose the **Build feature** button to complete the feature creation. The default trimetric view of the model after creating the fifth feature is shown in Figure 8-107.

Figure 8-106 Sketch with dimensions and constraints

Figure 8-107 Model after creating the top of the pencil

Advanced Modeling Tools-I

Writing the Text

1. Choose the **Sketch** button from the **Right Toolchest**; the **Sketch** dialog box is displayed.

2. Select the front face of the base feature as the sketching plane.

3. After entering the sketcher environment, create the text by using the **Text** button. Figure 8-108 shows the text written with dimensions.

4. Choose the **Done** button to exit the sketcher environment.

   The model after creating the text is shown in Figure 8-109.

Figure 8-108 Text with dimensions *Figure 8-109* Model after creating the text

Changing the Colors

You can apply colors and appearances to the surfaces in Pro/ENGINEER. Remember that the colors you apply are saved with the model and remain on the model until you clear them.

1. Choose the down arrow on the right of the **Appearance Gallery** button from the **View** toolbar in the **Top Toolchest**; a flyout is displayed.

2. Choose **More Appearances** from the flyout; the **Appearance Editor** window is displayed. Next, enter **Lead** in the **Name** edit box in this window.

3. Choose the swatch displayed in front of **Color** in the **Properties** area; the **Color Editor** is displayed. Set the RGB values to **0**. The color will be black. You need to apply this color to the tip of the pencil. You can also set the values of **Shine**, **Highlight**, **Reflection**, and **Transparency** to **0**.

   Note
   *You can also select an appearance icon from the **My Appearances** or **Library** area. Next, invoke the **Appearance Manager** to adjust the values as required. You can also add or remove textures to colors.*

4. Choose the **OK** button from the **Appearance Editor**; the cursor is modified to paint brush. Also, the **Select** message box is displayed and you are prompted to select surfaces to apply colors.

5. Select the **Surface** option from the filter drop-down list in the Status Bar.

6. Select the tip of the pencil and press the middle mouse button; the tip of the pencil turns black.

7. Similarly, assign other colors to other entities.

Saving the Model
1. Choose the **Save** button from the **File** toolbar and save the model.

> **Note**
> *Colors are not a feature of the model; therefore, they will not appear in the **Model Tree**.*

Tutorial 3

In this tutorial, you will create the blend feature shown in Figure 8-110. The two views of the blend feature are shown in Figure 8-111 with dimensions. After creating the model, you will redefine it such that the straight blending is changed into a smooth blending.

(Expected time: 30 min)

Figure 8-110 Isometric view of the model

Figure 8-111 Top and front views of the model

Advanced Modeling Tools-I

The following steps are required to complete this tutorial:

Examine the blend feature and determine the number of sections in this feature. The blend consists of four sections, refer to Figure 8-111.
a. Create the sketch for the first section of the blend feature, refer to Figure 8-112.
b. Create the sketch for the second section of the blend feature, refer to Figure 8-113.
c. Create the sketch for the third section of the blend feature.
d. Create the sketch for the fourth section, refer to Figure 8-114. Define the depth values between section numbers 1 and 2, 2 and 3, and 3 and 4.
e. Redefine the model to change the straight blending into a smooth blending, refer to Figure 8-116.

Make sure that the *c08* folder is the current Working Directory.

Starting a New Object File
1. Start a new part file and name it as *c08tut3*.

Three default datum planes are displayed in the drawing area.

Invoking the Blend Option
1. Choose **Insert > Blend > Protrusion** from the menu bar; the **BLEND OPTS** menu is displayed.

2. Choose **Parallel > Regular Sec > Sketch Sec > Done** from the **BLEND OPTS** submenu; the **ATTRIBUTES** menu is displayed and you are prompted to choose the **Straight** or **Smooth** option from this menu.

3. Choose **Straight > Done** from the **ATTRIBUTES** menu.

A **Smooth** blend will be created while redefining the model using the same sections that will be used to create the given model.

Selecting the Sketch Plane
1. Select the **FRONT** datum plane as the sketching plane. A red arrow points in the direction of feature creation and you are prompted to specify the direction of feature creation.

2. Choose **Okay** from the **DIRECTION** submenu displayed on selecting the sketching plane; the **SKET VIEW** submenu is displayed.

3. Choose **Top** from this menu and select the **TOP** datum plane present in the drawing area.

Drawing the First Section
The first section is a rectangle of 290x190 units.

1. Draw the sketch of the rectangular section and then add constraints and dimensions to it, as shown in Figure 8-112.

Figure 8-112 First rectangular section with dimensions

After drawing the rectangular section, you need to toggle the section and draw the next section.

Note
*While drawing the sections for the blend feature, the start point is very important. The start point should be similar to those shown in the figures 8-112, 8-113, and 8-114. If the start point is not at the desired point then select the point where you need the start point. Hold the right mouse button to invoke a shortcut menu, and then choose the **Start Point** option from it.*

Toggling the Section

Toggling of a section is required to sketch the next section. In this tutorial, four sections are used to create the required model; therefore, you need to toggle next section after you have finished drawing one section.

1. Choose **Sketch > Feature Tools > Toggle Section** from the menu bar. You can also hold the right mouse button to display the shortcut menu and choose the **Toggle Section** option from the shortcut menu.

When you choose **Toggle Section**, the previous section becomes inactive and appears gray in color.

Tip: *To toggle a section, simply right-click when you are in the selection mode. The selection mode in the sketcher environment can be invoked by choosing the **One-by-One** button.*

Drawing the Next Section

The next section is a circle.

1. Draw the sketch of the circular section, refer to Figure 8-113. Modify the diameter of the circle to 145.

Advanced Modeling Tools-I

As discussed earlier, the number of entities per section must be equal in a blend feature. Since a circle is a single entity, it should be divided at four points.

Dividing the Circular Section

The circular section should be divided at four points because the rectangle and square each have four entities. When you divide a circle at four points, the number of entities becomes four.

1. Choose the black arrow on the right of the **Delete Segment** button; a flyout is displayed. Choose the **Divide** button from the flyout.

2. Select the circle at four points, as shown in Figure 8-113.

As you select the points on the circle to divide it, some weak dimensions appear on the circle. Next, you need to apply constraints on the four points that were selected to divide the circle.

Applying Constraints on the Four Points

1. Choose the **Vertical** button from the **Sketcher Tools** toolbar and select the two divisional points on the left of the circle to lie in a vertical line. Similarly, select the two points on the right to apply the constraint.

2. Now, choose the **Horizontal** constraint button and select the two division points on the upper half and the lower half to lie in a horizontal line.

3. Modify the vertical dimension of the upper right division point, as shown in Figure 8-113. After the section is completed, the two sections with dimensions will be similar to the sections shown in Figure 8-113.

Figure 8-113 Two completed sections

4. Now, toggle the section and create the next section. The next section to be drawn is a square. After drawing the square section, draw the circular section. Divide the circular section into four entities similar to section 2 and then constrain and dimension it.

Figure 8-114 shows all completed sections with dimensions.

Figure 8-114 All four completed sections before giving depth

Note
In Figure 8-114, note the direction of the start points indicated by arrows. These arrows are important to avoid a twisted feature.

Applying Depth to the Sections

After the sketches of all sections are completed, you need to specify the depth value between each section. The dimensions for depth between each section can be referred to from Figure 8-111.

1. Choose the **Done** button from the **Sketch** mode; the **Message Input Window** appears and you are prompted to enter depth for section 2.

2. Enter **175** in the **Message Input Window** and press ENTER.

    Similarly, the **Message Input Window** appears again and you are prompted to enter depth for section 3. Enter **100** for section 3 and **100** for section 4.

Previewing the Blend Feature

The blend feature is completed and now it can be previewed.

1. Choose the **Preview** button from the **PROTRUSION: Blend, Parallel, Regular Sections** dialog box that is displayed at top right corner of the window.

2. Choose the **Default Orientation** option from the **Named View List** flyout; the model orients in the drawing area, as shown in Figure 8-115.

Advanced Modeling Tools-I

Figure 8-115 Trimetric view of the model

3. Now, choose the **OK** button from the **PROTRUSION: Blend, Parallel, Regular Sections** dialog box; the trimetric view of the model is displayed in the drawing area.

Saving the Model

1. Choose the **Save** button from the **File** toolbar and save the model.

Redefining the Blend Feature

After saving the straight blend feature, you need to redefine this feature so that it is converted to a smooth blend.

1. Select the model in the drawing area; the edges of the model turn red in color.

2. Press and hold down the right mouse button in the drawing area until a shortcut menu is displayed.

3. Choose the **Edit Definition** option from the shortcut menu; the **PROTRUSION: Blend, Parallel, Regular Sections** dialog box is displayed.

4. Select the **Attributes** option under the **Element** tab; the **Attributes** option is highlighted.

5. Choose the **Define** button from this dialog box; the **ATTRIBUTES** menu is displayed.

6. Choose **Smooth > Done** from the **ATTRIBUTES** menu.

7. Now, choose the **OK** button; the straight blend feature is converted into a smooth blend, as shown in Figure 8-116.

Figure 8-116 Smooth blend feature

Tutorial 4

In this tutorial, you will create the model of a tap shown in Figure 8-117. All dimensions for the three sections are shown in the figure. **(Expected time: 30 min)**

This model will be created by using the general blend. In general blend, each section should have a coordinate system. A coordinate system helps in the alignment of sections. Each section is dimensioned with its coordinate system.

The following steps are required to complete this tutorial:

Examine the model and determine the number of sections in the blend feature, refer to Figure 8-117.
a. Create the first section for the blend feature, refer to Figure 8-118.
b. Create the second section for the blend feature, refer to Figure 8-119.
c. Create the third section for the blend feature, refer to Figure 8-120.
d. Create the Shell feature, refer to Figure 8-112.

Starting a New Object File
1. Start a new part file and name it as *c08tut4*.

   The three default datum planes appear in the drawing area if they were not turned off in the previous tutorial.

Invoking the Blend Option
You need to create the model by using the general type of blend.

1. Choose **Insert > Blend > Protrusion** from the menu bar; the **BLEND OPTS** submenu is displayed.

Advanced Modeling Tools-I

Figure 8-117 Sectioned, left, front, and top views of the model

2. Choose **General > Regular Sec > Sketch Sec > Done** from this submenu; the **ATTRIBUTES** menu is displayed.

3. Choose **Smooth > Done** from the **ATTRIBUTES** menu; you are prompted to select a sketching plane.

4. Select the **TOP** datum plane and then choose **Okay** from the **DIRECTION** submenu; the **SKET VIEW** submenu is displayed. Choose the **Right** option from it and select the **RIGHT** datum plane; the system takes you to the sketcher environment.

Drawing the Sketch of the First Section of the Blend

The blend consists of three sections. The dimension values for the second section are half of the dimensions of the first section and the dimensions for the third section are one-third of the dimensions of the first section.

1. Draw the sketch of the first section.

2. Choose **Sketch > Coordinate System** from the menu bar; a reference coordinate system is attached to the cursor. Place the coordinate system at the intersection of the two planes by using the left mouse button; the coordinate system is automatically aligned with the two datum planes.

3. Apply constraints and modify the dimensions of the sketch, as shown in Figure 8-118.

4. Choose the **Done** button from the **Right Toolchest**; the **Message Input Window** is displayed and you are prompted to enter the x-axis rotating angle for section 2.

5. Enter **0** and press ENTER; you are prompted to enter the y-axis rotating angle for section 2. Enter **50** and press ENTER; you are prompted to enter the z-axis rotating angle for section 2. Enter **0** and press ENTER.

The sketcher environment is invoked and you are allowed to draw the sketch for the second section. Notice that the datum planes are not displayed even if they are turned on as they are not required now. The use of datum planes is to reference the sketch you draw. But, the second section that you will draw has already been referenced to the first section. Hence, the datum planes are not displayed and you can draw the next section anywhere in the drawing area.

Drawing the Sketch for the Second Section

1. Draw the sketch for the second section, insert a reference coordinate system, apply constraints and dimensions to the sketch, and modify the dimensions, as shown in Figure 8-119.

Figure 8-118 Sketch with dimensions and constraints for the first section

Figure 8-119 Sketch with dimensions and constraints for the second section

2. After completing the sketch, choose the **Done** button; the **Confirmation** message box is displayed and you are prompted to specify if you want to continue to the next section.

3. Choose **Yes** because you need to draw the third section of the blend feature. The **Message Input Window** is displayed and you are prompted to enter the x-axis rotating angle for section 3.

Advanced Modeling Tools-I

4. Enter **0** and press ENTER; you are prompted to enter the y-axis rotating angle for section 3. Enter **30** and press ENTER; you are prompted again to enter the z-axis rotating angle for section 3. Enter **0** and press ENTER.

The sketcher environment is invoked and you are allowed to draw the sketch for the third section.

Drawing the Sketch of the Third Section

1. Draw the sketch of the third section, insert a reference coordinate system, apply constraints and dimension to the sketch, and modify the dimensions, as shown in Figure 8-120.

2. After completing the sketch, choose the **Done** button; the **Confirmation** message box is displayed and you are prompted to specify if you want to continue to the next section.

3. Choose **No** because all sections needed to create the blend feature are completed.

The **Message Input Window** is displayed and you are prompted to enter the depth for section 2.

Specifying the Depths between Sections

1. Enter **100** in the **Message Input Window** and press ENTER. This depth is the distance between the first section and the second section. Now, you are prompted to enter the depth for section 3.

2. Enter **300** in this window and press ENTER. This depth is the distance between the second section and the third section.

The blend feature is complete and now you can preview it.

3. Choose the **Preview** button from the **PROTRUSION: Blend, General, Regular Sections** dialog box; the preview of the model is displayed. Now, choose **OK** to create the sweep feature. Next, choose the **Default Orientation** button from the **Named View List** button; the default trimetric view of the blend feature is created, as shown in Figure 8-121.

Creating the Shell Feature

1. Choose the **Shell** button from the **Engineering Features** toolbar; the **Shell** dashboard is displayed and you are prompted to select the surfaces to be removed from the part.

2. Select the one end surface of the swept feature by using the left mouse button and then select the other end surface using CTRL+left mouse button. The two selected surfaces are highlighted red in color.

Figure 8-120 Sketch with dimensions and constraints for the third section

Figure 8-121 The default trimetric view of the blend feature

3. Enter **3** as the thickness value of the shell in the dimension edit box present on the **Shell** dashboard and press ENTER.

4. Choose the **Build feature** button to create the shell feature.

   The default trimetric view of the shell feature is shown in Figure 8-122. You can use the middle mouse button to change the orientation of the model.

Figure 8-122 Trimetric view of the model for Tutorial 4

Saving the Model
1. Choose the **Save** button from the **File** toolbar and save the model.

Advanced Modeling Tools-I

Self-Evaluation Test

Answer the following questions and then compare them to those given at the end of this chapter:

1. The types of Protrusion in Pro/ENGINEER are different from those available for Cut. (T/F)

2. The **Cut** option is available only if a base feature exists. (T/F)

3. If the value of shell thickness is negative then the shell thickness is added outside the boundary of the face selected for shelling. (T/F)

4. When a trajectory is closed, the **Add Inn Fcs** and **No Inn Fcs** options are displayed. (T/F)

5. The procedure to create a sweep cut feature is the same as that of a sweep protrusion. (T/F)

6. The **Sweep** option extrudes a section along a _____.

7. The cross-section of a swept feature remains _____ throughout the sweep.

8. The sketching plane that you select becomes _____ to the screen when you draw the trajectory.

9. An _____ section and an open trajectory are not possible.

10. A quilt is a _____ feature.

Review Questions

Answer the following questions:

1. What is the maximum permissible angle for the rotation of sections in a **Rotational** blend?
    (a) 120 (b) 90
    (c) 180 (d) 45

2. What is the maximum possible draft angle that can be applied to a solid in Pro/ENGINEER?
    (a) 10-degree (b) 30-degree
    (c) 60-degree (d) 90-degree

3. What is the minimum number of sections required for a blend feature?
    (a) one (b) two
    (c) three (d) None of these

4. A trajectory of a sweep feature can be modified independent of the geometry of the section. (T/F)

5. In which of the following types of blend, sections are translated and rotated about the x, y, and z axes?

   (a) **Parallel** (b) **Rotational**
   (c) **General** (d) None of these

6. You can create a cut feature by using the **Sweep** option. (T/F)

7. You need to create a coordinate system while creating a **Rotational** or **General** blend, . (T/F)

8. In **General** blend, the section is rotated about the y-axis of the coordinate system. (T/F)

9. The **Rotational** blend option is the same as the **Parallel** blend option, if the rotational blend angle entered between the two sections equals to 0-degree. (T/F)

10. There must be an equal number of vertices in each section for blending. (T/F)

Exercises

Exercise 1

Create the foundation bolt shown in Figure 8-123. The dimensions of the foundation bolt are shown in Figure 8-124.

(Expected time: 30 min)

Figure 8-123 Model for Exercise 1

Figure 8-124 Dimensions for Exercise 1

Advanced Modeling Tools-I

Exercise 2

In this exercise, you will create the model shown in Figure 8-125. Figure 8-126 shows the top, sectioned front, and the right views of the solid model with dimensions. Note that the hidden lines are not displayed for clarity. **(Expected time: 45 min)**

Figure 8-125 Model for Exercise 2

Figure 8-126 Top, front, and right-side views of the model

Exercise 3

In this exercise, you will create the model of a soap case shown in Figure 8-127. Figure 8-128 shows the top, sectioned front, right, and detail views with dimensions.

(Expected time: 45 min)

Figure 8-127 Isometric view of the soap case

Figure 8-128 Top, sectioned front, right, and detail views of the soap case

Advanced Modeling Tools-I 8-61

Exercise 4

In this exercise, you will create the model of a carburetor cover shown in Figure 8-129. Figure 8-130 shows the sectioned top view, sectioned front view, sectioned right-side view, and the sectioned bottom view with dimensions. **(Expected time: 45 min)**

Figure 8-129 Isometric view of the carburetor cover

Hints

1. Create the sketch of the base feature that includes a rectangle of 125x50 and then extrude it.
2. Choose **Insert > Sweep > Cut** from the menu bar.
3. Select the **FRONT** datum plane as the sketching plane for sketching a trajectory.
4. Sketch a trajectory by using the **3-Point / Tangent End** button from the **Sketcher Tools** toolbar. The start point and the endpoint of the arc should be at a distance of 28 units from the bottom of the base feature, and the radius of the arc should be 100.
5. Exit the sketcher environment by using the **Done** button.
6. Choose the **Merge Ends** option from the **ATTRIBUTES** menu.
7. Again, enter the sketching environment to create the section for the sweep feature. Choose the **3-Point / Tangent End** button from the **Sketcher Tools** toolbar. The arc created should be tangent to the reference lines, and the endpoints of the arc should be aligned with the edges of the base feature and should have a radius of 35.
8. Choose **OK** from the **CUT: Sweep** dialog box.
9. Choose **Insert > Blend > Cut** from the menu bar.
10. Choose **Done** from the **BLEND OPTS** submenu.
11. Choose **Done** from the **ATTRIBUTES** menu.
12. Select the bottom face of the base feature as the sketching plane.
13. Choose **Okay** from the **DIRECTION** submenu.
14. Choose the **TOP** option from the **SKET VIEW** submenu and select the **RIGHT** datum plane.

Figure 8-130 Top, sectioned front, sectioned right, and sectioned bottom views of the carburetor cover

15. Create an ellipse of Rx12 and Ry8 by using the **Ellipse** button.
16. Choose **Sketch > Feature Tools > Toggle Section** from the menu bar.
17. Create another ellipse of Rx24 and Ry16.
18. Exit the sketcher environment by using the **Done** button.
19. Choose **Okay** from the **DIRECTION** menu.
20. Choose **Done** from the **DEPTH** menu, enter the depth value of cut in the **Message Input Window**, and then press ENTER.
21. Mirror the cut feature about the **RIGHT** datum plane.
22. Create a round feature on all edges except the edges enclosing the bottom planar surface of the base feature.
23. Choose the **Shell** option from the menu bar. Remove the bottom face of the base feature.
24. Using the bottom face of the base feature as the sketching plane, create three protrusion features that are the supporting structures for the screws. Extrude these features by using the **Extrude up to next surface** button.
25. Using the **Hole** dashboard, create a hole in the protrusion feature created earlier.

Answers to Self-Evaluation Test
1. F, **2.** T, **3.** T, **4.** T, **5.** T, **6.** trajectory, **7.** constant, **8.** parallel, **9.** open, **10.** surface.

Chapter 9

Advanced Modeling Tools-II

Learning Objectives

After completing this chapter, you will be able to:
• *Use various advanced options for creating complex models.*
• *Create features using the Variable Section Sweep option.*
• *Create features using the Swept Blend option.*
• *Create features using the Helical Sweep option.*
• *Create features using the Sect to Srfs option.*
• *Create features using the Srfs to Srfs option.*

ADVANCED FEATURE CREATION TOOLS

Pro/ENGINEER facilitates the design process with some advanced options that you can use to create complex features with greater ease. All these options are available in the **Insert** menu present in the menu bar.

Variable Section Sweep Option

The **Variable Section Sweep** option can be invoked from the **Insert** menu in the menu bar or you can choose the **Variable Section Sweep** button from the **Base Features** toolbar. This option is used to create a sweep feature in which the section of the sweep feature varies along the shape of the trajectories. This feature is created using more than one trajectory. The section is swept along the origin trajectory and the variation of the section is controlled by the X-trajectory and other trajectories. You can sketch the sweep trajectory using various sketcher tools. You can also select a previously created entity as the trajectory for sweep. The **Variable Section Sweep** option is available for both protrusion and cut options.

The following points should be remembered while creating a variable section sweep feature.

1. You should define the origin trajectory to which the section is normal.

2. After creating the origin trajectory, you have to create an X-trajectory that defines the horizontal vector of the section.

3. You can also define additional trajectories to facilitate the creation of a complex profile.

4. When you draw the section for the variable section sweep feature, the section should be aligned to the endpoints of the X-trajectory and the other trajectories. If the section is not aligned, then the feature will be created without following the trajectory path and will be similar to a feature created using the **Sweep** option.

When you choose this option, the **Variable Section Sweep** dashboard will be displayed, as shown in Figure 9-1. Remember that you should have the trajectories present in the drawing area so that they can be selected for the creation of the variable section sweep feature. This is because you cannot sketch the trajectories by using the **Variable Section Sweep** dashboard. However, you can draw the trajectories using the **Sketch** button. As mentioned earlier, the process of creating a datum feature when a feature creation tool is active is called datum-on-the-fly. The options in the **Variable Section Sweep** dashboard are discussed next.

Figure 9-1 The **Variable Section Sweep** dashboard

References Tab

When you choose the **References** tab, the slide-down panel will be displayed, as shown in Figure 9-2. The options available in this slide-down panel are discussed next.

Advanced Modeling Tools-II

Trajectories Collector

This collector is used for selecting the trajectories by clicking in the collector to activate it. It also lists the selected trajectories. The first trajectory that you select is by default listed as the origin trajectory.

Note that you need to first select the normal and X trajectories and then draw the sketch of the section. This is because the sketch plane will be oriented only if you have defined the normal trajectory. Also, since the sketch needs to pass through the endpoints of the X-trajectory, it is better to define the X-trajectory before drawing the section. This way you will have the reference point from which the sketch needs to pass.

*Figure 9-2 The **References** tab slide-down panel*

This collector has three columns and the selected trajectories are listed in the rows. The first column is **X**. The check box in this column, when selected, converts the trajectory to the X trajectory. The second column is **N**. The check box in this column, when selected, converts the trajectory in that row to the normal trajectory. Remember that only one trajectory can be a normal trajectory and only one trajectory can be a X trajectory. The third column is **T**. There are two check boxes available in this column and in each row. All these check boxes are gray in color. When you select the check box, the name of the trajectory is filled in that cell and the value T=0 appears on the trajectory in the drawing area. This value is displayed on both the ends of the trajectory. Initially, this value is 0. When you enter a value, the point of alignment of the section with the trajectory varies.

>**Section plane control Drop-down List**. The options in this list are used to specify the direction of the section in which it starts sweeping.
>
>>**Normal To Trajectory Option**. When you use the **Normal To Trajectory** option to create the variable sweep, the section is normal to the origin trajectory and is swept along the X trajectory. The section should be aligned with the X trajectory to sweep along it. If the section is not aligned with the X trajectory then this option works similar to the **Sweep** option and the section is swept along the origin trajectory only. Figure 9-3 shows the two trajectories and the section used to create the variable section sweep feature. Figure 9-4 shows the resulting variable section sweep feature.
>>
>>Now, in Figure 9-5, the X trajectory and the origin trajectory are interchanged. The resulting Variable Section Sweep feature is shown in Figure 9-6. Note the difference in the sweep features. In Figure 9-5, the section is normal to the selected origin trajectory and the curve is selected as the origin trajectory.

Figure 9-3 Two trajectories and a section

Figure 9-4 Variable section sweep feature

Figure 9-5 Two trajectories and a section

Figure 9-6 Resulting variable section sweep feature

Normal To Projection Option. The **Normal To Projection** option is used to create a variable section sweep feature in which the section is normal to the two-dimensional (2D) projection of trajectories. The swept section is normal to the origin trajectory and the variation in the section is controlled by the X-trajectory and the other trajectories. When you use this option, you need to select or sketch an origin trajectory, an X-trajectory, other trajectories if required, and the direction of projection. The direction of projection can be specified by using the default coordinate system.

Figure 9-7 shows the origin trajectory and the X trajectory. These two trajectories are used to create the variable section sweep feature shown in Figure 9-8.

Constant Normal Direction Option. The **Constant Normal Direction** option is used to create a variable section sweep in which the section to be swept is normal to an edge, normal to the selected plane, or an axis.

Advanced Modeling Tools-II

Figure 9-7 Trajectories and section

Figure 9-8 Resulting variable section sweep feature

When you select the origin trajectory and then select the **Constant Normal Direction** option, you are required to select or create a plane, an edge, a curve, an axis, or a coordinate system to define the constant normal direction. Select a datum plane and then sketch the section. The system takes you to the sketcher environment and automatically orients the sketch plane such that it is normal to the selected direction. Figure 9-9 shows the origin trajectory, the section, and the normal vector of the datum plane to which the section is perpendicular. Figure 9-10 shows the section that is normal to the origin trajectory. This figure explains the difference between the **Normal To Trajectory** option and the **Constant Normal Direction** option.

Figure 9-9 Sweep feature with section perpendicular to the datum plane

Figure 9-10 Sweep feature with section normal to the origin trajectory

Options Tab

When you choose the **Options** tab, the slide-down panel is displayed, as shown in Figure 9-11. The options in this slide-down panel are discussed next.

Figure 9-11 The **Options** slide-down panel

Variable section
This radio button is used to create a sweep feature whose section varies along the trajectory.

Constant section
This radio button is used to create a sweep feature whose section is constant throughout the trajectory. The feature created using this radio button is similar to the feature created using the **Sweep** option.

Sketch placement point Collector
By default, **Origin** is selected as the start point of the section. This is the reason you draw the section at the start point of the trajectory. However, if you click in this collector to activate it and then select a datum point that lies on the origin trajectory, the section will start from that point. This means that the selected datum point becomes the start point of the trajectory.

Note
*The options available on the **Variable Section Sweep** dashboard are the same as those available on the **Extrude** dashboard. Using these options, you can specify the type of feature you want to create such as solid, surface, or thin feature.*

Swept Blend

The **Swept Blend** tool is a combination of sweep and blend. The sweep feature needs a trajectory along which the section is swept. Similarly, to create a parallel blend, you need to have more than one sections, which have the same number of entities. These sections are then blended, which result in the blend feature. The combination of both these features results in a swept blend feature.

Choose **Insert > Swept Blend** from the menu bar; the **Swept Blend** dashboard will be displayed, as shown in Figure 9-12. It is recommended that you should have the trajectories present in the drawing area so that they can be selected for the creation of the swept blend feature. This is because using the options available in the **Swept Blend** dashboard, you cannot sketch the trajectories. However, you can draw curves that can be used as trajectories by using the **Sketch** button when the **Swept Blend** dashboard is active. The options in the swept blend dashboard are discussed next.

*Figure 9-12 The **Swept Blend** dashboard*

References Tab

When you choose the **References** tab, the slide-down panel will be displayed, as shown in Figure 9-13. The options available in slide-down panel are discussed next.

Advanced Modeling Tools-II

Trajectories Collector

This collector is used for selecting the trajectories. The trajectories that you select will be listed in this collector. The trajectory that you select is listed as the origin trajectory by default (also referred to as normal trajectory). Note that you need to select the origin trajectory and then draw the sketch of the section. This is because the sketch plane will be oriented only if you have defined the origin trajectory. This way you will have the reference point through which the sketch needs to pass. This collector has two columns and the selected trajectories are listed in rows. The first column is **X**. The second column is **N**. Remember that only one trajectory can be a normal trajectory.

Figure 9-13 The **References** tab slide-down panel

Section plane control Drop-down List

The options in this list are used to specify the direction of the section in which the sketch starts sweeping.

Normal To Trajectory Option

This option is used to sweep the section normal to the origin throughout the trajectory.

Normal To Projection Option

The **Normal To Projection** option is used to create a swept blend in which the section to be swept is normal to the 2D projection of the origin trajectory. On selecting this option, you will be prompted to select the direction to which the section is perpendicular. Select the required reference; the selected reference will be displayed in the **Direction reference** collector.

Constant Normal Direction Option

The **Constant Normal Direction** option is used to create a swept blend in which the section is perpendicular to the normal trajectory and is swept along the origin trajectory.

Figure 9-14 shows three rectangular sections. These three sections are connected to each other by connecting their vertices through a trajectory. The shaded view of the model after shelling is shown in Figure 9-15.

Figure 9-16 shows two sections and a trajectory that are used to create the feature shown in Figure 9-17. Note that the number of entities should be same in all sections.

Figure 9-14 Three sections in the swept blend   *Figure 9-15 Shaded view of the feature*

Figure 9-16 Two sections and a trajectory   *Figure 9-17 Resulting feature*

Sections Tab

When you choose the **Sections** tab, the slide-down panel will be displayed, as shown in Figure 9-18. The options in the slide-down panel are discussed next.

Selected Sections

This option is used to select the section that is used to create a swept blend.

Sketched Sections

This option is used to sketch the section that is used to create the swept blend.

*Figure 9-18 The **Sections** tab slide-down panel*

Advanced Modeling Tools-II

Options Tab

When you choose the **Options** tab; the slide-down panel will be displayed, as shown in Figure 9-19. The **Cap ends** check box, if selected, caps both the end faces of the feature. The **No blend control** radio button is selected by default. This radio button along with the **Set perimeter control** radio button allows you to control the related parameters of the swept blend feature.

*Figure 9-19 The **Options** tab slide-down panel*

> **Note**
> If you invoke the **Swept Blend** dashboard, the **Create a Surface** button is chosen by default. To create a solid swept blend feature, choose the **Create a Solid** button from the dashboard. Also, in the **Options** tab slide-down panel, the **Cap ends** check box will not be enabled if the **Create a Solid** button is chosen.

Helical Sweep

The **Helical Sweep** option is used to create helical sweep features. You have to define a trajectory that will specify the shape and height of the helix, a pitch value, and a cross-section to create a helical feature using this option. The distance of the trajectory from the center line defines the radius of the helical path and the length of the trajectory defines the length of the sweep feature.

The main use of this option is to create the helical springs and threads. When you choose an option from the **Helical Sweep** option from the **Insert** menu in the menu bar, the **ATTRIBUTES** menu is displayed, as shown in Figure 9-20. The menu options are discussed next.

Figure 9-21 shows the parameters to be defined for the helical sweep and Figure 9-22 shows the resulting helical sweep feature.

*Figure 9-20 The **ATTRIBUTES** menu*

Figure 9-21 Sweep trajectory, sweep section, and axis of rotation to create a helical feature

Figure 9-22 The resulting helical sweep feature

Constant

The **Constant** option is used to create a helical feature with constant pitch, as shown in Figure 9-23.

Variable

The **Variable** option is used to create a helical feature of varying pitch. While using this option, you have to define the start pitch and the end pitch. You can also define a pitch between the start point and the endpoint of the helix. This pitch value between the endpoint and the start point is specified by creating points on the sweep trajectory. The helical sweep feature with variable pitch is shown in Figure 9-24.

Figure 9-23 Helical sweep feature with constant pitch

Figure 9-24 Helical sweep feature with variable pitch

The brief procedure to create a variable pitch spring is discussed next.

1. Choose **Insert > Helical Sweep > Protrusion** from the menu bar and then choose **Variable > Thru Axis > Right Handed > Done** from the **ATTRIBUTES** menu.
2. Select the sketching plane and then orient it.
3. Draw the sketch of the sweep trajectory and the center axis.
4. Add points on the sweep trajectory by choosing the **Point** button. These points will be used later on to vary the pitch of the spring.
5. Exit the sketcher environment; you will be prompted to enter the pitch at the start point. After entering the pitch value at the start, you will be prompted to specify the pitch value at the end.
6. After specifying the pitch value at the two ends, a subwindow is displayed with a pitch graph.
7. Select a point on the trajectory from the main window; you are prompted to enter the pitch value at that point.
8. Enter the pitch value at the selected point. Similarly, specify the pitch values at other points that were defined on the trajectory while sketching it. It should be noted that a specified pitch value can be modified by selecting the **Change Value** option from the **DEFINE GRAPH** submenu. As you specify the pitch values to the points, the graph in the subwindow also changes.

Advanced Modeling Tools-II 9-11

9. After all pitch values are entered, choose the **Done/Return** option from the **DEFINE GRAPH** submenu and the **Done** option from the **GRAPH** menu. Now, enter the sketcher environment to draw the section of the spring.
10. Draw the section of the spring at the intersection of the two infinite yellow dotted lines.
11. Exit the sketcher environment and choose **OK** from the **PROTRUSION** dialog box.

Note
You can use any geometric entity such as spline, line, or arc to create the sweep trajectory.

Thru Axis
The **Thru Axis** option is used to create a helical feature around an axis.

Norm To Traj
The **Norm To Traj** option is used to create a helical feature perpendicular to the sketched trajectory.

Right Handed
The **Right Handed** option is used to create a helical feature in which the section is swept in the counterclockwise direction from the start sketch.

Left Handed
The **Left Handed** option is used to create a helical feature in which the section is swept in the clockwise direction from the start sketch.

Blend Section To Surfaces
The **Blend Section To Surfaces** option is used to blend a selected set of tangential surfaces with a sketched contour. You can invoke this option by choosing **Insert > Advanced > Blend Section To Surfaces** from the menu bar. The contour sketched to create the feature using this option must be closed. This option can be used to create a surface or a solid feature. Figure 9-25 shows the section to be blended with the selected set of tangential surfaces and Figure 9-26 shows the resulting blended feature.

Figure 9-25 Highlighted set of tangential surfaces and the contour sketch

Figure 9-26 Feature created using the **Blend Section To Surfaces** option

Blend Between Surfaces

The **Blend Between Surfaces** option is used to create a blending between two curved quilts, two curved solid surfaces, or a combination of both. The curved surfaces may be revolved features or spheres. You can invoke this option by choosing **Insert > Advanced > Blend Between Surfaces** from the menu bar. Figure 9-27 shows the two spheres to be blended and Figure 9-28 shows the resulting blended feature created using this option.

Figure 9-27 *The two spheres to be blended*   *Figure 9-28* *Resulting blended feature*

Figure 9-29 shows the two curved features to be blended and Figure 9-30 shows the resulting blended feature created using this option.

Figure 9-29 *The two curved features to be blended*   *Figure 9-30* *Resulting blended feature*

TUTORIALS

Tutorial 1

In this tutorial, you will create the model shown in Figure 9-31. This figure also shows the sectioned top, front, right-side, and isometric views of the model. **(Expected time: 45 min)**

Advanced Modeling Tools-II   9-13

Figure 9-31 Sectioned-top, front, right-side, and isometric views of the model

The following steps are required to complete this tutorial:

Examine the model and determine the number of features in it. The model is composed of five features, refer to Figure 9-31.

a. Create the first feature as a set of datum curves that will be drawn on the **FRONT** datum plane, refer to Figures 9-32 through 9-34.
b. The second feature is the datum curve that will be drawn on the **RIGHT** datum plane, refer to Figure 9-35.
c. Create the variable section sweep, refer to Figures 9-36 through 9-38.
d. Create the round feature, refer to Figures 9-39 and 9-40.
e. Create the shell feature of thickness 2, refer to Figures 9-41 and 9-42.

Make sure that the required working directory is selected.

Starting a New Object File
1. Start a new part file and name it as *c09tut1*.

The three default datum planes are displayed in the drawing area.

Creating the Trajectories

In this section, you need to draw the datum curves that will be selected as trajectories to create the variable section sweep feature. After selecting the sketching plane, draw the sketch for the origin trajectory and dimension it. Then, you need to draw the sketch for the X trajectory on the same plane and dimension it. The X trajectory defines the horizontal vector of a section. If the section is aligned with the X trajectory, the section varies along the path of the X trajectory. Similarly, two additional trajectories will be drawn to guide the section throughout the sweep.

1. Choose the **Sketch** button from the **Datum** toolbar; the **Sketch** dialog box is displayed.

2. Select the **FRONT** datum plane from the drawing as the sketching plane.

3. Select the **TOP** datum plane from the drawing area and then select the **Top** option from the **Orientation** drop-down list. Next, choose the **Sketch** button from the **Sketch** dialog box.

4. Once you enter the sketcher environment, create the sketch of the origin trajectory. The origin trajectory is a straight line segment aligned to the **RIGHT** datum plane and its start point is aligned to the **TOP** datum plane. The sketch of the origin trajectory is shown in Figure 9-32.

Note
In the sketcher environment, you will draw all three datum curves because they are on the same datum plane.

*You are drawing the datum curves as individual features because you cannot sketch the trajectories using the tools available in the **Variable Section Sweep** dashboard.*

5. After the sketch of the origin trajectory is complete, draw the sketch of the X trajectory. The X trajectory is drawn using three arcs. It is recommended that you start the sketch from the top arc. After drawing the first arc, dimension it and then modify its dimension.

6. Draw the second arc and then modify the dimension, as shown in Figure 9-33.

7. Next, draw the third arc. As evident from the sketch of the X trajectory, the center points of the bottom and the second arcs are aligned horizontally.

8. Create the sketch of the third trajectory, as shown in Figure 9-34. This trajectory is created using a single arc.

9. After the sketch is complete, choose the **Done** button to exit the sketcher environment.

10. Similarly, create another trajectory on the **RIGHT** datum plane and keep the **TOP** datum plane at the left. The sketch of the trajectory is shown in Figure 9-35.

11. After the sketch is complete, choose the **Done** button to exit the sketcher environment.

Advanced Modeling Tools-II 9-15

Figure 9-32 Sketch with dimension of the origin trajectory

Figure 9-33 Sketch with dimensions of the X trajectory

Figure 9-34 Sketch with dimensions of the third trajectory

Figure 9-35 Sketch with dimensions of the additional trajectory

12. Choose the **Default Orientation** option from the **Named View List** flyout in the **Top Toolchest** to view the trajectories that you have created, as shown in Figure 9-36. This view gives a better display of trajectories in 3D space.

Creating the Variable Section Sweep Feature

The four trajectories that will create the variable section sweep have been created. Now, you need to invoke the feature creation tool and select these trajectories to create the feature.

1. Choose the **Variable Section Sweep** button from the **Base Features** toolbar; the **Variable Section Sweep** dashboard is displayed.

2. Choose the **References** tab to invoke the slide-down panel. Select the origin trajectory that was the first datum curve drawn.

3. Use CTRL+left mouse button to select the X trajectory (second datum curve). Note that as you are selecting the trajectories, they are being listed in the **Trajectories** collector.

4. Use CTRL+left mouse button to select the remaining two trajectories. Select the check box under the X column for **Chain 1** row. This makes the trajectory that you select second in the row as the X trajectory.

5. Now, choose the **Create or edit sweep section** button from the dashboard to enter the sketcher environment.

6. Draw the closed sketch of the section and apply the dimensions, as shown in Figure 9-37.

Figure 9-36 Default view of the four trajectories   *Figure 9-37 Sketch of the section with dimensions*

Note that the section is aligned to the start points of all the trajectories that are displayed by crosses. The cursor will automatically snap to these points as you move it close to these points. In order to vary the section with the trajectories, it is necessary to align the section with the trajectories.

7. After the sketch is complete, choose the **Done** button to exit the sketcher environment.

The preview of the variable section sweep feature is displayed in the drawing area.

8. Choose the **Sweep as solid** button from the dashboard if the preview shows a surface feature.

9. Choose the **Build feature** button from the dashboard. Now, you need to hide the datum curves.

10. Choose the **Layers** button from the **Top Toolchest**. In the Navigator, the layers of the current model are displayed. Right-click on the **PRT_ALL_CURVES** to invoke the shortcut menu.

11. From the shortcut menu, choose the **Hide** option. Regenerate the model, if needed. All datum curves in the model will disappear.

Advanced Modeling Tools-II

The variable section sweep feature is completed, as shown in Figure 9-38. You can use the middle mouse button to orient the feature, as shown in the figure.

Creating the Round Feature

Now, you need to create round on the edges of the base feature.

1. Choose the **Round** button from the **Engineering Features** toolbar; the **Round** dashboard is displayed.

2. Select the edges shown in Figure 9-39. Remember that you need to use CTRL+left mouse button to select more than one edge.

Figure 9-38 Variable section sweep feature

Figure 9-39 Edges to be selected to round

3. Enter **20** in the dimension edit box present on the dashboard. Choose **Build feature** from the dashboard. The base feature after creating the round is shown in Figure 9-40.

Creating the Shell Feature

Now, you need to create the shell and remove the front and bottom faces of the base feature.

1. Choose the **Shell** button from the **Engineering Features** toolbar; you are prompted to select the surfaces to be removed.

2. Select the surfaces, as shown in Figure 9-41. Remember that to select more than one face you need to use the CTRL+left mouse button.

3. Enter **2** in the dimension edit box. Then, choose the **Build feature** button from the dashboard.

The model after creating the shell feature is shown in Figure 9-42.

Figure 9-40 Model after creating the round

Figure 9-41 Surfaces selected to be removed

Saving the Model

You need to save the model because you may need it later.

1. Choose the **Save** button from the **File** toolbar and save the model.

Figure 9-42 Final model after shelling

Tutorial 2

In this tutorial, you will create the solid model of a Upper Housing of a motor blower assembly shown in Figure 9-43. Figure 9-44 shows the left-side view, top view, front view, and the sectioned left-side view of the model. **(Expected time: 1 hr)**

The following steps are required to complete this tutorial:

Examine the model and determine the number of features in it. The model is composed of ten features, refer to Figures 9-43 and 9-44.
a. Create the base feature, refer to Figures 9-45 and 9-46.
b. Create the swept blend feature in which the section is normal to the origin trajectory, refer to Figures 9-47 through 9-51.
c. Create the round feature of radius 1.5, refer to Figures 9-52 and 9-53.
d. Create the round of radius 0.5, refer to Figures 9-54 and 9-55.
e. Create the shell feature of thickness 0.25, refer to Figure 9-56.
f. Create an extruded cut, refer to Figures 9-57 and 9-58.

Advanced Modeling Tools-II

Figure 9-43 Solid model of the Upper Housing

Figure 9-44 Left-side view, top view, front view, and the sectioned left-side view of the model

g. Create another extruded cut, refer to Figures 9-59 and 9-60.
h. Create the eighth feature as an extruded feature, refer to Figures 9-61 and 9-62.
i. Create a mirror copy of the eighth feature, refer to Figure 9-63.
j. Create the hole feature, refer to Figure 9-64, and pattern it, refer to Figure 9-65.

Starting a New Object File

1. Start a new part file and name it as *c09tut2*. Also, set the template to **inlbs_part_solid**.

   The three default datum planes and the **Model Tree** are displayed in the drawing area.

Creating the Base Feature

To create the sketch for the base feature, you first need to select the sketching plane for the base feature. In this model, you need to draw the base feature on the **RIGHT** datum plane.

1. Choose the **Extrude** button from the **Base Features** toolbar. Invoke the **Sketch** dialog box.

2. Select the **RIGHT** datum plane as the sketching plane.

3. Select the **TOP** datum plane from the drawing area and then select the **Top** option from the **Orientation** drop-down list.

4. Choose the **Sketch** button from the **Sketch** dialog box to enter the sketcher environment.

5. Once you enter the sketcher environment, create the sketch of the base feature and apply the required dimensions, as shown in Figure 9-45.

6. After the sketch is complete, choose the **Done** button to exit the sketcher environment.

   The **Extrude** dashboard gets activated and the **Extrude from sketch plane by specified depth value** button is chosen by default.

7. Choose the **Extrude on both sides of sketch plane by half the specified depth value in each direction** button from the depth flyout.

8. Enter the depth **8** in the dimension edit box present in the **Extrude** dashboard. Choose the **Build feature** button from the **Extrude** dashboard.

   The base feature is completed. The default trimetric view of the base feature is shown in Figure 9-46.

Creating the Trajectories for Swept Blend

You can use the **Sketch** button to create the sketch for the trajectories of the swept blend feature before or after invoking the **Swept Blend** dashboard. However, it is recommended that you create the trajectory before invoking the **Swept Blend** dashboard.

1. Choose the **Sketch** button from the **Datum** toolbar; the **Sketch** dialog box is displayed.

2. Choose the **Use Previous** button from the **Sketch** dialog box to enter the sketcher environment.

Figure 9-45 Sketch of the base feature

Figure 9-46 Default trimetric view of the base feature

3. Draw the sketch, as shown in Figure 9-47, and exit the sketcher environment.

Figure 9-47 Sketch of the origin trajectory

Creating the Swept Blend Feature

1. Choose **Insert > Swept Blend** from the menu bar; the **Swept Blend** dashboard is displayed.

2. Choose the **References** tab to display the slide-down panel.

3. Select the trajectory from the drawing area. Note that as you select the trajectory from the drawing area, it is added in the **Trajectories** collector. Also note that the first trajectory you select from the drawing area is considered as the normal trajectory.

4. Next, choose the **Sections** tab to display the slide-down panel. Select the start point of the arc as the start point for creating the first cross-section; the **Sketch** button is enabled in the **Sections** slide-down panel. Choose the **Sketch** button to enter the sketcher environment.

6. After entering the sketcher environment, create the sketch for the first cross-section, as shown in Figure 9-48.

7. Choose the **Done** button to exit the sketcher environment.

8. The **Swept Blend** dashboard is enabled and is displayed above the drawing area. Now, choose the **Insert** button from the **Sections** tab slide-down panel and select the second point on the trajectory which is at a distance of 8.15 from the **FRONT** datum plane. Choose the **Sketch** button from the **Sections** slide-down panel and create the sketch for the second cross-section, as shown in Figure 9-49 and exit the sketcher environment.

Figure 9-48 Sketch for the first cross-section with dimensions

Figure 9-49 Sketch for the second cross-section with dimensions

9. Now, choose the **Insert** button and select the other end point of the trajectory to create the third cross-section, as shown in Figure 9-50.

10. Exit the sketcher environment after sketching the third cross-section; the **Swept Blend** dashboard is enabled and displayed above the drawing area. Choose the **Create a Solid** button from the **Swept Blend** dashboard; the preview of the feature is displayed in the drawing area. Choose the **Build feature** button from the **Swept Blend** dashboard to exit the feature creation tool.

The model, similar to the one shown in Figure 9-51, is displayed in the drawing area.

Creating the Round Features

In this section, you need to create two round features. These features must be created before shelling because the rounds are also shelled along with the other faces of the model. The third feature to be created is a round of radius 1.5 and the fourth feature is also a round of radius 0.5.

1. Choose the **Round** button from the **Engineering Features** toolbar; the **Round** dashboard is displayed.

Advanced Modeling Tools-II

9-23

Figure 9-50 Sketch of the third cross-section with dimensions

Figure 9-51 Default view of the swept blend feature

2. Select all four longer edges of the swept feature shown in Figure 9-52 to round them. Remember that the first edge can be selected by using the left mouse button and the remaining edges can be selected by using the CTRL+left mouse button. The preview of the round is displayed in the drawing area along with the default radius value.

3. Click on the radius value, enter **1.5** in the edit box that appears, and then press ENTER.

4. Choose the **Build feature** button from the **Round** dashboard. The default view of the model after creating the round feature of radius 1.5, is shown in Figure 9-53.

Figure 9-52 Edges to round

Figure 9-53 Default view of the model after creating the round feature of radius 1.5

Note
The round of radius 0.5 cannot be created by adding a round set. This is because this round needs to be created on the geometry of the previous round. Therefore, until the first round with the radius 1.5 is created, you cannot create the second round.

The third feature of the model is completed and now you need to create the fourth feature, which is also a round feature of radius 0.5. For this purpose, you need to invoke the **Round** dashboard.

5. Choose the **Round** button from the **Engineering Features** toolbar; the **Round** dashboard is displayed.

6. Select the edge where the base feature and the swept feature join, as shown in Figure 9-54.

Figure 9-54 Edge selected to round

The preview of the round is displayed in the drawing area along with the default radius value.

7. Click on the radius value, enter **0.5** in the edit box that appears, and then press ENTER.

8. Choose the **Build feature** button from the **Round** dashboard. The default view of the model after creating the round feature of radius 0.5 is shown in Figure 9-55.

Creating the Shell Feature

You need to create a shell of thickness 0.25 on the swept blend feature.

1. Choose the **Shell** button from the **Engineering Features** toolbar; the **Shell** dashboard is displayed and you are prompted to select the surface to remove.

2. Using the left mouse button, select the front face of the swept blend feature and then use the CTRL+left mouse button to select the bottom face of the base feature.

3. Enter **0.25** in the dimension edit box available on the **Shell** dashboard and then press ENTER.

4. Choose the **Build feature** button from the **Shell** dashboard. The shell feature is created as shown in Figure 9-56.

Advanced Modeling Tools-II

Figure 9-55 Model after creating a round feature of radius 0.5

Figure 9-56 The model after shelling

Creating the Extruded Cut

The extruded cut is the sixth feature of this model. You need to create the cut on the front face of the base feature.

1. Choose the **Extrude** button from the **Base Features** toolbar; the **Extrude** dashboard is displayed.

2. Choose the **Remove Material** button from the dashboard.

3. Select the front face of the base feature as the sketching plane.

4. Select the **TOP** datum plane from the drawing area and then select the **Top** option from the **Orientation** drop-down list.

5. Choose the **Sketch** button to enter the sketcher environment.

6. Draw the sketch of the cut feature and apply dimension to it, as shown in Figure 9-57. You can use the **Concentric** button from the **Sketcher Tools** toolbar to draw the sketch.

7. After the sketch is complete, choose the **Done** button to exit the sketcher environment.

   The **Extrude** dashboard reappears above the drawing area. The **Extrude from sketch plane by specified depth value** button is chosen by default.

8. Choose the **Extrude upto next surface** button from the depth flyout.

9. Choose the **Build feature** button from the **Extrude** dashboard. The cut feature is created, as shown in Figure 9-58.

Figure 9-57 Sketch with dimension for cut feature

Figure 9-58 Model with cut feature at the front face

Similarly, create the next extruded cut feature at the back face of the base feature. Select the sketch plane, draw the sketch, apply dimension, and extrude the sketch using the **Extrude upto next surface** button. The sketch for the cut feature is shown in Figure 9-59.

The seventh feature of the model, which is a cut feature is created, as shown in Figure 9-60.

Figure 9-59 Sketch with dimension for cut feature

Figure 9-60 Model with cut feature at the back face

Creating the Extruded Feature

The eighth feature of the model is an extruded feature and it will be created on the front face of the base feature.

1. Invoke the **Extrude** tool and select the front face of the base feature as the sketching plane for the extrude feature. Once you enter the sketcher environment, draw the sketch and then apply constraints and dimensions to it, as shown in Figure 9-61.

2. After the sketch is complete, choose the **Done** button to exit the sketcher environment.

Advanced Modeling Tools-II 9-27

3. From the depth flyout, choose the **Extrude to selected point, curve, plane or surface** button and select the back face of the base feature.

4. Choose the **Build feature** button from the **Extrude** dashboard. The extruded feature is completed and is shown in Figure 9-62.

Figure 9-61 Sketch for the extruded feature

Figure 9-62 Model after creating the extruded feature

Creating a Mirror Copy of the Eighth Feature

You need to create a mirror copy of the extruded feature, as shown in Figure 9-63 and this will be the ninth feature of the model. The extruded feature will be mirrored about the **FRONT** datum plane.

1. Choose **Edit > Feature Operations** from the menu bar; the **Menu Manager** with the **FEAT** menu is displayed.

2. Choose the **Copy** option from the **FEAT** menu; the **COPY FEATURE** submenu is displayed.

3. Choose **Mirror > Select > Dependent > Done** from the **COPY FEATURE** submenu; the **Select** message box is displayed and you are prompted to select the features to be mirrored.

4. Select the previous extruded feature from the drawing area and choose **OK** from the **Select** message box; the **SETUP PLANE** dialog box is displayed and you are prompted to select a plane or create a datum plane to mirror about.

5. Select the **FRONT** datum plane as the mirror plane; the extruded feature is mirrored about this datum plane, as shown in Figure 9-63.

6. Choose **Done** from the **Menu Manager**.

Creating the Tenth Feature

The tenth feature is a through hole and will be created using the **Hole** dashboard.

1. Choose the **Hole** button from the **Engineering Features** toolbar; the **Hole** dashboard is displayed in which the **Create simple hole** button is chosen by default.

   Create the hole, as shown in Figure 9-64, by specifying the placement parameters. The placement parameters can be referred from Figure 9-44.

Figure 9-63 Model after mirroring the extruded feature

Figure 9-64 Model after creating the hole

Creating a Pattern of the Hole Feature

As evident from Figure 9-43, you need to create eight instances of the hole. The first instance is created by using the **Hole** dashboard and you can use the **Pattern** option to create the remaining seven instances. You need to create a rectangular pattern of the hole feature. You can also create all holes using the **Hole** dashboard and specifying the placement parameters for each of them. But to save time, you should create a pattern of the hole.

1. Select the hole feature from the **Model Tree** or from the model. Hold down the right mouse button to invoke the shortcut menu.

2. Choose the **Pattern** option from the shortcut menu; the **Pattern** dashboard is displayed and the dimensions are displayed on the hole feature.

3. Select the **General** regeneration option from the **Options** slide-down panel.

4. Click on the dimension value **1** from the drawing area. Enter **2** in the edit box and press ENTER.

5. Enter **4** in the **1** edit box present on the dashboard and press ENTER. Now, you need to enter dimension increment in the second direction.

6. Click on the collector that displays **Click here to add item** on the right of the **2** edit box.

Advanced Modeling Tools-II 9-29

Next, click on the dimension value **0.75** from the drawing area. Enter the value **13.5** in the edit box and press ENTER.

7. Enter **2** in the **2** edit box present on the dashboard and press ENTER.

8. Choose the **Build feature** button from the dashboard. You can use the middle mouse button to spin the model and display it, as shown in Figure 9-65.

Figure 9-65 Trimetric view of the completed model

Saving the Model
1. Choose the **Save** button from the **File** toolbar and save the model.

Tutorial 3

In this tutorial, you will create the model of the wheel of a car, as shown in Figure 9-66. Figure 9-67 shows the top view, sectioned front view, sectioned right view, detail view, and two blend sections with dimensions. **(Expected time: 45 min)**

Figure 9-66 Solid model of wheel

The following steps are required to complete this tutorial:

Figure 9-67 Top view, sectioned front view, sectioned right view, detail view, and two blend sections with dimensions

Examine the model and determine the number of features in it. The model is composed of four features, refer to Figure 9-66.

a. Create the base feature as a revolved feature, refer to Figures 9-68 and 9-69.
b. Create the swept blend feature in which the section is normal to the origin trajectory, refer to Figures 9-70 through 9-73.
c. Pattern the swept blend feature, refer to Figure 9-74.
d. Create the round of radius 30 and radius 10, refer to Figures 9-75 and 9-77, respectively.
e. Create the revolved cut, refer to Figures 9-78 and 9-79.

The working directory was already selected in Tutorial 1, and therefore, you do not need to select it again.

Starting a New Object File

1. Start a new part file and name it as *c09tut3*.

The three default datum planes and the **Model Tree** are displayed in the drawing area.

Creating the Base Feature

To create the sketch for the base feature, you first need to select the sketching plane. In this model, you need to draw the base feature on the **FRONT** datum plane.

1. Choose the **Revolve** button from the **Base Features** toolbar; the **Revolve** dashboard is displayed.

Advanced Modeling Tools-II

2. Select the **FRONT** datum plane as the sketching plane.

3. Select the **TOP** datum plane from the drawing area and then select the **Top** option from the **Orientation** drop-down list.

4. Once you enter the sketcher environment, create the sketch of the base feature and then apply constraints and dimensions to it, as shown in Figure 9-68. The sections must be closed and a geometry centerline must be drawn for revolution.

5. After the sketch is complete, choose the **Done** button to exit the sketcher environment; the **Revolve** dashboard is displayed.

6. Choose the **Build feature** button from the **Revolve** dashboard to exit it.

   The base feature is completed. The default trimetric view of the feature is shown in Figure 9-69.

Figure 9-68 Sketch with constraints and dimensions for the base feature

Figure 9-69 Default trimetric view of the base feature

Creating the Trajectory for the Swept Blend

1. Choose the **Sketch** button from the **Datum** toolbar; the **Sketch** dialog box is displayed.

2. Select the **FRONT** datum plane as the sketching plane.

3. Next, select the **TOP** datum plane from the drawing area and then select the **TOP** option from the **Orientation** drop-down list.

4. Once you enter the sketcher environment, you need to create the sketch for the origin trajectory using the **Spline** tool and then apply constraints and dimensions to it, as shown in Figure 9-70.

5. After the sketch is complete, choose the **Done** button to exit the sketcher environment.

Creating the Swept Blend Feature

The second feature of the model is a swept blend. This feature will require a trajectory which has been drawn previously.

1. Choose **Insert > Swept Blend** from the menu bar; the **Swept Blend** dashboard is displayed.

2. Choose the **References** tab to invoke the slide-down panel. Select the origin trajectory that was drawn previously.

3. Now, choose the **Sections** tab to invoke the slide-down panel. Ensure that the **Sketched sections** option is selected in the slide-down panel. Select one of the end points on the trajectory and then choose the **Sketch** button from the **Sections** tab slide-down panel to enter the sketcher environment.

4. Draw the sketch for the first section and add dimensions to it, as shown in Figure 9-71.

Figure 9-70 Sketch with dimensions for the origin trajectory

Figure 9-71 Sketch for section 1 with dimensions

5. After the sketch is complete, choose the **Done** button to exit the sketcher environment.

6. After you exit from the sketcher environment, the **Sections** tab is displayed again. Choose the **Insert** button from the slide-down panel. Now, select the other end point on the trajectory and choose the **Sketch** button to enter the sketcher environment.

7. Draw the sketch for the second section and add dimensions to it, as shown in Figure 9-72. The second section is also elliptical in shape. Now, choose the **Done** button to exit the sketcher environment.

8. After the sketch is complete, choose the **Create a Solid** button from the dashboard.

9. Choose the **Build feature** button from the dashboard. The default trimetric view of the swept blend feature with the base feature is shown in Figure 9-73.

Advanced Modeling Tools-II

Figure 9-72 Sketch for section 2 with dimensions

Figure 9-73 The trimetric view of the swept blend feature

Creating the Pattern of the Swept Blend Feature

Creating the swept blend features individually on the base feature will consume a lot of time. Therefore, you need to create a rotational pattern of the swept blend feature.

1. Select the swept blend feature from the **Model Tree** or from the model. Hold the right mouse button to display the shortcut menu.

2. Choose the **Pattern** option from the shortcut menu; the **Pattern** dashboard is displayed and the dimensions are displayed on the selected feature.

3. Choose the **General** option from the **Options** tab slide-down panel.

4. Select the **Axis** option from the **Dimension** drop-down list; you are prompted to select an axis for creating the pattern feature. Select the axis of the base feature; the preview of the pattern feature is displayed in the drawing area.

5. Enter **3** as the number of instances in the first direction and **120** as the angle between the pattern instances.

6. Choose the **Build feature** button from the dashboard; the rotational pattern is created, as shown in Figure 9-74.

Creating the Round Feature

The third feature to be created a round of radius 30.

1. Choose the **Round** button from the **Engineering Features** toolbar; the **Round** dashboard is displayed.

2. Select the edges shown in Figure 9-75 to round. You may need to spin the model to select the inner edges of the swept blend feature. Remember that the first edge can be selected by using the left mouse button and the remaining edges can be selected by using CTRL+left mouse button.

Figure 9-74 Model after creating rotational pattern

Figure 9-75 Edges selected to round

The preview of the round is displayed in the drawing area along with the default radius value.

3. Click on the radius value, enter **30** in the edit box that appears, and then press ENTER.

4. Choose the **Build feature** button from the **Round** dashboard.

The round feature is completed. The default trimetric view of the round feature is shown in Figure 9-76. Add another set of round of radius 10 as highlighted in Figure 9-77, using the same options.

Figure 9-76 Model after creating a round of radius 30

Figure 9-77 Model highlighting the round feature of radius 10

Advanced Modeling Tools-II

Creating the Revolved Cut Feature

You need to first select a sketching plane to draw the sketch of the cut feature and then specify the angle of revolution.

1. Choose the **Revolve** button from the **Base Features** toolbar; the **Revolve** dashboard is displayed. Next, choose the **Remove Material** button.

2. Select the **FRONT** datum plane as the sketching plane.

3. Select the **TOP** datum plane from the drawing area and then select the **Bottom** option from the **Orientation** drop-down list.

4. Once you enter the sketcher environment, draw a centerline aligned to the **RIGHT** datum plane. Draw the sketch of the revolved cut feature and add dimensions and constraints to it, as shown in Figure 9-78.

5. After the sketch is complete, choose the **Done** button to exit the sketcher environment; the **Revolve** dashboard is enabled again.

6. Choose the **Build feature** button from the **Revolve** dashboard to exit it. The revolve cut feature is shown in Figure 9-79.

Figure 9-78 Sketch for the revolved cut feature   *Figure 9-79* The model with the revolved cut feature

Saving the Model

You need to save the model because you may need it later.

1. Choose the **Save** button from the **File** toolbar and save the model.

Tutorial 4

In this tutorial, you will create the spring shown in Figure 9-80. Figure 9-81 shows the front view of the spring with its dimensions.   **(Expected time: 15 min)**

Figure 9-80 *Isometric view of the spring*

Figure 9-81 *Front view with dimensions of the spring*

The following steps are required to complete this tutorial:

Examine the spring and determine the specifications of the spring, refer to Figure 9-80.
a. Draw the trajectory using the sketcher tools and apply dimensions to it, refer to Figures 9-81 and 9-82.
b. Specify the pitch of the spring.
c. Draw the section of the spring, refer to Figure 9-83.

Make sure that the required working directory is selected.

Starting a New Object File
1. Start a new part file and name it as *c09tut4*.

The three default datum planes and the **Model Tree** are displayed in the drawing area.

Creating the Helical Sweep Feature
The spring that you have to create is a right-handed spring of constant pitch.

1. Choose **Insert > Helical Sweep > Protrusion** from the menu bar; the **PROTRUSION: Helical Sweep** dialog box as well as the **ATTRIBUTES** menu are displayed. The **Constant > Thru Axis > Right Handed** options are selected in the **ATTRIBUTES** menu, by default.

2. Choose **Done** from the **ATTRIBUTES** menu; you are prompted to select a sketching plane.

3. Select the **FRONT** datum plane from the drawing area; the **DIRECTION** submenu is displayed. Choose **Okay**; the **SKET VIEW** submenu is displayed.

4. Select the **Top** option from the **SKET VIEW** submenu and choose the **TOP** datum plane from the drawing.

Advanced Modeling Tools-II

5. Once you enter the sketcher environment, draw the sketch of the trajectory and dimension it, as shown in Figure 9-82. As is evident from Figure 9-81, the endpoint of the trajectory is aligned to the **TOP** datum plane.

   You need to draw a center line in the sketch about which the spring will be rotated. This is the axis of the spring.

   Figure 9-82 Sketch of the trajectory with dimensions

6. After you complete the sketch of the trajectory, choose the **Done** button from the **Right Toolchest**; the **Message Input Window** is displayed and you are prompted to specify the pitch of the spring.

7. Enter the value **10** in the **Message Input Window** and press ENTER. Now, you need to enter the sketcher environment to draw the section of the spring. You will notice that a yellow cross of infinite length appears on the screen. This cross consists of two perpendicular lines of infinite length. The intersection point of these lines is the start point of the trajectory.

8. Draw the section of the spring such that the center of the circle coincides with the intersection of the two perpendicular lines. Then, dimension it, as shown in Figure 9-83.

9. After completing the sketch, choose the **Done** button to exit the sketcher environment.

10. Choose the **OK** button from the **PROTRUSION: Helical Sweep** dialog box; the spring is created as shown in Figure 9-84.

Saving the Model
1. Choose the **Save** button from the **File** toolbar and save the model.

Figure 9-83 Sketch of the section with dimensions   *Figure 9-84 Isometric view of the spring*

Self-Evaluation Test

Answer the following questions and then compare them to those given at the end of this chapter:

1. You can create helical sweep features with constant as well as variable pitch. (T/F)

2. The **Helical Sweep** option is used to create cut as well as protrusion features. (T/F)

3. You can create a helical feature having 40 units pitch and 50 units as the diameter of the circular cross-section. (T/F)

4. You can add as well as delete points while specifying the pitch values during the creation of variable pitch helical sweep. (T/F)

5. The **Variable Section Sweep** option is available for both protrusion and cut options. (T/F)

6. While using the **Variable Section Sweep** option, the contour of the sweep feature depends on the shape of the _____.

7. While using the **Variable Section Sweep** option, when you draw the section for the sweep feature, the section should be _____ to the endpoints of the trajectories.

8. When you choose the **Done** option from the **BLEND OPTS** menu, the _____ menu is displayed.

9. When you use the **Normal To Trajectory** option to create the variable sweep, the section is _____ to the origin trajectory and is swept along the X trajectory.

10. The **Swept Blend** option is used to create a model that is a combination of _____ and _____.

Advanced Modeling Tools-II

Review Questions

Answer the following questions:

1. Which of the following menus is displayed when you choose the **Helical Sweep** option from the **Insert** menu in the menu bar?

   (a) **ADV FEAT OPT**   (b) **ATTRIBUTES**
   (c) **SWEEP OPTS**   (d) None of these

2. Which of the following options is used to create a helical feature with constant pitch throughout the sweep?

   (a) **Right Handed**   (b) **Constant**
   (c) **Thru Axis**   (d) None of these

3. Which of the following options in the **BLEND OPTS** menu is used to create a sweep in which the swept section is normal to the trajectory defined as the origin trajectory?

   (a) **Pivot Dir**   (b) **NrmToOriginTraj**
   (c) **Norm To Traj**   (d) None of these

4. Which of the following options in the **Relations** dialog box is used to add dimensions that appear on the screen?

   (a) **Insert > From Screen** (b) **Insert > Function**
   (c) **Insert > From List**   (d) None of these

5. Which of the following options is used to create a swept blend feature in which you need to select a plane, edge, curve, or axis to which the section to be swept is perpendicular?

   (a) **Pivot Dir**   (b) **Nrm To Traj**
   (c) **NrmToOriginTraj**   (d) None of these

6. The **Variable Section Sweep** option can be used to create a sweep in which the section of the sweep is constant throughout the sweep. (T/F)

7. The X trajectory, is used to guide the section of the sweep feature along it. (T/F)

8. When you choose the **Edit Rel** option, the relations are not checked for errors. (T/F)

9. The **Switch Dim** option of the **RELATIONS** submenu is used to toggle the symbols and the dimension value mode. (T/F)

10. The **Helical Sweep** option is also used to create a cut. (T/F)

Exercises

Exercise 1

Create the model shown in Figure 9-85. Its front view is shown in Figure 9-86.

(Expected time: 15 min)

Figure 9-85 Isometric view of the spring

Figure 9-86 Front view of the spring

Exercise 2

Create the model shown in Figure 9-87. The front and top views of the model are shown in Figure 9-88.

(Expected time: 30 min)

Hints to create the swept blend feature:
1. Select the **FRONT** datum plane as the sketching plane and select the top face of the base feature to be at the top while sketching.
2. Draw the arc of radius 50 and locate its center from the base feature.
3. Exit the sketcher environment by choosing the **Done** button.
4. Choose **Insert > Swept Blend**; the **Swept Blend** dashboard is displayed.
5. Choose the **Extrude as Solid** button from the dashboard.
6. Choose the **Reference** tab from the dashboard and select the arc drawn.
7. Choose the **Sections** tab and select the endpoint of the arc lying on the base feature, Choose the **Sketch** button from the **Sections** tab slide-down panel to enter the sketcher environment. Draw the rectangle of dimension 15 x 75. Exit the sketcher environment.
8. Choose the **Insert** button from the **Sections** tab slide-down panel and then select the other end point of the arc. Then, choose the **Sketch** button from the slide-down panel; this will again take you to the sketcher environment. Draw another rectangle with the dimensions 15 x 30. Exit the sketcher environment by choosing the **Done** button.

Advanced Modeling Tools-II

Figure 9-87 Solid model for Exercise 2

Figure 9-88 Front and top views of the model

Exercise 3

Create the model of the Helical Gear shown in Figure 9-89. Its views and dimensions are shown in Figure 9-90. **(Expected time: 30 min)**

Figure 9-89 Model of the Helical Gear

Sweep with 3 sketches size 100%, 75%, 50% with rotation angle of 15° between each sketch

The plane for drawing the second section is at an offset of 45 units from the first sketch. Plane for the third sketch is at an offset of 95 units from the first sketch

Figure 9-90 Views and Dimensions for the model

Answers to Self-Evaluation Test

1. T, **2.** T, **3.** F, **4.** T, **5.** T, **6.** X trajectory, **7.** aligned, **8. SWEEP TRAJ 9.** normal, **10.** sweep, blend.

Chapter 10

Advanced Modeling Tools-III

Learning Objectives

After completing this chapter, you will be able to:
• *Create toroidal bend.*
• *Create spinal bend.*
• *Create warp transformation by using various transformation tools.*

ADVANCED MODELING TOOLS

In this chapter, you will learn to create models using advanced modeling tools such as **Toroidal Bend**, **Spinal Bend**, and **Warp**. These tools will help you analyze and create complex models with greater ease.

Toroidal Bend

The **Toroidal Bend** tool is used to create features with curved surfaces, or the models which generally have a cut profile on a curved surface. For example, if you want to create a feature shown in Figure 10-1, you will first create a rectangular plate and cut the profile on it, as shown in Figure 10-2. Then using the **Toroidal Bend** tool, you will bend the rectangular plate through an angle of 360 degrees, refer to Figure 10-1.

Figure 10-1 The plate after creating the toroidal bend

Figure 10-2 Rectangular plate with a cut profile

Choose **Insert > Advanced > Toroidal Bend** from the menu bar to invoke the **Toroidal Bend** option; the **Toroidal Bend** dashboard will be displayed, as shown in Figure 10-3. You can specify the method of creating the toroidal bend as well as the angle of rotation of the bend.

Figure 10-3 The **Toroidal Bend** dashboard

The following steps explain the procedure to create the model, refer to Figure 10-1. It is assumed that you have created the rectangular plate of dimensions 300 X 500 X 20, refer to Figure 10-2.

1. Choose **Insert > Advanced > Toroidal Bend** from the menu bar to invoke the **Toroidal Bend** dashboard. Next, choose the **References** tab from the dashboard; a slide-down panel will be displayed. Now, choose the **Define** button from the **Profile Section** area.

2. Select the right face of the base feature (which is the longer face of the base plate) as the sketching plane and orient the sketch plane.

Advanced Modeling Tools-III

3. After entering the sketcher environment, draw the sketch, as shown in Figure 10-4. The sketch comprises of a line that is drawn from the left edge to the right edge. Also, a user-defined coordinate system will be placed at the midpoint of the line.

Figure 10-4 Sketch along with the reference coordinate system

4. Next, exit the sketcher environment.

Note
The sketch, shown in Figure 10-4, controls the bend profile of the **Toroidal Bend** *feature. If the sketch is a straight line, the side profile of the* **Toroidal Bend** *will be a line; else it will be an arc. The user-defined coordinate system acts as the neutral point in the bend.*

5. Choose the **References** tab; a slide-panel will be displayed. Select the **Solid geometry** check box from it.

6. Next, choose the **Options** tab to display a slide-down panel. Select the **Standard** radio button, if it is not already selected.

7. Choose the **Bend Radius** button from the dashboard; a flyout will be displayed. Next, choose the **360 degrees Bend** option from it; you will be prompted to select the two parallel planes to define the length of the bend.

8. Select the face that was selected as the sketching plane and then select the longer face which is parallel to it; the preview of the toroidal bend will be displayed.

9. Choose the **Build Feature** button from the dashboard; the **Toroidal Bend** will be created and the model similar to the one shown in Figure 10-2 will be displayed in the drawing area.

Spinal Bend

The **Spinal Bend** tool is used to bend solids or quilts about a curved spine by continuously repositioning cross sections along the curve. Cross-sections, which are perpendicular to an axis, are repositioned perpendicular to the sketched spine without any distortion.

The **Spinal Bend** option can be invoked by choosing **Insert > Advanced > Spinal Bend** from the menu bar. The **OPTIONS** menu that will be displayed is shown in Figure 10-5.

The **OPTIONS** menu allows you to either select a previously created spine or sketch a new spine as is the case, by using the **Select Spine** or **Sketch Spine** option, respectively. Choosing the **No Prop Ctrl** option bends the solid through a single cross-section. The **SecProp Ctrl** option adjusts the geometry according to the various cross-sections created at different points in the trajectory.

Figure 10-6 shows the base feature for creating the spinal bend. The procedure to create the model, shown in Figure 10-7, using the **Spinal Bend** tool is discussed next.

Figure 10-5 *The **OPTIONS** menu*

Figure 10-6 *Model before creating the spinal bend*   *Figure 10-7* *Model showing the spinal bend*

Note
*It is assumed that you have created the base feature before invoking the **Spinal Bend** tool. Also, a datum plane has to be created on the top face of the model.*

1. Choose **Insert > Advanced > Spinal Bend** from the menu bar to invoke the **OPTIONS** menu and then choose **Sketch Spine > No Prop Ctrl > Done** from it. You will be prompted to select a solid or a quilt to bend.
2. Select the solid geometry from the drawing area; you will be prompted to select the sketching plane.
3. Select the **FRONT** plane of the base feature as the sketching plane and orient the sketch plane.

Note
The trajectory sketched for the spinal bend should be tangent to the solid geometry.

4. After entering the sketcher environment, draw the trajectory, as shown in Figure 10-8.

Advanced Modeling Tools-III

5. Exit the sketcher environment; you will be prompted to select the plane to define the volume of the blend.
6. Select the datum plane created on the top face of the model. The model similar to the one shown in Figure 10-7 will be displayed in the drawing area.

Figure 10-8 Sketched trajectory for spinal bend

Warp

The **Warp** tool helps you study the design variations during the conceptual stage. With the **Warp** tool, you can visualize the form and shape of solids, quilts, facets, and curves. The **Warp** tool can be used only in the **Part** mode. Choose **Insert > Warp** from the menu bar; the **Warp** dashboard will be displayed, as shown in Figure 10-9. The tabs and buttons of the **Warp** dashboard are discussed next.

*Figure 10-9 The **Warp** dashboard*

References Tab

When the **References** tab is chosen from the **Warp** dashboard, the slide-down panel will be displayed, as shown in Figure 10-10.

The **References** area indicates the geometry and direction chosen to create the **Warp** transformation. If the **Hide Original** check box is selected, the original entity selected for the creation of the **Warp** transformation is not displayed in the drawing area. The **Copy Original** check box, if selected, will keep a copy of the original entity chosen for creating the **Warp** transformation.

*Figure 10-10 The **References** tab slide-down panel*

List Tab

The **List** tab, when chosen, displays a slide-down panel which lists all **Warp** transformations performed on the selected entity. You can select the required operation from the slide-down panel of the **List** tab, and then edit, preview, or delete it. The **List** tab slide-down panel is shown in Figure 10-11.

Options Tab

The **Options** tab is used to input various parameters for the **Warp** transformation. The slide-down panel, which will be displayed when the **Options** tab is chosen using the **Transform** tool, is shown in Figure 10-12. The uses of **Transform** tool will be discussed later in this chapter.

*Figure 10-11 The **List** tab slide-down panel*

This slide-down panel lists the various parameters which control a particular **Warp** transformation. In the above slide-down panel, you can enter the values through which the geometry has to be transformed in the X, Y, and Z axes. Similarly, the various parameters which control the particular **Warp** transformation can be edited using the **Options** tab.

*Figure 10-12 The **Move** area of the **Options** tab slide-down panel*

Marquee Tab

The **Marquee** tab is used to create the **Warp** transformation using the **Spine** tool. When the **Marquee** tab is chosen, the slide-down panel will be displayed, as shown in Figure 10-13. The **Marquee** tab provides you with the options to control the warping operation of an entity through a curve or a spine sketched before the **Warp** transformation is performed.

You can choose points from the grid in the drawing area and then drag them to get the required shape. Alternatively, you can enter the values for creating the **Warp** transformation in the slide-down panel of the **Marquee** tab.

Transform Button

*Figure 10-13 The **Marquee Size** slide-down panel*

The **Transform** button can be used for various transformation operations such as translating, rotating, and scaling a geometrical entity. The translate option translates the geometry in the required direction. The rotate option rotates the geometry based on the position of the **Jack** (a blue color coordinate system which appears in the center of the drawing area). The scale option scales the geometry to the required scale factor.

Advanced Modeling Tools-III   10-7

The following steps explain the procedure to translate a geometry using the **Transform** button, as shown in Figure 10-14.

1. Choose **Insert > Warp** from the menu bar to invoke the **Warp** dashboard.
2. Choose the **References** tab to display the slide-down panel. Select the solid geometry from the drawing area. Now, click once in the **Direction** collector and select the **FRONT** datum plane as the direction reference.
3. Choose the **Transform** button from the **Warp** dashboard.
4. Click anywhere in the drawing area and drag the mouse to place the geometry at the desired location. Choose the **Build feature** button from the **Warp** dashboard to complete the **Warp** transformation.

Figure 10-14 The preview of the translated feature along with the original feature

The following steps explain the procedure to rotate geometry using the **Transform** button.

1. Choose **Insert > Warp** from the menu bar to invoke the **Warp** dashboard.
2. Choose the **References** tab to display the slide-down panel. Select the solid geometry from the drawing area. Now, click once in the **Direction** collector and select the **FRONT** datum plane as the direction reference.
3. Choose the **Transform** button from the **Warp** dashboard; the **Jack** will be displayed in the center of the drawing area.
4. Click on the handles of the **Jack** and drag the mouse to rotate the geometry to the required orientation.
5. Alternatively, click on the handles of the **Jack** and then choose the **Options** tab from the **Warp** dashboard. Enter the angle of rotation in the **Angle** edit box and choose the **Build feature** button from the **Warp** dashboard to complete the **Warp** transformation.

Figure 10-15 shows the model before rotating the geometry and Figure 10-16 shows the model after rotating the geometry.

Note
*The **Jack** can be moved independent of the solid geometry. To do so, select **Jack** in the **Transform** drop-down list in the dashboard. Next, click on the **Jack** in the drawing area and drag to place it at the required location. Hold the right mouse button to invoke the shortcut menu. Choose **Center Jack** option from the shortcut menu; click and drag on the active handles of the **Jack** to rotate the geometry to the required orientation.*

The following steps explain the procedure to scale a geometry using the **Transform** button.

1. Choose **Insert > Warp** from the menu bar to invoke the **Warp** dashboard.
2. Click on the **References** tab to display the slide-down panel. Select the solid geometry from the drawing area. Now, click once in the **Direction** collector and the **TOP** datum plane as the direction reference.

Figure 10-15 Model before rotating the geometry   *Figure 10-16 Model after rotating the geometry*

3. Choose the **Transform** button from the **Warp** dashboard.
4. Click on any corner of the marquee and choose the **Options** tab from the **Warp** dashboard; the **Options** slide-down panel, shown in Figure 10-17, will be displayed.
5. Enter the scale factor in the **Scale** edit box. The two options in the **Toward** drop-down list are **Opposite** and **Center**. The **Opposite** option scales the corner opposite to the selected reference corner and the **Center** option scales the geometry with respect to the center of the geometry.

*Figure 10-17 The **Scale** area of the **Options** tab slide-down panel*

Figure 10-18 shows a scaled feature previewed along with the original feature.

Figure 10-18 The preview of the original geometry with the scaled geometry

Advanced Modeling Tools-III

Warp Button

The **Warp** button can be used for changing the shape of the geometry. Some of the operations that are possible using the **Warp** button are tapering the top or the base of the geometry, or dragging a corner or an edge toward or away from the center.

The following steps explain the procedure to apply wrap transformation using the **Warp** button.

1. Choose **Insert > Warp** from the menu bar to invoke the **Warp** dashboard.
2. Choose the **References** tab to display the slide-down panel. Select the solid geometry from the drawing area. Now, click once in the **Direction** collector and select the **TOP** datum plane as the direction reference.
3. Choose the **Warp** button from the **Warp** dashboard.
4. Move the cursor toward one of the marquee points of the solid geometry to display the arrows. Click on the arrow that is perpendicular to the edge and then choose the **Options** tab from the **Warp** dashboard; the **Options** tab slide-down panel will be displayed, as shown in Figure 10-19.
5. Select the **center** option from the **Constraint** drop-down list.
6. Enter the warping length in the **parameter** edit box; the preview of the warped feature appears in the drawing area. Choose the **Build feature** button from the **Warp** dashboard to complete the feature creation.
7. Alternatively, move the cursor to any of the control points to display the arrows. Select one of the arrows and drag it when the arrow on the control point changes its color to cyan.

*Figure 10-19 The **Edge** area of the **Options** tab slide-down panel*

Figure 10-20 shows the model before applying the warp transformation and Figure 10-21 shows the model after applying the warp transformation.

Figure 10-20 Model before applying the warp transformation

Figure 10-21 Model after applying the warp transformation

Note

When you move the cursor onto a control point of the marquee, six arrows will be displayed; three in purple color and the other three in yellow color. The arrows in yellow are used to warp the model along the selected edge and the arrows in purple are used to warp the model by moving the selected corner within the selected marquee face. In this process, the other two corners follow symmetricity to maintain the original corner angles. If you do not require the other two corners to follow symmetricity, press and hold the ALT key and then drag the selected corner.

If you press and hold the SHIFT and ALT keys together while dragging the marquee points, the warp will take place symmetrically from both the corners.

Spine Button

The **Spine** button reshapes the geometry by manipulating the defining points of a curve (also referred to as spine). The transformation using the **Spine** button can be created in the linear or radial direction.

The following steps explain the procedure to apply a warp transformation using the **Spine** button.

1. The transformation using the **Spine** button will be applied with reference to a curve (also referred as a spine). You need to create a curve before invoking the **Spine** button. The transformation will then be applied by dragging the control points of the spine to the required location.

Note

Remember that the spine you create needs to be sketched parallel to the plane on which you apply the warp transformation.

2. Choose **Insert > Warp** from the menu bar to invoke the **Warp** dashboard.
3. Choose the **References** tab to display the slide-down panel. Select the solid geometry from the drawing area. Now, click once in the **Direction** collector and select the plane, which was the sketching plane for the spine, as the direction reference.
4. Choose the **Spine** button from the **Warp** dashboard; the slide-down panel will be displayed, as shown in Figure 10-22. Now, click once in the **Spine** collector and select the sketched spine from the drawing area.
5. Click and drag on any of the control points displayed on the curve (spine) to the desired location. Choose the **Build feature** button from the **Warp** dashboard to complete the creation of the feature.

*Figure 10-22 The **References** tab slide-down panel*

Advanced Modeling Tools-III

Stretch Button

The **Stretch** button can be used to stretch geometry along the required direction. The range and scale of stretch can be controlled using the various options in the **Options** tab of the **Warp** dashboard.

The following steps explain the procedure to apply a warp transformation using the **Stretch** button.

1. Choose **Insert > Warp** from the menu bar to invoke the **Warp** dashboard.
2. Choose the **References** tab to display the slide-down panel. Select the solid geometry from the drawing area. Next, click once in the **Direction** collector and select the **FRONT** datum plane as the direction reference.
3. Choose the **Stretch** button from the **Warp** dashboard. You can apply the transformation by moving the cursor onto the small white rectangle which will be displayed in the drawing area and then dragging it to the required location.
4. Drag the rectangle to stretch the model. Alternatively, enter a desired value of stretch in the **Scale** edit box; the model will be stretched in the direction of axis displayed and the preview of the stretched feature will be displayed in the drawing area.
5. To stretch the model in the other direction, choose the **Switch to next axis** button; the axis and a small white rectangle will be displayed in the other direction. Now, you can drag the rectangle to stretch the model in that direction. You can reverse the direction of stretch by choosing the **Reverse axis direction** button.
6. To set the length of the axis, invoke the **Marquee** tab; a slide-down panel will be displayed, as shown in Figure 10-23. Enter the start and end points of the axis in the **Start** and **End** edit boxes, respectively.
7. Choose the **Build feature** button from the **Warp** dashboard to complete the creation of the feature.

Figure 10-24 shows the model before the stretching transformation and Figure 10-25 shows the model after the stretching transformation.

Figure 10-23 The **Marquee** tab slide-down panel

Figure 10-24 Model before stretching

Figure 10-25 Model after stretching

Note

*The **Proportional** marquee size is selected by default in the **Marquee** tab slide-down panel, thereby stretching the model relative to its previous position. You can select **Absolute** to stretch the model to the specified length. To specify the stretch from an offset distance, select the **Offset** marquee size.*

Bend Button

The **Bend** tool bends the geometry to the required orientation. The following steps explain the procedure to create a bend using the **Bend** button.

1. Choose **Insert > Warp** from the menu bar to invoke the **Warp** dashboard.
2. Choose the **References** tab to display the slide-down panel. Select the solid geometry from the drawing area. Now, click in the **Direction** collector once and select the **FRONT** datum plane as the direction reference.
3. Choose the **Bend** button from the **Warp** dashboard. The model will be displayed in the drawing area with marquee and a yellow line with a small rectangle at one end.
4. Move the cursor onto the small white rectangle and drag it until the desired orientation is achieved. Alternatively, enter the desired orientation value in the **Angle** edit box available in the dashboard; the preview of the bend will be displayed in the model area.
5. Next, choose the **Options** tab; the slide-down panel will be displayed, as shown in Figure 10-26.

The **Pivot** edit box in the **Bend** area of this panel is used to specify the fixed point of the bend and the **Tilt** edit box is used to specify the angle of the bend. Enter the desired values in the respective edit boxes. You can also set the range of bend, similar to stretch, by invoking the **Marquee** tab in the dashboard.

*Figure 10-26 The **Bend** area of the **Options** tab slide-down panel*

Figure 10-27 shows the geometry before creating the bend feature and Figure 10-28 shows the geometry after creating the bend feature.

Figure 10-27 Model before bending

Figure 10-28 Model after bending

Advanced Modeling Tools-III

The bend operation can also be controlled by using the buttons in the **Warp** dashboard.

Switch to next axis button
This button switches the axis of bend from one plane to another.

Reverse axis direction button
This button reverses the direction of the axis of the bend.

Increase tilt by 90 degrees button
This button increases the tilt or the bending angle by 90 degrees from the previously applied bend angle.

Twist Button

The **Twist** button is used to twist the geometry around an axis by the user specified angle.

The following steps explain the procedure to twist a geometry using the **Twist** tool.

1. Choose **Insert > Warp** from the menu bar to invoke the **Warp** dashboard.
2. Choose the **References** tab to display the slide-down panel. Select the solid geometry from the drawing area. Now, click once in the **Direction** collector and select the **TOP** datum plane as the direction reference.
3. Choose the **Twist** button from the **Warp** dashboard; the model will be displayed in the drawing area along with the marquee and a small white rectangle.
4. Move the cursor onto the small white rectangle and drag to twist the model to the required orientation. Alternatively, enter the angle of twist in the **Angle** edit box in the dashboard; the preview of twist is displayed in the drawing area.
5. You can define the range of the twist feature, similar to **Stretch** and **Bend**. To do so, invoke the **Marquee** tab; a slide-down panel will be displayed, as shown in Figure 10-29. The **Start** and **End** edit boxes in this slide down panel are used to define the range of twist.
6. Choose the **Build feature** button from the **Warp** dashboard to complete the creation of the feature.

Figures 10-30 shows the model before twisting and Figure 10-31 shows the model after twisting.

*Figure 10-29 The **Twist** area of the **Marquee** slide-down panel*

Note
*The direction of twist and the axis of twist can be reversed or switched by using the **Reverse axis direction** and **Switch to next axis** buttons respectively in the **Warp** dashboard.*

Figure 10-30 Model before twisting   *Figure 10-31 Model after twisting*

Sculpt Button

The **Sculpt** tool allows you to deform the geometry through a mesh. The following steps explain the procedure to create a sculpt transformation.

1. Choose **Insert > Warp** from the menu bar to invoke the **Warp** dashboard.
2. Click on the **References** tab to display the slide-down panel. Select the solid geometry from the drawing area. Now, click once in the **Direction** collector and select the top datum plane as the direction reference.
3. Choose the **Sculpt** button from the **Warp** dashboard.
4. Choose the **Options** tab from the **Warp** dashboard; the slide-down panel will be displayed, as shown in Figure 10-32.
5. Select the type of symmetry you want from the drop-down list in the **Symmetry** edit box.

*Figure 10-32 The **Sculpt** area of the **Options** tab slide-down panel*

> **Note**
> *The **Symmetry** drop-down list specifies the direction in which the selected group of points move while sculpting. The **None** option is selected by default in the **Symmetry** drop-down list. If the **Horizontal** option is selected from the drop-down list, then the points move symmetric to the centerline of the face parallel to the selected reference plane.*

6. Select the type of drag from the **Drag** drop-down list.

> **Note**
> *The **Drag** drop-down list specifies the constraints on the group of points being sculpted. The **Normal** option is selected by default and the points move normal to the selected face when the transformation is created. If the **Free** option is selected from the **Drag** drop-down list, then the points selected for sculpting move freely in the drawing area. The **Along Row/Column** option will be used to move the points selected for sculpting towards the neighboring rows or columns.*

7. Select the type of filter required from the **Filter** drop-down list.

Advanced Modeling Tools-III

> **Note**
> The **Filter** drop-down list specifies the behavior of the points being sculpted. The **Constant** filter is selected by default and the points selected for sculpting move to the same distance as the dragged point. If the **Linear** filter is selected, then the selected points drop-off linearly with respect to the dragged point. The **Smooth** filter drops off the selected points smoothly with respect to the dragged point.

8. Select one or more curves or points from the marquee displayed. (Hold down the CTRL button for multiple point selections). Drag the selected points to the required location. Choose the **Build feature** button from the **Warp** dashboard to complete the **Warp** transformation.

Figure 10-33 shows the model before applying the **Sculpt** transformation and Figure 10-34 shows the model after applying the **Sculpt** transformation.

Figure 10-33 Model before applying the **Sculpt** transformation

Figure 10-34 Model after applying the **Sculpt** transformation

You may also specify how the geometry is sculpted by choosing the buttons that will become available when the **Sculpt** button is chosen in the **Warp** dashboard. These buttons are discussed next.

Switch mesh orientation to the next marquee face button
This button helps you to align the mesh in the direction in which the geometry will be sculpted.

Apply to one side of selected items button
This button sculpts the selected face in only one direction and is chosen by default.

Apply to both sides of selected items button
This button applies the motion of selected face to the opposite face.

Apply symmetrically to both sides of selected items button
This button, if chosen, allows the geometry to be symmetric from its center.

> **Note**
> *The number of rows and columns in the marquee can be controlled by specifying the required value in the Rows and Columns edit boxes respectively in the dashboard.*

TUTORIALS

Tutorial 1

In this tutorial, you will create the model shown in Figure 10-35.   **(Expected time: 30 min)**

Figure 10-35 Model for Tutorial 1

The following steps are required to complete this tutorial:

a. Create the blend feature, refer to Figure 10-36.
b. Create the revolve feature, refer to Figure 10-37 and 10-38.
c. Create the round feature on the two ends of the blend feature, refer to Figure 10-39.
d. Create the shell feature by removing the front face of the model, refer to Figure 10-40.
e. Create the warp features using the **Spine** tool, refer to Figures 10-41 through 10-44.

When you start the Pro/ENGINEER session, the first task is to set the working directory. Make sure the required working directory is selected.

Starting a New Object File
Start a new part file and as name it *c10tut1*.

Invoking the Blend Option
1. Choose **Insert > Blend > Protrusion** from the menu bar; the **BLEND OPTS** menu is displayed.

Advanced Modeling Tools-III

2. Choose **Parallel > Regular Sec > Sketch Sec > Done** from this menu; the **ATTRIBUTES** menu is displayed.

3. Choose **Smooth > Done** from the **ATTRIBUTES** menu; you are prompted to select a sketching plane.

4. Select the **FRONT** datum plane and choose **Okay** from the **DIRECTION** submenu. From the **SKET VIEW** submenu, choose the **Default** option to enter the sketcher environment.

Creating Sections for the Blend Feature

In this section, you need to create three elliptical sections for the blend feature.

1. Choose the **Center and Axis Ellipse** button from the **Sketcher Tools** toolbar and draw an ellipse with the **Rx** dimension **20** and **Ry** dimension **5**.

2. Choose **Sketch > Feature Tools > Toggle Section** from the menu bar to create the second section. Alternatively, right-click in the drawing area and then choose the **Toggle Section** option from the shortcut menu to create the second section.

3. Draw the second section of the blend feature which is an ellipse with the **Rx** dimension **20** and the **Ry** dimension **10**.

4. Choose **Sketch > Feature Tools > Toggle Section** from the menu bar to create the third section.

5. Draw the third section which is also an ellipse with the **Rx** dimension **25** and the **Ry** dimension **20**.

6. Choose the **Done** button to exit the sketcher environment; you are prompted to specify the depth for section 2.

7. Enter **15**; you are again prompted to specify the depth for section 3; enter **150** and press ENTER. Next, choose the **OK** button from the **PROTRUSION: Blend, Parallel, Regular Sections** dialog box. The model, similar to the one shown in Figure 10-36, is displayed in the drawing area.

Figure 10-36 Isometric view of the Blend feature

Creating the Revolve Feature

1. Choose the **Revolve** button from the **Base Features** toolbar. Create the sketch for the revolve feature, as shown in Figure 10-37, and revolve the sketch through an angle of 360 degrees. The model, after creating the revolve feature, is shown in Figure 10-38.

Figure 10-37 Sketch for the revolve feature

Figure 10-38 Model after creating the revolve feature

Creating the Round Feature

1. Choose the **Round** button from the **Base Features** toolbar; you are prompted to select an edge or a surface to create the round. Create a round feature of radius 1.5 at the rear edge of the model and then create a round feature of radius **6** at the front-end of the model. The model, similar to the one shown in Figure 10-39, is displayed in the drawing area.

Figure 10-39 Model after creating the round feature

Advanced Modeling Tools-III

Creating the Shell Feature

1. Create the shell feature by removing the front face of the revolved feature and specify the wall thickness value as **1**.

   The model after creating the shell feature is shown in Figure 10-40.

Creating the Sketch for the Warp Feature

You need to use the **Spline** button to create the deformation in the tube. Therefore, you first need to create the curve which will be used to create the warp feature.

Figure 10-40 Model after creating the shell feature

1. Choose the **Sketch** button from the **Base Features** toolbar; the **Sketch** dialog box is displayed.

2. Choose the **RIGHT** plane as the sketching plane and select the **Top** option from the drop-down list in the **Orientation** tab. Next, choose the **Sketch** button to enter the sketching environment.

3. Choose the **Spline** button from the **Sketcher Tools** toolbar and draw the spline curve shown in Figure 10-41. Note that the dimensions of the spline are not important as this sketch will be used as reference for deciding the shape after deformation.

4. Choose the **Done** button to exit the sketcher environment.

Figure 10-41 Sketched spline curve

Applying the Warp Transformation by Using the Spine Tool

1. Choose **Insert > Warp** from the menu bar; the **Warp** dashboard is displayed.

2. Choose the **References** tab; the **Geometry** collector is enabled by default. Select the model from the drawing area.

3. Click in the **Direction** selection box; you are prompted to select a plane or a coordinate system to define the direction of the warp.

4. Select the **TOP** plane from the drawing area; you are prompted to select the deformation tool.

5. Choose the **Spine** button from the **Warp** dashboard; you are prompted to select a curve to define the deformation.

6. Select the sketched spine as the reference curve for the warp transformation. The model similar to the one shown in Figure 10-42 is displayed in the drawing area.

7. Select the control points on the reference curve and drag them until the required spinal deformation is obtained. The position of the control points after carrying out the deformation is shown in Figure 10-43.

Figure 10-42 *Figure showing the parameters for the warp transformation*

Figure 10-43 *Figure showing the deformed model*

Note
The control points for creating the deformation may be randomly selected based on the profile required.

8. Choose the **Build feature** button to create the feature. Figure 10-44 shows the final model after applying the warp transformation and hiding the spline created.

Saving the Model
1. Choose the **Save** button from the **File** toolbar to save the model.

Advanced Modeling Tools-III

Figure 10-44 Final model after applying the warp transformation

Tutorial 2

In this tutorial, you will create the model shown in Figure 10-45. **(Expected time: 30 min)**

Figure 10-45 Model for Tutorial 2

The following steps are required to complete this tutorial:

a. Create the revolve feature, refer to Figure 10-47.
b. Create the shell feature of thickness 8, refer to Figure 10-48.
c. Create the extrude feature, refer to Figure 10-49, and then pattern the extruded feature, refer to Figure 10-50.
d. Create the round feature, refer to Figure 10-51.
e. Create the warp transformations, refer to Figure 10-52.

Starting a New Object File
Start a new part file and name it as *c10tut2*.

Creating the Revolve Feature
1. Draw the sketch of the revolved feature in the **FRONT** datum plane, as shown in Figure 10-46.

2. Revolve the sketch through 360 degrees to create the base feature, as shown in Figure 10-47.

Figure 10-46 Sketch for the revolved feature

Figure 10-47 Model showing the base feature

Creating the Shell Feature
1. Create the shell feature with the wall thickness value **8** and the top face of the base feature removed, as shown in Figure 10-48.

Creating the Extrude Feature and its Pattern
1. Create the extrude feature similar to the one shown in Figure 10-49.

Figure 10-48 Model after creating the shell feature

Figure 10-49 Model after creating the extrude feature

Advanced Modeling Tools-III

2. Create the axis pattern of the extrude feature, refer to Figure 10-50.

Creating Round Features

1. Choose the **Round** button from the **Engineering Features** toolbar; you are prompted to select the edges to create the round.

2. Choose the edges, as shown in Figure 10-51.

   Note
   Hold the CTRL key to select multiple edges.

3. Enter **5** in the edit box available in the **Round** dashboard and then choose the **Build feature** button to exit the **Round** dashboard.

   The model after creating the round feature is shown in Figure 10-51.

Figure 10-50 Model after creating the pattern   *Figure 10-51* Figure showing the round feature

Applying the Warp Transformation by Using the Twist Tool

1. Invoke the **Warp** dashboard by choosing **Insert > Warp** from the menu bar; the **Warp** dashboard is displayed and you are prompted to select the solids or quilts to warp.

2. Select the model in the drawing area and then choose the **References** tab from the **Warp** dashboard. Click in the selection area for the **Direction** collector; you are prompted to select a plane or a coordinate system to select the direction of the warp.

3. Select the **TOP** datum plane in the drawing area; you are now prompted to select the deformation tool.

4. Choose the **Twist** button from the **Warp** dashboard.

5. Enter **120** in the **Angle** edit box in the **Warp** dashboard; the preview of the warp transformation is displayed in the drawing area.

6. Choose the **Build feature** button from the **Warp** dashboard to complete the creation of the feature.

The model after applying the warp transformation is shown in Figure 10-52.

Saving the Model
1. Choose the **Save** button from the **File** toolbar to save the model.

Figure 10-52 Model after applying the warp transformation

Tutorial 3

In this tutorial, you will create the model shown in Figure 10-53.   **(Expected time: 30 min)**

Figure 10-53 Model for Tutorial 3

The following steps are required to complete this tutorial:

a. Create the extrude feature, refer to Figure 10-54 and 10-55.
b. Create the second extrude feature, refer to Figure 10-56 and 10-57.

Advanced Modeling Tools-III

c. Create the third extrude feature and pattern it, refer to Figure 10-58 and 10-59.
d. Create the mirror feature, refer to Figure 10-60.
e. Create the toroidal bend feature, refer to Figure 10-61 and 10-62.
f. Create the round features, refer to Figure 10-63.
g. Change the color and appearance of the model, refer to Figure 10-64.

Starting a New Object File
Start a new part file and name it as *c10tut3*.

Creating the First Extrude Feature
1. Draw the sketch for the first extrude feature in the **FRONT** plane, as shown in Figure 10-54.

2. Extrude it to a length of **1200**, refer to Figure 10-55.

Figure 10-54 Sketch of the extrude feature   *Figure 10-55* Model showing the first extrude feature

Creating the Second Extrude Feature
1. Choose the **Plane** button from the **Sketcher Tools** toolbar; the **DATUM PLANE** dialog box is displayed and you are prompted to select the references to place the plane.

2. Select the **TOP** datum plane from the drawing area. Next, choose the **Offset** option from the drop-down list in the **References** selection area and enter **230** in the **Translation** edit box. Choose **OK**; the new datum plane is created with the default name **DTM1**.

3. Choose the **Extrude** button from the **Engineering Features** toolbar; the **Extrude** dashboard is displayed.

4. Choose **DTM1** as the sketching plane and create the sketch of the extrude feature, as shown in Figure 10-56.

Figure 10-56 Sketch of the extrude feature

5. Choose the **Remove Material** button from the **Extrude** dashboard.

6. Enter **20** in the **Enter the depth value for side 1** edit box.

7. Specify the correct direction of cut and choose the **Build feature** button to complete the creation of the feature.

   The model after creating the second extrude feature is shown in Figure 10-57.

Figure 10-57 Figure showing the second extrude feature

Creating the Next Extrude Feature

1. With the **DTM1** plane as the sketching plane and the **RIGHT** plane oriented to the **Right**, draw the sketch of the tread, as shown in Figure 10-58.

Advanced Modeling Tools-III

Figure 10-58 Sketch for the third extrude feature

2. Extrude and remove material from the tire to a depth value of 20. Note that the feature must be extruded into the model.

Creating the Pattern of the Tread

1. Select the extruded feature created in the previous step from the **Model Tree** or by clicking on it in the drawing area.

2. Choose the **Pattern** button from the **Edit Features** toolbar; the **Pattern** dashboard is displayed and you are prompted to select the dimension to vary in the first direction.

3. Choose the **Dimensions** tab in the **Pattern** dashboard and select the dimension value **30** from the feature. Enter **30** in the **Increment** edit box in the **Direction 1** selection area of the **Dimensions** tab slide-down panel.

4. Click in the **Direction 2** selection area of the **Dimensions** tab; you are prompted to select the dimension to vary in the second direction.

5. Select the dimension from the top edge of the base feature. Enter **40** in the **Direction 2** edit box.

6. Enter **30** in the **Enter the number of pattern members in the second direction** edit box in the dashboard.

7. Choose the **Build feature** button from the dashboard to exit from the **Pattern** tool.

The model after creating the pattern is shown in Figure 10-59.

Creating the Mirror Feature of the Patterned Feature

1. Mirror the tread pattern on the other side using the **RIGHT** datum plane, as shown in Figure 10-60.

Figure 10-59 Model after creating the pattern of the tread

Figure 10-60 Model after creating the mirror feature of the treads

Creating the Toroidal Bend Feature

1. Choose **Insert > Advanced > Toroidal Bend** from the menu bar; the **Toroidal Bend** dashboard is displayed.

2. Choose the **References** tab; a slide-down panel is displayed. Select the **Solid Geometry** check box. Also, choose **Define** from the slide-down panel; the **Sketch** dialog box is displayed.

3. Select the front face of the base feature as the sketching plane. Next, choose the **Sketch** button from the **Sketch** dialog box to accept the default orientation and enter the sketcher environment.

4. Draw the section for the toroidal bend feature, as shown in Figure 10-61.

5. Choose the **Geometry Coordinate System** button from the **Sketcher Tools** toolbar and place the reference coordinate system at the origin, as shown in Figure 10-61.

6. Choose the **Done** button from the **Sketcher Tools** toolbar to exit the sketcher mode; the **Toroidal Bend** dashboard is displayed again. Choose the **Options** tab and select the **Standard** radio button, if it is not already selected, in the **Curve Bend** area of the slide-down panel.

7. Choose the **Bend Radius** button; a flyout is displayed. Choose **360 degrees Bend** from the flyout; you are prompted to select two parallel planes to define the length of the bend.

Advanced Modeling Tools-III

Figure 10-61 Section created for the toroidal bend feature

8. Select the front face and then the back face of the base feature; the preview of the toroidal bend feature is displayed.

9. Choose the **Build Feature** button; the model similar to that shown in Figure 10-62 is created in the drawing area.

Figure 10-62 Model after creating the toroidal bend feature

Creating the Round Feature

1. Create a round feature of radius **5** units by selecting the edges, as shown in Figure 10-63.

Figure 10-63 Model showing the edges selected for creating the round feature

Changing the Color and Appearance of the Model

1. Choose the down-arrow on the right of the **Appearance Gallery** button from the **View** toolbar; a flyout is displayed.

2. Click on the **std-metals.dmt** located on the right of the **Library** head; a flyout is displayed.

3. Click on the **Misc.** node under the **Photolux Library**; a list of categories is displayed.

4. Choose **adv-rubber.dmt** from the categories displayed; the materials available in this category are displayed.

5. Choose the **adv-rubber-black** material; the cursor changes into a paint brush.

6. Select **Part** from the selection filter and then select the part created. Press the middle mouse button; the selected appearance is applied to the entire model.

Figure 10-64 shows the model after changing the color and appearance.

Saving the Model

1. Choose the **Save** button from the **File** toolbar to save the model.

Advanced Modeling Tools-III   10-31

Figure 10-64 Model after changing the color and appearance

Self-Evaluation Test

Answer the following questions and then compare them to those given at the end of this chapter:

1. The toroidal bend feature can be created only on one side of the sketching plane. (T/F)

2. To specify the length of the bend for a 360 degrees toroidal bend feature, you need to select two _____ planes.

3. The **Spinal Bend** tool bends solids or quilts along a sketched spine. (T/F)

4. The **Spinal Bend** tool is used to bend solids or quilts by continuously _____ the cross-sections along a sketched spine.

5. The **Transform** tool can be used to perform _____, _____, and _____ operations.

6. The **Spine** tool deforms the geometry in either the _____ or the _____ direction.

7. The **Sculpt** tool deforms the geometry through a _____.

8. The **Switch to next axis** button switches the axis of bend from one _____ to another.

9. While using the **Sculpt** tool, the _____ drop-down list is used to specify the direction in which the group of points selected move when sculpted.

10. The warp transformations can be performed only in the part mode. (T/F)

Review Questions

Answer the following questions:

1. What are the different tools through which a warp transformation can be carried out?

2. What is the maximum bend angle through which a geometry can be bent using the **Toroidal Bend** tool?

   (a) 90 degrees (b) 180 degrees
   (c) 270 degrees (d) 360 degrees

3. The trajectory for creating a spinal bend on geometry should be sketched _____ to the solid geometry.

4. The _____ tool is used to stretch the geometry along the required direction.

5. The _____ check box, if selected, keeps the original entity selected for the creation of warp feature in the drawing area along with the preview of the transformed feature.

6. The direction reference chosen for the creation of warp feature is any one of the _____ planes.

7. The **Spine** tool reshapes the geometry by manipulating the defining points of a _____.

8. A solid geometry can be rotated by clicking and rotating the active handles of the _____.

9. While using the **Toroidal Bend** tool, the user-defined coordinate system defines the _____ of the bend profile.

10. While creating a model using the **Toroidal Bend** tool, if the sketch defining the bend is a straight line, the profile of the model is a _____.

Advanced Modeling Tools-III

Exercises

Exercise 1

In this exercise, you will create the model shown in Figure 10-65. The dimensions for the model can be assumed. The dimensions given in the hint are suggestive.

(Expected time: 20 min)

Figure 10-65 Model for Exercise 1

Hint
1. Create the sketch of the base feature which is a rectangle of dimensions **500 X 300** and extrude it to a depth of **15**.
2. Create a new datum plane at a distance of **250** from the **RIGHT** datum plane.
3. Choose **Insert > Advanced > Spinal Bend** from the menu bar and select the **FRONT** datum plane as the sketching plane.
4. Create the trajectory for the **Spinal Bend** which should be tangent to the bottom face of the base feature. The shape of the trajectory needs to be in the form of steps with the corners rounded. The dimensions of the trajectory can be assumed.
5. Exit from the sketcher environment; you will be prompted to select a plane to define the volume of the bend.
6. Select the **DTM1** datum plane. The model similar to the one shown in Figure 10-65 is displayed in the drawing area.

Exercise 2

In this exercise, you will create the model shown in Figure 10-66. The dimensions for the base feature can be assumed. **(Expected time: 20 min)**

Figure 10-66 Model for Exercise 2

Answers to Self-Evaluation Test
1. F, **2.** parallel, **3.** T, **4.** repositioning, **5.** translate, rotate, scale, **6.** linear, radial, **7.** mesh, **8.** plane, **9. Symmetry**, **10.** T

Chapter 11

Assembly Modeling

Learning Objectives

After completing this chapter, you will be able to:
- *Understand the top-down assembly approach.*
- *Understand the bottom-up assembly approach.*
- *Assemble components of the assembly using assembly constraints.*
- *Understand the packaging of components.*
- *Create the simplified representations.*
- *Use the View Manager.*
- *Edit assembly constraints after assembling.*
- *Modify the components of the assembly.*
- *Create the exploded state of the assembly.*
- *Add offset lines to exploded components.*
- *Understand the Bill of Material in the assemblies.*

ASSEMBLY MODELING

An assembly is defined as a design consisting of two or more components bonded together at their respective working positions using the assembly constraints. These assembly designs are created in the **Assembly** mode of Pro/ENGINEER. To invoke the **Assembly** mode, choose the **New** button from the **Top Toolchest**; the **New** dialog box will be displayed. In this dialog box, select the **Assembly** radio button from the **Type** area and then select the **Design** radio button from the **Sub-type** area, as shown in Figure 11-1. Specify the name of the assembly in the **Name** edit box and choose **OK**; the **Assembly** mode is activated.

Figure 11-1 Invoking the **Assembly** mode from the **New** dialog box

Also, the initial screen appearance of the **Assembly** mode in Pro/ENGINEER Wildfire 5.0 will be displayed, as shown in Figure 11-2.

IMPORTANT TERMS RELATED TO THE ASSEMBLY MODE

Before proceeding further in this chapter, it is very important for you to understand the following terms.

Top-down Approach

This is the method of assembling the components in which the components of the assembly are created in the same assembly file. In this type of assembly modeling approach, the components are created in the assembly file and then assembled using the assembly constraints. Note that the parts you create in the **Assembly** mode are saved as separate *.prt* files.

Assembly Modeling

*Figure 11-2 Initial screen appearance of the **Assembly** mode*

Bottom-up Approach

This is the method of assembling the components that are created as separate parts in the **Part** mode and are saved as *.prt* files. Once all parts of an assembly have been created, you will create a new assembly file (*.asm*) and then assemble the parts using the assembly constraints available in the **Assembly** mode. Since the assembly file has information related only to the assembling of components, its size is small and therefore requires less hard disk space.

Remember that if any of these assembly components is moved from its original location on the hard disk, the assembly will not open the next time. This is because Pro/ENGINEER searches for the assembly component in the folder in which it was originally saved. If it does not find the name of the component in that folder, it will show an error while opening the assembly file and the **RESOLVE FEAT** menu will be displayed, as shown in Figure 11-3. Choose the **Quick Fix** option from this menu; the **QUICK FIX** submenu will be displayed, as shown in Figure 11-4. You can use the options in this submenu to locate the part file.

The other important thing that you need to remember while opening an existing assembly is that for example, Nut is a component that is common and used in most of the assemblies. Therefore, if the current Pro/ENGINEER session has already a component with the name Nut, it will use this component only when you open the assembly and not the original Nut used in the assembly.

*Figure 11-3 The **RESOLVE FEAT** menu*

*Figure 11-4 The **QUICK FIX** submenu*

Tip: *It is recommended that you create separate folders for all assemblies that you create in Pro/ENGINEER.*

Placement Constraints
The placement constraints are the constraints that are used to rigidly bind the components of the assembly to their respective positions in the assembly. These constraints are also called the assembly constraints. Generally, these constraints are used in combinations and you can constrain upto six degrees of freedom of a component.

Package
It is the state in which the component being assembled is not fully constrained and therefore, is not rigidly placed at its actual location.

CREATING TOP-DOWN ASSEMBLIES
As mentioned earlier, the top-down assemblies are those in which all components are created in the **Assembly** mode and in the same assembly file. The components created in the **Assembly** mode can be saved as separate *.prt* files. As you already know that to create components, you need the sketcher environment and to invoke the sketcher environment, you need the **Part** mode. You can invoke the **Part** mode from within the **Assembly** mode and create components using the tools in the **Part** mode. The method to create the component from within the **Assembly** mode is discussed next.

Creating Components in the Assembly Mode
To create a component in the **Assembly** mode, choose the **Create** button from the **Right Toolchest**; the **Component Create** dialog box will be displayed, as shown in Figure 11-5. Select the **Part** radio button from the **Type** area and the **Solid** radio button from the **Sub-type** area to create a *.prt* file. Enter the name of the component in the **Name** edit box and

*Figure 11-5 The **Component Create** dialog box*

Assembly Modeling

then choose the **OK** button; the **Creation Options** dialog box will be displayed. From this dialog box, select the method for creating the component.

CREATING BOTTOM-UP ASSEMBLIES

As discussed earlier, the bottom-up assemblies are created by inserting the part files one by one in the assembly file and then assembling them using the assembly constraints. When the first component is inserted in the **Assembly** mode, its three default datum planes are placed in the same orientation as that of the default datum planes of the **Assembly** mode. The method of inserting a component in the assembly is discussed next.

Inserting Components in an Assembly

When you enter the assembly environment, the three default assembly datum planes are displayed in the drawing area. If you do not want the default assembly datum planes in the assembly file, then while opening a new file, you need to clear the **Use default template** check box that is available in the **New** dialog box. It is recommended that you use the assembly datum planes as the first feature of the assembly and assemble the components of the assembly taking the reference of these datum planes. Using the datum planes as the first feature will help you during the modification of the assembly.

Some of the advantages of using the assembly datum planes are:

1. The components of the assembly can be redefined in such a way that the component placed later can be made the first component.

2. The first component can be replaced by some other component.

3. The placement constraint of the first component can be modified.

To insert a component, choose the **Assemble** button from the **Engineering Features** toolbar; the **Open** dialog box will be displayed. This dialog box is the same as the **File Open** dialog box that is used to open an existing file. Select the part that you need to insert into the assembly. You can also preview the component before adding it to the assembly. After the components are displayed in the drawing area in the **Assembly** mode, you need to specify constraints in order to assemble them by using the **Component Placement** dashboard. Even if you are placing the first component, you need to constrain it using the assembly constraints. Generally, the first component is assembled with the datum planes. Remember that no component is placed automatically; you need to specify its position manually.

ASSEMBLING COMPONENTS

The components in an assembly can be placed parametrically or non-parametrically. If the components are placed using the assembly constraints, it is called parametric assembly. On the other hand, if the components are packaged, it is called non-parametric assembly.

To assemble the components parametrically, choose the **Assemble** button; the **Open** dialog box will be displayed. Select the required component and choose the **Open** button from the **Open** dialog box; the **Component Placement** dashboard will be displayed, as shown in Figure 11-6.

*Figure 11-6 The **Component Placement** dashboard*

Using the **Component Placement** dashboard, you can apply constraints to assemble the components and also control the display of the component to be assembled in the same or separate windows. The options in the **Component Placement** dashboard are discussed next.

Displaying Components in a Separate Window

The **Show component in a separate window while specifying constraints** button is used to display the component to be assembled in a separate window. When you choose this button, a new window will open displaying the component to be assembled. Note that viewing the component to be assembled, and the assembly, in separate windows, prevents cluttering of the components in the assembly window.

However, there is a limitation when the assembly and the component to be assembled are displayed in separate windows. If the components are in the same window, they change their orientation as you apply the constraints, thus giving you an idea of the next constraint to be applied. In other words, you can easily find out which degree of freedom of the component is constrained and which needs to be constrained.

Displaying Components in the Same Window

The **Show component in the assembly window while specifying constraints** button is used to display the component to be assembled in the assembly window itself. This button is chosen by default when you invoke the **Component Placement** dashboard. As you apply constraints, the component in the assembly window changes its position accordingly.

Applying Constraints

As discussed earlier, the components are assembled using the assembly constraints. The assembly constraints are also called placement constraints. These constraints help in placing and positioning a component precisely with respect to the other components in the assembly. The Constraint Type drop-down list in the **Component Placement** dashboard contains different types of placement constraints, as shown in Figure 11-7. You can select the required constraints from this drop-down list to assemble components in the assembly. These constraints are also available when you choose the **Placement** tab of the **Component Placement** dashboard.

Figure 11-7 The Constraint Type drop-down list

Automatic

When you choose this constraint, Pro/ENGINEER assumes the constraint and applies it according to the type of entity selected. For example, if you select axes of two components to assemble, Pro/ENGINEER will assume that you want to apply the **Align** constraint and the **Align** constraint will be applied to the two components.

Mate

The **Mate** placement constraint allows you to make two selected planes, datum planes, faces, or a combination of a datum plane and a face coplanar to each other. The selected faces or datums may or may not be in contact with each other.

On selecting the **Mate** constraint, the Offset drop-down list is displayed next to it in the dashboard. This drop-down list is also displayed when you choose the **Placement** tab. Using the options in this drop-down list, you can specify the offset value (if any) for the placement constraint. It has three options: **Offset**, **Coincident**, and **Oriented** and can be used in combination with three options.

Offset

If you need to keep the two faces or planes at some distance apart, then you can use the **Mate** constraint with some offset value. The offset distance between the two coplanar faces can be a positive or a negative value. Figure 11-8 shows the faces selected to apply the **Offset** constraint. Figure 11-9 shows the component assembled at an offset distance from the selected face.

Figure 11-8 Faces selected to apply the **Offset** constraint

Figure 11-9 Components after assembling

Coincident

The **Coincident** constraint allows you to make two selected planes or faces coplanar to each other. Figure 11-10 shows the faces selected to mate. Figure 11-11 shows the components after assembling.

Figure 11-10 *Faces selected for the **Coincident** constraint*

Figure 11-11 *Components after assembling*

Oriented

The **Oriented** constraint is used when you want to mate two faces or planes or a combination of the two, and at the same time, you want to orient some other faces or planes of the two components to face in the same direction. Figure 11-12 shows the faces selected to mate and Figure 11-13 shows the components after assembling.

Figure 11-12 *Faces selected for the **Oriented** constraint*

Figure 11-13 *Components after assembling*

Align

The **Align** constraint is used to assemble two components by making the selected faces or planes coplanar such that the aligned faces or planes face in the same direction. Apart from planes and faces, you can also select datum axes, datum points, edges, or vertices for applying the **Align** constraint.

The **Align** constraint can also be used in combination with the following three constraints: **Offset**, **Coincident**, and **Oriented**. Note that these combinations can only be used with the **Mate** and **Align** constraints.

Assembly Modeling

Offset
The **Offset** constraint is used to align two entities with some offset distance between the aligning entities. The offset value can be positive or negative. Figure 11-14 shows the faces to align offset and Figure 11-15 shows the components after applying the constraints.

*Figure 11-14 Components before applying the **Offset** constraint*

*Figure 11-15 Components after applying the **Offset** constraint*

Coincident
The **Coincident** constraint is used to assemble two components by making the selected faces or planes coplanar such that the aligned faces or planes face in the same direction. Figure 11-16 shows the faces selected to align coincident. Figure 11-17 shows the components after assembling.

*Figure 11-16 Components before applying the **Coincident** constraint*

Figure 11-17 Components after assembling

Oriented
The **Oriented** constraint makes the two selected faces or planes, or the combination of both, face in the same direction. Figure 11-18 shows the constraints applied on the two components and Figure 11-19 shows the two components after applying the constraints.

Figure 11-18 Components before applying the ***Oriented*** constraint

Figure 11-19 Components after applying the ***Oriented*** constraint

Insert

The **Insert** constraint is used to assemble the revolved components. Applying this constraint allows the revolved component, holes, or a combination of both to share the same orientation of the central axis. Figure 11-20 shows the faces selected to be inserted and Figure 11-21 shows the components after assembling.

Figure 11-20 Components before assembling

Figure 11-21 Components after assembling

Coord Sys

The **Coord Sys** constraint aligns the coordinate system of the first component with the coordinate system of the second component.

Tangent

The **Tangent** constraint is used to make the selected circular face tangent to the other selected face or plane.

Pnt On Line

The **Pnt On Line** constraint is used to align the selected datum point or the vertex on the first part with the selected edge, datum axis, or datum curve on the second part.

Pnt On Srf
The **Pnt On Srf** constraint is used to align the selected datum point or vertex on the first part with the selected surface or datum plane on the second part.

Edge On Srf
The **Edge On Srf** constraint is used to align the selected edge of the first part with the selected surface or datum plane on the second part.

Fix
The **Fix** constraint is used to fix a component.

Default
The **Default** constraint is used to assemble the component in the assembly by aligning the default coordinate system of the component with the default coordinate system of the assembly. Also, the part datum planes are aligned with the assembly datum planes.

Change orientation of constraint Button

This button on the dashboard is used to change the orientation of the constraint applied to components. This button is used only after a constraint has been applied to the components. Initially, this button is not available when the **Component Placement** dashboard is invoked.

Status Area
The **Status** area in the **Component Placement** dashboard displays the placement status of the component in the assembly. If you choose the **Build feature** button from the **Component Placement** dashboard when the placement status is displayed as **Partially Placed**, then the component assembled will be displayed in the **Model Tree** with a small square on it. Also, the component is packaged.

The dashboard consists of four tabs; **Placement**, **Move**, **flexibility**, and **Properties**. In this chapter, you will learn about the **Placement** and **Move** tabs.

Placement Tab
The options in this tab are used to apply as well as edit constraints to the components to be assembled. When you choose the **Placement** tab, a slide-down panel will be displayed, as shown in Figure 11-22.

The Constraint Type and Offset drop-down lists have already been discussed. Rest of the options in the slide-down panel are discussed next.

New Constraint Option
This option is used to specify a new set of constraints to the assembly components.

Select component Item Collector
This collector displays the entities of a component that have been chosen to assemble it with the parent component.

*Figure 11-22 The **Placement** tab slide-down panel*

Select assembly Item Collector
This collector displays the entities of the parent component that have been chosen to create an assembly.

> **Note**
> *Most of the options displayed on the dashboard are also available in the shortcut menu, which is displayed on right-clicking when the command is active.*

Status Area
This area displays the placement status of the component in the assembly. Sometimes, after adding constraints, a few placement constraints are required to be assumed. This is the reason sometimes the **Allow Assumptions** check box will be displayed in the **Status** area.

Move Tab
The options in the **Move** tab can be used when the component to be assembled is displayed in the assembly itself. This tab is used to move or rotate a component along a degree of freedom that is not constrained. The **Move** tab slide-down panel is shown in Figure 11-23. The options in this tab are discussed next.

Motion Type Drop-down List
The options in the **Motion Type** drop-down list are discussed next.

*Figure 11-23 The **Move** tab slide-down panel*

Orient Mode
This option, if selected, orients the part in the assembly about its spin center.

Translate
This option, if selected, moves the component from its current location in the assembly.

However, remember that the component can be moved only along the degrees of freedom that are not constrained.

Rotate
This option, if selected, causes the component to rotate in the assembly around its available degrees of freedom.

Adjust
This option is used to pack a component with reference to the assembly. When you select this option, you will be prompted to select a surface on the packaged component to adjust the reference plane. The component is assembled according to the surface specified.

> **Tip**: *It is recommended that you use the CTRL+ALT+left mouse button to translate a component and CTRL+ALT+middle mouse button to rotate a component. It is always easier to use the above combinations to move the component rather than switching to a separate tab in the **Component Placement** dashboard and using its options to move a component. Moving the components using the keyboard shortcuts, can speed up the process of locating the component correctly in the assembly and establishing constraints.*

Relative in view plane Radio Button
When you invoke the **Move** tab slide-down panel, this radio button is selected by default. It moves the component relative to the viewing plane.

Motion Reference Radio Button
When this radio button is selected, you need to select a reference plane through which the component will be moved. After, selecting the reference plane, the **Normal** and **Parallel** options are activated.

Normal plane
This option moves the component in a plane normal to the selected reference plane.

Parallel plane
This option allows you to move the component in a plane that is parallel to the selected reference plane.

Relative
These boxes display the coordinates of the current position of the component.

PACKAGING COMPONENTS
Consider a situation when you do not know the exact location of a component in the assembly or you want to specify the exact location later. In such cases, you can non-parametrically place the component in the assembly. This method of non-parametrically placing the components in the assembly is called packaging. There are two methods to package a component in an assembly. The first method is to use the **Insert** menu in the menu bar. The second method is to exit the **Component Placement** dashboard before fully constraining the components to be assembled.

To package a component, choose **Insert > Component > Package** from the menu bar; the **PACKAGE** menu will be displayed, as shown in Figure 11-24. The options in this menu are discussed next.

Add

The **Add** option is used to add the component to be packaged. On choosing this option, the **GET MODEL** sub-menu will be displayed. Using the options of this sub-menu, you can open a new component, select the component from the assembly, or select the last component from the assembly to assemble again.

Figure 11-24 The PACKAGE menu

When you select the component from the **Open** dialog box, the **Move** dialog box will be displayed, as shown in Figure 11-25. The options in this dialog box are similar to those in the **Move** tab of the **Component Placement** dashboard. After you have specified the location of the component in the assembly file, choose **OK** to place the component and close the **Move** dialog box. Remember that you can move only the packaged component using this option.

Move

The **Move** option is used to move the packaged component to a new location. When you choose this option, the **Move** dialog box will be displayed, as shown in Figure 11-25.

Fix Location

The **Fix Location** option is used to fix the location of an existing packaged component. When you choose this option, you are prompted to select the component to be fixed. Select the component to be fixed.

Figure 11-25 The Move dialog box

Finalize

As mentioned earlier, the packaged components are not assembled parametrically. Hence, packaging does not relate the component with its neighboring components in the assembly. Once the location of the component is decided, then it can be finalized using the **Finalize** option. When you choose this option, you will be prompted to select the packaged component. Selected the packaged component, the **Component Placement** dashboard will be displayed. You can parametrically assemble the component by adding the placement constraints to the component by using this dashboard.

CREATING SIMPLIFIED REPRESENTATIONS

As you know, the assembly designs consist of a number of parts and subassemblies. In case of some complicated assemblies, such as a computer CPU, once the cover is assembled, the components inside it are not visible. So there have to be some means to temporarily remove certain components that are not desired at some point of time from the current display or force them to be displayed in the wireframe so that you can see through them. This process of removing some components or changing their type of display from the current display is called **Simplified Representation**.

Simplified representations can be created using the **View** menu or by using the **View Manager**. The only difference between them is that by using the **View Manager** you can give a name to the representation. To create a simplified representation by using the cascading menu, select a component from the **Model Tree** and then choose **View > Representation** from the menu bar; a cascading menu will be displayed, as shown in Figure 11-26.

Figure 11-26 The cascading menu

Using the Cascading Menu

The options available in the cascading menu are used to create a simplified representation without saving it. The simplified representation reduces the regeneration time of the assembly, especially the complex assemblies. The options in this menu are discussed next.

Exclude

When you choose this option, the selected component is removed from the display. You can even select more than one component from the **Model Tree** or from the assembly to remove it from the display. However, the component remains in the memory of Pro/ENGINEER and is even displayed in the **Model Tree**. This component can be, at any time, forced to be displayed again. To display the component again, choose the **Master** option from the cascading menu. Figure 11-27 shows a butterfly valve assembly, in which the body is removed from the current display. This kind of representation helps in assembling the components inside the body, like the plate and the screw, in this case.

Figure 11-27 Components removed from the assembly

Master

This option is used to restore the original representation of the assembly, thereby displaying all components in it. When you use this option, the components that were removed from the current display after using the **Exclude** option get redisplayed, see Figure 11-28.

Figure 11-28 Master representation of the assembly

Assembly Only

The **Assembly Only** option will be used to hide all components of an assembly except the components of the subassembly.

Geometry

In this type of simplified representation, the complete geometry of the components will be displayed in the current model display style. This type of simplified representation takes a long time for regeneration. The components that are not selected in this type of representation cannot be modified. However, these components can be redefined.

Tip: *When you create a simplified representation, some information regarding the type of representation will be displayed in the drawing area. To remove this information, choose **View > Shade** from the menu bar.*

Graphics

When you choose the **Graphics** option, the selected components will be displayed in wireframe, as shown in Figure 11-29. This type of representation is generally used for assembling the components inside some other components. This type of simplified representation also reduces the regeneration time for large assemblies. However, note that the components displayed as the wireframe model in the graphic representation cannot be modified, redefined, or referenced.

Assembly Modeling

Figure 11-29 The graphics representation of an assembly

Using the View Manager

The **View Manager** is used to create, modify, and switch between the simplified representations, exploded views, and orientation of the assembly. To invoke the **View Manager**, choose the **View Manager** button from the **Top Toolchest**; the **View Manager** dialog box will be displayed, as shown in Figure 11-30. Alternatively, you can invoke the **View Manager** dialog box by choosing the **View Manager** option from the **View** menu. The various uses of this dialog box and operations that can be performed on an assembly using this dialog box are discussed next.

Creating a Simplified Representation by Using the View Manager

When the **View Manager** dialog box is displayed, the **Simp Rep** tab will be chosen by default. The options under this tab are similar to those that were available in the cascading menu. The red arrow on left of **Master Rep** indicates that this representation is set currently. To set any of the listed representation types, select the representation and right-click to invoke the shortcut menu. Choose the **Set Active** option from the shortcut menu to set the display of the assembly to that type of representation or double-click on any one of the representation types.

Figure 11-30 The View Manager dialog box

To create a user-defined representation, choose the **New** button from the **View Manager** dialog box. Specify a name for the representation and press ENTER; the **EDIT** dialog box will be displayed, as shown in Figure 11-31. Using this dialog box, you can select the components that you want to include, exclude, and substitute from the display. You can also redefine the representation type. To do so, select a representation from the list and choose the **Edit** button; a shortcut menu will be displayed. From this shortcut menu, choose the **Redefine** option; the **EDIT** dialog box will be displayed. Using this dialog box, you can redefine the representation.

*Figure 11-31 The **EDIT** dialog box*

Creating a Display Style by Using the View Manager
To create a new display style from the **View Manager** dialog box, choose the **Style** tab. Two styles are available in the **Names** list of the dialog box. You can create a new style or redefine an existing style. You can create new display styles and redefine them using the **New** and **Edit** buttons in the **View Manager** dialog box.

Setting the Orientation of an Assembly by Using the View Manager
If you choose **Named View List** button in the **Top Toolchest**, a flyout will be displayed. Various orientations given in this flyout are used to display the assembly as viewed from different directions. Using the **View Manager**, you can invoke the **Orientation** dialog box to set a user-defined orientation. To invoke the **Orientation** dialog box, choose the **Orient** tab and create a new orientation by choosing the **New** button from the **View Manager** dialog box. Name the view and then redefine it to display the **Orientation** dialog box. Use this dialog box to set the orientation of the assembly and then save the orientation by giving it a name listed in the flyout displayed on choosing the **Named View List** button.

Creating X-section of an Assembly by Using the View Manager
You can create the section view of the assembly using the **View Manager**. Choose the **Xsec** tab from the **View Manager** dialog box and then choose the **New** button to create a new section. Name the section and press the middle mouse button to display the **XSEC OPTS** menu. Use this menu to select the options to create the required section.

Assembly Modeling

REDEFINING THE COMPONENTS OF AN ASSEMBLY

Sometimes, after you have assembled the components of the assembly, you may need to modify or redefine the location or the placement constraints of the components. To do so, select the component from the **Model Tree** and right-click to invoke the shortcut menu. Choose the **Edit Definition** option from the shortcut menu. You can also right-click on the component to be redefined in the drawing area and choose the **Edit Definition** option from the shortcut menu. All components assembled after the selected component will become invisible and the **Component Placement** dashboard will be displayed. You can modify the existing placement constraints or add new constraints using this dialog box.

REORDERING COMPONENTS

To change the order of assembling the components, choose **Edit > Component Operations** from the menu bar; the **COMPONENT** menu will be displayed, as shown in Figure 11-32. Choose the **Reorder** option from this menu; you will be prompted to select the component to be reordered. When you select a component to reorder from the **Model Tree** or from the drawing area and choose **Done**, a message will be displayed in the **Message Area** mentioning those components before which you can insert the selected component.

*Figure 11-32 The **COMPONENT** menu*

Tip: *You can also reorder the components in an assembly by using the **Model Tree**. This can be done by selecting the component in the **Model Tree** and then dragging it to the position where it can be placed. Note that this method of reordering does not inform you where the component can or cannot be placed. However, the parent component of the selected child component gets highlighted when you start dragging the child component. This means if a component has a parent, then the parent is also reordered with the child. Remember that in the **Model Tree**, the parent component will always be placed before its child component.*

SUPPRESSING/RESUMING COMPONENTS

If you do not want certain components of the assembly to appear in the current display or in the drawing views, you can suppress them. To suppress the components, select the component from the **Model Tree** or the drawing area and then choose **Edit > Suppress > Suppress** from the menu bar.

Similarly, the suppressed components can be resumed by choosing the **Resume** option from the same menu. The components can also be suppressed/resumed using the shortcut menu that will be displayed when you right-click on the component in the **Model Tree** or in the drawing area. In the shortcut menu, choose **Suppress** to suppress and **Resume** to resume the components.

REPLACING COMPONENTS

The existing components of an assembly that are assembled using the assembly constraints can be replaced with some other components, if necessary. To replace a component, choose **Edit > Replace** from the menu bar; the **Replace** dialog box will be displayed, as shown in Figure 11-33 and you will be prompted to select the components to be replaced. Select the component to be replaced from the drawing area or from the **Model Tree**. The new component can be assembled using the **Family Table**, **Interchange**, **Layout**, or by an **Unrelated Component** options available in the **Replace By** area. After you have selected one of these options, for example, the **Unrelated Component** check box. Next, click on the **Select New Component** collector; you will be prompted to select a model to replace the component. Choose the **Open** button available on the right of the **Select New Component** collector; the **Open** dialog box will be displayed. Select the required model from it; the name of the selected model will be displayed in the **Select New Component** collector in the **Replace** dialog box. Now, choose the **Apply** button and then the **OK** button from the **Replace** dialog box; the **Component Placement** dashboard will be displayed. Now, add the required placement constraints to the model using this dashboard.

*Figure 11-33 The **Replace** dialog box*

ASSEMBLING REPEATED COPIES OF A COMPONENT

Sometimes, the assembly design demands the assembling of a particular component more than once. One option is that you should assemble the component every time and add the placement constraints all over again. However, this is a very tedious and time-consuming process, especially in the assemblies that have a large number of similar components. To solve this problem, Pro/ENGINEER provides you with an option of assembling multiple copies of the components. To repeat a component in an assembly, select the component to repeat from the **Model Tree** or from the drawing area and then choose **Edit > Repeat** from the menu bar; the **Repeat Component** dialog box will be displayed, as shown in Figure 11-34. The options in the **Repeat Component** dialog box are discussed next.

Assembly Modeling

Component Area

The button in this area is used to select the component whose multiple copies are to be assembled. The name of the selected component will be displayed in the display box provided in this area.

Variable Assembly Refs Area

The **Variable Assembly Refs** area displays the placement constraints that are applied on the selected component. You can keep the placement constraints that need to be present for the new component and modify the remaining constraints by selecting them from this area. The field in this area consists of the following columns.

Type

The **Type** column displays the type of placement constraints that are applied to the selected component.

CompRef

The **CompRef** column displays the references that were used to assemble the component. In case you want to change this for the new component, select this constraint and then choose the **Add** button. Now, select a reference on the assembly. A copy of the selected component will be added to the assembly at a new location. Similarly, to add another copy, repeat this procedure.

*Figure 11-34 The **Repeat Component** dialog box*

AsmRef

The **AsmRef** column displays the reference on the assembly that was used to assemble the selected component.

Place Component Area

The **Placement Component** area displays the new references added for the newly placed copies of the selected component.

Add

The **Add** button is chosen to add the required references for the new copy of the selected component. This button will be available only when you select one of the constraints from the **Variable Assembly Refs** area.

Remove

The **Remove** button is chosen to remove the selected reference from the new component. This button is available only when you select one of the references from the **Place Component** area.

To create a repeated component in an assembly, select the required component and then invoke the **Repeat Component** dialog box. Next, select the constraint to be copied from the **Variable Assembly Refs** area in the dialog box and then choose the **Add** button. Now, select the new reference for the new copied component from the screen; the selected component will be copied to the new reference. Choose **Confirm** to accept the repeated copy of the component.

MODIFYING THE COMPONENTS OF AN ASSEMBLY

Sometimes, during or after the assembly of a component, you may need to modify the dimensions of the component. You can even redefine the selected feature in the **Assembly** mode itself. The methods used to modify and redefine the features are discussed next.

Modifying Dimensions of a Feature of a Component

The dimensions of a selected feature of the component can be modified by selecting the component from the **Model Tree** or from the drawing area. When the outline of the model turns red in color, right-click to invoke the shortcut menu. Choose the **Activate** option; the name of the component appears in the drawing area. Also a small green button appears on the active component in the **Model Tree**. Now, select the activated component from the **Model Tree** and right-click to display the shortcut menu. Select the **Open** option to open the component as a part file in a separate window and edit the features as required. After modifying the dimensions, regenerate the component, and save the part file. Next, close the part file and activate the assembly window and regenerate the assembly to incorporate the changes made in the component.

Redefining a Feature of a Component

You can redefine the features of a component in the **Assembly** mode. This saves time in opening the part in the **Part** mode and then redefining the features. To redefine the feature of a component, you need to select the component from the **Model Tree** and make it active. After the component is activated, select the feature that you need to redefine from the drawing area. Hold down the right mouse button to invoke the shortcut menu. Choose the **Edit Definition** option; the feature creation tool is activated and now you can redefine the feature.

CREATING THE EXPLODED STATE

In an assembly design, the components assembled inside other components may not be visible. This could be misleading and may confuse the viewer as he cannot view all components. To avoid this confusion, generally an exploded view is provided along with the assembled view. An exploded view is a state in which all components move from their original position so that they are visible, as shown in Figure 11-35.

The exploded state can be generated by choosing **View > Explode > Edit Position** from the menu bar. On choosing the **Edit Position** option, the default exploded state of an assembly will be displayed. Also, the **Explode Position** dashboard will be displayed, as shown in Figure 11-36.

Various options in this dashboard are discussed next.

Assembly Modeling

Figure 11-35 The exploded state of an assembly

*Figure 11-36 The **Explode Position** dashboard*

Translate
This button is used to move a component from its current location to a new location in the assembly. To move a component, choose this button; three axes will be displayed on it. Next, move the cursor on the desired axis. When the axis gets highlighted, click and drag the component.

Rotate
This button is used to rotate a component about a selected axis. To rotate a component, choose this button; you will be prompted to select a reference for rotation. Select a reference (edge, axis, planar face/datum plane, any 2 points, or coordinate system); a small white square will be displayed. Next, click on the square and rotate the component.

View Plane
The **View Plane** option is used to select the current view plane (that is, the computer screen) as the reference for exploding a selected component. Choose this button; a small square will be displayed. Click on the square and move the component to the desired location.

References Tab

The options in this tab allow you to select the components as well as define a reference for movement. Choose this tab; a slide-down panel will be displayed, as shown in Figure 11-37. The **Components to Move** collector allows you to select and display the name of the selected component. The **Movement Reference** collector allows you to select a reference to define the movement of the selected component. Note that you need to click in the collector so that it gets activated, thereby, enabling you to select the required entities.

Options Tab

Choose this tab to display a slide-down panel, as shown in Figure 11-38. The options in this slide-down panel are discussed next.

*Figure 11-37 The **References** slide-down panel*

*Figure 11-38 The **Options** slide-down panel*

Copy Position

This button is used to restore the exploded component to its original position. For example, when an assembly explodes, its components move away. To restore components to their original position; choose the **Copy Position** button from the **Options** slide-down panel; the **Copy Position** dialog box will be displayed. Click in the **Components to Move** collector to activate it and select the exploded component moved away from the assembly. Next, click in the **Copy Position From** collector to activate it and then select a component from the assembly that is at a similar location in the assembly. Choose the **Apply** button from this dialog box; the selected component will be assembled at its original position in the assembly.

Motion Increment

You can specify an increment value for movement as well as define a smooth motion using this drop-down list.

Move with Children

On selecting this check box, the selected component moves along with its child components.

> **Note**
> *If you have not generated the exploded view of an assembly, a default explode state will be available on choosing **View > Explode > Explode View** from the menu bar. To display the unexploded state of the assembly, choose **View > Explode > Unexplode** in the menu bar.*

Assembly Modeling   11-25

*Alternatively, you can invoke the **View Manager** and then choose the **Explode** tab. Now, double-click on the required state to activate it. Also, you can create new states, edit existing states, and switch between various states created.*

Explode Lines Tab

Explode lines are used to display the actual path and direction of the mating components. Generally, these lines are used for an easy visualization of the exploded components of the assemblies. The exploded state of an assembly with the offset lines is shown in Figure 11-39.

Figure 11-39 The exploded state of an assembly with the offset lines

Create cosmetic offset lines to illustrate movement of exploded component Button

To create explode lines, an exploded state should exist in which the explode lines will be created. Choose the **Create cosmetic offset lines to illustrate movement of exploded component** button from the slide-down panel that is displayed on choosing the **Explode Lines** tab; the **Cosmetic Offset Line** dialog box will be displayed, as shown in Figure 11-40. Using this dialog box, you can select the objects for creating the explode lines. The objects that can be selected are axis, surfaces, edge, or curve.

Reference 1
Click in this collector to activate it, and then select the first reference.

Reference 2
Click in this collector to activate it, and then select the second reference.

Next, choose the **Apply** button to accept the creation of the explode lines and continue for the next collection. Choose the **Close** button to close this dialog box.

> **Note**
> *The display of explode lines is automatically turned off once you display the unexploded state of the assembly.*

Edit the selected explode line

This button will be available in the **Explode Lines** tab only when you select the explode line created earlier. To modify the explode line created, select it and then choose this button; two handles will be displayed at both ends of the line. Next, click on the handle and drag it to extend or shorten the explode line segment. To exit the edit mode, right-click; a shortcut menu will be displayed. Choose **Clear** from this shortcut menu.

*Figure 11-40 The **Cosmetic Offset Line** dialog box*

Delete the selected explode line

To delete the selected explode line, select the exploded line created and then choose the **Delete the selected explode lines** button; the selected explode line will be deleted.

Edit Line Styles

You can edit the attributes of the selected exploded line by choosing the **Edit Line Styles** button. You can modify the attributes such as line style type, color of the line style, or copy the line style from an existing line type.

Default Line Style

Choose this button to set the default attributes of the explode line.

You can also add a jog to an existing explode line segment. A jog is a break given to the continuation of a line segment. To do so, move the cursor on the explode line and right-click; choose **Add jog** from the shortcut displayed.

> **Note**
> *To delete an offset line, select the explode line and right-click; a shortcut menu will be displayed. Choose **Remove Explode Line** from it. You can also set the line style for the offset lines that you create in an exploded view by using the shortcut menu.*

THE BILL OF MATERIALS

The Bill of Materials or BOM is the tabular representation of all components of the assembly, along with the information associated with them. The information can be the material of the components, the additional note with the components, and so on. Pro/ENGINEER Wildfire 5.0 provides you with a ready-made BOM that can be directly utilized. This BOM will be automatically updated during the assembly of the components. The BOM can be viewed by using the **BOM** dialog box shown in Figure 11-41, which will be displayed by choosing **Info > Bill of Materials** in the menu bar. The options in this dialog box are discussed next.

Select Model Area
The options in the **Select Model** area are used to select the type of assembly whose BOM has to be displayed. These options are discussed next.

Top Level
The **Top Level** radio button is used to select the top level assembly for displaying the BOM. In this case, the subassemblies inserted in the current assembly are considered as a component.

Figure 11-41 The BOM dialog box

Subassembly
The **Subassembly** radio button is used to list the components of the selected subassemblies, as individual components in the **BOM**. When you select this radio button, you will be prompted to select the subassembly.

Include Area
The options in this area are discussed next.

Skeletons
In the Skeleton model geometry, the assembly level features such as cuts and holes do not affect the geometry of the skeleton model. The **Skeletons** check box is selected so that the skeletons, if any, in the assembly could also be included in the BOM.

Unplaced
The **Unplaced** check box is selected to include the unplaced components in the BOM.

Designated Objects
The **Designated Objects** check box is selected to include the bulk items, if any, that are used in the assembly. Bulk items are items whose solid models are not created but they are used in the assembly. In Pro/ENGINEER, you can include the weight and other properties of these bulk items to calculate certain parameters related to the assembly like total weight of assembly. Examples of bulk items are paint, glue, cotton lace, and so on.

After you have selected the options in the **BOM** dialog box, choose **OK** to open the browser that displays the BOM for the selected assembly. The file of the Bill of Material is automatically saved with the name of the assembly. The extension of this file is *.bom*. You can later retrieve it in the **Drawing** mode to display the BOM in the drawing views of the assembly.

TUTORIALS

Tutorial 1

In this tutorial, you will create all components of the Shock assembly and then assemble them, as shown in Figure 11-42. Also, you will create an exploded state of the assembly, as shown in Figure 11-43. The BOM is shown in Figure 11-44. The dimensions of the components are shown in Figures 11-45 through 11-52. **(Expected time: 2 hrs)**

Figure 11-42 The Shock assembly

Figure 11-43 The exploded state of the Shock Assembly

Assembly Modeling

ITEM	QTY.	NAME	MATERIAL
1	1	BRACKET	STEEL
2	1	U-SUPPORT	STEEL
3	1	PIVOT	STEEL
4	2	BUSHING	BRONZE
5	1	SELF LOCKING NUT	0.625-11UNC
6	1	WASHER	USER DEFINED
7	1	HEXAGONAL BOLT	STEEL
8	1	CASTLE NUT	STEEL

Figure 11-44 The Bill of Material for the Shock assembly

Figure 11-45 Dimensions for the Bracket

Figure 11-46 Dimensions for the Pivot

Figure 11-47 Dimensions for the U-Support

Figure 11-48 Dimensions for the Bushing

Figure 11-49 Dimensions for the Self locking nut

Figure 11-50 Dimensions for the Washer

Figure 11-51 Dimensions for the Hexagonal bolt

Assembly Modeling

Figure 11-52 Dimensions for the Castle nut

Note
You can download the part files for the assembly from www.cadcim.com

The following steps are required to complete this tutorial:

a. Create all components of the assembly as separate part files in the **Part** mode.
b. Create a new file in the **Assembly** mode and then assemble the **U-Support** with the default datum planes.
c. Assemble the **Bushing** with the **U-Support** and then repeat the Bushing in the assembly, refer to Figures 11-53 through 11-55.
d. Assemble the **Pivot** with the **Bushing**, refer to Figures 11-56 and 11-57.
e. Suppress the two Bushings and the **Pivot**.
f. Assemble the **Bracket** with the assembly, refer to Figures 11-58 and 11-59.
g. Assemble the **Washer**, **Hexagonal Bolt**, **Castle nut**, and **Self locking nut** in the assembly, refer to Figures 11-60 through 11-62.
h. Unsuppress the suppressed components.
i. After assembling all components, create the exploded state of the assembly, refer to Figure 11-63.
j. Generate offset lines in the exploded state, refer to Figure 11-64.
k. Save the assembly and then exit the **Assembly** mode.

Before you start creating components, set the working directory to *C:\ProE-WF-5.0\c11\Shockassembly*.

Starting the Components of the Assembly

The given assembly is created by using the bottom-up approach. As mentioned earlier, in bottom-up approach assemblies, the components are created as separate files and are placed in the assembly file. Therefore, first you need to create the components of the assembly.

1. Create all components of the assembly as separate part files and save them in the current working directory.

2. Close the part files, if opened.

Creating a New Assembly File

You need to assemble all components that you have created in an assembly file having an extension *.asm*. You need to open a new assembly file to assemble the components.

1. Choose the **New** button from the **File** toolbar; the **New** dialog box is displayed.

2. Select the **Assembly** radio button in the **Type** area of the **New** dialog box. In the **Sub-type** area of this dialog box, the **Design** radio button is selected by default. Enter the name of the assembly in the **Name** edit box as **SHOCKASSEMBLY**.

   Note
   *Make sure that the **Use default template** check box is selected in the **New** dialog box. If this check box is not selected, you cannot use the template provided by Pro/ENGINEER. Therefore, in this case, you will need to create the default datum planes by choosing the **Plane** button from the **Right Toolchest**.*

3. Choose **OK** from the **New** dialog box; the assembly environment is invoked.

Assembling the U-Support with the Default Datum Planes

1. Choose the **Assemble** button from the **Engineering Features** toolbar; the **Open** dialog box is displayed.

2. Select the **U-Support** component from the **Open** dialog box and choose the **Open** button; the **Component Placement** dashboard is displayed and you are prompted to select any reference for auto type constraining.

   In the **Component Placement** dashboard, the **Automatic** constraint type and the **Coincident** offset type are selected by default in the **Constraint Type** drop-down list and the **Offset** drop-down list, respectively.

3. Choose the **Show component in a separate window while specifying constraints** button from the **Component Placement** dashboard to display the **U-Support** component in a separate window.

4. Now, select the **FRONT** plane from the drawing area in the **COMPONENT WINDOW** and select the **ASM_FRONT** plane from the drawing area in the assembly window. Now, these two datum planes are aligned.

5. Similarly, select the other two datum planes and align them. After all the three planes are aligned, the message **Fully Constrained** is displayed in the **Status** area of the dashboard.

6. Choose the **Build feature** button to complete the assembly of the first part.

Assembly Modeling

Note

*You can also assemble the first component in an assembly by selecting the **Default** option from the Constraint Type drop-down list in the **Component Placement** dashboard.*

Assembling the Bushing with the U-Support

The next component you need to assemble is the **Bushing**.

1. Choose the **Assemble** button to display the **Open** dialog box.

2. Select the **Bushing** component and then choose the **Open** button from the **Open** dialog box; the **Component Placement** dashboard is displayed. Choose the **Show component in separate window while specifying constraints** button from the **Component Placement** dashboard to display the **Bushing** component in a separate window, if it is not chosen by default.

   Tip: *Viewing the components in separate windows helps the user locate the references for the assembly constraints easily and also gives the user an independent viewing control over the two windows. You can spin, pan, and zoom the components in their respective windows.*

3. Select the axis of the **Bushing** component and the axis of the **U-Support** component, as shown in Figure 11-53.

4. Next, select the planar face of the **Bushing** component and the inner planar face of the **U-Support** component, as shown in Figure 11-53. Select the **Mate** option from the **Constraint Type** drop-down list and then the **Coincident** option from the **Offset** drop-down list (if not selected by default) in the dashboard. Choose the **Build Feature** button; the model, similar to the one shown in the Figure 11-54, is displayed in the drawing area.

Figure 11-53 Constraints and the location to apply them

Figure 11-54 Components after assembling

> **Note**
> *You may need to choose the **Change orientation of constraint** button from the **Component Placement** dashboard to assemble the **Bushing** components in the required orientation.*

5. The next instance of the **Bushing** can be placed directly by using the **Repeat** option. To repeat the **Bushing** component in the assembly, select it from the **Model Tree** or from the drawing area and then choose **Edit > Repeat** from the menu bar. On doing so, the **Repeat Component** dialog box is displayed and the **Align** and **Mate** constraints are displayed in the **Variable Assembly Refs** area.

6. Select the **Mate** constraint from this area and then choose the **Add** button.

7. Select the inner right face of the **U-Support** component as the mating face. The copy of the **Bushing** component is assembled, as shown in Figure 11-55. Choose **Confirm** from the **Repeat Component** dialog box.

Figure 11-55 Assembled Bushings and the U-Support

Assembling the Pivot with the Bushing

The next component that you need to assemble is the **Pivot**.

1. Choose the **Assemble** button to display the **Open** dialog box.

2. In this dialog box, select the **Pivot** component and then choose the **Open** button to display the **Component Placement** dashboard.

3. Choose the **Placement** tab to display the slide-down panel. Select the axis of the **Pivot** and then the axis of the hole of the **Bushing**, as shown in Figure 11-56, and align them.

4. Next, click on the **New Constraint** option in the **Placement** tab slide-down panel. Select the **Align** option from the **Constraint Type** drop-down list and then the **Oriented** option from the **Offset** drop-down list, respectively. You can also right-click to invoke the shortcut menu and then choose the **New Constraint** option from it.

Assembly Modeling

5. Select the top planar face of the **Pivot** and the planar face of the **U-Support**, as shown in Figure 11-56.

6. Now, select the planar face of the **Pivot** and the planar face of the **Bushing**, as shown in Figure 11-56; the **Mate** constraint is automatically applied between them and is displayed in the **Constraint Type** drop-down list by default. Also, select the **Coincident** option from the **Offset** drop-down list so that the selected faces are coincident.

Figure 11-56 Constraints and the location to apply them

7. Choose the **Build feature** button to complete the assembly. The model similar to the one shown in Figure 11-57 is displayed in the drawing area.

Figure 11-57 Assembled view of the **Pivot**, **U-Support**, and **Bushing**

Suppressing Components

Next, you need to suppress both the **Bushing** and the **Pivot**. This is because when the components in the assembly increase, some components may be hidden behind the others. As a result, it gets difficult to select them. Also, more the number of components, more are the datum planes. Therefore, it becomes difficult to make selections on the components. However, when you suppress a component, its datum planes are also suppressed and the complications in the drawing area are reduced.

1. Spin the model and select the first **Bushing** from the drawing area or from the **Model Tree** and then right-click; a shortcut menu is displayed. Choose **Suppress** from the shortcut menu to suppress the component.

   The **Suppress** message box is displayed. Choose **OK** from the message box; the **Pivot** gets suppressed because it was dependent on the first bushing.

2. Similarly, suppress the other **Bushing** to make the assembly of the other components easy. Choose **OK** from the **Suppress** window to exit.

Note
Very often you need to use the datum planes and datum axes to assemble the components. Therefore, you need to turn their display on or off from the Datum Display toolbar, whenever required.

Assembling the Bracket with the Assembly

The next component you need to assemble is the **Bracket**.

1. Choose the **Assemble** button from the **Engineering Features** toolbar to display the **Open** dialog box.

2. Select the **Bracket** component to open; the **Component Placement** dashboard is displayed.

3. Choose the **Placement** tab to display the slide-down panel and select the **Align** option from the **Constraint Type** drop-down list.

4. Select the axis of the **Bracket** and the axis of the **U-Support**, as shown in Figure 11-58.

5. Click on the **New constraint** option in the **Placement** slide-down panel and select the **Mate** option from the **Constraint Type** drop-down list. You can also invoke the shortcut menu and choose the **New constraint** option from it.

6. Now, select the faces to mate, as shown in Figure 11-58; the preview of the assembly is displayed.

7. Choose the **Build feature** button from the **Component Placement** dashboard to complete the assembly. The model similar to the one shown in Figure 11-59 is displayed in the drawing area.

Assembling the Washer with the Assembly

The next component that you need to assemble is the **Washer**.

1. Choose the **Assemble** button to display the **Open** dialog box.

Assembly Modeling

Figure 11-58 Constraints and the location to apply them

*Figure 11-59 Assembled view of the **Bracket** with the **U-Support***

2. Open the **Washer** to display the **Component Placement** dashboard.

3. Choose the **Placement** tab from the dashboard to display the slide-down panel and select the **Align** option from the **Constraint Type** drop-down list to apply the align constraint.

4. Select the axis of the **Washer** and then select the axis of the **U-Support** from the drawing area to align the axes of the two components.

5. Now, click on the **New Constraint** option in the **Placement** tab slide-down panel and select the **Mate** option from the **Constraint Type** drop-down list.

6. The **Coincident** option is selected by default in the **Offset** drop-down list. Select the top planar face of the **Washer** and then the bottom planar face of the **Bracket** to assemble the **Washer**; the message **Fully constrained** is displayed in the **Status** area of the dashboard.

7. Choose the **Build feature** button from the **Component Placement** dashboard to complete the assembly. The model similar to the one shown in Figure 11-60 is displayed in the drawing area.

*Figure 11-60 Assembled view of the **Washer** with the **U-Support***

Inserting the Hexagonal Bolt in the Assembly

The next component that you need to assemble is the **Hexagonal bolt**.

1. Choose the **Assemble** button to display the **Open** dialog box.

2. Open the **Hexagonal bolt** to display the **Component Placement** dashboard.

3. Choose the **Placement** tab to invoke the slide-down panel and select the **Align** option from the **Constraint Type** drop-down list to add the align constraint.

4. Select the axis of the **Hexagonal bolt** and then the axis of the hole on the **U-Support**. Now, the two axes are aligned.

5. Click on the **New Constraint** option in the **Placement** tab slide-down panel and then select the **Mate** option from the **Constraint Type** drop-down list.

6. Select the bottom planar face of the **Hexagonal bolt** and then select the left outer planar face of the **U-Support**; the preview of the assembly is displayed.

7. Choose the **Build feature** button from the **Component Placement** dashboard to complete the assembly. The model similar to the one shown in Figure 11-61 is displayed in the drawing area.

Assembly Modeling

Figure 11-61 Assembly after assembling the **Hexagonal bolt**

Assembling other Components

Assemble the **Castle nut** and the **Self locking** nut to the assembly.

Unsuppressing the Components

All components are assembled at their required positions. Now, you need to unsuppress the suppressed components.

1. Choose **Edit > Resume > Resume All** from the menu bar. The suppressed components appear in the assembly where they were assembled. The completed assembly is shown in Figure 11-62.

Figure 11-62 Completed assembly with all components

Creating the Exploded State of the Assembly

To view all components in an assembly clearly, you need to create the exploded state of the assembly.

1. Choose **View > Explode > Edit position** from the menu bar; the **Explode Position** dashboard is displayed. Also, the default exploded state of the assembly is displayed.

Now, you need to edit the position of the component in the exploded view.

2. Choose the **References** tab in the **Explode Position** dashboard and click in the **Movement Reference** collector on the dashboard; you are prompted to select a reference to define the direction of movement.

3. Select the vertical axis of the **U-Support** from the drawing area; you are prompted to select the component to move.

4. Select the **Self locking** nut from the drawing area; a direction handle is displayed. Move the cursor to the required direction handle and drag to place it at the required position. Similarly, select and move the **Washer** and the **Bracket** to the required positions.

   Now, you need to move the components in the top half of the assembly. These components are moved with reference to the axis of the hole on the **U-Support**. Therefore, you need to select this axis as the motion reference.

5. Click in the **Motion Reference** collector on the dashboard; you are prompted to select the motion reference. Select the axis of the hole on the **U-Support** from the drawing area as the motion reference; you are now prompted to select the components to move.

6. Select and move the **Hexagonal bolt**, **Pivot**, **Bushings** and **Castle nut** to the required locations in the drawing area.

   The model similar to the one shown in Figure 11-63 is displayed in the drawing area.

Figure 11-63 Exploded state of the assembly

Tip: *You can also view the default exploded state of an assembly by choosing **View > Explode > Explode View** from the menu bar.*

Assembly Modeling

Creating Offset Lines

1. Choose the **Create cosmetic offset lines to illustrate movement of exploded component** button from the **Component Placement** dashboard; the **Cosmetic Offset Line** dialog box is displayed.

2. Click in the **Reference 1** collector and then select the axis of the **U-Support**.

3. Next, click in the **Reference 2** collector and then select the axis of the **Self locking nut**; the blue colored explode line is created. Next, choose the **Apply** button from the **Cosmetic Offset Line** dialog box.

4. Similarly, create the offset lines by selecting the axis of the hole on the **U-Support,** then the **Bushing** and then the **Castle nut**. Similarly, create offset lines by selecting the axis of the hole on the **U-Support,** then the **Bushing** and then the **Hexagonal bolt**.

   The model similar to the one shown in Figure 11-64 is displayed in the drawing area.

5. Next, exit the **Cosmetic Offset Line** dialog box.

Figure 11-64 Offset lines displayed in the exploded state

Saving the Assembly File
1. Choose the **Save** button from the **File** toolbar and save the model.

Closing the Window
1. Choose **Window > Close** from the menu bar to close the assembly file.

Tutorial 2

In this tutorial, you will create all components of the Pedestal Bearing assembly and then assemble them, as shown in Figure 11-65. You will also create the exploded state, shown in Figure 11-66, displaying the offset lines. The dimensions of the components are shown in Figures 11-67 through 11-71. The BOM is shown in Figure 11-72.   **(Expected time: 2 hrs)**

Figure 11-65 Assembly of the Pedestal Bearing

Figure 11-66 The exploded state of the Pedestal Bearing

Assembly Modeling

Figure 11-67 Dimensions for the Casting

Figure 11-68 Dimensions for the Cap

Figure 11-69 Dimensions for the components of the assembly

Figure 11-70 Dimensions for the Brasses

S. NO.	NO. OFF	PART'S NAME	MATERIAL
1	1	BODY	CAST IRON
2	1	CAP	CAST IRON
3	1	BRASSES	GUN METAL
4	2	SQUARE HEADED BOLT	MILD STEEL
5	2	NUT	MILD STEEL
6	2	LOCK NUT	MILD STEEL

Figure 11-71 The Bill of Material for the Pedestal Bearing

The following steps are required to complete this tutorial:

a. Create all components of the assembly as separate part files in the **Part** mode.
b. Create a new file in the **Assembly** mode and then assemble the **Casting** with the default assembly datum planes.
c. Assemble the **Cap** with the **Casting**, refer to Figures 11-72 and 11-73.
d. Suppress the **Cap** from the assembly.
e. Assemble the **Brasses** with the **Casting**, refer to Figures 11-74 and 11-75.
f. Insert the **Square headed bolt**, **Nut**, and **Lock nut** in the assembly and assemble them, refer to Figure 11-76.
g. Resume the suppressed components.
h. Create the exploded state of the assembly, refer to Figure 11-77.
i. Save the assembly and close the file.

Set the working directory to *C:\ProE-WF-5.0\c11\Pedestalbearing*.

Assembly Modeling

Starting Components for the Assembly

To create the assembly, all components must be created first in the **Part** mode. Also, you need to use the bottom-up approach to create the assembly.

1. Create all components of the assembly as separate part files and then save them in the current working directory.

2. Close the part files, if opened.

Creating a New Assembly File

As mentioned earlier, all components created are assembled in an assembly file that has an extension *.asm*. Therefore, you need to open a new *.asm* file.

1. Choose the **New** button from the **File** toolbar to display the **New** dialog box.

2. Select the **Assembly** radio button in the **Type** area of the **New** dialog box. In the **Sub-type** area of the **New** dialog box, the **Design** radio button is selected by default. Enter the name of the assembly in the **Name** edit box as **PEDESTALBEARING**.

3. Choose the **OK** button to enter into the assembly modeling environment.

Assembling the Casting with the Default Datum Planes

In the new assembly file, the three default assembly datum planes are displayed in the drawing area and the **Model Tree** is displayed at the left of the drawing area. If the display of the **Model Tree** was turned off in the previous tutorial, it will not appear. Now, you can start assembling components.

1. Choose the **Assemble** button to display the **Open** dialog box.

2. Select **Casting** from the **Open** dialog box and choose the **Open** button; the **Component Placement** dashboard is displayed.

   Note
   *It is recommended to choose the **Show component in a separate window while specifying constraints** button to display the component to be assembled in a new window.*

3. Select the **FRONT** datum plane of the model and then select the **ASM_FRONT** plane from the assembly to align them. Similarly, align the other two default planes with the respective assembly datum planes.

   Note
   *If the datum planes are not displayed in the drawing area, you need to turn on their display by choosing the **Plane Display** button from the **Datum Display** toolbar. After assembling the first component, you may need to turn off the display of planes. This is because the datum planes clutter the drawing area and then the selection of the references for applying assembly constraints becomes difficult. You can turn their display on when the datum planes are required.*

Assembling the Cap with the Casting

At first, you need to assemble the **Cap** with the **Casting**.

1. Choose the **Assemble** button to display the **Open** dialog box.

2. Select the **Cap** file and then choose the **Open** button from the **Open** dialog box to display the **Component Placement** dashboard.

3. Choose the **Placement** tab to display the slide-down panel and select the **Align** option from the **Constraint Type** drop-down list.

4. Select the axis of the **Cap** and then the axis of the **Casting**, as shown in Figure 11-72.

Figure 11-72 Constraints used for assembling the components

5. Choose the **New Constraint** node from the **Placement** tab and then select the **Mate** option from the **Constraint Type** drop-down list in the **Placement** tab slide-down panel. Then, select the **Offset** option from the **Offset** drop-down list.

6. Select the two mating faces and enter **4** in the edit box in the **Component Placement** dashboard.

7. Choose the **Build feature** button from the **Component Placement** dashboard to complete the creation of the assembly. The model similar to the one shown in Figure 11-73 is displayed in the drawing area.

Suppressing the Cap from the Assembly

You need to suppress the **Cap** because the next component has to be assembled with the **Casting**. When you suppress the **Cap** from the assembly, it becomes easier to assemble the new component. The **Cap** will be unsuppressed later.

Assembly Modeling

*Figure 11-73 Model after assembling the **Cap** with the **Casting***

1. Select the **Cap** from the drawing area and press and hold the right mouse button to display the shortcut menu.

2. Choose the **Suppress** option from the shortcut menu; you are prompted to confirm the suppression. Choose the **OK** button.

Assembling Brasses with the Casting

Next, you need to assemble the **Brasses** with the **Casting**.

1. Choose the **Assemble** button to display the **Open** dialog box.

2. Select **Brasses** and choose the **Open** button; the **Component Placement** dashboard is displayed.

3. Choose the **Placement** tab to display the slide-down panel and select the **Insert** option from the **Constraint Type** drop-down list.

4. Select the surface of the **Brasses** and then the surface on the **Casting**, as shown in Figure 11-74.

Note
*You can choose the **Show component in separate window while specifying constraints** button from the dashboard to display the component in a separate window, which makes it easier to select the faces and then apply the constraints.*

5. Click on the **New Constraint** option in the **Placement** tab slide-down panel. Next, select the **Mate** option from the **Constraint Type** drop-down list and the **Coincident** option from the **Offset** drop-down list.

6. Select the faces of the **Brasses** and the **Casting**, as shown in Figure 11-74.

Figure 11-74 Constraints used for assembling the components

7. Click on the **New constraint** button in the **Placement** tab slide-down panel and select the **Mate** option from the **Constraint Type** drop-down list and then select the **Offset** option from the **Offset** drop-down list.

8. Now, select the **TOP** datum plane of the **Brasses** and then the face of the **Casting**, as shown in Figure 11-74. Next, enter **-4** as the offset value in the **Offset** edit box.

9. Check whether to change the orientation by choosing the **Change orientation of the constraint** button. Choose the **Build feature** button from the **Component Placement** dashboard; the assembly model similar to the one shown in Figure 11-75 is displayed in the drawing area.

Figure 11-75 Assembling the Brasses with the assembly

10. Now, unsuppress the **Cap** by choosing **Edit > Resume > Resume All** from the menu bar. Similarly, assemble the remaining components. The final assembly is shown in Figure 11-76. You can choose the **Repeat** option to copy the repeated items.

Assembly Modeling

Figure 11-76 The final Pedestal Bearing assembly

Creating the Exploded State of the Assembly

To view all components in an assembly clearly, you need to create its exploded state.

1. Choose **View > Explode > Edit Position** from the menu bar; the **Explode Position** dashboard and the default exploded state of the assembly are displayed.

   Now, you need to edit the position of the component in the exploded view.

2. Choose the **References** tab from the dashboard and then click in the **Movement Reference** collector; you are prompted to select a reference to define the direction of movement.

3. Select the vertical axis of the **Cap** from the drawing area; you are prompted to select the component to move.

4. Select the **Casting** from the drawing area; a direction handle is displayed. Move the cursor to the required direction handle and drag to place it at the required position. Similarly, place the **Cap**, two **Square headed bolts**, two **Lock nuts** and then two **Nuts**, at the required location.

   Now, you need to move the **Brasses** to the required location in the drawing area.

5. Click in the **Motion Reference** collector again; you are prompted to select the motion reference. Select the axis of the **Brasses** from the drawing area as the motion reference; you are now prompted to select the component to move.

6. Select and move the **Brasses** to the required location in the drawing area.

   The model similar to the one shown in Figure 11-77 is displayed in the drawing area.

Figure 11-77 The Exploded Pedestal Bearing assembly

Creating the Offset Lines

1. Choose the **Create cosmetic offset lines to illustrate movement of exploded component** button from the **Edit Position** dashboard; the **Cosmetic Offset Line** dialog box is displayed.

2. Click in the **Reference 1** collector and select the axis of the right hole on the **Casting**.

3. Next, click in the **Reference 2** collector and then select the axis of the **Square Headed bolt** on the right half of the **Casting** to display the explode line. Similarly, select the axes from the other components to create the offset lines between them.

   The model similar to the one shown in Figure 11-78 is displayed in the drawing area.

4. Close the **Cosmetic Offset Line** dialog box.

Saving the Assembly

1. Choose the **Save** button from the **File** toolbar and then save the assembly.

Closing the Window

Now, you have saved the assembly and the window can be closed.

1. Choose **Window > Close** from the menu bar to close the file.

Assembly Modeling

Figure 11-78 Exploded state of the assembly displaying the offset lines

Self-Evaluation Test

Answer the following questions and then compare them to those given at the end of this chapter:

1. When you select two faces for applying the **Mate** constraint, the selected faces will be coplanar to each other. (T/F)

2. An exploded view is a state in which all components are moved from their actual locations so that they are visible. (T/F)

3. Dimensions of a feature cannot be modified in the **Assembly** mode. (T/F)

4. You can display the unexploded state of the assembly by choosing **Unexplode View** from the **View** menu. (T/F)

5. Offset lines are invisible by default once you display the unexploded state of the assembly. (T/F)

6. In the _____ type of simplified representation, the components removed from the current display are redisplayed.

7. The _____ type of simplified representation reduces the regeneration time in case of large assemblies.

8. The _____ constraint is similar to the **Mate** constraint, with the only difference being that this constraint allows you to specify some offset distance between the two coplanar faces.

9. The _____ constraint is used to assemble circular components.

10. The _____ is a tabular representation of all components of the assembly along with the information associated with them.

Review Questions

Answer the following questions:

1. Which constraint is used to align the selected datum point or vertex on the first part with the selected surface or datum plane on the second part?

    (a) **Orient** (b) **Pnt on Srf**
    (c) **Edge on Srf** (d) **Tangent**

2. When the assembly is constrained fully, the message displayed in the **Placement Status** area of the **Component Placement** dashboard is:

    (a) **Partially constrained** (b) **Fully constrained**
    (c) **Completely constrained** (d) None of these

3. In which of the following types of simplified representation, the complete geometry of the components is displayed in the current model display style?

    (a) Geometry representation (b) Graphics representation
    (c) Master representation (d) None of these

4. Which constraint is used to assemble two components by making the selected faces or planes coplanar such that the mating faces or planes face in the same direction?

    (a) **Insert** (b) **Orient**
    (c) **Tangent** (d) **Align**

5. The unexploded state of an assembly can be displayed by choosing **Unexplode View** from which of the following menus in the menu bar?

    (a) **View** (b) **File**
    (c) **Info** (d) **Window**

6. A component of an assembly assembled by using the assembly constraints cannot be replaced with some other components. (T/F)

Assembly Modeling

7. A part of an assembly can be hidden from the assembly. (T/F)

8. Offset lines can only be created in the exploded state of an assembly. (T/F)

9. The order of assembling components in an assembly can be changed. (T/F)

10. Pro/ENGINEER provides you with a ready made BOM that you can directly use. (T/F)

Exercises

Exercise 1

In this exercise, you will create all components of the Crosshead assembly and then assemble them, as shown in Figure 11-79. Also, you will create an exploded state of the assembly, shown in Figure 11-80, which display the offset lines. The dimensions of the components are shown in Figures 11-81 through 11-85. **(Expected time: 2 hrs)**

Figure 11-79 The Crosshead assembly

Figure 11-80 The exploded state of the Crosshead assembly

Figure 11-81 Front view and right-side view of the Body

Assembly Modeling

Figure 11-82 Dimensions of the Keep Plate

Figure 11-83 Dimensions of the Piston Rod

Figure 11-84 Dimensions of the Brasses and Bolt

Figure 11-85 Dimensions of the Nut

Exercise 2

Create the assembly of the Radial Engine shown in Figure 11-86. The assembly in the exploded state is shown in Figure 11-87. The dimensions of various parts of this assembly model are given in Figure 11-88 through 11-92. **(Expected time: 4 hrs)**

Figure 11-86 The Radial Engine assembly

Assembly Modeling 11-57

Figure 11-87 Exploded state of the Radial Engine assembly

Figure 11-88 Positioning of the articulated Rods

Figure 11-89 Orthographic views and dimensions of the Master Rod

Assembly Modeling

Figure 11-90 *Orthographic views and dimensions of the Piston*

Figure 11-91 *Orthographic views and dimensions of the Articulated Rod*

Figure 11-92 Views and dimensions of the other components

Answers to Self-Evaluation Test
1. T, **2.** T, **3.** F, **4.** T, **5.** T, **6.** Master representation, **7.** Graphics representation, **8. Mate** offset, **9.** Insert, **10.** BOM.

Chapter 12

Generating, Editing, and Modifying the Drawing Views

Learning Objectives

After completing this chapter, you will be able to:
- *Create and retrieve the drawing sheet formats.*
- *Generate different drawing views of an existing part.*
- *Edit the existing drawing views and parameters associated with them.*
- *Modify the existing drawing views.*

THE DRAWING MODE

In the earlier chapters, you learned about creating the parts in the **Part** mode and assembling different parts in the **Assembly** mode. In this chapter, you will learn to generate the drawing views of the parts and assemblies created earlier. Drawing views are generated in the **Drawing** mode. One of the major advantages of working with this software package is its bidirectional associative nature. This is the property that ensures that any modifications made in the model in the **Part** mode updates its drawing views and vice-versa. In Pro/ENGINEER Wildfire 5.0, there are two types of drafting methods: Interactive drafting and Generative drafting. In this chapter, you will learn Generative drafting. To generate the drawing views, first you need to start a new file in the **Drawing** mode of Pro/ENGINEER Wildfire 5.0.

Choose the **New** button from the **File** toolbar to display the **New** dialog box. Select the **Drawing** radio button in the **New** dialog box, as shown in Figure 12-1.

Specify the name of the drawing in the **Name** edit box and then choose **OK** to display the **New Drawing** dialog box, as shown in Figure 12-2.

New Drawing Dialog Box

The **New Drawing** dialog box is used to specify the template that will be used while starting a new file in the **Drawing** mode. The options available in this dialog box are discussed next.

Default Model Area

The **Default Model** area is used to specify the name of the model whose drawing views you want to generate. You can specify the name of the model in the **Name** edit box or select the model using

*Figure 12-1 The **New** dialog box*

the **Open** dialog box that will be displayed when you choose the **Browse** button. If a part or assembly file is already opened in the current session then the name of that model will be displayed by default in the **Name** edit box of the **Default Model** area.

Specify Template Area

The **Specify Template** area is used to specify whether you want to use an empty sheet, predefined formats, or the default template available in Pro/ENGINEER. There are three radio buttons in this area. The **Use template** radio button is selected by default. When the **Empty with format** radio button is selected, the dialog box gets changed, as shown in Figure 12-3.

When you select the **Empty** radio button, the **New Drawing** dialog box is modified, as shown in Figure 12-4.

Orientation Area

The **Orientation** area is available only when you select the **Empty** radio button from the

Generating, Editing, and Modifying the Drawing Views 12-3

*Figure 12-2 The **New Drawing** dialog box with the **Use template** radio button selected*

*Figure 12-3 The **New Drawing** dialog box with the **Empty with format** radio button selected*

Specify Template area. The buttons in this area are used to specify the orientation of the sheet. You can select a standard size sheet with a portrait or a landscape orientation using the **Portrait** or the **Landscape** button. You can also specify a sheet with the user-defined size by choosing the **Variable** button.

Size Area

The options in the **Size** area are used to set the size and the units of the sheet. The **Size** area is available only when you select the **Empty** radio button from the **Specify Template** area. The options in this area are discussed next.

Standard Size

The **Standard Size** drop-down list is used to select a drawing sheet of standard size. This drop-down list is available only when you choose the **Portrait** or **Landscape** button from the **Orientation** area.

Inches and Millimeters Radio Buttons

These radio buttons are selected to set the standards for the user-defined sheets. You can set the size of the sheet in inches or in millimeters. These buttons are available only when you choose the **Variable** button from the **Orientation** area.

*Figure 12-4 The **New Drawing** dialog box with the **Empty** radio button selected*

Width and Height edit boxes

These edit boxes are used to specify the width and the height of the user-defined drawing sheets. These edit boxes are available only when you choose the **Variable** button from the **Orientation** area.

Format Area

The **Format** area is available only when you select the **Empty with format** radio button from the **Specify Template** area.

Format

The **Format** drop-down list is used to select the available formats.

Browse

The **Browse** button is chosen to display the **Open** dialog box for retrieving the drawing formats. By default, there are only eight standard system formats that can be retrieved. However, you can create your own user-defined formats that can be retrieved later.

Choose **OK** from the **New Drawing** dialog box to proceed to the **Drawing** mode; a drawing sheet of the specified size and orientation will be placed on which you can generate the drawing views. The Drawing user interface of Pro/ENGINEER 5.0 has been enhanced to simplify your tasks and make it easy to perform. Additionally, the **Ribbon** has been introduced to display all frequently used tools collected logically in various groups and tabs. If required, you can increase the drawing area by minimizing the **Ribbon**. To do so, right-click on a tab in the **Ribbon** and choose **Minimize the Ribbon**.

GENERATING DRAWING VIEWS

In Pro/ENGINEER Wildfire 5.0, the first view that you need to generate is the general view. This view mostly acts as the parent view for the remaining views. The method of generating various views in Pro/E Wildfire 5.0 is discussed next.

Generating the General View

The **General** view is the first view that is generated on the drawing sheet. This view can be the top, front, right, left, bottom, back, trimetric, isometric view, or any user-defined view of the model. To generate the general view, choose the **General** button from the **Model Views** group in the **Layout** tab of the **Ribbon**; the **Select Combined State** dialog box will be displayed, as shown in Figure 12-5. This dialog box will be displayed only if the selected model is an assembly model. If the selected model is a part model, then this dialog box will not be displayed and directly the **Drawing View** dialog box, as shown in Figure 12-6, will be displayed on specifying the center point. In the **Select Combined State** dialog box, if you select the **No Combined State** option from the **Combined state names** collector and then choose the **OK** button, you will be prompted to select a center point to place the drawing view in the drawing sheet. Select the center point; the preview of

*Figure 12-5 The **Select Combined State** dialog box*

Generating, Editing, and Modifying the Drawing Views 12-5

the drawing with unexploded view in the default orientation will be displayed in the drawing sheet and also the **Drawing View** dialog box will be displayed, as shown in Figure 12-6.

*Figure 12-6 The **Drawing View** dialog box*

If you select the **DEFAULT ALL** option from the **Combined state names** collector of the **Select Combined State** dialog box and choose the **OK** button, you will be prompted to select a center point to place the drawing view in the drawing sheet. Select the center point; the preview of the drawing, with the exploded view in the default orientation will be displayed in the drawing sheet and also the **Drawing View** dialog box will be displayed, as shown in Figure 12-6.

> **Note**
> *If you do not want to be prompted to select a combination state, select the **Do not prompt for Combined State** check box from the **Select Combined State** dialog box.*

The **Drawing View** dialog box contains the options that are required to generate a general view. The **Categories** list box in the dialog box lists all parameters that are required to generate a drawing view in Pro/ENGINEER Wildfire 5.0. The **View Type** option is selected by default in the **Categories** list box and its related options are displayed on the right side of the **Categories** list box. These parameters/options are discussed later in this chapter.

The procedure to generate a general view is given below:

1. Choose **Layout > Model Views > General** button from the **Ribbon**; you will be prompted to select a center point.

Tip: *If you have not specified any model in the **Default Model** area of the **New Drawing** dialog box and choose **Layout > Model Views > General** button from the **Ribbon**, the **Open** dialog box will be displayed. You can select the model from the **Open** dialog box.*

*Pro/ENGINEER automatically selects the model in the **Default Model** area of the **New Drawing** dialog box. This model is selected from the present session of Pro/ENGINEER. If the model selected automatically is not the required model, then change the model by choosing the **Browse** button in the **New Drawing** dialog box.*

Note
*If the model that you have selected is an assembly model, then in such cases after choosing the **General** button, the **Select Combined State** dialog box will be displayed, as discussed earlier.*

2. As soon as you select the center point, the **Drawing View** dialog box will be displayed and the default view of the model will be displayed on the drawing sheet. In the **Type** drop-down list, the **General** option is selected by default and in the **View orientation** area, the **Views names from the model** radio button is selected by default. This radio button allows you to select the standard orientations of the model from the **Model view names** list box. If you select the **Geometry references** radio button, you can select the planar faces or the datum planes to orient in a particular orientation.

3. Select the view that you need to generate as the general view from the list provided below the **Model view names** list box.

4. After selecting the required options, choose the **Apply** button and then choose the **Close** button from the **Drawing View** dialog box.

Tip: *To set the model orientation using the **Geometry references** radio button, select an option from the **Reference 1** drop-down list and then from the model, select the face or the datum plane that you need to see from that selected view. Similarly, select an option from the **Reference 2** drop-down list and then select a datum plane or a face from the model. For example, if you select **Top** from the **Reference 1** drop-down list, then from the model, you need to select the face or the datum plane that you need to keep in the top orientation in the drawing view.*

Generating the Projection View

The projection views are the orthographic views generated by projecting lines normal from an existing view, as shown in Figure 12-7. Before generating a projected view, you need to make sure that at least one parent view is already present on the drawing sheet. To generate a projected view, choose **Layout > Model Views > Projection** from the **Ribbon**. Now, move the cursor to a location where you need to place the view and specify a point on this location. Depending on the point selected to place the view, the resulting view will be top, front, right-side, or left-side view.

Generating, Editing, and Modifying the Drawing Views

The scale factor of these views will be the same as that of the parent view from which they are projected. If more than one view exists that can be the parent view of the projection view, then you will be prompted to select the parent view for the new view.

Generating the Detailed View

Detailed views are used to provide the enlarged view of a particular portion of an existing view. To generate a detailed view, choose **Layout > Model Views > Detailed** from the **Ribbon**; you will be prompted to specify the center point for detail on an existing view. Define a center point on the view whose detail needs to be generated; you will be prompted to sketch a spline without intersecting other splines to define an outline. Draw a closed spline to define the outline of the detail view and exit the drawing mode by clicking the middle mouse button. Next, you need to specify the placement point for placing the detail view. You can change the name, scale, or the reference point on the parent view and can also select the boundary type of the detailed view using the options from the **Drawing View** dialog box, which will be displayed when you double-click on the detailed view.

Figure 12-7 shows a drawing sheet with various drawing views.

Note

*After generating a view, you need to choose the **Current Sheet** button from the **Top Toolchest**. This is because sometimes the scale or the other information related to the generated view is not displayed along with it.*

Figure 12-7 Sheet with various drawing views

Generating the Auxiliary View

The auxiliary views are generated by projecting normal lines from a specified edge, axis, or datum plane of an existing view. The view scale will be the same as that of the parent view. To generate an auxiliary view, choose **Layout > Model Views > Auxiliary** from the **Ribbon**; you will be prompted to select an edge, axis, or datum plane from the front surface of the main view. Select the edge or surface normal to which you need to place the generated view; a rectangular box will be attached to the cursor. Select a point on the drawing sheet to place the view on the drawing sheet. Figure 12-8 shows the edge to be selected as reference to generate the drawing view and the resulting auxiliary view.

Figure 12-8 Resulting auxiliary view

Generating the Revolved Section View

A revolved section view is the view that is generated from an existing view by revolving the section through an angle of 90-degree about the cutting plane and then projecting it along the length. Remember that the cutting plane of the revolved section view is normal to the parent view. The procedure to generate a revolved section view is discussed next.

1. Choose the **Revolved** button from the expanded **Model Views** group in the **Layout** tab of the **Ribbon**; you will be prompted to select a parent view for the revolved section.

2. Select the view from the drawing sheet that will be defined as the parent view for generating the revolved view.

3. Next, you need to select a center point on the drawing sheet to place the view. Select a point anywhere on the drawing sheet; the **Drawing View** dialog box will be displayed. The **Create New** cross-section option is selected by default in the **Revolved view properties** area of the **Drawing View** dialog box. The **XSEC CREATE** menu is also displayed on the lower right corner of the screen.

Note
*The **Create New** option is selected by default in the **Revolved view properties** area of the **Drawing View** dialog box, only if there is no previously created revolved section present.*

Generating, Editing, and Modifying the Drawing Views

12-9

4. Choose **Planar > Single > Done** from the **XSEC CREATE** menu; the **Message Input Window** will be displayed prompting you to specify the name of the cross-section. Enter the name of the cross-section and accept it; the **SETUP PLANE** menu will be displayed and you are prompted to select a planar surface or datum plane.

5. Select the plane along which the view will be sectioned, as shown in Figure 12-9. The resulting section view will be placed in-line with the section plane.

6. Choose the **Apply** button and then choose the **Close** button to exit the **Drawing View** dialog box. The resulting sectioned view is shown in Figure 12-10.

Figure 12-9 Datum plane for the revolved section view   *Figure 12-10* Resulting revolved section view

Note
The copy and align view will be discussed later in this chapter.

Drawing View Dialog Box Options

The remaining types of drawing views that you can generate in Pro/ENGINEER Wildfire 5.0 require the options available in the **Drawing View** dialog box. Therefore, it is important for you to understand these options before proceeding further.

View Type Option

When you invoke the **Drawing View** dialog box, the **View Type** option is automatically selected in the **Categories** list box. The **View name** edit box is used to enter the name of the drawing view. The **View orientation** area lists the options to orient the drawing view. These options are the standard options of orienting the model.

Visible Area Option

The **Visible Area** option is used to set the display of the view. You can display a drawing view as a full view, partial view, a half view, and broken view. The **Drawing View** dialog box, after choosing the **Visible Area** option, will be displayed, as shown in Figure 12-11. The options in the **View visibility** drop-down list of this dialog box are discussed next.

*Figure 12-11 The **Drawing View** dialog box with the **Visible Area** option chosen*

Full View

The **Full View** option is selected by default in the **View visibility** drop-down list. This option can be combined with any view types to generate a drawing view displaying the complete view.

Half View

The **Half View** option can be used on the projection, auxiliary, or general views to generate a drawing view that displays only half view of the part. Generally, an existing view is selected to display the half view. For generating a half view, double click on an existing view to display the **Drawing View** dialog box. In the **Categories** list box, choose the **Visible Area** option to invoke the **Visible area options** area and then select **Half View** from the **View visibility** drop-down list. On doing so, you will be prompted to select a reference plane that will be used to remove half of the drawing view. The reference plane can be a datum plane or a planar surface, and must be normal to the screen in the selected view. Select the reference plane; an arrow will be displayed attached to the selected plane. This arrow indicates the portion of the view to be removed. You can also flip the direction of the arrow using the **Side to keep** button available below the **Half view reference plane** collector in the dialog box. Generally, this type of view is generated for symmetric parts. Therefore, you can specify the type of symmetry line using the **Symmetry line standard** drop-down list. Figure 12-12 shows the reference plane to be selected and Figure 12-13 shows the resulting half view.

Partial View

The **Partial View** option can be used on the projection, auxiliary, revolved, or general views to generate a view that displays a specified portion of the view. To convert an existing view to a partial view, double-click on that view. Choose the **Visible Area** option

Generating, Editing, and Modifying the Drawing Views

12-11

Figure 12-12 Reference plane to be selected to generate a half view

Figure 12-13 Resulting Half view

from the **Categories** list box and select the **Partial View** option from the **View visibility** drop-down list; you are prompted to draw a spline that will be the boundary of the portion of the view you want to display, see Figure 12-14. Select the center point on the view and then draw the spline. Press the middle mouse button and exit the spline creation. Now, choose the **Apply** button from the **Drawing View** dialog box. You will notice that only the area of the view inside the spline is retained and the rest of the portion of the drawing view is cropped, see Figure 12-15.

Figure 12-14 Spline drawn on the view

Figure 12-15 Partial view

Broken View

This type of view is used for the parts having a high length to width ratio. The **Broken View** option can be used on the projection or the general views to generate a view that is broken along the horizontal or the vertical direction using horizontal or vertical lines. To generate a broken view, select the **Broken View** option from the **View visibility** drop-down list. Choose the **Add break** button in the **Drawing View** dialog box to add break lines. Select any one edge from the view and move the cursor vertically and select a point on the screen to draw the first vertical break line. Move the cursor and select a point up to which you want to break the view, see Figure 12-16. You can also specify the style of the break line using the **Break Line Style** drop-down list available on the extreme right of the list box. Now, choose the **Apply** button from the **Drawing View** dialog box to create the resulting broken view and then choose the **Close** button to exit it. Figure 12-17 shows the resulting broken view.

Figure 12-16 References to break the view

Figure 12-17 Resultant broken view

Figure 12-18 shows various views that have already been discussed in this section.

Figure 12-18 The different drawing views

Scale Option

When you select the **Scale** option, the **Scale and perspective options** area will be displayed on the right of the **Categories** list box. The **Default scale for sheet** radio button is selected by default. Therefore, all generated views are scaled with the default sheet scale. The second radio button is **Custom scale**. This radio button, when selected, allows you to enter a scale for the drawing view. When you modify the scale factor of a view, the view associated with this parent view is also scaled.

Generating, Editing, and Modifying the Drawing Views 12-13

The third radio button is **Perspective**. This radio button is selected to generate a perspective view. After selecting the **Perspective** radio button, you can specify the distance from the eye and the diameter of the view circle. Figure 12-19 shows a perspective view.

Figure 12-19 A general perspective view

Sections Option

The section views are generally used for the views that are complicated from inside. As it is not possible to display the inside of the part using the conventional views, therefore these views are cut (sectioned) using a datum plane or a planar surface and the resulting section view is displayed. When you choose the **Sections** option from the **Categories** list box in the **Drawing View** dialog box, the **Section options** area will be displayed. The **No section** radio button is selected by default. Select the **2D cross-section** radio button and then choose the **Add cross-section to view** button to activate the options to create a section. The options in the **Section options** area and the methods of section plane creation are discussed next.

Full Section View

Consider a part that is cut throughout its length, width, or height and the cut portion is removed from the display. The remaining portion, when projected normal to the cutting plane, displays the full section view.

To generate a full section view, you first need to generate a projected view from one of the views existing on the drawing sheet. After generating the projected view, double-click on it to invoke the **Drawing View** dialog box. Choose the **Sections** option from the **Categories** list box. The options available for generating the section view are displayed on the right of the **Drawing View** dialog box. Select the **2D cross-section** radio button to define a section plane. Now, choose the **Add cross-section to view** button to add a section plane. Some options in the drop-down lists are invoked in the area provided below the **Add cross-section to view** button. The **Full** option in the **Sectioned area** drop-down list allows you to create a full section view.

When you choose the **Add cross-section to view** button, the **XSEC CREATE** menu will be displayed. Choose **Planar > Single > Done** from the **XSEC CREATE** menu; you will be prompted to specify the name of the cross-section. Specify the name of the cross-section in the **Message Input Window**. After choosing **OK** from the window, the **SETUP PLANE** menu will be displayed and you will be prompted to select a planar surface or a datum plane. Select the datum plane from the other view; the name of the section view will be displayed in the **Name** drop-down list. Scroll to the right in the dialog box and click once in the **Arrow Display** collector to invoke the selection mode and select the view to display the section view arrows. You can also flip the material side of the section view using the **Flip** button. Choose the **Apply** button from the **Drawing View** dialog box. Figure 12-20 shows the top view and section view.

Figure 12-20 Top view and section front view

In the above section, you have learned to generate a full section view by defining a planar section plane. Now, you will learn to generate a full section view by defining an offset section plane. You need to make sure that before generating a section view by defining an offset section plane, the part file of the current model should be closed.

Invoke the **Drawing View** dialog box by double-clicking on an already generated projected view. Now, choose the **Sections** option from the **Categories** list box on the left of this dialog box. Select the **2D cross-section** radio button and choose the **Add cross-section to view** button to define the section plane. If there are some existing section planes, select the **Create New** option from the **Name** drop-down list; the **XSEC CREATE** menu will be displayed. Choose **Offset > Both Sides > Single > Done** from the **XSEC CREATE** menu; the **Message Input Window** will be displayed. Specify the name of the cross-section.

The model will be displayed in a sub-window on the left of the screen. The **SETUP SK PLN** menu will also be displayed and you need to select a sketching plane for drawing the sketch that represents an offset section plane. Select the sketching plane from the subwindow. Choose **Okay** from the **DIRECTION** submenu. The **SKET VIEW** submenu will be displayed; choose **Default** from this submenu. Draw the sketch of the offset section using the sketch tools available in the **Sketch** menu of the subwindow, refer to Figure 12-21. After drawing the sketch, choose **Sketch > Done** from the menu bar to exit the sketcher environment.

Generating, Editing, and Modifying the Drawing Views 12-15

Click once in the **Arrow Display** collector to invoke the selection mode and then select the view in which the section arrows will be displayed. Choose the **Apply** button from the **Drawing View** dialog box. Figure 12-21 shows the top view, offset sectioned front view, and sectioned general view of a part.

Figure 12-21 The section views created using the offset section plane

To generate an isometric section view, generate the general view and switch the orientation of the general view to isometric. Now, select the **Sections** option from the **Categories** list box and sketch a section plane using the subwindow as discussed earlier. Note that you cannot select a datum plane to define the section plane for an isometric section view. Figure 12-22 shows the top, full section front, and full section isometric views.

Half Section View
Consider a part that is cut half way through the length, width, or height and the front cut portion (front quarter) is removed from the display. This part when projected is called the half section view. In this projected view, only half of the part will be displayed sectioned and the other half of the part will be displayed as it is. To generate the half section view, you need to select the **Half** option from the **Sectioned Area** drop-down list while specifying the parameters for sectioning the view. After selecting this option, you are prompted to select the reference plane for the half section creation. Select the plane from the drawing view; you are prompted to pick the side to keep. Select a point on the side of the section view that you need to keep. Select the parent view where the section arrow will be placed and choose the **Apply** button from the **Drawing View** dialog box. Figure 12-23 shows the resulting half section view.

Figure 12-22 Top view, full section front view, and full section isometric view

Figure 12-23 Top view, half section front view, and half section isometric view

Local Section View

The **Local** section view is used when you want to show a particular portion of the view in the section, and at the same time not section the remaining view. The local section area is specified by drawing a spline around it. To generate the local section view, you first generate the full section view, as discussed earlier. After generating the full section view, select the **Local** option from the **Sectioned Area** drop-down list. Next, you need to draw a spline that will define the area of the drawing that needs to be sectioned.

To draw a local section isometric view, you need to draw a section plane and then choose the **Local** option. Define a center point for the local section and sketch the spline. This method of generating the local section isometric view is similar to generating the other

Generating, Editing, and Modifying the Drawing Views

section isometric views. Figure 12-24 shows the local section front view and the local section isometric view.

Figure 12-24 Top view, local section front view, and local section isometric view

Model edge visibility

Pro/ENGINEER Wildfire 5.0 provides you with two options for displaying the edges of the section drawing views. The **Total** radio button when selected in the **Section options** area of the **Drawing View** dialog box creates a section view that displays all visible edges of the section view, in addition to the section area. This option can be combined with the full, half, local, full (unfold) and full (aligned) views. Figure 12-25 shows the front and total sectioned left view.

The **Area** radio button, when selected, displays only that area of the section view that is sectioned. No other edges of the view are displayed in the area cross-section view, as shown in Figure 12-26. This option can be combined with the full, half, local, full (unfold) and full (aligned).

Full(Aligned)

This view is used to section those features that are created at a certain angle to the main section planes. Align sections straighten these features by revolving them about an axis that is normal to the parent view. Generally for this section view, the section plane is sketched. Remember that the axis about which the feature is straightened should lie on all cutting planes. This means that the lines that are used to sketch the section plane should pass through the axis about which the feature will be revolved. Figures 12-27 and 12-28 show these views when the **Area** radio button is selected. Figures 12-29 and 12-30 show these views when the **Total** radio button is selected.

Figure 12-25 The front view and the total cross-section view

Figure 12-26 The front view and the area cross-section view

Figure 12-27 The area cross-section view with normal lines of projection

Figure 12-28 The area cross-section view with aligned lines of projection

Figure 12-29 The total cross-section view with normal lines of projection

Figure 12-30 The total cross-section view with aligned lines of projection

Full(Unfold)

The **Full(Unfold)** option is used to generate the section view by unfolding the section surface of an offset section view. This type of view is only generated using a general view. To generate this type of view, first you need to generate a general view in the required orientation. You can place this general view anywhere on the drawing sheet. Now, choose the **Sections** option from the **Categories** on the left of the **Drawing View** dialog box. Now, define the section plane using the offset option and specify the view in which you need to display the arrows. Now, choose the **Full(Unfold)** option from the **Sectioned Area** drop-down list and complete the creation of the full unfold section view. Figure 12-31 shows the model and the section plane. Figure 12-32 shows an offset section view and a full unfold section view.

Figure 12-31 The model and the section plane

Figure 12-32 Offset section view and full unfold section view

Once you have understood the main options of the **Drawing View** dialog box, you can generate the copy and align the view. This view is discussed next.

Generating the Copy and Align View

These are the aligned views that are generated from an existing partial view. Therefore, to generate this type of drawing view, it is necessary that first a partial view should be generated. You will learn more about the partial views later in this chapter.

The procedure to generate a **Copy and Align** view is discussed next.

1. To generate the **Copy and Align** view, choose **Layout > Model Views > Copy and Align** from the **Ribbon**; you will be prompted to select an existing partial view to be aligned with. Once you have selected a partial view, you are prompted to select a center point for the drawing view.

2. Select a point anywhere on the drawing sheet to place the view. The view is placed at the selected location. You will be prompted to specify a center point for detail on the current view and to sketch a spline to define the outline of the **Copy and Align** view.

3. Specify the center point of the spline and draw the spline. Press the middle mouse button

to finish sketching the spline. The drawing view will be cropped along the spline drawn; you will be prompted to select a straight line (axis, segment, datum curve) alignment on the current view.

4. Select an edge from the current view, as shown in Figure 12-33, to align it with the partial view. The copied view is aligned with its parent partial view, as shown in Figure 12-34.

Figure 12-33 Selecting an edge from the current view to align with the partial view   *Figure 12-34 Resulting copy and align view*

Generating the 3D Cross-Section View

The **3D Cross-section** allows you to display 3D sections in the drawing views. This type of sectioning may be required to show the complex cross-sections of a model. Note that the 3D cross-sections are created using zones. Therefore, you first need to create zones and then use them to create 3D cross-sections. The procedure to create zones and 3D cross-sections is discussed next.

1. Open the part file of the model and choose **View > View Manager** from the menu bar or choose the **View Manager** button from the **Top Toolchest**; the **View Manager** dialog box will be displayed.

2. Choose the **XSec** tab and then choose the **New** button to define a new cross-section in the model.

3. Enter the name for the new cross-section and press ENTER; the **XSEC CREATE** menu will be displayed, as shown in Figure 12-35.

4. Select the **Zone** option from the menu; a dialog box with the name you have specified for the new cross-section will be displayed, as shown in Figure 12-36.

Note
*In the example discussed above, the name for the new 3D cross-section is given as **Xsec0001**. Therefore, the dialog box shown in Figure 12-36 is named as **Xsec0001**.*

5. Now, you need to define the planes for the zone creation. Select the datum plane through which you want to create a zone.

Generating, Editing, and Modifying the Drawing Views 12-21

Figure 12-35 The **XSEC CREATE** menu

Figure 12-36 The **Xsec0001** dialog box

6. You can add multiple reference entities or datum planes for defining the zone by choosing the **Add a reference to the zone** button from the **Xsec0001** dialog box. You can also remove references specified for the zone by selecting the reference from the **zone scope** area and then choosing the **Remove a reference from the zone** button from the **Xsec0001** dialog box.

7. By default, the direction for creation of the zone is chosen as the negative side of the selected reference entity. You can change the orientation by choosing the **Change orientation** button from the **Xsec0001** dialog box.

8. After specifying all the references for the zone, choose the **Accept settings** button to finish the zone creation and exit the dialog box.

Note
*If you want to make the 3D cross-section active in the drawing area, select it from the **View Manager** dialog box and right-click to invoke the shortcut menu. Choose the **Set Active** option from the shortcut menu; the 3D cross-section will be activated in the drawing area.*

9. Start a new drawing file and insert a general view in the drawing sheet by choosing the **General** button from the **Top Toolchest**.

10. Choose the **Sections** option from the **Categories** list of the **Drawing View** dialog box. Next, select the **3D cross-section** radio button from the **Section options** area; the 3D cross-section with the name **Xsec0001** will be listed in the drop-down list.

11. The **Show X-Hatching** check box is not selected by default. If you need to display the hatching lines, then select the **Show X-Hatching** check box and choose the **Apply** button from the **Drawing View** dialog box. The 3D cross-section will be displayed on the drawing sheet.

Figure 12-37 shows the trimetric view and the 3D cross-section of a part model, inserted in an A4 drawing sheet.

Figure 12-37 The trimetric view and the 3D cross-section in an A4 drawing sheet

Note
*The model created in Exercise 4 of Chapter 7 is used to generate a 3D cross-section, as shown in Figure 12-37. The references for creating the zone are the **FRONT** and the **RIGHT** datum planes.*

*You can also display the 3D cross-section in the **Shading** mode.*

EDITING THE DRAWING VIEWS
With this release of Pro/ENGINEER, it has become very easy to edit a drawing view and the items in the drawing views. All options of modifying the drawing views or items related to it can be chosen from the shortcut menu that will be displayed when you right-click after selecting the view or the item. However, these options can also be invoked from the menus available in the menu bar. Pro/ENGINEER allows you to perform the following types of editing operations on the drawing views.

Moving the Drawing View
When a view is generated, its movement is locked by default. To unlock the drawing view, choose **Lock View Movement** either from the shortcut menu that will be displayed on right-clicking on the drawing view from the drawing or directly from the **Model Tree**. Alternatively, clear the **Lock View Movement** check box in the **Environment** dialog box that will be displayed on

Generating, Editing, and Modifying the Drawing Views

choosing **Tools > Environment** from the menu bar. When you select the drawing view, it will be displayed inside a boundary. To move the drawing view, select it and then drag it to the required location on the drawing sheet. Remember that if you select the view that has some child views, the child views will also move along with the parent view in order to maintain their alignment with the parent view. Also, the projected views can be moved only in the direction of projection.

> **Note**
> *The **General** and **Detailed** views can be moved to any new location because they are not the projections of any view.*

Erasing the Drawing View

The **Erase View** button available in the expanded **Model Views** group in the **Layout** tab of the **Ribbon** is used to temporarily remove the selected drawing view from the sheet. However, the view still remains in the memory of the drawing and can be resumed at any point of time. As the view is not completely removed from the memory, you can also erase a view that has some child views associated to it and it will not affect the child view. Once a view is erased, a box will be displayed in place of the view displaying the name of the view. To resume the view, choose the **Resume View** button from the expanded **Model Views** group of the **Ribbon**. Alternatively, select the erased drawing view from the drawing or the **Model Tree** and right-click. Choose **Erase View** from the shortcut menu displayed.

> **Note**
> *When you erase a view, the leaders and dimensions that were attached with the view are also erased. When you resume an erased view, the leaders and dimension values are displayed again.*

Deleting the Drawing View

To delete a drawing view from the drawing sheet, select the view from the drawing or from the **Model Tree** and hold down the right mouse button to invoke a shortcut menu. Choose the **Delete** option from the shortcut menu. Alternatively, you can select the drawing view to be deleted and then choose the **Delete** button in the **Top Toolchest**. Once the view is deleted, no information related to the deleted view remains in the memory of the drawing. Remember that if a view that has some child views associated with it is deleted, then before deletion Pro/ENGINEER informs you that views associated with this view will also be deleted. You can use the **Undo Delete** button from the **Top Toolchest** for restoring the deleted views.

Adding New Parts or Assemblies to the Current Drawing

You can also add more parts or assemblies, in addition to the default part or assembly, for generating the drawing views. This is done by choosing **Layout > Document > Drawing Models** from the **Ribbon**. Alternatively, choose **File > Drawing Models** from the menu bar; the **DWG MODELS** menu will be displayed, as shown in Figure 12-38.

Choose the **Add Model** option to add a model to the current drawing. When you choose this option, the **Open** dialog box will be displayed. You can select the new model to be added using this dialog box. Remember that the latest model added will be the current model and the drawing views generated will be of this model. You can change the current model by choosing the **Set Model** option from the **DWG MODELS** menu. Similarly, you can also delete a model from the current drawing. However, only the model that does not have any view generated from it can be deleted.

Figure 12-38 The **DWG MODELS** menu

MODIFYING THE DRAWING VIEWS

You can also make the following modifications in the existing drawing views.

Changing the View Type

Select the drawing view that needs to be modified and hold down the right mouse button to invoke the shortcut menu. Choose **Properties** from the shortcut menu; the **Drawing View** dialog box will be displayed, as shown in Figure 12-39. The **Drawing View** dialog box can also be invoked by double-clicking on the view to be modified. The **View Type** option in the **Categories** area is chosen by default. You can modify the view type by selecting one of the types from the list under **Model view names** collector. Remember that only the general, projection, and auxiliary view types can be modified using this option.

Figure 12-39 The **Drawing View** dialog box

Generating, Editing, and Modifying the Drawing Views

Changing the View Scale
The scale of a view can be modified using the **Scale** option from the **Categories** list box of the **Drawing View** dialog box. You can modify the scale factor of the views that are generated using the general view and detailed view options.

> **Note**
> *The scale factor represents the scaling of the drawing model. For example, if the scale is set to 0.25, Pro/ENGINEER scales the drawing views to one-quarter (1/4) of the actual size of the model.*

Reorienting the Views
Double click on the general view to be reoriented to display the **Drawing View** dialog box. You can use the options from this dialog box to change the orientation of the selected view. However, if some child view is associated with the general view, then the child view will also be reoriented accordingly.

Modifying the Cross-sections
You can flip the side of sectioning and replace, delete, or rename the sections in the views using the **Sections** option from the **Categories** list in the **Drawing View** dialog box.

Modifying Boundaries of Views
You can modify the boundaries of the detailed or partial views using the option in the **Drawing View** dialog box. To modify the boundary of a detailed view, double-click on it to invoke the **Drawing View** dialog box. The selection mode is invoked by default in the **Reference point on parent view** selection area. Therefore, you can specify the center point for the boundary of the detailed view. To sketch the boundary of the detailed view again, click once in the **Spline boundary on parent view** selection area and draw the boundary on the parent view. To modify the boundary of a partial view, invoke the **Drawing View** dialog box and choose the **Visible Area** option from the **Categories** list box. Using the options available on the right of this dialog box, you can modify the boundary of the detailed view.

Adding or Removing the Cross-section Arrows
If you have not specified the cross-section arrows while generating the section views, you can specify them by selecting the section view and holding down the right mouse button to invoke the shortcut menu. Choose the **Add Arrows** option from the shortcut menu; you will be prompted to select the view where the arrows should be displayed. Select the view in which you need to display the arrows.

To remove arrows, select them and choose the **Delete** button from the **Top Toolchest**.

Modifying the Perspective Views

Double-click on the perspective view to display the **Drawing View** dialog box and choose the **Scale** option from the **Categories** list box. The options related to the perspective are available. You can modify the eye point distance or the view diameter using these options.

MODIFYING OTHER PARAMETERS

Apart from modifying the drawing views, you can also modify other parameters related to the drawing views. For example, you can modify the size and the style of the text, scale factor of all drawing views, cross-section hatching, and so on. All this is done by selecting the item. When the item is highlighted in red color, hold down the right mouse button to invoke the shortcut menu. You can select the options from the shortcut menu to modify that item.

You can modify any parameter associated with the drawing views. Depending on the item selected to modify, the options related to it vary. The options displayed in the shortcut menu vary from item to item.

Editing the Cross-section Hatching

Select the hatching from a drawing view. When the hatching turns red in color, hold down the right mouse button to invoke the shortcut menu. Choose the **Properties** option from the shortcut menu; the **MOD XHATCH** menu will be displayed, as shown in Figure 12-40.

The parameters related to cross-section hatching that can be modified are: the spacing of the hatching, angle of the hatching lines, offset value, and the line style of the hatching lines. There are also some standard hatch patterns that are available in Pro/ENGINEER. You can retrieve these standard patterns by using the **Open** dialog box displayed upon choosing **Retrieve** from the **MOD XHATCH** menu.

*Figure 12-40 The **MOD XHATCH** menu*

TUTORIALS

Tutorial 1

In this tutorial, you will generate the drawing views of the model created in Exercise 4 of Chapter 7, as shown in Figure 12-41. Select the A4 size drawing sheet and generate all drawing views shown in Figure 12-42.   **(Expected time: 45 min)**

Generating, Editing, and Modifying the Drawing Views

12-27

Figure 12-41 Part for generating drawing views

Figure 12-42 The drawing views to be generated

The following steps are required to complete this tutorial:

a. Start a new drawing file and select the required drawing sheet.
b. Generate the top view, refer to Figure 12-44.
c. Generate the front view taking the top view as the parent view, refer to Figure 12-44.
d. Generate the sectioned right view by defining a plane on the top view of the model, refer to Figures 12-45 and 12-46.
e. Generate the default 3D view of the model, see Figure 12-46.
f. Generate the detail view from the 3D view, see Figure 12-47.

Before you start generating drawing views, set *C:\ProE-WF-5.0\c12* as working directory. Copy the model *c07exr4.prt* file from the *c07* folder and paste it in the folder named *c12*. The drawing generated in this tutorial will be saved in the *c12* directory with an extension *.drw*. The part file *(.prt)* and the drawing file *(.drw)* should lie in the same directory or folder.

Note
You cannot open a drawing file if the part file, from which the drawing view was generated, has been deleted. Also, if the part file is removed from the folder where its drawing file is placed or if you rename the part file after generating the drawing views, the drawing file will not open.

Starting a New Drawing File

To generate drawing views in Pro/ENGINEER Wildfire 5.0, you first need to start a new file in the **Drawing** mode.

1. Choose the **New** button from the **File** toolbar to display the **New** dialog box.

2. Select the **Drawing** radio button and then enter *c12tut1* as the name of the file.

3. Choose **OK** from the **New** dialog box to display the **New Drawing** dialog box.

4. Choose the **Browse** button and select *c07exr4.prt* for generating the drawing views.

5. Select the **Empty** radio button from the **Specify Template** area.

6. Choose the **Landscape** button from the **Orientation** area, if it is not chosen by default, as shown in Figure 12-43.

Figure 12-43 The New Drawing dialog box with the Landscape button chosen

7. Select **A4** from the **Standard Size** drop-down list. Choose **OK** to proceed to the **Drawing** mode.

An A4 size sheet with the landscape orientation is displayed in the drawing area.

Generating the Top View

You can generate any view as the first view on the drawing sheet. However, in this tutorial, you will generate the top view as the first view.

1. Choose **Layout > Model Views > General** from the **Ribbon**; you are prompted to specify the center point for the drawing view.

Generating, Editing, and Modifying the Drawing Views 12-29

2. Specify the center point for the first view, which is on the top left corner of the sheet, as shown in Figure 12-44. On specifying the center point, the **Drawing View** dialog box is displayed along with the preview of the drawing view in the default orientation. In the **Model view names** list box, select the **TOP** option and choose the **Apply** button. The default view is oriented as the top view.

Note
Although you can move a view anywhere on the sheet, yet you should try to place the drawing view inside the sheet and also leave space for the other views to be generated.

3. Choose the **Scale** option from the **Categories** list box in the **Drawing View** dialog box; the **Scale and perspective options** area is displayed. Select the **Custom scale** radio button and enter **0.075** as the scale factor for the view. Choose the **Apply** button; the scale of the view is modified.

4. Choose the **Close** button from the **Drawing View** dialog box to complete the placing of the top view.

5. Turn off the display of datum planes, axes, points, and coordinate system by choosing the respective buttons from the **Datum Display** toolbar in the **Top Toolchest**.

6. Change the model display to no hidden by choosing the **No Hidden** button from the **Model Display** toolbar. Next, choose the **Repaint** button from the **Top Toolchest** to repaint the screen.

Tip: *If the view that you have placed on the drawing sheet is not at the proper location, you need to move the drawing view. To do so, select the drawing view; the selected drawing view is enclosed in a red box. Next, right-click to display a shortcut menu. Choose **Lock View Movement** from the menu displayed and then press the left mouse button inside the box and drag it to place it at the required location.*

Generating the Front View

The front view of the model is generated from the top view, which is already placed on the drawing sheet.

1. Choose **Layout > Model Views > Projection** from the **Ribbon**; you will be prompted to specify a center point for the drawing view.

2. Specify the center point for the front view below the top view, as shown in Figure 12-44.

3. Click anywhere on the drawing sheet to clear the current selection set.

If the front view of the model is not similar to the one shown in Figure 12-44, then set the projection type to first angle. Next, you need to change the first angle projection to the third angle projection. To do so, choose **File > Drawing Options** from the menu bar; the **Options** dialog box will be displayed. Enter **Projection_type** in the **Option** text

Figure 12-44 The top and front views

box; its option will be displayed in the **Value** drop-down list. Select **third_angle** from the drop-down list and choose the **Add/Change** button. Next, choose the **OK** button to accept the changes and exit the dialog box.

> **Tip**: *It is recommended that you use the **Repaint** button available in the **View** toolbar to remove any temporary information in the drawing area and to refresh the screen.*

Generating the Section View

To generate a section view, a section must be defined on the model. You will sketch this section to generate the section view for this tutorial.

1. Choose **Layout > Model Views > Projection** from the **Ribbon**; you are prompted to select a projection parent view.

2. Select the top view as the projection parent view; you are prompted to specify a center point for the drawing view.

3. Specify the center point on the right side of the top view to place the view.

4. Once the view is placed, double-click on it to display the **Drawing View** dialog box.

5. Select **Sections** from the **Categories** list box in the **Drawing View** dialog box; the section options are invoked in the **Drawing View** dialog box.

6. Select the **2D cross-section** radio button and choose the **Add cross-section to view** button; the window area below it is activated. Select the **Create New** option from the **Name** drop-down list; the **XSEC CREATE** menu is displayed.

7. Choose **Offset > Both Sides > Single > Done** from the **XSEC CREATE** menu.

8. Specify the name of the cross-section as **X** in the **Message Input Window** and press ENTER.

Generating, Editing, and Modifying the Drawing Views

12-31

Once you have specified the name of the cross-section, a separate window displaying the part appears. Also, you are prompted to select a sketching plane.

Note
*If the model in the **Part** mode is opened in another window, the subwindow will not appear and you have to manually change the window. Choose the **Window** menu and select the part file that is opened. Now, you can continue with the sketcher environment.*

9. Choose the **Plane Display** button from the **Datum Display** toolbar in the original window to display datum planes. You may need to repaint the screen in the subwindow by choosing **View > Repaint** from the menu bar of the subwindow to view the datum planes.

10. Select the **TOP** datum plane from the subwindow. Choose **Okay** from the **DIRECTION** submenu; the **SKET VIEW** submenu is displayed.

11. Choose the **Bottom** option from the **SKET VIEW** submenu and select the **FRONT** datum plane from the subwindow.

12. Choose the **Sketch > Line > Line** from the menu bar and sketch the line, as shown in Figure 12-45. These lines define the section plane.

13. Align the lines and modify the angular dimension to **120**, as shown in Figure 12-45.

Figure 12-45 Sketch for generating the total aligned section view

14. Choose **Sketch > Done** from the menu bar of the subwindow.

15. Select the **Full(Aligned)** option from the **Sectioned Area** drop-down list; you are prompted to select an axis.

16. Select the central axis of the model from the front drawing view. You may need to turn on the display of the central axis if its display is turned off.

17. Scroll the bar in the **Drawing View** dialog box to the right edge. Click in the field below the **Arrow Display** column; you are prompted to pick a view for arrows where the section is perpendicular. Select the top view to display the arrows.

18. Choose the **Apply** button from the **Drawing View** dialog box and then exit the dialog box; the section view is displayed.

19. Turn off the display of the datum planes and the datum axes.

Tip: *If you do not want to display the section arrows in any view, you can use the middle mouse button (in case of three button mouse) to abort the creation of arrows.*

Modifying the Hatching

You need to modify the spacing between the hatch lines to make the hatching dense. In this section, you will select the filter from the **Filter** drop-down list to select the hatch lines.

1. Select the **X-Section** filter from the **Filter** drop-down list available in the **Status Bar** above the drawing area. Select the hatching from the drawing sheet; the hatching lines turn red.

2. Press the right mouse button to invoke the shortcut menu. Choose the **Properties** option from the shortcut menu; the **MOD XHATCH** menu is displayed. Alternatively, double-click on the hatching lines to invoke the **MOD XHATCH** menu.

3. In the **MOD XHATCH** menu, choose the **Spacing** option to display the **MODIFY MODE** submenu.

4. The spacing between the hatching lines needs to be reduced. To do so, choose the **Half** option twice and then choose **Done** in the **MOD XHATCH** menu. On doing so, the hatching appears more dense, refer to Figure 12-46.

5. Set the filter back to the **General** option using the **Filter** drop-down list.

Generating the General View

The **General** view needs to be generated to show a 3D view of the model, which is the trimetric view.

1. Choose **Layout > Model Views > General** from the **Ribbon**.

2. Specify the center point for placing the general view below the section view, as shown in Figure 12-46; the **Drawing View** dialog box is displayed.

3. Set the value of the scale for the new view to **0.05** using the **Scale** option from the **Drawing View** dialog box.

4. Choose the **Apply** button and then exit the dialog box.

Generating, Editing, and Modifying the Drawing Views

12-33

Figure 12-46 Different drawing views

Generating the Detail View

As mentioned earlier, the detail view is required to provide details of a particular portion of the drawing view. In this section, you need to give the details of one of the ribs of the model.

1. If the general view is selected (highlighted in red box), then you need to click once on the drawing sheet to exit the current selection set. Next, choose **Layout > Model Views > Detailed** from the **Ribbon**; you are prompted to select a center point for detail on an existing view. This center point will be the center of the detailed view.

2. Select the center point for the detail on one of the ribs in the trimetric view, refer to Figure 12-47.

   You will be prompted to sketch a spline about the center point that you selected.

3. Draw the spline and then press the middle mouse button to exit the spline tool.

4. Select the center point for the placement of the drawing view. The detailed view is generated and is selected by default.

5. Press and hold the right mouse button on the detail view to invoke a shortcut menu and choose the **Properties** option; the **Drawing View** dialog box is displayed.

6. Select **Spline** from the **Boundary type on parent view** drop-down list.

7. Choose the **Scale** option from the **Categories** list box. Set the value of the custom scale to **0.075**. Choose the **Apply** button and exit the dialog box.

A note is also displayed with an arrow attached to the trimetric view. You may need to move the note to a suitable position by selecting it and then dragging the cursor. The final sheet after generating all views is shown in Figure 12-47. If you are unable to select the note, then choose the **Annotate** tab from the **Ribbon**. On doing so, you will be able to select it and move it.

Figure 12-47 The drawing views for Tutorial 1

Tip: *If any view or the text on the drawing is overlapping or is not at the desired place on the sheet, select it and then move it by dragging the mouse.*

Saving the Drawing File
You need to save the drawing file that you have created as you may need it later.

1. Choose the **Save** button from the **Top Toolchest**; the **Save Object** dialog box is displayed with the name of the drawing file that you entered earlier.

2. Choose **OK** to confirm the action.

Closing the Drawing File
After saving the drawing file created, you need to close the drawing file.

1. Choose **Window > Close** from the menu bar to close the drawing window.

Generating, Editing, and Modifying the Drawing Views 12-35

Tutorial 2

In this tutorial, you will generate the drawing views of the part created in Tutorial 1 of Chapter 8. The part is shown in Figure 12-48. The drawing views that need to be generated are shown in Figure 12-49. **(Expected time: 45 min)**

Figure 12-48 Model for generating drawing views

Figure 12-49 Drawing views to be generated

Before you start generating drawing views, copy the file *c08tut1.prt* from the *c08* folder in the current directory.

The following steps are required to complete this tutorial:

a. Start a new drawing file and select the size of the drawing sheet.
b. Generate the top view, refer to Figure 12-50.
c. Generate the sectioned front view by defining the **FRONT** datum plane as the section plane, refer to Figure 12-50.
d. Generate the right view of the sectioned front view, refer to Figure 12-51.
e. Generate the isometric sectioned view. The section will be defined by drawing a line on the **TOP** datum plane, refer to Figures 12-52 and 12-53.

Before you start generating the drawing views, set the working directory to *C:\ProE-WF-5.0\ c12*. The part *(.prt)* file and the drawing *(.drw)* file should lie in the same directory or folder.

Starting a New Drawing File

To generate the drawing views, you first need to start a new drawing file.

1. Choose the **New** button from the **File** toolbar to display the **New** dialog box.

2. Select the **Drawing** radio button and then enter *c12tut2* as the name of the file.

3. Choose **OK** from the **New** dialog box to display the **New Drawing** dialog box.

4. Choose the **Browse** button to select *c08tut1.prt* from the *c08* folder for generating drawing views and then choose **Open**.

5. Select the **Empty** radio button from the **Specify Template** area.

6. Choose the **Landscape** button from the **Orientation** area.

7. Select **A4** from the **Standard Size** drop-down list. Choose **OK** from the **New Drawing** dialog box to proceed to the **Drawing** mode.

Generating the Top View

First, you need to generate the top view. All other views, except the sectioned isometric view, will be the child views of the top view. You need to generate the top view first because the required sectioned front view can be generated only from the top view. The right view can also be generated independently, but then this view will not help generate any other required view.

1. Choose the **General** button from the **Ribbon**; you are prompted to specify a center point for the placement of the view.

2. Specify the center point for the placement of the top view close to the upper left corner of the drawing sheet; the **Drawing View** dialog is displayed.

3. Select the **TOP** option from the **Model view names** list box and choose the **Apply** button.

Generating, Editing, and Modifying the Drawing Views

4. Choose the **Scale** option from the **Categories** list box. Select the **Custom scale** radio button and enter **0.065** in the edit box.

5. Choose **OK** to exit the **Drawing View** dialog box.

   If necessary, move the view, as shown in Figure 12-50, and choose **No Hidden** from the **Model Display** toolbar. You may also need to repaint the screen.

Generating the Sectioned Front View

The sectioned front view of the model is generated from the top view. Before proceeding further, use the **Plane Display** button from the **Datum Display** toolbar to turn on the display of datum planes and repaint the screen.

1. Choose **Layout > Model Views > Projection** from the **Ribbon**; you are prompted to specify a center point for placement of the projection view.

2. Specify the center point for the placement of the front view below the top view, as shown in Figure 12-50.

3. Select the newly generated view and invoke the shortcut menu. Choose the **Properties** option to display the **Drawing View** dialog box.

4. Select the **Sections** option from the **Categories** list box to display the section related options in the dialog box.

5. Select the **2D cross-section** radio button and choose the **Add cross-section to view** button; the window area below it gets activated. Select the **Create New** option from the **Name** drop-down list, if it is not selected; the **XSEC CREATE** menu is displayed.

6. Choose **Planar > Single > Done** from the **XSEC CREATE** menu.

7. Enter **A1** as the name of the cross-section in the **Message Input Window** and then press ENTER to display the **SETUP PLANE** submenu; you are prompted to select a planar surface or a datum plane.

8. Select the **FRONT** datum plane (the plane that cuts the part horizontally through the center of the cylindrical feature in the top view) from the drawing area.

9. Scroll the bar in the **Drawing View** dialog box to the right. Click on the field below the **Arrow Display** column; you will be prompted to pick a view for arrows where the section is perpendicular. Select the top view to display the arrows.

10. Choose the **Apply** button and then exit the dialog box.

Modifying the Hatching

The offset distance between the hatching lines in the front sectioned view is large. Therefore you need to reduce the distance between the hatching lines.

1. Select the **X-Section** filter from the **Filter** drop-down list in the **Status Bar**. Select the hatching lines from the sectioned front view in the drawing sheet; the hatching lines turn red. Hold the right mouse button to invoke the shortcut menu. Choose the **Properties** option from the shortcut menu; the **MOD XHATCH** menu is displayed.

2. In the **MOD XHATCH** menu, choose the **Spacing** option to display the **MODIFY MODE** submenu.

3. The spacing between the hatching lines has to be reduced. Choose the **Half** option twice and then choose **Done** in the **MOD XHATCH** menu. Now, the hatching appears more dense.

4. Click once in the drawing area to remove the X-hatch from the current selection set. The sheet after placing these two views should look similar to the one shown in Figure 12-50.

5. Set the selection filter back to **General**.

Figure 12-50 Drawing sheet after generating the top view and the sectioned front view with the display of datum planes turned on

Generating the Right View

The right view is the projection of the sectioned front view. Before proceeding further, turn off the display of the datum planes.

1. Choose **Layout > Model Views > Projection** from the **Ribbon**; you are prompted to select the projection parent view.

2. Select the sectioned front view as the parent view.

3. Specify the center point for the placement of the drawing view on the right of the sectioned front view. The right view of the model is placed, as shown in Figure 12-51.

Generating, Editing, and Modifying the Drawing Views

12-39

Figure 12-51 *The drawing sheet after generating the top, sectioned front, and right views*

Generating the Isometric Section View

The isometric section view is an independent view and it will be generated by using the **General** option.

1. Choose the **General** button from the **Ribbon**.

2. Specify the center point on the upper right corner of the drawing sheet for placing the view; the **Drawing View** dialog is displayed.

   The default view is a trimetric view but you need to display the isometric view to be displayed. Therefore, you need to change the orientation.

3. Select the **Isometric** option from the **Default orientation** drop-down list; the isometric view of the model is displayed on the drawing sheet.

4. Choose the **Scale** option from the **Categories** list box. Select the **Custom scale** radio button and enter **0.06** as the scale factor in the edit box displayed. Next, choose the **Apply** button.

5. Select the **Sections** option from the **Categories** list box to display the section options in the dialog box.

6. Select the **2D cross-section** radio button and then choose the **Add cross-section to view** button. The collector below it gets activated. Select **Create New** from the name drop-down list; the **XSEC CREATE** menu manager is displayed.

7. Choose **Offset > Both Sides > Single > Done** from the **XSEC CREATE** menu; the **Message Input Window** is displayed.

8. Enter **Z** as the name of the section in the **Message Input Window** and press ENTER. Once you have specified the name of the section, a separate window is displayed with the model.

9. Select the **TOP** datum plane from the subwindow. You may need to turn on the display of the datum planes. Choose **Okay** from the **DIRECTION** submenu; the **SKET VIEW** submenu is displayed.

10. Choose the **Right** option from the **SKET VIEW** submenu and select the **RIGHT** datum plane from the subwindow.

11. Choose the **Sketch > Line > Line** from the menu bar and draw a line, as shown in Figure 12-52. This line creates a section plane.

12. Choose **Sketch > Constraint > Coincident** from the menu bar and align both ends of the line to the edges.

13. Choose **Sketch > Done** from the menu bar.

14. Choose the **Apply** button to place the view and then exit the dialog box.

Figure 12-52 *The sketch for the section line with the constraint*

Note
If the drawing view placed on the sheet overlaps the boundary of the drawing sheet, then you can move the drawing view. To do so, select the drawing view; the selected drawing view is enclosed in a red box. Now, press the left mouse button inside the box and drag it to place it at the desired location.

Modifying the Hatching

The spacing between the hatching lines in the sectioned isometric view is large. Therefore, you need to reduce the distance between them. Use the same procedure that was discussed earlier in this tutorial to modify the spacing between the hatch lines. The sheet, after placing all views, should look similar to the one shown in Figure 12-53.

Saving the Drawing File

In this section, you need to save the drawing file.

1. Choose the **Save** button from the **Top Toolchest**; the **Save Object** dialog box is displayed with the name of the drawing file that you entered earlier.

2. Press ENTER to save the file.

Generating, Editing, and Modifying the Drawing Views 12-41

Figure 12-53 Different drawing views generated

Closing the Drawing File

After you have saved the drawing file, close the drawing file.

1. Choose **Window > Close** from the menu bar; the drawing window is closed.

Self-Evaluation Test

Answer the following questions and then compare them to those given at the end of this chapter:

1. The bidirectional associative nature of a software package implies that when one file related to the part model is modified, the modifications reflect in other related files as well. (T/F)

2. General view is the first view that is generated in the sheet. (T/F)

3. The **Full** section view is the most widely used section view. (T/F)

4. Section views are generally created for the models having features that are not clearly visible in the standard view. (T/F)

5. Broken views are used for the parts that have a high length to width ratio. (T/F)

6. The _____ view is used when you want to show a particular portion of the view in a section and at the same time, do not want to section the remaining view.

7. The _____ option allows you to temporarily remove the selected drawing view from the sheet.

8. The _____ option is used to redisplay the drawing views that are erased using the **Erase View** option.

9. Using the _____ dialog box, you can reorient the general view.

10. The cross-section hatching on the sectioned portion can be modified using the _____ menu.

Review Questions

Answer the following questions:

1. Which of the following options, when chosen, displays all the erased drawing views on the sheet?

    (a) **Delete**   (b) **Resume View**
    (c) **Move**   (d) **Erase**

2. Which of the following buttons in the **View** toolbar is used to refresh the screen?

    (a) **Zoom Out**   (b) **Zoom In**
    (c) **Redraw the current view**   (d) **None**

3. Which of the following options, when selected, displays only the area of the section view that is sectioned?

    (a) **Total**   (b) **Area**
    (c) **Align**   (d) **None**

4. Which of the following options is used to permanently remove a drawing view from the sheet?

    (a) **Resume**   (b) **Erase**
    (c) **Delete**   (d) **Move**

5. Which of the following options is used to modify the numeric value associated with the drawing views?

    (a) **Xhatching**   (b) **Any Item**
    (c) **Value**   (d) **None**

6. The view type of an existing view can be changed. (T/F)

7. You can reorient only the general views. (T/F)

Generating, Editing, and Modifying the Drawing Views 12-43

8. You can flip the side of the cross-section views. (T/F)

9. The **Orientation** area in the **New Drawing** dialog box is available only when you select the **Empty** radio button from the **Specify Template** area. (T/F)

10. The orientation of a model saved in the **Part** mode can be used to orient the drawing view in the **Drawing** mode. (T/F)

Exercise

Exercise 1

Generate the drawing views of the model created in Tutorial 3 of Chapter 8 on an A4 size sheet. The model is shown in Figure 12-54. The drawing views to be generated are shown in Figure 12-55. **(Expected time: 45 min)**

Figure 12-54 Part for generating the drawing views

Figure 12-55 Drawing views to be generated in Exercise 1

Answers to Self-Evaluation Test
1. T, 2. T, 3. T, 4. T, 5. T, 6. Local Section, 7. Erase, 8. Resume View, 9. Drawing View, 10. MOD XHATCH

Chapter 13

Dimensioning the Drawing Views

Learning Objectives

After completing this chapter, you will be able to:
- *Show or erase dimensions in drawing views.*
- *Add notes to drawings.*
- *Add dimensional and geometric tolerance to drawing views.*
- *Edit the geometric tolerance.*
- *Add balloons to exploded assembly views.*
- *Add reference datums to drawing views.*
- *Modify and edit dimensions.*

DIMENSIONING THE DRAWING VIEWS

Once you have generated the drawing views, you need to generate dimensions, add notes, symbols, balloons, and so on in the drawing views. These dimensions are assigned to each entity of sketches in the model or the features associated with the model. These dimensions are associative in nature and they can be used to modify or drive the dimensions of a part, therefore these dimensions are called driving dimensions. Dimensions can be generated using the **Show Model Annotations** dialog box, refer to Figure 13-1.

Note
*You can also create dimensions in the **Drawing** mode, but these dimensions cannot drive the dimensions of the part. Therefore, the dimensions that you create in Pro/ENGINEER Wildfire 5.0 are called driven dimensions.*

Tip: *You must have noticed that some options in the menus available in the menu bar are followed by dots. The dots indicate that after you choose any of these options, a menu, dialog box, or dashboard is displayed.*

Show Model Annotations Dialog Box

When you import a 3D model to a 2D drawing, by default, the dimensions and other information of the model are stored in the drawing but they remain invisible. You can let the required model information be shown or erased on a particular view by using the options in the **Show Model Annotations** dialog box. The visible items are referred to as, shown and the items that are not visible are referred to as, erased. The erased annotations are not permanently deleted from the model as they remain stored in the database. To invoke the **Show Model Annotations** dialog box, choose **Annotate > Insert > Show Model Annotations** from the Ribbon; the **Show Model Annotations** dialog box will be displayed, as shown in Figure 13-1. This dialog box enables you to generate various parameters related to the model in the drawing view. There are 6 tabs in this dialog box. These are **Show Model Dimensions**, **Show Geometric Tolerances**, **Show Model Notes**, **Show Surface Finish Symbols**, **Show 3D Symbols**, and **Show Datum Targets**. These tabs are discussed next.

Show Model Dimensions Tab

The **Show Model Dimensions** tab is chosen by default in the **Show Model Annotations** dialog box. The options in this tab enable you to generate parametric dimensions in the drawing views. The bidirectional associative nature of this software package enables you to modify the model by modifying the dimensions from the drawing or the 3D environment.

*Figure 13-1 The **Show Model Annotations** dialog box*

Dimensioning the Drawing Views   13-3

Type Drop-down List
This drop-down list contains options that can be used to specify which dimension you want to be displayed in the drawing. These options act as a filter to display the dimensions. The options displayed in this filter are **All**, **Driving Dimension Annotation Element**, **All Driving Dimensions**, **Strong Driving Dimensions**, **Driven Dimensions**, **Reference Dimensions**, and **Ordinate Dimensions**. By default, **All** is selected.

List box
This list box consists of the dimensions to be displayed, their names, and a check box on the left of each dimension. You need to select a check box to display the corresponding dimension value in the selected drawing view. By default, all check boxes are cleared. If you want all the dimensions to be displayed in that view, then choose the **Select All** button. If you want to erase all the dimensions displayed in the view, then you need to choose the **Erase All** button. These two buttons are displayed below the list box.

Show Geometric Tolerances Tab
On choosing this tab, a list box will be displayed with a list of the tolerances applied to the dimensions in the part or the assembly environment. In this case also, you can specify the options to show or erase the geometric tolerances as you did in case of the **Show Model Dimensions** tab.

Show Model Notes Tab
Choose this tab to show or erase the notes that were created in the **Part** mode. If any change is made to a note in the **Drawing** mode, the note in the **Part** mode is automatically modified. Similarly, if you modify this note in the **Part** mode, the modifications are reflected automatically in the **Drawing** mode.

Show Surface Finish Symbols Tab
Choose this tab to show or erase the surface finish symbols associated with the part shown in the drawing views.

Show 3D Symbols Tab
Choose this tab to show or erase any symbol associated with the model.

Show Datum Targets Tab
Choose this tab to show or erase the critical measurement locations on the drawing view.

After selecting the required parameters, choose the **Apply** button to accept settings and continue the selection process. Choose the **OK** button to accept the settings and exit the dialog box or choose the **Close** button to close the dialog box and cancel the settings performed.

Figure 13-2 shows some dimensioned drawing views.

Figure 13-2 Dimensioned drawing views

Various buttons in the **Insert** group of the **Annotate** tab of the **Ribbon** are discussed next.

Dimension-New References
This button is chosen to create dimensions with new references in the drawing views.

Surface Finish
This button is chosen to create the surface finish symbols in the drawing views. On choosing this button, the **GET SYMBOL** menu appears. Select the required symbol from this menu; you are prompted to specify the height for the new instance. Specify the height for the instance and place it at the desired location. On doing so, you are prompted to define the new name for the view. Define a name for the view; the symbol is created.

Reference Dimension
This button is chosen to generate reference dimensions in the drawing views.

Jog
This button is used to create a jog. On choosing this button, you are prompted to select a dimension or leader type to create a jog. Select the required entity to create a jog.

ADDING NOTES TO THE DRAWING
The notes added to the model in the **Part** mode can be easily displayed in the drawing views by using the **Show Model Annotations** dialog box. However, if you have not added any note to the model in the **Part** mode and want to add it in the drawing views, then you will have to create them. The notes can be created by choosing **Annotate > Insert > Note** from the **Ribbon**. On choosing this option, the **NOTE TYPES** menu will be displayed, see Figure 13-3. In this menu, choose the type of leader to be used, if required. Next, choose the **Make Note** option

Dimensioning the Drawing Views

from this menu; the **ATTACH TYPE** menu will be displayed. Choose the required option from the **ATTACH TYPE** menu. Next, using the left mouse button, select a point on the drawing where you want to attach the note and then using the middle mouse button select the location for placing the note. Enter the text in the **Message Input Window** and choose the **Accept value** button. On doing so, you are again prompted to enter a note in the **Message Input Window**. This time, choose the **Cancel input** button; the note will be placed at the selected point.

ADDING TOLERANCES IN THE DRAWING VIEWS

You can create geometric tolerances in the dimensions. Tolerance is defined as the difference between the maximum and minimum variations in the dimensions of the selected component. It is almost impossible to manufacture a component to the exact dimensions. In such cases, the tolerance value is added to dimensions to make sure that some variation that occurs during manufacturing can be taken care of. However, when you actually send a part for manufacturing, there are other parameters along with the dimension tolerances that may vary and require some tolerances. Depending upon these factors, the tolerances are divided into two types: dimensional tolerances and geometric tolerances.

Figure 13-3 The NOTE TYPES menu

Tip: *If the dimensional tolerance is not displayed, then you need to set the **tol_display** to **yes** in the configuration file. To invoke this file, choose **File > Drawing Options** from the menu bar; the **Options** window will be displayed. Next, select the **tol_display** option in the **These options control dimension tolerances** heading in the **Options** window. Now, select **yes** from the **Value** drop-down list available at the bottom of the window. Choose **Add/Change** button and then the **OK** button to accept the changes and exit.*

Dimensional Tolerances

These are the variation in the standard dimensional values. The dimensional tolerances can be displayed along with the dimensions in the drawing views by setting the value of **tol_display** to **yes** in the configuration file. You can select and modify the type of dimensional tolerance from the **Properties** tab of the **Dimension Properties** dialog box. The **Dimension Properties** dialog box is discussed later in this chapter. Figure 13-4 shows the drawing views with the tolerance added to the dimensions.

Geometric Tolerances

When you send a component for manufacturing, you have to provide various other parameters along with the dimensions, dimensional tolerances and geometric tolerances. These parameters can be the geometric condition, surface profile, material condition, and so on. All these parameters are defined using the geometric tolerances. The geometric tolerances (will be called **gtol** henceforth) can be added to the drawing using the **Geometric Tolerance** dialog

Figure 13-4 Dimensions with tolerances

box, shown in Figure 13-5. This dialog box will be displayed when you choose **Annotate > Insert > Geometric Tolerance** from the **Ribbon**. The options in the **Geometric Tolerance** dialog box are discussed next.

*Figure 13-5 The **Geometric Tolerance** dialog box with the **Model Refs** tab chosen*

Model Refs Tab

The options in this tab are used to select the model or drawing where the gtol have to be placed and also to specify the model references.

Model

This drop-down list is used to select the model to display the gtol. You can select the model from this drop-down list or by using the **Select Model** button.

Dimensioning the Drawing Views

Reference

The options in this area are used to select the reference for adding the gtol. The reference can be an edge, axis, surface, feature, datum, or an entity. You can select the reference type from the **Type** drop-down list or by choosing the **Select Entity** button.

Placement

The options in this area will be available only when you select a reference type for placing the gtol. These options are used to specify the placement type for the gtol. The placement type can be selected from the **Type** drop-down list.

Datum Refs Tab

The options in the **Datum Refs** tab, shown in Figure 13-6, are used to select the primary, secondary, or tertiary datum references for the gtol.

You can also specify the composite tolerances to the primary, secondary, or tertiary datum references by using the **Composite Tolerance** check box in this area. The **Composite Tolerance** check box is available only when the **Position** or **Surface Profile** buttons are chosen from the types of gtol buttons on the left of the **Geometric Tolerance** dialog box. The value of composite reference can be specified in the **Value** edit box that is available only when you select the **Composite Tolerance** check box. The datum reference for the composite tolerance can be selected using the **Datum Reference** drop-down list that is available only when you select the **Composite Tolerance** check box.

*Figure 13-6 The **Geometric Tolerance** dialog box with the **Datum Refs** tab chosen*

Tol Value Tab

The options in the **Tol Value** tab, shown in Figure 13-7, are used to specify the tolerance value and the material condition for the gtol.

You can specify the overall tolerance value or the per units tolerance value using the options in this tab. You can also specify the material condition using the **Material Condition** drop-down list.

*Figure 13-7 The **Geometric Tolerance** dialog box with the **Tol Value** tab chosen*

Symbols Tab

The options in the **Symbols** tab, shown in Figure 13-8, are used to specify the symbols for the gtol. The symbols and modifiers for the gtol can be selected from the **Symbols and Modifiers** area, whereas the projected tolerance zone symbol can be selected from the **Projected Tolerance Zone** area. The location of the projected tolerance zone symbol and its height can be specified using the options in this area. You can also specify the profile boundary symbol for the profile gtol from the **Profile Boundary** area that appears in the place of **Projected Tolerance Zone** area. The **Profile Boundary** area is available only if you choose the **Surface Profile** or the **Line Profile** button from the left of the **Geometric Tolerance** dialog box.

*Figure 13-8 The **Geometric Tolerance** dialog box with the **Symbols** tab chosen*

Additional Text Tab

The options in the **Additional Text** tab, shown in Figure 13-9, are discussed next.

Additional text above
Select the **Additional text above** check box; the **Text Symbol** box will be displayed. Using **Text Symbol** box, you can insert the required text symbols above the gtol control frame. You can also insert additional text above the gtol control frame using the **Enter additional text above the gtol control frame** edit box that is available below the **Additional text**

Dimensioning the Drawing Views 13-9

*Figure 13-9 The **Geometric Tolerance** dialog box with the **Additional Text** tab chosen*

above check box. The text symbols that you have selected from the **Text Symbol** will also be displayed in this edit box.

Additional text on right
Select the **Additional text on right** check box; the **Text Symbol** box will be displayed. You can insert the required text symbols on the right of the gtol control frame using the **Text Symbol** box. You can also insert additional text on the right of the gtol control frame using the **Enter additional text on the right of the gtol control frame** edit box that is available below the **Additional text on right** check box. The text symbols that you have selected from the **Text Symbol** will also be displayed in this edit box.

Prefix
The **Prefix** check box is used to insert text and text symbols in the gtol control frame. On selecting this check box, the text and text symbols are inserted as prefix to the geometric tolerance text.

Suffix
The **Suffix** check box is used to insert text and text symbols in the gtol control frame. On selecting this check box, the text and text symbols are inserted as suffix to the geometric tolerance text.

New Gtol

The **New Gtol** button in the **Geometric Tolerance** dialog box is chosen to accept the current gtol and place a new gtol.

Move

The **Move** button is chosen to change the location of the current gtol.

Figure 13-10 shows the drawing view with reference datums and gtol.

Figure 13-10 The drawing view with reference datums and gtol

EDITING THE GEOMETRIC TOLERANCES

The gtol added to the drawing views can be edited using the **Geometric Tolerance** dialog box. This dialog box will be displayed when you select the text of the tolerance from the drawing view and then right-click to display the shortcut menu. Choose the **Properties** option from the shortcut menu to display the **Geometric Tolerance** dialog box. All options in the various tabs of the **Geometric Tolerance** dialog box are similar to those discussed earlier.

ADDING BALLOONS TO THE ASSEMBLY VIEWS

The **Balloon** button is used to create balloons associated with the assembly in the drawing views. You can add balloon to the assembly drawing views by choosing **Annotate > Insert > Balloon** from the **Ribbon**. The procedure to place balloons is similar to that used to add notes to the drawing, see Figure 13-11.

Tip: *The notes or balloons can be modified and edited using the options in the shortcut menu that will be displayed when you select them using the left mouse button and holding the right mouse button.*

ADDING REFERENCE DATUMS TO THE DRAWING VIEWS

Reference datums are used as references for geometric tolerance. Datums are needed to be set before adding the geometric tolerance.

To create a reference datum, choose **Annotate > Insert > Model Datum Plane** from the **Ribbon**; the **Datum** dialog box will be displayed, as shown in Figure 13-12. You can rename the selected datum and then choose the second button from the **Type** area to enclose the datum

Dimensioning the Drawing Views   13-11

Figure 13-11 Drawing view with balloons and note

inside a feature control frame. You can place these reference datums freely in the drawing views or in a selected dimension. Figure 13-13 shows the drawing views with reference datums.

*Figure 13-12 The **Datum** dialog box*   *Figure 13-13 Drawing views with reference datums*

MODIFYING AND EDITING DIMENSIONS

Pro/ENGINEER allows you to edit and modify the dimensions assigned to the drawing views. There are various methods of editing and modifying the driving dimensions. Before these methods are discussed, it is important for you to learn the terminology used in these methods. Figure 13-14 shows the terminology that is used in the **Drawing** mode of Pro/ENGINEER Wildfire 5.0.

Figure 13-14 Parameters associated with dimensions

Tip: *To display dimensions in a 3D view, you will first have to set the value of **allow_3d_dimensions** to **yes** in the configuration file. If this value is set to **no**, then the dimensions will not be displayed in 3D views. To open the configuration file, choose **File > Drawing Options** from the menu bar; the **Options** window will be displayed. This window lists all variables that can be applied for the current session.*

Modifying the Dimensions Using the Dimension Properties Dialog Box

To modify the dimensions using this option, select the dimension and right-click to invoke a shortcut menu. Choose the **Properties** option from the shortcut menu; the **Dimension Properties** dialog box will be displayed, as shown in Figure 13-15. The options in this dialog box are discussed next.

Properties Tab
The options in this tab are discussed next.

Name
You can specify a name for the dimension in the **Name** edit box.

Dimensioning the Drawing Views   13-13

*Figure 13-15 The **Properties** tab of the **Dimension Properties** dialog box*

Value and Display Area
The options in this area are related to the display of dimensions in the drawing. You can set the nominal, override and tolerance values of dimensions, number of decimal places in the dimension, and whether to round the dimension value or not in this area.

Tolerance Area
The options in this area are related to the tolerance in the drawing.

> **Tolerance mode**. This drop-down list will be available only when the value of **tol_display** is set to **yes** in the configuration file. The options in this drop-down list are used to select the type of tolerance mode. Depending on the option selected from this drop-down list, the other options in this area change.

Format Area
The options in this area are discussed next.

> **Decimal**. Select the **Decimal** radio button to display the dimensions in the decimal format. You can set the number of decimal values in the **Value and Display** area.

> **Fractional**. Select the **Fractional** radio button to display dimensions in the fractional format. The largest denominator can be set in the **Value and Display** area using the **Largest denominator** edit box that will be displayed when you select the **Fractional** radio button.

Angular dimension units. This drop-down list is used to specify the angular units for dimensions.

Dual dimension Area

The options under the **Dual dimension** area will be available only when the value of **dual_dimensioning** is set to **yes** in the configuration file. The options in this area are used to specify the placement point for the dual dimensioning and the number of decimal places.

> **Tip**: *After you modify the nominal value of a dimension in the **Value and Display** area, you will have to regenerate the model using the **Current Sheet** button to view the effect of modifications. The modified dimension appears magenta in color.*

Display Tab

The options displayed on choosing the **Display** tab in the **Dimension Properties** dialog box are shown in Figure 13-16. The options in this tab are discussed next.

*Figure 13-16 The **Dimension Properties** dialog box with the **Display** tab chosen*

Display Area

The options in this area are discussed next.

Basic. This radio button, if selected, displays the dimension in a rectangular box.

Inspection. This radio button, if selected, displays the dimension in an elliptical box.

Dimensioning the Drawing Views 13-15

Neither. This radio button is used when you do not require the display of dimensions in the Basic or Inspection type.

Prefix. The **Prefix** edit box is used to add some additional text as prefix to the default dimension text.

Postfix. The **Postfix** edit box is used to add some additional text as suffix to the dimension text.

Flip Arrows. This button is used to toggle the display of arrows between inside and outside the dimension extension lines.

Set dimension text Box

The **Set dimension text** box displays the text of the selected dimensions. You can edit the text using this edit box.

> **Tip**: *The modifications made using the **Dimension Properties** dialog box are applied dynamically on the dimensions. You can view these modifications in the background by moving the **Dimension Properties** dialog box on the side of the screen.*

Text Style Tab

The options displayed on choosing the **Text Style** tab in the **Dimension Properties** dialog box are shown in Figure 13-17. The options in this tab are discussed next.

*Figure 13-17 The **Dimension Properties** dialog box with the **Text Style** tab chosen*

Copy from Area
The **Copy from** area displays the options to modify the text style of the dimension text. You can edit the text using this area.

Character Area
The **Character** area displays the options to modify the font style of the dimension text. Various parameters like height, font name, width of font, font style, and so on can be modified using the options available in this area.

Note/Dimension Area
The **Note/Dimension** area displays the options to modify the dimension or the text in the form of a note. The parameters that can be modified using this area are text justification, color, line spacing, angle, and so on.

Preview button
The **Preview** button is used to preview the changes that are made using the **Dimension Properties** dialog box.

Reset button
The **Reset** button is used to reset the default values.

In addition to the options in various tabs, the following five buttons are available at the lower portion of this dialog box.

Move
The **Move** button is chosen to move the dimension to a new location on the current sheet. You can also move the dimension by selecting it and then dragging it by moving the mouse.

Move Text
The **Move Text** button is chosen to move the dimension text to a new location on the screen. Remember that only the text will be moved. The witness lines and the dimension lines do not move from their original location.

Edit Attach
The **Edit Attach** button is chosen to replace an existing selected dimension with a new dimension in user-defined location.

Orient
The **Orient** button is chosen to redefine the orientation and the placement of dimension text.

Text Symbol
The **Text Symbol** button is chosen to display the **Text Symbol** dialog box. Using this dialog box, you can add special symbols to the default dimension text.

Modifying the Drawing Items Using the Shortcut Menu

When you select an item from a drawing view and right-click, a shortcut menu with various options will be displayed. These options depend on the item selected to modify. These options vary from item to item. Some of the items related to the drawing, which can be modified using the shortcut menu are discussed next.

Value

You can modify the dimension value by selecting a dimension value. When the dimension value and the arrows turn red, click on the dimension value. Notice that now only the value is highlighted in red. Right-click to invoke the shortcut menu. From the shortcut menu, choose the **Edit Value** option. The dimension value will be displayed in the edit box. Modify the value in the edit box and press ENTER. Alternatively, double-click on the value; an edit box will be displayed. Enter a new value and press ENTER. To view the effect of the modification, you will have to regenerate the drawing view using the **Current Sheet** button from the **Top Toolchest**. This option is also used to modify the scale of the drawing view and the tolerance values.

Text Style

The parameters that can be modified are the selected text line, entire text material, text height, text style, style library for the text, and the current style.

Miscellaneous Modifications

The modifications that can be made using the shortcut menu are: move a dimension, flip the arrows of the dimensions, switch the selected dimension from one view to the other, make a jog in the witness line, modify the values or text of the dimension, modify the arrow style, break the witness line, remove the break from the witness line, erase the witness line, show the erased witness line, or erase the selected dimension from the drawing view.

Number of Decimal Places

To modify the number of decimal values for the dimension text, choose **Annotate > Parameters > Decimal Places** from the **Ribbon**; you will be prompted to specify the number of decimal places in the **Message Input Window**. Specify the number of decimal places; you will be prompted to select the dimensions to be modified. Select the dimension using the left mouse button and then press the middle mouse button to view the change in the decimal places.

Cleaning Up the Dimensions

Generally, dimensions displayed in the drawing views are scattered and improperly placed. This, in turn, makes the drawing views look very confusing. Pro/Engineer Wildfire helps you to clear this confusion by using two methods. The first method is to place all dimensions manually at the appropriate location in the view. The second and more convenient method is to place these dimensions in a proper order by choosing **Annotate > Arrange > Cleanup Dimensions** from the **Ribbon**; the **Clean Dimensions** dialog box will be displayed and you will be prompted to select dimensions or individual views to clean. After you select the dimension to clean, press the middle mouse button; the options in this dialog box will be enabled, as shown in Figure 13-18. These options are discussed next.

Placement Tab

The options in this tab of the **Clean Dimensions** dialog box are used to place the dimensions in the required location. The distance between the two dimensions and the distance between the view boundary and the dimension are set under this tab. The options in this tab are discussed next.

Space out dimensions
This option is used to maintain the distance between two dimensions. Most of the other options in this tab are available only when you select this option.

Offset
The **Offset** edit box is used to specify the offset distance between the first dimension and the view boundary.

Increment
The **Increment** edit box is used to specify the offset distance between the two dimension lines.

Offset Reference Area
View outline. The **View outline** radio button is selected to specify the offset distances taking the outline of the view as reference.

*Figure 13-18 The **Clean Dimensions** dialog box with the **Placement** tab chosen*

Baseline. The **Baseline** radio button is selected to specify the offset distance taking a selected flat edge, datum plane, snap line, detail axis line, or view border as the reference. When you invoke this option, you will be prompted to select either of the above mentioned entities as the reference.

Create Snap Lines
The **Create Snap Lines** check box is selected to create the snap lines, which can be used to clean the dimensions. The snap lines will be created at the distances specified in the **Offset** and the **Increment** edit boxes. If this check box is cleared, the snap lines will not be created.

Break witness lines
The **Break witness lines** check box is selected to break the witness lines if some dimensions overlap each other.

Cosmetic Tab

The options in the **Cosmetic** tab of the **Clean Dimensions** dialog box, are used for determining the location of the dimension value with respect to the dimension line, refer to Figure 13-19. The arrows and the orientation of the dimension text can also be controlled using this tab.

Dimensioning the Drawing Views

Flip Arrows
The **Flip Arrows** check box is selected to flip the arrows of the dimensions that are not easily adjusted inside the dimension lines.

Center Text
The **Center Text** check box is selected to place the dimensions at the center of the dimension lines.

Horizontal and Vertical buttons
These buttons are used to specify the placement of the horizontal or vertical dimension text outside the dimension line if they do not fit.

Figures 13-20 and 13-21 explain the use of the **Clean Dimensions** dialog box.

Note
The system does not show a reference datum plane in a drawing view unless it is perpendicular to the drawing area.

Figure 13-19 The **Clean Dimensions** dialog box with the **Cosmetic** tab chosen

Figure 13-20 Drawing views with dimensions before cleaning

Figure 13-21 Drawing views with dimensions after cleaning

TUTORIALS

Tutorial 1

In this tutorial, you will generate the drawing views of the part shown in Figure 13-22. Generate the dimensions in the drawing views. The views to be generated are shown in Figure 13-23.

(Expected time: 45 min)

Figure 13-22 Model for generating drawing views

Dimensioning the Drawing Views

Figure 13-23 Drawing views to be created alongwith the dimensions

The following steps are required to complete this tutorial:

a. Create the model in the **Part** mode using the given dimensions and save the file.
b. Open a new drawing file in the **Drawing** mode and generate the top and front views of the model on the drawing sheet, refer to Figure 13-24.
c. Generate the dimensions in the views and clean them using the **Clean Dimensions** dialog box, refer to Figure 13-25.
d. Add geometric tolerance to the required entities, refer to Figure 13-26.

Before you start creating the model and the drawing views, set the working directory to *C:\ProE-WF-5.0\c13*. Make sure that the *c13* folder exists inside the *ProE-WF-5.0* folder.

Creating the Model
First, create the given model in the **Part** mode. Its views will be generated later.

1. Create a new **Part** file and name it as *c13tut1*.

2. Create the model in the **Part** mode and save this model.

Starting a New Drawing File
To generate drawing views, you need to start a new drawing file.

1. Choose the **New** button from the **File** toolbar; the **New** dialog box is displayed.

2. Select the **Drawing** radio button from the **Type** area and enter the name of the drawing as *c13tut1* in the **Name** edit box.

3. Choose **OK** from the **New** dialog box; the **New Drawing** dialog box is displayed.

4. If the name of the model is not displayed in the **Default Model** area, choose the **Browse** button and select the model. Select the **Empty** radio button from the **Specify Template** area, the **Landscape** button from the **Orientation** area, and the **A4** option from the **Standard Size** drop-down list.

5. Choose **OK** from the **New Drawing** dialog box to enter the **Drawing** mode. The **Drawing** mode is invoked and a new A4 size drawing sheet is displayed.

Generating the Drawing Views

You need to generate the top and front views of the model.

1. Choose **Layout > Model Views > General** from the **Ribbon**.

2. Specify the center point for the drawing view, refer to Figure 13-24. When you specify the point, the **Drawing View** dialog box is displayed.

3. Select the **TOP** option from the **Model view names** list in the **View orientation** area.

4. Choose the **Scale** option in the **Categories** area and edit the scale factor for the view to **0.06**.

5. Choose the **Apply** button and close the dialog box. The default view is oriented as the top view and scaled to the specified scale factor.

6. Choose **No Hidden** from the **Model Display** toolbar and repaint the screen using the **Repaint** button from the **View** toolbar. The top view is shown in Figure 13-24.

7. Choose **Layout > Model Views > Projection** from the **Ribbon**. Make sure that the angle of projection is in the third angle projection, else you will not get the desired result.

8. Select the center point for the drawing view below the top view, as shown in Figure 13-24.

The sheet after generating the two views is shown in Figure 13-24.

Renaming the Datum Planes

The datum planes need to be renamed because the gtol values will be applied to the inclined surface with their references. This is evident from Figure 13-23.

1. Choose the **Plane Display** button from the **Datum Display** toolbar to display the datum planes and then repaint the screen.

2. Choose the **Annotate** tab from the **Ribbon** and then select the **Datum Plane** from the Filter drop-down list in the Status Bar.

Dimensioning the Drawing Views

13-23

Figure 13-24 Top and front views of the model

3. Select the **RIGHT** datum plane in the top view and when it turns red, hold the right mouse button to display a shortcut menu.

4. Choose the **Properties** option from the shortcut menu; the **Datum** dialog box is displayed.

5. Enter **A** in the **Name** edit box and then choose the second button from the **Type** area to enclose the datum in the reference box. Make sure the **On Datum** radio button is selected in the **Placement** area. Choose **OK** to exit the **Datum** dialog box.

6. Repeat steps 3 and 4 to rename the **TOP** and **FRONT** datum planes as **B** and **C**, respectively.

Dimensioning the Drawing Views

1. Choose **Annotate > Insert > Show Model Annotations** from the **Ribbon**; the **Show Model Annotations** dialog box is displayed with the **Show Model Dimensions** tab chosen by default. Also, you are prompted to select a view to display its annotations.

2. Select the front view (the view at the bottom); all dimensions of this view are listed in the dialog box.

3. Choose the **Select All** button available below the list box; all dimensions are displayed as strong dimensions in the selected view.

4. Choose the **Apply** button to accept and continue the settings.

5. Now, select the top view from the drawing area; its dimension is listed in the **Show Model Annotations** dialog box.

6. Select the check box placed on the left of the dimensions listed; the dimension of the selected item is displayed in the drawing area as a strong dimension.

7. Choose the **OK** button from the dialog box to accept the settings and exit the dialog box.

Placing the Dimensions in Order

The dimensions displayed in the drawing views are scattered and improperly placed. You need to place the dimensions in proper order using the **Clean Dimensions** dialog box.

1. Choose **Annotate > Arrange > Cleanup Dimensions** from the **Ribbon** to display the **Clean Dimensions** dialog box; you are prompted to select the dimensions to clean.

2. Select all dimensions from both the views by using the window selection method; the selected dimensions are highlighted. Press the middle mouse button.

3. Enter **0.5** in the **Offset** edit box and **0.5** in the **Increment** edit box.

4. Clear the **Create Snap Lines** check box. Choose **Apply** and then choose **Close** to exit the **Clean Dimensions** dialog box.

5. After cleaning the dimensions, the drawing views should look similar to the ones shown in Figure 13-25. Select and move the dimensions, if necessary.

Figure 13-25 Top and front views of the model with dimensions and datum planes

Displaying the Geometric Tolerance

1. Choose **Annotate > Insert > Geometric Tolerance** from the **Ribbon** to display the **Geometric Tolerance** dialog box. You will notice that the name of the model *c13tut1.prt* is displayed in the **Model** drop-down list.

2. Choose the angularity geometric condition by choosing the **Angularity** button from the **Geometric Tolerance** dialog box.

3. Select the **Surface** option from the **Type** drop-down list in the **Reference** area and select the left-inclined edge in the front view.

4. Select **With Leader** from the **Type** drop-down list in the **Placement** area; the **ATTACH TYPE** menu is displayed and you are prompted to select an edge for attaching the leader.

5. Select the left-inclined edge from the front view and then click the middle mouse button at the desired position in the drawing area to place the note. Even if the note is placed at an improper position in the drawing area, you can move its location later.

6. Choose the **Tol Value** tab from the **Geometric Tolerance** dialog box.

7. Enter **0.001** in the **Overall Tolerance** edit box.

8. Select **LMC** from the **Material Condition** drop-down list.

9. Choose the **Symbols** tab and then select the **Statistical Tolerance** check box from the **Symbols and Modifiers** area in the **Geometric Tolerance** dialog box.

10. Select the **Below Gtol** radio button from the **Projected Tolerance Zone** area and then select the **Zone Height** check box. Enter **0.001** in this edit box displayed on selecting the **Zone Height** check box. Choose **OK** to exit the **Geometric Tolerance** dialog box.

11. The drawing views after adding the geometric tolerances should look similar to the ones shown in Figure 13-26. You need to move the note for the geometric tolerances to a location shown in Figure 13-27 by selecting and dragging it. Similarly, arrange all dimensions and datums on the drawing sheet, as shown in Figure 13-27.

Saving the Drawing File

Now, you need to save the drawing file that you have created.

1. Choose the **Save** button from the **Top Toolchest**; the **Save Object** dialog box is displayed with the name of the drawing file that you had entered earlier. Press ENTER to confirm the saving of the file.

Figure 13-26 *Top and front views of the model with dimensions, datum planes, and geometric tolerances*

Figure 13-27 *The required drawing views after arranging all dimensions and datums*

Dimensioning the Drawing Views

Tutorial 2

In this tutorial, you will generate the drawing views of the model shown in Figure 13-28. The dimensioned drawing views are shown in Figure 13-29. **(Expected time: 45 min)**

Figure 13-28 Model for generating drawing views

Figure 13-29 Drawing views to be generated in Tutorial 2

The following steps are required to complete this tutorial:

a. Create the model in the **Part** mode using the given dimensions and save the file.
b. Open a new drawing file in the **Drawing** mode and generate the top view, front, right, and detailed views of the model on the drawing sheet, refer to Figure 13-30.

c. Dimension the views and clean the dimensions using the **Clean Dimensions** dialog box, refer to Figure 13-31.

Make sure the working directory is set to *C:\ProE-WF-5.0\c13*.

Creating the Model

First, you need to create the model in the **Part** mode whose drawing views are to be generated.

1. Create the model in the **Part** mode using the given dimensions.

2. Save this model created in the **Part** mode with the name *c13tut2*.

Starting a New Drawing File

To generate the drawing views, you first need to start a new drawing file.

1. Choose the **New** button from the **File** toolbar; the **New** dialog box is displayed.

2. Select the **Drawing** radio button from the **Type** area and enter the name of the drawing as *c13tut2* in the **Name** edit box.

3. Choose **OK** from the **New** dialog box; the **New Drawing** dialog box is displayed. In this dialog box, the name of the model is displayed in the **Default Model** area.

4. If the name of the model is not displayed in the **Default Model** area, choose the **Browse** button and select the model.

5. Select the **Empty** radio button from the **Specify Template** area, choose the **Landscape** button from the **Orientation** area, and select the **A4** option from the **Standard Size** drop-down list.

6. Choose **OK** from the **New Drawing** dialog box; you enter the **Drawing** mode and a new drawing sheet of A4 size is displayed on the screen.

Creating the Drawing Views

First, the top view of the model needs to be generated and then the front view will be generated by projecting it from the top view. The right view will be projected from the front view. The detail view will be placed on the drawing sheet by specifying a scale for it.

1. Choose **Layout > Model Views > General** from the **Ribbon**.

2. Specify the center point for the drawing view on the top-left side of the sheet; the **Drawing View** dialog box is displayed.

3. Select the **TOP** option from the **Model view names** list in the **View orientation** area.

Dimensioning the Drawing Views

4. Choose the **Apply** button; the default view is oriented as the top view.

5. Choose the **Scale** option in the **Categories** display area and specify the scale factor for the view as **0.006**. Exit the dialog box and then choose **No Hidden** from the **Model Display** toolbar. Repaint the screen using the **Repaint** button from the **View** toolbar. The top view is shown in Figure 13-30.

   The front view of the model is generated from the top view.

6. Choose **Layout > Model Views > Projection** in the **Ribbon**. Specify the center point for the drawing view which is below the top view, as shown in Figure 13-30. Make sure that the angle of projection is the third angle projection; else the desired projection will not be displayed.

7. Similarly, place the right and detailed views on the drawing sheet, as shown in Figure 13-30.

Figure 13-30 Drawing views before adding dimensions

Dimensioning the Drawing Views

1. Choose **Annotate > Insert > Show Model Annotations** from the **Ribbon**; the **Show Model Annotations** dialog box is displayed with the **Show Model Dimensions** tab chosen by default. Also, you are prompted to select a view to display its annotations.

2. Move the cursor toward the round feature in the detailed view and click when the round feature gets highlighted; the dimensions of the radius of round feature are listed in the dialog box.

3. Choose the **Select All** button available below the list box; all the radial dimensions are displayed in the selected view as strong dimensions.

4. Choose the **Apply** button to accept the settings and continue.

5. Now, select all the three views; all dimensions of the three views are listed in the dialog box.

6. Choose the **Select All** button; all dimensions are displayed on the view as strong dimensions.

7. Choose the **OK** button to accept the settings and exit the dialog box.

Placing the Dimensions in Order

The dimensions displayed in the drawing views are scattered and improperly placed. You need to use the **Clean Dimensions** dialog box to place the dimensions in order.

1. Choose **Annotate > Arrange > Cleanup Dimensions** from the **Ribbon** to display the **Clean Dimensions** dialog box; you are prompted to select the dimensions to clean.

2. Select all dimensions from the top and front views by dragging a rectangle around them. Press the middle mouse button so that the options in the **Clean Dimensions** dialog box are displayed.

   When you select the dimensions, the radius dimensions in the drawing views are not selected. This means that the radius dimensions will remain unaffected by the values that you will enter in the **Clean Dimensions** dialog box.

3. Enter **0.4** in the **Offset** edit box and **0.3** in the **Increment** edit box.

4. Clear the **Create Snap Lines** check box. Choose **Apply** and then choose **Close** to exit the **Clean Dimensions** dialog box.

   After you clean the dimensions, you will notice that the dimensions are not placed in the required order. So, you need to manually place the dimensions in proper order.

5. Select the dimension and drag it to the desired location on the drawing sheet.

   Some dimensions are repeated. For example, the diameter of the hole feature is displayed twice in the drawing view. So, you need to erase the dimensions that are repeated and are not needed.

6. Select the dimension and hold down the right mouse button on the repeated dimensions to display a shortcut menu. Choose the **Erase** option from the shortcut menu.

   In some cases, the dimensions are displayed in the views in which you do not want them to be displayed. In such cases, you can switch those dimensions to the other views. To switch the dimension to other view, select it and hold the right mouse button; a shortcut menu is displayed. Choose the **Move Item to View** option from it.

Dimensioning the Drawing Views 13-31

After manually placing the dimensions, the drawing views should look similar to the views shown in Figure 13-31.

Saving the Drawing File

1. Choose the **Save** button from the **Top Toolchest**; the **Save Object** dialog box is displayed with the name of the drawing file specified earlier.

2. Press ENTER to confirm the saving of the file.

Figure 13-31 The required drawing views

Self-Evaluation Test

Answer the following questions and then compare them to those given at the end of this chapter:

1. The reference datum planes are used to display geometric tolerances in a drawing view. (T/F)

2. If you modify a dimension value in the **Drawing** mode and then regenerate the drawing view, the modification will also be applied to the model in the **Part** mode. (T/F)

3. The notes created on a model in the **Part** mode can also be displayed in a drawing view in the **Drawing** mode. (T/F)

4. When you select a drawing view to display dimensions, all dimensions are placed in proper order in the drawing view. (T/F)

5. Most of the editing operations in a drawing view can be done using the shortcut menu that is displayed when you hold the right mouse button on the item to be modified. (T/F)

6. The _____ dialog box is used to display dimensions in drawing views.

7. The dimension values can be modified by choosing the _____ option from the **Edit** menu in the menu bar.

8. The _____ dialog box is used to clean dimensions in drawing views.

9. You have to set the value of _____ to **yes** in the configuration file to display the dimensional tolerance in drawing views.

10. The configuration file can be opened by choosing _____ from the menu bar.

Review Questions

Answer the following questions:

1. Which of the following dialog boxes is used to display dimensions in a drawing view?

    (a) **Dimension Properties**   (b) **Clean Dimensions**
    (c) **Show / Erase**   (d) None

2. Which of the following dialog boxes is used to modify the properties of the text in a drawing view?

    (a) **Dimension Properties**   (b) **Clean Dimensions**
    (c) **Show / Erase**   (d) None

3. Which of the following dialog boxes is used to display the geometric tolerances in a drawing view?

    (a) **Geometric Tolerance**   (b) **Clean Dimensions**
    (c) **Show / Erase**   (d) None

4. Which of the following options in the shortcut menu is used to switch a dimension from one view to another?

    (a) **Erase**   (b) **Flip Arrows**
    (c) **Move Item to View**   (d) None

5. Which of the following radio buttons in the **Type** area needs to be selected in the **New** dialog box to open a new drawing file?

   (a) **Assembly** (b) **Sketch**
   (c) **Part** (d) None

6. The dimensions erased using the **Erase** option of the shortcut menu are also deleted from the model in the **Part** mode. (T/F)

7. Notes or balloons can be modified and edited using the options in the shortcut menu. (T/F)

8. The system does not show a reference datum plane in a drawing view unless it is perpendicular to the drawing area. (T/F)

9. Generally, dimensions displayed in the drawing views are scattered and improperly placed. (T/F)

10. You cannot move text dynamically on a drawing sheet. (T/F)

Exercise

Exercise 1

In this exercise, you will generate the drawing views of the model created in Exercise 2 of Chapter 7, as shown in Figure 13-32. Add dimensions to the views, as shown in the figure.

(Expected time: 45 min)

Note

In the given drawing views, the center lines are not generated automatically; but are created manually. After creating the center lines, you need to define a line style and then apply it on the center lines.

Figure 13-32 Solid model and its drawing views

Answers to Self-Evaluation Test
1. T, 2. T, 3. T, 4. F, 5. T, 6. Show / Erase, 7. Value, 8. Clean Dimensions, 9. tol_display, 10. File > Properties > Drawing Options

Chapter 14

Other Drawing Options

Learning Objectives

After completing this chapter, you will be able to:
- *Sketch in the Drawing mode.*
- *Modify sketched entities and other items in drawing views.*
- *Create a user-defined drawing format for drawing sheets.*
- *Add or remove sheets from the current drawing.*
- *Create tables in the current sheet.*
- *Generate associative Bill of Material in the Drawing mode.*

SKETCHING IN THE DRAWING MODE

Sketching is one of the most important tools available in the **Drawing** mode. Sketching in the **Drawing** mode is called drafting. As discussed earlier, there are two types of drafting techniques in Pro/ENGINEER Wildfire 5.0: Generative drafting and Interactive drafting. Any item on the drawing sheet that is not generated from a model is called a draft entity or a draft item. Drafting is extensively used for creating user-defined formats, drawing tables, and drawing title blocks in the formats. Sketching in the **Drawing** mode is almost similar to that in the other modes of Pro/ENGINEER. Sketching can be done by using the tools in the **Sketch** tab of the **Ribbon**. The tools used to sketch in the **Drawing** mode are discussed next.

Selecting Entities

There is no button available for selecting entities. However, you will be in the selection mode by default, or after you exit any active command. You can select the drawing views, sketched entities, dimensions, notes, and so on from the drawing by simply clicking on them with the left mouse button. This button is extensively used for moving the drawing views or the items in the drawing view. You can select the entity and drag using the left mouse button to move it.

> **Tip**: *To delete an entity or an item from a drawing view, you can select the item and then press the DELETE key. You can also select the entity and choose the **Delete** option from the shortcut menu that is displayed when you hold the right mouse button.*

Line

The **Line** button is used to draw line segments. To invoke this tool, choose **Sketch > Insert > Line** from the **Ribbon**; the **Snapping References** dialog box will be displayed, as shown in Figure 14-1. The options in this dialog box are discussed next.

Select references

When the **Select references** button is chosen from the **Snapping References** dialog box, you are prompted to select an entity to which the line is to be snapped.

*Figure 14-1 The **Snapping References** dialog box*

Remove

The **Remove** button is used to remove a selected entity from the **Snapping References** dialog box.

Circle

The **Circle** button is used to create circles. To create a circle, you need to specify a center point and a point on the circumference of the circle.

> **Note**
> *When you choose any sketching tool, the crosshairs of infinite length are displayed attached with the cursor.*

Arc

You can draw arcs in the drawing mode using the **Center and Ends** and **3-Point / Tangent End** buttons.

The other geometric entities that can be drawn by using the tools in the **Ribbon** are splines, construction circles and lines, ellipses, and points. You can also create a fillet and a chamfer between two entities. You can also use the edges of the model and also create offsets.

Chain

The **Chain** button is used when the object you want to draw consists of more than one entity. To invoke this button, choose **Sketch > Settings > Chain** from the **Ribbon**. For example, when you choose the **Line** button, you can draw a single line. But if you draw a line after choosing the **Chain** button, you can draw continuous chain of lines. This chain can be ended only by pressing the middle mouse button.

Parametric Sketch

The **Parametric Sketch** button is used to draw sketches by automatically applying constraints.

MODIFYING THE SKETCHED ENTITIES

There are various options to modify the draft entities. The operations or modifications that can be applied on the draft entities are discussed next.

Trimming the Draft Entities

The sketched or draft entities can be trimmed using the tools available in the **Trim** panel of the **Sketch** tab in the **Ribbon**. The tools in the **Trim** panel, shown in Figure 14-2, are discussed next.

*Figure 14-2 The tools in the **Trim** panel of the **Ribbon***

Divide at Intersection

The **Divide at Intersection** button is used to divide two selected entities at the point of intersection. When you choose this option, you are prompted to select the two entities. Select the two entities to divide them at the intersection point. When you select an entity, and if a warning message window is displayed, then choose **OK** from it. This prompt informs you that the command will break all parametric sketching references.

Divide by Equal Segments

This button is in the extended **Trim** panel and is used to divide the draft entities into segments of equal length. To do so, choose the **Divide by Equal Segments** button and then select the entities to divide. After selecting the entity or entities, press the middle mouse button; the **Message Input Window** will be displayed and you will be prompted to enter the number of equal segments. Enter the number of equal segments into which you need to divide the entity and press ENTER.

Corner
This button is the same as discussed in the **Sketch** mode. This option trims the two selected entities so that a corner is formed after trimming. Make sure to select the entities using the CTRL key.

Bound
This button is used for deleting or extending a portion of an entity by defining a bounding entity.

Length
This button will be available when the **Trim** panel is expanded. Using this button, you can trim or extend an entity up to a specified length.

Increment
This button will also be available when the **Trim** panel is expanded and is used to extend or shorten an entity in specified increments. To extend the entity, enter a positive increment value and to shorten the entity, enter a negative increment value.

Stretch
The **Stretch** button is used to stretch a sketched entity by selecting it using a window. The vertices of the sketched entity that are included inside the window will be moved from their original location and stretched, and the remaining vertices will remain stationary.

Transforming the Draft Entities
The tools in the **Arrange** panel of the **Sketch** tab of the **Ribbon** can be used to translate or move the draft entities. The tools in the **Arrange** panel are shown in Figure 14-3 and are discussed next.

Translate
The **Translate** button is used to move the selected entity or entities on the drawing sheet. To translate the entities, invoke this tool and select the required entities. Next, press the middle mouse button to confirm the selection;

Figure 14-3 The tools displayed in the Arrange panel of the Ribbon

the **GET VECTOR** menu along with the **GET POINT** submenu will be displayed, as shown in Figure 14-4. The options in the **GET VECTOR** menu are used to specify the direction of translation.

Translate and Copy
The **Translate and Copy** button is available when the **Arrange** panel is expanded. This button is used to translate the selected entity and at the same time make a copy of the entity. After selecting the entities, press the middle mouse button; the **GET VECTOR** menu and the **GET POINT** submenu will be displayed. After defining the translation distance and direction, you need to specify the number of copies you want to create.

Rotate

The **Rotate** option is used to rotate the selected entity from its actual location. When you choose this option, you will be prompted to select the entity that you want to rotate. After selecting the entity or entities, press the middle mouse button. You will be prompted to select the center point for rotation. After you select the center point, the **Message Input Window** will be displayed and you will be prompted to enter the rotation angle in the counterclockwise direction. The default direction of rotation will be counterclockwise. However, you can rotate the selected entity in the clockwise direction by specifying a negative rotation angle.

Rotate and Copy

The **Rotate and Copy** button will be available when the **Arrange** panel is expanded and is used to create a pattern of the selected draft entity. Choose this button

*Figure 14-4 The **GET VECTOR** menu with the **GET POINT** submenu*

and then select an entity and press the middle mouse button; you will be prompted to select the center point of rotation. Select the center point of rotation in the drawing. The **Message Input Window** will be displayed and you will be prompted to enter the rotation angle. Press the middle mouse button to accept the entered rotation angle value. Now, enter the number of copies in the **Message Input Window**; the rotated copies of the selected entity will be placed on the drawing sheet.

Scale

The **Scale** button is used to scale the selected entity. After choosing this option, when you select the entity to scale and press the middle mouse button; you will be prompted to select the origin point for scaling. The new scale factor can be specified in the **Message Input Window**. A scale factor greater than 1 will increase the size of the selected entity and a scale factor less than 1 will reduce the size of the selected entity.

Mirror

The **Mirror** button is available when the **Arrange** panel is expanded. This button is used to mirror the selected entities using an existing sketched line.

Grouping Entities

A draft entity can be grouped with other draft entity, with a note, a geometric tolerance (gtol), or a dimension. In Pro/ENGINEER, the note, gtol, and dimensions are called detail items. After grouping the draft entities, an operation applied on any one of them is also applied to the grouped entity. Choose **Edit > Draft Group** from the menu bar to form a group among draft entities like lines, arcs, circles, and so on. The operation performed on any one of the grouped entities is performed on all entities forming that group. When you choose this option, the **DRAFT GROUP** menu will be displayed, as shown in Figure 14-5. Use the required option from this menu to create the draft group.

*Figure 14-5 The **DRAFT GROUP** menu*

Relate

The draft entities can be related to the view so that the draft entities move or re-scale along with the related views, maintaining their position with respect to the related views. The options to relate can be invoked by choosing **Edit > Relate** from the menu bar. On doing so, the cascading menu will be displayed, as shown in Figure 14-6. The options in it are discussed next.

*Figure 14-6 Cascading menu displayed on choosing **Edit>Relate***

Set Default Relate View

This option is available only when the drawing view is selected and is used to set the draft view as the current view. The draft entities that are drawn after setting a default draft view are grouped with the current draft view. Now, if you move the draft view, then the grouped entities will also move with it.

Note
When you move a view that forms a group with draft entities, the draft entities also move. But when you move the entities, the draft view does not move.

Unset Default Relate View

This option is used to unset the current draft view and is activated only when a current draft view exists.

Relate to View

This option is used to relate a view with a draft entity or entities. This option is activated in the cascading menu only when a draft entity is selected. When you choose this option, you will be prompted to select a view to which you want to relate the draft entity. Select the drawing view from the drawing sheet.

Relate to Object

This option is used to relate notes, dimensions, gtols, and other objects to a drawing view. This option is activated in the cascading menu only when an object is selected. When you choose this option, you are prompted to select dim, dim arrow, gtol, note, or a symbol which will serve as the host.

Unrelate

This option is used to unrelate the previously related objects. This option is available in the cascading menu only when a related object is selected.

Drafting by Using the Drawing Views

You can use the generated drawing views to create an entity or the whole drawing view. To use a generated drawing view, choose the black arrow besides the **Use Edge** button in the **Insert** group of the **Sketch** tab of the **Ribbon**; a flyout will be displayed with two options: **Use Edge** and **Offset Edge**. These options are discussed next.

Use Edge

The **Use Edge** option is selected to draw a copy of the selected edge in the drawing view. This option will be available only when you have at least one drawing view in the current drawing sheet and if it is selected.

Offset Edge

This option is used to offset the selected edges to the specified offset distance. When you choose this option, the **OFFSET OPER** menu will be displayed, as shown in Figure 14-7. There are two options in this menu: **Single Ent** and **Ent Chain**. The **Single Ent** option is used to select a single entity from the drawing view, whereas the **Ent Chain** option is used to select a chain of entities from the drawing view. After choosing any one of the options from the **OFFSET OPER** menu, if you move the cursor over the drawing view, each edge of the model in the drawing view will be highlighted separately in cyan color. After selecting each edge of the model, you need to define the offset distance.

Converting a Generated View to a Draft View

To convert a generated view into a draft view, select the view to convert and choose **Layout > Model Views > Convert to Draft Entities** from the **Ribbon**. The **Convert to Draft Entities** button is available when the **Model Views** group is expanded. When you choose this button, the **SNAPSHOT** menu will be displayed, as shown in Figure 14-8. The options in this menu are used to select all views or the current view. After selecting the option from this menu, the **Confirm** dialog box will be displayed with the prompt that the selected view(s) will be broken up into draft entities. Choose the **Yes** button from this dialog box. After converting a generated view to a draft view, all objects in the view will be converted to individual entities.

*Figure 14-7 The **OFFSET OPER** menu*   *Figure 14-8 The **SNAPSHOT** menu*

USER-DEFINED DRAWING FORMATS

Pro/ENGINEER provides you with some standard drawing formats for generating drawing views. These standard formats have standard sheet sizes, tables, and title blocks. However, sometimes you may need to create a user-defined drawing format that is specifically designed as per your requirements, including sheet size, tables, and title block. Choose the **New** button from the **File** toolbar to display the **New** dialog box. In this dialog box, select the **Format** radio button from the **Type** area and then specify the name of the format in the **Name** edit box to create the user-defined format. When you choose **OK**, the **New Format** dialog box will be displayed, as shown in Figure 14-9.

You can set the size and orientation of the format sheet by using this dialog box. After setting the parameters, choose **OK** from this dialog box to proceed to the **Format** mode; the **Format** mode will be invoked.

You can create the desired entities in this format by using the **Sketch** tab of the **Ribbon**. You can also add the text material to the format by using the **Note** button in the **Insert** group of the **Annotate** tab of the **Ribbon**. Figure 14-10 shows a user-defined format created using the A4 size sheet. This format consists of the user-defined title block. Figure 14-11 shows the drawing views generated on the user-defined format.

Figure 14-9 The **New Format** *dialog box*

Figure 14-10 A user-defined format

RETRIEVING THE USER-DEFINED FORMATS IN THE DRAWINGS

For generating the drawing views, you can also retrieve the user-defined format. Once you have created the user-defined format, you can use it in the **Drawing** mode as a sheet for generating the drawing views. To retrieve the user-defined format, select the **Empty with format** radio button and choose the **Browse** button from the **New Drawing** dialog box to invoke the **Open** dialog box. A folder named **System Formats** will be displayed in the **Open** dialog box. Some

Figure 14-11 *Drawing views generated on the user-defined format*

predefined formats are given in this folder. You can retrieve these predefined formats or browse to the location where you have saved the user-defined format created earlier.

Note
*You can add or replace formats in the drawing by using the options in the **Sheet Setup** dialog box that will be displayed when you hold the right mouse button on the drawing sheet. You can add another sheet and then select the format from this dialog box.*

Tip: *The user-defined format that you create is saved in the .frm format. The location of this format will be the working directory that was selected at the time when the format was created.*

ADDING AND REMOVING SHEETS IN THE DRAWING

To add sheets in the current drawing, choose **Layout > Document > New Sheet** from the **Ribbon**; a new sheet will be displayed and added to the current drawing sheet. Also, the sheet number will be displayed at the bottom left of the screen. You can also click on the folder icon displayed at the bottom left of the screen to add new sheet to the current drawing. You can generate various views of a model on multiple sheets. All these drawing views on different sheets are contained in a single drawing file.

To remove the current sheet from a drawing, choose **Edit > Delete > Delete Sheets** from the **Ribbon**; the **Delete Selected Sheets Confirmation** message box will be displayed. Choose **Yes** from the message box to confirm the deletion of the current sheet. You can also right-click on the required Sheet tab available at the bottom of the drawing area to invoke a shortcut menu and then choose **Delete** from the shortcut menu to delete that particular sheet.

CREATING TABLES IN THE DRAWING MODE

You can create any kind of tabular representation in the **Drawing** mode easily by using the tools in the **Table** tab of the **Ribbon** as shown in Figure 14-12.

*Figure 14-12 The **Table** tab of the **Ribbon***

Table Option

To create a table, choose **Table > Table > Table** from the **Ribbon**. When you choose this option, the **TABLE CREATE** submenu will be displayed, as shown in Figure 14-13. Choose the required order of table creation, that is ascending or descending order of the rows progress, as well as set the order in the right or the left direction. Next, specify a location to form the inner boundary of the table by using the options in the **GET POINT** submenu. Specify the length and width of the cells by picking the points on the screen or by entering the required values. Note that you need to press ENTER twice to exit from the sequence row/column creation.

Table From File Option

To insert a table that already exists in the *.tbl* file format, choose **Table > Table > Table From File** from the **Ribbon**; the **Open** dialog box will be displayed. Browse and select a *.tbl* file from this dialog box to open it.

Add Column

The **Add Column** button is used to add a column to an existing table. Choose **Table > Rows & Columns > Add Column** from the **Ribbon**, you will be prompted to select a point inside the existing table to add a column. Specify a point; a column gets added to the table.

*Figure 14-13 The **TABLE CREATE** submenu*

Add Row

The **Add Row** button is used to add a row to an existing table. When you choose this button from the **Rows & Columns** group of the **Table** tab of the **Ribbon**, you will be prompted to select a point inside the existing table to add a row.

The following are the editing operations that can be performed on the tables:

1. To move a table, select it and then drag it by holding it from one of the points that are highlighted on the table.

2. To enter text in any of the cells of the table, you need to double-click inside the cell to display the **Note Properties** dialog box.

3. To delete a table from the drawing, click anywhere on the table and choose **Table > Select Table** from the menu bar. Hold the right mouse button and choose **Delete** from the shortcut menu. You can also choose the DELETE key after selecting the required items.

   To delete an individual row/column, move the cursor over the boundary of the required row/column; the entire row/column will be highlighted. Click when the entities are highlighted and then choose the DELETE key.

   > **Tip**: *To save a table with the .tbl file format, choose **Table > Table > Save as Table** from the **Ribbon**. The **Save as Table** option is available only when a table exists in the drawing sheet.*

GENERATING THE BOM AND BALLOONS IN DRAWINGS

The Bill of Material (BOM) is a representation of the components and their parameters that are used in the assembly. In the **Drawing** mode, the BOM is generated and is associative in nature. Therefore, any modification in the assembly, such as addition or removal of components is automatically reflected in the BOM.

The procedure to generate the BOM and Balloons in the **Drawing** mode is discussed next.

Consider a case in which you have started a new drawing sheet of standard size A with a user-defined format. Now, follow the steps discussed next to generate the BOM and balloons.

Creating a Table for the BOM

Before proceeding to generate the BOM, first you need to create a table for it. The items to be listed in the BOM will be displayed in this table.

1. Choose **Table > Table > Table** from the **Ribbon** to display the **TABLE CREATE** menu.

2. Choose **Descending > Leftward > By Length** from the **TABLE CREATE** menu. Choose **Pick Pnt** from the **GET POINT** menu.

3. Specify a point close to the upper right corner of the inner format boundary. Now, you need to enter the dimensions of the BOM table.

   > **Tip**: *In the **Drawing** mode, most of the modifications and editing can be done by using the shortcut menu that will be displayed when you select the item to modify and then hold the right mouse button. The options in this menu vary and depend on the item selected.*
   >
   > *It is recommended that you use the options in the **Table** tab of the **Ribbon** to create the title blocks in the formats. The text can easily be added to the title block by double-clicking in the cell.*

4. Enter the width of the first column as **0.5** in the **Message Input Window** and press ENTER. Similarly, enter the width of the second column as **3** and the width for third column as **1**. Now, press ENTER twice; you are prompted to enter the height for the first row.

5. Enter the height of the first row as **0.5** and of the second as **0.5** in the **Message Input Window**. Press ENTER twice.

Setting the Repeat Region

After creating the table for the BOM, you need to define the repeat region in this table. Repeat regions are smart cells that can expand depending on the amount of data inserted in the cell. The second row will be defined as the repeat region.

1. Choose **Table > Data > Repeat Region** from the **Ribbon**; the **TBL REGIONS** menu will be displayed.

2. Choose the **Add** option from the **TBL REGIONS** menu; you are prompted to locate the corners of the region.

3. Select the first cell of the second row and then the third cell of the second row to define the region. Next, press the middle mouse button twice to exit the menu.

Creating the Column Headers

After creating the table and setting the repeat region, you need to define the column headings in the table.

1. Double-click in the first cell of the first row; the **Note Properties** dialog box will be displayed. Enter **Index** and choose **OK** to exit the dialog box.

   Similarly, enter **Part Name** and **Qty** in the second and the third cells.

Assigning the Report Symbols in the Repeat Region

The information in the cells that are defined as repeat region is determined by the text that is written in the form of report symbols. These report symbols associate the information in the cells with the assembly file directly.

1. Double-click in the first cell of the second row; the **Report Symbol** dialog box will be displayed. Select **rpt** from the dialog box; the **rpt** options are displayed in the dialog box.

2. Select the **index** option from the dialog box.

3. Double-click in the second cell of the second row; the **Report Symbol** dialog box will be displayed. Select **asm** from the dialog box; the **asm** options are displayed.

4. Select the **mbr** option from the dialog box and then select the **name** option from the dialog boxes that appear. This will ensure that the names of the parts in the assembly are displayed in this column. The number of rows will be automatically modified depending on the number of parts in the assembly.

Other Drawing Options

5. Double-click in the third cell of the second row; the **Report Symbol** dialog box will be displayed. Select **rpt** from the dialog box; the **rpt** options are displayed. Select the **qty** option from the dialog box.

Generating the Exploded Drawing View

After setting all options, you need to generate the isometric view of the exploded state of assembly. Therefore, you should have created an exploded state of assembly. To generate the exploded drawing view, follow the steps listed next.

1. Choose **Layout > Model Views > General** from the **Ribbon**; you will be prompted to select the center point for the drawing view.

2. Select the point on the drawing sheet to place the view; the **Drawing View** dialog box will be displayed. Select the **Isometric** option from the **Default orientation** drop-down list in the **Drawing View** dialog box. Choose the **Apply** button. Specify the scale factor, if required.

3. Select the **View States** option from the **Categories** list box. Select the **Explode components in view** check box. Select the name of the exploded state from the **Assembly explode state** drop-down list and then choose the **Apply** button.

4. Close the **Drawing View** dialog box.

Note that the BOM automatically appears on the table by extending the repeat region. Also, note that the **Qty** column is empty. If the BOM is not displayed, choose **Table > Data > Update Tables** from the **Ribbon**.

Setting the No Repeat Option

If the assembly has more than one quantity of a component, the components are repeated in the BOM. Therefore, you need to set the option to omit the repeated instances in the BOM.

1. Choose **Table > Data > Repeat Region** from the **Ribbon**; the **TBL REGIONS** menu will be displayed.

2. Choose the **Attributes** option from the menu; you will be prompted to select a region.

3. Move the cursor over the table below the first row. All rows, except the first row, are highlighted in cyan. The highlighted portion is called region. Select the region; the **REGION ATTR** submenu will be displayed. Choose the **No Duplicates** option and then choose the **Done/Return** button.

4. Press the middle mouse button twice to exit the menu.

5. Choose **Table > Data > Update Tables** from the **Ribbon**, if the information is not updated in the table.

Generating Balloons

Next, you need to generate Balloons. Balloons are generated by using the repeat region. Before generating balloons, you need to set the repeat region for the generation of balloons.

1. Choose **Table > Balloons > BOM Balloons**; the **BOM BALLOONS** menu will be displayed. Also, the **BOM BAL TYPE** submenu will be displayed with the **Simple** option chosen by default. Now, you will be prompted to select a region.

2. Select the region that was selected earlier and then press the middle mouse button to confirm the selection.

3. From the **BOM BALLOONS** menu, choose the **Create Balloon** option; the **BOM VIEW** submenu will be displayed.

4. Choose the **Show All** option and exit the menu. Balloons are generated and attached to the components of the assembly.

TUTORIALS

Tutorial 1

In this tutorial, you will create a format of size A and add the title block in the format. Then you will retrieve the format in the **Drawing** mode and create the table for BOM. Next, you will generate the exploded isometric view of the **Pedestal Bearing** assembly created in Tutorial 2 of Chapter 11. Also, you will add the balloons to the drawing view, as shown in Figure 14-14.

(Expected time: 45 min)

The following steps are required to complete this tutorial:

a. Start a new file in the **Format** mode. Create the format of the drawing and then add the title block in the format, refer to Figures 14-15 and 14-16.
b. Save the format file and then close it.
c. Start a new drawing file in the **Drawing** mode. Select **Pedestal Bearing** as the model and retrieve the format that you have created.
d. Create the table and enter the headers.
e. Define the repeat region and then assign the report symbols, refer to Figure 14-19.
f. Generate the exploded isometric view of the assembly, refer to Figure 14-20.
g. Add balloons to the drawing, refer to Figure 14-22.

Copy the *Pedestal Bearing* folder from the *c11* folder to the *c14* folder. As this is the first tutorial of this chapter, therefore you need to create the *c14* folder inside the *ProE-WF-5.0* folder. Set the working directory to *C:/ProE-WF-5.0/c14/Pedestal Bearing*.

Starting the Format File

As evident from Figure 14-14, the exploded view of the Pedestal Bearing is generated on a drawing sheet with a customized format. Therefore, you need to create a format before generating the drawing view. This format will then be retrieved later.

Other Drawing Options

14-15

Figure 14-14 The drawing view of the assembly showing the BOM and balloons

1. Choose the **New** button from the **Top Toolchest**; the **New** dialog box is displayed.

2. Select the **Format** radio button from the **Type** area in the **New** dialog box and name the file as **Format1**. Choose **OK** from the **New** dialog box; the **New Format** dialog box is displayed.

3. In this dialog box, the **Empty** radio button in the **Specify Template** area is selected by default and the **Landscape** button in the **Orientation** area is chosen by default. If they are not selected and chosen respectively, you need to select them.

4. Select **A** from the **Standard Size** drop-down list in the **Size** area and then choose **OK**; the **Format** mode is invoked. Note that a sheet of size **A** is displayed on the screen. This is evident from the text displayed below the sheet on the screen.

Creating the Format

1. Choose **Sketch > Insert > Offset Edge** from the **Ribbon**; the **OFFSET OPER** menu is displayed. Choose the **Ent Chain** option from this menu and then select all the four border lines of the format by drawing a window around them. Press the middle mouse button after the selection has been made.

    An arrow is displayed pointing outward. This arrow displays the direction of the offset. To offset the lines in the opposite direction, specify a negative offset value.

2. Enter **-0.25** in the **Message Input Window** and press ENTER. Press the middle mouse button to exit the **OFFSET OPER** menu.

3. Choose **Table > Table > Table** from the **Ribbon** to display the **TABLE CREATE** menu and the **GET POINT** submenu.

4. Choose **Ascending > Leftward > By Length** from the **TABLE CREATE** menu and then choose **Vertex** from the **GET POINT** submenu.

5. Select the lower right corner of the new rectangle created by offsetting the border lines. The corner of the new rectangle is selected because the title block will be created such that it is attached to the new rectangle. Now, you need to enter dimension values for the title block.

6. Enter **1.2** as the width of the first column in the **Message Input Window** and press ENTER. Similarly, enter **2** as the width of the second column and **1.2** for the third column in the **Message Input Window** and press ENTER; you are prompted to enter the width for the next column. Press ENTER to exit the command; you are prompted to enter the height for the first row.

7. Enter the height of the first row as **0.5**, the second as **0.5**, and the third as **0.5** in the **Message Input Window**. Press ENTER again to exit the command.

   The title block created will be similar to the one shown in Figure 14-15. Note that the title block created is not the required one. Therefore, you need to modify it.

8. Click on any cell and choose **Table > Rows & Columns > Merge Cells** from the **Ribbon** to display the **TABLE MERGE** menu. By default, the **Rows & Cols** option is chosen in the **TABLE MERGE** menu.

9. Select the first column and the second column of the top row to merge. Similarly, merge the third column of the top row with the new merged column.

10. Now, merge the second column of the second row with the second column of the third row. Press the middle mouse button twice to exit this tool.

    The table after merging rows and columns should look similar to the one shown in Figure 14-16.

11. You need to set the alignment of the text that will be entered in the cells of the table later. Double-click on any of these cells to invoke the **Note Properties** dialog box.

12. In the dialog box, choose the **Text Style** tab.

13. In the **Note/Dimension** area of this dialog box, select the **Middle** option from the **Vertical** drop-down list. Exit the **Note Properties** dialog box by choosing the **OK** button.

14. Now, the text is aligned vertically to the middle and horizontally to the center. Similarly, set the alignment in all cells of the table individually.

Other Drawing Options

Figure 14-15 Format with the title block

Figure 14-16 Modified title block

Saving the Format File

You need to save the format file that you have created so that it can be used as a template in the **Drawing** mode where you will generate the exploded drawing view of the Pedestal Bearing. The file will be stored in the *.frm* file format.

1. Choose the **Save** button from the **Top Toolchest**; the **Save Object** dialog box is displayed with the name of the file that you entered earlier. Press ENTER.

2. Close the current window by choosing **File > Close Window** from the menu bar.

Starting a New Drawing File

You need to start a new drawing file to generate the exploded drawing view of the Pedestal Bearing.

1. Choose the **New** button from the **File** toolbar to display the **New** dialog box. In this dialog box, select the **Drawing** radio button and specify the name of the drawing as *c14tut1*. Choose **OK**; the **New Drawing** dialog box is displayed.

2. In the **New Drawing** dialog box, choose the **Browse** button from the **Default Model** area and select the assembly file named *pedestalbearing.asm*.

3. Select the **Empty with format** radio button from the **Specify Template** area in the **New Drawing** dialog box.

4. Select **Format1** from the **Format** drop-down list. If **Format1** is not available in the drop-down list, choose the **Browse** button to locate **Format1**. Then, choose **OK** to start a new drawing file with the selected format.

Creating the Table for BOM

1. Choose **Table > Table > Table** from the **Ribbon** to display the **TABLE CREATE** menu and the **GET POINT** submenu.

2. Choose **Descending > Leftward > By Length** from the **TABLE CREATE** menu. Next, choose **Pick Pnt** from the **GET POINT** submenu.

3. Specify a point close to the upper right corner of the inner rectangle of the border. Now, you need to enter the dimensions of the BOM table.

4. Enter **12.7** as the width of the first column in the **Message Input Window** and press ENTER. Similarly, enter **76.2** as the width of the second column and press ENTER; you are prompted to enter the width for next column. Enter **25.4** as the width of the next column and press ENTER twice. Now, you are prompted to enter the height for the first row.

5. Enter the height of the first row as **12.7** and the second row as **12.7** in the **Message Input Window**. Press ENTER twice.

Setting the Repeat Region

Repeat regions are the smart cells in a table that can expand, depending on the amount of data inserted in a cell. You need to define the second row as the repeat region.

1. Choose **Table > Data > Repeat Region** from the **Ribbon**; the **TBL REGIONS** menu is displayed.

2. Choose the **Add** option from the **TBL REGIONS** menu; you are prompted to locate the corners of the region.

3. Select the first cell of the second row and then select the third cell of the second row to locate the corners of the region. Press the middle mouse button twice to exit the menu.

Creating the Column Headers

Now, you need to create headings in the table.

1. Double-click in the first cell of the first row; the **Note Properties** dialog box is displayed. In the dialog box, enter **Index** and choose **OK** to exit.

2. Similarly, enter **Part Name** and **Qty** in the second cell and the third cell, respectively.

Assigning the Report Symbols in the Repeat Region

The information in the cells that are defined as repeat region is determined by the text written in the form of report symbols. These report symbols associate the information in the cells with the assembly file directly.

1. Double-click in the first cell of the second row; the **Report Symbol** dialog box is displayed, as shown in Figure 14-17. Select **rpt** from this dialog box; the **rpt** options are displayed, as shown in Figure 14-18.

2. Select the **index** option from the dialog box.

3. Double-click in the second cell of the second row; the **Report Symbol** dialog box is displayed. Select **asm** from this dialog box; the **asm** options are displayed.

4. Select the **mbr** option from the dialog box, and then select the **name** option from the dialog box that appear.

5. Double-click in the third cell of the second row; the **Report Symbol** dialog box is displayed. Select **rpt** from this dialog box; the **rpt** options are displayed.

6. Select the **qty** option from the dialog box.

If the text selected to enter in the cells is overlapping the other text or is extending beyond the cell, ignore it. This is because the BOM will be created in the repeat region where this text exists and after the BOM is created, the text of the BOM will fit inside the cells. The drawing sheet after creating the column headers and entering the report symbols is shown in Figure 14-19.

Figure 14-17 The **Report Symbol** dialog box

Figure 14-18 The **Report Symbol** dialog box with the **rpt** options

Figure 14-19 Drawing sheet after adding the report symbols

Other Drawing Options 14-21

Generating the Exploded Drawing View

In Tutorial 2 of Chapter 11, you created the exploded view of the Pedestal Bearing in the **Assembly** mode. The name of the exploded view that you created was **EXP1**. As a result, the exploded view of the Pedestal Bearing is integrated with the assembly file that you copied from the *c11* folder. Now, you will use this exploded state to generate the exploded drawing view.

1. Choose **Layout > Model Views > General** from the **Ribbon**; the **Select Combined State** dialog box is displayed.

2. Select the **Do not prompt for Combined State** check box and then choose **OK** to exit the dialog box. Next, you are prompted to select the center point for the drawing view.

3. Select the point on the left of the drawing sheet, refer to Figure 14-20; the **Drawing View** dialog box is displayed. Select the **Isometric** option from the **Default Orientation** drop-down list in the **Drawing View** dialog box and then choose the **Apply** button.

4. Select the **Scale** option from the **Categories** list box. Next, select the **Custom scale** radio button from the **Scale and perspective options** area. Enter the value **.025** in the edit box and then choose the **Apply** button.

5. Select the **View States** option from the **Categories** list box. Next, select the **Explode components in view** check box and select the **EXP1** from the **Assembly explode state** drop-down list. Next, choose the **Apply** button.

6. Close the **Drawing View** dialog box to complete the placement of the required view.

Figure 14-20 Exploded isometric view of the assembly

If the model is not placed properly inside the boundaries of the drawing sheet, unlock it and then drag the drawing view and place it, as shown in Figure 14-20. Note that the BOM automatically appears in the table by extending the repeat region and the Qty column is empty.

Note

If the BOM is not displayed, then choose **Table > Data > Update Tables** *from the* **Ribbon**.

Setting the No Repeat Option

As some components are repeated in the assembly, they are repeated in the BOM. The BOM needs to be set such that no part name is repeated.

1. Choose **Table > Data > Repeat Region** from the **Ribbon**; the **TBL REGIONS** menu is displayed.

2. Choose the **Attributes** option from the menu; you are prompted to select a region.

3. Move the cursor over the table below the first row. All rows, except the first row, are highlighted in cyan. The highlighted portion is called region. Select the region; the **REGION ATTR** submenu is displayed. Choose the **No Duplicates** option and then choose the **Done/Return** button from the submenu.

4. Press the middle mouse button twice and exit the menu. The drawing sheet appears, as shown in Figure 14-21.

Figure 14-21 The drawing view showing BOM with no duplicates

Other Drawing Options

5. If the information is not updated in the table, choose **Table > Data > Update Tables** from the **Ribbon** to update the information.

Generating Balloons

Balloons are generated by using the repeat region. Before generating the balloons, you need to set the repeat region for the balloon generation.

1. Choose **Table > BOM Balloons** from the **Ribbon**; the **BOM BALLOONS** menu is displayed. The **BOM BAL TYPE** submenu is also displayed with the **Simple** option chosen by default. Also, you are prompted to select a region.

2. Select the region and then press the middle mouse button.

3. From the **BOM BALLOONS** menu, choose the **Create Balloon** option; the **BOM VIEW** submenu is displayed.

4. Choose the **Show All** option from the **BOM VIEW** submenu. Balloons are attached with all parts in the exploded view. The balloons contain the index number so that the parts in the assembly can be referred to as BOM.

5. Choose **Done** to exit this menu.

6. Drag the balloons to place them appropriately on the drawing sheet, as shown in Figure 14-22. You can select a balloon and then hold the right mouse button to invoke the shortcut menu. From this menu, you can select the required options to modify the attachment points of balloons.

Figure 14-22 The drawing view of the assembly showing the BOM and balloons

Entering Text in the Title Block

The text alignment in various cells of the title block was defined while creating the format. As a result, when you enter the text, it will automatically be aligned to the middle left.

1. Double-click on the top cell in the table; the **Note Properties** dialog box is displayed.

2. In this dialog box, enter **Pedestal Bearing Assembly**. Next, choose the **Text Style** tab and select the **Default** check box at the right of the **Height** property and choose **OK**.

3. Double-click on the cell that is in the first column and the second row; the **Note Properties** dialog box is displayed.

4. In this dialog box, enter **Scale** and then press ENTER. Now, enter **0.025** and choose **OK**; the text Scale: 0.025 is entered in two lines in the title block.

5. Similarly, enter the text in all remaining cells one by one, as shown in Figure 14-23.

Figure 14-23 The drawing view of the assembly showing the title block, balloons, and the BOM

Saving the Drawing File

1. Choose the **Save** button from the **Top Toolchest** to save the drawing file; the **Save Object** dialog box is displayed. Now, save the file by pressing ENTER.

Closing the Window

The drawing file is saved and now you can exit the **Drawing** mode.

1. Choose **File > Close Window** from the menu bar to close.

Other Drawing Options

> **Note**
> The occurrence of components in BOM depends on the order in which they were assembled in the assembly. In other words, the component placed first will occur first in the BOM.

Tutorial 2

In this tutorial, you will create a format of size A and add the title block in the format. You will retrieve the format in the **Drawing** mode and generate the exploded isometric view of the **Shock Assembly** created in Tutorial 1 of Chapter 11. Also, add the associative Bill of Material and the Balloons to the drawing view, as shown in Figure 14-24. **(Expected time: 45 min)**

The following steps are required to complete this tutorial:

a. Start a new file in the **Format** mode. Create the format of the drawing and add the title block in the format, refer to Figures 14-25 and 14-26.
b. Save the format file and then close it.
c. Start a new drawing file in the **Drawing** mode, select *shockassembly.asm* as the model, and retrieve the format created earlier.
d. Create the table for BOM and enter the headers.
e. Define the repeat region and then assign the report symbols, see Figure 14-27.
f. Generate the exploded isometric view of the assembly and generate balloons in the drawing view, refer to Figures 14-28 and 14-29.
g. Add text in the title block, refer to Figure 14-30.

Copy the *Shock Assembly* folder from the *c11* folder to the *c14* folder and set the *Shock Assembly* folder as the working directory.

Figure 14-24 The drawing view of the exploded assembly with BOM

Starting the Format File

As mentioned in the tutorial description, you need to create a format of size A that will be retrieved later to create the drawing view of the Shock assembly.

1. Choose the **New** button from the **Top Toolchest**; the **New** dialog box is displayed.

2. Select the **Format** radio button from the **Type** area in the **New** dialog box and name the file as *Format2*. Choose **OK** from the **New** dialog box; the **New Format** dialog box is displayed.

3. Select the **Empty** radio button from the **Specify Template** area and the **Landscape** button from the **Orientation** area of the **New Format** dialog box, if they are not already selected.

4. Select **A** from the **Standard Size** drop-down list in the **Size** area and then choose **OK** to invoke the **Format** mode. Note that a sheet of size A is displayed on the screen. This is evident from the text displayed below the sheet on the screen.

Creating the Format

1. Choose **Sketch > Insert > Offset Edge** from the **Ribbon**; the **OFFSET OPER** menu is displayed. Choose the **Ent Chain** option and then select all four border lines of the format by drawing a window around them. Press the middle mouse button after the selection has been made.

   An arrow is displayed pointing outward. This arrow displays the direction of the offset. Since you need to offset the lines in the opposite direction, you will specify a negative offset distance.

2. Enter **-0.25** in the **Message Input Window** and press ENTER. Press the middle mouse button twice to exit the **OFFSET OPER** menu.

3. Choose **Table > Table > Table** from the **Ribbon** to display the **TABLE CREATE** menu.

4. Choose **Ascending > Leftward > By Length** from the **TABLE CREATE** menu and then choose **Vertex** from the **GET POINT** submenu.

5. Select the lower right corner of the new rectangle created by offsetting the border lines. The corner of the new rectangle is selected because the title block will be created such that it is attached to the new rectangle. Now, you need to enter the dimensions for the title block.

6. Enter **3.2** as the width of the first column in the **Message Input Window** and press ENTER. Similarly, enter **1.2** as the width of the second column and press ENTER; you are prompted to enter the width for the next column. Press ENTER to exit the command. Now, you are prompted to enter the height for the first row.

Other Drawing Options 14-27

7. Enter the height of the first row as **0.5**, the second row as **0.5**, the third row as **1**, and the fourth row as **0.7** in the **Message Input Window**. Press ENTER twice.

   The title block created will be similar to the one shown in Figure 14-25. Notice the difference between the title block shown in Figure 14-25 and the one shown in Figure 14-26. You need to modify the title block that you have created so that it is similar to the one shown in Figure 14-26.

   Figure 14-25 Format with the title block

8. Select a cell in the table and choose **Table > Rows & Columns > Merge Cells** from the **Ribbon** to display the **TABLE MERGE** menu. The **Rows & Cols** option is chosen by default in the **TABLE MERGE** menu.

9. Select the cell in the first row and the cell in the second row of the first column to merge. Exit the **TABLE MERGE** menu.

   The table after merging the rows and columns should look similar to the one shown in Figure 14-26. You need to set the alignment of the text that will be entered in the cells of the table later.

10. Double-click in a cell to invoke the **Note Properties** dialog box. In this dialog box, choose the **Text Style** tab.

11. In the **Note/Dimension** area of this dialog box, select the **Middle** option from the **Vertical** drop-down list. Next, choose the **OK** button to exit the dialog box.

Figure 14-26 Modified title block

Now, the text is aligned vertically to the middle and horizontally to the center. Similarly, set the alignment in all cells of the table individually.

Saving the Format File

You need to save the format file that you have created so that it can be used as a template in the **Drawing** mode. The file will be stored in the *.frm* file format.

1. Choose the **Save** button from the **Top Toolchest**; the **Save Object** dialog box is displayed with the name of the file entered earlier. Next, press ENTER to save it.

2. Close the current window by choosing **File > Close Window** from the menu bar.

Starting a New Drawing File

You need to start a new drawing file for generating the exploded drawing view of the Shock assembly and for generating the BOM.

1. Choose the **New** button to display the **New** dialog box. Select the **Drawing** radio button, specify the name of the drawing as *c14tut2*, and then choose **OK**; the **New Drawing** dialog box is displayed.

2. Choose the **Browse** button and select the assembly file named *shockassembly.asm*.

3. Select the **Empty with format** radio button in the **Specify Template** area of the **New Drawing** dialog box.

4. Select **Format2** from the **Format** drop-down list. If **Format2** is not available in the

Other Drawing Options

drop-down list, choose the **Browse** button to locate **Format2**. Next, choose **OK** to exit the **New Drawing** dialog box.

Creating the Table for BOM

1. Choose **Table > Table > Table** from the **Ribbon** to display the **TABLE CREATE** menu.

2. Choose **Descending > Leftward > By Length** from the **TABLE CREATE** menu and choose **Pick Pnt** from the **GET POINT** menu.

3. Select a point close to the upper right corner of the inner border rectangle to start creating the BOM table.

4. Enter **12.7** as the width of the first column in the **Message Input Window** and press ENTER. Similarly, enter **76.2** as the width of the second column and press ENTER. You are prompted to enter the width for next column. Enter **25.4** and press ENTER twice. Now, you are prompted to enter the height for the first row.

5. Enter the height of the first row as **12.7** and of the second row as **12.7** in the **Message Input Window**. Press ENTER twice.

Setting the Repeat Region

Repeat regions are the smart cells in a table that can expand depending on the amount of data inserted in the cell. The second row will be defined as the repeat region.

1. Choose **Table > Data > Repeat Region** from the **Ribbon**; the **TBL REGIONS** menu is displayed.

2. Choose the **Add** option from the **TBL REGIONS** menu; you are prompted to locate the corners of the region.

3. Select the first cell of the second row and then select the third cell of the second row to define the region. Press the middle mouse button twice to exit the menu.

Creating the Column Headers

Next, you need to create headings in the table.

1. Double-click in the first cell of the first row; the **Note Properties** dialog box is displayed. In this dialog box, enter **Index** and choose **OK** to exit.

2. Similarly, enter **Part Name** and **Qty** in the second cell and the third cell, respectively.

Entering the Report Symbols in the Repeat Region

As mentioned earlier, the information in the cells that are defined as the repeat region is determined by the text that is written in the form of report symbols. These report symbols associate the information in the cells with the assembly file directly.

1. Double-click in the first cell of the second row; the **Report Symbol** dialog box is displayed. Select **rpt** from this dialog box; the **rpt** options are displayed.

2. Select the **index** option from this dialog box.

3. Next, double-click in the second cell of the second row; the **Report Symbol** dialog box is displayed. Select **asm** from this dialog box; the **asm** options are displayed.

4. Select the **mbr** option from this dialog box and then select the **name** option from the options that appear.

5. Double-click in the third cell of the second row; the **Report Symbol** dialog box is displayed. Select **rpt** from this dialog box; the **rpt** options are displayed.

6. Select the **qty** option from this dialog box. The drawing sheet after adding the report symbols is shown in Figure 14-27.

Figure 14-27 Drawing sheet after adding the report symbols

Generating the Drawing View

In Tutorial 1 of Chapter 11, you created the exploded view of the Shock assembly in the **Assembly** mode. The name of the exploded view that you specified was **EXP1**. As a result, the exploded view of the Shock assembly has been integrated with the assembly file that you copied from the *c11* folder. Now, you will use this exploded state to generate the exploded drawing view in the **Drawing** mode.

1. Choose **Layout > Model Views > General** from the **Ribbon**; the **Select Combined State** dialog box is displayed.

Other Drawing Options 14-31

2. Select the **Do not prompt for Combined State** check box and then choose **OK** to exit the dialog box. Next, you are prompted to select the center point for the drawing view.

3. Select the point of the left on the drawing sheet; the **Drawing View** dialog box is displayed. Select the **Isometric** option from the **Default orientation** drop-down list in the **Drawing View** dialog box and then choose the **Apply** button.

4. Select the **Scale** option from the **Categories** list box. Also, select the **Custom scale** radio button from the **Scale and perspective options** area. Enter **.004** in the edit box and then choose the **Apply** button.

5. Select the **View States** option from the **Categories** list box. Select the **Explode components in view** check box. Select the **EXP1** option from the **Assembly explode state** drop-down list and then choose the **Apply** button.

6. Close the **Drawing View** dialog box by choosing **Close**; the exploded isometric view of the assembly is displayed.

If the model is not placed properly inside the boundary of the drawing sheet, unlock it and then drag the drawing view and place it, as shown in Figure 14-28. If the BOM is not displayed, choose **Table > Data > Update Tables** from the **Ribbon** to display it.

Figure 14-28 Exploded isometric view of the assembly

Setting the No Repeat Option

The Shock assembly consists of two instances of Bushing. Therefore, in the BOM, it is also repeated. But, the BOM needs to be set such that no part name is repeated.

1. Choose **Table > Data > Repeat Region** from the **Ribbon**; the **TBL REGIONS** menu is displayed.

2. Choose the **Attributes** option from the menu; you are prompted to select a region.

3. Move the cursor on the table below the first row. All rows, except the first row, are highlighted in cyan. Select the region; the **REGION ATTR** submenu is displayed. Choose the **No Duplicates** option and then choose the **Done/Return** option.

4. Press the middle mouse button twice to exit the menu. The drawing sheet appears, as shown in Figure 14-29.

5. If the information is not updated in the table, choose **Table > Data > Update Tables** from the **Ribbon** to update it.

Figure 14-29 The drawing view of the assembly showing the BOM and balloons

Generating Balloons

The balloons are generated by setting the repeat region. Therefore, before generating the balloons, you need to set the repeat region.

1. Choose **Table > Balloons > BOM Balloons** from the **Ribbon**; the **BOM BALLOONS** menu is displayed. Also, the **BOM BAL TYPE** submenu is displayed with the **Simple** option chosen by default and you are prompted to select a region.

2. Select the repeat region that was created earlier and then press the middle mouse button.

Other Drawing Options 14-33

3. Choose the **Create Balloon** option from the **BOM BALLOONS** menu; the **BOM VIEW** submenu is displayed.

4. Choose the **Show All** option from the **BOM VIEW** submenu. Exit the menu.

   Balloons are attached with all parts in the exploded view. The balloons contain the index number so that the parts in the assembly can be referred to the BOM.

5. Drag the balloons to place them appropriately on the drawing sheet, refer to Figure 14-29. You can select the balloon and then hold the right mouse button to invoke the shortcut menu. From this menu, you can select the options to modify the attachment points of the balloons.

Entering Text in the Title Block

1. Double-click in the cell formed by the first row and the second column; the **Note Properties** dialog box is displayed.

2. In this dialog box, enter **Shock assembly**. Next, choose the **Text Style** tab and select the **Default** check box at the right of the **Height** property and choose **OK**.

3. Now, select the cell from the second row and the second column. Enter **CADCIM Technologies** in the **Note Properties** dialog box and choose the **OK** button.

4. Similarly, enter the text in all remaining cells one by one, as shown in Figure 14-30.

Figure 14-30 The drawing view of the assembly showing the title block, balloons, and the BOM

Saving the Drawing File

1. Choose the **Save** button from the **Top Toolchest** to save the drawing file; the **Save Object** dialog box is displayed. Press ENTER to save the file.

Closing the Window

The drawing file is saved and now you can exit the **Drawing** mode.

1. Choose **File > Close Window** from the menu bar to close the window.

Self-Evaluation Test

Answer the following questions and then compare them to those given at the end of this chapter:

1. When you move a view that forms a group with draft entities, the draft entities also move. (T/F)

2. Pro/ENGINEER Wildfire 5.0 provides you with some standard drawing formats for generating drawing views. (T/F)

3. Pro/ENGINEER Wildfire 5.0 allows you to create the user-defined formats. (T/F)

4. The BOM generated by using the repeat region is associative. (T/F)

5. One drawing file has only one drawing sheet. (T/F)

6. The _____ button of the **Balloons** group in the **Table** tab of the **Ribbon** is used to generate balloons.

7. The _____ dialog box is displayed when you double-click on the cell of a table.

8. The _____ option is chosen to avoid repetition of components in BOM.

9. The _____ key can also be used to delete any draft entity.

10. The _____ button of the **Table** group in the **Table** tab of the **Ribbon** is used to draw tables in the **Drawing** mode.

Other Drawing Options   14-35

Review Questions

Answer the following questions:

1. Which of the following modes in Pro/ENGINEER Wildfire 5.0 is used to create an associative BOM?

   (a) **Part**   (b) **Format**
   (c) **Drawing**   (d) None of these

2. Which of the following dialog boxes is displayed, when you double-click in the repeat region cell?

   (a) **Drawing View**   (b) **Note Properties**
   (c) **Report Symbol**   (d) None of these

3. Which of the following buttons on the **Right Toolchest** enables you to draw geometric entities continuously?

   (a) **Line**   (b) **Circle**
   (c) **Chain**   (d) None of these

4. Which of the following radio buttons is selected in the **New** dialog box to create a user-defined format for the drawing sheet?

   (a) **Part**   (b) **Format**
   (c) **Drawing**   (d) None of these

5. Which of the following menus in the menu bar has the **Close** option to close the current window?

   (a) **Info**   (b) **Window**
   (c) **View**   (d) None of these

6. You can open more than one window in Pro/ENGINEER Wildfire 5.0. (T/F)

7. It is not possible to draw splines in the **Drawing** mode. (T/F)

8. There are two types of drafting in Pro/ENGINEER Wildfire 5.0: Generative drafting and Interactive drafting. (T/F)

9. You can import a text file into the **Drawing** mode. (T/F)

10. The **Draft Group** option in the cascading menu is used to add or remove notes, surface symbols, or gtols from the selected dimension. (T/F)

Exercise

Exercise 1

Create a format of size A and then retrieve it in the **Drawing** mode to place the top view, front view, and an exploded isometric view of the **Cross Head** assembly created in Exercise 1 of Chapter 11. Add the associative assembly BOM and the balloons to the drawing view, as shown in Figure 14-31. **(Expected time: 45 min)**

Figure 14-31 Drawing for Exercise 1

Answers to the Self-Evaluation Test
1. T, 2. T, 3. T, 4. T, 5. F, 6. BOM Balloons, 7. Note Properties, 8. No Duplicates, 9. DELETE, 10. Table.

Chapter 15

Surface Modeling

Learning Objectives

After completing this chapter, you will be able to:
- *Create an extruded surface.*
- *Create a revolved surface.*
- *Create a sweep surface.*
- *Create a blended surface.*
- *Create a swept blend surface.*
- *Create a helical sweep surface.*
- *Create a surface by blending boundaries.*
- *Create a surface by using variable section sweep.*
- *Create surfaces by using style environment.*
- *Understand surface editing tools.*

SURFACE MODELING

Surface models are a type of three-dimensional (3D) models with no thickness. These models are widely used in industries like automobile, aerospace, plastic, medical, and so on.

Surface models should not be confused with thick models, that is, models having mass properties. Surface models do not have thickness whereas thick or solid models have a user-defined thickness. In Pro/ENGINEER, the surface modeling techniques and feature creation tools are the same as those used in solid modeling. A solid model of any shape that is created can also be created using the surface modeling techniques. The only difference between the solid model and the surface model is that the solid model has mass properties but the surface model does not. Sometimes, complex shapes are difficult to create using solid modeling. Such models can be easily created using surface modeling and then the surface model can be converted into the solid model. It becomes easy for a person to learn surface modeling if he is familiar with solid modeling feature creation tools.

CREATING SURFACES IN Pro/ENGINEER

In Pro/ENGINEER, a sketch can be toggled between a solid model and a surface model. The two buttons that are used to toggle between the solid feature and a surface feature are available on dashboards.

Creating an Extruded Surface

To create an extruded surface, choose the **Extrude** button from the **Base Features** toolbar; the **Extrude** dashboard will be displayed, as shown in Figure 15-1.

Figure 15-1 The Extrude dashboard

In this dashboard, the **Extrude as solid** button is chosen by default. Choose the **Extrude as surface** button to extrude the sketch and create a surface model. All the attributes of a solid model that were discussed in Chapter 4 are the same for a surface model also. Some of the examples of these attributes are sketching plane, both-side or one-side extrusion, depth of extrusion, and so on.

A surface model can be extruded with capped ends or with open ends. Figure 15-2 shows the open ends surface model and Figure 15-3 shows the capped ends surface model. Remember that to create the capped end surface model, the sketch should be a closed loop. Otherwise, a surface can be created with the open sketch.

To create a surface with capped ends, select the **Capped Ends** check box in the **Options** slide-down panel.

Surface Modeling

Figure 15-2 Surface with open ends

Figure 15-3 Surface with capped ends

Creating a Revolved Surface

To create a revolved surface, choose the **Revolve** button from the **Base Features** toolbar; the **Revolve** dashboard will be displayed, as shown in Figure 15-4. This feature creation tool works in the same way as in the case of solid modeling.

Figure 15-4 The **Revolve** dashboard

The **Revolve as solid** button is chosen by default. Choose the **Revolve as surface** button to create a revolve surface. You can create a revolved capped end surface or an open end surface. The **Capped Ends** check box in the **Options** slide-down panel is available only when the sketch is closed and the angle of revolution is less than 360-degree. Figure 15-5 shows the revolved surface with open ends and Figure 15-6 shows the revolved surface capped ends.

Figure 15-5 Revolved surface with open ends

Figure 15-6 Revolved surface with capped ends

Creating a Sweep Surface

To create a sweep surface feature, choose **Insert > Sweep > Surface** from the menu bar; the **SURFACE: Sweep** dialog box and the **SWEEP TRAJ** menu will be displayed. The method to create a surface sweep feature is the same as that to create a solid sweep feature. To create a solid sweep feature, refer to Chapter 8. The additional option of capping the ends that was available in the **Extrude** and **Revolve** tools is also available in the **Sweep** tool.

Figures 15-7 and 15-8 show the sweep surfaces with the open and capped ends, respectively.

Figure 15-7 Sweep surface with open ends created using a closed sketch

Figure 15-8 Sweep surface with capped ends created using a closed sketch

Creating a Blended Surface

To create a surface blend, choose **Insert > Blend > Surface** from the menu bar. The **BLEND OPTS** menu will be displayed. The method to create a blended surface is the same as that to create a solid blend. To create a solid blend feature, refer to Chapter 8. Blended surfaces can be with open ends or capped ends. Figure 15-9 shows the blended surface with open ends and Figure 15-10 shows the blended surface with capped ends.

Figure 15-9 Blended surface with open ends

Figure 15-10 Blended surface with capped ends

Surface Modeling

Creating a Swept Blend Surface

To create a swept blend surface, choose **Insert > Swept Blend** from the menu bar. The **Swept Blend** dashboard will be displayed. Choose the **Create a surface** button to create a sweep surface. The method to create a swept blend surface is the same as that to create a solid swept blend feature. To create a solid swept blend feature, refer to Chapter 9. Figure 15-11 shows the swept blend with open ends and Figure 15-12 shows the swept blend with capped ends.

Figure 15-11 Swept blend surface with open ends

Figure 15-12 Swept blend surface with capped ends

Creating a Helical Sweep Surface

To create a surface helical sweep, choose **Insert > Helical Sweep > Surface** from the menu bar. The **Surface: Helical Sweep** dialog box and the **ATTRIBUTES** menu will be displayed. The method to create a helical sweep surface feature is the same as that to create a solid helical sweep feature. For more information on creating solid helical sweep features, refer to Chapter 9. Figure 15-13 shows the helical sweep surface with open ends and Figure 15-14 shows the helical sweep surface with capped ends.

Figure 15-13 Helical sweep surface with open ends created using an open sketch

Figure 15-14 Helical sweep feature with capped ends created using the closed sketch

Tip: *If you want to create a surface blend with capped ends, you need to create a closed sketch. Pro/ENGINEER does not accept an open sketch for a capped end blend surface.*

*If you want to create a surface blend with capped ends along with an open loop section, choose the **Open Ends** option and then sketch the open loop section. Give the blend depth and create the blended surface. Now, redefine the surface feature and modify the open ends attribute to capped ends. Choose **OK** from the **SURFACE** dialog box. The blended surface with the capped ends is created. This is also true with other features like extrude, revolve, sweep, and so on.*

Creating a Surface by Blending Boundaries

To create a surface by blending boundaries, datum curves, or points, choose the **Boundary Blend** button from the **Base Features** toolbar; the **Boundary Blend** dashboard will be displayed, as shown in Figure 15-15 and you will be prompted to select two or more curve chains to define a blended surface. The options and buttons in this dashboard are discussed next.

*Figure 15-15 The **Boundary Blend** dashboard*

Curves Tab

When you choose the **Curves** tab, the slide-down panel will be displayed. Choose a curve from the drawing area; the curve will be highlighted in red and both ends of the curve, the value **0.00** will be displayed. When you modify this value, the curve will change accordingly at the corresponding end. Press CTRL+left mouse button to select the second curve; the second curve will also get highlighted, as shown in Figure 15-16. These curves will be numbered as per the sequence of selection. The surface created by using these two blending boundaries is, shown in Figure 15-17.

Figure 15-16 Curves selected as the blending boundary

Figure 15-17 Surface created by Blending boundaries

Surface Modeling

The collector present above the **Curves** tab shows **2 Chains**. The number of curves selected in the first direction will be displayed in this collector.

Now, invoke the **Curves** slide-down panel and select **2 Chain** from the **First direction** collector; the slide-down panel will be displayed, as shown in Figure 15-18. The **Move up** and **Move down** buttons available in the slide-down panel can change the order of selection of the curves. The **Close blend** check box is used to close the surfaces.

*Figure 15-18 The **Curves** slide-down panel*

Tip: *To delete the curves from the collector, select the curve in the collector and right-click and choose the **Remove all** option from the shortcut menu; all the curves available in the collector will be deleted.*

Figure 15-19 shows the surface created after selecting the four curves and Figure 15-20 shows the surface created by selecting the **Close blend** check box.

Figure 15-19 Surface created after selecting the curves

*Figure 15-20 Surface created by selecting the **Close blend** check box*

The **Second direction** collector in the **Curves** slide-down panel is used to select curves in the second direction. The second direction curves are usually drawn in a direction other than that of the first direction. Figure 15-21 shows the first and second direction curves and Figure 15-22 shows the surface created after selecting the curves shown in Figure 15-21.

Figure 15-21 Datum curves

Figure 15-22 Surface created by selecting the curves in two directions

Creating a Surface by Using the Variable Section Sweep

To create a surface by using the variable section sweep, choose **Insert > Variable Section Sweep** from the menu bar. The **Variable Section Sweep** dashboard will be displayed. Choose the **Sweep as surface** button. To learn more about the variable section sweep, refer to Chapter 9. The procedure of creating a variable section sweep feature or surface is the same as was discussed in Chapter 9.

Figure 15-23 shows the section and trajectories used to create the variable section sweep surface. You have an option to keep the ends open or capped. This option is available in the **Options** slide-down panel.

Figure 15-23 Variable section sweep surface with open ends

CREATING SURFACES BY USING THE STYLE ENVIRONMENT OF Pro/ENGINEER

Style is an environment available in Pro/ENGINEER that is used to draw free style curves and create surfaces by joining them. The surfaces created using the **Style** environment are called Super features. This is because these features can contain any number of curves or surfaces. The Style surfaces can be joined with the Pro/ENGINEER surfaces. They can have the parent-child relationship among themselves and also with Pro/ENGINEER features.

To enter the **Style** environment, choose the **Style** button from the **Base Features** toolbar or choose **Insert > Style** from the menu bar. Figure 15-24 shows the appearance of the **Style** environment.

Figure 15-24 The Style environment

Style Tools Toolbar

Figure 15-25 shows the **Style Tools** toolbar in the **Style** environment. The buttons in this toolbar are discussed next.

Select Button

This button is used to select the surfaces, curves, planes, and so on in the **Style** environment. If you are in middle of a feature creation tool, you can choose the **Select** button to exit that tool.

*Figure 15-25 The **Style Tools** toolbar*

Set Active Plane Button

This button is used to select the datum plane on which the drawing or the editing operation needs to be performed. The datum plane that you select is highlighted by a mesh.

Internal Plane Button

This button is chosen by selecting the black arrow on the right of the **Set Active Plane** button. When you select this arrow, a flyout will be displayed. Choose the **Internal Plane** button from this flyout to create an internal datum plane in the **Style** environment. When you choose this button, the **DATUM PLANE** dialog box will be displayed. This dialog box is used to create a datum plane in a similar procedure that was discussed in Chapter 5. The datum planes are named as DTM1, DTM2, and so on.

It should be noted that the datum planes created by using this button will be displayed in the drawing area only when you are in the **Style** environment. Once you exit the **Style** environment, these datum plane become invisible. Any feature created in the **Style** environment will be displayed in the **Style Tree** as a style feature.

Curve Button

This button is used to draw curves. When you choose this button, the **Curve** dashboard will be displayed, as shown in Figure 15-26. The options in this dashboard are discussed next.

*Figure 15-26 The **Curve** dashboard*

Create a Free Curve
In the **Curve** dashboard, the **Create a Free Curve** button is selected by default. As a result, you are prompted to define the points for creating the curve. To create the curve, click

Surface Modeling

on the screen. A red point will be displayed at the location where you clicked. Now, again click to define the second point of the curve. The two points are joined. When you click to define the location of the third point, you will notice that the curve that you are drawing is defined by a spline. After defining the points, press the middle mouse button to create the curve. While specifying a point, if you press the SHIFT key, then the point is snapped to the entity already present on the screen.

Remember that the curve drawn using the **Create a Free Curve** button will lie on the active datum plane. To draw a 3D curve, you need to snap the point on the existing entity. You can also draw a 3D curve by choosing the **Show All Views** button from the **Style** toolbar and then selecting a point each from any of the two different windows. If the **Style** toolbar is not available in the **Right Toolchest**, then right-click on the **Right Toolchest** and choose **Style** from the shortcut menu displayed. When you choose **Show All Views** button, the four-window view is displayed. In Pro/ENGINEER, this type of display is called a 4-view display mode. The 4-view display mode shows the top, default, right, and front views. You can select a point in one window and then select the second point in the other window. By specifying points in different windows, the 3D curve can be drawn. To switch back to the single window display mode, choose the **Show All Views** button again.

> **Tip**: *To undo the last operation, choose the **Undo** button from the **Edit** toolbar or press CTRL+Z keys.*

Create a Planar Curve
This button, when selected, allows you to create the curve on the datum plane that is highlighted by the mesh. This datum plane is called the active plane. The active plane can be selected before invoking the **Curve** dashboard by choosing the **Set Active Plane** button from the **Style Tools** toolbar.

> **Tip**: *Using the **Planar** option, you can project a point of an existing entity on the active datum plane. This can be done by selecting the point on the entity using the SHIFT key. The selected point is projected on the active datum plane.*

Create a Curve On Surface
This button is used to draw curves on surfaces. The points that you define on a surface are constrained to that surface. When you click to define the location of the first point of the curve, the point is placed. Now, this surface will be selected and the points placed hereafter should lie on the same surface. If you click outside this surface, then the point is not placed on the surface. After the curve is drawn, press the middle mouse button. The red curve is converted to a white curve indicating that the curve is completed. The curve drawn on the surface is the child of the surface.

Edit this curve using control points
If this toggle button is chosen while drawing the curve, then on editing the curve the control points will be displayed.

Proportional Update
If you create a curve, when this check box is selected, then the curve created can be edited proportionally.

Tip: *Using the **Free** option, you can draw a curve on a surface. To draw a curve on a surface, press SHIFT to select a point on the surface. The surface will be highlighted as you select a point on it and then the point will be placed on it. This method of selecting points on a surface can be used to draw curves that join points on two separate surfaces.*

Circle Button

This button is used to create circles. To create circles, choose the black arrow on the right of the **Circle** button; a flyout is displayed. Choose **Circle** from the flyout; the **Circle** dashboard will be displayed. Click anywhere in the drawing area; a circle with default radius will be placed at that location. The circle thus created can be free or planar circle. By default, the **Create a Free Curve button** is chosen in the dashboard, and therefore the curve created will be a free curve. You can adjust the radius of the circle by dragging the handle or enter the radius value in the edit box. The circles can also be edited similar to curves. You can also select the **Proportional Update** check box to enable you to edit the circle proportionally.

Similarly, you can create arcs by choosing the **Arc** button from the flyout displayed on choosing the black arrow on the right of the **Circle** button

Curve Edit Button

This button is used to edit the curves that are created as style features. If you choose this button, the **Curve Edit** dashboard will be displayed, as shown in Figure 15-27 and you will be prompted to select a curve. Select the curve; the curve will be displayed in the collector of the **Curve Edit** dashboard.

*Figure 15-27 The **Curve Edit** dashboard*

The options in the **Edit curve** dashboard are discussed next.

Curve Collector
When you select a curve to edit, the id of the curve will be displayed in this collector.

Change to a Free Curve
This button or tool is used to change the selected curve into a free curve.

Change to a Planar Curve
This button or tool is used to change the selected curve into a planar curve.

Change to a Curve on Surface
If the curve selected for editing is drawn using the **Curve On Surface** option, then this button will be selected by default.

Proportional Update Check Box
If the curve selected for editing is drawn by selecting the **Proportional Update** check box, then the curve will be edited proportionately with the points.

Surface Modeling

Edit this curve using control points

If the curve that for editing is drawn using the **Edit this curve using control points** button, then the control points will be displayed on the curve. Using these control points, you can modify the shape of the curve. You can also choose this button to display the control points on a curve drawn without choosing this button.

Tangent

Choose the **Tangent** tab to define the nature of contact between the curve and the adjacent surface. Alternatively, select one of the end control points of the curve, the tangent vector of the curve will be highlighted in red color. Now, right-click on the red vector to display the shortcut menu, as shown in Figure 15-28.

By default, a curve has a natural contact with the adjacent surface. This is evident from the circle mark on the left of the **Natural** option in the shortcut menu. Figure 15-29 shows the curve that is connected to the adjacent surface using the **Natural** option. The curve is drawn using the **Free** option. The point on the cylindrical surface will be selected by using SHIFT+left mouse button and similarly another point will be selected on the surface at the base. Figure 15-30 shows the curve whose contact type is changed to the **Surface Tangent** option by choosing it from the shortcut menu.

Figure 15-28 Shortcut menu for the end control point of the curve

Figure 15-29 Curve joining the two surfaces

Figure 15-30 Curve joining the base surface tangentially

Drop Curve Button

Using this button, a curve created in the **Style** environment can be projected onto the selected surface.

Choose the **Drop Curve** button from the **Style Tools** toolbar to create COS's (Curve On Surface); you will be prompted to select the curve that you need to drop onto the surface.

Select the curve and press the middle mouse button. Now, you will be prompted to select the surface on which you need to drop the curve. Select the surface; you will be prompted to select the plane normal to which the curve will be dropped. Select the plane normal to which the curve will be projected and exit the dashboard.

Curve on Surface by Intersect

On choosing this button, a curve will be created at the intersection of two sets of surfaces. To invoke this tool, choose the black arrow on the right of **Drop Curve**; a flyout will be displayed. Choose **COS By Intersect** from the flyout; you are prompted to select the first set of surfaces. Select the required surfaces. Next, click the middle mouse button to accept the selection and then select the second set of surfaces or planes and choose the **Build Feature** button to create the COS at the intersection.

Surface Button

This button is used to create a surface among a closed boundary of curves. When you choose this button, the **Surface** dashboard will be displayed and you will be prompted to select three or four boundary curves to define a surface. Select these four curves with the CTRL key pressed, as shown in Figure 15-31. After selecting these four curves, press the middle mouse button; the surface will be created, as shown in Figure 15-32.

Figure 15-31 Four curves   *Figure 15-32* Surface created using the curves

Surface Connect Button

When you choose this button, the **Surface Connect** dashboard will be displayed and you will be prompted to select two surfaces. The Style surface can be connected to the Pro/ENGINEER surface. When you select these two surfaces, as shown in Figure 15-33, with the CTRL key pressed and press the middle mouse button, the connections will be automatically be applied to the two surfaces. These connections may be of two types: curvature and tangent. If the tangent connection is applied, then the arrow will be displayed and if the curvature connection is applied, then a dashed line will be displayed on the surfaces. Figure 15-34 shows the two surfaces where the tangent connection as well as the curvature connection has been applied.

Choose the **Surface Connect** button from the **Style Tools** toolbar; the **Surface Connect**

Surface Modeling

Figure 15-33 The two surfaces

Figure 15-34 Arrow and dashed line

dashboard will be displayed, as shown in Figure 15-35, and you will be prompted to select the two surfaces. Select the surfaces. To apply the connection, click on any one end of the dashed line; the dashed line will be converted to an arrow, indicating that the two surfaces are connected. To remove the connection, use SHIFT+left click on the arrow.

Figure 15-35 The **Surfaces Connect** dashboard

Figure 15-36 shows the style surface when it is connected by using curvature connection and Figure 15-37 shows the surface when it is connected tangentially.

Figure 15-36 Surface connected at top by using curvature connection

Figure 15-37 Surface connected at top by tangent connection

Note
To delete a curve, select the curve and when it turns red, press the DELETE key.

Surface Trim Button

This button is used to trim a surface. When you choose this button, the **Surface Trim** dashboard will be displayed and you will be prompted to select the surface(s) to trim. Select the surface to trim and then press the middle mouse button. Now, you will be prompted to select the curve that can be used to trim the surface. Select the curve and press the middle mouse button. The selected surface will be highlighted in two portions. Select the portion to delete. Choose the green check mark from the dashboard to exit the trim tool.

Figure 15-38 shows the surface and the curve that are selected for trimming. This figure also shows the surface divided into two portions. The portion defined by the curve will be selected to delete. Figure 15-39 shows the surface after trimming.

Figure 15-38 Surface and curve selected for trimming

Figure 15-39 Surface after trimming

Note
*After completing the Style feature creation, choose the **Done** button to exit the **Style** environment.*

SURFACE EDITING TOOLS

The surface editing tools help in decreasing the modeling time. They also help in creating complex surface models. The surface editing tools that you will be learning in the next section are as follows:

1. Mirror
2. Merge
3. Trim
4. Fill
5. Intersect
6. Offset
7. Thicken
8. Solidify
9. Vertex Round

Mirroring the Surfaces

The **Mirror** button is used to mirror the surface about a plane. This button is available in the **Edit Features** toolbar only when a surface is selected. When you choose this button, the **Mirror** dashboard will be displayed, as shown in Figure 15-40.

Surface Modeling

*Figure 15-40 The **Mirror** dashboard*

Click in the **Mirror plane** collector, you can choose the mirroring plane. The **Copy as dependent** check box in the **Options** tab is selected by default. This makes sure that the parent-child relationship is maintained between the mirrored and original surfaces. Figure 15-41 shows the mirror plane and Figure 15-42 shows the mirrored feature.

*Figure 15-41 **The** mirror plane and the surface to be mirrored*

Figure 15-42 Surfaces after mirroring and keeping the original surface

Merging Surfaces

The **Merge** button is used to merge two surfaces and make them a single surface. A surface is also known as a quilt. To convert a surface into a solid, it is necessary that the surfaces are merged. While merging the surfaces, this tool also trims them. This button is available in the **Edit Features** toolbar only when the two surfaces to be merged are selected. When you choose the **Merge** button, the **Merge** dashboard will be displayed, as shown in Figure 15-43.

*Figure 15-43 The **Merge** dashboard*

The following steps explain the procedure to merge the surfaces, as shown in Figure 15-44.

1. Select the **Quilt** option from the **Filter** drop-down list. Select the two surfaces and when they turn pink in color, choose the **Merge** button; the **Merge** dashboard will be displayed. While merging the two surfaces, the part of the surfaces that will be retained after the two surfaces are merged is highlighted by yellow dots on it. The yellow arrows point to the direction in which the surfaces are retained. The direction of yellow arrow can be toggled by clicking on them or by using the **Change side of first quilt to keep and** the **Change side of second quilt to keep** buttons in the **Merge** dashboard. You can also click on the yellow arrows to flip the direction in which the surfaces are retained.

2. Choose the **Change side of first quilt to keep** button and then choose the **Change side of second quilt to keep** button. Notice that the outer side of the surfaces are highlighted with yellow dots, as shown in Figure 15-45.

Figure 15-44 Two surfaces to merge

Figure 15-45 Arrows showing the part of the surface to retain

3. Choose the **Preview** button to verify the desired trim and then exit the dashboard by choosing the **Build Feature** button. The resulting merged surface is shown in Figure 15-46. This merged surface is a single surface and now can be converted to a solid feature.

The **Reference** tab of the **Merge** dashboard shows the selected quilts. In the **Options** tab, you can select between **Intersect** and **Join** options. The **Join** option can be used when the edge of one quilt lies on the other quilt.

Trimming Surfaces

As the name suggests, the **Trim** button is used to trim the selected surfaces by using a trimming object. Select the surface that you need to trim and then choose the **Trim** button from the **Edit**

Figure 15-46 Resulting merged surface

Features toolbar; the **Trim** dashboard will be displayed, as shown in Figure 15-47. Also, you will be prompted to select the trimming object. This trimming object can be a curve, plane, edge, or a surface.

The part of the surface that is to be retained is highlighted with yellow dots. A yellow arrow points in the direction of the surface to be retained after trimming. You can choose the **Flip between one side, other side, or both sides of trimmed surface to keep** button from the dashboard or click on the yellow arrow to toggle the direction of the yellow arrow. By default, the trimming surface is deleted after the surfaces are trimmed. If you need to keep the trimming object, select the **Keep trimming surface** check box from the **Options** slide-down panel.

Surface Modeling

*Figure 15-47 The **Trim** dashboard*

Figure 15-48 shows the surface selected as the trimming object, the trimming surface, and the yellow arrow. It is evident from this figure that the arrow is pointing toward the right; therefore, the right portion of the surface will be retained after trimming. Figure 15-49 shows the surface obtained after trimming.

Figure 15-48 Surface and object to be Trimmed   *Figure 15-49 Surface obtained after trimming*

Creating the Fill Surfaces

The **Fill** option is used to create a planar surface by sketching its boundaries. When you choose this option from the **Edit** menu in the menu bar, the **Fill** dashboard will be displayed, as shown in Figure 15-50.

*Figure 15-50 The **Fill** dashboard*

Choose the **References** tab; a slide-down panel will be displayed. Choose the **Define** button from it to select the sketching plane and draw the sketch. Figure 15-51 shows the sketch plane and Figure 15-52 shows the surface that is created by using the **Fill** option.

Creating the Intersect Curves

The **Intersect** option is used to create a curve at the intersection of two surfaces. The intersect curve can then be used for various purposes. The **Intersect** option is available in the **Edit** menu only when you have selected a surface. When you choose this option from the **Edit** menu, the **Intersect** dashboard will be displayed, as shown in Figure 15-53.

Figure 15-51 The sketch plane for creating the fill surface

Figure 15-52 Fill surface

Figure 15-53 The **Intersect** dashboard

When you select the second surface, the intersecting curve will be created, as shown in Figure 15-54. Make sure to select the second surface by holding the CTRL key. The curve created can be copied, moved, and so on. One of the uses of the intersect curve is shown in Figures 15-55 and 15-56.

In Figure 15-55, the intersecting curve is copied at a distance of 150. The **Boundary Blend** tool is used to create the surface shown in Figure 15-56. To create the boundary blend, the intersecting curve will be selected and then the curve edge of the surface will be selected. Both the curves are blended and the tangency is increased by dragging the handles.

Figure 15-54 Surfaces selected to create the intersecting curve

Surface Modeling

Figure 15-55 Copied curve

Figure 15-56 Boundary blend created using the intersecting curve

Creating the Offset Surfaces

A surface can be copied to an offset distance. To offset a surface, select the surface to offset and choose **Edit > Offset** from the menu bar; the **Offset** dashboard will be displayed, as shown in Figure 15-57. The **Offset** option is available only when you have selected a surface to offset.

Figure 15-57 The **Offset** dashboard

In Pro/ENGINEER, there are three methods to offset a surface. These methods are as follows:

1. Create the offset of the whole surface using the **Standard Offset Feature** option.
2. Sketch a section and offset the area inside the section with the draft using the **With Draft Feature** option.
3. Sketch a section and offset the area inside or outside the section using the **Expand Feature** option.

In the **Offset** dashboard, first you need to specify the type of offset surface you need to create. The types of offset that can be created in Pro/ENGINEER Wildfire 5.0 are as follows:

1. Standard Offset Feature
2. With Draft Feature
3. Expand Feature
4. Replace Surface Feature

Standard Offset Feature

The **Standard Offset Feature** button is present at the upper-left corner of the **Offset** dashboard and is chosen by default. You can enter the offset value in the dimension edit box.

This option can be used to offset the surface as a whole. From the drop-down list in the **Options** slide-down panel, the **Normal to Surface** option is selected by default. This option allows you to offset a surface normal to the surface. If you select the **Automatic Fit** option from the drop-down list, then Pro/ENGINEER automatically fits the surface, or controls the direction of the offset in the X, Y, and Z axes. If you select the **Controlled Fit** option from the drop-down list in the **Options** slide-down panel, you need to select a coordinate system and specify the direction to offset. You can also join the offset surface with the side surfaces by selecting the **Create side surface** check box. Figure 15-58 shows the original surface and the offset surface.

Figure 15-58 The original and the offset surfaces

With Draft Feature

The **With Draft Feature** button can be chosen from a list of buttons that appear by selecting the black arrow present on the right of the **Standard Offset Feature** button. Using this button, you can sketch the section and then give a draft angle to the side surfaces. Choose the **Define** button from the **References** slide-down panel to define a sketching plane and to create the sketch of the draft surface. Figure 15-59 shows the draft offset surface with the **Straight** radio button selected from the **Options** slide-down panel. The section drawn on the sketching plane was circular. Similarly, Figure 15-60 shows the draft offset surface with the **Tangent** radio button selected from the **Options** slide-down panel.

Figure 15-59 Draft offset surface with straight profile

Figure 15-60 Draft offset surface with tangent profile

Surface Modeling   15-23

Expand Feature

The **Expand Feature** button can be chosen from the list of buttons that appear by selecting the black arrow present on the right of **Standard Offset Feature** button. Using this option, you can sketch the section and then choose whether to offset the inside or the outside of the sketch. For this purpose, you need to choose the **Change direction of offset to the other side** button from the dashboard. Alternatively, click on the yellow arrow displayed on the model. Figure 15-61 shows the offset surface when the inside of the sketch is selected to offset. The section that was drawn on the sketching plane was rectangular. Choose the **Define** button from the **Options** slide-down panel to define the sketching plane and create the sketch. Figure 15-62 shows the draft offset surface when the outside of the sketch is selected to offset.

Figure 15-61 *Inside of the sketch selected to offset*   *Figure 15-62* *Outside of the sketch selected to offset*

Replace Surface Feature

The **Replace Surface Feature** button is used to replace a specified face of a solid with a quilt or datum plane. It can add or remove material from the solid. To create a replacement surface, select the face to be replaced and then choose **Edit > Offset** from the menu bar; the **Offset** dashboard will be displayed. Choose the black arrow present on the right of the **Standard Offset Feature** button; a list of buttons will be displayed. Choose the **Replace Surface Feature** button; you are prompted to select the surface or datum plane to replace. Select the replacement surface; the preview of the modified solid feature will be displayed. Choose the **Build Feature** button to accept the preview and create the feature. Figure 15-63 shows the face of the solid selected to be offset and the replacement surface. Figure 15-64 shows the preview of the modified solid feature.

Figure 15-63 *The offset and replacement surfaces*   *Figure 15-64* *Preview of the modified solid feature*

Adding Thickness to a Surface

To add thickness to a quilt or a surface, select the quilt and choose the **Thicken** option from the **Edit** menu; the **Thicken** dashboard will be displayed, as shown in Figure 15-65.

*Figure 15-65 The **Thicken** dashboard*

Drag the handle to set thickness of the quilt or enter the thickness value in the dimension edit box. You can even remove material from the quilt by choosing the **Removes material from inside thickened quilt** button from the dashboard.

Using the drop-down list in the **Options** slide-down panel, you can give thickness to the quilt normal to the surface, allow Pro/ENGINEER to automatically scale the surface along the axes, or scale and fit the original surface with respect to the coordinate system. If you select the **Controlled Fit** option from the drop-down list in the **Options** slide-down panel, you need to select a coordinate system and specify the direction to scale.

Figures 15-66 and 15-67 show the surfaces after adding thickness by controlling thickness by using the **Normal to surface** option and the **Automatic fit** option, respectively.

*Figure 15-66 Thickening the surface by using the **Normal to surface** option*

*Figure 15-67 Thickening the surface using the **Automatic fit** option*

Surface Modeling

Converting a Surface into a Solid

You can convert a closed surface into a solid by choosing **Edit > Solidify** from the menu bar. This option is available only when a closed surface with capped ends is selected. This option fills the hollow surface with material.

Creating a Round at the Vertex of a Surface

The vertices of a surface or quilt can be rounded by using the **Vertex Round** option. Choose **Insert > Advanced > Vertex Round** from the menu bar; the **SURFACE TRIM: Vertex Round** dialog box will be displayed, as shown in Figure 15-68. Also, you will be prompted to select the datum quilt to intersect. Select the surface; you will be prompted to select the corner vertex(s) to be rounded. Select the first vertex and then press the CTRL key to select the other vertex, as shown in Figure 15-69. After selecting the vertices, press the middle mouse button; the **Message Input Window** will be displayed. Type the radius of round and press ENTER. Choose the **OK** button from the **SURFACE TRIM: Vertex Round** dialog box; the vertices will be rounded, as shown in Figure 15-70.

Figure 15-68 The SURFACE TRIM: Vertex Round dialog box

Figure 15-69 Vertices selected to be rounded

Figure 15-70 Vertices after creating round

TUTORIALS

Tutorial 1

In this tutorial, you will create the surface model shown in Figure 15-71. The orthographic views of the surface model are shown in Figure 15-72. **(Expected time: 45 min)**

The following steps are required to complete this tutorial:

Examine the model and determine the number of features in it, refer to Figure 15-72.
a. Create the base feature, which is a blend surface, refer to Figures 15-73 through 15-75.

Figure 15-71 The surface model

Figure 15-72 Top, front, and right views of the surface model

Surface Modeling 15-27

b. Create the second feature, which is a blend feature, refer to Figures 15-76 and 15-77.
c. The third feature is a mirror feature. It will be created by mirroring the second feature about a plane that passes through the center, refer to Figure 15-78.
d. Create the fourth feature, which is also a blend feature, refer to Figures 15-79 and 15-80.
e. Select the surfaces individually and merge them, refer to Figures 15-81 and 15-82.
f. Remaining features are the fill features and they will be used to create surfaces on the blend features, refer to Figures 15-83 through 15-85.
g. Create rounds on the edges, refer to Figure 15-86.

Starting a New Object File

1. Start a new part file and name it *c15tut1*.

   The three default datum planes are displayed in the drawing area. The **Model Tree** is also displayed in the drawing area. Close the **Model Tree** by clicking on the sash present on its right edge.

Creating the Base Feature

You need to create the base feature by using the **Blend** option present in the menu bar on the top of the screen.

1. Choose **Insert > Blend > Surface** from the menu bar; the **BLEND OPTS** menu is displayed.

2. Choose **Parallel > Regular Sec > Sketch Sec > Done** from the **BLEND OPTS** menu; the **SURFACE** dialog box and the **ATTRIBUTES** menu is displayed.

3. Choose **Straight > Open Ends > Done** from the **ATTRIBUTES** menu; you are prompted to select the sketch plane.

4. Select the **RIGHT** datum plane; the **DIRECTION** menu is displayed.

5. Choose **Okay** from the **DIRECTION** menu; the **SKET VIEW** menu is displayed.

6. Select the **Top** option from the **SKET VIEW** menu and then choose the **TOP** datum plane.

7. Draw an arc and dimension it, as shown in Figure 15-73.

8. After drawing the first arc, press and hold down the right mouse button and choose the **Toggle Section** option from the shortcut menu displayed.

9. Draw the second arc and dimension it, as shown in Figure 15-74.

10. After drawing the sketch, choose the **Done** button to exit the **Sketcher** environment; the **DEPTH** menu is displayed.

Figure 15-73 Sketch of the first arc   *Figure 15-74* Sketch of the second arc

11. Choose **Blind > Done** from the **DEPTH** menu; the **Message Input Window** is displayed.

12. Enter **150** in the **Message Input Window** and press ENTER.

13. Choose **OK** from the **SURFACE** dialog box; the base feature is created, as shown in Figure 15-75.

Figure 15-75 Trimetric view of the base feature

Creating the Second Feature

To create the second blend feature, you need to create a datum plane that is at a distance of 150 from the **FRONT** datum plane and passes through the center of the base feature.

1. Choose **Insert > Blend > Surface** from the menu bar.

2. Choose **Parallel > Regular Sec > Sketch Sec > Done** from the **BLEND OPTS** menu; the **SURFACE** dialog box and the **ATTRIBUTES** menu is displayed

Surface Modeling

3. Choose **Straight > Open Ends > Done** from the **ATTRIBUTES** menu; you are prompted to select the sketch plane.

4. Choose the **Make Datum** option to display the **DATUM PLANE** menu. Select the **Offset** option from this menu and then select the **FRONT** datum plane.

5. Press the middle mouse button to confirm the selection. Now, select the **Enter Value** option from the **OFFSET** menu to display the **Message Input Window** and enter **150** in it. Next, press the middle mouse button.

6. Choose the **Done** option from the **DATUM PLANE** menu and then choose **Okay** from the **DIRECTION** menu.

7. Set the orientation of the sketching plane such that the **TOP** datum plane is at the top while sketching.

8. Sketch an arc of radius 25, and then after toggling the sketch, draw the another arc, as shown in Figure 15-76.

9. Exit the **Sketcher** environment; the **DEPTH** menu is displayed.

10. Choose **Thru Until > Done** from the **DEPTH** menu.

11. Select the **FRONT** datum plane. Choose **OK** from the **SURFACE** dialog box; a blend surface extruded up to the selected datum plane is created, as shown in Figure 15-77.

Figure 15-76 Sketch of the second feature

Figure 15-77 Second feature created

Creating the Mirror Copy of the Second Feature

The third blend feature is the same as the second blend feature. Therefore, a mirror copy of the second blend feature will be used to create the third feature.

1. Select the second feature and then choose the **Mirror** button; the **Mirror** dashboard is displayed and you are prompted to select a plane to mirror about.

2. Select the **FRONT** datum plane and exit the **Mirror** dashboard by choosing the **Build Feature** button. The mirror copy of the second feature is created, as shown in Figure 15-78.

Figure 15-78 Surface model after creating the third feature

Creating the Fourth Blend Feature

The fourth blend feature will be created on the top of the base feature. To create the blend feature, you need to create a datum plane at a distance of 150 from the bottom of the base feature.

1. Choose **Insert > Blend > Surface** from the menu bar.

2. Choose **Parallel > Regular Sec > Sketch Sec > Done** from the **BLEND OPTS** menu; the **SURFACE** dialog box and the **ATTRIBUTES** menu is displayed.

3. Choose **Straight > Capped Ends > Done** from the **ATTRIBUTES** menu; you are prompted to select the sketch plane.

4. Choose the **Make Datum** option to display the **DATUM PLANE** menu. Select the **Offset** option and create a datum plane at a distance of 150 from the **TOP** datum plane.

5. Select the **TOP** datum plane as the sketching plane. Next, set the orientation of the sketching plane such that the **RIGHT** datum plane is at the top while sketching.

6. Sketch a circle of diameter 50 and dimension it. Toggle the sketch and then draw the second circle of diameter 70, as shown in Figure 15-79.

7. Exit the **Sketcher** environment; the **DEPTH** menu is displayed.

8. Choose **Thru Until > Done** from the **DEPTH** menu.

9. Select the **TOP** datum plane. Choose **OK** from the **SURFACE** dialog box; the blend surface is extruded up to the selected datum plane, as shown in Figure 15-80. Check if you need to flip the direction.

Surface Modeling   15-31

Figure 15-79 Sketch of the fourth blend feature

Figure 15-80 Model after creating the fourth blend surface

Merging the Surfaces to Create a Quilt

To create a round on the edges, it is necessary to create a common edge where the two surfaces will join. For this purpose, the surfaces need to be merged.

Note
*The easier way to select two surfaces for merging is to select them from the **Model Tree**. You should remember that to select more than one surface, you need to press the CTRL key. When you select the surfaces from the **Model Tree**, their boundaries are highlighted in red, indicating that the surface is selected.*

*You can also select the **Quilt** option from the **Filter** drop-down list to select the surfaces. The **Filter** drop-down list is available in the **Status Bar** at the right corner above the drawing area.*

1. Select the blend surface at the left, press the CTRL key and then select the blend surface in the middle. When the two surfaces are highlighted, choose the **Merge** button; the **Merge** dashboard is displayed with two arrows showing the portion that will be retained after merging.

   Note
   *The **Merge** button will be available only when two surfaces are selected for merging.*

2. Choose the **Change side of first quilt to keep** button from the dashboard; the direction of the yellow arrow changes.

3. Choose the **Change side of second quilt to keep** button from the dashboard; the direction of the yellow arrow changes. The portion of the surface that is now highlighted will be retained after merging the surfaces.

4. Exit the dashboard by choosing the **Build Feature** button. The model after merging the two surfaces is shown in Figure 15-81.

   Using the above procedure, merge the blend surface on the right with the merged surface. After that, merge the top blend surface with the merged surface. Figure 15-82 shows the surface model after merging all surfaces and forming a quilt.

Figure 15-81 Surface model after merging the two surfaces

Figure 15-82 Surface model after merging the surfaces

Creating the Fill Surfaces

Four surfaces will be created to cap the ends of the blend surfaces. First, the left blend surface will be capped using the **Fill** option.

1. Choose the **Fill** option from the **Edit** menu; the **Fill** dashboard is displayed.

2. From the **References** slide-down panel, choose the **Define** button; the **Sketch** dialog box is displayed and you are prompted to select the sketching plane.

3. Choose the **Plane** button from the **Datum** toolbar; the **DATUM PLANE** dialog box is displayed.

4. Select the two vertices of the left blend surface. To select the second vertex, hold down the CTRL key and then select the **FRONT** datum plane.

5. Select **FRONT** from the **DATUM PLANE** dialog box; a drop-down list appears in the row where you clicked. Select the **Parallel** option from the drop-down list and then choose the **OK** button from the **DATUM PLANE** dialog box.

Surface Modeling

The datum plane is created and a yellow arrow pointing in the direction of viewing the sketch is displayed.

6. Choose the **Sketch** button to close the **Sketch** dialog box to enter the **Sketcher** environment.

7. Choose the **Use** button from the **Sketcher tools** toolbar and select the smaller semicircular edge of the blend surface. Next, close the sketch by drawing a horizontal line between the two ends, as shown in Figure 15-83.

8. Exit the **Sketcher** environment and then exit the **Fill** dashboard by choosing the **Build Feature** button; the fill surface is created, as shown in Figure 15-84.

Figure 15-83 Sketch for the fill surface   *Figure 15-84* Surface after creating the fill surface

Similarly, create the fill surfaces to cap the ends of the middle surface blend feature. Mirror the left fill surface to the right. Figure 15-85 shows the surface model after capping all the ends of the blend surfaces.

Figure 15-85 Surface model after creating the fill surfaces

Merging the Fill Surfaces

The fill surfaces that you have created should be merged with the other surfaces in order to create a round on their edges.

1. Hold the CTRL key to select the fill surface that is on the left and then the blend surface in the middle. When the two surfaces turn pink in color, choose the **Merge** button to display the **Merge** dashboard.

2. Exit the dashboard by choosing the **Build Feature** button.

   Using the same procedure, merge the remaining fill surfaces individually with the blend surface in the middle. To check whether all the surfaces have been merged, select the surface model thrice. If the whole surface model is highlighted in pink color then it indicates all the surfaces have been merged and they form a quilt.

Creating Rounds

When all the surfaces are merged, the edges form at the intersection of two surfaces. These edges need to be rounded. In the given surface model, note that there are rounds that have two different radius values. Therefore, you need to create two sets to define two values of rounds.

1. Choose the **Round** button from the **Engineering Features** toolbar.

2. Select the edges having radius value 12. Remember that to select more than one edge, you need to hold down the CTRL key.

3. After creating the rounds of radii 12, choose the **Sets** tab to display the slide-down panel.

4. Click on **New set**; a set with the name **Set2** is added.

5. Select the two edges that have radius of 22. After creating the rounds of radius 22, exit the **Round** dashboard.

   The surface model after creating the rounds is as shown in Figure 15-86.

6. Choose the **Save** button from the **File** toolbar and save the model.

Figure 15-86 Surface model after creating rounds

Surface Modeling

15-35

Tutorial 2

In this tutorial, you will create the surface model shown in Figure 15-87. The front and right views of the surface model are shown in Figure 15-88. **(Expected time: 45 min)**

Figure 15-87 Isometric view of the surface model

Figure 15-88 Front and right views of the surface model

The following steps are required to complete this tutorial:

First, examine the model and determine the number of features in it, refer to Figure 15-88.
a. Create the base feature, which is an extruded surface with open ends, refer to Figures 15-89 and 15-90.
b. Create the second feature, which is a blend feature created at an offset distance of 65 from the **RIGHT** datum plane, refer to Figures 15-91 and 15-92.

c. The third feature is a mirror copy of the second feature, refer to Figure 15-93.
d. The fourth feature is the cylindrical surface, refer to Figures 15-94 and 15-95.
e. Create the two fill surfaces that will cap the ends of the base surface, refer to Figures 15-96 through 15-98.
f. Merge all surfaces by selecting them individually, refer to Figures 15-99 through 15-101.
g. Create the round features, refer to Figures 15-102 through 15-104.

Creating the Base Feature

The base feature is a surface between two blend surfaces. The base feature is created on the **RIGHT** datum plane.

1. Choose the **Extrude** button from the **Base Features** toolbar.

2. Select the **Extrude as surface** button from the **Extrude** dashboard. Select the **RIGHT** datum plane as the sketch plane.

3. Select the **TOP** datum plane from the drawing area and then select the **Top** option from the **Orientation** drop-down list.

4. Choose the **Sketch** button to enter the **Sketcher** environment.

5. Once you enter the **Sketcher** environment, create the sketch of the base feature and apply dimensions, as shown in Figure 15-89.

6. After completing the sketch, choose the **Done** button to exit the **Sketcher** environment.

    The **Extrude** dashboard reappears above the drawing area. In this dashboard, the **Extrude from sketch plane by specified depth value** button is chosen by default.

7. Enter **240** in the dimension box present in the **Extrude** dashboard. Choose the **Build feature** button from the **Extrude** dashboard.

    The base feature is created and the default trimetric view of this feature is shown in Figure 15-90.

Creating the Blend Feature

The second feature is a blend surface and it will be created on the datum plane that is at an offset distance of 65 from the **FRONT** datum plane.

1. Choose **Insert > Blend > Surface** from the menu bar.

2. Choose **Parallel > Regular Sec > Sketch Sec > Done** from the **BLEND OPTS** menu; the **SURFACE** dialog box and the **ATTRIBUTES** menu are displayed.

3. Choose **Straight > Open Ends > Done** from the **ATTRIBUTES** menu; you are prompted to select the sketch plane.

Surface Modeling

Figure 15-89 Sketch of the base surface

Figure 15-90 Base surface with open ends

4. Choose the **Make Datum** option to display the **DATUM PLANE** menu. Select the **Offset** option and create a datum plane at a distance of 65 from the **FRONT** datum plane.

5. Select the **FRONT** datum plane as sketching plane. Next, set the orientation of the sketching plane such that the **TOP** datum plane is at the top while sketching.

6. Next, enter the **Sketcher** environment.

7. Sketch an arc of diameter 35, dimension it, and then draw another arc of diameter 55, as shown in Figure 15-91.

8. Exit the **Sketcher** environment; the **DEPTH** menu is displayed.

9. Choose **Thru Until > Done** from the **DEPTH** menu.

10. Select the **FRONT** datum plane. Choose **OK** from the **SURFACE** dialog box; the blend surface extruded up to the selected datum plane is created, as shown in Figure 15-92. Check if you need to flip the direction of blend.

Figure 15-91 Sketch of the blend surface

Figure 15-92 Blend surface

Mirroring the Blend Surface

Next, you need to mirror the blend surface about the **FRONT** datum plane.

1. Select the blend surface and then choose the **Mirror** button from the **Edit Features** toolbar; the **Mirror** dashboard is displayed.

2. Select the **FRONT** datum plane and exit the dashboard; the blend surface is mirrored about the selected datum plane, as shown in Figure 15-93.

Figure 15-93 Model after creating the mirror copy of the blend surface

Creating the Cylindrical Surface

The cylindrical surface will be created on the **TOP** datum plane.

1. Choose the **Extrude** button from the **Base Features** toolbar to display the **Extrude** dashboard.

2. Choose the **Extrude as surface** button from the **Extrude** dashboard.

3. Select the **TOP** datum plane as the sketching plane.

4. After entering the **Sketcher** environment, draw a circle and dimension it, as shown in Figure 15-94.

5. Exit the **Sketcher** environment and extrude the sketch to some appropriate depth, refer to Figure 15-95.

The model after creating the surface extrusion is shown in Figure 15-95.

Creating the Fill Surface

The fill surface will be created to cap the ends of the base feature.

1. Choose **Edit > Fill** from the menu bar; the **Fill** dashboard is displayed.

2. Choose the **Define** button from the **References** slide-down panel; the **Sketch** dialog box is displayed and you are prompted to select the sketching plane.

3. Select the **RIGHT** datum plane as the sketching plane. Choose the **Flip** button.

Surface Modeling

Figure 15-94 Sketch of the cylindrical surface

Figure 15-95 Cylindrical surface

4. Select the **Top** option from the **Orientation** drop-down list and select the **TOP** datum plane. Choose the **Sketch** button to enter the **Sketcher** environment.

5. Choose the **Use** button and select the edges of the base feature; the sketch is completed, as shown in Figure 15-96.

6. Exit the **Sketcher** environment and then exit the **Fill** dashboard by choosing the **Build Feature** button. On doing so, the fill surface is created, as shown in Figure 15-97.

Figure 15-96 Sketch of the fill surface

Figure 15-97 Model after creating the fill surface

7. Mirror the fill surface about the datum plane on-the-fly. This datum plane is at an offset distance of 120 from the **RIGHT** datum plane.

   After creating the mirror copy of the fill surface, the other end of the base feature is also capped, as shown in Figure 15-98.

Merging the Blend Surface with the Cylindrical Surface

The blend surface that was the second feature and the cylindrical surface will be merged to get the required circular slot.

1. Select the cylindrical surface and the blend surface by pressing the CTRL key.

2. Choose the **Merge** button from the **Edit Features** toolbar; the **Merge** dashboard is displayed and the surface that will be retained after merging is highlighted.

3. Choose the **Change side of second quilt to keep** button to change the direction of the yellow arrow.

4. Exit the **Merge** dashboard by choosing the **Build Feature** button. The model after merging the two surfaces is as shown in Figure 15-99.

Figure 15-98 Model after creating the mirror copy of the fill surface

Figure 15-99 Model after merging the surfaces

Merging the Blend Surface and the Extruded Surface

The blend surface and the extruded surface will be merged to build a single surface.

1. Select the base feature and then select the **Merge 1** feature from the **Model Tree**.

2. Choose the **Merge** button from the **Edit Features** toolbar; the **Merge** dashboard is displayed and the surface that will be retained after merging is highlighted.

3. Choose the **Change side of second quilt to keep** button to change the direction of the yellow arrow.

4. You can see the preview of the blend surface by choosing the **Preview** button in the dashboard. Exit the **Merge** dashboard by choosing the **Build Feature** button. The model after merging the two surfaces is shown in Figure 15-100.

5. Similarly, merge the mirrored feature and the base feature. The surface model after merging the mirrored surfaces is shown in Figure 15-101.

Merging the Fill Surfaces with the Base Surface

The fill surfaces that you have created should be merged with the base surface in order to create a single quilt or a single surface. After merging the surfaces, you need to round the edges formed in due to merging.

Surface Modeling 15-41

Figure 15-100 Model after merging the blend surface with the base surface

Figure 15-101 Model after merging the mirror copy of the blend surface with the base surface

1. Select the fill surface and then select the base surface.

   Note
   It is better to select surfaces to be merged from the Model Tree.

   To merge two surfaces, it is necessary that they intersect each other.

2. Choose the **Merge** button from the **Edit Features** toolbar and then choose the **Build feature** button to merge both the surfaces.

3. Similarly, merge the mirror copy of the first fill surface with the base surface.

Creating Rounds

You need to create rounds on the cylindrical slot or edges where the two blend surfaces merge, and on the edges of the base surface.

1. Choose the **Round** button from the **Engineering Features** toolbar. Select the edge of the cylindrical slot, refer Figure 15-102; the preview of the round is highlighted on the selected edge.

2. Enter **4** in the dimension edit box for the radius of the round.

3. Click on **New set** in the **Sets** slide-down panel to add a second set named **Set2**.

4. Select the four edges each of which has the radius 18. Among these edges, the two edges are the edges that are formed by merging the two blend surfaces with the base surface and the other two edges are the top corners of the base surface, refer Figure 15-102.

5. Choose the **Build feature** button from the **Round** dashboard to create rounds. The surface model after creating the rounds is shown in Figure 15-103.

Creating a Full Round

A full round will be created by selecting the two surfaces. These surfaces are the front and back faces of the base surface.

Figure 15-102 Edges selected to create rounds

Figure 15-103 Resulting model after creating rounds on the selected edges

1. Choose the **Round** button from the **Engineering Features** toolbar.

2. Select the two faces, front and back, of the base surface.

3. Invoke the slide-down panel by choosing the **Sets** tab. The selected surfaces are displayed in the **References** collector available in the slide-down panel. The **Full Round** button is chosen by default in the slide-down panel. Now, you need to select the surface to be removed.

4. Select the top face of the base surface; the preview of the round is highlighted on the selected surfaces. Exit the **Round** dashboard by choosing the **Build Feature** button. The round is created, as shown in Figure 15-104.

5. Choose the **Save** button from the **File** toolbar and save the model.

Figure 15-104 Completed surface model

Surface Modeling 15-43

Self-Evaluation Test

Answer the following questions and then compare them to those given at the end of this chapter:

1. You can create a surface with capped ends by drawing an open sketch. (T/F)

2. Surface models have no thickness. (T/F)

3. Style features have the parent-child relationship among themselves as well as with the Pro/ENGINEER features. (T/F)

4. In the **Style** environment, when you press the SHIFT key and select a point on a surface by using the **Free** option, the point is snapped on that surface. (T/F)

5. The procedure to create a helical sweep surface is the same as that of a solid helical sweep feature. (T/F)

6. A feature created in the **Style** environment is displayed in the **Model Tree** as a _____ feature.

7. To enter the **Style** environment, choose the _____ button in the **Base Features** toolbar.

8. The _____ button is used to merge two surfaces and form an edge.

9. In the **Style** environment, the _____ button is used to draw curves.

10. A quilt is a _____ feature.

Review Questions

Answer the following questions:

1. Which of the following feature creation tools contains the options like parallel, rotational, and general?

    (a) **Sweep** (b) **Blend**
    (c) **Extrude** (d) None of these

2. Which of the following editing tools is used to create a flat surface by drawing a sketch?

    (a) **Trim** (b) **Copy**
    (c) **Fill** (d) None of these

3. What is the minimum number of sections required for creating a blend feature?

   (a) one (b) two
   (c) three (d) None of these

4. Which of the following editing tools forms an edge between two intersecting surfaces?

   (a) **Merge** (b) **Intersect**
   (c) **Trim** (d) None of these

5. In which one of the following types of blend, sections are translated and rotated about the x, y, and z axes?

   (a) **Parallel** (b) **Rotational**
   (c) **General** (d) None of these

6. The **Intersect** option is used to create an intersect curve. (T/F)

7. In the **Style** environment, the **Curve Edit** button is used to project curves on surfaces. (T/F)

8. Surface models are the 3D models with no thickness. (T/F)

9. In the **Style** environment, the **Surface** button is used to select at least three or four curves and create a surface. (T/F)

10. To undo the last operation performed, choose the **Undo** button from the **Style** toolbar. (T/F)

Exercises

Exercise 1

In this exercise, you will create the surface model shown in Figure 15-105. The orthographic views of the surface model are shown in Figure 15-106. **(Expected time: 40 min)**

Note
*Create the base feature using the **Blend** option and the ends as revolve features.*

Surface Modeling   15-45

Figure 15-105 *Isometric view of the surface model*

Figure 15-106 *Top, front, right, and detailed views of the surface model*

Exercise 2

In this exercise, you will create the surface model shown in Figure 15-107. The orthographic views and the detailed view of the surface model are shown in Figure 15-108.

(Expected time: 55 min)

Figure 15-107 Surface model

Figure 15-108 Top, front, right, and detailed views of the surface model

Answers to Self-Evaluation Test
1. F, **2.** T, **3.** T, **4.** T, **5.** T, **6.** Style, **7. Style**, **8. Merge**, **9. Curve**, **10.** surface.

Chapter 16

Working with Sheetmetal Components

Learning Objectives

After completing this chapter, you will be able to:
- *Create unattached flat walls.*
- *Create reliefs in the sheetmetal component.*
- *Create a flat wall.*
- *Create the twist wall and the extend wall.*
- *Add flange walls to sheetmetal components.*
- *Bend a sheetmetal component.*
- *Unbend the sheetmetal component and bend back the sheetmetal component.*
- *Convert solid models to sheetmetal components.*
- *Create a flat pattern of the sheetmetal component.*

INTRODUCTION TO Pro/SHEETMETAL

A sheetmetal component is created by bending, cutting, or deforming a thin sheet of uniform thickness. The sheetmetal designs are created in the **Sheetmetal** mode of Pro/ENGINEER Wildfire 5.0. The **Sheetmetal** mode provides you the options to create primary and secondary walls and convert a solid model into a sheetmetal component.

INVOKING THE SHEETMETAL MODE

To invoke the **Sheetmetal** mode, choose the **New** button from the **File** toolbar; the **New** dialog box will be displayed. The **Part** radio button in the **Type** area and the **Solid** radio button in the **Sub-type** area are selected by default. Select the **Sheetmetal** radio button from the **Sub-type** area, as shown in Figure 16-1. Enter the name of the file in the **Name** edit box and choose the **OK** button from the **New** dialog box; the **New File Options** dialog box will be displayed. Select **inlbs_part_sheetmetal** from the dialog box and then choose the **OK** button; the **Sheetmetal** mode will be invoked.

*Figure 16-1 The **New** dialog box*

Figure 16-2 shows you the initial screen appearance in the **Sheetmetal** mode. The initial appearance of the screen in the **Sheetmetal** mode is similar to the initial appearance of the screen in the **Part** mode. The three default datum planes, **FRONT**, **TOP**, and **RIGHT** will be displayed in the drawing area. Also, they will be mutually perpendicular to each other. The **Model Tree** will be displayed to the left of the drawing area.

The process of creating sheetmetal components is similar to that of creating solid or surface protrusions. You first need to create the sketch of the base feature and then use various tools such as Flat, Flange, and so on to create sheetmetal components.

*Figure 16-2 The initial screen appearance in the **Sheetmetal** mode*

INTRODUCTION TO SHEETMETAL WALLS

A wall is any section of the sheetmetal material in your design. There are two types of walls in Pro/SHEETMETAL. They are discussed next.

Primary Walls

Primary walls are created as base features in Pro/SHEETMETAL and are independent entities. The different type of primary walls are unattached flat wall, unattached extruded wall, revolved wall, blended wall, offset wall, variable section sweep, swept blend, helical sweep, and so on.

Secondary Walls

Secondary walls are the walls that are dependent on at least one primary wall. They share a parent-child relation with the primary walls. Secondary walls include all the primary walls and also walls such as flat wall, flange wall, extend wall, twist wall, and so on.

To design a part from scratch, you need to create the primary wall as the base feature. The other features such as flange wall, extend wall, and so on can then be created with reference to the primary walls.

Creating the Unattached Flat Wall

The first feature created in a sheetmetal design will be the base feature. This base feature is known as the unattached flat wall. Choose **Insert > Sheetmetal Wall > Unattached > Flat** from the menu bar or choose the **Flat** button from the **Sheetmetal** toolbar to display the **Flat** dashboard, as shown in Figure 16-3.

*Figure 16-3 The **Flat** dashboard*

References Tab

When you choose the **References** tab, the slide-down panel will be displayed, as shown in Figure 16-4.

The **References** tab slide-down panel helps you to select the sketching plane to create the sketch. Choose the **Define** button to display the **Sketch** dialog box. Select the required sketching plane and orient it. Once you enter the sketcher environment, create the sketch for the wall and choose the **Done** button to exit the sketcher environment. Next, enter the thickness of the sheet in the edit box in the **Flat** dashboard. Finally, choose the **Build feature** button to complete the creation of the unattached flat wall. Figure 16-5 shows a sheetmetal model created using this method.

*Figure 16-4 The **References** tab slide-down panel*

Figure 16-5 Model of the unattached flat wall

Properties Tab

When you choose the **Properties** tab, a slide-down panel will be displayed. This slide-down panel displays the feature identity in the **Name** collector. The **i** button in the slide-down panel, when chosen, opens the browser that displays all information about the feature you are creating.

Note
*The **Options** tab will not be enabled when you are creating the unattached flat wall or any other primary wall. It will be enabled only when the secondary walls are being created.*

Creating the Unattached Revolve Wall

The unattached revolve wall is a feature created by revolving a sketched section about a centerline. The revolve wall can be a primary or a secondary wall. When you choose **Flat > Revolve** from the **Sheetmetal** toolbar, the **FIRST WALL: Revolve** dialog box and the **ATTRIBUTES** menu will be displayed, as shown in Figures 16-6 and 16-7.

Figure 16-6 The **FIRST WALL: Revolve** dialog box

Figure 16-7 The **ATTRIBUTES** menu

The sketch for the unattached revolve wall can be revolved on one side of the sketch plane by selecting the **One Side** option or both the sides of the sketch plane by selecting the **Both Sides** option from the **ATTRIBUTES** menu. Then, choose **Done** from the **ATTRIBUTES** menu; you will be prompted to select the sketching plane. Select and orient the sketching plane, as required. Now, create the sketch for the unattached revolve wall and choose the **Done** button to exit the sketcher environment. You will then be prompted to enter the thickness range and the angle of revolution. After entering the required thickness value and the angle of revolution, the unattached revolved wall will be displayed in the drawing area. The section for creating the revolve wall can be closed or open. Figure 16-8 shows a closed sketch for creating the revolve wall and Figure 16-9 shows the resulting unattached revolved wall.

Figure 16-8 Closed sketch for creating the revolved wall

Figure 16-9 Resulting revolved wall

Creating the Unattached Blend Wall

The **Blend** option connects two or more sections by combining the characteristics of each section. You can sketch multiple boundaries of wall sections and then connect them using the **Parallel**, **Rotational**, or **General** type of blend wall. The number of entities in each section of the unattached blend wall should be the same. For example, you cannot blend a circle with a rectangle. This is because a rectangle is made up of four entities, whereas a circle is made up of only one entity. Therefore, these two sections can be blended only if the circle is divided into four entities.

The **Blend** option is used where the component to be created has varying cross-sections. When you choose **Flat > Blend** from the **Sheetmetal** toolbar, the **BLEND OPTS** menu will be displayed, as shown in Figure 16-10. The options in this menu are discussed next.

Parallel Blend

Parallel blends have sections that are drawn parallel to each other with a specified distance between them. Choose **Parallel > Regular Sec > Sketch Sec > Done** from the **BLEND OPTS** menu; the **ATTRIBUTES** menu will be displayed, as shown in Figure 16-11. The options in this menu are discussed next.

*Figure 16-10 The **BLEND OPTS** menu*

*Figure 16-11 The **ATTRIBUTES** menu*

Straight

The **Straight** option is used to connect the vertices of all sections in a blend feature with straight lines.

Smooth

The **Smooth** option is used to connect the vertices of all sections in a blend feature with curves.

Figure 16-12 shows the sketch of three sections that are used to create the parallel blend feature. Figures 16-13 and 16-14 show the parallel blend features with straight edges and smooth edges, respectively. These features are created using the sections shown in Figure 16-12.

Working with Sheetmetal Components

Figure 16-12 The sketch showing three sections for creating the parallel blend feature

Figure 16-13 Parallel blend feature with straight edges

Figure 16-14 Parallel blend feature with smooth edges

Note
While drawing sections for creating an unattached blend wall, the start point of all sections should be in the same direction in order to avoid twisted blend features.

Rotational Blend

The rotational blends have sections that are rotated about the Y-axis up to a maximum of 120-degree and the distance between two sections is measured from the coordinate system. Between each section an angle, called the rotational blend angle, has to be defined. In this type of blend, each section has its own user-defined coordinate system. If the rotational blend angle entered between the two sections is equal to 0-degree, then the **Rotational** blend option functions the same way as the **Parallel** blend option.

Note that all nonparallel blends can be open or closed. Choose **Rotational > Regular Sec > Sketch Sec > Done** from the **BLEND OPTS** menu; the **ATTRIBUTES** menu will be displayed, as shown in Figure 16-15. The options in this menu are discussed next.

Open

The **Open** option is used when the blend feature to be created has to be kept open. Figure 16-16 shows the sections used to create the rotational blend feature. As evident, in Figure 16-16, two sections are used to create the rotational blend feature and these sections are at an angle of 90-degree to each other. It is also evident from the figure that the second section is dimensioned from the coordinate system that was defined in the first section. Figure 16-17 shows the shaded model of the blend feature.

Figure 16-15 The ATTRIBUTES menu

Figure 16-16 The two sections with dimensions used to create the rotational blend feature

Figure 16-17 Shaded model of the rotational blend feature using the Open option

Closed

The **Closed** option is used to create a closed blend feature. In this type of blend feature, Pro/ENGINEER closes the feature by blending the last section with the first section.

Tip: *It is recommended that the closed blend features should have at least three sections.*

General Blend

Using the **General** option, sections are translated and rotated about the X, Y, and Z axes. The sections are aligned using the user-defined coordinate system. The coordinate system has to be manually placed in every section sketch that constitutes the blend feature.

Creating the Unattached Offset Wall

The unattached offset wall is a reflection of a quilt or a surface set at a specified distance from the original wall. If you choose the **Offset** button from the **Sheetmetal** toolbar, the **Unattached Wall: Offset** dialog box will be displayed, as shown in Figure 16-18, and you will be prompted to select a quilt or a solid surface to offset.

Working with Sheetmetal Components

Select the surface that you want to offset; you will be prompted to enter the offset distance. Enter the required distance value in the **Message Input Window**. You can also define the type of offset wall using the options in the **OFFSETTYPE** menu. When you double-click on the **Offset Type** option in the **Unattached Wall: Offset** dialog box, the **OFFSETTYPE** menu will be displayed, as shown in Figure 16-19. The options in the menu are discussed next.

Normal to Surf
This option, when chosen, creates the offset wall normal to the quilt or selected surface. The **Normal to Surf** option is chosen by default.

Figure 16-18 The Unattached Wall: Offset dialog box

Figure 16-19 The OFFSETTYPE menu

Controlled Fit
This option, when chosen, creates the offset wall at a controlled distance.

Auto Fit
This option automatically fits the offset wall from the quilt or surface.

Figure 16-20 shows the offset wall created at a distance of 500 from the top surface of the primary flat wall.

Note
An offset wall cannot be the first feature in your design.

Creating Reliefs in Sheetmetal Components
The reliefs control the sheetmetal material behavior and prevent unwanted deformation. For example, consider a bend without a relief. It might not represent an accurate real life model due to the stretching of material. By adding the appropriate bend relief, the sheetmetal bend will meet your design intent and enable you to create an accurate flat model. Reliefs may be added to the model at various stages of its creation.

Note
*You will learn about the options in the **Reliefs** tab later in this chapter.*

The different types of reliefs are discussed next.

Figure 16-20 Model with the original wall and the offset wall

Stretch Relief
This type of relief stretches the material, where the bent area intersects the fixed area. The stretch relief is shown in Figure 16-21.

Rip Relief
This type of relief cuts the material at each bend endpoint. The cuts are made normal to the bend line. The rip relief is shown in Figure 16-22.

Figure 16-21 Model with the stretch relief   *Figure 16-22 Model with the rip relief*

Rectangular Relief
This option adds a rectangular relief at each bend endpoint. The rectangular relief is shown in Figure 16-23.

Working with Sheetmetal Components

Obround Relief
This option adds an obround relief at each bend endpoint. The obround relief is shown in Figure 16-24.

Figure 16-23 Model with the rectangular relief

Figure 16-24 Model with the obround relief

Creating A Flat Wall

A flat wall is a planar or an unbent section of the sheetmetal. To create a flat wall, first you need to create the primary wall. The creation of the primary wall (unattached flat wall) has been discussed earlier in this chapter. The flat wall can take any shape, but the surface adjacent to the attached edge must be planar.

To create a flat wall, choose **Insert > Sheetmetal Wall > Flat** from the menu bar; the **Flat Wall** dashboard will be displayed, as shown in Figure 16-25. The options in this dashboard are discussed next.

Figure 16-25 The **Flat Wall** dashboard

Placement Tab
When you choose the **Placement** tab, the slide-down panel will be displayed, as shown in Figure 16-26. The collector in this slide-down panel displays **Select 1 item** because the attachment edge has not yet been defined. When you select the attachment edge, the collector in the slide-down panel will display the edge selected. Also, a preview of the rectangular flat wall will be created perpendicular to the edge selected.

Figure 16-26 The **Placement** tab slide-down panel

Shape Tab
When you choose the **Shape** tab, the slide-down panel will be displayed, as shown in Figure 16-27. The shape tab indicates the predefined wall profiles and their default dimensions.

*Figure 16-27 The **Shape** tab slide-down panel*

By default, **Rectangle** is selected in the Profiles drop-down list in the **Flat Wall** dashboard. The different profiles of walls are **Rectangle**, **Trapezoid**, **L**, **T**, and **User Defined**. These profiles can be selected from the profiles list in the **Flat Wall** dashboard.

Offset Tab

The **Offset** tab, when chosen, creates the flat wall at a specified distance from the selected attachment edge. When you choose the **Offset** tab, the slide-down panel will be displayed, as shown in Figure 16-28. When you select the **Offset wall with respect to attachment edge** check box, the **Add to Part edge**, **Automatic**, and **By value** radio buttons will be enabled. These radio buttons are discussed next.

*Figure 16-28 The **Offset** tab slide-down panel*

Add to Part edge

If you select the **Add to Part edge** radio button, the wall gets appended to the attachment edge without trimming the height of the attachment edge.

Working with Sheetmetal Components

Automatic
The **Automatic** radio button, when selected, offsets the wall and maintains its original height.

By value
The **By value** radio button, when selected, offsets the wall at a specified distance from the attachment edge. You can also drag the graphic handle to adjust the offset value.

Relief Tab
The **Relief** tab allows you to choose the type of relief to be applied on the wall. When you choose the **Relief** tab, the slide-down panel will be displayed, as shown in Figure 16-29. When the **Define each side separately** check box is selected, the **Side 1** and **Side 2** radio buttons will be enabled. These options are discussed next.

Side 1
The **Side 1** radio button indicates the point on one side of the attachment edge on which the relief will be applied.

Side 2
The **Side 2** radio button indicates the point on the other side of the attachment edge on which the relief will be applied.

*Figure 16-29 The **Relief** tab slide-down panel*

Type Drop-down List
The **Type** drop-down list specifies different types of reliefs such as **No Relief**, **Rip**, **Stretch**, **Rectangular**, and **Obround**. By default, the **Rip** is selected in the **Type** drop-down list. The types of relief have already been discussed earlier.

Bend Allowance Tab
The **Bend Allowance** tab is used to calculate the undeveloped length of the sheetmetal required to create a bend of specified radius and angle. When you choose the **Bend Allowance** tab, the slide-down panel will be displayed, as shown in Figure 16-30. When the **A Feature Specific Set Up** check box is selected, the **By K factor**, **By Y factor**, and **By Bend table** options will be enabled. These options are discussed next.

*Figure 16-30 The **Bend Allowance** tab slide-down panel*

By K factor
K Factor is the ratio of distance between the neutral bend line and the inside bend radius to the thickness of the material.

By Y factor
Y Factor is the ratio between the neutral bend line and thickness of the material.

By Bend table
It controls the calculations required for the length of flat material (developed length) needed to create a bend.

Add Bend on the attachment edge Button

The **Add Bend on the attachment edge** button creates a bend between the existing sheetmetal wall and the newly created wall. There are two methods of specifying the bend parameters of the flat wall and these are discussed next.

Dimension the inner surface of the bend Button

On choosing this button, you can specify the dimension for the inner surface of the bend.

Dimension the outer surface of the bend Button

On choosing this button, you can specify the dimension for the outer surface of the bend.

Figure 16-31 shows the base wall and Figure 16-32 shows the flat wall created on the rear edge of the base wall.

Figure 16-31 Model of the base wall

Figure 16-32 Model with the flat wall

Creating a Twist Wall

A twist wall is a spiraling or coiling section of sheetmetal. The twist wall is formed around an axis running through the center of the wall, turning the ends of the wall in opposite directions by a relatively small specified angle. You can attach the twist wall to a straight edge or an existing planar wall. The twist wall typically serves as a transition between two areas of sheetmetal.

Choose **Insert > Sheetmetal Wall > Twist** from the menu bar to invoke the **TWIST** dialog box and the **FEATURE REFS** menu. The **TWIST** dialog box and the **FEATURE REFS** menu are shown in Figure 16-33 and 16-34, respectively.

Working with Sheetmetal Components

*Figure 16-33 The **TWIST** dialog box*

*Figure 16-34 The **FEATURE REFS** menu*

You will be prompted to select the attachment edge on which the twist wall is to be created. Select the attachment edge from the drawing area; the **TWIST AXS PNT** menu will be displayed, as shown in Figure 16-35.

The **TWIST AXS PNT** menu allows you to define a point on the attachment edge that will form the centerline of the twist wall. The two options of defining the start point for the twist wall are discussed next.

Select Point
This option allows you to choose an existing datum point on the attachment edge.

*Figure 16-35 The **TWIST AXS PNT** menu*

Use Middle
This option allows you to select the middle point of the attachment edge as the centerline for the twist wall.

After specifying the point that defines the twist axis, you will be prompted to specify the dimensions of the wall. These options are discussed next.

Start Width
This option will be used to specify the width at the start point of the twist wall.

End Width
This option will be used to specify the width at the end point of the twist wall.

Twist Length
This option indicates the length of the twist wall measured from the attachment edge to the end point of the twist axis.

Twist Angle
The **Twist Angle** option is used to specify the angle of twist for the twist wall.

Developed Length

This option indicates the length of the twist wall, when untwisted.

Figure 16-36 shows the twist wall attached to the base wall.

Figure 16-36 Model with the twist wall attached to the base wall

Creating an Extend Wall

The extend wall lengthens an existing wall. You can extend the wall from a straight edge on an existing wall to a planar surface or to a specified distance. When you choose the **Extend** button from the **Sheetmetal** toolbar, the **WALL Options: Extend** dialog box will be displayed, as shown in Figure 16-37, and you will be prompted to select a straight edge to extend. When you select the edge to extend, the **EXT DIST** menu will be displayed, as shown in Figure 16-38. The options in the **EXT DIST** menu are discussed next.

Figure 16-37 The WALL Options: Extend dialog box

Figure 16-38 The EXT DIST menu

Up To Plane

This option allows you to extend the wall up to a plane. The plane or face upto which a wall is to be extended can be an existing default datum plane, the flat face of another independent flat wall, or a new datum plane.

Working with Sheetmetal Components

Use Value
This option allows you to extend the wall to a specified distance. You can select a default value, enter a required value, or select two parallel edges to extend.

Figure 16-39 shows two independent unattached flat walls and Figure 16-40 shows the extend wall created between two flat unattached independent walls.

Figure 16-39 *Model with two independent unattached flat walls*

Figure 16-40 *Model with the extend wall between two independent unattached flat walls*

Creating a Flange Wall
A flange wall is a bent section of sheetmetal. Choose **Insert > Sheetmetal Wall > Flange** from the menu bar to invoke the **Flange Wall** dashboard. The **Flange Wall** dashboard is shown in Figure 16-41. The options in this dashboard are discussed next.

Figure 16-41 *The **Flange Wall** dashboard*

Placement Tab
The **Placement** tab indicates the reference edge chosen to create the flange wall. When you choose the **Placement** tab, the slide-down panel will be displayed, as shown in Figure 16-42.

Figure 16-42 *The **Placement** tab slide-down panel*

Shape Tab
The **Shape** tab indicates the profiles and dimensions of the predefined flange wall shapes such as **I**, **Arc**, **S**, **Open**, **Flushed**, **Duck**, **C**, **Z**, or **User Defined**. The predefined wall profile can be selected from the drop-down list in the **Flange Wall** dashboard. When you choose the **Shape** tab after selecting the predefined wall profile, the slide-down panel will be displayed with three buttons, as shown in Figure 16-43. The **Sketch** button in the slide-down panel can be used to draw the sketch for the user-defined profile. The **Open** button in the slide-down panel can be used to import sketch. Choose the **Open** button from this slide-down panel; the **Open** dialog box will be displayed. Using this dialog box, you can import the required sketch.

The **Shape Attachment** area determines the height of the wall. There are two radio buttons in this area: **Height dimension includes thickness** and **Height dimension does not include thickness**. On selecting the first radio button, the thickness of the sheetmetal is included while calculating the wall height whereas, on selecting the other radio button, the thickness is not included while calculating the wall height. The **Save As** button in the slide-down panel can be used to save the sketch so that you can import it later on.

Figure 16-43 The **Shape** *tab slide-down panel*

Length Tab

The **Length** tab allows you to extend the end faces of the **Flange Wall** independently. The edit boxes in the slide-down panel can be used to specify the distance through which the flange wall has to be extended in either direction. When you choose the **Length** tab, the slide-down panel will be displayed, as shown in Figure 16-44.

Figure 16-44 The **Length** *tab slide-down panel*

Working with Sheetmetal Components

Offset Tab
The **Offset** tab allows you to offset the flange wall to a specified distance from the selected attachment edge. When you choose the **Offset** tab, the slide-down panel will be displayed, as shown in Figure 16-45.

When you select the **Offset wall with respect to attachment edge** check box, the **Add to Part edge**, **Automatic**, and **By value** radio buttons will be enabled. These radio buttons are discussed next.

*Figure 16-45 The **Offset** tab slide-down panel*

Add to Part edge
If you select the **Add to Part edge** radio button, the wall will be appended to the attachment edge without trimming the height of the attachment edge.

Automatic
This radio button, when selected, offsets the flange wall and maintains its original height.

By value
This radio button, when selected, offsets the flange wall at a specified distance.

Miter Cuts Tab
When you choose the **Miter Cuts** tab, the slide-down panel will be displayed, as shown in Figure 16-46. Miter cuts are created to allow bending of two sheetmetal plates created in the same plane.

Relief Tab
The **Relief** tab allows you to choose the type of relief to be provided to the sheetmetal wall to prevent any unwanted deformation. This tab can also be used to create bend reliefs and corner reliefs. When you choose the **Relief** tab, the slide-down panel will be displayed, as shown in Figure 16-47.

*Figure 16-46 The **Miter Cuts** tab slide-down panel*

When the **Define each side separately** check box is selected in the **Relief** tab slide-down panel, the **Side 1** and **Side 2** radio buttons will be enabled. The bend reliefs in the **Relief Category** area are **Rip**, **Stretch**, **Rectangular**, and **Obround**. The corner reliefs available in this area are **V Notch**, **Circular**, **Rectangular**, and **Obround**.

Bend Allowance Tab
When you choose the **Bend Allowance** tab, the slide-down panel will be displayed, as shown in Figure 16-48. When the **A Feature Specific Set Up** check box is selected, the **By K factor** radio button, the **By Y factor** radio button, and the **Use Bend table** check box will be enabled. These options have already been discussed earlier in this chapter.

*Figure 16-47 The **Relief** tab slide-down panel*

*Figure 16-48 The **Bend Allowance** tab slide-down panel*

Properties Tab

When you choose the **Properties** tab, the slide-down panel will be displayed, as shown in Figure 16-49. This slide-down panel displays the feature identity in the **Name** collector. The **i** button in the slide-down panel, when chosen, opens the browser that displays the information about the feature you have created. This slide-down panel also indicates the thickness of the flange wall being created.

*Figure 16-49 The **Properties** tab slide-down panel*

Figure 16-50 shows a flange wall with a rectangular relief created on the primary unattached flat wall.

Figure 16-50 Model with the flange wall attached to the base wall

Working with Sheetmetal Components

Creating the Bend Feature

The **Bend** tool transforms the sheetmetal wall into an angular or roll shape. You need to sketch a bend line and determine the direction of the bend using the direction arrows or orienting the sketching view. The bend line is used as the reference for calculating the developed length and creating the bend geometry. Bends can be added at any time during the design process, as long as, a wall feature exists. You can add bends across form features, but you cannot add them where they cross another bend. Depending on where you place the bend in your sheetmetal design, you may need to add reliefs for the bend.

Choose **Insert > Bend Operation > Bend** from the menu bar or choose the **Bend** button from the **Sheetmetal** toolbar to invoke the **OPTIONS** menu, as shown in Figure 16-51. The options in this menu are discussed next.

*Figure 16-51 The **OPTIONS** menu*

Angle
This option creates a bend through a specified radius and angle. The direction arrows determine the bend location. You can create the angle bend on one side of the bend line or equally on both sides.

Roll
This option creates a bend through a specified radius. The direction arrows determine the bend location. You can create a roll bend on one side of the bend line or equally on both sides.

Regular Bend
The **Regular** option, when chosen, bends a sheetmetal wall around a neutral bend axis into angular or roll shapes. You need to sketch a bend line and determine the location of the bend with direction arrows or the sketching view. This type of bend will be used more frequently in creating various sheetmetal components. It has no transition surfaces. There are two types of regular bends and these are discussed next.

Angle
This option, when chosen, bends a sheetmetal wall through a specified radius and angle.

Roll
This option, when chosen, bends the sheetmetal wall through a specified radius, but the angle is determined by both the radius and the amount of flat material to be bent.

When you choose **Angle > Regular > Done** from the **OPTIONS** menu, the **BEND Options** dialog box and the **USE TABLE** menu will be displayed, as shown in Figures 16-52 and 16-53, respectively. The options in the **USE TABLE** menu are discussed next.

*Figure 16-52 The **BEND Options** dialog box*

*Figure 16-53 The **USE TABLE** menu*

Part Bend Tbl
The **Part Bend Tbl** option, if chosen, uses the default bend table to create a bend in that particular part.

Feat Bend Tbl
The **Feat Bend Tbl** option, if chosen, creates an independent bend table for the individual feature.

When you choose the **Done/Return** option from the **USE TABLE** menu, the **RADIUS SIDE** submenu will be displayed, as shown in Figure 16-54. The options in this submenu are discussed next.

Inside Rad
The **Inside Rad** option, if chosen, dimensions the bend radius from the inner surface of the sheetmetal wall.

*Figure 16-54 The **RADIUS SIDE** submenu*

Outside Rad
The **Outside Rad** option, if chosen, dimensions the bend radius from the outer surface of the sheetmetal wall.

After defining the side for the bend radius, choose **Done/Return** from the **RADIUS SIDE** menu; the **SETUP SK PLN** menu will be displayed and you will be prompted to select a sketching plane to define the bend line. Figure 16-55 shows a base wall and Figure 16-56 shows the model with an **Angle** bend created using the **Regular** option.

w/Transition Bend

The **w/Transition** (with transition) option shapes one section of a sheetmetal plane, leaving the other sections flat or with different bend conditions. When you choose the **Bend** button from the **Sheetmetal** toolbar, the **OPTIONS** menu will be displayed. Choose **Angle > w/Transition > Done** from the **OPTIONS** menu; the **USE TABLE** menu will be displayed, refer to Figure 16-53. Select the required option and choose **Done/Return**; the **RADIUS SIDE** submenu will be displayed, refer to Figure 16-54. Select the required option and choose **Done/Return**; the **SETUP SK PLN** menu will be displayed and you will be prompted to select the sketching plane. After defining the sketching plane and its orientation, you will first be prompted to

Working with Sheetmetal Components

Figure 16-55 Model of the base wall

Figure 16-56 Model with the angle bend

sketch the section defining the bend line, and then to sketch section to define the flat and bent sections. You can define one or more transition areas for the **w/Transition** bend.

The sketch for each transition area must consist of two lines. Therefore, you need to sketch two lines: one adjacent to the bend area and the other adjacent to the first one. Figure 16-57 shows the sketch you need to define to create a bend in a sheetmetal component using the **w/Transition** option.

There are two types bends that can be created using the **w/Transition** option. They are discussed next.

Angle
This option, when selected, bends the sheetmetal wall through a specified radius and angle.

Roll
This option, when selected, bends the sheetmetal wall through a specific radius, but the angle is determined by both the radius and the amount of flat material to be bent.

Figure 16-58 shows the model with an angle bend created using the **Regular** option and Figure 16-59 shows the model with an angle bend created using the **w/Transition** option.

Figure 16-57 Sketch for creating a bend using the w/Transition option

Note
*You cannot specify bend reliefs for bends created using the **w/Transition** option. If you need to create a cut in the transition area, create it before you create the w/Transition bend and then unbend the sheet. You will then need to bend back the component to satisfy the design intent.*

Figure 16-58 Model with an angle bend created using the **Regular** option

Figure 16-59 Model with an angle bend created using the **w/Transition** option

Planar Bend

A **Planar** bend forces the sheetmetal wall around an axis that is normal to the surface and the sketching plane. You need to sketch a bend line and form the planar bend around an axis using the direction arrows which will be displayed in the drawing area. Choose the **Bend** button from the **Sheetmetal** toolbar to invoke the **OPTIONS** menu. Choose **Angle > Planar > Done** from the **OPTIONS** menu; the **BEND Options** dialog box and the **USE TABLE** menu will be displayed. Choose the required option and then choose **Done/Return** from the **USE TABLE** menu.

You will next be prompted to select the sketching plane. Select the sketching plane and define its orientation. Sketch the bend line and specify the direction of the bend through the direction arrows, which appear in the drawing area. Figure 16-60 shows the bend line sketched on the base wall and Figure 16-61 shows a bend created on the base wall using the **Planar** option.

There are two kinds of **Planar** bends. These are discussed next.

Figure 16-60 Bend line sketched on the base wall

Figure 16-61 Bend created on the base wall

Working with Sheetmetal Components

Angle
This option, when selected, bends the sheetmetal wall through a specified radius and angle.

Roll
This option, when selected, bends the sheetmetal wall through a specified radius, but the angle is determined by both the radius and the amount of flat material to be bent.

Note

*You cannot copy a bend using the **Mirror** option. While you can generally unbend zero-radius bends, you cannot unbend the bends with cuts across them. If you do modify the developed length, remember that revising the developed length only affects the unbent geometry and not the bend back features.*

Creating the Unbend Feature

The **Unbend** option flattens any curved surface on the sheetmetal part. The curved surface may be a bend feature or a primary or secondary wall created previously. When you choose the **Unbend** button from the **Sheetmetal** toolbar, the **UNBEND OPT** menu will be displayed, as shown in Figure 16-62. The different types of unbend features in the **UNBEND OPT** menu are discussed next.

Regular
The **Regular** option, when chosen, creates an unbend that is generic and applies to almost all sheetmetal bends or wall surfaces. Note that the section chosen to create the unbend feature must be developable. When you choose **Regular > Done** from the **UNBEND OPT** menu, the **Regular Type** dialog box will be displayed, as shown in Figure 16-63.

*Figure 16-62 The **UNBEND OPT** menu*

*Figure 16-63 The **Regular Type** dialog box*

Also, you will be prompted to select the plane or edge which remains fixed while creating the feature. When you select the plane or edge to remain fixed, the **UNBENDSEL** menu will be displayed, as shown in Figure 16-64. The options in this menu are discussed next.

*Figure 16-64 The **UNBENDSEL** menu*

UnbendSelect
This option allows you to select specific bend surfaces to unbend.

Unbend All
This option allows you to unbend all bends and curved surfaces.

Figure 16-65 shows a model with a flat wall attached to the primary wall and a regular bend created at either ends. Figure 16-66 shows the unbend model created using the **Regular** option.

Figure 16-65 Model with the regular bend and a flat wall

Figure 16-66 Model after unbending

Creating the Bend Back

The **Bend Back** feature enables you to return the unbent areas to their formed positions. Remember that as a rule, you can bend back only the unbent features. When you choose the **Bend Back** button from the **Sheetmetal** toolbar, the **BEND BACK** dialog box will be displayed, as shown in Figure 16-67. Also, you will be prompted to select the edge or plane which remains fixed while creating the feature. After selecting the area to remain fixed, the **BENDBACKSEL** menu will be displayed, as shown in Figure 16-68. The options in the **BENDBACKSEL** menu are discussed next.

Figure 16-67 The BEND BACK dialog box

Figure 16-68 The BENDBACKSEL menu

Working with Sheetmetal Components

BendBack Sel
This option bends back the selected sections.

BendBack All
This option bends back all unbent sections.

Figure 16-69 shows the model with the surfaces selected for creating the bend back feature and Figure 16-70 shows the model created by using the **Bend Back** option.

Figure 16-69 Model with the surfaces selected for creating the bend back feature

Figure 16-70 Model after creating the bend back feature

Note
*The model shown in Figure 16-69 is a base wall, with flange walls attached to its front and rear edges. Both the flange walls are unbent, while the base wall is selected as the section to remain fixed. The **Bend Back** option is then applied on the model.*

Creating the Conversion

Converting solid parts to sheetmetal parts enables you to modify your existing solid design with sheetmetal industry features. The conversion can serve as a shortcut in your design process because you can use existing solid designs to reach your sheetmetal design intent. Also, you can include multiple features within a single conversion feature. After you convert a part to sheetmetal, the part behaves like any other sheetmetal component.

Basic conversion
The process of converting a solid model into a sheetmetal component by removing one of the surfaces or by making one of the surfaces of the solid model as the driving surface is known as creating the basic conversion.

Sheetmetal Conversion
If the converted part is not manufacturable, then you need to create a sheetmetal conversion by adding features such as rips, bends, and corner reliefs.

The basic conversion defines how you want to use the existing solid part in your sheetmetal design. You can create the shell feature on the solid model by selecting the surfaces to be removed, or you can make any one of the surface of the solid model as a driving surface (the driving side). Block-like parts mostly use the **Shell** option to convert to sheetmetal, while thin protrusions with constant thickness mostly use the **Driving Srf** option.

Figure 16-71 shows the solid model and Figure 16-72 shows the model after shelling and removing the bottom face.

Figure 16-71 Model of the solid part   *Figure 16-72* Model after converting it into sheetmetal component by removing the bottom surface

> **Note**
> *To covert the solid model into a sheetmetal component, first you need to create a solid model, shown in Figure 16-71. Then, choose **Applications > Sheetmetal** from the menu bar; the **SMT CONVERT** menu will be displayed with two options, **Driving Srf** and **Shell**. Choose any one option from the menu for the sheetmetal conversion.*

While converting a solid model into a sheetmetal component, you might need to add certain features such as point reliefs, edge rips, bends, and so on to make the component manufacturable. Choose **Insert > Conversion** or choose the **Conversion** button from the **Sheetmetal** toolbar to display the **SMT CONVERSION** dialog box, as shown in Figure 16-73.

The additional features are discussed next.

Figure 16-73 The **SMT CONVERSION** dialog box

Point Relief
This option creates reliefs at selected edges. These reliefs may also be datum points. This type of relief can be used under the conditions mentioned next.

Working with Sheetmetal Components

1. Defining a point break that divides an existing edge into two separate edges that can be partially ripped or partially bent.

2. Defining the end of a rip connection.

3. Defining point relief at vertices of bends and rips.

Edge Rip
A rip feature can be defined as a zero volume cut that tears or shears the sheetmetal walls. If the sheetmetal component you are designing is a continuous piece of material, you cannot unbend the component without creating the rips. This option creates rips along the selected edge, which enables you to unbend the sheetmetal part.

Rip Connect
The **Rip Connect** option connects existing planar rips with straight line rips. The rip connects are sketched as point-to-point connections, which require you to define rip endpoints. The endpoints can be datum points or vertices and must be the endpoints of a rip.

Bends
This option converts sharp edges to bends. By default, the inner radius of the bend is set to the thickness of the sheetmetal wall.

Corner Reliefs
This option creates reliefs in selected corners.

Figure 16-74 shows a solid model that has been converted into a sheetmetal component and Figure 16-75 shows the model with the edge rip, rip connect, and bend features.

Figure 16-74 The solid model after being converted into a sheetmetal component

Figure 16-75 Model with the edge rip, rip connect, and bend features

Creating Cuts in the Sheetmetal Component

The process of creating cuts in a sheetmetal component is similar to the one followed to create cuts in a solid model. The **Extrude** button in the **Sheetmetal** toolbar can be used to create cuts in a sheetmetal component. Choose the **Extrude** button from the **Sheetmetal** toolbar to invoke the **Extrude** dashboard; the **Extrude** dashboard will be displayed, as shown in Figure 16-76.

Figure 16-76 The Extrude dashboard

Notice that the **Remove Material** button in chosen by default in the **Extrude** dashboard. This happens only when you have created a primary wall in your design and intend to create cuts on it. The other options in the **Extrude** dashboard have the same functionality as discussed in earlier chapters.

The cut features in sheetmetal components are created with reference to the driving surface or the offset surface. Driving surface is the surface on which you create the base feature. When you turn the model display to the **No hidden** mode, the surface highlighted in green color is the driving surface. The offset surface is created by adding material to the driving surface equal to the thickness of the sheetmetal component. When you turn the model display to the **No hidden** mode, the surface highlighted in white color is the offset surface. When you invoke the **Extrude** dashboard, the **Remove material normal to surface** button is chosen by default. There are three options through which you can create cuts in a sheetmetal component.

Remove material normal to both Driven and Offset surfaces Button

This button, if chosen, removes material normal to both the driving and offset surfaces.

Remove material normal to Driven surface Button

This button, if chosen, removes material normal to the driven surface. This button is selected by default.

Remove material normal to Offset surface Button

This button, if chosen, removes material normal to the offset surface.

Creating the Flat Pattern

The **Flat Pattern** tool is equivalent to the **Unbend All** feature. This feature flattens any curved surface, whether it is a bend feature or a wall. But the most distinctive characteristic of the **Flat Pattern** tool is that it automatically places itself at the end of the **Model Tree** to maintain the flat model view. If new features are added to your design, the flat pattern is suppressed but is automatically resumed after the features are added. If you do not want to flip between the flat pattern and the solid views for each new feature, manually suppress and resume the flat pattern as required. You can create a flat pattern at any point in

Working with Sheetmetal Components

your design because of the property that the feature jumps to the end of the **Model Tree** to maintain the flat model view.

> **Note**
> *You can create only one flat pattern per part. Once you create a flat pattern, the option is disabled.*

To create a flat pattern, choose **Insert > Bend Operation > Flat Pattern** from the menu bar or choose the **Flat Pattern** button from the **Sheetmetal** toolbar; you are prompted to select the edge or plane that will remain fixed during the process of creating the feature. Select the surface you want as fixed and the flat pattern of the model is created in the drawing area.

Figure 16-77 shows a sheetmetal component chosen to create the flat pattern. Select the primary wall surface that needs to remain fixed and the model similar to the one shown in Figure 16-78 will be displayed in the drawing area.

Figure 16-77 Model used for the flat pattern   *Figure 16-78 Model after creating the flat pattern*

TUTORIALS

Tutorial 1

In this tutorial, you will create the sheetmetal component of the Holder Clip shown in Figure 16-79. The flat pattern of the component is shown in Figure 16-80. The dimensions are shown in Figures 16-81 and 16-82. The thickness of the sheet is 1 mm. After creating the sheet metal component, create its flat pattern.   **(Expected time: 45 min)**

Figure 16-79 Model for Tutorial 1

Figure 16-80 The flat pattern of the component

Figure 16-81 Top view of the Holder Clip

Figure 16-82 Front view of the Holder Clip

The following steps are required to complete this tutorial:

a. Create the base feature, refer to Figures 16-83 and 16-84.
b. Create the flange walls on the right and left edges of the base wall, refer to Figures 16-85 through 16-89.
c. Create the next flange wall on the front edge of the base wall, refer to Figure 16-91. Next, create a cut feature on it, refer to Figures 16-92 and 16-93.
d. Create a flat wall attached to the flange wall created in the previous step, refer to Figure 16-94 and Figure 16-95.
e. Create the next flange wall, refer to Figure 16-96 and Figure 16-97.
f. Create the next flange on the other front edge of the base wall, refer to Figure 16-99.
g. Create the round feature and the chamfer feature, refer to Figures 16-100 and 16-101.
h. Create the hole features on the top and bottom walls, refer to Figures 16-102 and 16-103.
i. Create the flat pattern of the model, refer to Figure 16-104.

Working with Sheetmetal Components

Starting a New Object File

1. Start a new file in the **Part** mode and select the **Sheetmetal** from the **Sub-type** area. Next, enter *c16tut1* in the **Name** edit box.

2. Set the template to **mmns_part_sheetmetal**.

Creating the Base Wall

1. Choose the **Flat** button from the **Sheetmetal** toolbar; the **Flat** dashboard is displayed and you are prompted to select a closed sketch.

2. Choose the **References** tab from the **Flat** dashboard to display the slide-down panel and then choose the **Define** button from the slide-down panel; the **Sketch** dialog box is displayed and you are prompted to select a sketching plane.

3. Select the **TOP** datum plane from the drawing area and then choose the **Sketch** button from the **Sketch** dialog box.

4. Draw the sketch for the base wall, as shown in Figure 16-83, and choose the **Done** button to exit the sketcher environment.

Figure 16-83 The sketch for the base wall

5. Enter **1** in the edit box of the **Flat** dashboard and choose the **Build feature** button from the dashboard to complete the creation of the feature. The model similar to the one shown in Figure 16-84 is displayed in the drawing area.

Creating the First Flange Wall

1. Choose the **Flange** button from the **Sheetmetal** toolbar; the **Flange Wall** dashboard is displayed and you are prompted to select the edge to attach the wall.

2. Select the right edge of the base wall, as shown in Figure 16-85; the preview of the flange wall is displayed in the drawing area. The **I** profile is selected by default in the selection box above the **Placement** tab in the **Flange Wall** dashboard. The dimension, indicating the bend radius at the attachment edge, is also displayed in the drawing area and the default value is selected as 1, which is dimensioned from the inner surface of the bend.

Figure 16-84 Model of the base wall

Figure 16-85 The attachment edge for the flange wall

3. Choose the **Shape** tab from the **Flange Wall** dashboard to display the slide-down panel and then double-click on the default height value in the slide-down panel. Next, enter **41**. The angle at which the wall is created with respect to the base wall is selected as 90-degree by default. You can also drag the handles and adjust the values dynamically. Alternatively, double-click on the values displayed on the model; the edit boxes will be displayed where you can enter new values as per your requirement.

4. Choose the **Dimension the outer surface of the bend** button from the **Flange Wall** dashboard and enter **2** in the edit box; the preview of the wall is displayed in the drawing area.

5. Choose the **Build feature** button from the **Flange Wall** dashboard to complete the creation of the wall; the model similar to the one shown in Figure 16-86 is displayed in the drawing area.

Figure 16-86 Model with the flange wall

Creating the Next Flange Wall

1. Select the attachment edge, which is the inner edge of the previously created flange wall, as shown in Figure 16-87, and create a flange wall as discussed earlier, with **21** as its height value and **2** as its radius value. The model similar to the one shown in Figure 16-88 is displayed in the drawing area.

Working with Sheetmetal Components

Figure 16-87 The attachment edge chosen for the flange wall

Figure 16-88 Model with the flange wall

Creating the Flange Walls on the Left Edge of the Base Wall

1. Create the flange walls on the left edge of the base wall by following the similar procedure that you used for creating the flange walls on the right edge. The model after creating the flange walls on the left edge of the base wall is shown in Figure 16-89. You can also mirror the left side flange walls about the RIGHT plane.

Figure 16-89 Model after creating the flange wall on the left edge

Creating the Next Flange Wall on the Front Edge of the Base Wall

1. Choose the **Flange** button from the **Sheetmetal** toolbar; the **Flange Wall** dashboard is displayed and you are prompted to select the edge to attach the wall.

2. Select the front edge of the base wall, as shown in Figure 16-90. The preview of the flange wall is displayed in the drawing area.

3. Choose the **Shape** tab to display the slide-down panel. Specify **41** as the value of height of the wall in the edit box in the slide-down panel. You can also double-click on the height value displayed on the model and enter the new value. The angle at which the wall is created with respect to the base wall is selected as 90-degree by default.

4. Choose the **Dimension the outer surface of the bend** button from the **Flange Wall** dashboard and enter the value **2** in the edit box. The preview of the flange wall is displayed in the drawing area.

5. Choose the **Build feature** button from the **Flange Wall** dashboard; the model, similar to the one shown in Figure 16-91, is displayed in the drawing area.

Figure 16-90 The attachment edge for the flange wall

Figure 16-91 Model with the flange wall

Creating the Cut Feature on the Front Flange Wall

1. Choose the **Extrude** button from the **Sheetmetal** toolbar and select the front face of the front flange wall as the sketching plane. Make sure that the **Remove Material** button is chosen.

2. Draw the sketch for the extruded cut feature, as shown in Figure 16-92.

3. Exit the sketcher environment and extrude the sketch through all faces in the model. The sheetmetal component after creating the cut feature is shown in Figure 16-93.

Figure 16-92 The sketch for the extruded cut feature

Figure 16-93 Model after creating the cut feature

Working with Sheetmetal Components

Creating the Flat Wall

1. Choose the **Flat** button from the **Sheetmetal** toolbar; the **Flat Wall** dashboard is displayed and you are prompted to select the attachment edge to create the wall.

2. Select the attachment edge, as shown in Figure 16-94; the **Rectangle** profile of the wall is selected by default and the preview of the wall is displayed in the drawing area.

3. Select the **Flat** option from the angle drop-down list in the **Flat Wall** dashboard.

4. Choose the **Shape** tab from the **Flat Wall** dashboard; the slide-down panel is displayed with the default dimensions of the flat wall. Specify **21** as the value for the height of the wall and specify **-21** as the offset distance from the bottom edge of the flange wall in the first edit box available at the bottom left of the slide-down panel. The preview of the flat wall is displayed in the drawing area.

5. Choose the **Build feature** button from the **Flat Wall** dashboard to complete the feature creation. The model similar to the one shown in Figure 16-95 is displayed in the drawing area.

Figure 16-94 The attachment edge for the flat wall

Figure 16-95 Model after creating the flat wall

Creating the Next Flange Wall

1. Choose the **Flange** button from the **Sheetmetal** toolbar; the **Flange Wall** dashboard is displayed and you are prompted to select the attachment edge to create the wall.

2. Select the attachment edge, as shown in the Figure 16-96; the preview of the flange wall is displayed in the drawing area.

3. Choose the **Shape** tab from the **Flange Wall** dashboard to display the slide-down panel. Specify **30** as the value for the height of the wall in the edit box in the slide-down panel. The angle at which the wall is created with respect to the front flange wall is selected as 90-degree by default.

4. Enter **2** as the dimension for creating the bend at the attachment edge which is dimensioned from the outer surface of the bend.

5. Choose the **Build feature** button from the **Flange Wall** dashboard to complete the creation of the feature. The model similar to the one shown in Figure 16-97 is displayed in the drawing area.

Figure 16-96 The attachment edge for the flange wall

Figure 16-97 Model showing the flange wall

Creating the Next Flange Wall on the Front Edge of the Base Wall

1. Create the next flange wall on the front edge of the base wall by selecting the attachment edge, as shown in Figure 16-98, and specifying the height of the wall as **19**. The model similar to the one shown in Figure 16-99 is displayed in the drawing area.

Figure 16-98 The attachment edge for the flange wall

Figure 16-99 Model showing the flange wall on the front edge of the base wall

Creating the Round and Chamfer Features

1. Create the rounds with radius 7, as shown in Figure 16-100.

2. Create the edge chamfer, as shown in Figure 16-101. For the dimensions of the edge chamfer, refer to Figure 16-82.

Figure 16-100 Model after creating the round feature

Figure 16-101 Model after creating the chamfer feature

Creating the Hole Features on the Top and Bottom Walls

1. Choose **Insert > Hole** from the menu bar; the **Hole** dashboard is displayed.

2. Select the top surface of the base wall and specify the placement parameters for the hole, refer to Figure 16-81.

3. Choose the **Build feature** button from the **Hole** dashboard to exit it. The model after creating the hole feature on the top surface of the base wall is shown in Figure 16-102.

4. Similarly, create the hole feature on the bottom flange wall by specifying the placement parameters shown in Figure 16-81. The model after creating the hole feature on the bottom flange wall is shown in Figure 16-103.

Figure 16-102 Model with the hole feature on the base wall

Figure 16-103 Model with the hole feature on the bottom flange wall

Creating the Flat Pattern of the Model

1. Choose the **Flat Pattern** button from the **Sheetmetal** toolbar; the **Select** message box is displayed and you are prompted to select the plane or the edge that remains fixed while creating the feature.

2. Select the top surface of the base wall; the flat pattern of the model is created with the 3D notes.

3. To clear the 3D notes, choose **Tools > Options** from the menu bar; the **Option** dialog box is displayed. Enter **smt_bend_notes_dflt_display** in the **Option** edit box and then select **no** from the **Value** drop-down list.

4. Choose the **Add / Change** button from the dialog box and then choose **OK** to exit. The flat pattern of the model is displayed, as shown in Figure 16-104.

Figure 16-104 Model after creating the flat pattern

Saving the Model

1. Choose the **Save** button from the **File** toolbar to save the model.

Tutorial 2

In this tutorial, you will create the sheet metal component shown in Figure 16-105. The dimensions are shown in Figures 16-106, 16-107, and 16-108. The flat pattern of the component is shown in Figure 16-109. The thickness of the sheet is 1 mm, Bend Radius is 1 mm, Relief Type is Rectangular, and width value is equal to thickness. After creating the sheetmetal component, create its flat pattern. **(Expected time: 45 min)**

Figure 16-105 *Model for Tutorial 2*

Figure 16-106 *Top view of the model*

Figure 16-107 *Left-side view of the model*

Figure 16-108 *Front view of the model*

Figure 16-109 *Flat pattern of the component*

The following steps are required to complete this tutorial:

a. Create the base feature, refer to Figures 16-110 and 16-111.
b. Create the hole feature on the top surface of the base wall, refer to Figure 16-112 and pattern the hole feature, refer to Figure 16-113.
c. Create a flange wall on the right edge of the base wall, refer to Figure 16-114.
d. Create the cut feature, refer to Figure 16-115 and Figure 16-116.
e. Create the next flange wall attached to the wall created previously, refer to Figure 16-118.

f. Create the two flange walls along with the cut feature on the left side of the base wall as created previously, refer to Figure 16-119.
g. Create the flat wall on the front edge of the base wall, refer to Figure 16-121.
h. Create the flat pattern of the component, refer to Figure 16-122.

If required, set the working directory to *C:\ProE-WF-5.0\c16*.

Starting a New Object File
1. Start a new file in the **Sheetmetal** mode and name it as *c16tut2*.

2. Set the template to **mmns_part_sheetmetal**.

Creating the Base Wall
1. Choose the **Flat** button from the **Sheetmetal** toolbar; the **Flat** dashboard is displayed and you are prompted to select a closed sketch.

2. Choose the **References** tab from the **Flat** dashboard to display the slide-down panel. Choose the **Define** button from the slide-down panel; the **Sketch** dialog box is displayed and you are prompted to select a sketching plane.

3. Select the **TOP** datum plane from the drawing area and choose the **Sketch** button from the **Sketch** dialog box.

4. Draw the sketch for the base wall, as shown in Figure 16-110, and choose the **Done** button to exit the sketcher environment.

5. Enter the value **1** in the edit box in the **Flat** dashboard and choose the **Build feature** button from the dashboard to complete the creation of the feature. The model similar to the one shown in Figure 16-111 is displayed in the drawing area.

Figure 16-110 The sketch for the base wall   *Figure 16-111 Model of the base wall*

Creating the Hole Feature
1. Create a hole on the lower right corner of the base wall, as shown in Figure 16-112 by specifying the dimensions shown in Figure 16-106.

Working with Sheetmetal Components

Creating the Pattern of the Hole Feature
1. Create the rectangular pattern of the hole, as shown in Figure 16-113

Figure 16-112 Model after creating the hole feature

Figure 16-113 Model after creating the pattern of the hole feature

Creating the First Flange Wall
1. Choose the **Flange** button from the **Sheetmetal** toolbar; the **Flange Wall** dashboard is displayed and you are prompted to select the edge to attach the wall.

2. Select the right edge of the base wall; the preview of the flange wall is displayed in the drawing area.

3. Choose the **Shape** tab from the **Flange Wall** dashboard to display the slide-down panel and specify **50** as the value for the height of the wall in the edit box.

4. Choose the **Dimension the outer surface of the bend** button from the **Flange Wall** dashboard and enter **2** as the value in the edit box; the preview of the wall is displayed in the drawing area.

5. Choose the **Build feature** button from the **Flange Wall** dashboard to complete the creation of the wall. Figure 16-114 shows the model after creating the flange wall.

Creating the Cut Feature
1. Choose the **Extrude** button from the **Sheetmetal** toolbar and select the front face of the flange wall as the sketching plane. Also, make sure that the **Remove Material** button is chosen.

2. Draw the sketch for the cut feature on the front face of the previous flange wall, as shown in Figure 16-115.

3. Extrude the sketch through all faces of the model to create the cut feature, as shown in Figure 16-116.

Figure 16-114 Model with the flange wall

Figure 16-115 The sketch for the cut feature   *Figure 16-116 Model with the cut feature*

Creating the Next Flange Wall

1. Choose the **Flange** button from the **Sheetmetal** toolbar; the **Flange Wall** dashboard is displayed and you are prompted to select the edge to attach the wall.

2. Select the attachment edge, as shown in Figure 16-117; the preview of the flange wall is displayed in the drawing area.

3. Select the **Open** option from the Wall profile drop-down list in the dashboard; the preview of the wall is displayed in the drawing area.

4. Accept the default parameters in the **Shape** tab slide-down panel and choose the **Build feature** button from the **Flange Wall** dashboard to complete the creation of the wall.

   Figure 16-118 shows the model with the flange wall.

Figure 16-117 The attachment edge for the flange wall

Figure 16-118 Model with the flange wall

Creating the Flange Walls on the Left Edge of the Base Wall

1. Create the flange walls on the left edge of the base wall by following the same procedure that was used for creating the first two flange walls on the right edge of the base wall, refer to Figure 16-119. You can also mirror the flange walls with respect to the RIGHT plane.

Creating the Cut Feature on the Left Flange Wall

1. Create the cut feature on the left flange wall by following the procedure used for creating the cut on the right flange wall. The model after creating the cut feature is shown in Figure 16-119.

Figure 16-119 Model after creating the flange walls on the left edge of the base wall and the cut feature on the left flange wall

Creating the Flat Wall

1. Choose the **Flat** button from the **Sheetmetal** toolbar; the **Flat Wall** dashboard is displayed and you are prompted to select the attachment edge to create the wall.

2. Select the front edge of the base wall; the **Rectangle** profile of the wall is chosen by default and the preview of the wall is displayed in the drawing area.

3. Choose the **Rectangle** option from the dashboard; a flyout is displayed. Choose the **User-Defined** option from the flyout.

4. Choose the **Shape** tab from the **Flat Wall** dashboard to display the slide-down panel. Choose the **Sketch** button from the slide-down panel; the **Sketch** dialog box is displayed.

5. Orient the model such that the top face of the base wall is at the top and draw the sketch for the user-defined flat wall, as shown in Figure 16-120. Note that the sketch drawn should be open at the top. Choose the **Done** button to exit the sketcher environment.

Figure 16-120 The sketch for the flat wall

6. Choose the **Relief** tab from the **Flat Wall** dashboard to display the slide-down panel and then select the **Rectangular** option from the **Type** drop-down list. Accept the default parameters for the relief. If required, you need to choose the **Flip** button.

7. Choose the **Build feature** button from the **Flat Wall** dashboard to complete the creation of the flat wall. The model similar to the one shown in Figure 16-121 is displayed in the drawing area.

Creating the Flat Pattern of the Model

1. Choose the **Flat Pattern** button from the **Sheetmetal** toolbar; the selection box is displayed and you are prompted to select the plane or the edge to remain fixed while unbending or bending back.

2. Select the top surface of the base wall; the flat pattern of the model is created and the model similar to the one shown in Figure 16-122 is displayed in the drawing area.

Saving the Model

1. Choose the **Save** button from the **File** toolbar to save the model.

Figure 16-121 Model after creating the flat wall *Figure 16-122 Model after creating the flat pattern*

Self-Evaluation Test

Answer the following questions and then compare them to those given at the end of this chapter:

1. What are the different kinds of walls in the **Sheetmetal** environment of Pro/E?

2. What are the different types of unattached walls in the **Sheetmetal** environment of Pro/E?

3. _____ , _____ , and _____ are three different types of unattached blend walls.

4. The rotational blend walls have sections that can be rotated about the Y-axis upto a maximum angle of 90-degree. (T/F)

5. The _____ in a sheetmetal component control the material behavior and prevent the unwanted deformation.

6. In the **Sheetmetal** environment of Pro/E, the _____ wall can be a primary or a secondary wall.

7. The _____ wall button can be used to lengthen an existing wall.

8. The _____ is a reference point for calculating the developed length and creating the bend geometry.

9. The _____ option flattens any curved surface, whether it is a bend feature or a curved wall.

10. A _____ feature can be defined as a zero-volume cut.

Review Questions

Answer the following questions:

1. While creating an unattached blend wall, the _____ option is used to connect vertices of all sections in the blend feature with straight lines.

2. Parallel blends have sections that are drawn _____ to each other.

3. If the rotational blend angle between two sections is equal to 0-degree, then the rotational blend option functions in the same way as the parallel blend option. (T/F)

4. While creating a flange wall, the _____ tab is used to specify the dimensions of the predefined wall profiles.

5. The bend feature can be created on the area that was previously bent. (T/F)

6. The _____ feature bends back only unbent features.

7. The _____ feature is defined as a zero volume cut that tears or shears the sheetmetal walls.

8. To convert a solid model into a sheetmetal component, you first need to _____ the solid model.

9. The flat pattern can be created only once on a sheetmetal component. (T/F)

10. When you choose the **Extrude** button to create a cut on a sheetmetal component, the **Remove Material** button is chosen by default. (T/F)

Exercises

Exercise 1

Create the sheetmetal component shown in Figure 16-123. The dimensions of the model are shown in Figures 16-124 and 16-125. The flat pattern of the component is shown in Figure 16-126. Assume the missing dimensions.   **(Expected time: 30 min)**

Working with Sheetmetal Components

Figure 16-123 Model for Exercise 1

Figure 16-124 Top view of the component

Figure 16-125 Front view of the component

Figure 16-126 Flat pattern of the component

Exercise 2

In this tutorial, you will create the sheet metal component shown in Figure 16-127. The flat pattern of the component is shown in Figure 16-128. The dimensions of the model are shown in Figure 16-129. The material thickness, bend radius, relief depth, and relief width is 1mm. Assume the missing dimensions. **(Expected time: 30 min)**

Figure 16-127 *Sheet metal part for Tutorial 1*

Figure 16-128 *Flat pattern of the part*

Figure 16-129 *Dimensions of the sheet metal part*

Answers to Self-Evaluation Test
1. Primary wall and Secondary wall, **2. Flat**, **Revolve**, **Blend**, and **Offset**, **3.** Parallel, Rotational, General, **4.** F, **5.** reliefs, **6.** flat, **7. Extend**, **8.** bend line, **9.** flat pattern, **10.** rip

Index

Symbols

3D Cross-Section 12-20

A

Activates Sketcher to create section button 6-9
Add 11-14
Adding and Removing Sheets 14-9
Adding or Removing the Cross-section
    Arrows 8-3
Adding tolerances to the drawing views 13-20
Add Inn Fcs option 6-8
Add Jogs 11-26
Adds counterbore 6-11
Adds countersink 6-11
Adds tapping 11-13
Add to Favorites 4-22
Add to Part edge 16-12
Advantages of Nesting the Sketches 1-18
Align Constraints 11-8
All Versions 5-25
Angles Tab 8-27
Angular Dimensioning 11-21
Angular Dimensioning an Arc 11-2
Arc 11-16
Array of Datum Points from a Coordinate
    System 5-24
Assembling Repeated Copies 11-20
Automatic Constraints 11-7

B

Backup 1-19
Backup dialog box 1-19
Balloons in Drawings 14-11
Base features 6-15
Base Features toolbar 10-13
Basic conversion 16-27
Basic Rounds 6-14
Bend Back 16-26
BEND BACK dialog box 16-26
BENDBACKSEL menu 16-26
Bend Button 10-12

BEND Options dialog box 16-22
Bidirectional Associative Property 8-8
Blend Between Surfaces 8-8
Blended Surface 15-4
Blend features 9-12
BLEND OPTS menu 16-6
BLEND OPTS submenu 4-9
Blend Section to Surfaces 9-11
Boundry Chain 11-2
BOM dialog box 11-27
Bottom-up Approach 11-3
Bottom-up Assemblies 11-5
Bound 14-4
Break witness lines 13-18

C

Chain button 14-3
CHAMFER (CORNER) dialog box 6-24
Chamfer dashboard 6-25
Change orientation of constraint button 11-11
Changing the View Scale 12-25
Changing the View Type 12-24
Circle 2-7, 14-2
Circular fillets 3-3
Cleaning Up the Dimensions 13-17
Collection 5-5
Column Headers 14-12
Column Option 14-10
Common Folders and Folder Tree 1-12
Component Area 11-21
Component Create dialog box 11-4
Component Placement dashboard 11-6
Constant Normal Direction 9-4
Constant section 9-6
Constant Thickness Shell 8-14
Constraint 1-8
Constraint Type drop-down list 11-6
Construction Circle 3-9
Control Points Check Box 15-11
Conversion 16-27
Converting a Generated View to a Draft
    View 14-7

Converting a Surface to a Solid 15-25
Coordinate Dimensioning 3-7
Coordinate System 7-14
Coord Sys 11-10
Copy Feature submenu 7-15
Copying Features 7-15
Copy Pos 11-24
Corner 14-4
Corner Chamfer 6-23
Cosmetic Tab 13-18
Create defining dimension 2-14
Creating a Blended Surface 15-4
Creating a Helical Sweep Surface 15-5
Creating an Extruded Surface 15-2
Creating a Protrusion 4-2
Creating a Reference Coordinate System 8-7
Creating a Revolved Surface 15-3
Creating a Spline 6-22
Creating a Surface by Blending
    Boundaries 15-6
Creating a Surface Using Variable Section
    Sweep 15-8
Creating a Sweep Cut 3-3
Creating a Sweep Surface 15-4
Creating a Swept Blend Surface 15-5
Creating a Variable Radius Round 6-24
Creating base features 3-3
Creating Chamfers 6-23
Creating Circular Fillets 11-4
Creating Components in the Assembly
    Mode 5-26
Creating Constant Thickness Shell 8-14
Creating Cuts 5-25
Creating Datum Curve by Sketching 8-19
Creating Datum Planes 7-2
Creating draft features 8-25
Creating Feature Patterns 6-31
Creating Fillets 7-2
Creating Holes 6-14
Creating Patterns 6-2
Creating Ribs 6-30
Creating Round at the Vertex of a Surface 15-25
Creating Rounds 6-13
Creating Simplified Representations 8-5
Creating Straight Holes 8-2
Creating Surfaces in Pro/E 15-2

Creating Surfaces using Style environment of
    Pro/E 15-9
Creating Sweep Feature by Selecting a
    Trajectory 8-7
Creating Swept Protrusions 11-23
Creating Tables 14-10
Creating the Bend 16-21
Creating the Bend Back 16-26
Creating the Column Headers 14-12
Creating the Conversion 16-27
Creating The Exploded State 11-22
Creating the Fill Surfaces 15-19
Creating the Flat Pattern 16-30
Creating the Intersect Curves 15-19
Creating the Offset Lines 11-25
Creating the Offset Surfaces 15-21
Creating the Table for BOM 14-11
Creating the Unbend 16-25
Creating Thin Sweep Protrusion 15-10
Cuts in the Sheetmetal Component 16-30

D

Datum Axes 5-14
DATUM AXIS dialog box 5-15
Datum Axis Normal to a Plane 5-17
Datum Axis Passing Through an Edge 5-16
Datum Axis Passing Through a Point and
    Normal to plane 5-17
Datum Axis Passing Through the Center of a
    Round Surface 5-18
Datum curves 8-16
Datum dialog box 13-11
Datum Display Toolbar 1-23
Datum Options 5-5
DATUM PLANE dialog box 5-6
Datum Planes 5-5
Datum Planes Created On-The-Fly 5-13
Datum Point at the Center of a Curved
    Edge 5-22
Datum Point at the Intersection of Three
    Surfaces 5-21
Datum Point by Clicking 5-24
DATUM POINT dialog box 5-20
Datum Point on an Edge or a Curve 5-23
Datum Points 5-19
Datums 5-2
Datum toolbar 5-5

Index

Default Constraint 11-11
Default Datum Planes 4-3
Default Model Area 12-2
Deleting a Feature 2-20, 6-36
Deleting a Pattern 7-15
Deleting the Drawing View 12-23
Deleting the sketcher entities 6-5
Detailed View 12-7
Diameter Dimensioning 1-8
Diameter dimensioning of the hole 3-2
Dimension 3-2
Dimensional Tolerances 13-5
Dimensioning 3-8
Dimensioning a Sketch Using the Baseline Option 2-13
Dimensioning of Splines 2-15
Dimensioning options 2-14
Dimensioning Revolved Sections 3-8
Dimensioning the basic sketched entities 2-12
Dimensioning the Drawing Views 13-2
Dimensioning the Endpoints 7-3
Dimensioning the sketch 2-13
Dimension Patterns 7-4
Dimension Properties dialog box 13-12
Dim Orientation dialog box 4-22
Direction Patterns 2-21
Disabling the Constraints 8-25
Disadvantages of Nesting the Sketches 4-23
Displaying the Components in a Separate Window 11-6
Displaying the Components in the Same Window 11-6
Divide at Intersection 14-3
Divide by Equal Segments 14-3
Draft dashboard 2-6
Draft features 8-25
DRAFT GROUP menu 14-5
Drafting Using the Drawing Views 14-7
Draft surfaces Collector 8-25
Drawing a Centerline 2-6, 2-9
Drawing a Circle 2-7
Drawing a Line 2-5
Drawing an Arc 2-23
Drawing an Ellipse 2-10
Drawing a Rectangle 2-21
Drawing a sketch using the sketcher tools toolbar 12-5

Drawing display options 12-9
Drawing View dialog box 12-24
Drawing View Dialog Box 13-8

E

Edge Chamfer 6-24
Edge On Srf 11-11
Editing Definition 6-33
Editing features of a model 6-32
Editing the Cross-section Hatching 12-26
Editing the Drawing Views 12-22
Editing the Geometric Tolerances 13-10
Ellipse Radius dialog box 3-6
Ellipse Using the Ellipse Button 2-10, 2-9
Elliptical Fillets 3-5
Entity 1-8
Erasing the Drawing View 11-16, 12-23
Exclude 11-15
Explicit Relationship 4-22
Exploded Drawing View 14-13
Exploded State 11-22
Explode Position dialog box 11-24
Extend Wall 16-16
Extrude as surface 4-8
Extrude dashboard 4-5
Extrude Dashboard 4-5
Extruded Surface 15-2

F

FEAT menu 6-34
Feature-Based Nature 1-2
Field Datum Point 5-24
File formats 3-13
File Toolbar 7-6
Fill dashboard 15-19
Fill Patterns 5-4
Filter drop-down list 11-15
Finalize 11-14
Fix constraint 11-11
Fix Location 11-14
Flange Wall 16-17
Flange Wall dashboard 16-17
Flat Wall 16-11
Flat Wall dashboard 16-11
Free Ends 6-20
Full (Aligned) 12-17

Full Round Button 6-19
Full section view 12-17
Full(Unfold) 12-19

G

General Blend 8-12, 16-8
General Pattern 7-14
Generating Balloons 14-14
Generating Drawing Views 12-4
Generating the Auxiliary View 12-8
Generating the BOM 14-11
Generating the Copy and Align View 12-19
Generating the Detailed View 12-7
Generating the General View 12-4
Generating the Projection View 12-6
Geometric Tolerances 13-5
Geometry 11-16
GET POINT submenu 14-5
Getting Started 1-7
GET VECTOR menu 14-5
Graphics Only 11-16

H

Half section view 12-15
Half View 12-10
Helical Sweep 9-9
Helical Sweep Surface 15-5
Help Button 1-24
Hole Dashboard 6-2

I

Identical Pattern 7-12
Implicit Relationship 4-22
Important Points to Remember While Creating a Hole 6-13
Increment Button 14-4
Insert Constraint 11-10
Inserting Components in the Assembly 11-5
In Session 1-16
Intent Chain 8-7
Intersect Curves 15-19
Intersect Option 8-19
Invoking the Sheetmetal Mode 16-2
Invoking the Sketch Mode 2-3

L

Length Button 14-4
Line 14-2
Linear 6-3
Linear Dimensioning a Line 2-14
Linear Dimensioning of the Hole 6-4
Local section view 12-16

M

Managing files 1-20
Marquee Tab 10-6
Master Rep 11-16
Mate 11-7
Menu manager 7-17
Merge dashboard 15-17
Merge Ends 2-21
Merging Surfaces 15-17
Mirror 7-16
Mirroring a Geometry 7-18
Mirroring the sketcher entities 2-18
Mirroring the Surfaces 15-16
Miscellaneous Modifications 13-17
Model Display Toolbar 2-19
Model edge visibility 12-17
Model Tree 6-36
Modify Dimensions dialog box 3-9
Modifying a Dimension by Double-Clicking 2-19
Modifying a Feature 2-18
Modifying and Editing Dimensions 13-12
Modifying a Spline 3-10
Modifying Boundaries of Views 12-25
Modifying Components of the Assembly 11-22
Modifying Dimensions Dynamically 7-16
Modifying other Parameters 12-26
Modifying the Cross-sections 12-25
Modifying the Dimensions of a Feature of a Component 11-22
Modifying The dimensions of a sketch 11-15
Modifying the Dimensions of the Spline 11-12
Modifying the Drawing Items 13-17
Modifying the Drawing views 12-24
Modifying the Perspective Views 12-26
Modifying the Sketched entities 12-22
Move 7-17

N

Navigator 1-9, 1-26
Need for datums in modeling 5-2
Nesting of Sketches 4-22
New Constraint Option 11-11
New dialog box 1-13, 12-2, 16-2
New Drawing dialog box 12-3
New Drawing Dialog Box 12-2
New File Options dialog box 1-14
New Format dialog box 14-8
New Gtol 13-9
New Refs 7-15
No Inn Fcs option 8-4
No Repeat Option 14-13
Normal Constraint 5-9
Normal To Projection 9-4
Normal To Trajectory 9-3
NOTE TYPES menu 13-5
Number of Decimal Places 13-17

O

Offset Constraint 5-12
Offset dashboard 1-18
OFFSET OPER menu 14-7
Offset Surfaces 5-13
Old Versions 1-14
One By One 3-14
On-The-Fly 1-11
Open dialog box 8-2
Organize Button 11-13

P

Package 11-4
PACKAGE menu 11-14
Packaging the Components 11-13
Parallel Blend 8-8
Parallel Blend 16-6
Parallel Constraint 5-10
Parameter 1-8
Parametric Nature 1-6
Parametric Sketch 14-3
Partial View 12-10
Part mode 4-2
Pattern dashboard 7-3
Patterns 7-2
Pick Point 6-24

Pieces slide-up panel 6-21
Placement Constraints 11-4
Placement Tab 11-11
Placement tab slide-up panel 4-8
Placing a Point 2-5
Planar Bend 16-24
Pnt On Line 11-10
Pnt On Srf 11-11
Point 1-16
Preview Button 4-9
Primary Walls 16-3
Projection View 12-6
Project Option 8-21
Properties Tab 4-4
Pro/Sheetmetal 16-2

R

Radial Dimensioning 2-15
Radial dimensioning of the hole 6-4
RADIUS SIDE submenu 16-22
Rectangle 2-7
Rectangular Relief 16-10
Redefining a Feature of a Component 11-22
Redefining Features 6-33
Redefining the Components 11-19
Reference Patterns 7-8
Refit object 2-23
Regular bend 16-21
Regular Type dialog box 16-25
Relate to Object 14-6
Relate to View 14-6
Relation 1-9
Reliefs in Sheetmetal Components 16-9
Relief Tab 16-13
Remove Button 14-2
Remove from Favorites 1-12
Removing Material by Extruding a Sketch 5-25
Removing Material by Revolving a Sketch 5-26
Rename dialog box 1-19
Reordering Features 6-33
Reordering the Components 11-19
Reorder submenu 6-34
Reorienting the Views 12-25
Repaint 2-23
Repeat Component dialog box 11-21
Repeat Region 14-12
Replacing Components 11-20

Replacing the Dimensions 3-3
Rerouting Features 6-35
Reset button 13-16
Resolve Sketch dialog box 2-19, 4-15
Retrieving the User-Defined Formats 14-8
Revolve dashboard 12-8, 14-5
Revolved Section View 4-14
Revolved Surface 15-3
Revolving a Sketch 4-15
Revolving a Sketch as a Solid 4-16
Revolving a Sketch with Thickness 6-30
Ribs 6-29
Rip Relief 16-10
Rotate 6-15
Rotate and Copy 14-5
Rotating the Features 7-17
Rotational Blend 8-10, 16-7

S

Same Refs 7-16
Save 1-18
Save a Copy 1-18
Saved view list 4-14
Scale Option 12-12
Scale Rotate dialog box 3-13
Sculpt Button 10-14
Secondary Walls 16-3
Section of the Solid Model 7-18
Sections Option 12-13
Select assembly Item Collector 11-12
Select Button 15-9
Select component Item Collector 11-11
Selected Items dialog box 5-4
Select Feat submenu 6-34
Selection Method 5-3
Select Model Area 11-27
Select references 14-2
Select Traj 8-4
Sets tab slide-up panel 6-17
Setting the Repeat Region 14-12
Sheetmetal Conversion 16-27
SHEETMETAL Walls 16-3
Shell 8-13
Show Instances 4-6
Simple Holes using Standard Hole Profile 4-12
Simplified Representation Using the View
    Manager 11-17

Sketch dialog Box 2-2, 4-13
Sketcher environment 9-6
Sketcher Tools toolbar 8-2
Sketching in the Drawing Mode 14-2
Sketch mode 3-7
Sketch placement point collector 12-3
Sketch Traj Option 10-3
Smooth 16-6
Snapping References dialog box 14-2
SNAPSHOT menu 14-7
Sort By 10-11
Specify Template Area 12-2
Spinal Bend 1-9
Spine Button 10-10
Splines 6-11
Split by draft hinge 8-26
Split by split object 8-27
Standard Hole 6-10
Straight 16-6
Stretch 14-4
Stretch Button 10-11
Stretch Relief 16-10
Strong Constraints 11-20
Strong Dimensions 8-7
Style Environment of Pro/ENGINEER 15-9
Style Tools Toolbar 15-9
Suppressing Features 6-35
Suppressing/Resuming 11-19
Surface by Blending Boundaries 15-6
Surface Modeling 15-2
Surface Trim Button 15-16
Surf Chain 8-2
Sweep Cut 9-6
Sweep features 6-16
Sweep Protrusions 6-16
Sweep Surface 15-4
SWEEP TRAJ menu
Swept Blend 15-5

T

TABLE CREATE submenu 14-10
Table From File Option 14-10
Table Option 14-10
Table Patterns 7-9
Tables in The Drawing mode 14-10
Tangency 3-8
Tangent 11-10

Index

Tangent Constraint 5-13
Tangnt Chain 8-6
Text Style 13-17
Text dialog 3-11
Text Style Tab 13-15
Text Symbol 13-16
The Bill Of Material 11-26
The Drawing Mode 12-2
The Sketch mode 2-2
Thicken dashboard 15-24
Thicken Sketch 4-11
Through Constraint 5-7
Through Curve Button 6-20
Tolerance mode 13-13
Tol Value Tab 13-7
Toolbars 1-22
Top-down Approach 11-2
Top-down Assemblies 11-4
Toroidal Bend 10-2
To Selected option 4-9
Trajectories collector 9-3
Transform Button 10-6
Transforming the Draft Entities 14-4
Translate 11-12
Translate and Copy 14-4
Translating the Features 7-17
Trim dashboard 15-19
Trimming Surfaces 15-18
Trimming the Draft Entities 14-3
Trimming the lines 2-21
Trimming the sketcher entities 2-20
Twist Button 10-13
Twist Wall 16-14
Type Drop-down List 1-11

U

Unattached Blend Wall 16-6
Unattached Flat Wall 16-4
Unattached Flat Wall dashboard 16-4
Unattached Offset Wall 16-8
Unattached Revolve Wall 16-5
Unbend 16-25
UNBEND OPT menu 16-25
UNBENDSEL menu 16-25
Understanding the orientation of
    datum planes 4-16
Undo 2-19

Unrelate 14-6
Unset Default Relate View 14-6
Up One Level 1-12
Uses of Patterns 7-2
USE TABLE menu 16-22
Using Blend Vertex 8-12
Using the Edit Menu 2-18
Using the Navigator 11-17

V

Value 13-17
Variable Angle Drafts 8-28
Variable Assembly Refs Area 11-21
Variable Pattern 7-13
Variable section 9-6
Variable Section Sweep 9-2, 15-8
Variable Section Sweep dashboard 9-2
Variable Thickness Shell 8-15
View Manager 11-17
View Manager dialog box 7-19
View Type Option 12-9

W

Warp 10-5
Warp Button 10-9
Weak Constraints 1-9
Weak Dimension into a Strong Dimension 2-13
Weak Dimensions 1-9
With Draft Feature 15-22
Working Directory 1-9
Working with Constraints 2-16
Working with Splines 3-7
Working with the Sketch in the Sketch
    mode 2-4
Work Region Method 7-19
Wrap 8-23
Writing text in sketcher environment 3-11
w/Transition bend 16-22

X

Xsec0001 dialog box 12-21
XSEC CREATE menu 12-21

Z

Zoom Out 2-23

Other Publications by CADCIM Technologies

The following is the list of some of the publications by CADCIM Technologies. Please visit www.cadcim.com for the complete listing.

Computer Animation Textbooks
- Autodesk 3ds Max Design 2010: A Tutorial Approach
- Autodesk 3ds Max Design 2009: A Tutorial Approach
- Autodesk Maya 2010: A Comprehensive Guide
- Autodesk Maya 2009: A Comprehensive Guide
- Autodesk 3ds Max 2009: A Comprehensive Guide
- 3ds Max 2008: A Comprehensive Guide

Computer Programming Textbooks
- Learning Oracle11g
- Learning ASP.NET AJAX
- Learning Java Programming
- Learning Visual Basic.NET 2008
- Learning C++ Programming Concepts
- Learning VB.NET Programming Concepts

Autodesk Revit Textbooks
- Autodesk Revit Architecture 2010 for Architects & Designers
- Autodesk Revit Architecture 2009 for Architects & Designers
- Autodesk Revit Architecture 2008 for Architects & Designers
- Autodesk Revit Building 9 for Designers & Architects
- Autodesk Revit Building 8 for Designers & Architects

AutoCAD Civil 3D Textbook
- AutoCAD Civil 3D 2009 for Engineers

Autodesk Alias Textbooks
- Learning Autodesk Alias Design 2010
- Autodesk AliasStudio 2009 for Designers

Autodesk Inventor Textbooks
• Autodesk Inventor 2010 for Designers
• Autodesk Inventor 2009 for Designers
• Autodesk Inventor 2008 for Designers
• Autodesk Inventor 11 for Designers
• Autodesk Inventor for Designers, Release 10
• Autodesk Inventor for Designers, Release 9

Solid Edge Textbooks
- Solid Edge ST for Designers
- Solid Edge V20 for Designers
- Solid Edge V19 for Designers
- Solid Edge V18 for Designers
- Solid Edge for Designers, Version 16
- Solid Edge for Designers, Version 15

NX Textbooks
- NX 6 for Designers
- NX 5 for Designers
- NX 4 for Designers
- NX 3 for Designers

SolidWorks Textbooks
- SolidWorks 2010 for Designers
- SolidWorks 2009 for Designers
- SolidWorks 2008 for Designers
- SolidWorks 2007 for Designers
- SolidWorks for Designers, Release 2005

CATIA Textbooks
- CATIA V5R19 for Designers
- CATIA V5R18 for Designers
- CATIA V5R17 for Designers
- CATIA V5R16 for Designers
- CATIA V5R15 for Designers

EdgeCAM Textbooks
- EdgeCAM 11.0 for Manufacturers
- EdgeCAM 10.0 for Manufacturers

Pro/ENGINEER Textbooks
- Pro/ENGINEER Wildfire 4.0 for Designers
- Pro/ENGINEER Wildfire 3.0 for Designers
- Pro/ENGINEER Wildfire for Designers Release 2.0
- Pro/ENGINEER Wildfire for Designers

AutoCAD LT Textbooks
- AutoCAD LT 2010 for Designers
- AutoCAD LT 2009 for Designers
- AutoCAD LT 2008 for Designers
- AutoCAD LT 2007 for Designers
- AutoCAD LT 2006 for Designers

ANSYS Textbook
- ANSYS 11.0 for Designers

AutoCAD Electrical Textbook
- AutoCAD Electrical 2010 for Electrical Control Designers

Mechanical Desktop Textbook
- Mechanical Desktop Instructor, Release 5

Paper Craft Book
- Constructing 3-Dimensional Models: A Paper-Craft Workbook

Textbooks Authored by CADCIM Technologies and Published by Other Publishers

AutoCAD Textbooks (US Edition)
- AutoCAD 2010: A Problem-Solving Approach
  DELMAR CENGAGE Learning
- Customizing AutoCAD 2010
  DELMAR CENGAGE Learning
- AutoCAD 2009: A Problem-Solving Approach
  DELMAR CENGAGE Learning
- Customizing AutoCAD 2009
  DELMAR CENGAGE Learning
- AutoCAD 2008: A Problem-Solving Approach
  Autodesk Press
- Customizing AutoCAD 2008
  Autodesk Press
- AutoCAD 2007: A Problem-Solving Approach
  Autodesk Press
- Customizing AutoCAD 2007
  Autodesk Press

3D Studio MAX and VIZ Textbooks
- Learning 3ds max5: A Tutorial Approach
  (Complete manuscript available for free download on *www.cadcim.com*)
- Learning 3DS Max: A Tutorial Approach, Release 4
  Goodheart-Wilcox Publishers (USA)
- Learning 3D Studio VIZ: A Tutorial Approach
  Goodheart-Wilcox Publishers (USA)
- Learning 3D Studio R4: A Tutorial Approach
  Goodheart-Wilcox Publishers (USA)

CADCIM Technologies Textbooks Translated in Other Languages

CATIA Textbooks
- CATIA V5R18 for Designers (Serbian Edition)
  Mikro Knjiga Publishing Company, Serbia
- CATIA V5R18 for Designers (Korean Edition)
  Onsolutions, South Korea

SolidWorks Textbooks
- SolidWorks 2006 for Designers (Russian Edition)
  Piter Publishing Press, Russia
- SolidWorks 2008 for Designers (Serbian Edition)
  Mikro Knjiga Publishing Company, Serbia
- SolidWorks 2006 for Designers (Serbian Edition)
  Mikro Knjiga Publishing Company, Serbia
- SolidWorks 2006 for Designers (Japanese Edition)
  Mikio Obi, Japan

NX Textbooks
- NX 6 for Designers (Korean Edition)
  Onsolutions, South Korea
- NX 5 for Designers (Korean Edition)
  Onsolutions, South Korea

Pro/ENGINEER Textbooks
- Pro/ENGINEER Wildfire 4.0 for Designers (Korean Edition)
  HongReung Science Publishing Company, South Korea
- Pro/ENGINEER Wildfire 3.0 for Designers (Korean Edition)
  HongReung Science Publishing Company, South Korea

3ds Max Textbook
- 3ds Max 2008: A Comprehensive Guide (Serbian Edition)
  Mikro Knjiga Publishing Company, Serbia

AutoCAD Textbooks
- AutoCAD 2006 (Russian Edition)
  Piter Publishing Press, Russia
- AutoCAD 2005 (Russian Edition)
  Piter Publishing Press, Russia
- AutoCAD 2000 Fondamenti (Italian Edition)
- AutoCAD 2000 Tecniche Avanzate (Italian Edition)
- AutoCAD 2000 (Chinese Edition)

Coming Soon: New Textbooks from CADCIM Technologies
- Character Animation: A Tutorial Approach
- NX 7 for Designers
- Solid Edge ST2 for Designers
- AutoCAD Map 3D 2010 for Geospatial Professionals
- Autodesk Maya 2011: A Comprehensive Guide
- Autodesk 3ds Max Design 2011: A Tutorial Approach
- Autodesk Revit Architecture 2011 for Architects & Designers
- AutoCAD Civil 3D 2011 for Engineers
- Autodesk Inventor 2011 for Designers
- AutoCAD LT 2011 for Designers
- Autodesk Revit Structure for Structural Designers & Detailers
- CATIA V6R2010 for Designers

Online Training Program Offered by CADCIM Technologies

CADCIM Technologies provides effective and affordable virtual online training on various software packages including computer programming languages, Computer Aided Design and Manufacturing (CAD/CAM), animation, architecture, and GIS. The training will be delivered 'live' via Internet at any time, any place, and at any pace to individuals, students of colleges, universities, and CAD/CAM training centers. For more information, please visit the following link: **http://www.cadcim.com**

Printed in Great Britain
by Amazon.co.uk, Ltd.,
Marston Gate.